HISTORY
OF
LOUISIANA.

HISTORY

OF

LOUISIANA.

THE AMERICAN DOMINATION.

BY

CHARLES GAYARRÉ.

WITH CITY AND TOPOGRAPHICAL MAPS OF THE STATE, ANCIENT AND MODERN,

WITH

A BIOGRAPHY OF THE AUTHOR,

BY

GRACE KING.

BIBLIOGRAPHY

BY

WM. BEER,

LIBRARIAN NEW ORLEANS PUBLIC LIBRARY,

TOGETHER WITH AN EXHAUSTIVE INDEX.

FIFTH EDITION.

IN FOUR VOLUMES.

VOL. IV.

A FIREBIRD PRESS BOOK

PELICAN PUBLISHING COMPANY
Gretna 1998

Entered according to Act of Congress in the year 1882
By Charles Gayarre

In the clerks office of the District Court of the United States for
the Southern District of New York.

Copyright 1903
by F. F. Hansell & Bro., Ltd

Reprinted 1965
by Pelican Publishing Company

Second printing—1974
ISBN 1-56554-655-5

Manufactured in the United States of America
Published by Pelican Publishing Company, Inc.
1000 Burmaster Street, Gretna, Louisiana 70053

CONTENTS.

CHAPTER I.

CESSION OF LOUISIANA TO THE UNITED STATES.—1803-1804.

Effects of the Cession—Feelings of the Inhabitants—Organization of the Territory—Powers of Governor Claiborne—Act of Congress about Slavery—Laussat's Dispatch—His Views and Predictions—Affrays and Tumults—Unpopularity of the Cession—Secession of the Western States — The Louisiana Bank — Condition of the Militia — Public Meetings — Insurrection above Manchac — Kemper and his Followers —Opposition to the Government—Judicial Organization—Adoption of Laws — Governor Claiborne Sworn into Office — Spanish Intrigues—A Political Pamphlet—Popular Excitement—Governor Claiborne's Vindication—Two Hundred Frenchmen Ordered Away—Garcia and Morgan—Arrest of Garcia—Casa Calvo's Complaints—Claiborne's Answers—Importation of Slaves—First Legislative Assembly—Belief in Re-cession—The Yellow Fever—Prevention of Yellow Fever—Debates in Congress—Reflections on the Debates . . . .

CHAPTER II.

GOVERNOR CLAIBORNE'S ADMINISTRATION.—1805.

Petition of the Louisianians—John Randolph's Report—Congressional Legislation—Claiborne to Madison—New Territorial Government—Grants of Land by Morales—Casa Calvo and his Body-Guard—Quarrels between Morales and Casa Calvo—Desired Departure of the Spaniards —Increase of Spanish Armaments—Apprehensions of Spanish Hostilities—Suspected Spanish Agents—Aaron Burr Arrives in New Orleans —Claiborne's Secret Correspondence—The Spaniards Unwilling to Depart—Claiborne's Remonstrances—Claiborne and Casa Calvo—Departure of Casa Calvo—Casa Calvo Goes to Texas—Claiborne Prepares for War—Suspicious Movements of Casa Calvo—Claiborne Asks for Reinforcements—Organization of the Militia—Negotiations with Spain—Pinckney and Cevallos—Monroe Sent to Spain—France Unfavorable to the U. S.—Negotiations with Spain—Ultimatum of the United States

iv CONTENTS.

—Negotiations with Spain at an End—Attacks Against Claiborne—Claiborne's Self-Vindication—Claiborne not on a Bed of Roses—New Orleans Incorporated—Religious Quarrels—Claiborne and his Enemies—Sauvé, Destréhan, and Derbigny—Claiborne's Report to Madison—Important Manuscript Found—The Ursuline Nuns put on the Stage—Meeting of the Legislature—Claiborne's Message—Father Walsh and Father Antonio—A Schism among the Catholics—The Fortifications of New Orleans—Claiborne and Land Titles—List of the Public Buildings—Conflict of Civil and Military Authority—Condition of the Judiciary. 58

CHAPTER III.

GOVERNOR CLAIBORNE'S ADMINISTRATION.—1806.

Military Resources of the Territory—Secretary Graham to Madison—The Spaniards still Linger in Louisiana—Claiborne's Alarms—The Mulatto Corps—Claiborne to Casa Calvo—Battalion of Orleans Volunteers—Indifference to the Right of Suffrage—Expulsion of Morales—Expulsion of Casa Calvo—High Charges in Louisiana—Internal Improvements—Claiborne on Education—Increase of Troops Required—Hostile Acts of the Spaniards—John Randolph and Claiborne—Regulations on Citizenship—Governor Claiborne's Veto—Claiborne's Opinion of the Natives—Another Veto by Claiborne—Claiborne and the French Consul—Election of D. Clarke to Congress—Emigration from Louisiana—Causes of Discontent—Claiborne and the Lady Abbess—Judicial Decision on Allegiance—Celebration of the Fourth of July—Claiborne and General Herrera—Claiborne's Military Measures—Arrival of Wilkinson—Father Antoine Suspected—Father Antoine Swears Allegiance—Claiborne's Conflicting Opinions—Claiborne's Despondency—Wilkinson Denounces Burr—Daniel Clarke Suspected—Commotion in New Orleans—Claiborne and Martial Law—Wilkinson and Martial Law—Claiborne and the Embargo—Proposed Impressment of Sailors—Wilkinson and Aaron Burr—Claiborne and Wilkinson Disagree—Cowles Meade on Burr—Arrest of Citizens—Swartwout and Ogden—Claiborne and Judge Workman—The Embargo Repealed. 122

CHAPTER IV.

GOVERNOR CLAIRBORNE'S ADMINISTRATION.—1807-1808.

Arrest of Workman and Kerr—Suspicious Movements of Folch—Claiborne to Cowles Meade—The Legislature and Wilkinson—Arrest of Aaron Burr—Claiborne on the Plans of Burr—Claiborne and the Habeas Corpus—Military Interference with Slavery—Claiborne and the Batture—Edward Livingston and the Batture—Riots about the Batture Claim—Claiborne and the Rioters—Proceedings of the Rioters—Governor Claiborne on the Judiciary—The President and the Batture—Claiborne's Instructions to a Judge—Demolition of Fort St. Louis—Digest of Civil Law—Circular to Militia Officers—Riots and Disturbances—

CONTENTS. v

Claiborne on the Civil Law—Reflections on the Civil Law—Proceedings in Courts—Aversion to Militia Duty—Negroes Running Away to Texas. 174

CHAPTER V.

CLAIBORNE'S ADMINISTRATION.—1809-1810.

Claiborne on Public Schools—Criminal Jurisprudence and Punishments—Claiborne on Foreign Relations—Surrender of Runaway Negroes—Arrival of United States Troops—Violent Feuds in Pointe Coupée—Admission into the Union Demanded—Census of Inhabitants—Opposition to State Government—French Emigration from Cuba—Claiborne and the French Emigrants—Claiborne Checking Immigration—Arrival of too Many Strangers—Sickness Among the U. S. Troops—Mortality Among the U. S. Troops—Encouragement to Domestic Industry—The Yellow Fever and Health Laws—Necessity of Public Education—Claiborne on Public Appointments—Hostility of Claiborne Increasing—Claiborne's Noble Letter—Smuggling of Slaves and Merchandise—Heroism of Louis Grandpré—A Declaration of Independence—Convention of West Florida—West Florida Annexed—The President's Proclamation—Instructions to Claiborne—Address to the Floridians—Great Britain's Protest—New Parishes Formed. 204

CHAPTER VI.

CLAIBORNE'S ADMINISTRATION.—1811-1812.

Debates in Congress—Mr. Miller's Speech—Mr. Rhea's Speech—Josiah Quincy's Speech—Poindexter's Speech—Mr. Gold's Speech—A Convention Called—Conditions of Admission as a State—Insurrection of Negroes—The Negroes Defeated—Livingston and Fulton—Meeting of the State Convention—Speech of Poydras—Proceedings of the Convention—The Constitution of Louisiana. 244

CHAPTER VII.

ADMINISTRATION OF GOVERNOR CLAIBORNE.—1812-1813.

Debates in Congress—Enlargement of the State—State Government Organized—War with Great Britain—Aversion for Public Life—A Want of Men for Offices—A number of Resignations—Madison's Inaugural Address—The Smugglers of Barataria—Danger of Indian Hostilities—Conflagrations and Overflows—F. X. Martin on the Constitution—Credit of U. S. Impaired—Inadequate Protection from the U. S.—The Militia to be called out—Judicial Decision on the Batture—Massacres by the Indians—Claiborne's Indian Talk—Proclamation Against Smugglers—John and Pierre Lafitte—Deeds of the Buccaneers—The Baratarians—Anxieties of the Public Mind. . . . 276

vi   CONTENTS.

CHAPTER VIII.

CLAIBORNE'S ADMINISTRATION.—1814.

Effects of War—Suggested Ameliorations—Too Much Legislation—The Baratarians—F. X. Martin on the Constitution—Projected Invasion of Texas—Requisition on the Militia—Insubordination of the Militia—Danger of a Civil War—Claiborne and the Militia—Unpopularity of Militia Duty—The Militia Refractory—Federal Requisition Rejected—Claiborne on the Press—Claiborne's Appeal—Danger of Invasion Increasing—Claiborne to be impeached—Peace with the Creeks—Louisiana's Destiny—The Free Men of Color—Claiborne's Military Orders—English Proclamation—British Colonel Nicholls—Colonel Nicholls to his Troops—Claiborne's Apprehensions—Claiborne to General Jackson—Claiborne to the Louisianians—Public Meeting—Patriotic Resolutions—Committee's Address to Louisianians—Claiborne to Mayor Girod—Attack on Fort Bowyer—The British Repulsed—General Jackson's Proclamation—Jackson to the Colored Men—Colonel Nicholls to John Lafitte—Sir W. H. Percy to John Lafitte—John Lafitte and British Emissaries—John Lafitte to Blanque—John Lafitte to Claiborne—Pierre Lafitte to Blanque—Expeditions against the Baratarians—Claiborne on the Colored Men—Claiborne trusts the Louisianians—Claiborne on Smuggling—Smuggling no Crime—Sympathy for Smugglers—Jackson and the Spaniards—Pensacola Taken—the French Consul Insulted—Extra Session of the Legislature—Claiborne to the Legislature—Call for the Whole Militia—Claiborne on the Legislature. . 308

CHAPTER IX.

GOVERNOR CLAIBORNE'S ADMINISTRATION.—1814.

The Banks Suspend Payment—Arrival of General Jackson—General Jackson's Character—Defenceless Condition of the State—Jackson's Preparations—Importance of Louisiana—General Jackson's Oath—Claiborne's Military Claims—Clairborne to the Senate—Literature in Louisiana—Approach of the British—Debates in the Legislature—Louaillier's Report—Action of the Legislature—Effects of Jackson's Presence—Battle on Lake Borgne—Federal Neglect of Louisiana—Claiborne's Pithy Message—Martial Law Proclaimed—Jackson's Address to the Citizens—Jackson's Military Measures—Savary, the Colored Man—Jackson's Address to the Militia—Jackson's Military Orders—Services of Lafitte Accepted—A Stay Law Enacted—Arrival of Tennesseeans—Feelings in New Orleans—Forces of the Invaders—Bayou Bienvenu—The Fishermen's Village—Treachery of Fishermen—Landing of the British—Jackson Marching—Skirmishes with the Enemy—Attack by the Carolina—Attack by General Jackson—Battle of the 23d of December—Jackson's Report—General D. Morgan's Corps—Excitement in New Orleans—Reflections—United as One Man.   379

CONTENTS. vii

CHAPTER X.

GOVERNOR CLAIBORNE'S ADMINISTRATION.—1814–1815.

Preparations of the British—Cutting of the Levee—The Carolina Blown up—Attack of the 28th of December—Death of Colonel Henderson—The Congreve Rockets—Artillery Duel—Effective Firing from the Louisiana —Americans Strengthening their Lines—British Black Troops—The Rifle and the Dirty Shirts—Our Mode of Warfare—Cannonade on the 31st of December—Battle of the 1st of January—British Redoubts— Movements of the Enemy—Arrival of the Kentuckians—The Women of Louisiana—Arrival of British Reinforcements—Description of our Lines—Admirable Behaviour of Our Troops—Full Preparations on Both Sides—Battle of the 8th of January—Comments on the Battle—Marshal Soult's Opinion—Military Commentaries—Tribute to Our Troops— Sympathy for the Wounded—Colored Nurses of New Orleans—Incapacity of General D. Morgan—Condition of Morgan's Troops—The Kentuckians Demoralized—Mayor Arnaud's Command—Defeat of General Morgan—Kentuckians Justifying Themselves—Colonel Thornton's Expedition—Thornton Not Arriving in Time—Jackson to Morgan's Defeated Troops—General Humbert—Condition of Morgan's Troops— Suspension of Hostilities—Attack on Fort St. Philip—Evacuation of the British Army—Retreat of the British—Jackson visits the British Camp—Jackson Orders a Thanksgiving—Jackson to his Army—The Results Obtained—Compliments to the Baratarians—General Jackson's Report—Report of a Court-Martial—Reception of Jackson in New Orleans—Address of Abbé Dubourg—Jackson's Answer to Dubourg. . 441

CHAPTER XI.

GOVERNOR CLAIBORNE'S ADMINISTRATION.—1815

Jackson Displeased with Claiborne—Surrender of Fort Bowyer—Admiral Cochrane's Complaint—General Keane's Sword — Abducted Negroes Claimed—British Infatuation—Abducted Slaves Claimed—Arbitration of Russia—Historic Contrast—Major Lacoste and his Slaves—British Love of Plunder—Booty and Beauty—Jackson and the Legislature— Jackson's Answer to the Legislature—Claiborne's Answer to the Legislature—Colonel Fortier's Testimony—Abner Duncan's Testimony— Major Davezac's Testimony—Colonel Déclouet's Testimony—Character of Déclouet—Guichard's Testimony—The Committee of Investigation— No Thanks Voted to Jackson—General Coffee to the Legislature— Jackson to the Mayor of New Orleans—Reflections—Skipwith to Jackson—Thibodaux to Skipwith—Blanque's Letter to the Citizens—Reflections. 511

CHAPTER XII.

CLAIBORNE'S ADMINISTRATION.—1815.

Jackson's Quarrel with the French in New Orleans—Jackson's Address to

CONTENTS.

the Militia—General Jackson and the French—Louaillier's Publication
—Arrest of Louaillier—Arrest of Judge Hall—Firmness of Duplessis
—Arrest of Dick and Hollander—The Militia Disbanded—Jackson on
Popularity—Claiborne and Jackson on Bad Terms—Claiborne to Mazu-
reau—Claiborne to Jackson—Large Meetings of Citizens—Livingston's
Inconsistencies—Trial of Louaillier—Jackson on Martial Law—Martial
Law Revoked—Jackson's Farewell Address—The Uniform Companies
to Jackson—Jackson to the Uniform Companies—Trial of General
Jackson—Jackson's Noble Speech—Jackson's Violent Temper—Federal
Compliments to Louisiana—The President's Pardon Proclamation—
Claiborne Vindicating Himself—Washington's Advice. . . . 578

SUPPLEMENTAL CHAPTER.

1816—1861.

Death of Governor Claiborne—Governor James Villeré—Governor T. Bolling Robertson—Governor Henry Johnson—Governor Peter Derbigny—
Governor A. B. Roman—Governor E. D. White—Governor A. B. Ro
man—Governor Alexander Mouton—Governor Isaac Johnson—Govern-
or Joseph Walker—Governor P. O. Hebert—Governor Robert C. Wickliffe—Governor T. O. Moore—The Doom of Louisiana. . . . 632

HISTORY OF LOUISIANA.

AMERICAN DOMINATION.

CHAPTER I.

CESSION OF LOUISIANA TO THE UNITED STATES — FORMATION OF THE TERRITORIAL GOVERNMENT OF ORLEANS — FEELINGS OF THE INHABITANTS — DEBATES IN CONGRESS.

1803—1804.

ON the 20th of December, 1803, the colony of Louisiana had passed from the domination of Spain into that of the United States of America, to which it was delivered by France after a short possession of twenty days, as I have related in a former work.* Its inhabitants, of French or Spanish descent, and almost all the foreigners who resided in the province, either permanently or temporarily, were discontented and gloomy. To them the change of government, or nationality, was extremely distasteful, for reasons as various as the habits, tastes, prejudices, passions, disappointments and hopes of each individual. A few Americans, who were almost lost in the vast numerical superiority of the rest of the population, and who had just expectations to profit, in every way, by the great event of the cession, were alone to feel and to manifest any degree of exultation. The immediate

* History of Louisiana. Spanish Domination. Redfield, Publisher. New York, 1854.

effect of that cession was to vest all the powers of the defunct government (a sort of Gallic and Spanish hybrid) in Governor Claiborne, until Congress should legislate on the organization of the government of the new territory. Thus this officer, as he informed the inhabitants in a set proclamation, had suddenly become the Governor-General and the Intendant of Louisiana, uniting in his person all the authority severally possessed by those two functionaries under the despotic government of Spain. Well might he be astonished at the strange position in which he was placed; for he, a republican magistrate, found himself transformed into an absolute proconsul, in whom centered all the executive, judicial and legislative authority lately exercised, in their respective capacity, by the superseded Spanish dignitaries. Moreover, he was to wield those extraordinary powers in maintaining and enforcing the laws and municipal regulations of Spain, which were to remain in vigor until modified by the Government of the United States, and of which he was entirely ignorant. Not only were they unknown to him, but they were written in a language with which he was not acquainted, and they were thoroughly impregnated with a spirit completely foreign to his inclinations—to the atmosphere in which he was born and had grown up to manhood—and to the very moral and political training of his mind. Besides, he was to construe and to execute those laws in their application or adjustment to the wants of a population of which he knew nothing. These were circumstances which could not but startle him by their novelty, and by the danger with which they were fraught. Surely it is not to be wondered at, if the colonists looked at their new ruler with a jealous eye, and if they awaited with nervous apprehension the course which he was to pursue. He himself must have felt that his situation was such as to require that he should tax to the utmost all the knowledge, talent, sagacity, prudence and firmness which he might possess, and that no time was to be lost in his giving a decided manifestation of his being gifted with these qualifications.

His first measure was to organize the judiciary, and he established, on the 30th of December, 1803, a Court of Pleas, composed of seven justices. Their civil jurisdiction was limited to cases not exceeding in value three thousand dollars, with the right of appeal to the Governor, when the amount in litigation rose above five hundred dollars. That tribunal was also vested with jurisdiction over all criminal cases in which the punishment did not exceed two hundred dollars and sixty days' imprisonment. Each of those seven justices was clothed, individually, with summary jurisdiction over all debts under one hundred dollars, reserving to the parties an appeal to the Court of Pleas, that is, to the seven justices, sitting together in one court.

In confirmation of what I have written on the discontent existing among those whose allegiance was now to be claimed by the United States, I quote Judge Martin's views on the same subject, as expressed in his History of Louisiana. "The people of Louisiana, especially in New Orleans," says this learned jurist, who came to the territory shortly after the cession, "were greatly dissatisfied at the new order of things. They complained that the person whom Congress had sent to preside over them was an utter stranger to their laws, manners and language; and had no personal interest in the prosperity of the country—that he was incessantly surrounded by newcomers from the United States, to whom he gave a decided preference over the Creoles and European French in the distribution of offices—that in the new Court of Pleas, most of the judges of which were ignorant of the laws and language of the country, proceedings were car ried on in the English language, which Claiborne had lately attempted to introduce in the proceedings of the municipal body, and that the suitors were in an equally disadvantageous situation in the Court of the Last Resort, in which he sat as sole judge, not attended, as the Spanish Governors were, by a legal adviser. That the errors in which he could not but help falling* were without redress. They urged that, under the former government, an appeal lay from the Governor's decision to the Captain-General of Cuba, from thence to the Royal Audience in that island, and in many cases from thence to the Council of the Indies at Madrid." Thus Claiborne was at the same time the Governor, the intendant and the supreme judge of Louisiana. There could not be under the sun a more perfect despotism.

It is true that this state of things did not last beyond the time which was strictly necessary for Congress to modify it. On the 26th of March, 1804, an act was passed to organize the newly acquired province, and to divide it into two parts: the one called "Territory of Orleans," and the other "District of Louisiana," and their executive, judicial and legislative organization was provided for.† But that act was so framed that it proved to be a fresh source of discontent, instead of a healing ointment on festering wounds. The severing of Louisiana into two distinct fragments turned out to be a very unpopular measure, and was keenly resented by the old population. It had always been a unit in the hands of France and Spain. Now that it was relieved from the burden of its colonial vassalage, and was promised the speedy possession of sovereignty, it should not have been afflicted, in the opinion of the Louisianians, with

---

* Considering that he was administering Spanish laws, which he hardly comprehended.
† See the Appendix.

this odious partition, which was evidently destined, they thought, to diminish their importance, and to retard the advent of that sovereignty which had become the object of their desires. They maintained that Congress had no right to curtail Louisiana of the magnificent proportions which it possessed when ceded, and that it was with those proportions, and not in a state of mutilation, that it was to be received into the Confederacy, *as soon as possible*, according to the very terms of the treaty of cession.

The Louisianians, who had objected to the immense power possessed by Claiborne as Governor, intendant and judge in the last resort, did not think that a sufficient guarantee had been given to them by the slight change made in the recent act of Congress for the organization of the Territory. Thus, by that act, the Supreme Court had been made to consist of three judges, it is true, but one of them was sufficient to constitute the court; so that, according to circumstances, the change might amount only to this: that one man, called "Judge," could dispossess them of their property, tarnish their honor, and hang them at will, instead of the man formerly called "Govérnor."

There was another feature in that act which was exceedingly unpalatable. It was the prohibition to import slaves, except by those American citizens who should come to settle in good faith in the Territory, with such slaves as they owned in their former domicile. This was looked upon as a blow purposely aimed at the old inhabitants, who, by such legislation, were deprived of the means of increasing that manual labor which was so much needed for the development of their resources. It may not be amiss to state that a Convention "for promoting the abolition of slavery and improving the condition of the African race," had assembled at Philadel phia on the 13th of January, and had called, through "resolutions," submitted to Congress on the 26th of that month, the attention of that body "to the utility and propriety of passing such laws as should prohibit the importation of slaves into the Territory of Orleans." They appealed to the solemn declaration made by the United States, that "all men were born free and equal," and hence they argued, "that our Government could not authorize man to enslave unoffending man." Such was their language. They also urged other magniloquent considerations which have become familiar to the American mind, from the persevering zeal with which they have ever since been pressed into the service of ambitious demagogues, or of praiseworthy patriots and philanthropists, according to the different views taken of the subject by their respective friends and supporters. Be it as it may, on this occasion, the importation of slaves was partially prohibited in conformity with the wishes of the petitioners against slavery. The Louisianians were greatly mortified. They thought that it was an encouragement to further interference, and some predicted that it was but an entering-wedge.

There was also in that act a provision which excited the ire of the former colonists. It was one which declared that certain concessions of lands made by the Spanish Government were "null and void." This was considered as a demonstration of hostility, and as a threatening indication that something else would soon be forthcoming in violation of what the Louisianians believed to be their rights and privileges. An intense anxiety was produced by the authority granted to the President of the United States to appoint "Registers and Recorders of Land Titles," who were to receive and to record all titles acquired under the Spanish and French Governments, and also commissioned to take cognizance of all claims to land, and to decide on them in a summary way, and with such proceedings as they might deem best to adopt—which proceedings and decisions were to be reported to the Secretary of the Treasury, and laid before Congress for their final judgment. The people thought that this was a complicated machinery to dispossess them of all their broad and fertile acres. They trembled at the consequences which they foresaw—such as arbitrary spoliations, or ruinous litigation, with an endless train of troubles and vexations which were dolefully predicted to them by those who pretended to read the dark pages of futurity.

Such was the state of feelings which prevailed among the former subjects of Spain and France, when the Colonial Prefect Laussat, who had been the agent of France in delivering the territory to the United States, and who had remained in it several months after the cession, departed for the island of Martinique, not without having addressed to his Government some interesting observations, which show that he sagaciously appreciated, to a certain extent at least, some of the results which were to follow from the cession, at no distant time. "The Americans," he said, "have given fifteen millions of dollars for Louisiana; they would have given fifty, rather than not possess it. They will receive one million of dollars for duties at the custom-house in New Orleans during the present year,—a sum exceeding the interest of the money they have paid for the acquisition, without taking into consideration the value of the very great quantity of vacant lands. As to the twelve years during which our vessels are to be received on the footing of national ones, they present but an illusive prospect, considering the war,[*] and the impossibility of our being able to enter into competition with their merchantmen. Besides, all will

[*] The war of France with England.

in a short time turn to the advantage of English manufactures, on account of the great facility which this place will exclusively enjoy, from its situation, to supply the Spanish colonies as far as the Equator. In a few years, the country, as far as Rio Bravo, will be in a state of cultivation. New Orleans will then have a population of about thirty to fifty thousand souls; and the new territory will produce sugar enough for the supply of North America and part of Europe. Let us not blind ourselves; in a few years the existing prejudices will be worn off; the inhabitants will gradually become Americans by the introduction of native Americans and Englishmen—a system already begun. Many of the present inhabitants will leave the country in disgust; those who have large fortunes will retire to the mother-country; a great proportion will remove into the Spanish settlements, and the remaining few will be lost among the new-comers. Should no fortunate amelioration of political events intervene, what a magnificent New France have we lost! The Creoles and French established here unite in favor of France, and cannot be persuaded that the convention for the cession of Louisiana is anything but a political trick; they think that it will return under the dominion of France."* It is important to remark, for the better understanding of the history of Louisiana, in its future developments, that the representative of France seemed to admit the possibility of what he mysteriously and quaintly called "the intervention of a fortunate amelioration of political events," by which the territory which his country had reluctantly relinquished might be recovered, and that the Creoles and the European French remaining in that territory thought that the cession was a "political trick," and that they would return "under the dominion of France."

* Martin's History of Louisiana, 2d vol., p. 244.

Before his departure, Laussat caused to be distributed among such of the inhabitants of Louisiana as had shown themselves most zealous in favor of the French Government, as a feeble testimonial of the satisfaction and goodwill of that Government, seven hundred and sixty-five pounds of powder, which, " being French," he said," was much appreciated by the inhabitants, who are ardent sportsmen."*

In another dispatch, he gives the most graphic description of the condition in which he leaves the ceded province, and comments harshly on the organization of the territorial government, which was to go into operation on the 1st of October, in compliance with the act of Congress passed on the 26th of March. He also reflects in no measured terms on the blunders which he attributes to the agents of the new proprietors of Louisiana, in taking possession of their magnificent acquisition.

" The Louisianians," he writes, " have seen themselves, with much regret, rejected for the second time from the bosom of their mother-country. At first, on their being made aware of that event, their interpretations of the cession and their comments on it showed but too clearly the extreme bitterness of their discontent. In this disposition they were secretly encouraged by the Spaniards, ... who, besides, were marvelously assisted by the natural antipathy which the Louisianians entertain for the Americans.

" Nevertheless, on the approach of the change of domination, partly from the love of novelty, partly from the hope of those advantages which were depicted to them, and perhaps also from a forced resignation to a fate which they could not avoid, they had become tolerably well disposed toward passing under the Government of the United States.

---

* Chasseurs passionnés. See the Appendix.

" But hardly had the agents of that Government taken the reins in hand, when they accumulated errors on errors, and blunders on blunders. I will refrain from enumerating them in detail to Your Excellency, Citizen Minister, but I will only, in a few words, mention the leading characteristics of their administration, such as the sudden introduction of the English language, which hardly anybody understands, into the daily exercise of public authority, and in the most important acts of private life—the affrays and tumults resulting from the struggle for pre-eminence, and the preference shown for American over French dances at public balls— the invasion of bayonets into the halls of amusement and the closing of the balls—the active participation of the American General and of the Governor in those quarrels— the inconsiderate proceedings which ensued—the revolting partiality exhibited in favor of native Americans or of Englishmen, both in the audiences granted by the authorities and in the judgments rendered—the marked substitution of American to Creole majorities in all administrative and judicial bodies—the arbitrary mixture of old usages with new ones, under the pretext of a change of domination—the intemperate speeches—the injurious precautions—the bad advisers*—the scandalous orgies —the savage manners and habits—the wretched appointments to office--what more shall I say, Citizen Minister? It was hardly possible that the Government of the United States should have a worse beginning, and that it should have sent two men† more deficient in the proper requisites to conciliate the hearts of the Louisianians. The first, with estimable qualities as a private man, has little intellect,‡ a good deal of awkwardness, and is extremely beneath the position in which he has been placed. The

---

* Mauvais entourage.   † Governor Claiborne and General Wilkinson.
‡ Peu de moyens et beaucoup de gaucherie.

second, who has been long known * here in the most unfavorable manner, is a rattle-headed fellow, full of odd fantasies.† He is frequently drunk, and has committed a hundred inconsistent and impertinent acts. Neither the one nor the other understands one word of French, or Spanish. They have, on all occasions, and without the slightest circumspection, shocked the habits, the prejudices and the natural dispositions of the inhabitants of this country. The gazettes of Philadelphia have lately published, I do not know by what mistake, a confidential dispatch of Governor Claiborne to President Jefferson, in which he speaks of the Louisianians as of ignorant but kindly disposed beings, in the treatment of whom everything could be dared with impunity, and who, unable to appreciate the value of the American institutions, are not susceptible of self-government.

"As if it were to drive them into extremities, copies of the late act of Congress to organize the Territory have recently been brought to their perusal. . . . . . Your Excellency might hear on all sides the utterance of such sentiments as these : 'Is it in this way that we are secured the benefits that were to result to us from the cession of Louisiana by France? Are these the liberties of which she seemed to have guarantied to us the preservation by an express clause of the treaty? Is it thus that she calls us to the enjoyment of the rights, advantages and immunities of citizens of the United States?'"

Laussat further speaks of the excitement as being so intense, that, at night, placards, in which insurrection was openly preached, were put up at all the corners of the streets. Crowds gathered round and copied them, preventing also their being torn away. Even public officers who attempted it were driven off. In the country, par-

---
* Connu ici de longue main sous de vilains rapports.
† Un brise raison à boutades.

ticularly in the districts of the Attakapas and of the Opelousas, which were the most populous, and which, says Laussat, "had always distinguished themselves by their ardent love for France," the dispositions which were manifested were not more favorable. "I contented myself," continues Laussat, "with observing everything in silence, or if I was provoked into breaking it at all, I did so by speaking in favor of the treaty of cession, and by representing that henceforth it would be impossible to do away with such an act. It is what the Louisianians absolutely refuse to be convinced of. They complacently feed on the idea that the First Consul has merely yielded to temporary circumstances, but that when peace shall come, and when he shall have humbled the insolence of Great Britain, he will recede from the treaty of cession. They arrange this political question in their own way, and they firmly adhere to what they have thus settled in their own minds. They make no concealment of it; they have expressed on the subject their sentiments to me, and also to the Governor, and to the American General. . . . . . .

"With regard to myself, Citizen Minister, I am very far from having such a belief. It is a dream, which I do not rank among the things which are possible. I think, on the contrary, that Louisiana being once emancipated from her colonial fetters, it would be unnatural to expect that she should ever willingly resume them and give up her new position."

He then asserts that the animosity which prevailed at the time against the Government of the United States would soon die away, unless unskillfully kept alive by the faults of the Administration. "These people," he added, "are naturally gentle and docile, although touchy, proud and brave. Besides, they are few in number, and scattered about, without experience, and without any rallying-point. The Spanish Government made it its policy to keep them entirely disconnected with public affairs, which it has accustomed them to consider with indifference, and even with a sort of abnegation. The Louisianians will not for a long time recover from such a training, and in the mean while they will gradually make up their minds to their change of circumstances, because, although their new chiefs should go astray and commit blunders, yet there are advantages inherent to the Constitution and to the situation of the United States, of which it is impossible to prevent these people from experiencing the salutary influence.

"But, on the other side, if this country is entirely abandoned to the impulsion which will be given to it, I consider it from this time as no longer existing for France. The Americans in general detest us. Those amongst them who have the least of English nature in them, are more English than French, notwithstanding their hypocritical and pompous protestations. There is not a day on which they have not proved it to me here. Add to this disposition on their part the temptations offered them by the resources of English commerce. There is no doubt that Louisiana is a vast field which England will work to its own profit. . . . . . . This probable turn of affairs might be counteracted by the innate attachment and the natural sympathy of the Louisianians for France, but one of the most prompt effects of the change of domination will be a complete revolution in the elements composing the population of this country. In less than ten years the greater portion of what is now considered as private property will have changed hands. Cause will be given to the old colonists to be disgusted with their new condition; they will be set aside, expropriated and expelled. The Government of the United States is not blind to the fact that Lower Louisiana is the key which answers for the security of their finest and most extensive possessions. They will have no rest until they shall have succeeded, either by open force, or by secret and skillful contrivances, in putting that key in the hands of full-hearted and full-blooded Americans.

"If our Government should ever look back to this country, it should be, in my opinion, only with a view of entirely detaching the Western States from the rest of the Confederacy. Such a scheme, far from being extravagant, would have, on the contrary, innumerable chances of success. Time alone will one day bring on this scission. But what is important for the French Republic is, that this scission be operated under the protection of France, and whilst generations of Frenchmen and French spirit retain their ascendency in these regions. The consequences of such a revolution would then turn infinitely to the advantage of our nation, and Louisiana, in such a state of political independence and filial alliance, would be to France of a far more inestimable value than the most important colonies."

To those who may become familiar with what I have related in my work on the "Spanish Domination in Louisiana," and in the preceding pages, and with what I shall recite in the sequel of this history, the famous Burr conspiracy, which was to convulse the public mind two years after, and which has remained to this day a mooted mystery, may not appear an altogether baseless fabric. General Wilkinson, who was destined to act in it a conspicuous part, and who had been commissioned, jointly with Claiborne, to take possession of Louisiana, departed a short time after Laussat, and sailed for New York, leaving the few companies of the United States troops which he had brought with him, distributed at the following points: New Orleans, Natchitoches, Pointe Coupee and Fort Adams.

Nothing is more apt to produce discontent in any community than the want of a circulating medium; and where discontent exists from any other sources, nothing is more powerful in contributing to bring it to its climax than this very cause. So it was in Louisiana at that time. The distress in the province had become very great from the scarcity of money. The flow of silver from Vera Cruz, which was so refreshing under the Spanish Government, had ceased with the change of dominion, and Spain showed no prompt disposition to redeem a large quantity of paper which she had set afloat in the late colony under the name of "liberanzas," and which had fallen into considerable depreciation. It became necessary to find a remedy for the evil, and Claiborne sought it in the establishment of a bank styled "The Louisiana Bank," with a capital which was susceptible of extension to two millions of dollars. Were the people pleased? Not in the least. On the contrary, this measure excited lively apprehensions. A Bank! Such an institution was entirely new to them. Many thought that it would turn out to be nothing else but legalized robbery. Was it not to issue paper money, and had they not already greatly suffered from the depreciation of French and Spanish paper? What better results could be expected from American paper? They believed it to be the renewal of what the "assignats" had been in the worst times of the French Republic. Hence the general impression was, that the country would be ultimately ruined, rather than benefited, by the newly devised plan of relief.

The militia, which was quite a respectable corps under the Spanish Government—which Laussat had partially, and with considerable difficulty, succeeded in keeping together—and which Claiborne had been attempting to retain in existence, had at last become entirely disorganized. On the other hand, most of the individuals who were flocking from all parts of the United States, had eagerly formed themselves into companies of various denominations, under the cheerfully granted patronage of Claiborne, who hoped that it would stimulate some of the natives to enroll themselves. But such was not the case. They stood apart, and looked with sullen displeasure on the new military associations, of which they were keenly jealous. Resenting the conduct of the late colonists, the Americans showed perhaps a want of policy in parading, more than was necessary, through the streets of New Orleans, with ostentatious display, and with what was thought to be an expression of defiance. The dissatisfaction was increased, a more marked estrangement from the new order of things ensued, and a line still more distinct was drawn between the two populations.

But these causes of discontent paled before those which arose from the 4th section of the act providing for the temporary government of the Territory of Orleans. By that section they were flatly denied any participation whatever in that government, as the members of their Legislative Council were to be annually selected by the President, and as all the other civil and military officers were to be appointed either by the President or by the Governor, who were authorized to choose them, if they should deem it advisable, from among those who had resided only one year in the province, and who were therefore utter strangers to the old population.* Thus it is seen that Congress was then very far from suspecting that there could exist any sovereignty whatever in

---

* As to the Legislative Council, that body could not even take the initiative in legislation, but was only to deliberate on such subjects as might be laid before them by Claiborne.

territories, not even that squatter sovereignty which has since become so famous in the vocabulary of politicians. At last, the dissatisfaction rose to such a pitch that it manifested itself in open and public acts. In the name of some of the most influential merchants of the city and of the wealthiest and most respected planters in its neighborhood, a public meeting was called for the 1st of June, in which it was unanimously determined to apply to Congress for the repeal of so much of their late act as related to the partition of Louisiana and the restriction on the importation of slaves. It was further resolved to ask for the immediate admission of Louisiana, in its original entirety, into the Union, in accordance with what was deemed the obvious intention of the treaty of cession. A committee was appointed to prepare and submit to the next public meeting the draft of a memorial to Congress. That committee was composed of Jones and Livingston, Americans, Pitot, a Frenchman, and Petit, a Creole. The second meeting, which was held in the beginning of July, was much more numerous than the first, and an enthusiastic approval was given to the report of the committee. Twelve individuals were chosen to circulate copies of it in parishes and to procure the signatures of the most notable inhabitants, without forgetting, at the same time, to collect voluntary contributions for paying the expenses of the deputies who were to be sent to Washington City with their list of grievances and their memorial for redress. The last and third meeting took place on the 18th of July. A deputation of three was resolved upon, and its members were: Derbigny and Sauvé, European French, and Destréhan, a native of Louisiana. It is evident that, in this choice, the Louisianians were guided more by their sense of outraged dignity and violated rights, than by prudential considerations of policy. Violent prejudices were to be removed; and in order to obtain this object, three deputies, with French habits, French minds and a French tongue, could not be called a judicious selection.

In the mean time, if the inhabitants below Manchac and on the right bank of the Mississippi, were adverse to the change which had taken place in their destinies by the transfer of their allegiance from the French flag to the flag of the United States, the population of that district included in the present parishes of West and East Feliciana and of East Baton Rouge, being of English descent, and composed of settlers who had originally come from the old Thirteen States, were extremely anxious for annexation to the kindred race from which they had been severed, as Spain still retained possession of the territory in which they lived, and refused to acknowledge that it was comprehended within the cession. They were incensed at the omission, on the part of the commissioners of the United States, to claim them as an integral portion of the recent acquisition, and at their abstaining to enforce that claim by physical means if necessary. In the hope of giving a pretext for an intervention in their behalf, or under the belief that they could achieve for themselves the liberation which they desired, they raised the standard of revolt against the Spanish authorities; they assembled to the number of about two hundred men, and resolved to attack the Spanish fort at Baton Rouge. But it was an ill-concerted scheme; some disagreement took place among the leaders, who had to give up the enterprise, and who took refuge across the line in the Mississippi territory. Such of their followers as relied for protection on their obscurity, or insignificancy, returned peacefully to their respective homes.*

* The repression of this insurrection cost the Spanish Government a pretty considerable outlay. As soon as the news reached Pensacola, Governor Folch

This insurrection had been preceded by one which had been headed by Kemper, one of the most redoubtable enemies of the Spaniards. To compel the release of some of his friends imprisoned by the Government which he hated, he had seized the persons of Don Vincente Pintado, a militia captain, and of the Alcalde Juan Ocono, and was threatening to attack the fort at Baton Rouge. Order was restored without bloodshed by the prudence and firmness of the ex-governor of Louisiana, Marquis of Casa Calvo, who was still lingering in the territory, and who sent troops and an armed vessel to the seat of these disturbances.*

On the 1st of October, the territorial government which had been decreed by the act of Congress of the 26th of March, went into operation, with Clairborne as Governor, and Brown as Secretary.

Boré, Bellechasse, Cantrelle, Clark, De Buys, Dow, Jones, Kenner, Morgan, Poydras, Roman, Watkins and Wikoff had been appointed members of the Legislative Council by the President.

Duponceau, a Frenchman, who subsequently obtained great celebrity in Philadelphia as a jurist, Kirby, and Prevost, a stepson, I believe, of Vice-President Aaron Burr, were appointed Judges of the Superior Court. D. Hall, an Englishman by birth, was commissioned District Judge of the United States, with Mahlon Dickens as District Attorney, and Lebreton D'Orgenoy as Marshal. Duponceau declined, Kirby died, and Prevost opened the first territorial court, alone, on the 9th of November.

departed at the head of 150 men, of infantry and cavalry, and soon reached Bayou Manchac through the lakes. But he found that tranquillity had been restored by the efforts of Governor Grandpré. (See the dispatch of Intendant Morales to Miguel Cayetano Soler, one of the Spanish ministers, dated New Orleans, Sept. 26th, 1804, and also the same to the same, October 31st, 1804. State Archives, Baton Rouge.)

* Morales to Cayetano Soler, 19th August, 1804. State Archives at Baton Rouge.

Boré, Bellechasse, Jones and Clark had been the leaders of the opposition which had arisen in the territory; they had acted the most conspicuous part in the meetings of the inhabitants; they had been the most zealous in stimulating their fellow-citizens to remonstrate against the form of government which had been forced upon them; they could not, therefore, with any consistency, aid in establishing that very government against which they had protested, and they declined accepting the proffered seats in the Legislative Council. On the 8th of October, Jones wrote on the subject to Governor Claiborne a very spirited letter, in which he said: "I cannot accept of any office under a law of which I have, from the beginning, so openly expressed my disapprobation, and which, for the happiness of my fellow-citizens, forgive me if I add, for the honor of my native country, I ardently wish to be annulled.

"When calm reflection shall have taken the place of passion and of party spirit, I flatter myself that my conduct on the present occasion will be approved. I was born an American. I glory in the name. In defence of that happy land which gave me birth my life and my fortune shall always be staked, but I cannot consent, for any consideration, to do an act which I think subversive of the rights and liberties of my fellow-citizens."

This refusal to take their seats, on the part of these gentlemen, had considerable influence on the other members, who held back in dubious suspense, without declining, but without accepting. Two months nearly elapsed, and no council could be formed, notwithstanding the incessant efforts of Claiborne to soothe and conciliate the refractory tempers he had to deal with. What was to be done in this perplexing emergency? It happened that the President, not knowing the first names of the persons whom he had selected, had contented himself with designating them by their surnames, and had sent blank commissions to be filled on the spot. Claiborne, thinking himself authorized by the necessity of the case, and anxious to avoid the mischief which would have resulted from further delay, assumed the responsibility of appointing Dorcière, Flood, Mather and Pollock in the place of the four gentlemen who had declined the President's appointment.* In this way a mere quorum was obtained on the 4th of December.†

The Territory was divided by this Legislative Council into twelve counties, with an Inferior Court for each, composed of one judge, and the practice therein was provided for, as well as in the Superior Court. Suits were to be instituted by a petition in the form of a bill in chancery. These words, "A bill in Chancery," grated strangely on the ears of the old inhabitants of Louisiana. What was meant by chancery? What was a bill in chancery? The attempt to enlighten them on the subject would have been ludicrously futile; hardly any one would have understood the explanation, and no explanation or instruction was sought, or given. The definition of crimes and the mode of prosecution in criminal cases, according to the common law of England,

---

* Martin's History of Louisiana, p. 252, 2d vol.

† Julien Poydras, of Pointe Coupée, one of the most influential and wealthiest men in the Territory, had greatly contributed by his efforts to the formation of the Council. In his letter of acceptance to Claiborne he had used this language: "The President of the United States having appointed me a councilor, I conceive it a duty to accept. If those who have great interest in the country should decline serving it when called upon, their conduct would be unwarrantable. I could offer many plausible excuses, such as age, insufficiency of talents, self-interest, &c. But in so doing I should not act the part of a patriot. A beginning must be made; we must be initiated into the sacred duties of freemen and the practices of liberty." This reasoning, however, had no influence on Cantrelle, who also refused a seat in the Council. Commenting on the course pursued by Poydras, Governor Claiborne said: "His acceptance is a fortunate occurrence, and his conduct and reasoning form a happy contrast to the part acted by Jones, Clark and others."

were adopted, and were not more intelligible to the people. Common Law! What was it? They were told that it was "unwritten law." Unwritten law! That, indeed, was something new under the sun for those who had always been governed by precise laws, regulations and ordinances! How could law be unwritten? Where was it to be found? They were answered, it was "that law which draws its binding force from immemorial usage and universal reception in England." Is it to be wondered at if they shook theirs heads in utter bewilderment? But when it was added, for a clearer elucidation of the matter, that they might, if they pleased, take it to be " a body of rules, principles and customs, which derived their authority and sanctity from their filtration for centuries through the thick strata of successive British generations, and which, originating in natural justice and equity, or local customs, were only to be evidenced by the records of judicial decisions scattered through hundreds of volumes written in a language which they did not comprehend, the only distinct impression which such an explanation left on their minds was, that the common law was the most unfathomable of all laws, and some mysterious and complicated engine of oppression, which would certainly be used to their detriment. They much better understood the provision which was made for the inspection of flour, pork and beef. They also understood the charter of incorporation which was given to the city of New Orleans, and other acts relating to the formation of a public library and to the establishment of navigation and insurance companies. The creation of a university, which was intrusted with the locating of schools in each county, was also within their comprehension; but as no appropriation of funds was made for those seminaries of learning, the people were sadly puzzled to discover how the views of the Legislature were to be carried into execution for the education of their children. Some may have thought that the "Common Law," in its amplitude, had provided for the statutory omission, and that some relief for the projected schools might be found in a "chancery bill." But vain was the hope, if it ever existed; and this first attempt to educate the population proved an absolute failure.

The Council adjourned in February, 1805, after having appointed a committee to prepare a civil and a criminal code, with the assistance of two professional men, for whose remuneration five thousand dollars were appropriated. A moderate remuneration for such a work, if worthily done!

After this sketch of the proceedings of the Council, it will not be out of place to make a rapid review of the acts of the Governor. As before stated, the new territorial organization went into operation on the 1st of October, and Claiborne was sworn into office[*] on the 3d of that month, by Pitot, mayor of the city. On that very day, giving information of the fact to Mr. Madison, Secretary of State, he said, "Mr. Brown, Secretary of the Territory, is at Natchez, and does not propose adventuring into New Orleans until about the close of this month; and I think this is a very wise precaution, for the city is not yet free from that dreadful scourge, the yellow fever." In the proclamation which he issued a few days after, to convene the Legislature, he used this language: "In the course of my late administration, which, from a variety of circumstances, was accompanied with peculiar difficulties, I received from the officers, civil and military, a zealous and able co-operation in all measures for the public good, and from the people in general an indulgence and support which encouraged harmony and in-

---

[*] Claiborne's dispatch to Madison, on the 3d of October, 1804.

sured the supremacy of the law." This document must have been very acceptable to the Louisianians, for it put them in possession of a direct official contradiction, proceeding from the best and most authentic source, of those offensive suppositions and apprehensions which had been entertained against them by that Congress who had voted the odious territorial organization to which they were to be subjected after the 1st of October.

On the 18th of August, Mr. Madison had written to Claiborne* that the continuance and conduct of the Spanish officers at New Orleans justly excited attention; that, in every view, it was desirable that those foreigners should be no longer in a situation to affront the authority of the United States, or to mingle by their intrigues in the affairs of the Territory; and that the 1st of October, the day fixed for the inauguration of the territorial government, would be an epoch which might be used for letting it to be understood that their stay, so much beyond the right and the occasion for it, was not seen with approbation, leaving the mode and manner of the intimation to the discreet judgment of the Governor. In answer to this communication, Claiborne wrote on the 5th of October: "There is no doubt with me but that the Spanish officers encourage the discontents which arise here," and on the 9th he hastened† to communicate to the Marquis of Casa Calvo the instructions he had received from the Secretary of State in relation to his desired departure and that of his followers.

An able pamphlet,‡ written in French, and entitled

---

* State Archives at Baton Rouge. † State Papers at Baton Rouge.

‡ Esquisse de la situation politique et civile de la Louisiane depuis le 30 Novembre 1803 jusqu'au 1er Octobre 1804, par un Louisianais. Diverso intercà miscentur mænia Luctu. Virg. Æneid. A la Nouvelle Orléans, de l'imprimerie du Télégraphe, chez Beleurgey et Renard, rue Bourbon.

"A Sketch of the Political and Civil Situation of Louisiana from the 30th of November, 1803, to the 1st of October, 1804, by a Louisianian," had been widely circulated, and had produced so great a sensation, that Claiborne thought it of sufficient importance to make it the subject of a special communication to Mr. Madison. This pamphlet contained an almost complete review of all the grieveances of which the Louisianians complained, and the tone of moderation and conviction in which it was conceived added to its force and effect. It attacked unsparingly the conduct of the American Government and some of the acts of Claiborne. But, at the same time, it spoke respectfully of that magistrate's character, and rendered unequivocal justice to his integrity and to the purity of his intentions. This is the more remarkable, from the fact that the excitement then prevailing among all the classes of that population for whose perusal it was intended had been carried to its utmost point of intensity. Claiborne's communication* to Madison is an elaborate vindication of himself against the charges specified in the pamphlet, and if not a refutation, it is at least a positive denial of many of the assertions contained in it, and in a document of which, however, he was ignorant,—that is, the dispatch of Laussat to the French Government on the state of the late colony, and which is inserted in the preceding pages. Claiborne's defence seems imbued with the spirit of a man who is conscious of having done nothing but what was right; and in perusing it, the reader can hardly refrain from coming to the conclusion that the Governor, whether correct or not in his views, was at least in earnest, and believed every line which he wrote.

On the 19th of October, as an instance of the inflam-

* Claiborne to Madison, 16th of October, 1804, p. 8 of the Executive Journal at Baton Rouge, vol. 1.

mable temper of the population, Claiborne informed Madison that a private affair—the caning of a Frenchman in the street by an Englishman—had nearly produced a very serious affray, in which the Americans had sided with the Englishman, and the French or those of French extraction with his adversary. "This city," he said, "requires a strict police; the inhabitants are of various descriptions, many highly respectable, and some of them very degenerate. Great exertions have been made (and with too much success) to foment differences between the native Americans and the native Louisianians — every incident is laid hold of to widen the breach, and to excite jealousy and confusion—the intrigues of certain late emigrants from France, and some of the satellites of the Spanish Government, have tended considerably to heighten the discontents in this quarter. Everything in my power has been done to counteract these intrigues, but with little success. The fact is, that the affections of many of the Louisianians for their mother-country are warm, and others seem attached to the Spanish Government. I have to complain also of some of the native Americans; they are rash, and very imprudent. The newspaper publications likewise add to my embarrassments; they give inquietude to the Louisianians and trouble to me. The present state of things here mortifies me excessively, but I hope that good order will be preserved, and harmony soon restored. These objects shall constitute my first and greatest cares."

Another of his communications to the Secretary of State at Washington, dated on the 26th of the same month, contains these sagacious observations: "Although there has been much discontent manifested in New Orleans and its vicinity, yet I do not believe that the disaffection is of a serious nature, or that it is extensive. That some difficulty should attend the introduction of American government and laws, was to have been expected. On every change of dominion, discontents, more or less, invariably ensue; and, when we take into view the various and rapid transitions and transfers which have taken place in this territory, we may indeed felicitate ourselves on the great share of good order which has been preserved. The most arbitrary governments find advocates, and the most unprincipled despot is seldom without friends. When despotism reigns, silence (produced by fear) is received as the test of contentment, and a tame submission to injustice as proof of the public sanction. Had an administration, rigid, coercive and unjust, been introduced into the ceded territory, under the authority of the United States, I am persuaded there would have been less murmuring, and a delusive appearance of popular approbation. But under a mild and just government, which admits of freedom of speech and of opinion, the man, indeed, must be little acquainted with human nature who would expect to find in Louisiana union in expression and sentiment."

On the next day, in another communication which he intended to be in justification of his course of administration, he observed: "My object has been to avail the public of the services of the well-informed and deserving citizens, and as there are many native Americans of this description residing in Louisiana, it ought not to be a matter of surprise that some of them should have received offices. The ancient Louisianians hold as many appointments as their numbers and qualifications entitle them to, and therefore they ought not to complain."

On the 3d of November, Claiborne received the information that a vessel, with near two hundred French men on board, who had been prisoners of war to the British Government, but who had successfully risen against their captors on the high seas, had entered the

Mississippi, with the design of coming up to New Orleans with their prize.* He immediately wrote to Capt. Samuel Davis: "If this statement be correct, no refuge or shelter can be given in any port of this Territory to the said vessel, and she must depart as soon as possible. You will therefore proceed immediately to Plaquemine, where you will find that vessel detained, and ascertain how far the statement made to me be true. If you find that the vessel is a prize, or that she was captured in the manner described, you will hand the letter herein inclosed to the person who shall appear to have command of said vessel, and urge her immediate departure." On the same day, giving information of this fact to Madison, he said: "I determined that, under the treaty, it would be improper to permit this vessel to find an asylum here, and I was further convinced that the sudden arrival of so many Frenchmen in this city (whose habits and situation are not, probably, calculated to render them useful members of society) might disturb the harmony of our community."

But Claiborne's intentions were completely defeated. The two hundred Frenchmen who had captured the vessel had no idea of going back to sea in her, and many of them deserted her and found their way to the city. Finally, she and her cargo were seized by the U. S. Marshal at the request of British claimants, and the case had to be adjudicated upon by judicial authority. As to those Frenchmen who had thus made their escape, Claiborne wrote to Madison, "that they had already proved themselves unworthy members of society, and that he was therefore the more desirous to prevent the men remaining on board from landing." †

The arrival of those two hundred Frenchmen with

---

* Claiborne to Davis, 3d November, 1804, p. 21, Executive Journal, vol. 1.
† Claiborne to Madison, 15th Nov., 1804, p. 27. Do.

the vessel "Hero," which they had captured, to the great contentment of the Louisianians, who had no friendly feelings for the English, had produced some degree of agitation, which was greatly increased by another incident. On the 15th of November, the Sheriff, Louis Kerr, had received an order from the Superior Court to hold to bail Captain Manuel Garcia, a Spanish officer, at the suit of D. B. Morgan, in the sum of six hundred dollars and upward. Morgan was a native citizen of the United States, and had been for some time past employed as a surveyor for Spain in West Florida. For some cause or other he had been arrested by the Spanish authorities on Spanish ground, and with the property in his possession had been put on board of a Spanish galley commanded by Garcia and bound to Pensacola. On her way down the lakes, the galley anchored at the mouth of Bayou St. John, from which Morgan made his escape to New Orleans. On his arrival, he applied to Folch, the Governor of Florida, who was then in New Orleans on his way to Pensacola, in order to obtain the restoration of his property, which was detained on board of the galley. But his application not having been attended to, Morgan had recourse to judicial process against Garcia, who also happened to have come to the city, and against whom a writ was issued. This Spanish officer, on his being waited upon by the Sheriff, refused to be taken into his custody, or in lieu thereof, to give bail, although several gentlemen offered to go security for him. He declined their services, on the ground that such were his orders from his superior officers, and declared that he would submit only to force. He requested, however, the Sheriff to await the arrival of Governor Folch, whom he had sent for and expected every moment To this the Sheriff gave his assent; but Governor Folch, being confined to his room by indisposition, sent his son, who directed Captain Garcia not to give bail, and to resist by force any attempt to remove him from the house in which he was. This youth was excited, and in giving these orders, used some intemperate language. By this time the room in which this scene took place had become crowded, principally by Spaniards, many of whom were armed. The Sheriff was about ordering in a few men whom he had left in the street, when he was entreated to desist a few minutes longer, and to see Governor Claiborne, the Marquis of Casa Calvo and Governor Folch, between whom it was presumed that this affair could be amicably arranged, on the plea that, in virtue of Governor Claiborne's permission to the Spanish officers generally to pass through the ceded territory from Baton Rouge to Pensacola, Captain Garcia thought himself protected by the law of nations and the good faith of the American Government from arrest. Leaving Garcia in the hands of his friends, the Sheriff called on Judge Prevost, and related to him the circumstances of the case. The Judge's stern answer was, that the writ must be executed, or that the Sheriff would have to abide the consequences of its non-execution. This officer, therefore, had nothing else to do but to obey, and on his way back to Garcia's house, being informed that a large concourse of people, at least two hundred in number, had gathered round it in a state of great excitement, he thought it advisable to add to his constabulary escort the reinforcement of a corporal and three men whom he took from the guard-house. But on his making his appearance where Garcia was, swords were drawn by his opponents, and he found himself too weak to effect the arrest which he had contemplated. Finally, Garcia surrendered to a detachment of the United States troops commanded by Lieutenant Wilson.*

* L. Kerr's report to Claiborne, 17th Nov., 1804. Executive Jour., p. 29, vol. 1

The Spanish authorities were much excited by this outrage, as they considered it, and the Marquis of Casa Calvo wrote to Governor Claiborne a letter, in which he expressed his feelings of indignation, and maintained that Captain Garcia could not be made liable on American territory for what he had done by the command of his superiors in the Spanish dominions. Claiborne was no less irritated by the tone assumed toward him, and returned, on the 16th of November, this spirited answer to Casa Calvo: "I have read with respectful attention your Excellency's letter of this evening, and in reply I have only to state, that the Spanish officer you allude to is in arrest in virtue of a process regularly issuing from the Superior Court of this territory. Upon what grounds it may have been issued, or how far it may have been irregular, it is not within my province to inquire. The powers of the Judiciary are derived immediately from the General Government of the United States. The court is independent, and not subject to my control. If the arrest of the officer be illegal, the court will certainly direct his liberation on a proper application to that effect. I cannot perceive in this transaction any just cause for the agitation which has been discovered on the part of your Excellency, and of Governor Folch. In a verbal message to me from your Excellency, expressions are conveyed derogatory to the Government which I represent, as well as personally offensive to me, and I learn with regret that Governor Folch has used language equally exceptionable. Your Excellency can easily conceive my feelings on receiving such communications. No threats of this nature, you may be assured, can induce me to swerve from my duty; and permit me to add, that the power does not exist which can *shake* the authority of *my country* over this territory."

A long correspondence ensued on the subject between

Casa Calvo and Claiborne, and it was at last agreed to leave the case in the hands of the judiciary, as appears by a communication of the 22d of November, in which Claiborne said to Casa Calvo : "I learn with pleasure that you are at last convinced that the affair of Captain Garcia is placed on the only footing which the existing laws of this territory can admit of. How far my permission for Governor Folch and suite to pass by this route to Pensacola entitles Captain Garcia to exemption from arrest, is matter for the consideration of the court, and on this question there is no doubt but the decision will be a proper one."

But as soon as one difficulty was settled another would spring up, and Claiborne was never allowed to enjoy long any degree of undisturbed tranquillity. Thus he had hardly got rid of the Garcia controversy, when another arose between him and Casa Calvo, in consequence of his refusing to carry into execution certain judgments which had been rendered against certain individuals by the Spanish authorities. Casa Calvo bitterly complained of this refusal, which made it impossible for him to collect "the arrears of the king's revenue." At last Claiborne put an end to it by addressing to the Marquis this final note on the subject: " A mere acquaintance* with the laws of the United States, sir, would be sufficient to inform you that they will suffer no judgment to be executed, but those rendered in their own courts; that in those courts foreign judgments, however respectable the tribunal which rendered them, are only evidence, and require the confirmation of an American judgment before any execution can flow therefrom. I have therefore only to add, that in all cases of this nature, the courts of this Territory are open to you, and

---

* Claiborne to Casa Calvo, 22d of November, 1804. Executive Journal, page 89, vol. 1.

are vested with the power (no longer in my hands) of redressing any grievances which you may have occasion to complain of."

Another source of tribulation to Claiborne was the necessity of soon preventing altogether that slave-trade to which the ancient population was accustomed, and which could not continue under the new *régime*. It was a task which, had he been so disposed, it would have been impossible, for the present, to perform strictly and effectually. Negroes were daily smuggled into the Territory through the Spanish possessions, by the way of the lakes, Borgne, Pontchartrain and Maurepas, to the districts of East Baton Rouge and Feliciana, and also through the innumerable bayous which empty into Barataria Bay and other sea outlets. At the North, Claiborne was accused of conniving at the trade, and he had to defend himself against the accusation. In a communication* of the 25th of November to the President, he says: "The late admission of foreign negroes has also been a subject of complaint against me. The Searcher of all hearts knows how little I desire to see another of that wretched race set his foot on the shores of America, and how from my heart I detest the rapacity that would transport them to us. But, on this point, the people here were united as one man. There seemed to be but one sentiment throughout the province. They must import more slaves, or the country was ruined forever. The most respectable characters could not, even in my presence, suppress the agitation of their temper, when a check to that trade was suggested. Under such circumstances, it was not for me, without the authority of previous law, or the instructions of my government, to prohibit the importation."

---

* Page 48, vol. 1, Executive Journal.

On the 27th of November, the peace of New Orleans was disturbed by a quarrel between the city militia and the troops of the United States, arising from a feeling of jealousy which had sprung up between them, and Claiborne was again called upon to settle this difficulty, on a formal complaint laid before him by the City Council against Lieutenant Wilson, the same who had arrested Captain Garcia. A court-martial had to be convened, which took cognizance of the charges brought by the city authorities against the lieutenant, and the affair was finally settled, not without leaving, however, some ill blood fermenting on both sides.

The new Legislative Council, which it had been so difficult to form, met on the 4th of December, as before stated, and Claiborne addressed to them an appropriate message on that important occasion, which was the harbinger in Louisiana of the era of self-government by the people. He particularly recommended to them the subject of education: "Let exertions then be made," he said, "to rear up our children in the paths of science and virtue, and to impress upon their tender hearts a love of civil and religious liberty. Among the several States of the Union an ingenuous emulation happily prevails, in encouraging literature and literary institutions, and some of these are making rapid strides toward rivaling the proudest establishments of Europe. In this sentiment, so favorable to the general good, you, gentlemen, I am certain, will not hesitate to join."

Shortly after this paragraph comes this passage, which, no doubt, was designed to quiet some anxiety then existing among the clergy, as to their position under the new order of things: "As connected with the education of youth," he remarks, "every constitutional encouragement should be given to ministers of the Gospel. Religion exalts a nation, whilst sin is the reproach of any people. It prepares us for those vicissitudes which so often checker human life. It deprives even misfortune of her victory. It invites to harmony and good-will in this world, and affords a guaranty for happiness hereafter." This was certainly very acceptable to the religious-minded part of the community, but any political body, attempting to act on such a recommendation from the Executive, and to determine what kind of constitutional encouragement, under our institutions, can be given by legislation to ministers of the Gospel, would probably find the subject fraught with considerable difficulties.

It is a curious fact that, when thus going through the solemnity of opening, with commendable dignity and with apparent reliance on those he addressed, the first Legislative Assembly in Louisiana, Claiborne was aware that there was among the population very little faith in the duration of the system of government which he was gravely introducing to their supposed grateful acceptance. This is proved by his communication of the 11th of December to Madison :* "The President's Message,' he says, "has been translated into the French language, and I will take care to have it circulated among the people. It will tend to remove an impression which has heretofore contributed greatly to embarrass the local administration, to wit—that the country west of the Mississippi would certainly be re-ceded to Spain, and perhaps the whole of Louisiana. So general has been this impression, particularly as it relates to the country west of the Mississippi, that many citizens have been fearful of accepting any employment under the American government, or even manifesting a respect therefor, lest at a future time it might lessen them in the esteem of

* Page 55, Executive Journal, vol. 1.

Spanish officers. This opinion as to re-cession has been greatly encouraged by the Marquis of Casa Calvo and Governor Folch, who are really so uninformed of the strength of the United States, as to suppose that the Spanish monarch could readily acquire and maintain possession of Louisiana, and I doubt not but they have made such representations to their court."

The yellow fever had, in the autumn of this year, been very fatal in New Orleans, and in connection with other remarks on this subject, Claiborne, in a message to the Legislative Council, on the 14th of December, had called the attention of that body to a plan devised by Jefferson to prevent the recurrence of such a calamity. Referring to the probable growth of New Orleans, the President said: "The position of New Orleans certainly destines it to be the greatest city the world has ever seen. There is no spot on the globe to which the produce of so great an extent of fertile country must necessarily come. It is three times greater than that on the eastern side of the Alleghanies, which is to be divided among all the seaport towns of the Atlantic States. In the middle and northern parts of Europe, where the sun rarely shines, they may safely build cities in solid blocks without generating disease; but under the cloudless skies of America, where there is so constant an accumulation of heat, men cannot be piled on one another with impunity. Accordingly, we find this disease confined to the solid-built parts of our towns, and the parts on the water-side, where there is most matter for putrefaction, but rarely extending into the thin-built parts of the towns, and never into the country. In these latter places it cannot be communicated. In order to catch it, you must go into the local atmosphere where it prevails. Is not this, then, a strong indication that we ought not to contend with the laws of nature, but should decide at once that all our cities shall be thin-built?"

After these introductory observations, the President expressed the opinion that, in building cities in the United States, the people should take the checker-board for their plan, leaving the white squares open and unbuilt forever and planted with trees. "As it is probable,"* he observed to Claiborne, " that New Orleans must soon be enlarged, I inclose you this same plan for con sideration. I have great confidence that, however the yellow fever may prevail in the old part of the town, it would not be communicated in that part which should be built on this plan, because this would be like the thin-built parts of our towns, where experience has taught us that a person may carry it after catching it in its local region, but can never communicate it out of that. Having very sincerely at heart that the prosperity of New Orleans should be unchecked, and great faith, founded, I think, on experience, in the effect of this mode of building against a disorder which is such a scourge to our close-built cities, I could not deny myself the communication of the plan, leaving it to you to bring it into real existence, if those more interested should think as favorably of it as I do. For beauty, pleasure, and convenience, it would certainly be eminent." It must be apparent to all those who may look at the map of the city of New Orleans as it stands at this time, in 1859, that thus far, in its ever progressive enlargement, the plan recommended by Jefferson has met with very little attention.

Toward the end of December, the elements of discord which had distracted the country seemed to come to a temporary truce, and to be disposed to allow the expiring year to make in peace its exit from the stage; for Clai

---

* Executive Journal, vol. 1, page 56.

borne wrote to Madison on the 31st: "I have* never witnessed more good order than at present pervades this city, and, as far as I can learn, the whole Territory. I discover also, with great pleasure, the existence of a friendly understanding between the modern and the ancient Louisianians. The winter amusements have commenced for several weeks; the two descriptions of citizens meet frequently at the theatre, at the balls and other places of public amusement, and pass their time in perfect harmony. A great anxiety exists here to learn the fate of the memorial to Congress. The importation of negroes continues to be a favorite object with the Louisianians; and I believe the privilege of electing one branch of the Legislature would give very general satisfaction. Immediate admission into the Union is not expected by the reflecting part of society, nor do I think there are many who desire it." But this roseate hue, which had spread over the horizon, flattering Claiborne with halcyon days, was soon to give way to the darkening shades of a stormy sky. Claiborne had suffered himself to be blinded by a pleasing delusion. The discontent which was rankling in many hearts was too deep and too bitter to be soothed by the occasional amenities of social intercourse in the public places to which he refers. That discontent arose from feelings which were proof against the fascinations of the ball-room, the attractions of theatrical performances, the bewitching influence of musical entertainments, or the sparkling bowls of the festive board. It was hardly possible that it should have been otherwise; for if the act of Congress, dividing Louisiana into two territories, and providing for the temporary government thereof, had excited the indignation of its inhabitants, and if Boré, Bellechasse, Jones, Cantrelle and Clark,

---

* Executive Journal, vol. 1, page 61.

when refusing to take their seats in the newly appointed Legislative Council, and to aid in carrying into execution "an act" which they had proclaimed to be an infringement of the rights and dignity of those to whom it was to be applied, had been approved by the immense majority of their fellow-citizens, it is due to them to say that the debates in Congress, on the discussion of that very act, had been of such a nature as to wound their just susceptibilities. Many members of that body, who had opposed its passage, had taken of it the same view in which it presented itself to the people of Louisiana. In relation to the power vested in the Governor "to convene and prorogue the Legislative Council, whenever he might deem it expedient," Mr. Leib, in the House of Representatives, had said "that it made that body the most dependent in the United States; and that, when the power of prorogation vested in the Governor was duly considered, it seemed to him that the people of the Territory would be much better without such a body. It was a royal appendage." . . . .

Not only did Mr. Gregg agree with Mr. Leib, as to the objectionable feature that gentleman had pointed out, but he was also opposed to the power given to the President to appoint the members of the Council. "It was a burlesque. How was the President to know anything of their qualifications? From whom was he to derive that information except from the Governor? And why, therefore, should not that officer himself be at once the appointing power?" Mr. Varnum was of opinion that they were establishing a kind of government hitherto unknown in the United States. "Why not make provision for the election of a legislative body by the people? Policy, justice, propriety and the obligations of the treaty of cession required it at their hands." Mr. Elliot declared that, "to authorize the President to appoint the members of the Legislative Council, was neither consistent with the spirit of the Constitution, nor with the treaty."

"It is extremely difficult," said in reply Mr. Eustis of Massachusetts," to form any system of government for this Territory consonant with our ideas of civil liberty under the Constitution of the United States. Before we determine the principle on which the Council is to be formed, it is necessary distinctly to understand the genius, the manners, the disposition and the state of the people to be governed. The treaty has been resorted to by my colleague, to show that they are entitled to elect their own Legislature. It says: *The inhabitants of the ceded territory shall be incorporated in the Union of the United States, and admitted as soon as possible, according to the principles of the Federal Constitution, to the enjoyment of all the rights, advantages and immunities of citizens of the United States.* Are the people of Louisiana admitted into the Union at this time, or not, with all the rights of citizens of the United States? If they are so admitted, they are undoubtedly entitled to all the rights of citizens of the United States. If not, there remains another inquiry: Are they qualified from habit, and from the circumstances in which they are placed, to exercise those high privileges? If they are both entitled and qualified to enjoy them, we can have no hesitation in pronouncing the bill grounded on a wrong principle, and that it ought to be rejected. But I do not consider the subject in this light. The people are, in my opinion, unprepared for, and undesirous of, exercising the elective franchise. The first object of the Government is to hold the country. How? By protecting the people in all their rights, and by administering the Government in such a manner as to prevent any *disagreement* among them—to use *no other term.* Suppose the people called upon to choose those who are to make laws for themselves, does the information we possess justify the belief that this privilege could be so exercised as to conduce to the peace, happiness and tranquillity of the country? I apprehend not.

"According to this bill, the Governor and Council are to make the laws. Suppose the Council is in session and the Governor possesses no power to prorogue them. Suppose they should engage in acts subversive of their relation to the United States, would not this power be of essential utility? It appears to me indispensably necessary that a vein of authority should ascend to the Government of the United States, until the people of the territory are admitted to the full enjoyment of State rights. From that knowledge of this people which I have been able to acquire, I have formed an opinion that authority should be constantly exercised over them, without severity, but in such a manner as to secure the rights of the United States and the peace of the country.

"The government laid down in this bill is certainly a new thing in the United States; but the people of that country differ materially from the citizens of the United States. I speak of the character of the people at the present time. When they shall be better acquainted with the principles of our Government, and shall have been desirous of participating in our privileges, it will be full time to extend to them the elective franchise. Have not the House been informed from an authentic source, since the cession, that the provisions of our institutions are inapplicable to them? If so, why attempt, in pursuit of a vain theory, to extend political institutions to them for which they are not prepared? I am one of those who believe that the principles of civil liberty cannot suddenly be engrafted on a people accustomed to a *régime* of a directly opposite hue. The approach of such a people to liberty must be gradual. I believe them at present totally unqualified to exercise it. If this opinion be erroneous, then the principles of this bill are unfounded; if, on the contrary, this opinion is sound, it results that neither the power given to the President to appoint the members of the Council, nor to the Governor to prorogue them, are unsafe, or unnecessary.

"The extension of the elective franchise may be considered by the people of Louisiana a burden instead of a benefit. I have understood that there is none of that equality among them which exists in the United States; grades are there more highly marked, and they may deem it rather a matter of oppression to extend to them the privilege which we deem inestimable, and with the value of which we have been long familiar.

"Before we decide this principle, it is absolutely necessary to consider the relation of these people to the United States. I consider them as standing in nearly the same relation to us as if they were a conquered country. By the treaty they are, it is true, entitled to the enjoyment of all the rights, advantages and immunities of citizens of the United States, and to be incorporated into the Union as soon as possible, according to the principles of the Federal Constitution—but can they be admitted now? Are they at this moment so admitted? If not, they are not entitled to these rights; but if they were, I should doubt the propriety of extending to them what might be misused.

"It is very natural and honorable to gentlemen o liberal minds to be desirous of extending to these people the privilege enjoyed by our own citizens; but sentiments of this kind, however liberal and praiseworthy, may be carried in the face of facts, and may operate injuriously on those they are intended to benefit. Upon the whole, as the bill only purports to provide for a temporary government, and as, in the course of a year, we shall have more information respecting the country, when it will be in our power, in case such information shall justify it, to extend all the privileges which gentlemen seem so desirous to grant, I hope the Committee will not agree to strike out this section."

Mr. Lyon said in reply, that the bill contained many traits which were exceedingly disgusting to him. "I think," he continued, "that these people have a right, by nature and by treaty, to have some concern in their own government; and although they may not be entirely qualified for self-government, and we may not be willing to put them on the same footing with the people of a free and independent state, I know of no reasons why they may not be allowed, by their representatives, to come before the Governor in an organized way, with an expression of their wishes and of their wants, and to propose for his adoption laws which they may think fitting and salutary for their country. I am not ready to say with Mr. Leib, the gentleman from Pennsylvania, that I wish to take from the Governor the power of convening and proroguing the Legislative Assembly or Council. I am willing, for the present, that he should have that power, as well as an unqualified negative on their bills. In that case, how can the representatives of that people injure our government? It is the business of the Governor, appointed by the President, to watch over them for the interest of the nation. His power will be ample for the protection of that interest. When they ask his assent to those things that are fitting and proper, he will give it, I hope; when they ask it for those things which are not fitting or proper, he will, no doubt, refuse it; and if they should at any time become troublesome, he will prorogue them, and tell them to go home about their business. I cannot refuse these people the humble boon, the pitiful specimen of liberty which consists in laying before the Governor, by their representatives, for his consent, the bills they wish passed into laws for their local accommodation and for their satisfaction with respect to their rights and their property; neither would I mock their feelings by a Legislative Council appointed by the President. I do not think it fits his character. How is he to divine who it is best to appoint? I would as soon compliment Bonaparte with that power. I dare say he is better acquainted with the people there. But the gentleman from Massachusetts seems to think these people are not desirous of exercising the power of electing their Legislative representatives. If that is the case, do we not owe something on this score to principle—to consistency—to the national honor pledged by treaty? If there is danger on that score (which I am pretty certain there is not), let the government be so organized that it can go on without the representatives of those districts who neglect or refuse to elect."

"But the most ludicrous idea I have heard expressed on the subject is, that these people must be kept in slavery until they are taught to think and behave like freemen. Establish the government proposed, it is said, and let them learn under that to enjoy the rights and benefits of freemen. I wonder how much longer this probationary slavery it to last, in order to bring about the purpose proposed? For my part, I believe they have had it longer than has done them any good. I really wish to know how much longer this apprenticeship is to continue, and what are the symptoms by which we are to know when slaves are fitted to be freemen."

Mr. Lucas seemed to have taken up the strange idea that the United States were bound by the treaty of cession, only to secure to the people of Louisiana as large a portion of liberty, and as full an enjoyment of their rights, as they would have been permitted to possess, had they remained under the Government of France or Spain. "But the United States," he said, "had done more than they were bound. For instance, the privilege of the Habeas Corpus had been extended to the inhabitants of the Territory—a privilege which they had never possessed when they were connected either with France or Spain. An argument was drawn from the treaty, that these people are to be admitted to the absolute enjoyment of the rights of citizens; but gentlemen would not deny that *the time when*, and the *circumstances* under which this provision of the treaty was to be carried into effect, were submitted to the decision of Congress. It has been remarked, that this bill establishes elementary principles of government never previously introduced in the organization of any Territory of the United States. Granting the truth of this observation, it must be allowed that the United States had never had devolved upon them the obligation of making provision for the government of any people under such circumstances. Legislators must not rest on theory, but must raise their political structures on the basis of the moral and intellectual state of the people for whom they are to be made. He did not wish to reflect on the inhabitants of Louisiana, but he would say that they were not prepared for a government like that of the United States. They had been governed by Spanish officers, exercising authority according to their whim, which was supported by military force, and it could not be maintained that a people thus inured to despotism were prepared on a sudden to receive the principles of our government. It was questionable whether there was in Europe a nation to whom these principles would be so advantageous as they were to us.

"It should be recollected by gentlemen who so strenuously advocated the abstract principle of right, that the people of Louisiana had not been consulted in the act of cession to this country, but had been transferred by a bargain made over their heads. As a proof that this act had not been received with approbation by them, it must be borne in mind, that, when they saw the American flag hoisted in the room of the French, they shed tears. Was it not a proof that they were not so friendly to our government as some gentlemen imagined? He was persuaded that the people of the Mississippi Territory would not have acted in this manner. There is no doubt but that after they shall have experienced the blessings of a free government, they will wonder at their having shed tears on this occasion; but they must, in the first instance, feel those blessings."

Mr. Macon's first objection to the bill was, that it created a species of government unknown to the laws of the United States. "I believe," he added, "that the territorial government, as established by the ordinance of the old Congress, is the best adapted to the circumstances of the people of Louisiana, and that it may be so modified as best to promote their convenience. The people residing in the Mississippi Territory are now under this kind of government. Is it not likely that the people of Louisiana will expect the same form of government and laws with their neighbors; and is it not desirable for the general peace and happiness that there should be a correspondence between them? If they are as ignorant as some gentlemen represent them (and of this I know nothing), will they not expect the same grade of government with the inhabitants of the Mississippi Territory, with whom they will have a constant intercourse? Although the Mississippians lived previously under the Spanish Government, when formed into a Territory, no inconvenience resulted from having granted to them the privileges which we desire to extend to Louisiana. It is said, in reply to this observation, that a large number of inhabitants of that Territory were Americans. It is true that many of them were native Americans, but some also were Spanish.

"The simple question is, what kind of government is better fitted to this people? It is extremely difficult to legislate for a people with whose habits and customs we are unacquainted. I, for one, declare myself unacquainted with them; nor would I, in fixing the government, unless for the safety of the Union, do an act capable of disgusting the people for whom it is adopted. It will be a good policy to avoid whatever is calculated to disgust them. My opinion is that they will be better satisfied with an old-established form of government, than with a new one. Why? Because they have seen it established in the adjacent Territory of Mississippi, and know the manner in which it operates. If there are bad men in Louisiana, will anything be more easy than to disgust the people against the General Government, by showing that they have given one kind of government to the people of the Mississippi Territory, and a different kind to them? In my mind, it is sound policy to give them no cause of complaint. We ought to show them that we consider them one people."

Mr. Campbell was very energetic in his denunciations of the bill. "On examination," said he, "it will appear that it really establishes a complete despotism; that it does not evince a single trait of liberty; that it does not confer one single right to which they are entitled under the treaty; that it does not extend to them the benefits of the Federal Constitution, or declare when, hereafter, they shall receive them. I believe it will, on investigation, be found difficult to separate liberty from the right of self-government; and hence arises the question now to be decided, whether we shall countenance the principle of governing by despotic systems of government, or support the principle that they are entitled to be governed by laws made by themselves, and to expect that they shall, in due time, receive all the benefits of citizens of the United States under the Constitution.

"By section 4, all legislative power is vested in a Governor and thirteen Councilors appointed by the President. The people have no share in their choice. The members of the Council are only to aid the Governor; they have no right to make laws themselves. The words of the section are:

"'*The Governor, by and with the advice and consent of said Legislative Council, or of a majority of them, shall have power to alter, modify, or repeal the laws which may be in force at the commencement of this act.*'

"That is, the *Governor* makes the laws by and with the advice of the Council. They are not to deliberate on what shall be law; but he, like some ancient potentates, is to suggest to them what, in his opinion, is proper to be law. This is the proper construction of this section, or I do not understand it. *He* is to make; *they* are not to make the laws, and submit them for his approbation. He makes them, and asks his creatures whether they will agree or not to them. I hope that we are not prepared to establish such a system as this.

"If then the proposed system be despotic, it is proper in the next place to inquire why it is erected over the people of Louisiana? Is their condition such as not to qualify them for the enjoyment of any of the blessings of liberty? Are they blind to the difference between liberty and slavery? Are they insensible to the difference of laws made by themselves, and of laws made by others? We have no evidence that this is the case. If we retrace the progress of liberty among other nations, I would ask gentlemen where they find reason for the opinion that the people of Louisiana are unfitted for the enjoyment of its blessings? They will find that it has, in many cases, arisen among people far less enlightened. I trust, therefore, we shall not determine that, because the people of that country have not investigated the full value of free government, they are not qualified to enjoy any freedom. I ask gentlemen to point out, when they talk of the abuse of the elective franchise, a solitary instance where the people have abused the rights they acquired under it. They will find it hard to point one. Whereas I ask them for a single instance, in the annals of mankind, where despotism has not been abused. This they will find it difficult to adduce. One principle cannot be denied: when power is vested in the people, they exercise it for their own benefit, and to the best of their skill. They have no object in abusing it; for they are to be the first victims of its improper exercise. I ask them, where is the danger of placing in the hands of the people the right of choosing those who are to regulate their own internal concerns? Surely, when gentlemen depicted the great danger of this investiture of power, they did not consider that the very act before us subjects all laws to the control of Congress, and that in all cases wherein Congress shall negative them, they will have no validity. Where, then, is the danger? Will it be injurious to the United States that the Legislature of the territory, chosen by the people, should make laws for their own accommodation, without prejudice to the Union? It cannot. I feel surprised when I hear gentlemen say, 'We ought to be cautious in giving power, lest it should be used in opposition to the interests of the Union.' How can this be, when this Government has the appointment of all the officers, and particularly the Governor and judges, and when to the Legislature is only confided the management of internal concerns, when they have no authority to form connections with foreign powers, or to form any coalition with their neighbors, in opposition to the measures of the General Government? If the people are already hostile to the United States, it is evident that it is not the severity of despotism that will make them friendly. I ask, how are we to account for this change in our deportment toward them? Not long since, these people were congratulated on their releasement from a despotic government, and were invited into the arms of a government ready to extend to them all the blessings of self-government. Now, we are about to damp all their hopes, and to send forth a few creatures to lash them with despotism and to make all their laws. We go further. We do not even hold forth the idea that, on a future day, they shall make their own laws. Our language is, if, notwithstanding the despotism we extend over you, you patiently bear your chains like good subjects, we may withdraw them, and let you govern yourselves. If this is not the language of gentlemen, I do not comprehend it.

"It is stated by a gentleman from Massachusetts (Mr Eustis) that it is difficult to form a government for such a people; and that it is necessary previously to consider the habits and manners of the people to be governed. I am sorry, at this enlightened day of the world, to hear arguments in favor of despotism, so often used before. How does a despot govern his subjects? He tells them and makes them believe that they are ignorant, and unqualified to govern themselves. Considering their ignorance, he tells them he does them a favor by governing them, and that they have nothing to do but to obey. This is the doctrine on which monarchy and despotism rose. In proportion as it prevails, despotism prevails; and in proportion as it is destroyed, the principle of liberty prevails. Let us not say that the people are too ignorant to govern themselves. No, give them an opportunity, and they will acquire knowledge, at least sufficient to make a proper choice of those best qualified to superintend their public concerns. This will act as a stimulus to those who expect to be chosen, to make themselves qualified. But I never knew before this day, that for a people to be fit for the enjoyment of liberty, they must, for a certain time, be under the scourge of despotism.

"The same gentleman inquires, In case the elective franchise shall be withheld, what hold have we on the people of Louisiana? This inquiry is readily answered. We shall have power to repeal all laws they make; and a governor appointed by us will have the nomination of all military and civil officers who administer the government. If this is not a hold and a check upon them, I know not what it is. While examining this point, it may not be improper to inquire what is the best way of making these people most attached to the United States; and whether that end will be answered by denying them all liberty, and by making a radical difference between their government and that of territories similarly situated with themselves? Let me for once observe, that it is the true policy of this Government to conciliate the people to us, to our manners and laws, to show them that, considering them as a part of the Union, they have the right to expect the enjoyment of privileges unknown to them before, instead of disappointing their hopes and compelling them to serve a long quarantine before they are admitted to a participation of those rights which we ourselves possess.

"It has been intimated that these people are unfit to

govern themselves; but I am acquainted with no information that warrants this inference. I believe that information of a different nature derived from other gentlemen is more to be relied on, because those who give it are better informed. As to their interests, I cannot conceive what can have rendered them so different from those of the Mississippi Territory. They were once the same people and under the same government, and they cannot have since become unfit for self-government. The best information assures me that a considerable proportion of the population is composed of American citizens, amounting, perhaps, to one-fourth or one-fifth of the whole. There are in it, also, many British subjects, not so ignorant as to be entirely insensible to the benefits of a free government.

"Is there, too, anything in the Spanish Government whose effects are so degrading as to disqualify a man from enjoying freedom? If this were the case, it would have been an argument against accepting the country at all. Have we not, however, understood that this great measure has been effected with a double view of accommodating the United States, and benefiting the people of Louisiana, by extending to them the advantages of a free government? Shall we consider ourselves at liberty to barter them, to view them as cattle, and govern them as such? I hope not.

"One idea relied on by gentlemen is worthy of notice. It takes for granted that the people do not wish for a free government. I ask gentlemen if they are really serious in this remark? If they are, the argument will be conclusive in giving them, if they choose, an absolute despotism. In that case, if we knew it were the desire of the people to have a king, whatever might have been our opinions of the benefits of liberty, it would be our duty to give them one. Gentlemen cannot think so, nor would they suffer the United States to degrade their character by such an act. I conceive the United States bound to give them a republican form of government, and to consider, therefore, not what they may desire, but what will suit their ultimate interest, while it promotes the interest of America at large. One gentleman observes that we ought to consider the people of Louisiana as totally distinct from, and as not possessed of any similar habits with ourselves. I trust, however, we shall consider them as a part of the human species. I believe the gentleman will find the human character the same in different parts of the globe. If this principle had been pursued, liberty had never flourished; if the people had never enjoyed liberty till they were ripe for it, how many ages of darkness would have passed away? But the fact is, the people suffer oppression to an astonishing degree—despotism grinds them till human nature can endure no more, and then they break their chains in a revolt. I therefore can see no force in the argument of waiting till they are ripe for liberty. How ripe? If they have never tasted its benefits, how can they know them? I trust, therefore, that we shall extend to them the same rights as are enjoyed by the other Territories, and that it shall not be said that we have met to make laws for a people whom we have called our friends and brothers, different from the laws which we have made for ourselves."

Mr. Jackson succeeded Mr. Campbell on the floor, and was proceeding to attack the bill on the same grounds with his predecessors on his side of the question, and was objecting to certain injurious reflections cast on the people of Louisiana by Huger of South Carolina, who had intimated that, in his opinion, the Louisianians were no better than negroes, and consequently were to be treated as that degraded race, when he was interrupted by

Mr. Huger, who explained that his meaning was not such as the gentleman's language implied, and declared that he had spoken barely by way of comparison, to show that nothing was more dangerous than to pass from the extreme of slavery to perfect liberty.

"I will not pretend to say," resumed Mr. Jackson, "that I accurately comprehend the meaning of the gentleman. His words were: *they ought to be looked upon as a certain portion of people among us and treated as such.* If he did not allude to slaves, I do not know to whom he did allude. But as he says he did not allude to them, I will avoid any remark that may implicate him in such an allusion."

When Mr. Jackson took his seat, up started Mr. Holland. "Gentlemen maintain," he said, "that if we deny the people of Louisiana the right of self-government, we deny them everything. But before they are permitted to make laws, ought they not to understand what law is? If we give power to these people, will they not choose persons as ignorant as themselves? It is a fact that many of the most respectable characters in Louisiana conceive the principle of self-government a mere bubble, and they will not consider themselves aggrieved if it is not extended to them. Does the history of nations show that all men are capable of self-government? No such thing. It shows that none but an enlightened and virtuous people are capable of it; and if the people of Louisiana are not sufficiently enlightened, they are not prepared to receive it. For what are they prepared? To remain in a passive state, and to receive the blessings of good laws; and receiving these, they have no reason to complain."

Many more members of the House of Representatives than those whose names are here mentioned took their share in these debates. The subject was also fully discussed in the Senate, and Congress, after the most lengthy deliberations, voted by a large majority for the passage of the bill, which, however, had been strongly opposed in that body, and with as vehement language as could be desired by the Louisianians, to whom it was so objectionable.

These debates, and their final result, it must be admitted, were of a character to wound deeply the just susceptibilities of the people of Louisiana, and to keep up that excitement of which I have already related some of the baleful effects. Huger, of South Carolina, a gentleman of French descent, had been understood to say on the floor of the Capitol, notwithstanding his subsequent explanations of a retractive nature, that the French of Louisiana were hardly above the standard of a certain portion of the population of the United States, which was, with propriety, deprived of all political rights. Another, without going so far, had said that they ought to be treated as a conquered people. Many had maintained that it was impossible to suppose that a population long subjected to the debasing governments of France and Spain were fit subjects to be intrusted with the dangerous possession of liberty, without a gradual training and a slow process of emancipation. The whole length and breadth of the debate was narrowed down to this question: "*Are the people of Louisiana capable of self-government?*" "If they are, and if we are convinced of it," said the warmest advocates of the bill, "we give it up; for we admit that it establishes a form of government hitherto unknown to us, and at variance with our other institutions. We admit that it would be an infamous act of tyranny if applied to any other people, but we are persuaded that it is demanded by the necessities of the case." This was avowedly the basis on which stood "the bill to organize the government of the Territory of Orleans, and that bill, notwithstanding the extraordinary features which it was admitted to possess, was voted a law by an immense majority in Congress—which law was readily sanctioned by the President of the United States. Thus the Louisianians, a few months after they had been delivered to the warm embraces and paternal protection of that great Republic which invited all mankind to the enjoyment of liberty, had the intense mortification of being branded, before the whole world, with a solemn official declaration that they were incapable of self-government—a declaration which derived an additional humiliating pungency from the circumstance that it was made by a democratic Congress, and promulgated by Thomas Jefferson, that great apostle of universal liberty, and the immortal author of that celebrated document in which all men are proclaimed to be born 'free and equal.'"

These debates, of which I have here given a short abridgment, deserve to be studied with care, and possess much interest, particularly when taken in connection with the projected annexation of Mexico, Cuba, Nicaragua and other Territories, and with the probable expansion of the protection, if not of the government, of the United States, over nations whose vitality is threatened with destruction, and who, it is believed, are destined to seek shelter under the strong eagle wing of their colossal neighbor.

It will also be remarked that no one, in those days, seems to have imagined that there could exist any degree of sovereignty, not even squatter sovereignty, in the people of a territory of the United States, and that the introduction and advocacy of a doctrine which was destined in after years to assume proportions of great magnitude in the politics of the country, would then have probably been looked upon, how ever sound and correct it might be, as nothing short of a monstrous heresy.

Before dismissing from further consideration this bill for the organization of the ceded province of Louisiana, it may not be improper to notice a feature in it which is important in itself, but which is entitled to still greater importance from its connection with a question which perhaps overshadows every other on the political map of the country. It is that Congress, in 1804, when it passed that bill, exercised the contested power of preventing the importation of slaves into territories, for it regulated, on that memorable occasion, the slave-trade between the slave States and a slave Territory. To give that act its due weight, one must recollect that it was sanctioned by Thomas Jefferson, and by that party which had lately defeated the Federal party, and had proclaimed itself pledged to a strict construction of the Constitution, and to an uncompromising opposition to the assumption of powers not expressly delegated to the General Government. Should the adversaries of slavery, as it exists in some of the States of our Confederacy, ever obtain the ascendency in both Houses of Congress, it is probable that they will attempt to legislate on the slave-trade between the States, and that this act to organize the Territory of Orleans in 1804, will afford a precedent of which they will avail themselves with that pertinacity of purpose and that fanatical vigor of intellect they have ever displayed in assailing that institution, which the South considers as its very life-blood and the indispensable condition of its existence, and also as the very breath and essence of its prosperity.

CHAPTER II.

GOVERNOR CLAIBORNE'S ADMINISTRATION.

1805.

ON the 4th of January, 1805, the petition of "the merchants, planters, and other inhabitants of Louisiana," signed by Destréhan, Sauvé and Derbigny, their delegates, had been read and referred in the Senate of the United States. It was an able review of the grounds upon which rested the organization of the territorial government, which was declared to be oppressive and degrading. " Misrepresented and insulted," said the Delegates, " it cannot be deemed improper to show how groundless * are the calumnies which represent us in a state of degradation, unfit to receive the boon of freedom. How far any supposed incapacity to direct the affairs of our own country would release the United States from their obligation to confer upon us the rights of citizenship, or upon what principle they are to become the judges of that capacity, might, we believe, fairly be questioned; for we have surely become not less fit for the task since the signature of the treaty than we were before that period; and that no such incapacity was then supposed to exist, is evident from the terms of that instrument, which declares that we are to be admitted as soon as possible according to the principles of the Con

---

* Annals of Congress, 8th C., 2d S. Gales & Seaton, page 1601.

stitution. If the United States, then, may postpone the performance of this engagement until, in their opinion, it may be proper to perform it, of what validity is the compact; or can that be called one, of which the performance depends only on the will of the contracting party? . . .

"To deprive us of our right of election, we have been represented as too ignorant to exercise it with wisdom, and too turbulent to enjoy it with safety. Sunk in ignorance, effeminated by luxury, debased by oppression, we were, it was said, incapable of appreciating a free constitution, if it were given, or feeling the deprivation if it were denied. The sentiments which were excited by this humiliating picture may be imagined, but cannot be expressed consistent with the respect we owe to your Honorable Body. . . .

"We could not imagine what had produced the idea of our effeminacy and profusion; and the laborious planter, at his frugal meal, heard with a smile of bitterness and contempt the descriptions published at Washington of his opulence and luxury.

"As to the degree of information diffused through the country, we humbly request that some more correct evidence may be produced than the superficial remarks that have been made by travelers, or residents, who neither associate with us, nor speak our language. Many of us are native citizens of the United States, who have participated in that kind of knowledge which is there spread among the people; the others generally are men who will not suffer by comparison with the population of any other colony. Some disadvantages as to education in the higher branches of literature have lately attended us, owing to the difficulty of procuring it, but the original settlement of the province was marked by circumstances peculiarly favorable in this respect. It was made at no distant date, at a period when science had obtained a great degree of perfection, and from a country in which it flourished; many individuals possessing property and rank which suppose a liberal education, were among the first settlers; and, perhaps, there would be no vanity in asserting that the first establishment of Louisiana might vie with that of any other in America for the respectability and information of those who composed it. Their descendants now respectfully call for the evidence which proves that they have so far degenerated, as to become totally incompetent to the task of legislation.

"For our love of order and submission to the laws, we can confidently appeal to the whole history of our settlement, and particularly to what has lately passed in those dangerous moments, when it was uncertain at what point our political vibrations would stop; when national prejudice, personal interest, factious views, and ambitious designs, might be supposed to combine for the interruption of our repose; when, in the frequent changes to which we have been subject, the authority of one nation was weakened before the other had established its power. In those moments of crisis and danger, no insurrection disturbed, no riot disgraced us; the voice of sedition was silent; and before a magistrate was appointed, good morals served instead of laws, and a love of order instead of civil power. It is then as unjust to task us with turbulence, as it is degrading to reproach us with ignorance and vice."

The delegates, in this memorial, energetically insisted on the rights of the inhabitants of Louisiana to be promptly admitted into the Confederacy as the citizens of a Sovereign State, and ably discussed the 3d section of the treaty of cession on which they relied in support of their pretensions.

"The inhabitants of the ceded Territory," they observed, "are to be *incorporated into the Union of the United States*. These words can in no sense be satisfied by the act in question. A territory governed in the manner it directs may be a province of the United States, but can by no construction be said to be incorporated into the Union. To be incorporated into the Union must mean to form a part of it. But to every component part of the United States the Constitution has guaranteed a republican form of government, and this, as we have already shown, has no one principle of republicanism in its composition. It is, therefore, not in compliance with the letter of the treaty, and is totally inconsistent with its spirit, which certainly intends some stipulations in our favor. For if Congress may govern us as they please, what necessity was there for this clause, or how are we to be benefited by its introduction? If any doubt, however, could possibly exist on the first member of the sentence, it must vanish by a consideration of the second, which provides for our admission to the rights, privileges and immunities of citizens of the United States. But this territorial government, as we have shown, is totally incompatible with those rights. Without any vote in the election of our Legislature, without any check upon our Executive, without any one incident of self-government, what valuable *privilege* of citizenship is allowed us? What *right* do we enjoy, of what *immunity* can we boast, except, indeed, the degrading exemption from the cares of legislation and the burden of public affairs?"

They further argued that the words "as soon as possible" of the treaty, which stipulated their admission into the Union, could never be so construed as to allow Congress the right of deferring that admission indefinitely. If it might be procrastinated for two years, no reason could be seen why it might not be postponed for twenty, or a hundred, or totally omitted. It could not be supposed that the United States had only bound themselves to admit Louisiana into the Union as soon as they should think proper, and no more; for a treaty implies a compact; and what compact can arise from a reservation to perform, or not to perform, as one of the parties should deem expedient? Hence they had no doubt that the words "as soon as possible" meant, as soon as the laws necessary for the purpose could be passed.

In connection with that part of the act which restricted the importation of slaves into the Territory, the delegates said: "To the necessity of employing African laborers, which arises from the climate and the species of cultivation pursued in warm latitudes, is added a reason in this country peculiar to itself. The banks raised to restrain the waters of the Mississippi can only be kept in repair by those whose natural constitution and habits of labor enable them to resist the combined effects of a deleterious moisture and a degree of heat intolerable to whites. This labor is great; it requires many hands, and it is all-important to the very existence of our country. If, therefore, this traffic is justifiable anywhere, it is surely in this province, where, unless it is permitted, cultivation must cease, the improvements of a century be destroyed, and the great river resume its empire over our ruined fields and demolished habitations.

"Another evil," they said, " not indeed growing out of this act, but of great moment to us, is the sudden change of language in all the public offices and administration of justice. The great mass of the inhabitants speak nothing but the French. The late government was always careful, in the selection of officers, to find men who possessed our own language, and with whom we could personally communicate. Their correspondence with the interior parts of the province was also carried on chiefly in our own language. The judicial proceedings were indeed in Spanish, but being carried on altogether in writing, translations were easily made. At present, for the slightest communication an interpreter must be procured. In more important concerns, our interest suffers from not being fully explained. A phrase, a circumstance, seemingly of little moment, and which a person not interested in the affair will not take the trouble to translate, is frequently decisive, and produces the most important effects. That free communication so necessary to give the magistrate a knowledge of the people, and to inspire them with confidence in his administration, is by this means totally cut off, and the introduction of *vivâ voce* pleadings in the courts of justice subjects the party who can neither understand his counsel, his judge, nor the advocate of his opponent, to embarrassments the most perplexing, and often to injuries the most serious."

The delegates concluded their address in this earnest and pathetic strain:

"Duly impressed, therefore, with a persuasion that our rights need only to be stated to be recognized and allowed; that the highest glory of a nation is a communication of the blessings of freedom; and that its best reputation is derived from a sacred regard to treaties; we pray you, Representatives of the people, to consult your own fame and our happiness by a prompt attention to our prayer; we invoke the principles of your revolution, the sacred, self-evident and eternal truths on which your governments are founded; we invoke the solemn stipulations of treaty; we invoke your own professions and the glorious example of your fathers, and we adjure you to listen to the one and to follow the other, by abandoning a plan so contradictory to everything you have said, and they have taught—so fatal to our happiness and the reputation of your country. To a generous and free people we ought not to urge any motive of interest, when those of honor and duty are so apparent; but be assured that it is the interest of the United States to cultivate a spirit of conciliation with the inhabitants of the Territory they have acquired. Annexed to your country by the course of political events, it depends upon you to determine whether we shall pay the cold homage of reluctant subjects, or render the free allegiance of citizens attached to your fortunes by choice, bound to you by gratitude for the best of blessings, contributing cheerfully to your advancement to those high destinies to which honor, liberty and justice will conduct you, and defending, as we solemnly pledge ourselves to do, at the risk of fortune and life, our common constitution, country, and laws."

The President, in his annual message, delivered on the 8th of November, 1804, to Congress, had called the attention of that body to the practicability of ameliorating the form of the territorial government of Louisiana. On the 25th of January, 1805,* John Randolph, chairman of the committee appointed to take into consideration this part of the message, and to whom had also been referred the memorial here partly recited, the original of which was in the French language, but with an English translation annexed to it, made a report on the subject in the House of Representatives. He said that it was only " under the torture" that the 3d article of the treaty of cession could be made to speak the language ascribed to it by the memorialists, or could countenance, for a mo-

---

* Eighth Congress, 2d Section, p. 2014, Gales & Seaton.

ment, the breach of good faith which they had conceived themselves justified in exhibiting against the Government. "But because," said he, "the memorialists may have appreciated too highly the rights which have been secured to them by the treaty of cession, the claim of the people of Louisiana on the wisdom and justice of Congress ought not to be thereby prejudiced. Relying on the good sense of that people to point out to them that the United States cannot have incurred a heavy debt in order to obtain the Territory of Louisiana, merely with a view to the exclusive or special benefit of its inhabitants, your committee, at the same time, earnestly recommend that every indulgence, not incompatible with the interests of the Union, may be extended to them." Whereupon the committee submitted the following resolution: "*Resolved*, That provisions ought to be made by law, for extending to the inhabitants of Louisiana the right of self-government." The committee, before coming to this conclusion, had given permission to the delegates of the inhabitants of Louisiana to address to them such remarks as they might conceive to be favorable to the elucidation of the question which was so interesting to their constituents. Availing themselves of the privilege conceded to them, the Louisiana delegates submitted to the committee an elaborate and able argument in support of the views which they had taken of the rights of those whom they represented, and particularly insisted on the injustice of "procrastinating the incorporation of the *present* inhabitants of Louisiana into the Union," begging the committee, at the same time, "to make some allowance for the disadvantage under which they labored to express themselves in a language which was not altogether familiar to them."

Notwithstanding their zeal and the ability which they displayed, Derbigny, Sauvé and Destréhan were not as successful in their efforts as was desired. On the 2d of March, however, an act was approved, "providing for the government of the Territory of Orleans," by which the President was authorized to establish therein a government, in all respects similar to that of the Mississippi Territory, in conformity with the ordinances of the old Congress in 1787, except so far as related to the descent and distribution of estates, and the prohibition of slavery. As to the inhabitants of the Territory, they were authorized, as soon as the number of its free population should reach sixty thousand souls, to form for themselves a constitution and State government, in order to be admitted into the Union upon the footing of the original States, "in all respects whatever," provided that Congress "should be at liberty, at any time prior to the admission of the inhabitants of the said Territory to the right of a separate State, to alter the boundaries thereof as they might think proper."

Twenty-five representatives were to be elected by the people—which was something gained—instead of the thirteen members chosen by the President, and who heretofore had constituted the legislative body. These representatives, who were to be elected for two years, were to be convened by the Governor in the city of New Orleans, on the 1st Monday of November, 1805. Certain qualifications as to residence and citizenship were required, with a fee simple estate of two hundred acres of land. The upper House, to which was given the name of "Legislative Council," was composed of five members,* to be chosen by the President of the United States, with the advice and consent of the Senate, out of ten individuals selected by the House of Representatives of the Territory. Their period of service was five

---

* Judge Martin's History of Louisiana, 2d vol., p. 260.

years, but as they could, at any time, be removed by the President, it is evident that they were under his control to a considerable extent. The only qualification required from them was a freehold estate of five hundred acres of land. This was about the amount of modification made to the first act of territorial organization which had excited so much discontent, and it is evident that this modification was not sufficiently liberal to afford much gratification, for the little of self-government which was granted to the Louisianians carried with it so many checks and curbs, that it was a mocking shadow rather than a pleasing and substantial reality.

In relation to this subject, Claiborne, on the 21st of April, thus wrote to Madison: "The law of Congress for the government of this Territory will not give general satisfaction. The people had been taught to expect greater privileges, and many are disappointed. I believe, however, as much is given them as they can manage with discretion, or as they ought to be trusted with until the limits of the ceded territory are acknowledged, the national attachments of our new brothers less wavering, and the views and characters of some influential men here better ascertained. I particularly attend to those persons who were formerly in the Spanish service, and are permitted by their Government to remain in Louisiana as pensioners, or in the enjoyment of their full pay." And on the 4th of May, he said: "The agents,[*] Messrs. Sauvé, Destréhan and Derbigny, are preparing for publication a pamphlet in which I fear much will be said which will tend to agitate the public mind. I have seen Messrs. Sauvé and Derbigny, and find the latter much disappointed and dissatisfied...... For my own part, I am still convinced that an early introduction of the

---

[*] Executive Journal, 2d vol., p. 145.

entire representative system in Louisiana would be a hazardous experiment." So anxious was he, however, to do away with that general feeling of discontent, that, in a circular addressed to the sheriffs of the Territory on the 9th of May, he says: "I am fully aware that many parts of your duty will be unpleasant, and may subject you to the ill-will of those who may, through your public agency, be made to feel the energy of the law. But there is a manner of discharging an unpleasant duty which never fails to soften resentment, and most generally begets the friendship of those with whom we act. I will only recommend the observance at all times of the utmost equanimity of temper and politeness of conduct."

Claiborne had been reappointed Governor; Graham had been appointed Secretary, and Sprigg and Mathews Judges of the Superior Court, with Prevost, who was already on the bench.

On the 4th of November, the House of Representatives met in New Orleans, and selected the ten individuals out of whom the President of the United States was to form a Legislative Council for the Territory. Their choice fell on Bellechasse, Bouligny, D'Ennemours, Derbigny, Destréhan, Gurley, Jones, Macarty, Sauvé and Villeré. The President selected Bellechasse, Destréhan, Macarty, Sauvé and Jones, thereby giving ample satisfaction to the Louisianians, as he had thus allowed the creole element to preponderate in that important body.

On the same day, when the act " further providing for the government of the Territory of Orleans" became a law, the President approved another act, " for ascertaining and adjusting the titles and claims to lands within the Territory of Orleans, and the District of Louisiana." This act was a Godsend to the lawyers, who, to the dismay of the litigation-hating population of Louisiana, were flocking from all quarters to settle in its bosom, and who eagerly tendered their services to those who were in need of their assistance.

The act above alluded to applied only to the confirmation of such grants or sales of land as had been made by the Spanish and French Governments in territories of which they were in actual possession. In the mean time, Morales, whose presence in New Orleans was so obnoxious to the Government of the United States, on account of his continuing to exercise his functions of Spanish Intendant on American territory, and particularly on account of his numerous grants and sales of land in that part of West Florida claimed as included in the acquisition of Louisiana, and against which the act of the 2d of March was aimed, had been in vain endeavoring to retire to Pensacola, wherein he conceived himself entitled to carry on his functions of Intendant. But Folch, the Governor of Florida, hated Morales, and denied his pretensions. Morales appealed to the Captain-General of Cuba, who decided in his favor, and cited orders of the king in support of his opinion. But Folch, who seems to have been countenanced by the Marquis of Casa Irujo, the Spanish Minister to the United Sates, disregarded the alleged orders from the King, and set at defiance the Captain-General. He sent Don José de Clouet with a detachment of troops, with which he was to watch Morales at Dauphine Island and Mobile Point, and arrest him on his way to Florida. The Governor further instructed * the officer in command of fort Barrancas, at Pensacola, to imprison Morales in that fortress, should he succeed in eluding the grasp of De Clouet, and arrive at the spot where his presence was not desired. He also threatened Carlos Grandpré, Governor of the Baton Rouge district, to deprive him of his command, if

---

* Dispatch of Morales, New Orleans, 9th November, 1805, to Don Miguel Cayetano Soler, Ministro de Hacienda, Madrid.

he recognized Morales as Intendant. All that he contented himself to do for the relief of that officer, was to offer him, as an asylum for himself and his employees, the fort of Mobile, where he would be permitted to deposit his archives.

Yielding to the complaints of the Government of the United States, the Marquis of Casa Irujo, the minister sent to them by Spain, had remonstrated with Intendant Morales on the concessions and sales of land which he was daily making in the Territory in dispute between the two governments, and had advised him to suspend his proceedings. On the 20th of December, Morales, who still styled himself "Intendant of Louisiana," wrote from New Orleans a dispatch to Casa Irujo, in which he said that, by virtue of the royal ordinance of the 22nd of October, 1798, concerning the Spanish Colonial intendencies, he possessed the exclusive power, freely and without any interference from any authority in America, however exalted, to make concessions, grants, distributions, and sales of land as he might think best conducive to the interest of his Majesty, which both of them had so much at heart; therefore, that he could, without giving any just cause of offence, refuse to have any communication with the minister on the subject, but that, as he was convinced that the minister did not intend to assume an authority to which he could have no pretensions, but was merely volunteering advice with the best of motives, he,* Morales, would not hesitate to make known to him the reasons why he pursued the course which he had adopted.

"In a ministerial dispatch of the 20th of last February, 1805,"† says Morales, "I was informed that the

---

* Archives of State, Baton Rouge. Extracts from the Archives of Indies in Seville.

† Antes y en el interim que se efectua la cesion ó traspaso de su soberania.—Ministerial Dispatch.

King expected *that I should draw from this branch of revenue (the sale of lands), with my well-known zeal, all the profits of which it was susceptible for the royal treasury.*" He then alludes to several other communications, from which it clearly results, that the King wished him to make for the royal exchequer as much money as he could out of the public lands in the ceded provinces, whilst they were yet in a state of transit from one government to another. Such instructions were, certainly, unworthy of the royal majesty, as it could hardly be denied that they were of a fraudulent character. In another passage of the same dispatch, he says to Casa Irujo,* that it would be good policy to encourage the idea that all that part of West Florida, including the District of Baton Rouge, as far as the western bank of the Rio Perdido, in which he had been making large sales of land, would be finally abandoned to the United States, because without the prevalence of such an idea, and if it was believed that Spain would retain possession of that territory, the lands would become valueless. "Not only," says the shrewd and money-making Intendant, " it would be expedient to allow this belief (creencia) to circulate, but it would be still more profitable to persuade the people that, when the cession shall be allowed to take place, Spain, before making it, will take care to stipulate for the confirmation of all the sales or grants of land previously made by her officers in all the ceded territories, and will thereby secure her former colonists against the hard conditions imposed on them by Congress in the above recited Act of the 2nd

---

* Si, Señor Marques, como hombre puedo equivocarme en mi juicio, pero vivo en la creencia de que el momento que se pretenda persuader es errada la de que la Florida Occidental pertenecerá a los Estados-Unidos, y que el Rey la conservará como parte integrante de sus dominios, en el mismo momento debe renunciarse á sacar utilitad alguna de sus tierras. Certainly, **a very poor compliment paid by the Intendant to his master.**

of March, with regard to the verification and settlement of land claims in the Territory of Orleans and District of Louisiana.*

In this very interesting dispatch,† he begs leave to call the attention of the Marquis of Casa Irujo to the fact, that all the sales and concessions of land made by the Governors, or other Spanish authorities in Louisiana, during thirty years, did not bring a maravedi into the royal exchequer, and he boastingly remarks that, whilst his jurisdiction as Intendant was questioned, and whilst he was awaiting to be re-clothed with the powers appertaining to his office, he had skillfully availed himself of the circumstances offered by the cession of Louisiana, which, of course, gave immediate value to what had hitherto possessed none whatever, and had succeeded in putting into the King's coffers fifty thousand dollars—a sum which would have been much greater, he affirmed, if he had not been counteracted and checked by Claiborne, the American Governor, and by the Spanish Governor Folch, who ruled at Pensacola.

The Intendant concludes his dispatch in these words: "The royal treasury has not had to disburse anything in relation to those lands, because the purchasers assumed the expenses of survey and all other costs, which have not been inconsiderable, and which, therefore, may be looked upon as a part of the product of those sales. This sum ought to be considered (to use a common saying)

---

* Para que las ventas y concesiones hechas por el Gobierno Español no queden sujetas á las duras condiciones que pusó el Congreso en su acto, ó decreto de 2 de Marso de este año para arreglar y verificar los titulos y pretenciones de los poseedores de tierras en el territorio de Orleans y distrito de la Luisiana.

† Yo causante de que la intendencia fuese reintegrada en lo que le correspondia, aprovechando de la circonstancia que ofreció la cesion de la Luisiana he conseguido hayan entrado en cajas Reales mas de cincuenta mil pesos. Habrá sido mucho mas sin los embarazos del Gobierno Americano y del comandante Folch.

as a windfall. Had it not been believed that the Territory of Baton Rouge would become a possession of the United States, its inhabitants being accustomed to get lands without paying a cent for them, it would have been impossible to obtain from that source any funds for the royal treasury; and nevertheless, the way in which I managed it is criticised—which management consisted in secretly circulating the report that Spain would soon part with that Territory; obstacles and embarrassments are thrown in my way by those who should protect me, with a view to prevent me from obtaining all the results which I should get without such opposition; and, finally, indefatigable efforts are used to diminish my merits in these transactions, and weaken the credit which I should be entitled to claim, thus rendering painful to me what should have been a cause of gratulation. This is, however, the fate of the man who thinks of nothing but the strict accomplishment of his duties; but, fortunately, if I do not succeed in putting down the false charges brought against me, one consolation shall never be wanting, and it is that which I shall draw from my conscience."* It must not be forgotten, whilst reading this curious dispatch, that when the Intendant was thus secretly circulating the report that Spain would soon abandon the

* .... La Real Hacienda no ha tenido desembolso alguno, pues los compradores han satisfecho los gastos de apeo, medida, &c., que han sido de bastante consecuencia, y que pueden considerarse parte del producto de las tierras. Dicha suma, como se dice vulgarmente, debe mirarse caida del cielo. Sin la creencia que el Territorio de Baton Rouge iba á ser possecion de los Estados-Unidos, estando como estaban acostumbrados estos habitantes á conseguir tierras sin desembolso, nada habria producido este ramo de Real Hacienda, y á pesar de ello, se critica mi manejo, se me ponen obstaculos y embarazos por los que deben protegerme, para que no consega todo lo que sin tales inconvenientes habria logrado, y por ultimo se practican diligencias y establecen recursos para diminuir el merito, y aun para que me produzca pena y desagrado lo que habrá de proporcionarme satisfaciones. Disgracia grande del hombre que trabaja y se esmera en llenar sus deberes! Pero me quedo el recurso de que si mis descargos no fueron suficientes, &c.

district of Baton Rouge, the Spanish Government was loudly and bitterly complaining of the grasping and unjust arrogance of the United States in claiming it as comprehended within the ceded Territory.

Thus Morales was still lingering in New Orleans, much to the annoyance of Claiborne. As to the Marquis of Casa Calvo, he was preparing to make an excursion through the colonial provinces of Spain in the neighborhood of the United States as far as Chihuahua; and the remainder of the Spanish troops had at last been removed to Pensacola. The intended departure of the Marquis was a great relief to Claiborne and to others, to whom his presence had been very unacceptable. The Spanish guard which Caso Calvo retained about his person had been an object of complaint. Claiborne had requested him to dispense with that unnecessary display, and that officer having acceded to it, Claiborne had written to him a note, on the 4th of January, to thank him for having complied with his wishes. "The existence of your guard," said he, "was not considered an object of serious concern, since I was well assured that your Excellency would disapprove and repress any interference on their part with the citizens. But, as complaints were made, I thought that it would conduce to harmony to have your guard withdrawn from the streets. The protection due to your Excellency is prescribed by our laws, and every officer of this government will be happy to render it." * The importance attached by the complainants to the Marquis's guard can hardly be conceived, and the bombastic Resolutions which were introduced in the City Council on this subject by a member of that body, become almost ludicrous, when contrasted with the naked fact, that those Spanish troops which were represented

---

* Executive Journal, p. 68, vol. 1.

in those Resolutions "as dangerous to the peace of the city and to the sovereignty of the United States," consisted only of a corporal and four men posted at the dwelling of the Marquis.*

Another cause of annoyance to Claiborne was the rivalry and hatred existing between the ex-Intendant Morales and the ex-Governor Casa Calvo, whilst they remained in Louisiana to wind up the affairs of the King of Spain. In their conflicts, they constantly appealed to the American governor, who, of course, declined all interference, and had even to check them whenever they pretended to exercise any authority over matters which, by the change of sovereignty, had been withdrawn from their jurisdiction. Claiborne † also complained more than once, that Edward Livingston and Daniel Clark, moved by their hostility to him and by dangerous political views, "had injured the interest and character of the Government in the Territory." These two gentlemen seem to have sided with the Spanish authorities in their quarrels, and their interference was a source of infinite mortification and irritation to the American Governor. As to the Marquis of Casa Calvo, Claiborne seems, nevertheless, to have entertained a favorable opinion of him, for he says: "I find no difficulty in transacting business with the Marquis. He possesses a great share of Spanish pride, and a warm, irritable temper, which sometimes betrays him into imprudencies, but his disposition is generous and accommodating, and his general deportment that of a gentleman." His relations, however, with Governor Folch of Florida do not appear to have been of the same pleasant character. "Of Governor Folch," ‡ he remarked, "I cannot speak as favorably. He has more temper than

---

* Claiborne to Madison, 5th June, 1805, Executive Journal, p. 64, vol. 1.
† Claiborne to Madison, 19th January, 1805, Executive Journal, p. 70, vol 1.
‡ Claiborne to Madison, Executive Journal, p. 114, vol. 1.

discretion, more genius than judgment, and his general conduct is far from being conciliatory."

On the 10th of February, the Spanish officers, although notified that their presence in the Territory was unpalatable, clung, under various pretences, and with a sort of mysterious and inexplicable fondness, to the province which their government had ceded to France, and France to the United States. "It seems the evacuation is not yet completed," wrote Governor Claiborne,[*] "and that several Spanish officers continue in this city; some have been permitted to retire on half pay." As to the Marquis of Casa Calvo, his plea for remaining was,[†] that "he expected shortly to be employed in defining the boundary line between the United States and the Mexican possessions." In the mean time, war had broken out between Spain and England, and the news of that war, together with the opening of the port of Havana to neutral vessels,[‡] had greatly benefited the commerce of New Orleans. The levee became crowded with flour and salted provisions, red wines and dry goods destined for exportation. Nevertheless, the Spaniards gave great uneasiness to Governor Claiborne. Their forces in Pensacola and West Florida amounted to nine hundred effective men; besides, two hundred were stationed at Baton Rouge, about eighty at Mobile, and according to common report, the number of the troops in Texas had been considerably augmented. At the Bay of St. Bernard they had been erecting a fort, and the coast was studded with their garrisons. It was even believed that, at a point distant only two hundred and forty miles from the mouth of the Sabine, they had concentrated two thousand troops.[§]

---

[*] Claiborne to Madison, Executive Journal, p. 88, vol. 1.
[†] Claiborne to Madison, Executive Journal, p. 102, vol. 1.
[‡] Claiborne to Madison, Executive Journal, p. 95, vol. 1.
[§] Claiborne to Madison, Executive Journal, vol. 1, page 118.

What made it worse, was the impression generally spread among the population, "that they were shortly to fall again under the dominion of Spain;" and the Spanish officers in Louisiana and in Pensacola took frequent occasions to remark, "that West and East Florida would be given in exchange for the territory west of the Mississippi; and that on no other condition would the cession be made." *

These reports of the increase of the Spanish armaments induced Claiborne to demand explanations of the Marquis of Casa Calvo. At the interview which took place, Claiborne said, " that the President had been desirous that, pending the negotiations between the two governments, the present state of things should not be innovated on by either party, and particularly that no new positions, or augmentations of military force, should take place on either side, within the territory claimed by both eastward of the Mississippi; that the President was anxious that the existing differences should be amicably adjusted, and entertained strong hopes that such would be the result." The Marquis replied, "that the forces of his Catholic Majesty had not been augmented at Baton Rouge, Mobile, or Pensacola, in any other manner than by concentrating at these places the troops which had been withdrawn from the various parts of Louisiana now in possession of the United States." They finally parted † from each other with reciprocal assurances of personal consideration, and of their great solicitude for the preservation of a good understanding between their two nations." This interview had taken place on the 19th of April. On the 21st, Casa Calvo called on Claiborne, and in the course of conversation, expressed his surprise

---

* Claiborne to Madison, 5th April, 1805, Executive Journal, vol. 1, page 120.
† Claiborne to Madison, 19th April, 1805. Ex. Jour., p. 124, vol. 1.

at the desire of the American Government to extend their limits. " He introduced," said Claiborne,* " the old hackneyed argument that a republican form of government could not long exist over extensive territories. He, however, seemed to think that the issue of the mission † would be favorable to the wishes of the President. There is no doubt but the great object of the Spanish Government will be to limit the possessions of the United States westwardly by the Mississippi, and to attain which, East and West Florida and other considerations would cheerfully be offered. I form this opinion from my various conversations with the Marquis, with Governor Folch, and other Spanish officers. Indeed, many persons here yet believe that the country west of the Mississippi will be ceded to Spain. The Marquis, in his private conversations, encourages such opinions, and until the issue of Mr. Monroe's mission is known, the Louisianians will not consider their political destiny as fixed. I have always told you that the foreign agents here saw with pleasure, and secretly countenanced, the discontents of the people, and I am persuaded that they have been mentioned to the Court of Spain as evidences of the favorable impressions which the former masters of Louisiana had left behind them. Fearing that these discontents would tend to encourage Spain in her pretensions to West Florida, and to lessen the interest which France might otherwise take in effecting an accommodation and thus embarrass our administration, I saw with regret and surprise the unnatural part which three or four apostate Americans of talents were acting here. But there are men whose hearts are so organized, that no consideration, not even the interest of their country, would induce them to forego the pleasure of gratifying

---

* Claiborne to Madison, p. 128. Ex. Jour., vol. 1.
† Mr. Monroe's Special Mission to Spain.

their personal resentment, and there are others in whose breast a spirit of avarice and self-aggrandizement has acquired such an ascendency as to have stifled every honest emotion. But it is unnecessary to enlarge further on this head. In every community there are degenerate characters, and it affords me consolation to assure you that the great body of the Americans here are useful, worthy members of society, and faithful to the interest of their country. I can add with like sincerity that the Louisianians, generally speaking, are a virtuous, amiable people, and will, in a short time, become zealous supporters of the American Union."

In the mean time, whilst Claiborne was thus looking round to guard against danger from foreign and intestine foes, the news which he frequently received from two individuals in the Western District of Louisiana, who had his entire confidence, Dr. Sibley and Captain Turner, were far from being of an encouraging character. Captain Turner was persuaded that Spanish agents had endeavored to alienate the affections of certain Indian tribes from the United States, and had soured the minds of the people of Natchitoches against the American Government, impressing them, at the same time, with the belief that Louisiana, or at least that part of it which lay west of the Mississippi, would shortly return under the dominion of Spain. Turner's statements to Claiborne were confirmed by Dr. Sibley. Both united in informing him " that the intrigues of the priests at Natchitoches had had an injurious tendency, inasmuch as they had weakened the allegiance of the citizens by giving currency to an opinion that they would soon become Spanish subjects, and excited hatred against the American Government by representing that it afforded no protection to religion, and that an association with infidels (meaning the Americans) would dishonor the memory of their ancestors, who had lived and died in the true faith. "A character calling himself the bishop of one of the interior provinces of Mexico," says Claiborne,* "lately made a visit to Natchitoches. He traveled with great dispatch and in much pomp. He appeared to be a man of great literature and of considerable address. He kept a journal, and took the latitude of many places through which he passed. His inquiries as to the geographical situation of Louisiana were minute, and from his general conduct it would seem that his visit was rather with political than religious views. The bishop was received by the Commandant at Natchitoches with respectful attention, and after resting a few days in the vicinity of that post, took his departure for the city of Mexico, to which place there is said to be from Natchitoches a plain direct road, that can be traveled with facility at any season of the year." When such was the state of things on the frontiers of Texas, large sums of silver were coming to New Orleans from Vera Cruz, consigned to the Marquis of Casa Calvo, ostensibly for the payment of pensions to Spanish officers allowed to reside in Louisiana, and to meet the expenses which the Marquis might have to incur as Commissioner of Limits.†

At this conjuncture of affairs, Aaron Burr, on whose brow the result of his duel with Hamilton seems to have put the seal of Cain's curse and fate, arrived in Louisiana with letters of introduction from Wilkinson, the pensioner and the tool of Spain, who, "to expedite his voyage, had fitted out for him an elegant barge, sails, colors and ten oars, with a sergeant and ten able, faithful hands," ‡ and who wrote to Daniel Clarke that "that great and honorable man would communicate to him

---

* Claiborne to Madison, 6th June, 1805. Ex. Journal, vol. 1, p. 176.
† Claiborne to Madison, 15th June, 1805. Ex. Journal, vol. 1, p. 187
‡ Purton's Life of Burr, p. 391. New York, eleventh edition, 1858.

many things improper to letter, and which he would not say to any other." * Claiborne alludes to this event with remarkable laconism in a letter addressed to Madison on the 26th of June, 1805 : " Col. Burr," says he, "arrived in this city on this evening"—and he only returns to the subject to say, in a letter of the 14th of July to Jefferson : " Col. Burr continued in this city ten or twelve days, and was received with polite attention. He has departed for St. Louis, and proposes to return to New Orleans in October next." Purton, his late biographer, writes that Burr was received everywhere in that city as *the great man*, and was " invited by Governor Claiborne to a grand dinner, given to him, and which was attended by as distinguished a company as New Orleans could assemble." † Whether Burr swelled the number of those "dangerous Americans who sympathized with the Spaniards," and of whom Governor Claiborne complains, does not appear, but it is to be presumed that the "*great man*," the friend and protégé of Wilkinson at the time, could not but have given to the Spaniards some satisfactory intimation of what had brought him to New Orleans, or Wilkinson, their pensioner and spy, would not have countenanced him so openly in those critical circumstances, when so many dark intrigues were evidently on foot. Whatever they were, it seems that Claiborne's apprehensions had recently been much allayed, for, on the 27th of July, he wrote to Madison that the police of the city having become vigilant, and the civil authorities throughout the province being thoroughly organized, he could no longer see any necessity for the stationing of regular troops in the interior of the colony. " In this city," said he, " one company might be usefully employed as a guard for the public property, but a

---

* Purton's Life of Burr, p. 393.   † Do. do., page 393.
‡ Claiborne to Madison, Ex. Journal, vol. 1, page 217.

greater number appears to be unnecessary. The strengthening of the forts at Plaquemines, or the erecting of a new fort at some strong position on the Mississippi below New Orleans, I consider an object worthy the attention of the administration, and in this way a part of the troops now here might be well employed, I think, and others might with propriety be sent to some frontier post. To guard, however, against difficulties with Spain, it might be advisable to have a regular force so posted as to enable them to act with promptitude and effect, as well in attacking the Floridas as in defending this city, and I know of no position more eligible than Fort Adams."

But it is worthy of notice, that during the sojourn of Burr in New Orleans, from the 26th of June to the 14th of July, it was determined at Washington that there was a sufficient cause for a secret correspondence between Claiborne and the Department of State, and to accomplish that purpose, a cipher was sent to the Governor, who acknowledged the receipt thereof on the 12th of August. What had happened, and what was it which it was deemed proper to conceal from the public eye, from that time to the present day? Nothing is left here for us to explore but the unsafe field of conjecture; and the circumstantial evidence of probabilities is to be accepted, instead of the positive information derived from well-ascertained facts. It is but too often that the historian, when consulting official documents, discovers that there are secret ones which will never meet his eye, and without which the events which he investigates cannot be thoroughly sifted and fully appreciated.

However secure Claiborne seemed to be at this time, and however gratified he might have been by the disposition shown by Casa Calvo to oblige the American Government on several occasions—such, for instance, as the granting of passports to an American exploring expedition, which, under the command of Dunbar, was to go up Red River into the Spanish Provinces—and such as the surrender of slaves who had run away from the Natchitoches District into Texas—still he had not ceased to be exceedingly anxious that the Spanish officers should remove out of the Territory. But not only did those officers seem to forget the invitation to depart, which they had received on the 9th of October, 1804, but they even objected to being taxed, with the rest of the citizens, for slaves and other property which they had in the Territory. To their remonstrances on the subject Claiborne replied: "For myself," he said in a letter to Casa Calvo, "I cannot see with what propriety the individuals generally claiming to be officers of Spain, and who reside in this Territory, can claim any exemption from the municipal laws. How far your Excellency, and the gentlemen attached to your family, to whom I am disposed to pay every attention in my power, may be entitled to any peculiar exemption from the operation of the municipal laws of this Territory, is a question on which I shal solicit the opinion of the Secretary of State of the United States." He also availed himself of this occasion to remind the Marquis that, by the treaty of the 30th of April, 1803, a period was prescribed within which the forces of his Catholic Majesty should be withdrawn from the ceded Territory. "Subsequently to the expiration of that period," said he, "your Excellency was urged to direct the departure of certain officers who had continued in the Territory so long beyond the right and the occasion for it. But they, nevertheless, remain stationary, and the circumstance furnishes ground to believe that some of them contemplate a permanent residence." Commenting on the subject in a dispatch to Madison[*] dated

[*] Executive Journal, vol. 1, p. 230.

August 7th, 1805, Claiborne observed: "You, no doubt, will be surprised to see so many foreign officers in the city. The fact is, that they are wedded to Louisiana, and necessity alone will induce them to depart." But Casa Calvo had winning ways, and there was a charm in his deportment which mollified Claiborne, and almost compelled him, notwithstanding his complaints, to show great forbearance to the Spanish officers. This is demonstrated by the letter* which, on the 14th of August, he wrote to Casa Calvo: "Permit me to assure your Excellency of the satisfaction I have had in the various communications which have occasionally passed between us. There is a frankness and sincerity in your letters which entitle them to high consideration on my part. Therefore, although I have complained, and not without cause, of the great delay of the Spanish authorities in this Territory beyond the time prescribed for their departure, I have, nevertheless, been disposed to make great allowance for the difficulties which you have suggested, and am fully persuaded of the disposition of your Excellency to execute, as far as may depend upon your agency, with promptitude and in good faith, the stipulations of the treaty."

Notwithstanding these pleasant relations, and the favorable dispositions existing between these two officers, the report of the retrocession to Spain of the country west of the Mississippi was gaining so much ground, that Claiborne, becoming alarmed at the consequences which might follow, called on the Marquis, and asked him if he knew on what authority this report was circulated. The Marquis answered in the negative, and added that he understood that the negociations had been suspended in Spain, and that Mr. Monroe had left Madrid. He further said, that the Minister of State, Cevallos, had in

* Executive Journal, vol, 1, p. 241.

formed him (Casa Calvo) that the desire of the Court of Spain was to make the Mississippi the boundary, and that their expectation was to obtain this object in due time. "The Marquis," said Claiborne to Madison,* "delivered himself in the French language. From my imperfect knowledge of French, it is possible that I may have misunderstood some of his expressions, but I am sure I gave you the substance of what he said. The prospects of a retrocession of the west bank of the Mississippi is now, and has always been, the theme of the Spanish officers who remain in the Territory, and many citizens seem to view it as an event likely to happen; an impression which I greatly regret, since it tends to lessen their confidence in the American Government, and to cherish a Spanish party among us. Next, therefore, to a final adjustment of limits with the Spanish Government, I most desire to see every Spanish officer removed from the ceded Territory. There must certainly be a power existing somewhere vested, to cause to be executed the clause in the treaty which directs the Spanish forces to be withdrawn within three months from the ceded Territory, and I should be pleased to have it hinted to me that, in my character as commissionor or Governor, I could, on this occasion, take, if necessary, compulsory measures."

The Government of the United States, however, had not, so far, shown itself disposed to pursue such a course, and Claiborne, on the 20th of August, departed from New Orleans,† on a journey to several of the counties of the Territory. In undertaking this excursion, he had two objects in view: the one was to benefit his much-impaired health; and the other, to assist personally in

---

* Executive Journal, vol. 1, p. 253.
† Executive Journal, vol. 1, p. 253.

organizing the militia—an object of the utmost importance, considering the hostile attitude which the Governments of Spain and of the United States had taken toward each other. On the 26th, Claiborne arrived at Baton Rouge, and partook of the hospitality of the Spanish Governor, Don Carlos de Grandpré. "I was introduced," wrote Claiborne to Madison,* "into a fort where the Governor has resided for several months, from an apprehension that Kemper and his associates still meditated an attack against his government. The fort of Baton Rouge has lately been repaired, but the works are ill-constructed, and could not be defended from assault by a less number than one thousand men; the seat has also been injudiciously selected, for it is commanded by ground not more than a quarter of a mile distant." On his return to New Orleans, Claiborne informed Madison † "that he had found everything tranquil, and did not apprehend any event in which the people of the Territory would take an agency which would subject the government to embarrassments." But he added, "that a rupture between the United States and Spain was esteemed here as highly probable, and excited much anxiety."

At last, on the 15th of October, the Marquis of Casa Calvo departed from New Orleans, in accordance with a previous notice which he had given to Claiborne, explanatory of his intentions, which were—to pass through Bayou Lafourche and the Bayou Tèche to the sea,‡ and thence to the mouth of the Sabine, which he proposed to ascend as far as the old Post of Adais. In making this excursion, the Marquis stated that he had two objects in view: the one to enjoy the

---

* Executive Journal, vol. 1, p. 254.
† Do. Vol. 1, p. 261. Dispatch of the 5th October, 1805.
‡ Do. Vol. 1, p. 255. Dispatch of the 14th October, 1805.

amusement of hunting ; the other, to acquire some geographical knowledge of the country, and in particular, to ascertain the latitude of the Post of Adais, and to make an examination for some stone posts, which were said to have been deposited somewhere in its vicinity, and immediately on the line which was formerly established between the French and Spanish possessions west of the Mississippi. "I expressed to the Marquis a wish," wrote Claiborne, "that, on his arrival at the Post of Adais, he should be joined by an American officer from the garrison of Natchitoches, who should witness his proceedings, and make report to me thereof. To which proposition the Marquis having assented, Captain Turner, who speaks the French language, has been selected to accompany him." One of the instructions to Turner was to ascertain the longitude and latitude of several points in the country to be visited, and also the line of demarcation which had formerly existed between the Spanish and French Territories. He was further requested to collect whatever other information might be useful for the Government, "although it did not come within his instructions."*

On the 24th of October, Claiborne's apprehensions of an attack on Louisiana from the Spaniards had become much keener, and were founded on information which he had lately received, and which he thought correct. Thus he believed that four hundred Spanish troops had recently arrived at Pensacola, and that a larger number was daily expected; that three hundred men had been ordered to Baton Rouge, and that eight hundred had been posted in Texas, near the frontiers of Louisiana. He was well assured that a Spanish agent had contracted for the delivery at Mobile of four thousand barrels of

---

* Executive Journal. Claiborne to Turner, 14th October. Vol. 1, p. 264.

flour, and that the same agent, not being enabled to procure by contract the delivery of four thousand pairs of shoes at the same point, had purchased a quantity of leather. So convinced was Claiborne of impending danger, that he wrote to Robert Williams, Governor of the Mississippi Territory, to give him timely notice of the coming storm.* "I am persuaded," says he, "that the Spanish agents in our vicinity calculate on an immediate rupture, and that they are making all the preparations which their means permit, to commence the war in this quarter with advantage. Until, therefore, we have information of an amicable settlement of differences, or some strong assurances that hostilities will not be resorted to, permit me to advise that you remain at your post. I well know that, if you were to depart for North Carolina, and any difficulties should arise in your absence, you would be extremely mortified, and, therefore, although I strongly hope that peace may with honor be preserved, yet, as war may speedily commence, I should regret your absence from a position where you might be among the first to partake of the danger and the glory of defending our country." These were noble sentiments, and Claiborne proceeded to act in accordance with them, by providing himself and his friend, the Governor of Mississippi, with that weapon which every brave hand longs to grasp, when laurels are to be won; for he concludes the communication, from which I have made the preceding extract, with these words:—"I have purchased for you an elegant sword; it is similar to one I have purchased for myself, and is said to be the kind of small-arms at present worn by the generals in France."

On the 30th of October, Claiborne was confirmed in

---

* Claiborne to Williams, 24th October, Executive Journal, vol. 1, p. 276.

his apprehensions of a rupture between Spain and the United States. A governor-general of the province of Texas had arrived at San Antonio, and as he was a brigadier-general and was said to possess military talent, the fact was looked upon as not without signification. Besides, a fort had been erected on the Trinity River, and occupied by a garrison of two hundred men, the greater part cavalry. "The conduct of the Spaniards in this quarter," wrote Claiborne to Dearborn, Secretary of War, "is highly exceptionable, and manifests a hostile disposition." At the same time, heavy duties were levied by the Spanish authorities in Mobile on all American vessels navigating up the Tombigbee River from the ocean. Claiborne strongly remonstrated in a* communication to Governor Folch against the vexations thus inflicted, and which were calculated to weaken the good understanding which should have existed between the two nations. He further complained of the considerable armaments of the Spaniards, and demanded explanations on the subject, considering, said he, "that negotiations between our respective governments are still in train."

Claiborne kept his eyes always vigilantly open on Florida and Texas, and was somewhat solicitous about the movements of Casa Calvo in the latter territory. New Orleans was fruitful in reports on the subject. It was generally believed that the Marquis had taken with him a considerable sum of money. Some said that he was to meet on the frontiers of Texas three thousand troops, of which he was to take the command; others that he was engaged in sowing discontent among the people of the western part of Louisiana; many were under the impression that the money carried away by the Marquis was destined to conciliate the Indians to the

---

* Executive Journal, page 282, vol. 1.—Dispatch of the 31st Oct., 1805.

Spanish interest in case of a rupture with the United States. There were some who suspected that all these objects together were within the compass of his journey. Various, indeed, were the conjectures,* and the news which Claiborne received from time to time was not such as to quiet the excitement of the public mind. "Some troops," wrote Dr. Sibley to him, "have arrived at Nacogdoches—it is said two hundred; and it is likewise said they are going to fortify, in a short time, within five or six leagues of Natchitoches. Considering the attachment to them of their militia, and the contrary toward us of our militia, they are stronger than we are, counting numbers." In such an emergency, Claiborne hastened to write to Madison: † "The regular troops here are few in number, nor can I rely with certainty on the body of the militia. I believe that many of the creoles of the country would be faithful to the American Government, but perhaps a majority of them would remain neutral, and I am inclined to think that most of the Frenchmen, and all the Spaniards who reside here, in the event of war, would favor the Spanish interest. These are my impressions, and I deem it a duty to impart them to you."

After having given this information, Claiborne urged the sending of reinforcements to him as soon as possible. He advised that Fort St. John and Plaquemines be repaired and placed in a state of defence; that the troops at Fort Adams be removed to Pointe Coupée; and that the troops in New Orleans, leaving only a necessary guard for the public stores and barracks, be posted at Fort St. John, and above and below the city of New Orleans at suitable positions, not more than six miles distant from the city. He thought that, by these measures,

---

* Executive Journal, Claiborne to Madison, 5th November, vol. 1, p. 285.
† Executive Journal, vol. 1, page 285.

the passage of a hostile army by way of the lakes, or from Baton Rouge, or from the mouth of the river, might be opposed, and that, in this manner, "various rallying-points would be presented for the patriotic citizens of the militia." The vigilance of Claiborne continued to rise in proportion with the increase of danger, and, on the 7th of November,* he wrote to the Secretary of War: "I have no doubt but that we have a few Spanish soldiers in this city, who have disguised their outward garb. The inclosed deposition will give some information concerning them; their movements will be watched, and such measures adopted as their conduct may justify."

When hostilities were thus within the range of probabilities, Claiborne felt himself compelled to give much attention to the organization of the militia. Conspicuous among the different corps was the battalion of Orleans, which was composed of Americans, and of creoles of Louisiana, who, wrote Claiborne † to Madison, "possess a great share of military ardor." But Graham, the Secretary of the Territory, seems to have had but an indifferent opinion of the efficacy of the militia. In a communication to the Secretary of War at Washington he said: ‡ "My own opinion is that it is not, nor ever will be, equal to the defence of the Territory. The climate, the nature of the country, which does not admit of a thick population, and above all, the number of negroes, will ever make this a feeble part of the Union, even if the Creoles should be tempted to shoulder their muskets and feel as Americans. In this city there are some volunteer corps which might, I believe, be depended upon, and no doubt, in case of an emergency, others might be raised, but these

* Executive Journal, vol. 1, p. 289.
† Executive Journal, vol. 1, p. 291.
‡ Executive Journal, vol. 2, p. 19, 26th December, 1805.

would consist of men who could not leave the city for any length of time."

After having taken a view of what was occurring between the Spaniards and Americans in Louisiana, and in the neighboring provinces, it is proper now to examine the course pursued by the two governments at Madrid and Washington. On the 4th September, 1803, Casa Irujo, the Spanish Minister at Washington, had protested in the name of his Government against the cession of Louisiana to the United States;* but, on the 10th of February, 1804, he had informed the Government of the United States that he had received orders to declare that his Catholic Majesty "had thought fit to renounce his opposition to the alienation of Louisiana made by France, notwithstanding the solid reasons on which it was founded, thereby giving a new proof of his benevolence and friendship toward the United States;" and, on the 15th of May, the minister had repeated the same declaration, coupled with the hope "that the United States would correspond, with a true reciprocity, with the sincere friendship of the king, of which he, the king, had given so many proofs."

There were pending, however, between the two Governments, questions which were soon destined to test their mutual forbearance and friendship. The principal ones were those originating in the claims of the United States concerning the limits of Louisiana and the injuries done to American commerce by France, with the assent or acquiescence of Spain, and for which therefore she was held responsible. These questions were discussed with great ability on both sides, and the arguments would fill up a large volume, but did not lead to any satisfactory conclusion. At last, on the 5th of July, 1804, the

---

* Gayarre's Spanish Domination in Louisiana, p. 584.

American Minister at Madrid wrote to Cevallos, the Spanish Minister of Foreign Affairs, a note which was couched in the terms of an ultimatum, and in which he said, " I wish to have your Excellency's answer as quickly as possible, as on Tuesday I send a courier with circular letters to all our consuls in the ports of Spain, stating to them the critical situation of things between Spain and the United States, the probability of a speedy and serious misunderstanding, and directing them to give notice thereof to all our citizens, advising them so to arrange and prepare their affairs as to be able to move off within the time limited by the treaty, should things end as I now expect. I am also preparing the same information for the commander of our squadron in the Mediterranean for his own notice and government, and that of all the American merchant vessels he may meet.* On the 8th Cevallos replied by a note, in which he remonstrated against the menace implied in the American Minister's communication, and said, "The King, my master, cannot persuade himself that such language is conformable to the moderation which he appreciates in the American Government." On the 14th, Mr. Pinckney disclaimed all idea of having intended to take a menacing tone toward Spain, but, at the same time, maintained that the position he had assumed was justified by the extraordinary language used, and the extraordinary course pursued by the Spanish Government. He said, "I have repeatedly told your Excellency that, as to the two questions of abandoning the French claims,† or consenting to anything to affect the limits of Louisiana, my instructions are as positive as possible never to abandon the one, or enter into any contract, or even negotiation, respecting the other." And he further held this em-

---

* Appendix to Gales & Seaton's 8th Congress, 2d Session, p. 1316.
† For which French claims Spain was held responsible.

phatic language: "In all the differences between Great Britain and France, the United States have uniformly maintained their rights with a firmness that has done them honor in the opinion of every nation; and as I have often told your Excellency, it is not to Spain, or any other nation, they will yield them." This lofty tone was met with a corresponding spirit by Cevallos, and both Ministers, with equal tenacity, seemed determined not to yield an inch to each other.

Such a turn of affairs rendered it expedient, in the opinion of the President, to send a special envoy to Madrid, with a view of making a last effort to arrange matters amicably with Spain, and he selected Mr. Monroe, who was instructed to proceed from London to Madrid, and, on his route, to avail himself in Paris of every opportunity which might present itself for ascertaining and turning to just account the dispositions of the French Government with regard to the questions depending between the United States and Spain. In his instructions of the 26th of October, 1804, given to Monroe, the Secretary of State said, "Notwithstanding the rumor which appears to have spread in Europe of an impending rupture between Spain and the United States, there is nothing in the avowed sentiments of the Spanish Government, and certainly nothing in the sound policy of Spain, to justify an inference that she wishes to be no longer at peace with us. It may reasonably be expected, therefore, that you will meet with a friendly reception. In return, you are authorized by the President to give every proper assurance of the desire of the United States to maintain the harmony and to improve the confidence between the two nations; and with this view to hasten, by frank elucidations and equitable accommodations, a removal of every source from which discord might arise." Mr. Monroe, in passing through Paris, had no difficulty in ascertaining that the French Government took of the questions depending between Spain and the United States a very different view from that which was expected or desired by the President; for, on the 21st of December, 1804, Talleyrand had made to General Armstrong, the American Minister at Paris, a communication which left no doubt on the subject, and in which he used this very significant language: "His Imperial Majesty has seen with pain the United States commence their differences with Spain in an unusual manner, and conduct themselves toward the Floridas by acts of violence, which, not being founded on right, could have no other effect but to injure its lawful owners. Such an aggression gave the more surprise to his Majesty, because the United States seemed in this measure to avail themselves of their treaty with France as an authority for their proceedings, and because he could scarcely reconcile with the just opinion which he entertains of the wisdom and fidelity of the General Government, a course of proceedings which nothing can authorize toward a Power which has long occupied, and still occupies, one of the first ranks in Europe."

This communication shows that time had made no alteration in the determination of the French Government; for General Armstrong, in a dispatch of the 12th of March, 1804, had written to Mr. Monroe long before he, Monroe, had been requested to proceed to Madrid to settle these Spanish difficulties :* "The moment I received your letters of the 15th and 26th of February, I took measures to sound this Government on the present posture of things at Madrid, which, on the authority of your communication, I represented as strongly indicating a rupture between the United States and Spain. . . . To the question, what would be the course of this Gov-

---

* Gales & Seaton, p. 1362.

ernment in the event of a rupture between us and Spain, they answered: 'We can neither doubt nor hesitate; we must take part with Spain.' In another dispatch of the 18th, he said: 'Another experiment has been made, but without producing any result propitious to our objects. Nay, the more this subject is discussed, the more determined are they in maintaining the doctrines, and pursuing the conduct indicated in my letter of the 12th.'" On the 23d of May, 1805, Mr. Madison,* alluding to these two communications from General Armstrong, wrote to Mr. Monroe: "From these communications it appears that France has arrayed herself on the side of Spain in such a manner that Spain will neither be disposed nor be permitted to bend to our claims, either with respect to West Florida, or the French spoliations."

In the mean time, Monroe and Pinckney had jointly resumed the suspended negotiations at Madrid, but they had no favorable results. On the contrary, they seemed to have exacerbated the feelings of irritation already existing, as appears by a joint note addressed† by Monroe and Pinckney to Cevallos on the 9th of April, 1805, in which they said, "The undersigned have the honor to inform his Excellency that they expect an early answer to this communication, and that by it will their future conduct be governed. They consider the negotiation as essentially terminated by what has already occurred; and if they pursue it, it will be only on the proof of such a disposition on the part of his Majesty's Government as shall convince them that there is just cause to conclude that it will terminate to the satisfaction of the United States. Having acquitted themselves, in every particular, of what was due to the just, the pacific and friendly policy of their Government, it remains that they

---

* Gales & Seaton, p. 1353   † Gales & Seaton, p. 1429.

should not be unmindful of what they owe to its honor, its character and its rights. If his Majesty is disposed to adjust these important concerns by an amicable arrangement between the two nations, on fair and equal terms, it may be easily and speedily done. Each party knows its rights, its interests, and how much it ought to concede, in a spirit of conciliation, to accomplish the objects of the negotiation. The undersigned feel the force of that sentiment, and will not fail to respect it. Should his Majesty's Government, however, think proper to invite another issue, on it will the responsibility rest for the consequences. The United States are not unprepared for, or unequal to, any crisis which may occur. The energy which they have shown on former occasions, and the firmness of their past career, must prove that, in submitting with unexampled patience to the injuries of which they complain, and cherishing with sincerity the relations of friendship with his Catholic Majesty, no unmanly or unworthy motive has influenced their conduct."

This note failed to produce its desired effect, and after repeated efforts on both sides to come to an understanding, Pinckney and Monroe, on the 12th of May, submitted to Cevallos the following ultimatum:

"On condition that Spain will cede, on her part, the Territory to the east of the Mississippi, and arbitrate her own spoliations conformably to the convention of August 11, 1802, the United States will cede, on their part, their claim to territory west of a line to be drawn from the mouth of the Colorado to its source, and from thence to the northern limits of Louisiana, in such a manner as to avoid the different rivers and their branches which empty into the Mississippi.

"They will establish a Territory of thirty leagues on both sides of this line, which shall remain unsettled for-

·-er, or of thirty leagues on their own side, if Spain desires to extend her settlement to the Colorado.

"They will also relinquish their claim for French spoliations, which amounts to one hundred and sixty-four vessels, by undertaking to satisfy the parties themselves in a sum specified.

"They will relinquish, likewise, their claim to compensation for the suppression of the deposit at New Orleans."

On the 15th, Cevallos sent his reply, which he concluded in these words:*

"In this view of the subject, it cannot be concealed from the penetration of your excellencies, that, as a consequence of the propositions you have made by your note of the 12th, Spain would cede to the United States, not only the Territories which indisputably belong to her to the east of the Mississippi, that is, the two Floridas, but also others equally her own, in the interior province of New Spain, without receiving anything in return but the renunciation of a right which she does not acknowledge in the United States—which is, to reclaim for the damages arising from the suspension of the deposit, and for those occasioned by the French privateers on the coast and in the ports of Spain during the last war, when, on the contrary, Spain thinks she has shown that she is in no manner liable for the same.

"The justice of the American Government will not permit it to insist on propositions so totally to the disadvantage of Spain; and, however anxious his Majesty may be to please the United States, he cannot, on his part, assent to them, nor can he do less than consider them as little conformable to the rights of his crown."

Three days after, on the 18th of May, the negotiation

---

* Gales & Seaton, p. 1458.

being considered as at an end by the foregoing answer of the Spanish Minister of Foreign Affairs, Mr. Monroe, whose duty it became to repair immediately to London, where he was Resident Minister of the United States, asked for his passport, which was granted, and, on the 21st, he had his final audience of the King, to take leave in the usual form. On the 23d, Monroe and Pinckney, jointly, wrote from Aranjuez to Madison: "We are sorry to inform you that the negotiation with which we were charged by the President with the Government of Spain is concluded, after failing in all its objects, notwithstanding our unwearied and laborious exertions, for so great a length of time, to procure for it a different result." On the 3d of December, the President informed Congress, in his annual message, of the complete failure of negotiations with Spain, and of the injuries perpetrated by her and others of the belligerent powers in Europe against American commerce. " In reviewing," said he, " those injuries from some of the belligerent powers, the moderation, the firmness and the wisdom of the Legislature will all be called into action. We ought still to hope that time and a correct estimate of interest, as well as of character, will produce the justice we are bound to expect. But should any nation deceive itself by false calculations, and disappoint that expectation, we must join in the unprofitable contest of trying which party can do the other most harm. Some of these injuries may, perhaps, admit a peaceable remedy. Where that is competent, it is always the most desirable. But some of them are of a nature to be met by force only, and all of them may lead to it." Thus the year 1805 closed for the United States with a lowering horizon, portending of war and its concomitant calamities.

As to those events appertaining merely to the internal condition of the Territory, a succinct recapitulation of them will complete the history of this year. Early in January, Claiborne had informed Madison of the revulsion which had taken place in the temper of the people concerning the establishment of a Bank, which had been so violently opposed in the beginning. But, at last, its incipient capital had been subscribed, and an election of Directors had been proceeded to. "I had hoped," he wrote * to Albert Gallatin, "that this measure would not have been carried into effect, since it had been disapproved of at the Seat of Government. But the spirit of adventure, which, for a length of time, was dormant, has been revived by the exertions of a few individuals, and it seems that the people are determined to put the Bank in motion."

Claiborne had not found the Executive Chair one of ease and repose in Louisiana. Severe strictures were constantly published on his administration, his public character, and even his private life. On the 19th of January, he thought himself bound, in duty to himself and to the Government he represented, to forward to Madison the papers which contained those strictures, with observations on the principal accusations brought against him. "My accusers," he† said, "take great care to impress the public with an opinion that my government commenced here under the most favorable auspices—an assertion contradicted by every circumstance of the times," &c. .

When possession of Louisiana was received, the aspect of affairs was not such as promised either a pleasing administration, or a happy result. The people were split into parties, divided in their affections, and the sport of foreign and domestic intriguers. The functions of government were nearly at a stand, and much was wanting to produce system in, and restore order to, the different

---

* Claiborne to Albert Gallatin, Jan. 6, p. 65, vol. 2, **Executive Journal**.
† Executive Journal, p. 67, vol. 1

departments. Great changes were expected under the new order of things, and more was required, to conciliate and attach the general sentiment to the American Government, than my resources permitted, or the energies of any man could accomplish. The honest distrust which I entertained of my talents, the sincere diffidence with which I entered upon the duties of my office, my constant reluctance to exert any of the large discretionary powers intrusted to me, except when urged by imperious necessity, or the strong pressure of political expediency, and my anxious solicitude for a speedy termination of the Provisional Government, are all known to you.

. . . .

That I committed errors I readily admit, but I am not sensible of having been betrayed into any material measure that I can reflect on with self-accusation. It is true that I did not do so much as some seem to have expected, nor was my administration marked with any of those strong traits which some would call energy, but others, more properly, oppression. A charge of tyranny on the one part, or imbecility on the other, was equally an object of dread," &c. . . . .

As to the reproach laid at his door for having permitted the Spanish troops to remain so long in the Territory, he observed that the taking of any other than conciliatory measures of persuasion to hasten their departure would not have been authorized by anything which had occurred, and he added: "I doubt, even had we had the authority, whether we had the force necessary to carry any compulsory measures into effect. As to the Marquis of Casa Calvo having retained a sentinel at his house, it never gave me any uneasiness, and indeed I knew not until lately that it was even considered as an object of jealousy by any of our citizens. I, however, communicated the circumstance to you, and conceiving from your silence that you viewed it, as I did, in a very unimportant light, I did not interfere on the subject till lately, on a complaint made againt the guard for an outrage on a citizen, and the sentinel was discontinued at my request." . . . .

The Intendant Morales and the Marquis of Casa Calvo hated each other thoroughly, and as both officers, within their respective departments, still pretended to exercise authority over those Spaniards who remained in the Territory, and over the property they held therein, there had arisen between them bitter conflicts, which had involved Claiborne, to whom both appealed, in repeated difficulties. On this subject, in the same communication to Madison to which I have already referred, he said: "Viewing the contest from the beginning as one arising altogether out of the private animosities of two foreign officers, in which neither I, nor my country, was anywise interested, I was unwilling that my name or authority should be used on the occasion, and was also desirous that the affair might terminate without troubling our Government, or involving its officers in the question. As soon as I discovered that the Marquis proceeded to unauthorized lengths, and called upon me to carry into execution his decrees between persons answerable only to the Territorial tribunals, my conduct was immediately such as a knowledge of the rights of my country dictated. . . . .

"The injurious and ill-founded allusions made to the influence of the Marquis over my conduct deserve no notice. The truth is, that nothing but a formal intercourse of civilities ever existed between us, and even this has been discontinued since the affair of Don Manuel Garcia, in which, though exclusively a judicial proceeding, the Spaniards, through ignorance of our Government, have supposed me to have been concerned.

"It may, perhaps, be to you a matter of curiosity to know the nature and extent of the party to which I am indebted for those unfriendly attacks. I have therefore no hesitation to tell you that they proceeded originally from the resentment of Mr. Daniel Clark, who, conceiving himself entitled to the confidence of the President, and possibly to some distinguished place in the administration here, is mortified to find himself so entirely overlooked. To his party Mr. Edward Livingston, who, as prudence ought to have suggested, probably at first intended no interference with the politics of the country, was too easily persuaded to attach himself, and his opposition to me, and to the acts of the Government I represent, speedily ensued. I early discovered the political views of these gentlemen; they went, in my opinion, to injure the interest and character of our Government in this country, and I therefore pursued such a line of conduct toward them and their measures as my duty required. I might, I believe, name another gentleman, late of New York, as attached to this party, from whom I did not expect opposition. But the party are few in number, and, but for the standing their talents give them, could not be considered as formidable. For my part, the plain and economical habits in which I have been educated and hitherto lived, united to an unsuspicious disposition, qualify me but badly for a personal competition with those whose manners have been formed on a model better calculated for the etiquette of this city, and who, from long practice, are more conversant with the arts of intrigue. To what lengths the opposition to me may be carried I know not, but I am inclined to think that nothing will be left unsaid which can wound my feelings, and that my public and private character will be cruelly misrepresented."

Claiborne was right in his apprehensions; for the

animosity of his enemies went so far as to accuse him of having used his authority to favor the elopement and the subsequent marriage of Lieutenant Doyle, of the United States Army, with a young Creole girl. This accusation seems to have assumed so much importance, that he thought proper to vindicate himself in a formal communication to Mr. Madison, dated January 26, 1805. "Mr. Doyle's marriage," said he, "was not with me an object of any concern. I knew the young man only by name. His folly I regretted, but the elopement being effected, I thought it best, to prevent the girl from being dishonored, to permit the marriage. A license, however, was not granted, until the father solicited it, and the part I acted was alone dictated by benevolence." Claiborne was truly what he represented himself—a benevolent man, but benevolence seldom disarms malignity; and the Governor had to learn it from bitter personal experience. He thus expressed himself on the 6th of February: "The press in this city is, indeed, becoming licentious; it even menaces the tranquillity of private life. But, hitherto, the Executive of the Territory has been the principal object of abuse. I am happy, however, to add, that the Louisianians have no concern in the abusive publications, and very generally disapprove of them. The discontented party are composed principally of natives of the United States, and I am inclined to think their number very inconsiderable."

Unfortunately, this state of things led to quarrels, and quarrels to duels. One of them was fatal, and Claiborne had to deplore the death of his brother-in-law and private secretary, Micajah G. Lewis. Claiborne felt the blow so keenly, that he made it the subject of a special communication to the President of the United States,* and it is impossible, on reading it, not to

---

* Dispatch of the 17th of February, 1805, Executive Journal, p. 91, 2nd vol

sympathize with his wounded spirit. "You have, no doubt," he said, "discovered that, like most men who fill exalted stations, it has been my misfortune to have attracted the envy, and excited the malevolence and ill-will of a portion of society, and I presume you are apprised of the persecution I am suffering here, through the vehicle of the licentious press. Every circumstance, as well of a private nature as of my official conduct, that calumny could torture into an accusation against me, has been brought into public view, and exhibited in every shape that malignant wit could devise. I early discovered that these ungenerous attacks excited generally the susceptibility of Mr. Lewis, and with the most anxious solicitude for his welfare, I used every argument to induce him to view with calmness the tempestuous sea to which my political elevation had exposed him. On one occasion, I had accommodated a dispute in which his sympathies had involved him, and I had persuaded myself that my advice, united to his mild and pacific disposition, would have insured his future safety. But unfortunately for me, and unfortunately for my poor brother, even my misfortunes became the sport of party spirit, and the ashes of his beloved sister were not suffered to repose in the grave. She was raised from the tomb to give poignancy and distress to my feelings. He sought and discovered the author of the cruel production. A duel was the consequence, and my amiable young friend received a bullet through his heart at the second fire. I hope the assurance to you is unnecessary, that this melancholy affair was kept a secret from me; and that the news of the fatal result was the first intimation I received of it. Gladly would I have made bare my own bosom to the shock, before any friend of mine, and particularly one so dear to me as Mr. Lewis, had fallen a victim in this cause."

On the 28th of February, Claiborne transmitted to Madison a copy of the act to incorporate the city of New Orleans. "The provision," he said, "which allows the citizens to elect aldermen is very popular. It will be the first time the Louisianians ever enjoyed the right of suffrage, and I persuade myself that they will, on this occasion, use it with discretion." On the 8th of March he resumed the subject, and wrote: "The late election for city aldermen was conducted with great order, but the apathy of the people on the occasion astonished me. But few voted, and none appeared interested as to the issue. I have appointed James Pitot Mayor, and Doctor John Watkins Recorder of the city. The former is a French gentleman of talents and respectability, who has resided here for many years. The character of the latter is known to you."

Causes to irritate or excite the public mind seemed at that time to grow up with wonderful exuberance. Even religious quarrels were not wanting, as is shown by a communication* from Claiborne to Madison, on the 18th of March: "A dispute," he wrote, "has arisen among the members of the Catholic Church in this city. Mr. Walsh, who claims to be the Vicar-General of Louisiana, took upon himself to dismiss a priest who had care of this parish. The priest appealed to his parishioners, who have disavowed the authority of Mr. Walsh, and elected (amidst many hurras) the dismissed priest their pastor. The subject excites much interest among the Catholics, but it is probable will not eventuate in any unpleasant consequences." This appeal of the priest from the decree of his superior, to what he must have considered the higher tribunal of his parishioners, and his subsequent election by them, are cer-

* Executive Journal, p. 102, vol. 1.

tainly very curious facts in the history of the Catholic Church in Louisiana. Claiborne, in a later communication, returned to the subject in these words: "The schism among the Catholics of the Territory increases. The Vicar-General, who claims precedence in the Church, is about publishing a pastoral letter, and proposes to give it a general circulation. I very much regret this religious controversy, &c. Mr. Walsh is an Irishman, and his principal opponent, Mr. Antonio, a Spanish priest.* The Marquis of Casa Calvo is said to take great interest in favor of the latter, but I have no evidence of this fact." Later, however, he discovered that the Marquis took an active part in these religious disputes, and he made up his mind to address† a letter to that gentleman on the subject, suggesting the indelicacy and impropriety of any interference on his part.

As it has been already mentioned in the preceding pages, the law remodeling the Territorial Government of Louisiana was not such as to give any degree of satisfaction to those who had so bitterly complained of the original act of organization. "The people," said Claiborne‡ to Madison, "had been taught to expect greater privileges, and many are disappointed. I believe, however, as much is given them as they can manage with discretion, or as much as they ought to be trusted with, until the limits of the ceded territory are acknowledged, the national attachments of our new brothers less wavering, and the views and character of some influential men here better ascertained. I particularly attend to those persons who were formerly in the Spanish service, and are permitted by their Government to remain in Louis-

---

* Antonio de Sedella, the same who had attempted to introduce the Inquisition into Louisiana in 1789.
† Executive Journal, p. 122, vol. 1.
‡ Claiborne to Madison, 21st April, 1805, p. 132, vol. 1.

iana as pensioners, or in the enjoyment of their full pay." In this communication he again pours out the anguish of his soul under the incessant attacks of his enemies. "I confess, sir," he says, "that the opposition, the cruel opposition I have experienced, has harrowed up my feelings excessively. But I have found powerful consolation in an approving conscience, and in a well-founded hope that my superiors, to whom the difficulties I have combated are known, would approbate a conduct which has, throughout, been directed by the purest motives of honest patriotism."

Such was the excited state of the Territory with its motley population, when an event which took place at the mouth of the river warmed up the native pride of the Americans, and raised their Government in the estimation of those whose dispositions toward it were not friendly, and who delighted in depreciating its power and its character. For some time two British privateers had been, with impunity, cruising off the mouth of the Mississippi, and were in the habit of boarding every vessel coming in or going out. At length they had the audacity to capture an American schooner, bound in, within view of the Block-House, and not more than three miles distant from land. The captain of the revenue cutter which was stationed there thought it his duty to rescue the vessel, which he did after an engagement of one hour, and conveyed her safely into the river. During the engagement the cutter sustained little or no damage.*

If Claiborne felt deeply the blows which his enemies aimed at him, he was much soothed and relieved by the assurances of continued confidence and esteem which it pleased the President to give him. In answer to such assurances he wrote † to the Chief Magistrate, on the 4th

---

* Claiborne to Madison, 22d April, 1805. Ex. Jour., p. 135, vol. 1.
† Claiborne to Jefferson. Ex. Jour., p. 144, vol. 1.

of May: "I have received your favors of the 10th and 14th of March, and am indeed happy to find that the ungenerous attacks to which I had been subjected have not made on your mind impressions unfavorable to me. I am aware that abuse, much abuse, is the constant attendant on office under our Government. I had endeavored to meet it with composure, but when I perceived a political conduct represented as vicious which I know to have been guided by the purest motives of honest patriotism, and acts which *in truth* were benevolent and praiseworthy, represented as dishonorable—and all this done by a faction, who had recourse even to subornation and perjury in order to sully my reputation, I must confess that my feelings received a wound which alone could be healed by conscious rectitude and a belief that the confidence of the Executive in me was not diminished."

On the 4th of May, the Legislative Council was prorogued by Claiborne to the 20th of June. In giving information of this fact to Madison, Claiborne* said, "The agents, Messrs. Sauvé, Destréhan and Derbigny, are preparing for publication a pamphlet, in which, I fear, much will be said which will tend to agitate and divide the public mind. I have seen Messrs. Sauvé and Derbigny, and find the latter greatly disappointed and dissatisfied. He considers the treaty as violated, and supposes that the Government was uncandid to the agents, and unjust to the Louisianians. He, however, expressed a hope that his fellow-citizens would be contented, and reconciled to the government which Congress had prescribed. I nevertheless fear that, in the pamphlet preparing by the agents, some imprudent observations may be introduced. For my own part, I am still convinced that

---

* Ex. Jour., p. 145, vol. 1. † Ex. Jour., p. 158, vol. 1.

an early introduction of the entire representative system into Louisiana would be a hazardous experiment, and I seriously doubt whether the second grade of government will be conducted with discretion."

After having prorogued the Legislative Council, Claiborne had departed from New Orleans on a visit to some of the distant parishes of the State. In the course of his journey he found, as he reports, the inhabitants contented and apparently well disposed to the American Government. "A few designing, ambitious men," he wrote on the 18th of May, "would wish to create disturbances, but it is probable they will not succeed. I was pleased to learn that the late Congress had made provision for ascertaining the legal titles of land in the Territory, inasmuch as an early division thereon will promote the interests of the United States, as well as of individuals. We abound here in land speculators, and the present state of things is not unfavorable to their views."

On the 31st of May Claiborne had returned to New Orleans, after having proceeded as far up as Pointe Coupée, and made many appointments under the new judiciary system. His excursion was a pleasant one, and the friendly welcome which he met everywhere was particularly agreeable to him."*

Claiborne, on the 6th of June, sent to Madison the expected pamphlet from the pen of Derbigny, Destréhan and Sauvé, with these observations on his part: "You will find in this production evidences of discontent—a want of information and of prudence on the part of the agents—but I believe the publication will excite but little interest in the Territory, and be productive of no mischief. It may, therefore, be best to permit it unmo

---

* Claiborne to Madison, 31st of May, 1805. Executive Journal, p. 160, vol. 1.

lested to sink into oblivion. We have among us men who would sacrifice the interest of any country, or the happiness of any people, to the gratification of their ambition. That such men should be discontented with the present state of things, need not be a matter of surprise, but I am persuaded the great body of the citizens of Louisiana cannot be shaken in their allegiance, or be made to think that they are not greatly benefited by their annexation to the United States. There has been a rumor that certain discontented persons have contemplated a mission to France, with a view of soliciting the attention of the Emperor to the affairs of this Territory, and praying that he may interfere in their favor."

In June, Governor Claiborne learned from Dr. Sibley and Captain Turner, that they had seen a manuscript purporting to be the official journal of a French officer,* who, in the year 1719, was instructed to erect a fort on the Bay of St. Bernard. Claiborne communicated this fact to Madison, saying: "In this journal there are letters from official characters which show that, at that period, the extent of Louisiana was a source of jealousy to Spain, that a dispute as to limits had arisen between the subordinate agents of France and Spain, but that the claims of the former extended from the Perdido to the Rio Bravo, and were bottomed upon a treaty referred to in the correspondence, called the treaty of Cambrai. Viewing this manuscript as an important document, I shall solicit Dr. Sibley, in whose possession it now is, to cause a copy thereof to be taken, and to transmit the original to me for the purpose of being deposited among the records of Louisiana. The copy I will request the Doctor to forward to the Department of State." This

---

* Bernard de la Harpe.

important document was effectually secured, preserved, and subsequently published.

If the attention of Claiborne had been called only to such objects, or merely to objects of general importance, his task would have been, comparatively, less annoying; but he was constantly wearied by applications for redress, or protection, in matters which belonged exclusively to the police department, or to the judiciary. For instance, on the 8th of June, he felt himself constrained to write this letter* to James Pitot, the Mayor of New Orleans: "I have received a letter from the Lady Abbess of the Ursuline Nuns in this city, in which it is stated, that in a late performance at the theatre, their community had been held up to the public as an object of derision, and that the last act was marked with peculiar indecency and disrespect, and that it is proposed to be renewed on Tuesday next, and she solicits the protection of the civil authority. For myself, I consider the police of the theatre as falling more immediately under the police of the City Magistrate, and that on yourself, as Mayor of New Orleans, particularly devolves the duty of checking the irregularities of the stage. The Society of Nuns in this city is under the protection of the law, and their peculiar situation must interest in their favor the feelings of every heart." As to the religious dispute between the Vicar-General Walsh and Father Antonio de Sedella, it seemed to grow, and to luxuriate in its growth, in proportion to its prolongation. On the 15th of June, Claiborne informed Madison that the parties had resorted to a suit at law, to determine the right of possession to the church, and that it was expected that "a great show of zeal and acrimony would be made."

* Executive Journal, p. 179, vol. 1.

On the 3d of July, Claiborne prorogued again the Legislature, which had reassembled in June, after its first prorogation on the 4th of May. In his address to its members on that occasion, he said: "In a Territory whose citizens are, for the most part, either natives, or descendants of the natives of France and Spain, who had long cherished a fond remembrance of the country of their forefathers—in a Territory that had been controlled by the will of arbitrary chiefs for near a century, and harassed by frequent changes of allegiance, where the ties of birth, affinity and language, the influence of habit and past favors had made those impressions which like causes everywhere produce—that man, indeed, must be little acquainted with human nature who had supposed that, in a Territory thus situated, the principles of the American Government could have been introduced without difficulty, or that the public functionaries could have discharged their duties in such a way as to have conciliated the good opinion of all." He then went on reviewing and defending all the acts of his administration, and passing from that subject to the legislative labors of those he was addressing, he remarked: "With a period so limited as that of your sessions, and with such a diversity of duties before you, more could not have been expected, and it is a subject of congratulation that so much has been done, and done so well. Another important change in the nature of our Government now awaits us. The Congress of the United States, ever just to their engagements, and faithful to the interests of all within their protection, have assigned the period at which Louisiana is to become one of the sovereign and independent States of the American Union. In the mean time, the right of self-government is extended to this district under the like restrictions which have been laid on our fellow-citizens in the other Territories of the

United States. This species of temporary government has been found commensurate to the protection of society, and the advancement of the general weal, and is certainly well calculated for the gradual introduction of those representative principles on which the future Constitution of the State (when erected) must necessarily be predicated. But possibly there may be many whom this new form of government will fail to satisfy. It would, indeed, be a presumption unwarranted by experience, to calculate on universal approbation of any measure. The best of men may occasionally differ in political sentiments, and the investigation of their opinions leads to truth, and may be considered one of the salutary incidents of political freedom. But, unfortunately, society is sometimes infested with members who argue not to enlighten, but to mislead their fellow-citizens, and who, from motives of disingenuous ambition, or from malice, labor incessantly to raise themselves on the ruin of others. That there have been, and still are, a few individuals among us of that disposition, is, I fear, too true. Under their patronage, calumny may recommence its efforts. It may distort the most innocent actions, and pervert error into crime. It may enter the household of domestic life, harrow up private feelings, and produce private distress. But the distrust of the discerning, and the contempt of the good, will, sooner or later, drive the authors into obscurity.   .   .   .   .   .   .

.   .   .   .

"We have heard idle reports of various kinds, respecting territorial divisions, and partial, and sometimes total, retrocessions to foreign Powers, but these seem to be the fanciful chimeras of unreflecting minds. My firm belief is, that the Mississippi will cease to flow, ere she ceases to behold Louisiana attached to the empire of American freedom. A disposition to encroach on the *territories of others* is foreign to the nature of our Government; but the perfect preservation of *its own* is one of its vital principles. Just to the rights of others, the American nation will preserve *their own* inviolate, or perish with them.

Referring to this address, of which he sent a copy to the Department of State at Washington, Claiborne said* to Madison, "Perhaps you will perceive on my part a greater share of feeling than ought to have been manifested, but the late state of party here was such that I could not well have omitted to notice it, and I am persuaded that the allusions made to the efforts of calumniators may have a good effect, not on them, for they are callous to every virtuous impulse, but with the people, who, I trust, will not for the future be as easily imposed upon by pretended patriots."

On the 11th of July, Vicar-General Walsh wrote to Claiborne a letter, in which he complained " of the interruption of public tranquillity which had resulted from the ambition of a refractory monk, supported in his apostasy by the fanaticism of a misguided populace, and by the countenance of an individual,† whose interference was fairly to be attributed less to zeal for the religion he would be thought to serve, than to the indulgence of private passions and the promotion of views equally dangerous to religion and to civil order." He further informed Claiborne that two individuals had gone to Havana, with the express intent of procuring a reinforcement of monks to support Father Antonio de Sedella in "his schismatic and rebellious conduct," and prayed for such relief and assistance as the Executive could afford him. Claiborne replied, "that under the American Government, where the rights of conscience

---

* Claiborne to Madison, 6th July, 1805. Ex. Journal. p. 201, vol. 1.
† Probably the Marquis of Casa Calvo.

are respected, and no particular sect is the favorite of the law, the civil magistrates were bound carefully to avoid interference in religious disputes, unless, indeed, the public peace should be broken, or menaced, and then it became their duty to act." He then recommended harmony and tolerance to the priest; "for," observed he, "if those who profess to be the followers of the meek and humble Jesus, instead of preaching brotherly love and good will to man, and enforcing their precepts by example, should labor to excite dissension and distrust in a community, there is indeed ground to fear that the Church itself may cease to be an object of veneration."

At this time, Claiborne received a very flattering proof of the President's unshaken confidence, by the renewal of his commission as Governor of Louisiana, which circumstance, he said in a letter of the 22d of July, "had excited in his breast the liveliest emotions of gratitude and pleasure."

The late act of Congress in relation to the land claims and titles in the Territory had produced, as mentioned before, great anxiety in the public mind, so much so that it was deemed expedient to send John W. Gurley, the Register of the Land Office, on a tour through the several counties of the Territory, to give explanations as to its bearings and effects, "and to defeat," said Claiborne, "the machinations of those few wicked men among us, who labor incessantly to embarrass and injure the administration." He strenuously recommended* to Gurley "to spare no pains to acquire for the Government the general confidence of the citizens, and in particular to convince them that their rights to land would be liberally confirmed according to the equity of their situation, and not to rigorous law."

---

* Executive Journal, p. 209, vol. 1.

James Pitot had resigned his commission as Mayor, and Watkins had been appointed in his place. The new City Council went actively to work and to plan improvements. It passed Resolutions requiring the evacuation of the forts around the city, which were occupied by the troops of the United States, their speedy destruction, and the filling up of the ditches which surrounded the forts and New Orleans. Claiborne partially complied with their request. In a communication of the 2d of August, he said to them, " I am so strongly impressed with the opinion that the stagnant water which accumulates in the old fortifications must prove injurious to the health of the city, that I cheerfully consent to the leveling of them all, except those of Forts St. Charles and St. Louis. These two forts are garrisoned by troops of the United States, and cannot be evacuated, but in pursuance of orders emanating from the President. Desirous, however, of co-operating with the City Council in all measures which may conduce to the health of the city, I have no objection to the draining of the ditches in the vicinity of St. Charles and St. Louis, under an impression that it can be done without injury to the works."

In relation to the public buildings, a controversy arose as to their possession. Colonel Freeman, the Commander of the United States troops, was in possession of some of them, which were claimed by the city. Claiborne sided with the civil authorities, but Freeman refused to obey Claiborne. This gave rise to a sharp correspondence between them, and the whole matter had to be referred to the President of the United States.

In August, Claiborne undertook a journey through the several counties of the Territory, and, on the 23d of that month, he wrote to Madison, from the County of Acadia, sixty miles above New Orleans, in relation to the late land act of Congress: "To meet the convenience of the citizens," said he,* "and to render them justice, I am inclined to think that some amendment to the late act of Congress relative to the titles of land in this Territory will be found advisable, and upon this subject I shall hereafter do myself the honor to write you fully. I will at this time only observe, that some indulgence ought to be given to the owners of lands on the Mississippi; and particularly, that they should be secured in a right of pre-emption to a certain quantity of acres on the rear of their present possessions. Under the Government of Spain, it was customary to grant from six to twenty acres in front and forty in depth. The cypress swamps which approach near the lands now in cultivation were seldom included in the grant, but from time immemorial the timber has been at the disposition of the inhabitant who owned the lands in front, and he was considered by the Spanish Government as possessing an equitable right to the swamp. If Congress should not make some special provision on this point, much discontent will arise. Large cypress swamps, which at present limit the valuable farms on the Mississippi, will be monopolized by speculators, and the present settlers greatly injured."

In the beginning of autumn, and when Claiborne was in Concordia,† a Frenchman, who had, no doubt, brought from France his mad notions about liberty, made an attempt to excite the negroes to insurrection, and considerable alarm ensued in consequence of it; but the Frenchman was arrested, and the uneasiness soon subsided.

On the 13th of September, Claiborne sent to Albert Gallatin, Secretary of the Treasury, an estimate of the expenses of the Government of the Territory of Or-

---

* Executive Journal, p. 252, vol. 1.
† Claiborne to Madison, **p. 257,** vol. 1.

leans for the coming year, 1806, and that estimate shows the economy with which that Government was carried on, for it amounted* to only $18,650.

From a communication† made by Claiborne to the President of the United States on the 23d of October, it appears that the buildings which were considered as property devolving upon the United States, were:— First—The Government House, very ancient and out of repair. Second—The Military Barracks, a row of brick buildings, sufficiently large to accommodate twelve or fifteen hundred men, and needing only some inconsiderable repairs. Third—The Military Hospital, a large brick building adjoining the Barracks, and in good repair. Fourth—The Public Stores, two large brick buildings, and very valuable. Fifth—the Cavalry Barracks, consisting of two brick buildings, much out of repair. Sixth—The old Custom-House, a large wooden building, unfit for any public purpose. Seventh—The Lower Custom-House, a small wooden building. Eighth—The Priests' House, a small wooden edifice, heretofore appropriated for the residence of the Head of the Church in Louisiana. Ninth—The Powder Magazine, a brick building, near the bank of the Mississippi, and opposite the City of New Orleans. Tenth—The Public School-House, a brick building, and well calculated for its purposes. "The Principal, or City Hall," said Claiborne, "a very beautiful and commodious building, is claimed by the City Council as the property of the city, and being under the impression that their claim is a good one, I have committed it solely to their disposition."

If the continued presence of the Spanish troops had been unpalatable to the Government of the United States, to Governor Claiborne, and to some of the inhabi-

---
* Claiborne to Gallatin, p. 259, vol. 1.
† Claiborne to Jefferson, p. 272, vol. 1.

tants of the Territory, the United States troops in New Orleans became as great a subject of annoyance to its citizens. It is but very seldom that civil and military authorities can harmonize, and that conflicts of jurisdiction do not arise wherever they are brought in close proximity. It proved to be the case in New Orleans, as everywhere else. The Mayor of the city got into a sharp quarrel with Colonel Freeman, the Commander of the United States troops, and, on the 6th of November,* Claiborne advised the President of the United States to remove the troops from New Orleans. "The troops situated here," he said, "have, I believe, conducted themselves as well as an army ever did, similarly situated, but it is impossible for any commander to maintain discipline among men posted in a city, where the temptations to dissipation are so various, and the means of evading the attention of officers so easy."

On the 20th of November, Claiborne had the satisfaction to forward to the Secretary of State at Washington the copy of an address from the House of Representatives of the Territory to the President, which had been unanimously adopted, "and which," he said, "evidenced a degree of patriotism which, he hoped, would have a good effect." He further remarked, that he had of late observed a favorable change in the public sentiment. "No man," he continues," † "entertains a greater regard for the ancient inhabitants of Louisiana than myself, or more appreciates their many private virtues, and I entertain strong hopes that, in a few years, they will become very zealous members of the American Republic."

Claiborne had commissioned Colonel Hopkins to organize the militia throughout the Territory; and among other very judicious instructions, he had specially rec-

---

* Executive Journal, p. 287, vol. 1.
† Executive Journal, p. 294, vol. 1.

ommended to him, in selecting captains and subalterns, "to endeavor to make an equal distribution, where the population would permit it, among the ancient and modern Louisianians; but, in all appointments, to consider a fair reputation as an essential qualification, and an attachment to the Government of the United States as a great recommendation."

The Judiciary being the great conservative element in our institutions, the importance of securing for the Bench the services of men distinguished for their moral and intellectual worth has always been deeply felt, but, at the same time, no adequate salary for such services has ever been provided for to this very day. The evil is coeval even with our Territorial organization; for, on the 27th of November, 1805, Claiborne wrote as follows to the Secretary of State, Mr. Madison: "The economy observed in the salaries of the judicial officers of this Territory will, I fear, affect the respectability of our Judiciary. The compensation of a Supreme Judge is really inadequate to a comfortable support. Judge Hall, although by no means extravagant in his mode of living, cannot, I am sure, make his salary meet his expenses; and as for Judge Prevost, who has a large family to maintain, he cannot possibly avoid making inroads on his private fortune."

Whether or not it was owing to these inadequate salaries that Claiborne had not been able to secure proper men to sit in the inferior courts which had been created by the Legislative Council, it is no less certain that, according to his declaration, "they neither commanded, in the discharge of their functions, for the law, or for themselves, the public respect." Forgetting even the impartiality of judges, it seems that they took an active part in quarrels, disputes, and other contests, from which they ought to have kept themselves aloof. Thus closed the year 1805.

CHAPTER III.

GOVERNOR CLAIBORNE'S ADMINISTRATION.—AARON BURR'S CONSPIRACY.

1806.

CLAIBORNE, in the beginning of December, 1805, had been compelled to visit the populous county of Attakapas, with a view of putting an end, in person, to disturbances which had almost assumed the proportions of a civil war, and which arose from the assassination of a Frenchman named St. Julien, who was connected by marriage with one of the most influential families of that section of the Territory. Another object of Claiborne's journey was to examine the means of defence on which he could rely, should he be attacked by the Spaniards. During his absence, the administration of the Government devolved upon Secretary Graham, who, on the 2d of January,* wrote to Madison: "This day we received by a ship in a very short passage from New York the President's Message of the 3d of December to the Senate and House of Representatives. A copy was immediately sent to the Governor, and if he receives it, I am sure it will hasten his return to the city, unless he finds it expedient to remain a little longer where he is, *to make some arrangements for the defence of our western frontiers.* He may probably think this the more necessary, as a report has gone abroad that the Marquis of Casa Calvo has been tampering with the Indians in that quar

---

* Executive Journal, page 20, vo'. 2.

ter. Whatever he may have done, his journey, I apprehend, must have been undertaken from motives different from those he assigned to the Governor, for he has not yet, I am told, gone where he stated he should go, and he has been already longer absent than he led us to believe he would be. I should unwillingly raise in your mind any improper suspicions against this gentleman, but my opinion is, that he ought not to be permitted to remain in this country. His manners and his character must give him influence, and that influence must be used against us, whenever an occasion for doing so may present itself. If we could get clear of every Spaniard in the country, I should rejoice; for we should then be freed from our most dangerous enemies. From the report made to the Mayor, there are about two hundred and thirty of these people here. They are generally of that description who would be ready to seize any moment of disturbance to commit the vilest depredations; and, whether in peace or in war, they are a nuisance to the country.

"As the President's Message induces me to believe that a rupture with Spain is not an improbable event, I have felt it my duty (the Governor being absent) to ascertain, for your information, what are our present probable means of defence. From the best accounts I can get, we have in this city and its vicinity about three hundred and fifty men, other than French, Spanish, or natives, on whose good wishes we may rely. In this estimate are included *all* the Americans, and, in fact, all those whose language is not French, or Spanish. I speak of inhabitants. To these we may add a hundred, or perhaps one hundred and fifty sailors, and the regular troops in garrison, from all of which I calculate that we could not draw in a few days more than five hundred men fit for service. In making this estimate, it is far from my intention to insinuate that there are not many among the natives, and some among the French, who would join us; but, at present, it is impossible for me to form anything like a conjecture *how many* would do so. From what I hear, and from what I see, I am induced to think that the prevailing disposition among these two classes of people is to remain neutral, in case of a war between Spain and the United States. Yet I believe this disposition would be more or less general according to the measures pursued by the Americans here. If we show a determination to resist any attack that may be made, many of them, I calculate, will join us—some from principle, and more from a conviction that we must ultimately succeed. But if we do not form a rallying-point for them, they will, I believe, do nothing themselves. Under this impression, the Mayor and myself are endeavoring to draw all our countrymen into a military association for the defence of the city, if it should be attacked by the Spanish forces now on our western and eastern frontiers. . . . . This association will be put into no regular form until the return of the Governor. He will then give it that which seems to him most proper. The object of it is to draw out, under the exigency of the moment, and to put in military array, men who would not otherwise subject themselves to the inconvenience of doing military duty. The expedient will answer but for a time, and I fear but for a very short time; for the Spanish forces are increasing in our neighborhood, and might, even with their present number, if they are brave, bear down any opposition we could make. This is, at least, the prevailing opinion, and the very circumstance of its being so is alarming, for we have few men here who would take what they supposed to be the weakest side. To save their property would be the great object of nearly all, and to take arms on the weakest side might be supposed as the readiest means of losing it. The peculiar circumstances attending the mulatto corps will require much delicacy of management. I have, therefore, thought it most prudent not to say anything to them until the Governor's return."

Claiborne's return was not long delayed, for he arrived on the 5th of January, and he informed Madison, on the 7th, that he had long regretted* the prolonged residence of the Marquis of Casa Calvo and other Spanish officers in the Territory, because their intrigues weakened the attachment of our citizens to their government, engendered discontent, and were made the ground for belief that the country west of the Mississippi would speedily return to Spain. He added that, for these reasons, he received with pleasure the official communication of the President's determination to urge them to a final departure, and he gave the assurance that he would endeavor to convey this order in the same spirit with which it was sent to him, so as to leave no room for discussion. But the Marquis was still absent, and some uncertainty prevailed as to the place where he might be found. "In the course of to-morrow," wrote Claiborne, "I will endeavor to obtain correct information on this point, and will communicate to the Marquis, by express, the order for his departure. I think it best that the Marquis should not again visit this city. It is not probable that the order for the departure of the Spanish officers will excite any commotion in the interior of the Territory, or that it would occasion regret to other persons than the connections of the individuals concerned. But in New Orleans there are many adherents to the Spanish interest, a few of respectable standing in society, but for the most part

---

* Executive Journal, p. 27, vol. 2.

composed of characters well suited for mischievous and wicked enterprises. I do not believe that, under existing circumstances, the Marquis would encourage acts of violence and hostility; but as his influence here is considerable, and might, if used on the occasion, give rise to a commotion which could not be checked without bloodshed, I have thought it prudent early to apprise him of the President's orders. I shall, indeed, be sorry if the excursion of the Marquis should have subjected me to the smallest share of censure. I did not suppose that his real objects were unfriendly to the United States, nor did I accredit assurances to the contrary, which he so readily gave me. But as I doubted my authority to prevent his excursion, I thought it best to state no objections to it."

Claiborne's visit to several of the counties of the Territory had been attended with satisfactory results. Some of the civil authorities, whose regular action had been impeded, had been again set in motion, and gave fair promise to answer the Governor's expectations. He had commissioned many militia officers; he had given on the land laws such explanations as were suited to check the rising discontent; and he had made successful efforts, as he believed, to attach the citizens to the Government of the United States. He was not, however, without considerable alarm; for, on the 8th, he informed the Department of State* that, in the present crisis of affairs, the regular troops in the Territory were too few in number to give confidence to the well-disposed citizens, or to deter the treacherous from forming mischievous machinations. "The Louisianians," he said, "are a timid people, and so little acquainted are they with the strength of the United States, that the issue of

---

* Executive Journal, p. 30, vol. 2.

a contest with Spain is esteemed by them as doubtful, and, therefore, they (or many of them) would probably be disposed to remain neutral, as the surest means of preserving their property. If war should be deemed inevitable, I esteem it my duty to suggest the propriety of raising and organizing a respectable corps of horse. The country west of the Mississippi is interspersed with immense prairies, and an army could not act to advantage in that quarter without the support of cavalry.

" With respect to the Mulatto corps in this city, to which Mr. Graham alluded in his communication, I am, indeed, at a loss to know what policy is best to pursue. Their organization during the late temporary government was not liked by the ancient Louisianians, nor were there wanting Americans who, with a view to my injury, reprobated the proceeding, both by speaking and writing. Indeed, so much was said on the subject, that the late Legislative Council thought it prudent to take no notice of the Mulatto corps in the General Militia Law. This neglect has soured them considerably with the American Government, and it is questionable how far they would, in time of danger, prove faithful to the American standard. I shall, however, procure a census of the free people of color who reside in and near this city. Those capable of bearing arms may probably amount to about five hundred, and, while proper exertions shall be made to conciliate the goodwill of all, I have little doubt but that those among them who possess property and a fair reputation will, in any event, prove faithful in their allegiance."

On the 10th of January, Claiborne dispatched Capt. Ross in search of the Marquis of Casa Calvo, with a letter informing the Marquis that the President of the United States had directed him and all other persons holding commissions from, or retained in the service of, his Catholic Majesty, to quit the Territory of Orleans as soon as possible. He further informed the Marquis that this proceeding had been resorted to as a measure of precaution, rendered the more expedient from the rejection by Spain of the proposals submitted by the Envoy Extraordinary of the United States for an amicable adjustment of existing differences—from the reinforcements lately landed at Pensacola—from similar movements on our western frontier—and from the recent acts of aggression committed by the Spanish troops in that quarter. "I repeat to your Excellency," said Claiborne, "that this is only a measure of precaution dictated by the circumstances of the times, and not intended as an act of offence toward your nation, or of rigor against yourself and the other gentlemen attached to the service of his Catholic Majesty.

"In making this communication to your Excellency, it may be proper further to inform you, that you have never been accredited by the President of the United States as a Commissioner of Limits; that no proposal has been made on the part of Spain for setting such a commission on foot, nor indeed can it be considered as necessary, so long as the present difference of opinion continues respecting the lines to be run."

The next day, the 11th, he communicated a similar order to Intendant Morales, who was then in New Orleans, and who immediately remonstrated against the enforcement of such a measure. But Claiborne replied, that he had no power to deviate from his instructions, and that if his Catholic Majesty wished an accredited agent to reside at New Orleans, the proper channel of application would be, through his Minister, to the President of the United States. Claiborne was determined this time to get rid, cost what may, of the presence of these dangerous guests, and even instructed Major Porter, who was in command of Fort Claiborne, in the District of Natchitoches, to use force, if necessary, to prevent the return of Casa Calvo, should that officer attempt, as was expected, to pass through that section of the Territory on his way back to New Orleans.*

Under such circumstances, and when it was still a matter of doubt how the Spanish officers would take this abrupt dismissal from the Territory, where they were lingering with such persevering and mysterious fondness, Claiborne learned, with great displeasure, that General Wilkinson had given a special order to detach one full company from New Orleans to Fort Adams. The regular troops in the city did not exceed two hundred and eighty men at the time, including officers, and of these about sixty were on the sick-list. To withdraw a whole company from such a small effective force was, therefore, a matter of considerable importance.† Claiborne requested Colonel Freeman, the commanding officer in New Orleans, to suspend the execution of Wilkinson's order. But the Colonel refused, on the ground that he had no such discretionary power. In a case of emergency, Claiborne would, therefore, have had to rely chiefly on the militia, which was far from having yet a proper organization, with the exception of the Battalion of Orleans Volunteers, represented by Claiborne as composed‡ of "active, gallant young men, who possessed much military ardor, and who would, if the occasion required it, support with firmness the interest and honor of their country." He also wrote to Madison: "The native citizens of the United States who reside in this city have of late manifested a great share

---

* Executive Journal, p. 40, vol. 2.
† Executive Journal, p. 42, vol. 2.
‡ Executive Journal, p. 42.

of military ardor, and I perceive with satisfaction that a true spirit of patriotism animates many of the young Creoles." * But he did not express himself so favorably as to the interest taken by the population in the exercise of their right of suffrage; for he thought proper to call the attention of Madison to the " great degree of political apathy" which had prevailed in the community in relation to an election for the House of Representatives, which had been held on the 21st of January.

Perhaps this indifference shown to the Government which had been lately implanted in Louisiana was, to some degree, due to the apprehension on the part of many of displeasing the Spanish authorities still present, by appearing to harmonize with the new possessors of the soil, and to appreciate their institutions; for it must not be forgotten that, in the opinion of many, the cession of Louisiana was far from being irrevocably settled. Hence Claiborne spared no effort to accelerate the departure of these agents of the Government of Spain. Morales, who was anxious to remain where he was, had alleged to Claiborne, as a reason for the delay he solicited, that he was expecting from the Viceroy of Mexico a large sum of money, about four hundred thousand dollars, to pay the debts of his Catholic Majesty to certain citizens of the Territory, which could not be done in his absence. This was intended as a strong argument, from which much was to be hoped; but Claiborne met it in these words: " Should, sir, the money arrive here before a Spanish agent is accredited in this city by the President of the United States, I shall lose no time in forwarding to you at Pensacola a blank passport, in which you may insert the name of such person as you may think proper to vest with authority to receive it, and to

---

* Executive Journal, p. 46.

liquidate and discharge the aforesaid debt." This was not all; and Claiborne, not trusting entirely to the force of his logic to produce on the stubborn pertinacity of Morales the effect which he desired, added this significant paragraph : " I esteem it a duty to remind you that the departure from this Territory of yourself and the gentlemen attached to your department will be expected in the course of the present month." This was allowing very little breathing-time to Morales; for this note was dated on the 25th of January, and to it was annexed a passport couched in the most courteous terms.* It was no longer possible for the Intendant to expostulate, and, on the 1st of February, he departed for Pensacola.

Thus the obnoxious Intendant had at last been driven out. There remained the lordly Casa Calvo to be also dismissed without delay. Claiborne was anxious to have done with this unpleasant duty; the more so, that every day something occurred which rendered more desirable the complete absence of all Spanish influence in the Territory. For instance, on the 29th of January, Stephen, a free black man, had appeared before Claiborne and declared on oath that the people of color had been tampered with, and that some of them were devoted to the Spanish interest, which declaration Claiborne believed to be true.† Stephen's information was also corroborated by that of a white man called Horatio Gerel, which was not without effect on Claiborne's mind, although he did not credit, on the whole, the statement of the deponent.

Fortunately, Claiborne's anxiety was relieved by the arrival of Casa Calvo, on the evening of the 4th of February. The Marquis had come from Nacogdoches, through Natchitoches, but without having met with Captain Ross. On the 6th, Claiborne hastened to express

* Executive Journal, p. 49, vol. 2.
† Executive Journal, p. 53, vol 2.

to him, as politely as possible, "the wish that his departure might not be delayed beyond a few days." The Marquis was shocked, and remonstrated; but Claiborne replied that he could not doubt, nor could discuss, the propriety of the orders of the President of the United States; that they served as a rule for his conduct; and that on the present occasion, the only duty devolving upon him was to see them executed. Wherefore he required that the Marquis and all other persons holding commissions from, or retained in the service of, his Catholic Majesty, should quit the Territory of Orleans as soon as possible, and he "tendered such services as might be in his power to facilitate their embarkation." The Marquis was far from being pacified by the urbane tone of this communication. He retorted that he looked on the treatment inflicted on him as a shameful act of violence, and an insult to the King his master. "On the contrary," replied Claiborne, on the 11th of February, "the residence of so many Spanish officers in this Territory having been permitted by the President, so long beyond the time prescribed by treaty for their departure, is a proof of his respect for his Catholic Majesty, and of his liberal indulgence toward those employed in his service; an indulgence which, I am sorry to perceive, is not sufficiently appreciated by all who experience it." Then followed a request that the Marquis should depart on or before the 15th day of the present month, with all the officers of Spain remaining in the Territory. The next day, the 12th, he sent to the Marquis a passport, inclosed in a short note, expressing "his best wishes for the health and happiness of the nobleman whose presence had become so unacceptable." Casa Calvo, like Morales, felt that he could no longer tarry, and departed on the day fixed by Claiborne, but full of wrath and indignation.

On the 13th of February, Claiborne informed Jefferson

that the public sentiment, if he was not greatly mistaken, had of late undergone a change highly favorable to the American Government. "The natives of Louisiana," he said, " are for the most part attached to the Government of the United States, and I am persuaded that most of the men of property would, in the event of war, rally around the American standard." Toward the close of this month, Claiborne rendered to Albert Gallatin, Secretary of the Treasury, an account of his expenses, with his remarks and comments on the subject, among which is a passage depicting a state of things which has continued to this day: " You will probably be surprised at the high charge of printing for the Executive Department; but it is only in unison with every other charge for public or private services in the city; and if my expenditure should wear the aspect of extravagance, I pray you to attribute it to the character of the place where I reside, and not to the want of a disposition, on my part, to bring my disbursements within the limits of a prudent economy."

The dismissal of Morales and Casa Calvo from New Orleans gave new fuel to the already existing hostility of the Spaniards to the Americans, and that hostility showed itself repeatedly, in different ways, whenever the opportunity occurred. Thus, on the 15th of March, Claiborne was informed that, for the future, the mail of the United States would not be permitted by Governor Folch, of Florida, to pass either by land or by water through that part of the dominions of his Catholic Majesty; that the fortifications of Mobile were undergoing repairs, and that the Spaniards were at work among the numerous tribes of the Choctaws, with the hope, in case of need, to induce them to join in a war against the United States. This information excited the apprehensions of Claiborne, and, on the 18th of March, he[*] wrote to the

[*] Executive Journal, p. 87, vol. 2.

President: "The presence of a respectable force is essential to the safety of New Orleans. I suppose that, at this time, there cannot be less than two millions of dollars in this city, which, together with the merchandise in the numerous private warehouses, would furnish a rich booty for a successful enemy."

According to a proclamation of the Governor concerning an early session of the Legislature, that body met on the 24th of March. Claiborne, in his message, congratulated them on the prosperous condition of the Territory, whose interests were committed to their care. "The late Legislative Council," he said, "did much for the preservation of order in society, and for the advancement of the general weal; but much as that assembly did, still much is left for the present Legislature to accomplish. . . . . . In the infancy of our political career, we should consider our laws as experiments, and they should undergo such improvements as reason and experience may suggest." He then recommended a revision of the judiciary system, certain improvements to be made in the criminal code, the establishment of a penitentiary with solitary confinement, the creation of work-houses for vagrants, houses of correction for the dissolute, houses of refuge for the destitute, and provisions for the trial of slaves by summary process. He also called the attention of the Legislature to the necessity of facilitating the means of internal commercial intercourse, and of improving navigation on those watercourses which led from the counties of Attakapas and Opelousas to the river Mississippi. The want of that proper care which should have been bestowed on roads and levees was commented upon, and legislative interference demanded. As to the important subject of education, he said, "It is with regret I have to inform you that the law passed by the Legislative Council, entitled

'An Act to establish a University in the Territory of Orleans,' does not promise to advance the interest of literature with the rapidity which was contemplated. . . . . . The doctrine which prevailed in an ancient Republic of Greece, with respect to their youth, is one which, in my opinion, ought always to be cherished by a free people. The youth should be considered as the property of the State, their welfare should constitute a primary care of the Government, and those in power should esteem it an incumbent duty to make such provisions for the improvement of the minds and morals of the rising generation as will enable them to appreciate the blessings of self-government, and to preserve those rights which are destined for their inheritance. I am one of those who admire the plan adopted by some of the States of the American Union: that of establishing a school in every neighborhood, and supporting it by a general tax on the society. I should, indeed, be happy to see a similar policy pursued in this Territory, and a tax which would bear alike on every individual, in proportion to his wealth, levied for the purpose." He enlarged on the necessity of organizing the militia in the most effective manner, which was of importance at all times, but more particularly " at a period when the United States were experiencing from foreign powers injuries which, if not promptly redressed, must be avenged." He wound up with recommending an increase of taxes to meet the expenses of the new Government.

On the 27th of March, Claiborne wrote to Madison: " I am anxious to learn the real state of affairs between the United States and foreign nations, and particularly so as it relates to Spain. The free navigation of the Mobile by American vessels is still prohibited, and our fellow-citizens on the Tombigbee are experiencing therefrom the most serious inconveniences; their articles of exportation are of no value, and many of the necessaries of life, which were hitherto received by the Mobile, are in great scarcity; in short, sir, if the present state of things should continue for six months longer, the settlement would be ruined, and perhaps abandoned. The American citizens on the Tombigbee have entered into an agreement not to traffic, or to have any intercourse with the Spaniards, so long as the free navigation of the Mobile is denied. But this agreement only proves the spirit and patriotism of our fellow citizens; it will produce no injury on their oppressors." Commenting on this state of things, he drew the inference from passing events, and from those which were expected, that American interests required that there should be at least twelve hundred troops in the Territory of Orleans. "The presence of such a force," he remarked, "would not only deter the Spanish agents in our vicinity from venturing on acts which are calculated to irritate, but, what is infinitely of more consequence, it would give our new fellow-citizens a confidence in the American Government which, I am sorry to say, many of them, at this time, do not possess. I have labored to infuse among the people here a martial spirit, and to keep up a degree of military ardor, but I perceive, with regret, that the spirit which was for awhile roused is declining, and that a general apathy is prevailing. The native Americans declare that the Government neglects them, and the ancient Louisianians, seeing no military preparations, are impressed with an opinion that the United States are either unable, or unwilling, to contend with the power of Spain."

Claiborne was not without reasons for desiring a reinforcement. The news from Natchitoches were of an unpleasant nature.* Spanish troops, to the number of

---

* Executive Journal, p. 104, vol. 2.

four hundred, accompanied by some Indians, had assembled on the Sabine, threatening to advance, and to resume the same position near to Natchitoches from which a small Spanish guard had lately been driven by Captain Turner, under the orders of Major Porter. This movement on the part of the Spaniards had excited much alarm on the western frontier, and should they persevere in their design, it was doubted whether it would be in the power of Major Porter to oppose them with success, inasmuch as his force did not exceed two hundred effective men. Major Porter, however, was not intimidated by this hostile demonstration, and had stationed* a company of infantry in advance of Natchitoches, and within the limits assigned by the Spanish agents to the province of Texas.

Meanwhile, Governor Folch, of Florida, being under the impression that a war between the United States and Spain was a probable event, and that France would not view, without concern, a contest in which the interest of her ally was involved, wrote to Mr. Desforgues, the French Consul at New Orleans, and advised the immediate transportation to Mobile of a park of artillery belonging to France, and still remaining in the Territory. Mr. Desforgues refused to conform to the wishes of Governor Folch, and replied that he would not deliver the artillery, either to the agents of Spain, or of the United States, without the orders of his Government. He confidentially communicated this correspondence to Governor Claiborne, to convince him of his disposition to act a just and candid part toward the United States, and he expressed the hope that it would also be received as an evidence of his confidence in the Governor, and of his personal esteem for him.†

---

* Executive Journal, page 110, vol. 2,
† Executive Journal, p. 110, vol. 2. Claiborne to Madison, 8th of April, 1806.

To the mortification of Claiborne, the Territorial Legislature, which he had convened in an extraordinary session, made* but little progress in the dispatch of business. "The ancient Louisianians," said he in a communication to Jefferson, "are greatly jealous of the native Americans who are in the House of Representatives, nor are there wanting some designing malcontents out of office and confidence, who have recourse to every expedient to disseminate the seeds of distrust and discontent. I am at present on excellent terms with the two Houses of Assembly, but I fear this good understanding will not continue throughout the session; many laws will be offered for my approbation, and my duty will compel me to reject several. Then commences a jealousy of the Executive, and the base intriguers will spare no pains to widen the breach."

On the 16th of April, Claiborne was much gratified at being informed that the Spanish force had been withdrawn from the Sabine, and that the orders to cross that river and establish a post near Natchitoches were countermanded by the Governor-General of Texas. But, at the same time, he was much annoyed by an attack made against him in Congress by John Randolph, who, with his usual acerbity of temper, accused his administration of being marked with weakness and imbecility. Commenting on this attack in a letter to Madison, dated 29th of April,† he said: "The correspondent of Mr. Randolph has made him to speak in language the reverse of truth. This Government is not an imbecile one! it is sufficiently strong for all good purposes! I ask Mr. Randolph and his friend to produce proof of its imbecility. I ask if the laws are not enforced? if personal rights are not secured and good

---

* Executive Journal, p. 118, vol. 2.
† Executive Journal, p. 119, vol 2.

order preserved? I do not know, nor do I believe, that the Government is odious. If there are persons who would have preferred another system, it does not follow that the present one deserves their odium. . . .
. . . With regard to the discontents of the people, I by no means consider them as general or as serious as is represented. That the Louisianians have a great partiality for France as their mother country; that former habits had attached many of them to the Spanish system of government, and that the intrigues of a few artful, designing men had promoted discontent and occasioned me much trouble, are facts of which I have long apprised you; but so far from admitting that the Louisianians are prepared to receive with open arms an invader, I am impressed with an opinion that, in the event of war, many of the creoles of the country would be found faithful to the United States. Perhaps a disposition to remain neutral might become prevalent, as the surest means of preserving their property."

Some difficulties having arisen as to the evidences of citizenship and the enjoyment of the rights which it conferred, Claiborne issued, on the 30th of April, a circular to the notaries public and the clerks of the Superior Court, who then were empowered to receive testimony on the subject, in which he informed them that the Governor, for the future, would give a certificate of citizenship to no person who should not prove his right to the same by his own oath and that of two citizens of the Territory—which citizens should either be the owners of real property within the same, or engaged in some particular business which promised a continuance of their residence in the Territory. They were instructed to notify this regulation to persons claiming citizenship, and to call their special attention to the fact that care would be taken to detect such person as might depose falsely touching the claim of citizenship for himself or others, and to bring him to that punishment which the law prescribes for the crime of perjury.*

Those disagreements which Claiborne had foreseen as destined to arise between the Legislature and himself, were not slow in making their appearance. An act had been passed " to establish certain conditions necessary to be a member of either house of the Legislature of the Territory of Orleans." Claiborne vetoed the bill, on the ground that its operation would be revolutionary, and that it would deprive of their seats several members of the present Legislature. "It seems to me," said he, "that a member possessed of the qualifications required by the ordinance for our Government has a right to continue his functions during the period of which he was elected; and that a law which shall impose other qualifications than those pointed out in the ordinance cannot be constitutional, unless its operation shall be prospective, and not permitted to affect the sitting members." This was on the 2d of May. On the 8th, he inclosed to Madison a copy of the bill, with a copy of the message in which he had expressed his disapprobation of it, and remarked: "The ancient Louisianians in the Legislature are impatient of control, and will illy receive a check from the Executive authority, but I must do my duty, and shall, on every occasion, act the part which my judgment approves. By pursuing this course, I may present my enemies fresh materials to work upon, and render myself unpopular, but my conscience will be tranquil, and I shall sleep the better at night." On the 14th he added:† "The Territorial Legislature will, I fear, do little good during

---

* Executive Journal, p. 121, vol. 2.
† Executive Journal, p. 125, vol. 2.

the present session. They are divided, and one party—the strongest—seems to be greatly influenced by a few men in this city, whose politics and views are, in my opinion, in opposition to the interests of the United States." He resumed the subject in a communication of the 16th of May, in these words: "The difference in language and the jealousy which exists between the ancient and modern Louisianians are great barriers to the introduction of that harmony and mutual confidence which I so much desire. . . . . .

"There are, no doubt, several minor causes of discontent in this quarter; but the most fruitful sources are the introduction of the English language in our courts of justice—the judicial system generally—and particularly the trial by jury—and the admission of attorneys. The pride as well as the convenience of the Louisianians are opposed to any innovation on their language; the trial by jury is by many considered as odious, and the lawyers as serious nuisances. . . . .
. . . .

"When our disputes with Spain are adjusted, and the citizens induced to think that their political destiny is fixed; when the English language is generally spoken, and a knowledge of the principles of the American Government diffused, then I shall be disappointed, if the Louisianians should not be among the most zealous and virtuous members of our Republic. But, at the present crisis, and with the present population, disturbed by the intrigues of adventurers—unprincipled adventurers from every country—it is not in the power of any man to put down distrust and dissatisfaction."

A few days after, on the 26th of May, he vetoed another bill, entitled "An Act declaring the laws which continue to be in force in the Territory of Orleans, and the authors which may be recurred to as authorities within the same." He had previously notified the Department of State at Washington of the course which he had intended to pursue, saying, "This measure was probably supported by some of the French lawyers, and has become a favorite one with the majority of the two Houses. Its rejection will, therefore, excite perhaps some discontent;" and he denounced Daniel Clarke and Evan Jones as being among the intriguers who were the most active in opposing him. "The first, from disappointment," he said, "is greatly soured with the General Administration; and the latter, from principle, is inimical to the General Government. They both cordially unite in doing the Governor here all the injury in their power."* These two gentlemen were wealthy and influential members of the old population of Louisiana, among which they had long resided; therefore they easily proved to be no despicable thorns in Claiborne's political ribs. Claiborne's veto of this last bill produced almost a commotion. Destréhan, Sauvé and Bellechasse, members of the Council, resigned in disgust; but, influenced by the entreaties of Claiborne, Bellechasse withdrew his resignation. The Council itself had passed a Resolution proposing a dissolution of the General Assembly, and assigning as one of their reasons for advocating such a measure, "that the Governor had rejected, and continues to reject, their best laws."

In a communication to Madison sent on the same day he vetoed the bill, Claiborne used the following language: "I consider the bill in question as improper, and it was my duty, therefore, to reject it. If, by the ordinance and laws of Congress, the civil law is recognized, the bill was useless. The Judges of the Superior Court can determine the authorities on which to rely. Their selection

---

* Executive Journal, p. 133, vol. 2.

would likely be more judicious than any which the Legislature could make. I profess myself uninformed of the merits of the bill, and to know not the consequences which might flow from it. In any event, I thought it but right to disapprove the measure." But was it not a very improper stretch of authority on the part of Claiborne to reject a bill, when "he professed himself uninformed of its merits," and thus to defeat a measure which he stated to be "a great favorite" with the representatives of the people? It is not astonishing, therefore, that he found himself the object of harsh censure, and that he produced a great deal of irritation.

Whilst the two Houses were in a state of violent excitement, and discussing the propriety of pronouncing their own dissolution as a political body, a storm arose from another quarter. The French Consul and the French citizens were infuriated by an attack made in one of the newspapers of the city on their beloved Emperor, Napoleon I.; and the Consul, Mr. Desforgues, addressed a formal complaint to Claiborne on the subject. The Governor very properly replied, that the Government had no power over the press; that its licentiousness was seen and regretted, but that a remedy had not yet been devised; that it was not in his power to take any measure on the occasion; that the Judiciary of the county could alone interfere; and that the French Consul should apply to the District Attorney, Mr. Brown, for advice. "Mr. Desforgues," wrote* Claiborne to Madison, "was greatly irritated, and, among many observations, stated that the French citizens would have risen in mass, and massacred the printer, had it not been for his interference. I thanked him for his good intentions, but assured him that there was no necessity for his in-

* Executive Journal, p. 138, vol. 2.

terference, since the Government was adequate to the preservation of order, and to the protection of its citizens from violence. I fear Mr. Desforgues is a violent man, and that he is intriguing with the Louisianians. His movements, however, shall not escape my observation."

Claiborne hastened to lay before the President of the United States the resignations of Destréhan and Sauvé, accompanied with this observation: "The services of an ancient Louisianian in the Legislature cannot with certainty be calculated on. Few are disposed to make any sacrifice of private interest for the public good." These harsh words, into which Claiborne was betrayed, notwithstanding his gentle and kind nature, show that he had permitted himself to be goaded into some degree of resentment. What had contributed to increase his vexations was the election to Congress, as a Delegate, of Daniel Clarke, his personal enemy, which took place about that time. But, on the 28th of May, Claiborne had the satisfaction to inform Madison that the House of Representatives had rejected the resolution of the Council to cease all legislation, and that both Houses "were conducting business with dispatch and concord." *

This dispatch and concord did not prevent the issuing of an address to the people of the Territory, which was signed by certain members of the Legislative Council and of the House of Representatives, and which reflected on the course pursued by Claiborne toward the Legislature. The Governor sent a copy of it to Madison, saying: "That † this publication will raise the popular sentiment in favor of the signers is, perhaps, probable; but I am persuaded its effects will soon pass away. For myself, I only regret the proceeding on ac-

* Executive Journal, p. 153, vol. 2.
† Executive Journal, p. 168, vol. 2, 3d June, 1806.

count of the precedent. An appeal to the people in this way tends to bring the constituted authorities into disrepute, and may lead to anarchy." On the 7th of June, the Legislature adjourned. "The last seven days of the session," said Claiborne to Madison, "the Legislature transacted much business, and separated in harmony. The most perfect good order prevails, and the people seem to take but little interest in the proceedings of their representatives." Several discontented members of the House of Representatives had also resigned after the example of Sauvé and Destréhan, such as Joseph Landry, for the County of Acadia; S. Croizet, for the County of Pointe Coupée; Louis Fonteneau, for the County of Opelousas; and Claiborne had to issue his proclamation for new elections.

In relation to the County of Opelousas, Claiborne was informed that a considerable emigration was about to take place from that county to the Spanish settlement on the River Trinity,* where great encouragement was given to settlers. He gave notice of the fact to Madison in a letter of the 15th of June. "I am informed," said he, "that the ancient inhabitants of Louisiana are much dissatisfied with our judicial system; that the trial by jury is not approved; and that the lawyers are execrated. It is not in my power to remove this cause of dissatisfaction. I never admired the system of county courts. The old plan of commandants was, in my opinion, best suited to the present state of the Territory; but the Legislative Council preferred the immediate introduction of a judiciary on American principles—and I reluctantly acquiesced in the measure. . . . . . . The conduct of the lawyers in the interior counties is a source of great discontent. They are said to be extravagant in their charges; to encourage litigation; and to

* Executive Journal, p. 182, vol. 2.

speculate on the distresses of their clients. I fear there is too much truth in this statement. . . . . Among the emigrants to this Territory there is a description of people which I consider the greatest pests that can afflict any honest society. They are those avaricious speculators who go about with a little ready cash to seek whom they may devour. Some of these hungry parasites have, I am told, fastened on the labors of those ancient Louisianians who have emigrated, and are about to emigrate to Trinity. It is probable that many persons will also emigrate to the Trinity from the counties of Natchitoches and Rapides. They are dissatisfied with our court system, fear taxation, and are made to believe by Spanish partisans that their fortune will be benefited by a removal."

Another cause of dissatisfaction was, that, at the sales of property taken under execution, the sheriffs themselves were frequently the purchasers. To put an end to this evil, Claiborne had to issue a monitory circular to these officers.*

Under the preceding Governments of France and Spain, the Governor of the province of Louisiana, being the representative of the King, was looked upon as the fountain of honor, the seat of justice, the shield of protection on every occasion, and the general and supreme redresser of all wrongs. This impression could not be easily effaced from the mind of the population; hence Claiborne was annoyed by constant appeals to the power which he was supposed to possess. It has been already related that, in the preceding year, a comedy had been acted on the New Orleans stage, which had wounded the feelings of the Ursuline Nuns. They had complained to Claiborne, and the offence having been re-

---

* Executive Journal, p. 185, vol. 2, 18th June, 1806.

peated this year, they again had turned to the Governor to screen them against the derision and ridicule which was aimed at their religious order. Claiborne's answer is given here as completing an episode, which is illustrative of the feelings, manners, and tone of the epoch. Such details, apparently trifling, have been too much neglected by historians, as unworthy of the dignity of their subject. Would not a letter from a Roman Consul to the High Priestess of the Vestals be interesting, if it made us better acquainted with the social life of that age? Battles and great political convulsions are generally the main features to be found in the historical portrait of a nation, but there are small lineaments which should not be omitted to complete its physiognomy. Claiborne's answer to the Lady Abbess must, therefore, be received as one of those light touches of the painter's brush which he deems necessary to the finishing of his work. That answer ran thus: "Holy Sister, the representations at the theatre of which you complain are to me sources of regret; and I beg you to be assured that all my influence will a second time be used with the Mayor of this city (to whom more properly belongs the duty of checking the abuses of the stage) to prevent a repetition of those exceptionable pieces. I am sorry that these representations should have given affliction to the community over which you preside. They may have amused the thoughtless, but cannot, I am sure, be approved by the reflecting part of society. The sacred objects of your Order, the amiable characters which compose it, and the usefulness of their temporal cares, cannot fail to command the esteem and confidence of the good and virtuous. I pray you, holy sister, to receive the assurances of my great respect and sincere friendship."

At this time an event took place which is worthy of

notice, in consequence of a question which arose in the trial, and of the decision thereon by the Superior Court. An inhabitant of the Territory, a Spaniard by birth, was arraigned on the charge of murder.* The counsel for the prisoner demanded, in conformity with the principles of common law, a jury composed in part of his countrymen. It was conceded that the prisoner was an inhabitant of Louisiana at the period of the cession to the United States, and was still an inhabitant thereof; but, inasmuch as he had not taken the oath of allegiance to the United States, it was contended that he was, in fact, an alien, and a subject of the King of Spain. "I am happy, however," wrote Claiborne to Madison, "to inform you that the demand was not acceded to by the court; and although the judges did not give in detail their reasons for rejecting the claim of the prisoner, yet it was understood to be the opinion of the court, that all persons who resided here at the period of the cession, and did not withdraw from the province with the Spanish or French authorities, could not otherwise be considered than as citizens of the United States. I rejoice at the decision, since it has removed from my mind a cause of some inquietude. Certain American lawyers who are settled here have doubted whether the people could be considered as American citizens, until they had taken the oath of allegiance to the United States, or could be convicted of treason, should they enter the armies of a power at war with the United States. I always thought this opinion erroneous. It seemed to me that the allegiance of the inhabitants of the ceded Territory to Spain and France having ceased, it must, of necessity, attach to the power that protected them. I never considered the administration of the oath as a necessary measure. But,

---

* Executive Journal, p. 194, vol. 2.

since lawyers of some eminence professed to entertain a contrary doctrine, I am happy to find my opinion supported by a decision of the Supreme Court." It is worthy of remark, that this decision supports the course pursued by General O'Reilly, in 1769, toward those who rebelled against the Spanish authorities after the cession of Louisiana by France, and who, when put on their trial, excepted to the jurisdiction of the court, on the ground that they were French subjects—which exception was overruled by O'Reilly.*

On the 5th of July, Claiborne informed the Secretary of War that, on the celebration of the 4th, the citizens of New Orleans had exhibited a degree of patriotism which had afforded him much pleasure. " All the stores of the city," said he, " were closed by order of the City Council, and the inhabitants generally suspended their usual avocations. High Mass was performed in the forenoon at the churches, and a *Te Deum* sung at night; a new tragedy, called 'Washington, or the Liberty of the New World,' was performed, and much applauded by a numerous audience, consisting, for the most part, of ancient Louisianians. The tragedy being finished, the company repaired to the public ball-room, and the evening was closed with dancing. As was usual, federal salutes were fired from the forts, and the Battalion of Orleans Volunteers paraded on the occasion. From these particulars you will observe that the American feeling is not in exile from this Territory. There are, indeed, some ancient prejudices which it is difficult to remove, and there are some local parties encouraged by a few designing men, whose native language is English—which, in some measure, stifles the germ of patriotism; but I persuade myself that the time is not far distant when the Louisian-

---

* Gayarre's History of Louisiana. French Domination, p. 338, vol. 2.

ians generally will be zealous members of our Republic."

In the beginning of July, Claiborne departed from New Orleans, partly to avoid a residence in the city during the sickly season, and partly to attend in person to the better organization and disciplining of the militia in the several counties of the Territory. Whilst in the County of Attakapas, on the 29th of July, he learned that the Spaniards were again making threatening demonstrations on the Sabine. This intelligence induced him to journey, through the County of Opelousas, to Natchez, where he might be better able to provide for any emergency of danger which might arise. There he was informed, on the 17th of August, that a considerable Spanish force had actually crossed the Sabine,* and had advanced within a few miles of Natchitoches, to Bayou Pierre, where they contemplated establishing a garrison. In consequence of this information, Claiborne, after having had an interview with Cowles Meade, Governor of the Mississippi Territory, and obtained from him a promise of assistance in case of need, departed immediately for the County of Rapides, on his way to Natchitoches, where, on the 26th of August, he addressed to Herrera, the commander of the Spanish force, a long letter, in which he complained of several acts of hostility committed by the Spaniards, and, among others, of this recent violation of a Territory which he hoped to have seen respected as neutral ground, at least pending the negotiations between their respective Governments for an amicable adjustment of the limits of Louisiana. Herrera, as a matter of course, demurred to this accusation, and defended, to the best of his argumentative powers, the course which he, or the other Spanish authorities,

---

* Executive Journal, p. 228, vol. 2.

had pursued. In the mean time,* Claiborne wrote to the Secretary of War: "I have found the Americans who are settled in the frontier counties devoted to the country, and solicitous to be called into service. . .
. . I am sorry, however, to add, that the same degree of patriotism does not exist among the French part of our society; many of the ancient Louisianians are still attached to the Spanish Government, and others are so fully impressed with an opinion that the United States are unable to resist *the mighty power of Spain*, that, in the event of war, they would probably be disposed to take a neutral stand, as the safest course."

Whilst Herrera and Claiborne were thus occupying an almost hostile position to each other, the Spanish General was attacked with a dangerous illness. Claiborne, having been apprised that he was destitute of medical attendance, sent him Doctor Hayward, on the 2d of September, with a kind note, expressing his wishes for the speedy recovery of his health, and tendering such other friendly civilities as might be in the power of the American Governor.† This act of high-toned courtesy on the part of Claiborne produced the most favorable impression on the proud-spirited and sensitive Spaniards. Herrera's sickness, however, suspended for awhile all negotiations, and matters stood still. In the mean time, Claiborne was strengthening himself, by calling the militia to the assistance of the troops which, under Colonel Cushing, were in front of the Spaniards. The Governor had required one hundred men of the County of Rapides; two hundred and fifteen offered their services, and among them a number of the ancient Louisianians—" a circumstance," said Claiborne, " which affords me singular satisfaction." Claiborne wished to take the offensive against

---

* Executive Journal, p. 240. Dispatch of the 28th of August, 1806.
† Executive Journal, p. 253, vol. 2.

the Spaniards, but Colonel Cushing objected, on the ground that this would be contrary to the instructions which had been left with him by General Wilkinson, who was then absent. Claiborne was somewhat nettled at this inactivity of the regular troops, and thus wrote to Cowles Meade, the Secretary and acting Governor of the Mississippi Territory: "Perhaps the inactivity of our troops in this quarter may not have been improper —perhaps our dispute with Spain may at this time be amicably and honorably adjusted, and if so, we shall all rejoice that blood was not shed; but my present impression is, that '*all is not right*.' I know not whom to censure, but it seems to me that there is wrong somewhere."* Seeing that there was not any probability of active operations, and thinking that his presence was unnecessary, as the Spaniards, instead of advancing, had fallen back to a place where they seemed disposed to remain quiet, Claiborne departed for the County of Rapides, to urge in person the organization of those reinforcements and the sending of those supplies which Colonel Cushing might ultimately want. There, having heard of the arrival of General Wilkinson at Natchez, he determined to remain, in the expectation of seeing him on his way to Natchitoches. Whilst sojourning at the spot where he was awaiting Wilkinson, he corrected the false impression which he had given the Secretary of War in relation to the French part of the population of Natchitoches.† "On my arrival at Natchitoches," he said, "I was led to believe that the French inhabitants were very generally disaffected; but my present impression is very different. I do now believe that, if an opportunity offers, many of them will evince their fidelity to the Government."

* Executive Journal, p. 269, vol. 2. Dispatch of the 9th of September.
† Executive Journal, p. 278, vol. 2. Dispatch of the 15th of September.

Wilkinson arrived on the 19th of September, at the place where Claiborne was expecting him, and immediately addressed the Governor in writing, to ascertain the number of militia who could be relied on from the Territory, in case of a conflict with the Spaniards. Claiborne replied that he could not promise the support of more than four hundred men, officers included.* "You will recollect," said he, "the extent of this frontier, and, indeed, the vulnerable position of the whole Territory. I am unwilling, therefore, to draw to any one point a large portion of my militia, lest, by doing so, I should invite attack in some other quarter." On the 22d, Claiborne departed for the County of Opelousas, in order to organize and stimulate its militia. There he found an unwillingness on the part of the ancient population to furnish volunteers as he desired. This feeling greatly exasperated those Americans who had settled in that region, and the excitement became so intense that Claiborne thought proper to address Judge Collins on this subject in a written communication, in which he said: "The reluctance of the ancient Louisianians to rally at the call of their country is seen and regretted, but I pray that this conduct may not occasion reproach from the native Americans, but, on the contrary, that they may continue to extend toward them every act of civility and kindness. I am disposed to make great allowances for the unwillingness of the Louisianians to enter, at this crisis, into the service of the United States. They have been educated in a belief that the Spanish monarchy was the most powerful on earth; and many of them are impressed with an opinion that the United States will fall an easy prey to the Spanish arms. Hence arises their neutral stand, as the surest means of safety to their per-

* Executive Journal, p. 283, vol. 2.

sons and property. There are other excuses which may be made for the recent conduct of some of the Louisianians, but it is unnecessary to recite them. I am persuaded of your disposition to cultivate harmony, and I am sure that by your example and precept you will discourage any proceedings which might lead to disunion, or what I should consider the greatest calamity that could befall the Territory."*

Claiborne returned to New Orleans on the evening of the 6th of October, and on the 8th he informed the Secretary of War that the number of militia from the frontier counties, who had marched for Natchitoches, exceeded five hundred men, and that a detachment of one hundred regulars, having in charge such military stores as could be obtained, and might be required by General Wilkinson, would set out in a few days. "But, " added he, "there is in this city a degree of apathy, at the present moment, which mortifies and astonishes me; and some of the native Americans act and discourse as if perfect security everywhere prevailed. . . . .
I fear the ancient Louisianians of New Orleans are not disposed to support with firmness the American cause; I do not believe they would fight against us; but my present impression is, that they are not inclined to rally under the American standard. We have a Spanish priest here who is a very dangerous man; he rebelled against the Superiors of his own church, and would even rebel, I am persuaded, against this Government, whenever a fit occasion may serve. This man was once sent away by the Spanish authorities for seditious practices, and I am inclined to think that I should be justifiable, should I do so likewise This seditious priest is a Father Antoine; he is a great favorite of the Louisiana ladies·

---

* Executive Journal, dispatch of the 24th of September, p. 296, vol. 2.

has married many of them, and christened all their children; he is by some citizens esteemed an accomplished hypocrite, has great influence with the people of color, and, report says, embraces every opportunity to render them discontented under the American Government."*

Claiborne, in consequence of these apprehensions, requested the Catholic priest to attend at the Government House, and in the presence of the Mayor of the city, and of Colonel Bellechasse, of the Legislative Council, mentioned to him the reports which were afloat concerning his conduct. The priest listened to them with much humility and solemnly affirmed his innocence, avowing his determination to support the Government and to promote good order. "I, nevertheless, thought it proper," wrote Claiborne, " to administer to him the oath of allegiance, and shall cause his conduct to be carefully observed." He then added, with his usual good-nature, as if it were to mitigate the effect of his harsh suspicions: "The priest declared the reports to have originated in the malice of his enemies. The division in the Catholic Church has excited many malignant passions, and it is not improbable that some injustice has been done to this individual." †

Whilst the Spaniards were so troublesome on the frontiers of Texas, they were remarkably quiet at Baton Rouge, Mobile and Pensacola. Was it a preconcerted plan, and was it their intention to draw all the American forces far to the West? Even at Mobile favorable concessions to American trade had been made. The intractable Governor Folch was no longer in the way. In consequence of a triumph which his rival Morales had obtained over him in an appeal to the Captain-General of Cuba, he had given up, for the present, the Government of

---

* Executive Journal, p. 305, vol. 2. Claiborne to Secretary of War, Oct. 8.
† Executive Journal, p. 310, vol. 2.

Pensacola, and it had devolved upon Colonel Howard, an Irish gentleman of talents, who had long been in the service of Spain, and who showed himself much more conciliating than Folch, in relation to the navigation of the Mobile River by the Americans.

Claiborne's correspondence with the General Government shows how changeful were his impressions, and consequently how wavering he was in the expression of his opinions. This was due to his proneness to listen to rumors and accusations. He seemed constantly to forget that there was a very strong and very natural jealousy between the ancient Louisianians and the new-comers, who were anxious to get the ascendancy in a territory which they considered their exclusive property by purchase, and where they were impatient to implant their laws and habits, with all their ideas and views in ethics, religion and politics. That class of men looked with extreme displeasure in many cases, and, in others, with considerable resentment, at the resistance offered by the old population, who, on their side, considered the native Americans as unprincipled intruders, coming to deprive them of their language, their religion, their lands, their time-honored legislation, their manners and customs—in fact, everything they held dear and sacred. Hence accusations and recriminations on both sides, particularly from many active, restless, and not overscrupulous Americans, who flocked to this new field of enterprise which had opened to them, and where they hoped to secure wealth and political power. Claiborne was constantly permitting himself to share in suspicions that drew from him assertions, or opinions, which he was afterward obliged to retract. Thus, in relation to the organization of the Attakapas militia, which soon held itself in readiness to march, at a moment's warning, to the seat of the expected conflict, he wrote to the Secretary of War on the

12th of October: "I had feared that some difficulty would be experienced in executing my orders, but I am agreeably disappointed. The citizens discovered a great share of patriotism, and avowed their determination to defend with their lives their country. Whatever may be the local discontent of the Louisianians, I begin now to think that they will generally rally at the call of Government. When I first went to Natchitoches, I did distrust the fidelity of the Louisianians in that quarter; and, indeed, every American residing there, with whom I conversed, agreed in opinion that the French part of the society was generally disaffected, but I trust we shall all be disappointed." Again, on another occasion, he had complained of the apathy and want of patriotism in New Orleans, and, on the 17th of October,* he said to the Secretary of War: "I hasten to announce to you the patriotism of the citizens of New Orleans and its vicinity. At a muster, this morning, of the 1st, 2d and 4th Regiments of militia, every officer, non-commissioned officer and private present, made a voluntary tender of their services for the defence of the Territory generally, and more particularly for the defence of the city. This display of patriotism affords me much satisfaction, and has rendered this among the happiest of my life." He also called, with much commendation, the attention of the Secretary of War to the patriotic address made to the militia on that occasion by Colonels Bellechasse and Macarty.

But, on the 7th of November, Claiborne's faith in the Louisianians had again been shaken. A relapse had occurred, and the chronic old fever of suspicion had fastened upon his mind with renovated vigor. The militia had not turned out as he had expected. He was even in bad humor with the native Americans. As ap-

* Executive Journal, p. 314, vol. 2.

peared by information received from General Wilkinson, the Concordia Militia had failed to repair to their post. "I know not," says Claiborne, "how to account for the delinquency. Concordia is settled exclusively by Americans."* As to those constant objects of distrust and jealousy—the Louisianians—he adds: "You will observe that the General places but little confidence in the French who are settled at Natchitoches; perhaps I may be too sanguine in my expectations; but I continue to think that those of the Louisianians who are not for us, will not be against us. I do believe they will be inclined to take a neutral stand."

As to the city militia, he remarked that their late conduct in tendering their military services had perhaps made on his mind a more favorable impression than it deserved. "I find," said he, "that their enthusiasm has in a great measure passed away, and the society here is now generally engaged in what seems to be a primary object—the acquisition of wealth. Indeed, the love of money seems to be the predominant passion; and that virtue called patriotism finds but few votaries. I nevertheless continue of the opinion that a great majority of the Louisianians, I mean the natives of the country, would resist any invader. But I have not equal confidence in all the foreigners who are settled in this Territory. On the contrary, from a part of these we have everything to fear. A few days since, we had news of peace in Europe, and immediately some of the Frenchmen among us began to speak of the probability of Bonaparte's again taking possession of Louisiana, and of the facility with which it might be accomplished. . . . At present, the Louisianians do not appear to be unfriendly to the Government; but I have, on other occa-

---

* Executive Journal, p. 329, vol. 2.

sions, witnessed the facility with which designing men could lead them astray."

On the 15th of November, Claiborne was still in a state of despondency. "Everything is tranquil," he wrote to Wilkinson from New Orleans; "the body of the citizens lately discovered some share of patriotism ; but the accustomed apathy of the country again prevails, and I begin to despair of making the militia an efficient force." On the 25th, he said to the Secretary of War: "You are apprised* of the difficulty of organizing and disciplining the militia of any country, but the peculiar situation of this Territory has rendered it here an Herculean task. . . . . . How far the militia generally are attached to the United States, and would, in the hour of peril, rally around our standard, must be left to time and events to prove. But my opinion as to the native Louisianians has always been the same ; a majority are well disposed, and were it not for the calumnies of some Frenchmen who are among us, and the intrigues of a few ambitious, unprincipled men, whose native language is English, I do believe that the Louisianians would be very soon the most zealous and faithful members of our Republic. But until a knowledge of the American Government, laws, and character, is more generally diffused among the people, you cannot with certainty count upon their fidelity. Ambitious, unprincipled men have acquired confidence in this quarter, and will, I fear, for some time, maintain their influence."

On the 25th of November, General Wilkinson arrived in New Orleans, after having made with the Spaniards on the Sabine arrangements which secured the United States against hostilities in that quarter.

---

* Executive Journal, p. 340, vol. 2.

But before this event occurred, and whilst he was confronting the Spaniards, apparently with many chances of a speedy collision, Samuel Swartwout, an emissary of Burr, had arrived at the General's camp on the 8th of October, and had delivered to him a confidential letter—such a letter as conspirators only send to accomplices.* Wilkinson received Swartwout with great favor, and detained him until the 18th, when that emissary departed for New Orleans. On the 21st of October, Wilkinson determined to denounce Burr. Forthwith he dispatched a messenger, who arrived in Washington on the 25th of November, and delivered to the President the dispatches with which he had been intrusted. On the 27th, Jefferson issued his famous proclamation, which made known to the country the traitorous enterprise afoot, and nipped it in the bud.† What were Wilkinson's reflections, or what were his secret acts and dealings between the 8th and the 21st of October, which was the time he ostensibly took to deliberate on the course he had to pursue, it is impossible to ascertain. But it is well known that, after the sending of his denunciatory dispatch to the President on the 21st, he, on the 29th, sent a written message to the Spanish Commander-in-Chief, in which he proposed that, without yielding any pretension, ceding a right, or interfering with discussions which belonged to their superiors, the state of things existing at the delivery of the province to the United States should be restored, by the withdrawal of the troops of both Governments from the advanced posts they occupied to those of Nacogdoches and Natchitoches respectively.‡ The Spaniards, who had been thus far so intractable, suddenly became

---

* Purton's Life of Aaron Burr, p. 426, vol. 2.
† Purton's Life of Aaron Burr, p. 432.
‡ Martin's History of Louisiana, p. 271, vol. 2.

very accommodating, and accepted the propositions. Having patched up this kind of truce, Wilkinson had hurried down to New Orleans.

The time had come for Claiborne to be seriously alarmed, and with better cause than had ever been given him by the Spaniards. He was advised from several respectable quarters that the Union of the States was seriously menaced, that the storm would probably break out in New Orleans, and that in this plot, headed by the notorious Vice-President, Aaron Burr, thousands were engaged.* In expressing his alarm to the Secretary of State on this subject, Claiborne said : " If this be the object of the conspirators, the delegate to Congress from this Territory, Daniel Clarke, is one of the leaders. He has often said that the Union could not last, and that, had he children, he would impress early on their minds the expediency of a separation between the Atlantic and Western States. Dr. John Watkins and Mr. J. W. Gurley have heard these sentiments expressed *by that gentleman*." But, a few days after, he took back this charge against Clarke in these words : " Upon further inquiry, I find nothing to justify an opinion that he is a party in the existing conspiracy . . . . In a late conversation with Dr. Watkins, he informs me that since the election of Mr. Clarke to Congress, he has heard him deliver some patriotic sentiments, and his former sentiments the Doctor now seems to attribute *more* to the impulse of some momentary passion than to deliberate reflection. It is due to justice to acquaint you of these particulars; and justice I will render to every man—even my greatest enemy." † After having had a conference with Wilkinson to devise the means which it might become necessary to adopt " to support the

---

* Executive Journal, p. 347, vol. 2.
† Executive Journal, p. 352, vol. 2, 5th Dec., 1806.

honor and welfare of the country," he informed Madison "that he had no doubt that a conspiracy was formed highly injurious to the interest of the United States, and that characters of high standing were concerned in it, although he was not yet advised of the particulars." Meanwhile, the City of New Orleans had been suddenly thrown into the wildest state of excitement and perturbation. The cry was, that Burr was coming down with a large force to take possession of it, with a variety of designs attributed to him, which were multiplied or magnified by fear, and which became of a more alarming character, as they were conveyed from lip to lip, after having passed through heated imaginations which added more vivid colors to the original tale of invasion. Claiborne requested Captain Shaw, of the United States Navy, to have all the force under his command ready for immediate service * to meet the threatening danger. That force consisted of two bomb-ketches and four gunboats. Wilkinson went to work in great haste to repair the old fortifications, and even "contemplated picketing in the city." † On the 5th of December, Claiborne wrote to Madison: "If General Wilkinson is not greatly deceived, the safety of the Territory is seriously menaced. . . . . . . From the firmness and the bravery of the army and navy on this station much may be expected; but as regards the *support* which the militia may render, I cannot hazard an opinion. . . . . I have had so many proofs of the influence of unprincipled men, and the prevalence of wicked political principles, that I know not in what portion of the militia to confide. General Wilkinson tells me that he had heretofore received hints of a Mexican expedition, and from the characters who, it seems, are the leaders of the pres-

---

* Executive Journal, p. 349, vol. 2.
† Executive Journal, Dispatch 4th Dec., 1806, p. 350, vol. 2.

ent plot, but had attached no consequence to their conversations, under an impression that, unless sanctioned by the Government, no men of reputation and talents could seriously contemplate an object of the kind." Claiborne's embarrassments were increased by the absence of instructions, or even of information of any kind from the General Government, for he had received no official communication from Washington since July. On the 5th of December he sent a messenger to the General Government with dispatches, which he declared to be of "very great importance," and he recommended to the messenger that "he should mention to no one the objects of his journey, or the place of his destination, as this reserve might be essential to his safety."* On the 6th, Claiborne was startled by Wilkinson's demand that he, the Governor, should proclaim martial law. The reasons which Wilkinson assigned for it were expressed in his usually florid, and characteristic style. "The dangers," said he, "which impend over this city and menace the laws and Government of the United States from an unauthorized and formidable association must be successfully opposed at this point, or the fair fabric of our independence, purchased by the best blood of our country, will be prostrated, and the Goddess of Liberty will take her flight from this globe forever."

"Under circumstances so imperious, extraordinary measures must be resorted to, and the ordinary forms of our civil institutions must, for a short period, yield to the strong arm of military law.

"Having exposed to you, without reserve, the authentic grounds on which I found my apprehensions, you can readily comprehend the high, solemn and important considerations by which I am moved, when I most ear-

---

* Executive Journal, p. 357, vol. 2.

nestly entreat you to proclaim martial law over this city its ports and precincts. For unless I am authorized to repress the seditious and arrest the disaffected, and to call the resources of the place into active operation, the defects of my force may expose me to be overwhelmed by numbers; and the cause and the place will be lost. The idea you offered me this morning of calling forth the militia and taking a position for the protection of your territory above is utterly inadmissible, because you could not for a moment withstand the desperation and superiority of numbers opposed to you, and the brigands, provoked by the opposition, might resort to the dreadful expedient of exciting a revolt of the negroes. If we divide our force, we shall be beaten in detail. We must therefore condense it here, and, in concert with our watercraft, rest our main defence at this point."

Whilst waiting for Claiborne's answer, Wilkinson, among his other military preparations, made arrangements with the French Consul to receive possession of the French artillery remaining in the Territory, as soon as its value should be estimated, and informed Claiborne that he had received such intelligence as induced him to believe that Burr would be at Natchez on the 20th of December, with two thousand men. On the 7th, Wilkinson renewed his application to Claiborne for the proclaiming of martial law, saying: "I believe I have been betrayed, and therefore shall abandon the idea of temporizing or concealment, the moment after I have secured two persons now in this city. Our measures must be taken with promptitude and decision, regardless of other consequences or considerations than the public safety, for I apprehend Burr, with his rebellious bands, may soon be at hand."*

* Executive Journal, p. 363, vol. 2.

Although "having entire confidence in the firmness and patriotism of General Wilkinson, and although disposed most cordially to co-operate with him," Claiborne refused acceding to his request to proclaim martial law, on the ground that, preparatory to the adoption of such a measure, the suspension of the Writ of Habeas Corpus would be necessary, and that this high prerogative could alone be exercised by the Territorial Legislature, which was not then in session. But, at the same time, he declared that, if the danger should augment, and if the privilege of the Habeas Corpus should, by impeding the arrest of the suspected, be found to favor the escape of the guilty, it was probable that he should, by proclamation, "direct its suspension, and plead in justification the necessity of the case." On the 9th, the members of the New Orleans Chamber of Commerce met, on request, at the Government House, Paul Lanusse being in the chair as President, and Richard Relf as Secretary. They were apprised by Wilkinson and Claiborne of the just causes existing for the apprehension of danger, and they were asked to furnish sailors to man the small American fleet which was on the station. Whereupon it was unanimously agreed that a general and immediate embargo of the shipping in port be recommended to the Governor, as the best means of obtaining the desired effect. Claiborne acted without delay in conformity with this recommendation, and orders were issued that no vessel, without the permission of Claiborne, or Wilkinson, should depart from New Orleans. At the same time, several thousand dollars were subscribed by the merchants to supply with clothes and other necessaries the sailors who should enter the service of the United States.* When the merchants were thus showing so much patriotism at

---

* Executive Journal, pp. 870, 871, vol. 2.

the cost of so great a sacrifice of private interest, they learned with extreme surprise that Wilkinson insisted on enlisting their sailors for six months, which would have completely paralyzed all commercial operations for that length of time. Why an enlistment for six months? Why an embargo for six months? What necessity could there be for it? The danger, if it existed, could only be momentary; a *coup de main* was all that could be apprehended; and therefore no reasons could be discovered by the merchants in justification of Wilkinson's extraordinary pretensions, which would have subjected them to immense losses, if not to utter ruin. Claiborne was of their opinion, and expostulated with Wilkinson. "I learn," he wrote to the General, "that the term of service is the greatest obstacle. It is proposed to enlist the sailors for six months; this length of time is objected to. Do you not think that two months, unless sooner discharged, would answer our objects? I am sorry you should think me wanting in decision," continued he, "to assist Captain Shaw in obtaining men. I have authorized an embargo—an act of authority which can alone be exercised legally by the General Government, and this act of mine, I fear, the Collector will not long submit to, lest, by withholding clearances, he may subject himself to personal actions."[*]

But Wilkinson was not a man to care much for Claiborne's scruples. Sailors having refused to enlist for six months, he called in person on Claiborne to request "an impressment"—from which high-handed measure Claiborne shrunk. "I submit it to your cool reflection," he said to Wilkinson, "whether *at this time* I could be justifiable in compelling men by force to enter the service. Many good-disposed citizens do not appear to

---

[*] Executive Journal, p. 378.

think the danger considerable, and there are others who (perhaps from wicked intentions) endeavor to turn our preparations into ridicule." On the 15th of December, Wilkinson sent to Claiborne a communication, in which he attempted to meet his objections and answer his questions, particularly as to the length of time for which the seamen should be engaged. "It is my opinion," he said, "that the men should be engaged for the shortest period consistent with the public safety; but, as I believe Mr. Burr's conspiracy is more profound and widely spread than his numerous agents, friends and well-wishers here will admit, I think the contract should be so qualified as to insure the service of the seamen until his machinations are destroyed in the Western States, or his attempt has been defeated in this quarter; and, for this purpose, I would propose that they should be shipped without any specification of service—to resist the attack of Aaron Burr and his lawless banditti from the Ohio River against the Territory. the laws and government of the United States. . . . .

"It is my cool and deliberate judgment, from my knowledge of Burr's character and desperation, and from the tenor of the information you have received, and the apparent toleration and support which he receives in Kentucky and Tennessee, that we have reached an extremity in our public affairs, which will not only justify, but which imperiously demands, the partial and momentary dispensation of the ordinary course of our civil institutions, to preserve the sanctuary of public liberty from total dilapidation. I believe it to be wise and just to inflict temporary privations for permanent security, and that justice being previously done to the seamen, they should be compelled to serve the country which gave them birth and gives them protection, on the very liberal terms which are proffered to them. Give me leave, and in three hours our vessels shall be manned.

"Having put my life and character in opposition to the flagitious enterprise of one of the ablest men of our country, supported by a crowd of coequals, ceremony would be unseasonable and punctilio unprofitable. I therefore speak from my heart when I declare, that I verily believe you are sincerely desirous to co-operate with me in all my measures, but pardon the honest candor which circumstances require and my situation demands, when I observe that, with the most upright and honest intention, you suffer yourself to be unduly biased by the solicitations of the timid, the capricious, or the wicked, who approach you and harass you with their criticisms on subjects which they do not understand, and with their opposition to measures which they do not comprehend, or which, understanding, they are desirous to prevent, or to defeat. What will our alertness import, without force and energy to support it? And can we be prepared without means? Shall our reverence for our civil institutions produce their annihilation, or shall we lose the house because we will not break the windows?" But, notwithstanding Wilkinson's pressing solicitations, Claiborne still continued to refuse to order the impressment of the sailors, the suspension of the writ of Habeas Corpus, the declaration of martial law, and the arrest of suspected persons. He said that he knew of no precedent for it in any State of the Union, or in any of its Territories, and added, "the Judiciary of the Territory, having exclusive cognizance of offences, is the only tribunal to which I can refer you, nor can any acts of mine arrest, or suspend their powers."

Whilst Claiborne and Wilkinson were thus on terms of friendly disagreement as to these measures, the former received from the Acting Governor, Cowles Meade, of

Mississippi, a letter in which he said, "We want arms and ammunition; we have men, and those men are patriots. But, sir, we are badly provided. I can only promise to make the stand and fight the battle of Leonidas. Burr may come—and he is no doubt desperate—but treason is seldom associated with generous courage, or real bravery. Should he pass us, your fate will depend on the General, not on the Colonel. If I stop Burr, this may hold the General in his allegiance to the United States. But if Burr passes this Territory with two thousand men, I have no doubt but the General will be your worst enemy. Be on your guard against the wily General. He is not much better than Catiline. Consider him a traitor, and act as if certain thereof. You may save yourself by it."*

Wilkinson, having acquired the conviction that he could not drive Claiborne into joining him in those arbitrary measures which he meditated, determined to act without him, and assumed responsibilities which were justified, in his opinion, by the imminence of the danger which he imagined to exist. On the 7th of December, he had dispatched Lieutenant Swann, of the army, to Jamaica, with a letter to the officer commanding the British naval force on that station, informing him of Burr's plans, and of the circulation of a report that the aid of a British naval armament had been either promised, or applied for, and warning him and all British officers that their interference, or any co-operation on their part, would be considered as highly injurious to the United States, and as affecting the present amicable relations between the two nations. The communication concluded with the expression of a hope that the British Government would refrain from any interference or co-operation, and prevent

---

* Ex. Jour., p. 386, vol. 2. Cowles Meade to Claiborne, 24th December, 1806.

any individual from affording aid to the conspirators. This communication seemed to take the British officers by surprise. Admiral Drake stiffly observed in reply that, from the style and manner in which the communication had been made, he hardly knew how to answer it, but declared that he availed himself of this opportunity to assure Wilkinson that British ships of war would never be employed in any improper service.*

On Sunday, the 14th of December, Dr. Erick Bollman, a German, who had acquired some celebrity for his attempt to liberate Lafayette from his prison of Olmutz, had been arrested by order of Wilkinson and confined in some unknown place. On the evening of the following day, a writ of Habeas Corpus was sued for on his behalf before Sprigg, one of the Judges of the Superior Court. Sprigg declined acting until he could consult his colleague, Mathews. But Mathews was nowhere to be found. On the 16th, however, the writ was obtained; but Bollman had, in the mean time, been put on board of a vessel and sent down the river. On the same day, application was made to Workman, the Judge of the County of Orleans, for a writ of Habeas Corpus in favor of two men, Ogden and Swartwout, who had been arrested, a few days before, by order of Wilkinson, at Fort Adams, and who had arrived at New Orleans on board of a bomb-ketch of the United States, where they were detained. Workman granted the writ without hesitation, and called on Claiborne for support. But the Governor refused to interfere.†

The alarm, and even the terror which prevailed in the city, where everybody feared for his own personal safety, was such, that no boat could be procured to take the officer of the Court on board of the ketch, which was

---

* Martin's History of Louisiana, pp. 235 and 277, vol. 2.
† Martin's History of Louisiana, p. 280, vol. 2.

lying in the middle of the river. It was only on the next day that, for the tempting consideration of a large sum of money, for the payment of which the Judge pledged the responsibility of the county, a boat was obtained. The writ being at last served, Captain Shaw stated, in his return to it, that Swartwout was no longer in his hands, but produced Ogden, who was liberated. As to Wilkinson, on whom a writ of Habeas Corpus had also been served in relation to Bollman, he replied, on the 18th, that he took on himself all responsibility for the arrest of Bollman, charged with misprision of treason against the Government of the United States, and that "he would act with the same energy, *without regard to standing or station*, against all individuals who might be discovered as participants in Burr's lawless combination." This return was afterward amended by an averment that, at the time of the service of the writ, Bollman was not in the power or possession of Wilkinson.*

Hardly had Ogden been liberated when he was again arrested, together with another individual named Alexander. On the application of Livingston, Judge Workman issued writs of Habeas Corpus for both prisoners. Instead of a return in due form, Wilkinson sent a written message to Workman, begging him to accept his return, such as it was, to the Superior Court, as applicable "to the two traitors who were the subjects of the writs." Whereupon, Livingston obtained a rule on Wilkinson to make a further and more explicit return to the writs, or show cause why an attachment should not issue against him.† Judge Workman, before acting, made a second application to Claiborne, to ascertain whether he would assist the Court in the execution of its decree against Wilkinson. But that appeal was ineffectual, although backed

---
* Martin's History of Louisiana, p. 280, vol. 2.
† Martin's History of Louisiana, p. 281, vol. 2.

by Judge Hall and Judge Mathews. On the 26th, Wilkinson having refused to modify his former return, Livingston moved for an attachment against him. Before granting it, Judge Workman applied for the third time to Claiborne, addressing him in writing, and officially— in which communication he observed that a common case would not require the step he was taking in his judicial capacity, but that, on this extraordinary occasion, he deemed it his duty, before any order from his tribunal was attempted to be enforced against a man who had all the regular forces of the United States at his command, and, in pursuance of the promulgated will of the Governor, a great part of the armed force of the Territory, to ask whether the Executive had the ability to enforce the decree of the Court, and, if he had, whether he would deem it expedient to do so. "Not only the conduct and power of Wilkinson," said the Judge, "but various other circumstances, peculiar to our present situation, the alarm excited in the public mind, the description and character of a large part of the population of the country, might render it dangerous, in the highest degree, to adopt the method, usual in ordinary cases, of calling to the aid of the Sheriff the posse comitatus, unless it were done with the assurance of being supported by the Governor in an efficient manner." Thus pressed, the Governor wrote a note to Wilkinson, advising him to yield to the civil authorities. But the General peremptorily refused; and Claiborne declining to employ force against him, Workman resigned,* on the ground that the Court and its officers should no longer remain exposed to the contempt or insults of a man whom they were unable to punish or resist. This was acknowledging the fact that Wilkinson was supreme

---

* Martin's History of Louisiana, p. 284, vol. 2.

dictator, and that henceforth his will was to be the law. In consequence, the general alarm was daily becoming more intense in the city, when, on the 31st of December, Claiborne recalled, greatly to the satisfaction of the merchants, the order which he had granted on the 9th, at the request of Wilkinson, to prevent the departure of vessels from New Orleans.

In the mean time, on the 2d of this month (December) the President had sent his annual message to Congress, in which, speaking of the inhabitants of the Territories of Mississippi and Orleans, he said, "I inform you with great pleasure of the promptitude with which the inhabitants of those Territories have tendered their services in defence of their country. It has done honor to themselves, entitled them to the confidence of their fellow-citizens in every part of the Union, and must strengthen the general determination to protect them efficaciously under all circumstances which may occur."

CHAPTER IV.

GOVERNOR CLAIBORNE'S ADMINISTRATION—DOINGS OF AARON BURR AND WILKINSON.

1807—1808.

MUCH to the satisfaction of the people of New Orleans in these exciting times, the Legislature met in that city on the 12th of January. Two days after, General Adair arrived from Tennessee, passing through the Choctaw Territory, and was the first to herald his own arrival, which took everybody by surprise. He reported that Colonel Burr, attended by a servant only, would be in New Orleans in three days.* Whatever were the intentions of Adair, he had not much time left him to execute them. In the afternoon of his arrival, whilst he was resting from his journey, the hotel where he had stopped was surrounded by one hundred and twenty men of the United States troops, commanded by Lieutenant-Colonel Kingsbury, accompanied by one of Wilkinson's aids. General Adair was dragged from the dining-table, and conducted to headquarters, where he was put in confinement, to be shipped as soon as the opportunity should present itself.† Strong patrols paraded through the streets, and several other persons were arrested, among whom were Workman, Kerr and Bradford. The commotion produced in the city may easily be imagined.

---

* Claiborne's communication to several members of Congress, p. 3, Executive Journal, vol. 3.
† Martin's History, p. 284, vol. 2.

Wilkinson, however, ordered Bradford to be released without further delay, and, on the following day, Workman and Kerr were discharged on a writ of Habeas Corpus granted by the District Court of the United States. On the 15th, Claiborne communicated these facts officially to the Legislature, and said: "The state of things here for some time past has been most unpleasant; the judges are greatly dissatisfied, and there are many persons who much censure the General, and also myself for not opposing his measures with force. There are others again, perhaps a majority of the inhabitants of the city, who applauded the measures pursued, and think them such as could alone insure the general safety. For myself, I believe the General is actuated by a sincere disposition to serve the best interest of his country; but his zeal, I fear, has carried him too far. . . . .

"My apprehensions of Mr. Burr and his associates have, in a great measure, subsided; but the security I now feel may be attributed to the preparations which have been made here to meet danger. My impressions are strong that there are many dissatisfied persons in this city. There are a few citizens whom I believe to be unjustly implicated—others to whom a charge of imprudence alone ought, probably in truth, to attach; but there is good reason to suppose that some persons here (from whose standing in society a contrary course was expected) meditated much mischief. They, however, are now unable to produce any."

On the 19th of January, the Governor sent to General Wilkinson a long communication, in which he submitted to him his plans to secure the complete protection of New Orleans.* "From the influence of the President's proclamation," he said, "and of the present friendly dis-

---

* Executive Journal, p. 6, vol. 2.

position toward the General Government of the people of Kentucky and Ohio, as manifested by some late proceedings of their Legislatures, united with the preparations for offence and defence in this city, my impressions are that Colonel Burr will not descend the Mississippi in considerable force. . . . . . It seems to me that Colonel Burr, abandoning (from necessity) the idea of moving in force, may endeavor to introduce into this city and its vicinity (unobserved and as private adventurers) a number of partisans for the purpose of carrying the place by surprise. In this event, the regulations herein proposed must prove salutary." . .

It is a remarkable fact that, at this critical conjuncture, Governor Folch, who had always been so inimical to the Americans, happened to arrive from Pensacola at the mouth of Bayou St. John, with four hundred men, ostensibly on his way to Baton Rouge, and wrote to Claiborne to obtain permission to proceed to New Orleans with the officers of his suite, and hence to continue his route to his place of destination. Claiborne replied: " I am sorry to oppose any obstacle to your Excellency's desires, but in the present state of affairs in this Territory, and to avoid all causes for rumors which, although unfounded, may add to that agitation in the public mind which has been occasioned by the news, this moment received, of the arrival of Burr and his associates in the Mississippi Territory, I am constrained to request that your Excellency would continue your voyage by water."*

On the same day, Claiborne and Wilkinson wrote jointly to the acting Governor of the Territory of Mississippi, Cowles Meade, in these terms: " Understanding

---

* Executive Journal, p. 10, vol. 3.

that Aaron Burr has taken post within the Territory over which you preside, we cannot but express our solicitude, lest his *pretensions* to innocence, and *the arts which he may employ to delude and seduce our fellow-citizens from their duty to their country*, may be partially successful. We rely with confidence on your exertions to seize the arch-conspirator, and having done so, permit us to suggest for your consideration the expediency of placing him without delay on board one of our armed vessels in the river, with an order to the officers to descend with him to this city. Otherwise, if his followers are as numerous as they are represented to be, it is probable it may not be in your power to bring him to trial. We take this occasion to advise you confidentially to keep a strict eye upon the Spaniards. Governor Folch is proceeding to Baton Rouge with four hundred men."

On the 22d of January, the Legislative Council, in their response to the message by which the Governor had opened their session, said: "It is indeed difficult to believe that, in the bosom of a Government the most free that exists on earth, plots, the success of which must be fatal to liberty, should have been formed. If, however, it be true that the ambitious and depraved men who have conceived such criminal projects have found proselytes, the Legislative Council are convinced that it is not amongst the ancient inhabitants of this Territory, and that, notwithstanding the dissatisfaction which they once manifested openly when they thought themselves aggrieved, there is no perfidy, no treason to be apprehended from them by the General Government. If they do not yet possess all the privileges enjoyed by the American citizen, they already set so much value on the rights which have been granted to them, that their late privation of those rights in the present stormy circumstances have created among them the most serious alarms." The Council thus alluded to the high-handed measures lately enforced by General Wilkinson, and to his arbitrary arrest of citizens who were under the ægis of those civil authorities which military power had attempted to supersede. A more marked tone of discontent pervaded the address which the House of Representatives sent to Claiborne on the 26th of the same month: "With regard to the extraordinary measures," they said, "which have taken place for some time past in this Territory, although your Excellency has not thought proper to reveal to the Legislature the reasons which have led to them, yet this House considers it as a sacred duty which they owe to themselves and their fellow-citizens, fully to investigate those measures and the motives which have induced them, and to represent the same to the Congress of the United States."

Claiborne thus commented on these two addresses in a communication to the Secretary of State :* "You will perceive by these two documents that the Legislature partakes in a great measure of that agitation which at present pervades the public mind, and that, although the measures lately pursued here, with a view to the public safety, are not openly censured, yet they are not approved. We, however, are assured of the fidelity of the ancient Louisianians to the United States, and of their attachment to the General Government. For myself, I believe that this declaration is correct so far as relates to a majority of the ancient Louisianians, and perhaps *the whole*, so far as to exempt them from all participation in Burr's conspiracy, but of that portion of our society whose native language is English, I cannot speak so favorably. Of the patriotism of many I have had abundant proofs; but there are others (and the

* Executive Journal, p. 19, vol. 3.

number, I fear, is not inconsiderable) who, I verily believe, would most cordially have supported the views of Burr."

In the mean time, the news reached New Orleans that Burr had been arrested at Natchez, and had given bond for his appearance before the Territorial Court at its next term. Claiborne expressed again on this occasion his apprehension that the issue of the trial would be "most unfortunate." He said:† " His acquittal will probably ensue, and this dangerous man will be left to continue (undisturbed) in this remote and exposed quarter his wicked intrigues against the Government of his country. I find that in Natchez also, as in this city, a considerable hue and cry is raised about the violation of the Constitution of the United States. I am persuaded that many good citizens complain from the very best motives, and with full conviction that there is just cause; but among the most clamorous are men who, I have some reason to believe, would not regret a dismemberment of the Union, or withhold their aid in the subversion of the Government and laws. These men, however, are now most profuse in their professions of attachment to constitutional rights, and many good people hang around them with the same affection as if they really possessed the merits of a Hampden or a Sydney."

On the 10th of February, Claiborne received a letter from John Graham, the Secretary of the Territory of Orleans, written from Frankfort in Kentucky, in which he was informed that Blannerhasset (made immortal by a celebrated passage in Wirt's speech on the trial of Aaron Burr), who had gone down the Ohio with about two hundred men and twenty boats, had proposed, in September, 1806, to one of Graham's friends, in whose verac-

---

* The history of his subsequent trial and acquittal at Richmond in Virginia is well known.

ity the fullest confidence was to be placed, to join him, Blannerhasset, and Colonel Burr, in a plan to bring about a dissolution of the Union, and that, after pointing out the advantages which would result to leading men from the erection of a separate government on this side of the Alleghanies, and after observing that the people were ripe for such a measure, he had said that their plan would be to go with an armed force to New Orleans, to seize that place, and after getting the money in the banks, the military stores and French artillery which had been left there, to force the country into a separation from the Atlantic States by operating on its commerce.*

"My solemn belief is," wrote Claiborne to the Governor of the Territory of Mississippi, "that the seizure of this city and her riches was the primary object of the conspirators, and the dismemberment of the Union the ultimate end of the leaders. I believe the horrible plot has been promoted by foreign influence; that Spain has furnished Burr with his pecuniary means; that the agents of that power in our vicinity were advised of his movements, and that the late events on the Sabine were intended to draw the attention of our Government from the real point of attack. The expedition to Mexico I believe to have been suggested by *the arch leader*, with a view of covering the real design, and inducing men (whose hearts would have revolted at the idea of arming against their country) to receive his orders. You will have seen by the Kentucky papers a disclosure of the project of the Spanish Court, in 1797, to sever the Western from the Atlantic States, and the means which were proposed to effect it. In 1797, the Spanish Court desired to narrow the Western limits of the United States; in 1807, her object is the same; and to accom

---

* Executive Journal, p. 23, vol. 3.

plish it, she endeavors to excite among us intestine divisions."

"Under these impressions," continued he, "I do not consider the danger as passed; and while it becomes us to guard against the arts of domestic traitors, we should also watch with care the movements of our Spanish neighbors." *

Apprehending such dangers, Claiborne sent a message to the Territorial Legislature, recommending to their consideration the expediency of suspending the privilege of the writ of Habeas Corpus. He immediately informed the Secretary of State, at Washington, of the step he had taken, and said to him:† "If I can acquire possession of Burr, Blannerhasset, or Tyler, I shall take means to convey them to the City of Washington, for it is *there* that these great offenders will probably meet the punishment they deserve. The trial of Burr at Natchez will determine in his acquittal, and I shall be disappointed if (as was the case in Kentucky) the jury do not eulogize his conduct." Ten days later, returning to the subject, he wrote to the same functionary:‡ "I have good reason to believe that Irujo, the Spanish Minister, under an impression that Burr's sole object was a division of the American Union, *did give countenance and aid to the traitor*. I am told by a person attached to the Spanish service that Irujo, early in the last year, advised the Governors of Havana, Pensacola and Baton Rouge of the designs of Burr, and that Folch and Grandpré were advised to place at the disposition of Burr such cannon, muskets, and ammunition as they could conveniently spare. My informer gives it as his opinion that, had Burr appeared before Baton Rouge three weeks ago,

---

* Executive Journal, p. 24, vol. 3.
† Executive Journal, p. 25.
‡ Executive Journal, p. 27.

the fort would immediately have been surrendered to him; but that Irujo's last dispatches had given great alarm to the Spanish agents, and had put them upon their guard against the traitorous adventurers."

Much to the mortification of Claiborne, the Territorial Legislature refused to suspend, or to put under any restriction whatever, the writ of Habeas Corpus, on the ground that it would be a violation of the Federal Constitution. On the 3d of March, however, he was relieved by the news that Burr, who had fled from the Territory of Mississippi, had been again arrested near Fort Stoddard, in Alabama, by Lieutenant Gaines. But he retained a considerable degree of alarm as to the effect which his course of action might have produced on many influential men in the United States, whose opposition or animadversion, he was not willing to encounter—among others, Andrew Jackson, since so famous, to whom he wrote on the 31st of March: "Doctor Claiborne can also state the reasons which influenced my conduct during the late interesting crisis. I have been the more solicitous to advise the Doctor of particulars, in order that he might the more readily assure my friends of Tennessee that the purest motives of honest patriotism continue to direct all my acts." *

He was particularly solicitous about justifying his application to the Legislature for the suspension of the writ of Habeas Corpus, and thus attempted to conciliate the approbation of Andrew Jackson, whose future importance he seems to have foreseen: "The inclosed paper will furnish you with copies of the addresses and answers referred to in my last letter, as also a copy of my message of the 10th of February to the Legislature, recommending a suspension of the writ of Habeas Cor-

* Executive Journal, p. 43, vol. 8.

pus. This message will probably draw down upon me the censure of some whose good opinion I am solicitous to retain, but the man who (regardless of personal consequences) will not do that which his judgment approves, is unworthy of confidence, either public, or private. You should judge of my conduct by the magnitude of the danger as it appeared to me, not as it has turned out to be. Thus keep this consideration in view, and I am fully persuaded that you will be among those of my friends who will not condemn me. With respect to the expediency of suspending the Habeas Corpus at the period the message was communicated, and with regard to the powers of the Legislature to do so, I have no doubt. The judges, however, and the District Attorney, Mr. Brown, say, they have examined the ordinance by which the Territory is governed, and unite in opinion that the Legislature thereof has not the power to suspend the writ of Habeas Corpus. But, if the gentlemen had carried their researches a little further, and examined also the Constitution of the United States, I am inclined to think that their opinion would have been otherwise. The ordinance was passed in 1787; its language is: *That the people shall always be entitled to the privilege of the writ of Habeas Corpus and the trial by jury.* It is therefore conceded that, until the Constitution was adopted and became the supreme law of the land, the power nowhere existed to suspend the Habeas Corpus in the North-western Territory. But the Constitution declares that *the Habeas Corpus shall not be suspended except in times of rebellion, or danger of invasion.* Here then a power to suspend is recognized, nor is it among those powers exclusively delegated to Congress, or prohibited to the States hence it follows that (by the amendments to the Constitution) the power is reserved to the States. If a State, there fore, can suspend the Habeas Corpus, I contend that a Territorial Legislature can do likewise, for their powers extend to all the rightful subjects of legislation, and those are rightful which the supreme law of the land (the Constitution) recognizes." It is evident from what precedes that there was in those days an approximation to that doctrine of Territorial embryo Sovereignty, which has lately been the subject of so much discussion. Claiborne addressed also a letter of the same import to George Poindexter, whose approbation of his course he was desirous to obtain in the Burr conspiracy.

On the 2nd of April, Claiborne forwarded to the Secretary of the Treasury a list of the public buildings, and lots owned or claimed in New Orleans by the United States.*

He added, that he would endeavor to procure a survey of the lots, accompanied with a drawing which would show their situation, and that he would forward the same in due time.

The excitement produced by Burr's conspiracy and by the arrests made by the military power in New Orleans was beginning to subside, when the same power soon gave rise again to a great deal of discontent, which came very near generating tumults and disorder. Several gun-boats of the United States were anchored in the Mississippi, opposite to New Orleans, and near to the western bank. On the 4th of July, a planter in their vicinity was correcting a female slave, whose cries being heard by the officers and crews of the gun-boats, three of the young officers, accompanied by a few sailors, entered the planter's inclosure, and released by force his slave. The effect produced in the community by such an act may easily be supposed, and the public efferves-

---

* Executive Journal, p. 47, vol. 3.

cence could, at first, hardly be kept down, but fortunately, the appeals made to the sober judgment of the people prevailed against passion, and the case was calmly submitted to the investigation and decision of a court of justice.

New Orleans, in those days, was never long in a state of quietude, and it was soon again thrown into commotion. Edward Livingston, a native of New York, a man who had speedily risen to be at the head of the bar of New Orleans, and whose acknowledged talents, coupled with his supposed rapacity, gave great uneasiness to the community at the time, early after his arrival in the Territory had become concerned in the purchase of a parcel of ground fronting the upper suburb of New Orleans, and commonly called the *Batture*—a piece of land of comparatively recent alluvial formation. It had been occupied as a common by the city for many years previous, and the title which the city had to it was, in the opinion of the inhabitants, unquestionable. It had happened, however, that Livingston had prosecuted with success his claim, and, in pursuance of a decree of the Superior Court of the Territory, the plaintiff had been put in possession by the sheriff. A few days afterwards, Livingston employed a number of negroes to commence the "digging of a canal" which he projected to make in a part of the land decreed to him by the court, but the citizens assembled in considerable force and drove him off. On the day following, Livingston went again to the land in question with a view of exercising his rights of ownership, but was again opposed by the citizens. These events had taken place during a temporary absence of Claiborne from the city. On his return, which was on the 1st of September, he found the public mind in a great state of agitation. Livingston immediately claimed the Governor's interference in his favor, and the

City Council, on the other hand, passed a Resolution requesting that functionary to lose no time in taking measures to prosecute the claim of the United States to the *Batture*, which was considered by the Council as indisputable.

"I must confess," wrote Claiborne to the Secretary of State, on the 3d of September,* "that I feel much embarrassed what course to pursue. The opposition on the part of the people to a decision of the court is in itself so improper, and furnishes a precedent so dangerous to good order, that it cannot be countenanced. But the opposition on the present occasion is so general, that I feel myself compelled to resort to measures the most conciliatory, as the only means of avoiding still greater tumult, and, perhaps, bloodshed. For myself, I have supposed that the court was in error in awarding the property in question to the plaintiff. My opinion is, that the title is in the United States, but the court, probably, are better acquainted than myself with the merits of the case. Mr. Brown, the attorney for the United States, was one of Mr. Livingston's counsel in the cause, and may feel a delicacy in prosecuting the claim of the United States, but, under existing circumstances, I have esteemed it my duty to urge his doing so."

"The assembly of the people on the *Batture* was unlawful, and the opposition to Mr. Livingston and his negroes may be considered as a riot—an offense properly cognizable by our courts, and as they are open, I see no real necessity for Executive interference, unless, indeed, I should think proper to issue a proclamation advising the people to desist from further opposition to Mr. Livingston's claim, and warning them of the consequences

---

* Executive Journal, page 102, vol. 3,

—a measure much desired by the claimant—but I have as yet declined doing so for several reasons, one of which is, it might make an impression in the United States that the people were disposed for insurrection, which is not true.

"In my next letter I will acquaint you more particularly with the merits of the Batture case. It is indeed a question highly interesting to the inhabitants of this city. From it (the batture) has been taken all the earth for constructing the *Levee* that protects New Orleans from the inundations of the river. It has also furnished the earth used in public and private buildings and for improving the streets."

"In high water the Batture is entirely covered. If reclaimed, it is feared the current of the Mississippi will in some measure change its course, which will not only prove injurious to the navigation, but may occasion depredations on the levees of the city, or those in its vicinity."

In the meantime Livingston had instituted civil actions against the most prominent citizens who had opposed his taking possession of the Batture. But still the people retained that possession, and, on the 15th of September, the Governor went in person to persuade the mout of the course which they were pursuing. At noon of that day, ten or twelve white laborers, employed by Livingston who seemed determined not to shrink before any exhibition of popular fury, began to work on the Batture. At 4 o'clock, the sound of a drum was heard in the streets, the excited citizens rushed out of their houses, and collected to the number of several hundred, most of them being natives of Louisiana, or France. Being early advised by the sheriff of the assemblage of the people, and in consequence of the sheriff's apprehension that the public peace would be greatly disturbed, the Governor repaired to the spot, and addressed the multitude in these words: "Permit me, fellow-citizens, to claim your attention, and, as your governor and your friend, to submit to your consideration a few observations:

"Whatever may be the redress desired, believe me, the mode you have adopted is improper. It cannot possibly avail you, and, if you persist in it, will injure yourselves and your cause.

"It is the duty of us all to yield submission to the laws. The Superior Court of this Territory has pronounced this Batture to be the property of Mr. John Gravier, and he, Mr. Livingston, (who claims under Gravier) has been put peaceably in possession thereof by the sheriff. The Supreme Court derives its authority from the government of the United States, and *its decrees must therefore be obeyed.*

"It is no less my duty than sincere desire to promote by all the means in my power, the interests of my fellow-citizens. To the President of the United States who expects from me a faithful relation of whatever concerns the welfare of this Territory, I have already transmitted such information as I could obtain relative to the conflicting claims to the Batture, nor will I omit laying before him such further representations on the subject as may be furnished me. The decision of the Supreme Court is for the present conclusive; it does not preclude (in my opinion) all further inquiry as to the right of property to the Batture. But such inquiry must be commenced and conducted in submission to the Government and conformably to the laws.

"I have come among you singly and with confidence. I look to yourselves for support; we must all aid in the preservation of good order. I am persuaded that no individual in this assembly could wish to raise his arm against the Government, and when, fellow-citizens, your

Chief Magistrate unites to a command an earnest en treaty that you should forthwith retire in peace to your respective homes, no one, I am certain, will be found in opposition." *

The Governor was received and heard with respectful attention. After this discourse, Colonel Macarty, who stood near him, proceeded to state the serious uneasiness which the decision of the Court had excited; the long and undisturbed possession of the Batture by the city, as well under the French as the Spanish Government; and the great injury which would result to the inhabitants if the land should be built upon and improved." The Governor replied "that the decision of the Court could not be controlled by him, that its authority was sanctioned by the Government, and that its decrees must not be opposed by the people." A person in the crowd observed, "And in the mean time no work must be done on the Batture." Many voices exclaimed, "That is the general wish." Claiborne took the occasion to observe, "That the American Government was wise and just—that it was a government of laws and not of men—that the laws reigned and the citizens must be subservient thereto—that he was ready and desirous to transmit to the Government such representations as should be furnished him relative to the conflicting claims to the Batture." Colonel Bellechasse, another influential man, who also stood near Claiborne, stated in a concise manner his reasons for believing the Batture to be the property of the public. He expressed his readiness to go to Pensacola in search of documents to prove that the Batture had always been considered by the Spanish Government as Spanish property—and asked whether the Governor had any objection to the people nominating an agent to carry

---

* Executive Journal, vol. 8, page 110.

to the President of the United States a statement of their grievances. "None," answered the Governor, "provided the representation should be respectful." "Will you recommend our agent to the President?" was the immediate inquiry. Claiborne assured the crowd that he would, provided the agent should be a man of respectability, and Colonel Macarty was then chosen by universal acclamation. It being now understood that the whole management of the affair was left to Colonel Macarty, the citizens withdrew in peace to their respective homes.

Claiborne, in relation to this popular excitement, during which he had behaved with commendable forbearance and judgment, addressed these reflections to Mr. Madison, the Secretary of State: "It is deemed a misfortune that the Superior Court of the Territory should be a court of dernier resort. I wish not to reflect upon our Territorial Judges. But I do think that the citizens can justly claim of Congress provision for appeals, in certain cases, from the Court of this Territory to the Supreme Court of the United States, or if this be considered improper, that a High Court of Appeals, with official powers for this and the adjoining Territory, be created by law. In these two Territories suits of immense importance are frequently brought, involving many intricate questions of law, and in the determination of which all Judges may sometimes err." But whilst the case was pending before the Federal Government, Livingston had quietly taken possession of the Batture, and in the month of November was making improvements on it.

In the month of December, war rumors became current in New Orleans, and a collision was daily expected between the United States and England, on the questions of impressment of sailors, the right of search, and the protection claimed to be afforded by the American flag to those vessels which sailed under it. Claiborne wrote to Madison, strongly approving the course of the administration in resisting the pretensions of Great Britain, and said: "I consider the Louisianians very generally as being well affected to the Government, but, in the event of an English war, they will with enthusiasm rally round our standard."

During this year, Claiborne, in the exercise of certain prerogatives which he thought belonged to the Executive, had come into conflict with the judiciary. He seemed to have felt it keenly, and thus addressed the Secretary of State: "In cases of collision between the judiciary and the Executive, where the former shall evidence a manifest disposition to embarrass the Executive, and to prevent the execution of a law enacted by the Territorial Legislature, must the Executive yield implicit obedience to the judiciary, or is he authorized to take measures to carry (the opinion of the judges notwithstanding) the will of the Legislature into effect? Your opinion, sir, on this subject will be thankfully received." The inquiry was a curious one, and it would have been interesting to see the answer of Madison, but it has not been my good fortune to lay my hands on that document.

On the 29th of December, 1807, Claiborne wrote to the Secretary of State: "General Moreau is expected here in a few days. For myself, I attach no suspicion to the movements of that great but unfortunate man, etc..
. . . . . General Dayton is on his way hither, and Bollman is said to be near the city. I fear we shall have 'so many choice spirits' among us during the winter, that it will be found expedient to order to New Orleans a greater number of regular troops."

1808. On the meeting of the Territorial Legislature, Claiborne, on the 18th of January, said to them in the annual Executive Message with which the sessions of such bodies are generally opened: "A University has been established by law, but is left to the precarious support of private bounty. In behalf of so valuable an institution, the liberality of the citizens was with confidence appealed to, but without the smallest success." He advised the Legislature to provide for this neglect, and he recommended also the establishing of one or more free schools in each parish, under the direction of a board of trustees.*

On the 24th (January), Claiborne received a communication from the President of the United States in relation to the Batture, which was taken possession of, in obedience to received instructions, by the Marshal of the United States. Many of the Americans, among whom Livingston had many partisans, affected to censure severely the orders of the Federal Executive, but the Louisianians, on the contrary, were much gratified, and the Legislature passed a vote of thanks to the President. The Batture became a source of an endless and protean litigation which occupies a conspicuous place in the annals of our jurisprudence.

From the beginning of the organization of the Territorial Government the Louisianians had been restive under the obligation of paying taxes to which they were not accustomed, and the Legislative Council, addressing Claiborne on his late message, made these observations: "The Council has learned with pleasure that the actual impositions are more than sufficient to defray the public expenses. The people of Louisiana, formerly accustomed to pay none apparently, felt the establishment of taxes as a great hardship, and would probably see the augmentation of them with concern."

---

* Executive Journal, p. 151, vol. 3.

On appointing one of his own kinsmen to office, Major Richard Claiborne, the Governor sent him written instructions which do equal credit to the mind and heart of their author.* "You are about entering" said he, on an arduous task. The duties which your office enjoins require reflection and attention rather than labor. The members of a community are more concerned in the jurisprudence of a country than perhaps in any other part of the Government. The business transacted in courts of justice comes home to every man's feelings and fireside, and the petty contests and domestic broils which arise in a village or neighborhood excite more interest than all the differences of whatever kind in which the rest of the world may be engaged. . . . .

"Recollect that the people among whom you are going to reside differ from those with whom you have been accustomed to associate—differ from each other. The population of that, as well as of every other, part of this Territory, is composed of Creoles, Europeans and emigrant citizens of the United States, all of them adhering to the peculiar prejudices acquired in their respective countries. Perhaps among materials so jarring and discordant it may be difficult to preserve harmony and mutual good-will. But to this end all your efforts must tend. Exert yourself to render them satisfied with each other—satisfied with yourself. Mildness in the administration of the laws, a general acquiescence in their received and usual habits, are of the most essential importance. Where principle is not concerned, indulge even their follies and prejudices. As this, on the one hand, will exempt you from a charge of fastidiousness, so on the other, it will insure respect and consideration, when you shall find it necessary to act in opposition to their wishes.

* Executive Journal, p. 166, vol. 3.

"In deciding upon the rights and liberties of the citizens, let your conduct be marked with deliberation and firmness, eradicate from your bosom, as far as the fallibility of our nature will allow, those passions and prepossessions often unjust in private life, but always fraught with ruin and misery when influencing our public acts. Cultivate a general acquaintance with the people, instruct them in the principles of our Constitution and inculcate an attachment to the Union. Be yourself on your guard, and warn them against the designs of base men who pervade the Territory in all directions, poisoning the community with false and malignant statements, and industriously fomenting distrust and dissatisfaction toward the American Government."

In the month of March, the City Council requested the Governor to consent to the demolishing of Fort St. Louis and the filling up of the trenches surrounding it, "inasmuch as it impeded the communication between the town and the suburb St. Mary, and the trenches were receptacles of stagnant water and of all manner of filth which engender disease—and the further request was that the materials of said fort be left at the disposal of the Council for the use of the city." Claiborne consented to the first part of the request, but ordered that the materials of the demolished fort be left at the disposal of the military agent of the United States who would employ them elsewhere for public uses.*

Claiborne informed the Secretary of State, on the 14th of March, that the Legislature of the Territory was still in session, but that "they had done little, and were not likely to do more;" that New Orleans, the seat of faction and intrigue, was illy calculated for the residence of the legislative body, and that a "resolution" had passed

* Executive Journal, p. 181, vol. 3.

the House of Representatives to remove the seat of government to a little village on the Mississippi, about one hundred miles above the city, but that he feared the measure would not be approved by the Council.

On the 31st of March the Legislature adjourned, after having adopted a Digest of the civil laws then in force in the Territory of Orleans, with alterations and amendments adapted to the present form of Government. It had been prepared by Moreau Lislet and Brown, two distinguished members of the bar, who had been appointed, in 1805, to that effect. "This work," wrote Claiborne to Madison, " will be of infinite service to the magistrates and the citizens. Heretofore a knowledge of the laws by which we were governed was extremely confined. The lawyers who avowed themselves to be civilians told the judges what the law was, and the citizens, in the most common transactions of life, needed the aid of counsel; but this state of insecurity and uncertainty will, for the future, be in a great measure remedied."

His approbation, however, was far from being unqualified, for he added: "I see much to admire in the *Civil Law;* but there are some principles which ought to yield to the Common Law doctrine. Indeed it has been with me a favorite policy to assimilate as much as possible the laws and usages of this Territory to those of the States generally, but the work of innovation could not be pursued hastily, nor with safety, until the existing laws were fully presented to our view."

Considering the probability of a war between the United States and Great Britain, the Federal Government thought of erecting fortifications to protect the entrance of the Mississippi, and consulted Claiborne on the subject. "Calculate," said he to the Secretary of War, " the expense of a similar work in any State of the

Union, and then make an addition of fifty per cent., and you will fall far short of the real expenditure at Plaquemine. A work at the English Turn is desirable. The Fort at Plaquemine may, with a leading breeze and under cover of the night, be passed. But, under no circumstances, could a vessel evade a battery at the English Turn."

By this time the celebrated "embargo measure," adopted by the United States in consequence of their foreign unfriendly relations, was in full operation, and Claiborne, in addressing the President of the United States on that subject, said: "The provisions of the new Embargo Act are calculated to give efficacy to a measure the most dignified and the most salutary which, under existing circumstances, could have been resorted to, for, as you have well observed, in replying to the Columbian Order of New York: *There can be no question in a mind truly American, whether it is best to send our citizens and property into certain captivity and wage war for their recovery, or to keep them at home.*"

The militia of the Territory had relapsed into a state of great inactivity and indifference, which was particularly to be regretted at a time of apprehended collisions with foreign nations. To rouse the Louisianians from their apathy and revive their military ardor, Claiborne bethought himself of sending a circular to all the officers who were in command of regiments. It was a spirited address, and invited all those who were subject to militia duty, to repair with pleasure and promptitude to the field of exercise, "for," said he, "without some previous military discipline and knowledge of tactics, a band of citizen-soldiers, however courageous and patriotic, are illy calculated to combat with success veteran armies. This Territory, from its peculiar local situation, is exposed on all sides to perilous casualties, and in the first moments of danger, whether from within, or without, we must depend upon ourselves for the means of defence. Adequate succor would most unquestionably be promptly afforded from the Western and Atlantic States, but, in our remote and isolated position, it behooves us to be prepared to resist the first onset."

In the beginning of August, there were again in New Orleans several riots and disturbances which gave some anxiety to Claiborne. They consisted in serious affrays between the American sailors and the French, Spaniards and Italians of the same class. They appeared on the Levee in battle array, and had skirmishes which were severe, and in which considerable damage was done to life and limb. Many supposed that the foreign sailors had been stimulated to this quarrel with a view of covering a more dangerous conspiracy. The Mayor even designated to the Governor a person supposed to be in the pay of a foreign government, who had in the city a complete company of men ready to obey his orders. At one time the situation of the city became really alarming,* and Claiborne wrote to Colonel Sparks, who was in command of the United States troops in the Mississippi Territory, to have additional companies of regulars sent down to New Orleans. These disturbances had happened during the absence of Claiborne, who had been on a visit to the County of Opelousas. He speedily returned, and, on the 31st of August, he wrote to the Secretary of State that the city was quiet, "but," said he, "we have, however, to lament the residence among us, and particularly in this city, of a number of abandoned individuals who render the greatest vigilance on the part of the police essential to the general safety. Among those individuals are many persons who have

---

* Executive Journal, p. 283, vol. 8.

deserted the service of Spain, or fled from the punishment which awaited their crimes."

The "Digest of the Civil Laws" having at last been printed and being ready for delivery, Claiborne sent a copy of it to every Parish Judge, with this circular, dated on the 22d of October :* "Previous to the receipt of this letter, there will have been delivered to you a copy of the 'Digest of the Civil Laws.' It being understood by our courts of justice that the principles of the civil law (except in criminal cases) were in force throughout the Territory, it became expedient to place them before the public. Heretofore, few citizens had a knowledge of the civil law. It was spread over innumerable volumes, and was for the most part written in a language which few could read. The uncertainty of the law was a source of great embarrassment, not only to private individuals, but to the magistrate who was to administer it. By the adoption of the digest one desirable object is at least effected. The laws are rendered more certain, and, if in their operation they should be found unjust, the Legislature will, I am persuaded, lose no time in making the necessary amendments.

"Indispensable as (under existing circumstances) has been the adoption of the 'Digest,' it will, nevertheless, (I suspect) be much censured by many native citizens of the United States who reside in the Territory. From principle and habit they are attached to that system of jurisprudence prevailing in the several States under which themselves and their fathers were reared. For myself, I am free to declare the pleasure it would give me to see the laws of Orleans assimilated to those of the States generally, not only from a conviction that such laws are for the most part wise and just, but from the

---

* Executive Journal, p. 308, vol. 8.

opinion I entertain that in a country where a unity of government and interests exists, it is highly desirable to introduce throughout the same laws and customs. We ought to recollect, however, the peculiar circumstances in which Louisiana is placed, nor ought we to be unmindful of the respect due the sentiments and wishes of the ancient Louisianians who compose so great a proportion of the population. Educated in a belief of the excellencies of the civil law, the Louisianians have hitherto been unwilling to part with them, and, while we feel ourselves the force of habit and prejudice, we should not be surprised at the attachment which the old inhabitants manifest for many of their former customs and local institutions. The general introduction, therefore, into this Territory of the American laws must be the effect of time; the work of innovation must progress slowly and cautiously, or otherwise much inconvenience will ensue, and serious discontents will arise among a people who have the strongest claims upon the justice and the liberality of the American Government.

"I fear you will continue to experience difficulty in the faithful discharge of your official duties. The aversion of the ancient Louisianians to our courts of justice, and particularly their dislike of lawyers, *the mutual jealousy* between the French and American population, together with the great dislike of the latter to the principles of the civil law (which will for the present be your guide) cannot fail to render your situation unpleasant. But I must pray you to persevere in your honest endeavors to render the Government acceptable to the people, and to administer the laws with justice and in mercy."

In relation to the adoption of the "Digest of Laws" by the Territorial Legislature, Judge Martin, whose opinion on the subject is entitled to so much authority, remarks in his History of Louisiana :* "Although the Napoleon Code was promulgated in 1804, no copy of it had as yet reached New Orleans; and Moreau Lislet and Brown availed themselves of the project of that work, the arrangement of which they adopted, and, *mutatis mutandis*, literally transcribed a considerable portion of it. Their conduct was certainly praiseworthy; for, although the project is necessarily much more imperfect than the code, it was far superior to anything that any two individuals could have produced early enough to answer the expectations of those who employed them. Their labor would have been much more beneficial to the people than it has proved, if the Legislature to whom it was submitted had given it their sanction as a system, intended to stand by itself, and be construed by its own context, by repealing all former laws on matters acted upon in this Digest.

"Anterior laws were repealed so far only as they were contrary to, or irreconcilable with, any of the provisions of the new. This would have been the case, if it had not been expressed.

"In practice, the work was used as an incomplete digest of existing statutes which still retained their empire; and their exceptions and modifications were held to affect several clauses by which former principles were absolutely stated. Thus the people found a decoy in what was held out as a beacon.

"The Fuero Viejo, Fuero Juzgo, Partidas, Recopilaciones, Leyes de las Indias, Autos accordados and Royal Schedules remained parts of the written law of the Territory, when not repealed expressly, or by a necessary implication.

"Of these musty laws the copies were extremely rare.

* Martin's History of Louisiana, p. 291, vol. 2.

A complete collection of them was in the hands of no one, and of very many of them, not a single copy existed in the province.

"To explain them, Spanish commentators were consulted, and the corpus juris civilis and its own commentators were resorted to; and to eke out any deficiency, the lawyers who came from France or Hispaniola, read Pothier, D'Aguesseau, Dumoulin, etc.

"Courts of Justice were furnished with interpreters of the French, Spanish and English languages. These translated the evidence and the charge of the court when necessary, but not the arguments of the counsel. The case was often opened in the English language, and then the jurymen who did not understand the counsel were indulged with leave to withdraw from the box into the gallery. The defence being in French, they were recalled, and the indulgence shown to them was enjoyed by their companions who were strangers to that language. All went together into the jury-room—each contending the argument he had listened to was conclusive, and they finally agreed on a verdict in the best manner they could."

In the month of November, the community of Pointe Coupée, an important settlement, had gradually become so divided into parties, and the jealousy between the American and Creole population had become so intense, that Claiborne endeavored to allay the excitement. His appointment, as sheriff, of an individual named Petrony had been a cause of great discontent to the Americans, or rather to the "modern Louisianians," as Claiborne called them in contradistinction to the "ancient Louisianians." In the hope of restoring harmony, Claiborne wrote in the following strain to Charles Morgan, one of the most prominent citizens of Pointe Coupée: "As relates to the Sheriff, Mr. Petrony, I can only say that he came well recommended to me, as a man of honesty, probity and good demeanor. The circumstance of his not having been born 'an American' is not considered an objection to him. I certainly feel for my countrymen, the native citizens of the United States, a sincere and ardent attachment, nor is it possible for me, in any situation, or under any circumstances, to be unjust toward them. But, in my official character, I can acknowledge no other distinction between the inhabitants of the Territory who, by birth, or the treaty of cession, are entitled to the rights of citizenship, than personal merit. In making appointments, therefore, I have been desirous to select the most worthy and the most capable, keeping in view the expediency of dividing the offices as near as may be between the ancient and modern Louisianians, as one means of lessening the existing jealousy and distrust between these two descriptions of citizens." This occurrence shows a state of feeling which was almost universal in the Territory. *Ex uno disce omnes.*

A quota of militia having been required of the Territory by the President of the United States, which were preparing for an anticipated war, Claiborne wrote to the Secretary of State on the 27th of December: "I hope and believe that the number called for may be obtained by voluntary enlistment; but I nevertheless perceive a reluctance on the occasion, which mortifies me exceedingly. It arises, on the part of the Creoles, from an apprehension that they may probably be ordered out of the Territory, and on the part of the native Americans, from a fear lest they may be placed under the command of officers of the regular army; and these impressions are much encouraged by the opinions and discourse of a wretched, discontented faction (composed principally of the partisans of Burr) which has so long infested this Territory."

Ever since the cession of Louisiana to the United States, great losses had been experienced by the inhabitants of those parts of the Territory which bordered on Spanish possessions, and principally on Texas, in consequence of the frequent flight of negroes who ran away from their masters, and resorted to the protection of a foreign flag, under which they were induced to believe that their condition would be improved. This had given rise, every year, to a long correspondence between Claiborne and the Spanish Governors, but no satisfactory result had been obtained, so that the discontent in Louisiana grew every day greater as to this state of things, and, on the 14th of December, Doctor Sibley, of Natchitoches, wrote to Governor Claiborne: "Nothing important has occurred here lately since the desertion of about thirty negroes; things cannot long remain in this state; it would be better (the people say) for them to be under the Government of Spain than thus situated. How long their allegiance to our Government will remain without protection, I know not. The negroes were furnished with Spanish cockades at Nacogdoches, a dance given them, and since they have been marched off to the Trinity River, singing 'Long live Ferdinand the Seventh.'"

CHAPTER V.

CLAIBORNE'S ADMINISTRATION — ARRIVAL OF MANY EMIGRANTS FROM ST. DOMINGO — TERRIBLE EPIDEMIC AMONG THE U. S. TROOPS — FORT BATON ROUGE TAKEN BY INSURGENTS — THE STATE OF WEST FLORIDA — NEGROES SMUGGLED INTO LOUISIANA — ANNEXATION OF WEST FLORIDA TO THE UNITED STATES.

1809—1810.

As time progressed and the prospect of war increased, Claiborne became more anxious about the organization of the militia, and, in a communication sent to the Secretary of State on the 1st of January, he expressed his views on the subject as follows : " The militia here is an inefficient force. My best and incessant exertions to introduce order and discipline have been attended with but little success. They are, moreover, badly armed, and, indeed, in case of an attack, the negroes are so numerous in the settlements on the Mississippi, that it might be dangerous to draw a considerable detachment of militia to any one point. I have no reason to believe that the great body of the people of the Territory are otherwise than friendly to the American Government. I do fear, however, that unless supported by a strong regular force, they would not, in case of attack, manifest that patriotic ardor in defence of the country which is essential to its preservation. You are not uninformed of the very heterogeneous mass of which the society in New Orleans is composed. England has her partisans ; Ferdinand the Seventh some faithful subjects ; Bonaparte his admirers ;

and there is a fourth description of men commonly called *Burrites*, who would join any standard which would promise rapine and plunder. There are, nevertheless, many *virtuous citizens*, in whose honesty and patriotism I fully confide, and with a respectable regular force around which to rally, they would prove themselves worthy of reliance in the hour of danger. . .

. . . .

" New Orleans could not afford to an European power the booty which was found at Copenhagen; but in these rapacious days, the vast sums of money known to be deposited in the two banks of this city, together with the quantity of cotton, etc., here stored, may present a lure too tempting to be resisted ! "

Returning to the subject, he said to the Secretary of War on the 10th of January :* " In order to comply with the President's late requisition, I have given orders for a draft. In New Orleans no companies have yet volunteered their services. This circumstance mortifies me exceedingly. But I still flatter myself that, in the interior, more patriotism may be displayed."

The Legislature of the Territory having resumed their annual sessions, Claiborne, when informed that they were ready to proceed to business, sent his message on the 14th of January. In that document he informed them, with regret, that the act to provide for the means ot establishing public schools in the parishes of the Territory, which they had passed at their last session, was not likely to produce the desired effect; that, in the Parish of Pointe Coupée, provision had been made for the support of two or more public schools, but that the other parishes did not seem disposed to imitate so worthy an example. " I have observed with pleasure," said he,

---

* Executive Journal, p. 26, vol. 4.

"that schools for private instruction have of late greatly increased, and that fathers of families seem impressed with the importance of educating their offspring. The instruction of our children in the various branches of science should be accompanied with every effort to instill into their minds principles of morality; to cherish their virtuous propensities; to inspire them with ardent patriotism, and with that spirit of laudable emulation, which '*seeks the esteem of posterity for good and virtuous actions.*' Youth thus reared into life become the pride of their parents, the ornaments of society, and the pillars of their country's glory."

Passing to another subject of considerable importance, he observed, "Your criminal jurisprudence requires revision. Punishments are not proportioned to crimes, and, in some cases, offenders are imprisoned for life, whose reformation might probably be effected by a less rigorous suffering. The jail of New Orleans is the common receptacle for convicts sentenced to hard labor. But no means being pointed out for their employment, these unfortunate victims of the law herd together in idleness, until their vices become contagious. Their support, moreover, is a serious charge upon the Treasury, so much so that a view to political economy has had an influence in pardoning offenders whose claims for mercy were very doubtful. For these and other considerations, which will readily occur, you will be convinced of the expediency of erecting a Penitentiary House, and of prescribing such rules for its internal police as may be best calculated to reclaim the wicked and dissolute."*

Referring to the hostile attitude taken by foreign powers against the United States, Claiborne thus stimulated the patriotism of the Legislature: "At this epoch, when

---

* Executive Journal, p. 37, vol. 4.

what are termed the civilized nations of Europe vie in acts of atrocity with the piratical States of Barbary, a people, to hope for safety, must be armed and united. The Government of the United States has made repeated efforts to restore an amicable intercourse with England and France. Nothing has been demanded of the belligerents which the immutable principles of justice did not sanction; no conduct of theirs was objected to but such as was in violation of our rights as a free and independent people. The language of remonstrance and complaint has been exhausted, and our wrongs remain unredressed. There seems to be no alternative but war, or a continuance of the embargo. Advert to the history of the American nation from the commencement of its existence to the present day! What triumphs have been achieved! What examples of fortitude, of firmness, of prudence have been afforded! A national character acquired by the blood of heroes, and maintained by the wisdom of illustrious statesmen, must and will be preserved. Our honor will never be sullied by receiving the commands of France; nor our independence prostrated by paying tribute to Great Britain. The embargo imposes privations, which a magnanimous people will cheerfully bear. It may be the means of avoiding still greater ills. But, however things may eventuate, whether in inevitable war, or honorable peace, the good citizens of this Territory will unite hand and heart in the support of the Government and in the defence of their country."

In their reply, the Legislature said to Claiborne: "Tell the Federal Government that the Louisianians, proud to belong to the great family, are ready to vie in zeal, in efforts and in sacrifices for the defence of their country."[*]

---

[*] Executive Journal, p. 43, vol. 4.

In transmitting these sentiments to the Secretary of State, Claiborne observed: "This answer may be considered as conveying the political sentiments of the great majority of the people of the Territory. Indeed, Sir, the Louisianians are becoming every day more attached to the American Government, and I am persuaded that, when the occasion serves, they will prove themselves worthy members of the American family. I have nevertheless to regret the residence among us of some foreigners, faithful friends of England, of Spain and of France, and the existence also of a faction in New Orleans (the remnants of Burrism) whose object is to embarrass the administration and to excite discontents."

In the mean time, Governor Claiborne succeeded at last in obtaining from Salcedo, the Governor of Texas, the surrender of some of the negroes who had fled to that province. This circumstance, being calculated to prevent the recurrence of an evil which had been of so long duration, gave great satisfaction in Louisiana. Claiborne assured Salcedo that a like conduct would be pursued in relation to such slaves as might fly from their Spanish masters and take refuge in the Territory of Orleans, and he informed him that, in order that no difficulty whatever might arise, the Legislature had enacted a special law on the subject, a copy of which he transmitted to him. "Your Excellency," said he to Salcedo, "will recognize (I trust) in the provisions of this law those just and liberal principles which should always characterize the intercourse between neighboring and friendly governments."

Julian Poydras, a very wealthy planter of Pointe Coupée, who was avowedly friendly to the general and local administration, was, much to Claiborne's gratification, elected by the Territorial Legislature a delegate to Congress for the ensuing two years. This was the more satisfactory to Claiborne from the fact of there being in New Orleans a pretty strong party opposed to him, and to all his friends and supporters. On the 13th of February, Claiborne had informed the Federal Government that there was in the city a base faction, composed principally of Burrites and Englishmen, who were making every exertion to excite disunion and disorder. "A paper called *La Lanterne Magique*," said he, "is devoted to their views, and I much fear that, among a people (like the Louisianians) who are still for the most part strangers to our government, laws and language, the libelous publications which wickedly appear against the government and its officers will make some unfavorable impressions. The Legislature, however, are almost unanimous in approving the measures of Government, and I am happy to add that, without the city of New Orleans, little or no dissatisfaction is expressed."

On the 26th of March, New Orleans was becoming crowded with United States troops. More than fourteen hundred of them were then in the city, and several hundred more had entered at the Balize. General Wilkinson, their commander, was daily expected from the North. The number soon amounted to about two thousand, and the public Barracks not being sufficient for their accommodation, many of the companies were comfortably, but expensively, quartered in different parts of the city.

In the month of April, Claiborne went up to the Parish of Pointe Coupée with the view of allaying a feud between the Parish Judge, Dormenon, and L'Abbé Lespinasse, the Parish priest, which had divided the citizens into two factions greatly embittered against each other, and almost disposed to engage in a petty civil war. These two leaders of the two contending parties were both Frenchmen by birth. The former was supported by Poydras, the delegate elect to Congress, and a majority of the planters of the Parish. The latter was patronized by a few respectable Creole families, by almost all the women, and by some native Americans who had recently emigrated to the Parish. The Judge and his partisans wished the removal of the Parish Priest; the Abbé and his friends desired the dismissal of the Judge. "My powers," said Claiborne to the Secretary of State, "did not permit me to act in either case, and my inclination led me to take no other notice of the dispute than to advise all parties to preserve good order, and to add that any breach of the public peace would be noticed by the civil authority. The Sheriff of the District is said to be so friendly to the Judge as to evidence great partiality in the selection of jurors, and a great clamor has been raised against him. This cause of complaint, which I believe to be not altogether unfounded, shall be removed so soon as I can find a capable and honest man, indifferent to both parties, willing to accept the office. I should be at no loss to select an individual from among the citizens of Pointe Coupée, both honest and capable. But they have so generally taken part in this contest, that it will be advisable to appoint as sheriff some person who has not heretofore resided in the Parish." This incident, insignificant in itself, but not an exceptional one, is deserving of notice, as illustrating the curious social condition then existing in the Territory.

In such a social condition, Claiborne had soon found out that, among his manifold duties, the most delicate and disagreeable was that of appointing to office. He informed the President that, to conciliate the population generally, and indeed to be just to the old inhabitants, he was bound to fill a portion of the offices of honor and profit with those whose native language was French. "But," said he to the Secretary of State, "this policy is much censured by some of my fellow-citizens, and made a cause of opposition to my administration. You will find inclosed a list of the most important civil and military officers of the Government, and in which are noticed the several places of nativity. From this list you will find that, if there is any favoritism, *it is toward native Americans.*"

The Legislature, in their last session, had adopted a memorial to Congress, the object of which was to obtain the early admission of the Territory into the Union as a member of the Confederacy, on the same footing with the original States. This memorial was transmitted by Claiborne to the Secretary of State at Washington on the 18th of May, but with a letter which he wrote in opposition to their wishes, and which is too interesting a document not to be reproduced here at length.*

" I am not from principle," said he, " an advocate for Territorial systems of government, nor during my agency in their administration have I experienced so much satisfaction, as to have created a personal bias in their favor; but it really seems to me that the system, as it relates to this District, cannot yet be done away without hazarding the interest of the United States, and the welfare of this community. I can bear testimony to the good intentions and amiable character of a majority of the inhabitants, to their industrious habits, to their obedience to the laws, and growing attachment to the American Government; but they nevertheless are not prepared for self-government to the extent solicited by the Legislature. The Government of the Territory in its present shape is with some difficulty administered; and as much power has been vested in the people as is, for the present, likely to be used with discretion. Our population is a mixed one, and composed of very discordant materials; the mass of

---

* Executive Journal, p. 82, vol. 4.

the inhabitants still entertain strong prejudices in favor of their ancient laws and usages, and, should the immediate control of the General Government over this Territory be withdrawn, those great principles of jurisprudence, so much admired in the United States, would not meet here that patronage which the general interest would require.

"In 1806, a census of the inhabitants of this Territory was taken, and I believe with great accuracy. There were then 52,998 souls, of which 23,574 were slaves, and 3,355 free people of color, leaving a white population of 26,069; of these at least 13,500 are natives of Louisiana, for the most part descendants of the French; about 3,500 natives of the United States, and the residue, Europeans generally, including the native French, Spaniards, English, Germans and Irish.

"I have no document which enables me to state with certainty the number of the several descriptions of persons composing the white population. But the above is, I am sure, very near correct. Since the year 1806, the emigration has not been considerable; it may have given us an increase of between three and four thousand free persons, two-thirds of whom are native Americans. But it is understood that many of the unfortunate people lately banished from Cuba will seek an asylum in this Territory, and that, in a few weeks, the French population may receive an addition of several thousand.

"The memorial met with considerable opposition in the House of Representatives, and, on its final passage, the votes were eleven in the affirmative and seven in the negative. I much doubt whether, *if a question as to the early reception of the Territory into the Union as a State* was submitted to the people, there would be found a majority in its favor. Of one fact I am assured—that a great majority of the native citizens of the United States residing here are against the measure, as are also many of the native Louisianians. I was the other day in conversation on the subject with a very respectable and influential planter, and, among other objections to the prayer of the memorial, he stated *that the time was ill-chosen; that when the Spanish possessions in our vicinity were on the eve of a revolution, and we knew not in what manner the United States, and this Territory in particular, might be affected by the war now raging, the period was not favorable for organizing a State Government: that the taxes already imposed by the Territorial authorities were as great as the people could conveniently meet, and that no change was for the present desirable, which would be accompanied with an accumulation of expenses.* He noticed, also, *the negligence of his fellow-citizens in making use of the privilege already conferred on them, and doubted whether they were yet sufficiently informed on political matters to conduct a State Government.* These remarks were just. The time is indeed illy chosen. There is, moreover, a want of information among the body of the people; the rights of the citizen are not generally understood, and his duties (more particularly political) often neglected. The apathy which prevails at our elections has been remarkable. In counties where there are more than two hundred voters there are instances of persons being returned as Representatives to the General Assembly by a lesser number than thirty suffrages, and hitherto it has seldom happened that, at any election, however contested, a majority of the voters have attended the polls.

"On transmitting a copy of this memorial to the Department of State, I have to regret, Sir, that my sentiments as to its object should not accord with those of a majority of the members of the Legislative Council and House of Representatives, for whose integrity of character I feel the highest respect, and in whose good intentions I fully confide. But whilst my judgment assures me that it would at this time be inexpedient to admit this Territory into the Union as a member State, I should be wanting in duty were I not to suggest the necessity of amending the ordinance of Congress of 1787, which has been extended to the Territory of Orleans, and more specially as relates to our Supreme Judiciary. I believe, also, that an increase of the members of the Legislative Council* would meet the interest and wishes of the citizens."

The revolution of St. Domingo had caused a French emigration into the island of Cuba, and the ruthless invasion of Spain by France was the cause of another exodus of those same refugees, who sought in Louisiana an asylum which was denied them in the country where they had become objects of hatred and suspicion. In the month of June, many of those emigrants had already arrived in New Orleans, some with their slaves and with whatever other property they could bring with them, and others utterly destitute. The negroes, having been introduced in violation of law, were seized, but it was thought to be one of those hard cases when humanity required that the law should be permitted to sleep, or at least that it should not be strictly and rigorously enforced. It was supposed that Congress, being appealed to, would, from sympathy for the fugitives, modify the law so as to permit them to retain what was with most of them their only means of securing a livelihood in their new home, and would not deprive those who had been twice the victims of an adverse fate, of the few remaining wrecks of their former fortunes. Acting in conformity with this spirit of compassion, and in anticipation of the

---

* They were only five in number.

expected course to be pursued by the Federal Government, Claiborne wrote to the Mayor of New Orleans:

"The Collector of the District of Orleans having requested me by a letter bearing date on this day, 19th of June, to name some persons to whom he may deliver, *conformably to the provisions of the act of Congress, passed on the 2d day of March, 1807, to prohibit the importation of slaves,* certain negroes arriving here from Cuba, I must beg you to have the goodness to receive the same, and to place them in the possession of their respective owners, provided they previously enter into bond, with sufficient security to the Governor of the Territory and his successors in office, with a condition that the negroes so placed in their possession shall be held subject, and, at all times after ten days' notice, be forthcoming at the office of the Mayor of the City of New Orleans, there to abide such further and other dispositions as the Governor of the Territory of Orleans, or his successors in office, or the President and Congress of the United States may think proper to make or direct. . . . .
. . . .

"In the event that there be any persons, claiming negroes, who cannot give the security required, you will then be pleased to hire the negroes to some citizen who will give the necessary surety for their delivery at your office as aforesaid, and to pay over the proceeds of the hire to the respective owners."

Two days after, Claiborne communicated to the Secretary of State what he had done in this matter, and said, "I am not certain, Sir, that the temporary disposition I have made of these poor people will, upon investigation, be found correct. The letter of the law may not have been adhered to. But, under all circumstances, I trust the measures I have already directed will be approved. The case is a peculiar one. It was not anticipated by the Government, and may not perhaps be considered as fully provided for under the acts of Congress. The emigration of the French from Cuba was compulsory, and their misfortunes, under the general law of nations, recommend them to the greatest indulgence. An accredited agent of the United States, the Consul of St. Yago, had moreover encouraged them to hope, as appears from his letter to me, *that in their peculiar situation, the Government, as regards the slaves, may have the power and the inclination to grant them some relief from the precise rigor of established statutes,* and in this expectation they entered the waters of the Mississippi. Of the wretched condition of these unfortunate exiles I am well assured. The enclosed petition from them is calculated to awake the sympathy of all who can feel for private distress.

"The vessels coming from Cuba with slaves are all under seizure, and detained to the great loss of the owners. These vessels are American and Spanish bottoms, and I have been assured by the several captains, that had not the feelings of humanity induced them, of their own accord, to bring away the exiled French, the Spanish authorities would have forced them to do so.

"Several other vessels from St. Yago have entered at the Balize with passengers, but I am not informed of their numbers. The French already arrived here are represented, for the most part, to be men of fair characters and industrious habits. The great majority of the people of color, emigrating hither, are women and children; and the negroes who have been introduced are said to consist of faithful domestics, who have adhered to their masters in all the vicissitudes of their fortunes, and of a few Africans purchased by the French during their residence in Cuba."

These emigrants, whose sufferings entitled them to so

much sympathy, and even to indulgence, if they had needed it, for impropriety of behavior, for persistency in defective habits, or for the conspicuousness of morals not entirely free from blame, did not find favor, however, with some of those at whose doors they were knocking for hospitable reception. For, on the 18th of July, Claiborne wrote to the Secretary of State: "Considerable exertions have been made and are now making, through the medium of a paper called the *New Orleans Gazette*, to excite prejudices against those unfortunate strangers, and to impress society with an opinion that my conduct in relation to them and their slaves has been in direct opposition to the laws and the best interests of the United States. According to the newspaper writers, those strangers are, very generally, men of the basest character, who, for the last few years, have committed many wanton and cruel depredations on the commerce of the United States, and their stay in the Territory would endanger its peace and safety.

"For myself, Sir, I would have preferred that the space in our community which these emigrants have filled, had been occupied by native citizens of the United States. But I really see no cause for that uneasiness and alarm which have been expressed. There are, doubtless, among them some worthless individuals. But, upon inquiry, I find that the great majority are men of fair reputations and industrious habits, who deserve a greater portion of happiness than has heretofore been allotted to them. As regards myself, the newspaper abuse is a matter of no consequence. Assured of the rectitude of my conduct, and that the President will not condemn me unheard, I bid defiance to my enemies. But as regards the strangers whom misfortune has thrown upon our shores, I am sorry to find them so much abused; it can only tend to lessen the gratitude for the asylum afforded them. There are, certainly, many excellent Americans who are dissatisfied with so considerable a foreign population. But the persons the most noisy on the occasion are those who participate in all the Spanish and English resentment against the French nation, and of whose breasts prejudice has taken such complete possession as to extinguish all sense of feeling for private distress." *

Notwithstanding the hostility shown to them by a portion of the population of Louisiana, the flood of emigrants had continued to pour in, and on the 18th or July, their number amounted to 5,754, of whom 1,798 were white people, 1977 free colored and black, and 1,979 slaves.

Referring to this subject, Claiborne said to the Secretary of State on the 29th of July: "These trials," (alluding to the trials of some Frenchmen on the charge of piracy,) and the newspaper publications in which the refugees from Cuba are represented as the basest of men, and dangerous to the tranquillity of the territory, have produced here a great share of agitation. The foreign Frenchmen residing among us take great interest in favor of their countrymen, and the sympathies of the creoles of the country (the descendants of the French), seem also to be much excited. The native Americans and the English of our society, on the contrary, with some few exceptions, appear to be prejudiced against these strangers, and express great dissatisfaction that an asylum in this territory was afforded them. I have endeavored to impress reflecting men with the propriety of observing moderation in their language and conduct. But we have here many warm, rash individuals, whose imprudent expressions aid considerably the views of a

* Executive Journal, p. 113, vol. 4.

few base characters whose sole object is to produce confusion, and who seize on every opportunity to bring into contact the discordant materials of which this community is composed."*

Although strongly sympathizing with the French refugees, Claiborne thought it prudent to check that kind of immigration, and wrote as follows to Mr. Anderson, the American Consul at Havana. "The refugees from Cuba who have arrived in this territory have experienced the most friendly hospitality. But their number is becoming so considerable as to embarrass our own citizens, and I fear they will not be enabled much longer to supply, as fully as they would wish, the wants of these unfortunate strangers. You will, therefore, render a service to such of the French as may not have departed from Cuba, by advising them to seek an asylum in some other district of the United States.

"As regards the people of color who have arrived here from Cuba, the women and children have been received, but the males above the age of fifteen have, in pursuance of the Territorial Law, been ordered to depart. I must request you, Sir, to make known this circumstance, and also to discourage free people of color, of every description, from emigrating to the Territory of Orleans. We have already a much greater proportion of that description than comports with the general interest." He addressed the same letter to Maurice Rogers, United States Consul at St. Yago de Cuba. But the colored people who had been ordered to depart contrived to evade the order, and remained in New Orleans, where they have left a numerous posterity. Even others of the same class subsequently arrived, and, notwithstanding a show of opposition, were permitted to glide into a quiet residence in the territory.

* Executive Journal, p 121, vol. 4.

The perturbed state of the world at that time was the cause that many individuals whose condition became unsettled were looking round for places where they could better their fortunes, and not a few of them were daily arriving in New Orleans from almost every quarter of the horizon which embraced the civilized portion of the earth, and particularly from Jamaica, Guadeloupe, and the other West India Islands. British aggressions and conquests in those regions had disposed many of their French inhabitants to seek for refuge elsewhere. "At all times," said Claiborne to the Secretary of State, on the 4th of November, "the utmost vigilance on the part of the officers of Government in this Territory is essential, but it is particularly so at the present period, when so many strangers are daily arriving among us, of whom many are of doubtful character and of desperate fortunes, and many, probably, would become willing instruments in the hands of those unprincipled, intriguing individuals who would wish to disturb the peace and union of the American States. That there are such individuals in this territory I have long since known, and I have no reason to believe that their hostility to the interests of the United States has in the least abated."

In consequence of the steady tide of emigration which was flowing towards Louisiana, chiefly from the shores of San Domingo, Cuba, Jamaica, and Guadeloupe, house rent in New Orleans and the price of provisions had become so extravagantly high that, in the month of November, families who had but limited resources began to find them drawing to an end, and the number of the poor and destitute were daily augmenting.*

It has already been stated that, in the month of May, about two thousand troops of the United States had

---

* Executive Journal, p. 167, vol. 4.

been concentrated in New Orleans. General Wilkinson, who was their commander, had arrived in that city from the North, on the 19th of April, after having stopped at Havana and Pensacola. Immediately after his return, he reconnoitered the country around New Orleans in search of a spot from which the troops might readily be brought into action in case of an attack, and where they might in the meanwhile enjoy as much health and comfort as the climate would allow. His choice fell on an elevated piece of ground on the left bank of the Mississippi, about eight miles below the city, near the point where the road leading to the settlements of Terre aux Bœufs leaves that which runs along the river. A large detachment was sent to Terre aux Bœufs to make the necessary preparations, and the rest of the troops gradually followed. On the 13th of May, seven hundred non-commissioned officers and privates had assembled at that spot.*

They had hardly been three weeks encamped, when the most peremptory order from the department of war was received by Wilkinson, directing him to embark his whole force immediately, leaving only sufficient garrisons at New Orleans and Fort St. Philip, and to proceed to higher grounds in the rear of Fort Adams and of Natchez, and by an equal division of his men to form an encampment at those localities.†

From the difficulty of procuring boats and from other circumstances, the troops did not begin to ascend the river before the 15th of September. Their progress lasted forty-seven days, during which, out of nine hundred and thirty-five men who embarked six hundred and thirty-eight were sick, and two hundred and forty died.

* Martin's History of Louisiana, p. 294, vol. 2.
† Martin's History of Louisiana, p. 295, vol. 2.

It is sad to relate that, of the nineteen hundred and fifty-three regulars who had been sent to New Orleans seven hundred and ninety-five died, and one hundred and sixty-six deserted, so that the total loss was almost one-half of the whole. The greatest sickness was in the month of August, when five hundred and sixty-three men were on the sick list.*

This disaster produced a profound sensation in the United States, and a great clamor arose against Wilkinson, who had already been so long suspected of being in the pay of Spain, and to whose misconduct his opponents attributed what had happened on this occasion. So loud was the hue and cry against him, that James Madison, who had succeeded Jefferson as President of the United States, thought proper to call him to the seat of Government to justify himself, and General Wade Hampton was appointed to take the command in his place.

1810. Claiborne, in the annual message which he delivered at the opening of the session of the Legislature, in January, 1810, complimented them on the new-born interest which the people of the Territory had exhibited in the recent elections for members of their body. "Their indifference on former occasions," he said, "to the right of suffrage was cause for serious concern. It was apprehended that such apathy would in the end prove injurious to their best interests. But, by the recent returns from the several counties, it is apparent that the body of the people are becoming sensible of the importance of the elective franchise and that its exercise is justly considered to be a duty." He further observed, that the embarrassments to commerce necessarily resulting from the condition of the foreign relations of the United States having diminished the value of most of

---

* Martin's History of Louisiana, p. 296, vol. 2.

the surplus productions of the Territory, and augmented considerably the price of all articles of foreign importation, therefore the strongest considerations of interest invited the Louisianians to the exercise of a prudent economy, and to seize on a moment so auspicious as the present, to encourage domestic manufactures and to lessen their dependence on a foreign market for articles of necessity and comfort.

"It is submitted to you," he said, "whether some legislative encouragement may be advisable. To what extent you can best determine. But, were only an honorable premium awarded for the samples of cotton and woollen cloths exhibited from the different Parishes, it could not fail to produce a laudable emulation. I have observed in the prairies of Attakapas and Opelousas some flocks of sheep whose fleece appeared to me to be of good quality. The improvement of the breed of that useful animal is an advisable object. In climates not very dissimilar to that of this territory he is reared to advantage, and I am persuaded that, with due care, his welfare will be equally sure in our extensive western prairies. The Merino sheep, whose wool is held in such high estimation, were a few years since imported into the Atlantic States, and promise to contribute greatly to their real wealth and convenience. I submit, therefore, to the legislature the expediency of introducing into this territory, at the public expense, as many of that improved breed as may be sufficient to make the experiment how far the climate is adapted to their prosperity. The great and necessary consumption of woollen manufactures in this territory makes it important that we should early resort to means to acquire at home those supplies which we, so sparingly, and at so enhanced a price, receive from abroad, and of which resource, it is probable, we may soon in a greater degree be deprived."

In relation to the administration of justice he judiciously said: "There are, doubtless, necessary amendments which may occur to you, but I trust they will not be numerous. A disposition for frequent change of judicial systems should not be encouraged; it often proves injurious. Multiply your laws and they become less known—the more uncertain—and the citizen finds it better to endure, than to seek a redress for grievances."

In consequence of the frequent ravages of the Yellow-fever, particularly in the autumn of the past year, he recommended to the Legislature the policy of making "some general health laws which should enforce cleanliness, and subject the shipping entering the Mississippi to those quarantine regulations which at other places had proved salutary.*

In a communication to the Secretary of the Treasury, bearing date, January 17, Claiborne recommended that Congress be invited to make some appropriation to support, under the direction of the Territorial Legislature, the establishment of public schools in the Territory of Orleans. "I am sorry," he said, "to observe that the education of the youths of this district has been, and is still, greatly neglected; nor do I expect ever to see as liberal an appropriation for public schools as the present state of this society demands, unless Congress shall deem them objects worthy their patronage. Donations have been made, I believe, by Congress, to most of the Territories, with a view to the encouragement of education, and I am persuaded a like generosity will be observed toward the Territory of Orleans. The donation I recommend would enable the Territorial Legislature immediately to establish seminaries of learning in the sev

---

* Executive Journal, p. 219, vol. 4.

eral counties, where the children of the native Louisianians and the native Americans, of the native Frenchmen and the native Spaniards, now inhabiting this Territory, might be instructed in useful knowledge, and the effects of whose early intercourse and friendship would probably be such as to induce the rising generation to consider themselves one people, and no longer to feel that jealousy and want of confidence which exists among their fathers."*

This jealousy and this want of confidence of which Claiborne complains was a stumbling block in the way of his administration, and proved to him a constant source of trouble and anxiety, as may be seen from his dispatch of the 23d of January to the Secretary of State, to whom he expressed his sentiments in these terms: " To give general satisfaction to the inhabitants of this Territory, among the several descriptions of which so much jealousy and dislike exists, I have found impracticable. My sole object is now, and ever has been, to be just to them all, and to conciliate as much as possible the minds of the ancient inhabitants of the Territory to the American Government. As one means of doing so, I have occasionally invited them, in common with the native citizens of the United States, to partake in the administration of the local government. I have had no reason to regret this policy, and I hope and believe that it is approved by the President of the United States. The ancient inhabitants (I mean the natives of Louisiana, or those who were settled here previous to the cession), possess a great share of the wealth of the District, and of course pay a very considerable proportion of the Territorial tax. To exclude them from a participation in the affairs of the Territory would, to say the least of it, be an act of injustice.

* Executive Journal, p. 232, vol. 4.

"From the list of appointments enclosed you will find that, next to the native Americans, the natives of Louisiana enjoy the greatest share of my patronage. Men who were born in this country, and where also their fathers are entombed, I never can treat as aliens. But my mode of thinking and acting has made me some bitter enemies. Not an office is created, or becomes vacant, but the number of my foes increases, and if my choice should happen to fall on a citizen whose native language is French, I am immediately charged with being too friendly to French interests."

Claiborne also informed the General Government that, as long as the Floridas should remain in the possession of a foreign power, all the laws prohibiting the importation of slaves would be evaded. "It is confidently reported," he said, "that two or three vessels have lately sailed from Pensacola for the Coast of Africa, and design to return with a cargo of negroes. These will be carried to the rich settlement of Baton Rouge, and such as cannot be sold there will probably be conveyed across the Mississippi and disposed of in the Territory of Orleans."*

I have already mentioned that Wade Hampton had succeeded General Wilkinson in his military command. Claiborne, in a note of the 27th of January, suggested to him the expediency of leaving at New Orleans, as a garrison, three or four complete companies, "because," as he remarked, "you are doubtless advised of the very heterogeneous mass of which the society in New Orleans is composed, and that we have among us men of every nation and character. Heretofore, nothing has occurred to threaten the public peace. But with a population so mixed, and becoming more so every day by the press of emigration from Cuba and elsewhere, I must confess I am not

---

* Executive Journal, p. 237, vol. 4.

without apprehensions that disorders and disturbances may arise. The free-men of color, in and near New Orleans (including those recently arrived from Cuba), capable of carrying arms, cannot be less than eight hundred. Their conduct has hitherto been correct. But in a country like this, where the negro population is so considerable, they should be carefully watched. Until the militia of the Territory is rendered an efficient force, I should be sorry to see less than three or four companies of regular troops in New Orleans, or in its vicinity. I have not been wanting in efforts to better the condition of the militia. But many obstacles are in my way."

It is remarkable, that the antagonism which in the Legislature of Louisiana has so long existed between the representatives of New Orleans and its vicinity, and those of the rest of the country, had a contemporaneous origin with the formation of the Territorial Government; for, on the 17th of February, Claiborne informed the Secretary of State that "the Territorial Legislature was still in session; that a great difference of opinion had arisen between the members from the Western counties and those from New Orleans and its vicinity, and that the parties were so nearly divided, that few, if any, laws of general concern would probably pass."

In the mean time, the opposition to Claiborne's administration was becoming more intense on the part of his enemies, and the Attorney-General of the Territory thought it his duty to institute judicial proceedings against a virulent libel which had been published against the Executive. On being informed of it, the Governor wrote a very noble letter to the Attorney-General, requesting him to stop the prosecution. "An officer whose hands and motives are pure," he said, "has nothing to fear from newspaper detraction, or the invectives of angry and deluded individuals. My conduct in life is the best answer I can return to my enemies. It is before the public, and has secured, and will, I am certain, continue to secure me the esteem and confidence of that portion of society whose approbation is desirable to an honest man.

"The lie of the day gives me no concern. Neglected calumny soon expires; notice it, and you gratify your calumniators; prosecute it, and it acquires consequence; punish it, and you enlist in its favor the public sympathy. The liberty of the press is all important to a free people; but its licentiousness in the United States has become a curse to my country. It destroys all the benefit which its liberty would otherwise produce. The press, in former days, kept bad men in check; but in these times its denunciations afford no evidence of demerit, for we all know that they are directed as well against the virtuous as the wicked. Judicial interference is not, in my opinion, the best means of putting down that licentiousness. It can alone be effectually done by the people themselves. When they shall think proper to withdraw their patronage from the vehicles of slander, and not until then, will the libelers of the laws of the Government, its officers, and honest citizens, disappear."*

In the month of May, Claiborne, having obtained leave of absence, departed from New Orleans for Baltimore, and the Government was left in the hands of Th. Bolling Robertson, the Secretary of the Territory.

On the 6th of September, Robertson issued the following circular to all those whom it might concern in the Territory: "You have no doubt heard of the late introduction of African slaves among us. Two cargoes have been already smuggled into this Territory by the way of Barataria and Lafourche, and I am fully convinced

* Executive Journal, p. 252, vol. 4.

from a variety of circumstances which have come to my knowledge, that an extensive and well laid plan exists to evade or to defeat the operation of the laws of the United States on that subject. The open and daring course which is now pursued by a set of brigands who infest our coast, and overrun our country, is calculated to excite the strongest indignation in the breast of every man who feels the slightest respect for the wise and politic institutions under which we live. At this moment, upwards of one hundred slaves are held by some of our own citizens in the very teeth of the most positive laws, and notwithstanding every exertion which has been made, so general seems to be the disposition to aid in the concealment, that but faint hopes are entertained of detecting the parties and bringing them to punishment. Confiding in your zeal, I have thought it advisable to state to you my impressions on this all-important subject, and to call upon you to use all the means in your power to give efficacy to a system of law founded on the purest principles of humanity and the soundest views of enlightened policy."

It is true that, for some considerable time before official notice was taken of the fact, smuggling had been carried on to some extent in relation to Africans, and as to every other sort of merchandize, to an immense amount, not only through Barataria and Lafourche, but also through Bayou Teche in Attakapas.

In the neighborhood of Bayou Sara and in the adjacent country there was a large settlement of native Americans, who resolved to avail themselves of the impotency to which Spain was reduced by its war with France, and to secure their political independence. During the summer, having obtained the assistance of their countrymen who dwelt near them in the contiguous counties of the Territory of Mississippi, they suddenly flew to arms, embodied themselves into a small army of insurgents, and marched on Baton Rouge. In the fort which commanded the town, Delassus, the Spanish Governor of the district, used to reside, but he was absent at the time, and the fort had been left in charge of a youth, Louis Grandpré, the son of Carlos de Grandpré, the former Governor. Grandpré had under him only a score or two of old soldiers, most of whom were cripples, and the fort itself was in such a condition, that it would have been deemed incapable of defence by any military man. The forces by which Grandpré was attacked were so overwhelming, that he ought to have surrendered rather than attempt an impossibility and fruitlessly expose his own life and that of the corporal's guard he had with him, but he had received no instructions to meet the case, and he chivalrously thought that he was not, under any circumstances whatever, to give up what had been intrusted, for safe keeping, to his fidelity and honor. Therefore, when summoned by the insurgents to lower his flag, he resolved to die, and replied in the negative. The result was not long delayed; a loud shout of mutual encouragement on the side of the Americans, a simultaneous rush, and they went pell-mell into the fort. They had been met, sword in hand, but by one single man, and he alone perished. It was Grandpré who had thus hopelessly confronted his multitudinous foes. There was no defence made except by him, and it is to be regretted that his enemies, being hundreds to one, had not the magnanimity, or the opportunity, to spare the life of this young hero.

The insurgents, soon after their success, had a Convention which purported to be composed of the representatives of the people of West Florida, and they issued a declaration of independence, in which they solemnly made known to the world that the several districts constitu ting the province of West Florida, had assumed the rank, then and hereafter, of a free and independent State. It is remarkable that in this document, in which they give their reasons for operating this revolution, they show no hostility to Spain, but, on the contrary, take care to record "the fidelity with which they had professed and maintained allegiance to their legitimate sovereign, while any hope remained of receiving from him protection for their property and their lives." They seem to have been solicitous to proclaim that they had not taken arms against their King, for whom they professed to have always entertained an inviolable attachment, which had also extended to Spain as *the parent country, whilst so much as a shadow of legitimate authority remained, to be exercised over them.* Here is this curious document, signed by John Rhea, President of the Convention, and Andrew Steele, Secretary, on the 26th day of September:

"By the Representatives of the people of West Florida, in Convention assembled:

"A DECLARATION.

"It is known to the world with how much fidelity the good people of this Territory have professed and maintained allegiance to their legitimate Sovereign, while any hope remained of receiving from him protection for their property and their lives.

"Without making any unnecessary innovation in the established principles of the Government, we had voluntarily adopted certain regulations, in concert with our First Magistrate, for the express purpose of preserving this Territory, and showing our attachment to the Government which had heretofore protected us. This compact, which was entered into with good faith on our part, will forever remain an honorable testimony of our upright intentions and inviolable fidelity to our King and parent country, while so much as a shadow of legitimate authority remained to be exercised over us. We sought only a speedy remedy for such evils as seemed to endanger our existence and prosperity, and were encouraged by our Governor with solemn promises of assistance and co-operation. But those measures which were intended for our preservation he has endeavored to pervert into an engine of destruction, by encouraging, in the most perfidious manner, the violation of ordinances sanctioned and established by himself as the law of the land.

" Being thus left without any hope of protection from the mother country, betrayed by a magistrate whose duty it was to have provided for the safety and tranquillity of the people and Government committed to his charge, and exposed to all the evils of a state of anarchy, which we have so long endeavored to avert, it becomes our duty to provide for our own security, as a free and independent State, absolved from all allegiance to a Government which no longer protects us.

" We, therefore, the Representatives aforesaid, appealing to the Supreme Ruler of the world for the rectitude of our intentions, do solemnly publish and declare the several districts composing this Territory of West Florida to be a *free and independent State;* and that they have a right to institute for themselves such form of government as they may think conducive to their safety and happiness; to form treaties; to establish commerce; to provide for their common defence; and to do all acts which may, of right, be done by a sovereign and independent nation; at the same time declaring all acts, within the said Territory of West Florida, after this date, by any tribunals or authorities not deriving their powers from the people, agreeably to the provisions established by this Convention, to be null and void; and calling upon all foreign nations to respect this our declaration, acknowledging our independence, and giving us such aid as may be consistent with the laws and usages of nations."*

This declaration of independence was transmitted to the President of the United States with the utmost speed, through Governor Holmes, of the Mississippi Territory, and on the 10th of October, John Rhea, the President of the West Florida Convention, addressed the following communication to the Secretary of State at Washington, in which he prayed for the annexation of that District to the United States, and took the opportunity to claim, in full ownership, on behalf of the Commonwealth of West Florida, all the unlocated lands within its limits, to which he pretended that they were entitled on several grounds, *and particularly as a reward for having wrested the government and country from Spain at the risk of their lives and fortunes.*

"The Convention of the State of Florida," said Rhea to Robert Smith, Secretary of State, on the 10th of October, "have already transmitted an official copy of their act of independence, through His Excellency Governor Holmes, to the President of the United States, accompanied with the expression of their hope and desire that this Commonwealth may be immediately acknowledged and protected by the Government of the United States, as an integral part of the American Union. On a subject so interesting to the community represented by us, it is necessary that we should have the most direct and unequivocal assurances of the views and wishes of the American Government without delay, since our weak and unprotected situation will oblige us to look to some foreign Government for support, should it be refused to

---

* Annals of Congress, by Gales & Seaton, Appendix, p. 1254, 11th Congress, 3d Session.

us by the country which we have considered as our parent State.

"We therefore make this direct appeal through you to the President and General Government of the American States, to solicit that immediate protection to which we consider ourselves entitled; and, to obtain a speedy and favorable decision, we offer the following considerations: 1st. The Government of the United States, in their instructions to the Envoys Extraordinary at Paris, in March, 1806, authorized the purchase of East Florida, directing them at the same time to engage France to intercede with the Cabinet of Spain to relinquish any claim to the Territory which now forms this Commonwealth. 2d. In all diplomatic correspondence with American ministers abroad, the Government of the United States have spoken of West Florida as a part of the Louisiana cession. They have legislated for the country as a part of their own territory, and have deferred to take possession of it, in expectation that Spain might be induced to relinquish her claim by amicable negotiation. 3d. The American Government has already refused to accredit any minister from the Spanish Junta, which body was certainly more legally organized as the representative of the sovereignty, than that now called the Regency of Spain. Therefore, the United States cannot but regard any force or authority emanating from them, with an intention to subjugate us, as they would an invasion of their territory by a foreign enemy. 4th. The Emperor of France has invited Spanish Americans to declare their independence rather than to remain in subjection to the old Spanish Government; therefore, an acknowledgment of our independence by the United States could not be complained of by France, or involve the American Government in any contest with that power. 5th. Neither can it afford any just cause of complaint to Great Britain, although she be the ally of Spain, that the United States should acknowledge and support our independence, as this measure was necessary to save the country from falling into the hands of the French exiles from the Island of Cuba, and other partisans of Bonaparte, who are the eternal enemies of Great Britain.

"Should the United States be induced by these, or any other considerations, to acknowledge our claims to their protection as an integral part of their territory, or otherwise, we feel it our duty to claim for our constituents an immediate admission into the Union as an independent State, or as a Territory of the United States, with permission to establish our own form of government, or to be united with one of the neighboring Territories, or a part of one of them, in such manner as to form a State. Should it be thought proper to annex us to one of the neighboring Territories, or a part of one of them, the inhabitants of this Commonwealth would prefer being annexed to the Island of Orleans; and, in the meanwhile, until a State government should be established, that they should be governed by the ordinances already enacted by this Convention, and by their further regulations hereafter.

"The claim which we have to the soil or unlocated lands within this Commonwealth will not, it is presumed, be contested by the United States, as they have tacitly acquiesced in the claim of France, or Spain, for seven years; and the restrictions of the several embargo and non-intercourse laws might fairly be construed, if not as a relinquishment of their claim, yet as at least sufficient to entitle the people of this Commonwealth (who have wrested the Government and country from Spain at the risk of their lives and fortunes) to all the unlocated lands. It will strike the American Government that the moneys arising from the sales of these lands, applied as they will be to improving the internal communications of the country, opening canals, etc., will, in fact, be adding to the prosperity and strength of the Federal Union. To fulfill with good faith our promises and engagements to the inhabitants of this country, it will be our duty to stipulate for an unqualified pardon for all deserters now residing within this Commonwealth, together with an exemption from further service in the army or navy of the United States."*

In consequence of these events, the President of the United States resolved to take immediate possession of the District of West Florida, and, on the 27th of October, issued this proclamation :

"Whereas the Territory south of the Mississippi Territory, and eastward of the River Mississippi, and extending to the River Perdido, of which possession was not delivered to the United States, in pursuance of the treaty concluded at Paris on the 30th of April, 1803, has, at all times, as is well known, been considered and claimed by them as being within the colony of Louisiana, conveyed by the said treaty, in the same extent that it had in the hands of Spain, and that it had when France originally possessed it ;

"And whereas the acquiescence of the United States in the temporary continuance of the said Territory under the Spanish authority, was not the result of any distrust of their title, as has been particularly evinced by the general tenor of their laws, and by the distinction made in the application of those laws between that Territory and foreign countries, but was occasioned by their conciliatory views, and by a confidence in the justice of their cause, and in the success of candid discussion

---

* Annals of Congress, p. 1252, 11th Congress, 3d Congress.

and amicable negotiation with a just and friendly power;

"And whereas a satisfactory adjustment, too long delayed, without the fault of the United States, has for some time been entirely suspended by events over which they had no control; and whereas a crisis has at length arrived subversive of the order of things under the Spanish authorities, whereby a failure of the United States to take the said Territory into its possession may lead to events ultimately contravening the views of both parties, whilst in the mean time the tranquillity and security of our adjoining Territories are endangered, and new facilities given to violators of our revenue and commercial laws, and of those prohibiting the introduction of slaves;

"Considering, moreover, that under these peculiar and imperative circumstances, a forbearance on the part of the United States to occupy the Territory in question, and thereby guard against the confusions and contingencies which threaten it, might be construed into a dereliction of their title, or an insensibility to the importance of the stake: considering that, in the hands of the United States, it will not cease to be a subject of fair and friendly negotiation and adjustment: considering, finally, that the acts of Congress, though contemplating a present possession by a foreign authority, have contemplated also an eventual possession of the said Territory by the United States, and are accordingly so framed as, in that case, to extend in their operation to the same:

"Now, be it known, that I, James Madison, President of the United States of America, in pursuance of these weighty and urgent considerations, have deemed it right and requisite that possession should be taken of the said Territory in the name and behalf of the United

States W. C. C. Claiborne, Governor of the Orleans Territory, of which the said Territory is to be taken as part, will accordingly proceed to execute the same, and to exercise over the said Territory the authorities and functions legally appertaining to his office. And the good people inhabiting the same are invited and enjoined to pay due respect to him in that character, to be obedient to the laws, to maintain order, to cherish harmony, and in every manner to conduct themselves as peaceable citizens, under full assurance that they will be protected in the enjoyment of their liberty, property, and religion."

On the same day, the Secretary of State sent the following instructions to Claiborne:*

"As the district, the possession of which you are directed to take, is to be considered as making part of the Territory of Orleans, you will, after taking possession, lose no time in proceeding to organize the militia; to prescribe the bounds of parishes; to establish parish courts; and finally, to do whatever your legal powers, applicable to the case, will warrant, and may be calculated to maintain order; to secure to the inhabitants the peaceable enjoyment of their liberty, property, and religion; and to place them, as far as may be, on the same footing with the inhabitants of the other districts under your authority. As far as your powers may be inadequate to these and other requisite objects, the Legislature of Orleans, which it is understood will soon be in session, will have an opportunity of making further provisions for them, more especially for giving, by law, to the inhabitants of the said Territory, a just share in the representation in the General Assembly; it being desirable that the interval of this privation should not be

* Annals of Congress, by Gales & Seaton, p. 1256, 11th Congress, 3d Session.

prolonged beyond the unavoidable necessity of the case.

"If, contrary to expectation, the occupation of this Territory on the part of the United States should be opposed by force, the commanding officer of the regular troops on the Mississippi will have orders from the Secretary of War to afford you, upon your application, the requisite aid; and should an additional force be deemed necessary, you will draw from the Orleans Territory, as will Governor Holmes from the Mississippi Territory, militia in such numbers and in such proportions from your respective territories, as you and Governor Holmes may deem proper. Should, however, any particular place, however small, remain in possession of a Spanish force, you will not proceed to employ force against it, but you will make immediate report thereof to this Department.

"You will avail yourself of the first favorable opportunities that may occur to transmit to the several governors of the Spanish provinces in the neighborhood copies of the President's proclamation, with accompanying letters of a conciliatory tendency."

The same functionary, on the 15th of November, sent to Governor Holmes the view which the Federal Government took of the claims of the inhabitants of West Florida to the unlocated lands in that district. "To repress," he said, "the unreasonable expectations therein indicated in relation to the vacant land in that Territory, it is deemed proper to lose no time in communicating to you and to Governor Claiborne the sentiments of the President on the subject.

"The right of the United States to the Territory of West Florida, as far as the River Perdido, was fairly acquired by purchase, and has been formally ratified by treaty. The delivering of possession has, indeed, been deferred, and the procrastination has been heretofore acquiesced in by this Government, from a hope, partially indulged, that amicable negotiation would accomplish the equitable purpose of the United States. But this delay, which proceeded only from the forbearance of the United States to enforce a legitimate and well-known claim, could not impair the legality of their title; nor could any change in the internal state of things, without their sanction, however brought about, vary their right. It remains, of course, as perfect as it was before the interposition of the Convention. And the people of West Florida must not for a moment be misled by the expectation that the United States will surrender, for their exclusive benefit, what had been purchased with the treasure and for the benefit of the whole. The vacant land of this Territory, thrown into common stock with all the other vacant land of the Union, will be a property in common, for the national uses of all the people of the United States. The community of interests upon which this Government invariably acts, the liberal policy which it has uniformly displayed toward the people of these Territories (a part of which policy has ever been a just regard to honest settlers), will, nevertheless, be a sufficient pledge to the inhabitants of West Florida for the early and continued attention of the Federal Legislature to their situation and their wants."

The Secretary of State further requested Governor Holmes to keep in mind, and to inform the memorialists, "that the President could not recognize in the Convention of West Florida any independent authority whatever to propose, or to form a compact with the United States."

England, who was then the faithful ally of Spain, and who was engaged with her in that gigantic and ever memorable national struggle known as the "Peninsular

War," remonstrated against the course pursued by the United States in relation to West Florida.

"I deem it incumbent upon me," said Mr. Morier, Great Britain's representative at Washington, to the Secretary of State, on the 15th of December, "considering the strict and close alliance which subsists between His Majesty's government and that of Spain, to express to the Government of the United States, through you, the deep regret with which I have seen that part of the President's message to Congress, in which the determination of this Government to take possession of West Florida is avowed.

"Without presuming to discuss the validity of the title of the United States to West Florida (a title which is manifestly doubtful, since, according to the President's proclamation, it is left open to discussion, but which has, nevertheless, been brought forward as one of the pleas to justify the occupation of that province), may it not be asked why that province could not have been as fairly a subject of negotiation and adjustment in the hands of the Spaniards, who possess the actual sovereignty there, as in the hands of the Americans, who, to obtain possession, must begin by committing an act of hostility toward Spain?

"But it may be said that the Spanish forces in Mexico, in Cuba, or at Pensacola, are unequal to quell the rebellious association of a band of desperadoes who are known here by the contemptuous appellation of land-jobbers. Allowing as much, (which you will agree with me, sir, is allowing a great deal,) would it not have been worthy of the generosity of a free nation like this, bearing, as it doubtless does, a respect for the rights of a gallant people at this moment engaged in a noble struggle for its liberty—would it not have been an act, on the part of this country, dictated by the sacred ties of good neighborhood and friendship which exist between it and Spain, to have simply offered its assistance to crush the common enemy of both, rather than to have made such interference the pretext for wresting a province from a friendly Power, and that in the time of her adversity?

"For, allow me, Sir, to inquire how can the declaration in the President's proclamation, *that, in the hands of the United States, that Territory will not cease to be a subject of fair and friendly adjustment*, be made to accord with the declaration in his Message to Congress, (implying permanent possession,) *of the adoption of that people into the bosom of the American family?*

"The act, consequently, of sending a force to West Florida to secure by arms what was before a subject of friendly negotiation, cannot, I much fear, under any palliation, be considered other than as an act of open hostility against Spain.

"While, therefore, it is impossible to disguise the deep and lively interest which His Majesty takes in everything that relates to Spain, which would, I am convinced, induce him to mediate between Spain and the United States on any point of controversy which may exist between them, with the utmost impartiality and good-will toward both parties, I think it due to the sincere wish of His Majesty to maintain unimpaired the friendship which at this moment happily exists between Great Britain and the United States, to say that such are the ties by which His Majesty is bound to Spain, that he cannot see with indifference any attack upon her interests in America. And as I have no doubt that the Government of the United States will attribute this representation to the most conciliatory motives, I am induced to request, in answer to it, such explanation on the subject, as will at once convince his Majesty's Government of the pacific disposition of the United States toward his Maj esty's allies the Spaniards, and will remove the contrary impression, which, I fear, the President's Message is likely to make." *

Acting in conformity with his instructions, Claiborne had hastened to Natchez; and, putting himself at the head of a corps of militia, he marched to St. Francisville in the District of West Florida, where, on the 7th of December, he hoisted the flag of the United States without opposition, and, in their behalf, took formal possession of the country. The inhabitants cheerfully submitted to his authority, and *the State of West Florida* ceased its ephemeral existence. It was annexed to the Territory of Orleans by a special proclamation, and, by subsequent ones, Claiborne instituted in this new part of the Territory the parishes of Feliciana, East Baton Rouge, St. Helena, St. Tammany, Biloxi and Pascagoula. From a census taken, this year, by the Marshal of the United States, according to Congressional legislation, it appears that the population of the Territory of Orleans, without counting that of these new parishes, amounted to seventy-six thousand five hundred and fifty-six souls.

* Annals of Congress by Gales & Seaton, p. 1261. 11th Congress, 3d session.

CHAPTER VI.

CLAIBORNE'S ADMINISTRATION — PROPOSED ADMISSION OF LOUISIANA INTO THE UNION — VIOLENT OPPOSITION — DEBATES IN CONGRESS — JOSIAH QUINCY'S SPEECH — INSURRECTION OF NEGROES — ADOPTION OF A STATE CONSTITUTION.

1811—1812.

THE course pursued by the President in relation to West Florida was as warmly approved by many, as it was bitterly censured by some, in the Congress of the United States. "If my recollection is accurate," said an orator in the Senate, who spoke in favor of the administration,* " all parties had agreed we ought to have the country. They only differed as to the mode of acquiring it. The President, influenced by that policy which has hitherto guided the present administration, of avoiding making this nation a party in the present European war, in the exercise of the discretionary power vested in him by the act of Congress passed on the 24th of February, 1804, which had solemnly asserted our right to this Territory, and authorized the President to take possession of it, and establish a port of entry on the Mobile, whenever he should deem it expedient, did not think proper to seize upon it by force, but to wait for the occurrence of events to throw it into our hands without a struggle. The expediency of taking possession of this Territory cannot, it appears to me, admit of a doubt. If the President had refused or hesitated to meet the wishes

* Annals of Congress. Gales & Seaton, p. 40, 11th Congress, 3d Session.

of the people of West Florida, by extending to them the protection of the American Government, and if they had sought security in the arms of a foreign Power, what should we have heard? He would have been charged with imbecility, and fear of incurring responsibility. He would have been denounced as unworthy of the station his country had assigned to him. Let it be remembered that the Orleans Territory is our most vulnerable part—remote from our physical force—a climate more fatal to our people than the sword of a victorious enemy —and that an enemy in possession of West Florida can with great facility cut off New Orleans from the upper country. If the fortunate moment had not been seized, this province would have fallen into the hands of a foreign power; or, if time had been given for intrigue to mature itself, another Burr-plot would probably have risen from the ashes of the first, more formidable to the integrity of this empire. Burr, like Archimedes, fancied that if he had a place to stand upon—a place beyond the jurisdiction of the United States to rally his followers, he could overturn the Government. He has, it is true, fled from the frowns of an indignant country, but he was not alone. Let an opportunity be afforded, and a thousand Burrs would throw off the mask and point their arms against the Federal Union."

Referring to the President's proclamation, which has already been recorded in the pages of this History, another orator opposed to the administration exclaimed: " This proclamation is not only a declaration of war, but it is an act of legislation, too. It annexes the territory in question to the Orleans Territory: it creates a Governor; it enacts laws, and appropriates money; it gives the Governor of the Orleans Territory all the authorities and functions over this particular territory which he possesses by virtue of his office as Governor of the former."

After having argued that the President had no power under the Constitution to issue that proclamation, he said: "What has Spain recently done to provoke this act of aggression upon her territory? What new offence has she given the United States? Is it her determination to resist the usurpation of France, or is it, that she has lately sent a minister to express her friendly disposition to treat with you for both the Floridas, and pay what she owes us for spoliations? Do you calculate that France will conquer Spain? This, in my humble opinion, she will not do. France is not now contending with an armed soldiery, but she fights an armed people—a people struggling for their liberty, their religion, and their laws, and resolved not to survive them. With such a cause, and such a resolution, neither France nor the combined powers of the earth can subdue them. What are to be the consequences of this measure—a measure adopted at a time particularly calculated to excite the resentment of Spain and her allies—at a time when that nation is pressed on all sides by its enemy, when its strength is prostrated, when it bleeds at every pore and is almost in the act of fainting? What are we to expect but its indignation and retaliation?"

He concluded his remarks as follows: "The honorable gentleman from Kentucky has told us that Europe is now in a state of barbarism, and has emphatically asked: *Are we to sit here and cavil about questions of right?* What if Europe has become barbarous? Is that a reason why Americans should become so too—why we should depart from the great system of conduct which has been the pride, the safety and the boast of our country—of faith—of justice—of peace? Is this a reason why we should violate our treaty with Spain—not one of those barbarous powers—but one of the victims of those powers? Is this a reason why we should commit an act of injustice and violence toward a people who have proffered you their friendship? Is this a reason why we should embroil the nation in war?"

Notwithstanding this acrimonious opposition, the President was firmly sustained by a large majority.

On the 4th of January, the House of Representatives in Congress assembled, having resolved itself into a Committee of the Whole on the Bill for admitting the Territory of Orleans into the Union as an independent and sovereign State; lengthy discussions ensued, and a violent opposition was made to the Bill on constitutional grounds, and on grounds of policy. It was maintained, among many other reasons given, that the Territory of Orleans was not within the limits of the United States when the Constitution was adopted, and therefore could not be incorporated into the Union of those States; that the population of the Territory was not sufficiently numerous; and besides, that it was not American in its feelings. "Without intimating," said Mr. Miller, "how far this last consideration may have influence on my mind, under the circumstances in which that country has been lately placed, I cannot, however, but remark that it is natural for man to carry his feelings and prejudices about him. I was born in Virginia, and I have not yet lost some of my Virginia feelings, notwithstanding an absence of fifteen years, and I cannot see why we should expect the people of New Orleans to act and feel differently from other people, more particularly when the French nation is towering so far above the other nations of the earth. They will have a sacred pride in their glory, they will have some attachments, to what extent I cannot say. But, inasmuch as we know that, if we send Paddy to Paris, Paddy he will come back, the idea is certainly not unworthy of our consideration.

"The bill on your table has another feature of some

weight with me in relation to its policy. You propose to do them a favor by granting them admission to the rank of the other States before they can legally demand it, and, at the same time, you propose terms beyond which they cannot go. This resembles very much a polite invitation to walk in, but under an injunction to see that your feet are well cleaned, and your toes turned out. It is a niggardly sort of policy that I am sorry to see engrafted in the bill. If you design to be liberal, be so; do not destroy your liberality by an ungenerous sentiment.

"Again, there are objections to the bill as presented, that render it impossible for me to give it my sanction. It will be seen that the bill proposes to annex that portion of West Florida in dispute between this and the Spanish Government, to the State to be formed out of the Territory of Orleans. The President has declared to the world that this portion of the country, in our hands, shall be subject to mutual arrangements hereafter to be entered into between the two governments. But, once annex it to a State, and the power to negotiate ceases. What power have we to negotiate about the territory of any of the States? We have none."

Mr. Rhea, of Tennessee, observed in reply: "It has been with extreme regret that I have heard so often, and upon so many former occasions, as well as in the present debate, the charges of French influence and disaffection to this Government, made either in express terms, or else intelligibly insinuated, against the people of New Orleans. Suffer me to ask where are the evidences to support these imputations? Certainly not before the House. Gentlemen may have received from extraneous sources such impressions on their own minds. But if we examine the history of these people since their connection with us, abundant testimony will be found, not only to exonerate them from the charge of disaffection, but to demonstrate their fidelity to the American Government. When, on the acquisition of that country, the most radical innovations upon its laws, customs, usages, and civil proceedings were introduced, these people peaceably submitted, without any symptom of insurgency. When they saw many of their dearest rights endangered, or prostrated by new and imprudent modes of judicial proceedings, and by the chicanery of desperate adventurers, they made no unlawful appeals for redress."

On the 14th of January, the subject was resumed in the House of Representatives, and met with the same unrelenting opposition. Josiah Quincy, one of the favorite sons of Massachusetts, and one of the ablest and most influential men of that State, rose, and thus gave vent to his feelings, with more than his usual emphasis of manner: "I address you, Mr. Speaker, with an anxiety and distress of mind with me wholly unprecedented. The friends of this bill seem to consider it as the exercise of a common power—as an ordinary affair—a mere municipal regulation, which they expect to see pass without other questions than those concerning details. But, Sir, the principle of this bill materially affects the liberties and rights of the whole people of the United States. To me, it appears that it would justify a revolution in this country; and that, in no great length of time, it may produce it. When I see the zeal and perseverance with which this bill has been urged along its parliamentary path, when I know the local interests and associated projects which combine to promote its success, all opposition to it seems painfully unavailing. I am almost tempted to leave, without a struggle, my country to its fate. But while there is life, there is hope. So long as the fatal shaft has not yet been sped, if Heaven so wills it, the bow may be broken, and the vigor of the mischief-meditating arm withered.

"If there be a man in this House, or nation, who cherishes the Constitution under which we are assembled, as the chief stay of his hope, as the light which is destined to gladden his noonday, and to soften even the gloom of the grave, by the prospect it sheds over his children, I fall not behind him in such sentiments. I yield to no man in attachment to this Constitution, in veneration for the sages who laid its foundation, in devotion to those principles which form its cement and constitute its proportions. What then must be my feelings—what ought to be the feelings of a man cherishing such sentiments, when he sees an act contemplated which lays ruin at the root of all these hopes; when he sees a principle of action about to be usurped, before the operation of which the bonds of this Constitution are no more than flax before the fire, or stubble before the whirlwind? When this bill passes, such an act is done, and such a principle usurped.

"There is a great rule of human conduct, which he who honestly observes, cannot err widely from the path of his sought duty. It is, to be very scrupulous concerning the principles you select as the test of your rights and obligations; to be very faithful in noticing the result of their application; and to be very fearless in tracing and exposing their immediate effects and distant consequences. Under the sanction of this rule of conduct, I am compelled to declare it as my deliberate opinion, that, *if this bill passes, the bonds of the Union are virtually dissolved; that the States which compose it are free from their moral obligations, and that, as it will be the right of all, so it will be the duty of some, definitely to prepare for a separation, amicably if they can, violently if they must.*"

Mr. Quincy was here interrupted and called to order

by Mr. Poindexter, the delegate from Mississippi, but with a loud voice, and more accentuated intonations, he repeated the remarks which he had made; he justified and vindicated their propriety and correctness ; and, to save all misapprehension, and secure their being preserved forever, he fearlessly committed them to writing and handed the paper to the Clerk of the House.

This language and the other features of this incident, extraordinary as they were, produced only a *little confusion*, according to the report of the debates.*

Mr. Poindexter required the decision of the Chair whether it was consistent with the propriety of debate to use such expressions. He said it was radically wrong for any member to use arguments going to dissolve the Government, and tumble their body itself into dust and ashes. The question he wished to propound to the Chair was this : " Whether it be competent in any member of this House to invite any portion of the people to insurrection, and, of course, to a dissolution of the Union ?" " And I," replied Mr. Quincy, " will make this question : Is it not the duty of a member to state the consequences of a measure which appears injurious to him ? And the more pregnant the measure is with evil, is not the duty of stating it the more imperious ?" The Speaker decided that a great latitude in debate was generally allowed ; and that, by way of argument against the bill, the first part of the gentleman's observation was admissible; but that the latter member of the sentence, *that it would be the duty of some States to prepare for a separation, amicably if they can, violently if they must,* was contrary to the order of debate.

Mr. Quincy having appealed from this decision, and required the yeas and nays on the appeal, the decision of the Chair was reversed, and, therefore, the observations

* Annals of Congress, Gales & Seaton, p. 525, 11th Congress, 3d Session.

of the orator declared to be in order. With a face beaming with satisfaction, and with an exulting tone and manner, he resumed his speech, in the course of which he said: "The bill which is now proposed to be passed has this assumed principle for its basis—that the three branches of this National Government, without recurrence to Conventions of the people in the States, or to the Legislatures of the States, are authorized to admit new partners to a share of the political power, in countries out of the original limits of the United States. Now, this assumed principle I maintain to be altogether without any sanction in the Constitution. I declare it to be an atrocious and manifest usurpation of power; of a nature dissolving, according to undeniable principles of moral law, the obligations of our national compact; and leading to all the awful consequences which flow from such a state of things.

"Touching the general nature of the instrument called the Constitution of the United States, there is no obscurity—it has no fabled descent, like the Palladium of ancient Troy from the heavens. Its origin is not confused by the mists of time, or hidden by the darkness of past unexplored ages; it is the fabric of our day. Some now living had a share in its construction—all of us stood by and saw the rising of the edifice. There can be no doubt about its nature. It is a political compact. By whom, and about what? The preamble to the instrument will answer these questions.

"*We, the people of the United States, in order to form a more perfect union, establish justice, insure domestic tranquillity, provide for the common defence, promote the general welfare, and secure the blessings of liberty to ourselves and our posterity, do ordain and establish this Constitution for the United States.*

"It is, *we, the people of the United States, for ourselves*

and our posterity, not for the people of Louisiana, nor for the people of New Orleans, or of Canada. None of these enter into the scope of the instrument. It embraces only *the United States of America.* Who those are, it may seem strange in this place to inquire. But truly, our imaginations have, of late, been so accustomed to wander after new settlements to the very end of the earth, that it will not be time ill-spent to inquire what this phrase means, and what it includes. These are not terms adopted at hazard; they have reference to a state of things existing anterior to the Constitution. . .
. . . .

"As the introduction of a new associate in political power implies, necessarily, a new division of power, and a consequent diminution of the relative proportions of the former proprietors of it, there can, certainly, be nothing more obvious than that, from the general nature of the instrument, no power can result to diminish, and give away to strangers, any proportion of the rights of the original partners. If such a power exist, it must be found, then, in the particular provisions of the Constitution. . . . .
. . . .

"Have the three branches of the Government a right, at will, to weaken and outweigh the influence respectively secured to each State in this compact, by introducing, at pleasure, new partners situate beyond the old limits of the United States? The question has no relation merely to New Orleans. The great objection is to the principle of the bill. If this bill be admitted, the whole space of Louisiana, greater, it is said, than the whole extent of the old United States, will be a mighty theatre in which this Government assumes the right of exercising this unparalleled power; and it will be; there is no concealment; it is intended to be exercised. Nor will it stop until the very name and nature of the old partners be overwhelmed by new-comers into the Confederacy. The question goes to the very root of the power and influence of the present members of this Union. . . . .

. . . .

"This is not so much a question concerning the exercise of sovereignty, as it is who shall be sovereign— whether the proprietors of the old United States shall manage their own affairs in their own way, or whether they, and their Constitution, and their political rights, shall be trampled under foot by foreigners, introduced through a breach of the Constitution. The proportion of the political weight of each sovereign State constituting this Union depends upon the number of the States which have a voice under the compact. This number the Constitution permits us to multiply at pleasure within the limits of the original United States, observing only the expressed limitations in the Constitution. But when, in order to increase your powers of augmenting this number, you pass the old limits, you are guilty of a violation of the Constitution in a fundamental point, and in one also which is totally inconsistent with the intent of the contract, and the safety of the States which established the association. What is the practical difference to the old partners, whether they hold their liberties at the will of a master, or whether, by admitting exterior States on an equal footing with the original States, arbiters are constituted, who, by availing themselves of the contrariety of interests and views which in such a confederacy necessarily will arise, hold the balance among the parties which exist and govern us, by throwing themselves into the scale most conformable to their purposes? But the last is the more galling, as we carry the chain in the name and garb of freemen. . . .

"But, says the gentleman from Tennessee (Mr. Rhea), *these people have been seven years citizens of the United States.* I deny it. As citizens of New Orleans, or of Louisiana, they never have been, and by the mode proposed they never will be, citizens of the United States. They may be girt upon us for the moment, but no real cement can grow from such an association. What the real situation of the inhabitants of these foreign countries is, I shall have occasion to show presently. But, says the same gentleman, *if I have a farm, have I not a right to purchase another farm in my neighborhood, and settle my sons upon it, and in time admit them to a share in the management of my household?* Doubtless, Sir. But are these cases parallel? Are the three branches of this Government owners of the farm called the United States? I thank Heaven that they are not. I hold my life, liberty, and property, and the people of the State from which I have the honor to be a representative, hold theirs, by a better tenure than any this National Government can give. Sir, (addressing the speaker,) I know your virtue, and I thank the Great Giver of every good gift, that neither the gentleman from Tennessee, nor his comrades, nor any, nor all the members of this house, nor of the other branch of the Legislature, nor the good gentleman who lives in the palace yonder, nor all combined, can touch these my essential rights, and those of my friends and constituents, except in a limited and prescribed form. No. We hold them by the laws, customs, and principles of the Commonwealth of Massachusetts. Behind her ample shield we find refuge, and feel safety. I beg gentlemen not to act upon the principle that the Commonwealth of Massachusetts is their farm.

"But the gentleman adds: *What shall we do if we do not admit the people of Louisiana into our Union—our children are settling that country?* Sir, it is no concern of mine what he does. Because his children have run wild and uncovered in the woods, is that a reason for him to break into my house, or the houses of my friends, to filch our children's clothes, in order to clothe his children's nakedness? This Constitution never was, and never can be strained, to lap over all the wilderness of the West, without essentially affecting both the rights and convenience of its real proprietors. It was never constructed to form a covering for the inhabitants of the Missouri, and the Red River country; and whenever it is attempted to be stretched over them, it will rend asunder. I have done with this part of my argument. It rests upon this fundamental principle, that the proportion of political power subject to the internal modifications permitted by the Constitution, is an inalienable, essential, intangible right. When it is touched, the fabric is annihilated. For on the preservation of these proportions depend our rights and liberties.

. . . .

"The debates on the Constitution will show that the effect of the slave vote upon the political influence of this part of the country, and the anticipated variation of the weight of power to the West, were subjects of great jealousy to some of the best patriots in the Northern and Eastern States. Suppose then that it had been distinctly foreseen that, in addition to the effect of this weight, the whole population of a world beyond the Mississippi was to be brought into this and the other branch of the Legislature, to form our laws, control our rights, and decide our destiny; can it be pretended that the patriots of that day would for one moment have listened to it? They were not madmen. They had not taken degrees at the hospital of idiocy. They knew the nature of man, and the effect of his combinations in political societies. They knew that when the weight of particular sections of a confederacy was greatly unequal, the resulting power would be abused; that it was not in the nature of man to exercise it with moderation. The very extravagance of the intended use is a conclusive evidence against the possibility of the grant of such a power as is here proposed. Why, Sir, I have already heard of six States, and some say there will be, at no great distance of time, more; I have also heard that the mouth of the Ohio will be far to the East of the centre of the contemplated empire. If the bill is passed, the principle is recognized. All the rest are mere questions of expediency. It is impossible that such a power be granted. It was not for those men that our fathers fought; it was not for them this Constitution was adopted. You have no authority to throw the rights and liberties and property of this people into a *hotch-pot* with the wild men on the Missouri, nor with the mixed, though more respectable race of Anglo-Hispano-Gallo-Americans who bask on the sands at the mouth of the Mississippi. I make no objection to them from the want of moral qualities, or political light. The inhabitants of New Orleans are, I suppose, like those of all other countries, some good, some bad, some indifferent.

. . . .

" I will add only a few words in relation to the moral and political consequences of usurping that power. I have said that it would be a virtual dissolution of the Union; and gentlemen express great sensibility at the expression. The true source of terror is not the declaration I have made, but the deed you propose. Is there a moral principle of public law better settled, or more conformable to the plain suggestions of reason, than that the violation of a contract by one of the parties may be considered as exempting the other from its obligations? Suppose, in private life, thirteen form a partnership, and ten of them undertake to admit a new partner without the concurrence of the other three, would it not be at their option to abandon the partnership after so palpable an infringement of their rights? How much more in the political partnership, where the admission of new associates, without previous authority, is so pregnant with obvious dangers and evils? Again, it is settled as a principle of morals, among writers on public law, that no person can be obliged beyond his intent at the time of the contract. Now, who believes, who dares assert that it was the intention of the people, when they adopted this Constitution, to assign eventually to New Orleans and Louisiana a portion of their political power, and to invest all the people those extensive regions might hereafter contain, with an authority over themselves and their descendants? When you throw the weight of Louisiana into the scale, you destroy the political equipoise contemplated at the time of forming the contract.

. . . .

"Do you suppose the people of the Northern and Atlantic States will, or ought to, look on with patience and see Representatives and Senators from Red River and Missouri, pouring themselves upon this and the other floor, managing the concerns of a seaboard fifteen hundred miles at least from their residence, and having a preponderancy in councils, into which, constitutionally, they could never have been admitted? I have no hesitation upon this point. They neither will see it, nor ought to see it, with content. It is the part of a wise man to foresee danger, and to hide himself. This great usurpation which creeps into this House under the plausible appearance of giving content to that important point, New Orleans, starts up a gigantic power to control the nation. . . . . . .

"New States are intended to be formed beyond the Mississippi. There is no limit to men's imaginations on this subject, short of California and Columbia River. When I said that the bill would justify a revolution, and would produce it, I spoke of its principle and its practical consequences. To that principle and those consequences I would call the attention of this House and nation. If it be about to introduce a condition of things absolutely insupportable, it becomes wise and honest men to anticipate the evil, and to warn and prepare the people against the event. The extension of this principle to the States contemplated beyond the Mississippi, cannot, will not, ought not to be borne; and the sooner the people contemplate the unavoidable result, the better; the more likely that convulsions may be prevented ; the more hope that the evils may be palliated, or removed.

"What is this liberty, of which so much is said? Is it to walk about this earth, to breathe this air, and to partake of the common blessings of God's providence? The beasts of the field and the birds of the air unite with us in such privileges as these. But man boasts a purer and more ethereal temperature. His mind grasps in its view the past and the future, as well as the present. We live not for ourselves alone. That which we call liberty, is that principle on which the essential security of our political condition depends. It results from the limitations of our political system prescribed in the Constitution. These limitations, so long as they are faithfully observed, maintain order, peace and safety. When they are violated in essential particulars, all the concurrent spheres of authority rush against each other, and disorder, derangement and convulsions are, sooner or later, the necessary consequences.

"With respect to this love of our Union, concerning

which so much sensibility is expressed, I have no fear about analyzing its nature. There is in it nothing of mystery. It depends upon the qualities of that Union, and it results from its effects upon our, and our country's, happiness. It is valued for that *sober certainty of waking bliss* which it enables us to realize. It grows out of the affections, and has not, and cannot be made to have, anything universal in its nature. Sir, I confess it; the first public love of my heart is the Commonwealth of Massachusetts. There is my fireside; there are the tombs of my ancestors.

> "Low lies that land, yet blest with fruitful stores,
> Strong are her sons, though rocky are her shores;
> And none, ah! none, so lovely to my sight,
> Of all the lands which Heaven o'erspreads with light."

"The love of this Union grows out of my attachment to my native soil, and is rooted in it. I cherish it because it affords the best external hope of her peace, her prosperity, her independence. I oppose this bill from no animosity to the people of New Orleans, but from the deep conviction that it contains a principle incompatible with the liberties and safety of my country. I have no concealment of my opinion. The bill, if it passes, is a death-blow to the Constitution. It may afterward linger; but, lingering, its fate will at no very distant period be consummated."

Mr. Poindexter, in reply, maintained the constitutionality of the bill in all its bearings and features. As to its expediency, or policy, he observed: "But it is said that the rights of State sovereignty ought to be withheld from the people of the Territory of Orleans, because a majority of the population is composed of emigrants from France, and the descendants of Frenchmen; that among these, there exists a predominant attachment to the government of France. I shall not attempt to controvert the fact, that there are individuals of wealth and influence in that Territory, who from early habits and education have imbibed a strong predilection for French laws, customs and manners. No lapse of time, no change of situation, can obliterate the impressions which the mind receives from early precept and example. Is it to be expected that a people whose laws and usages, from time immemorial, have been materially different from those which constitute the rule of conduct in this country, and whose ignorance of our political institutions results from the very nature of the government under which they have lived, can suddenly transfer their affections from that system of jurisprudence which has been handed down from their ancestors, to a government whose laws they do not understand, either in theory, or in practice? Such a transition cannot be reconciled without the aid of practical experience, by which the blessings of our free Constitution are demonstrated in the security which it affords to the life, liberty and property of the citizen. How far the original inhabitants of Louisiana are liable to the charge of French partiality, I am not prepared to say; but believe them to be an orderly class of society—well disposed toward the Government of the United States. Those who manifest the greatest regard for France are to be found amongst the emigrants, whose views and expectations carry them beyond the simplicity of a republican form of government. But while I admit the existence of French influence in that quarter of the Union to a certain extent, I cannot make it the basis on which to justify a refusal to emancipate the great body of the people from the trammels of territorial vassalage.

. . . .

' From the influence of France nothing need be feared.

The distance by which we are separated from that great Power is a sufficient guarantee that no attempt will be made on her part to subvert our authority in Louisiana. France is not in a situation to assail us, if such a disposition existed in her ruler. The want of naval power will, for many years to come, form an insuperable barrier to the introduction of a French army into the United States. But the people of the Territory of Orleans can never be prevailed on to commit their destinies to an adventurer; they enjoy, not only the necessary comforts, but the luxuries of life in abundance; their increasing wealth furnishes a certain pledge of future greatness. The Government of which they now form a component part, though in many particulars different from that in whose laws they have been educated, exempts them from the desolating storm which carries misery and distress into every region of the whole world; and under the auspices of our mild and salutary Constitution, they may repose in full confidence that their political connection will not depend on the whim or caprice of the tyrants of Europe. It cannot be forgotten that, in the situation of colonies, they were bought and sold like herds of cattle, at the will of foreign nations, without regard to their feelings or wishes. With these insuperable ties on the allegiance of the people of the Territory of Orleans, I consider it an act both of justice and policy to receive them as brothers in the great American family."

In relation to Josiah Quincy's threats of a dissolution of the Union, Mr. Poindexter said: " On all the great questions which have been discussed in this House for four years, a war with England and a separation of the Western States from the Union have been constantly thrown in the way to obstruct the measures of the Administration. Why these subjects have gone hand in hand, I leave gentlemen who are in the secret to explain.

It ought not to be forgotten that, on a proposition to repeal the embargo, at a time when its effects were severely felt both in Great Britain and her colonies, the gentleman from Massachusetts told us that the people of New England were prepared for insurrection and revolt, unless that measure of resistance to the aggressing belligerents was relinquished; and, contemporaneously with these opinions uttered on the floor of the House of Representatives, the British Minister, resident in the United States, made a confidential communication to his Government, in which a dissolution of the Union was deemed a probable event, should the commercial embarrassments of this country continue. From whom that Minister received his information, no gentleman acquainted with the history of that transaction can doubt."

Mr. Gold sided with Josiah Quincy in the main points of his arguments, and even justified the language which that distinguished member of the House had used, when recommending a dissolution of the Union, should the Bill pass. He said : " In the Parliament of Great Britain, a country so often stigmatized on this floor, will be found examples of free debate fully equal in ardency, vehemence and invective to all that fell from the eloquent member from Massachusetts. We have there witnessed the old Earl Chatham, at a crisis all important to the British Empire (the commencement of the great contest for American rights), sounding the alarm at the measures of administration; pronouncing the war in America founded in wrong and injustice, and arraigning the known *favorite* measures of the King in a strain of angry and terrible invective that can scarce find its parallel in the English language. Shall this House, in all the fullness of freedom secured by the Constitution, be afraid to follow such examples? It is here, Sir, on this floor, that free debate is consecrated. Here different opinions are to mingle in conflict. To repress this freedom, would touch the vital principles of the Constitution."

After animated debates prolonged through many sittings of the House, the Bill passed at last by a vote of 77 yeas to 36 nays, and was approved by the President on the 20th of February. By that act of Congress, all free white male citizens of the United States, who had arrived at the age of twenty-one years, and had resided within the said Territory at least one year previous to the day of election, and had paid a territorial, county, or district, or parish tax; and all persons having in other respects the legal qualifications to vote for Representatives in the General Assembly of the said Territory, were authorized to choose Representatives to form a Convention—which Representatives were to be apportioned amongst the several counties, districts, and parishes in the said Territory of Orleans, in such manner as the Legislature thereof should direct. The number of Representatives could not exceed sixty. The election for those Representatives was to take place on the 3d Monday of September, and the members of the Convention were authorized to determine by a majority of the whole number elected, whether it was expedient or not, at that time, to form a Constitution and a State Government; and, in case of a vote in the affirmative, then the Convention was, in like manner, to declare that it adopted the Constitution of the United States, whereupon the Convention was authorized to form a Constitution and a State Government for the people of said Territory.

The conditions annexed to this grant of authority were: That the Constitution should be republican, and consistent with the Constitution of the United States; that it should contain the fundamental principles of civil and religious liberty; that it should secure to the citizen the trial by jury in all criminal cases, and the privilege

CONDITIONS OF ADMISSION AS A STATE.

of the writ of Habeas Corpus conformable to the provisions of the Constitution of the United States; that the laws enacted by the new State should be promulgated, and all its records of every description preserved, and its judicial and legislative written proceedings conducted, in the language in which the laws and the judicial and legislative proceedings of the United States were published and conducted; that the said Convention should provide by an ordinance, irrevocable without the consent of the United States, that the people inhabiting the said Territory agreed and declared that they forever disclaimed all right or title to the waste or unappropriated lands lying within the said Territory; that the same should be and should remain at the sole and entire disposition of the United States; that each and every tract of land sold by Congress should remain exempt from any tax laid by order or under the authority of the State for any purpose whatever, for the term of five years from and after the respective days of the sales thereof; that the lands belonging to citizens of the United States residing without the said State should never be taxed higher than the lands belonging to persons residing therein; and that no taxes should be imposed on lands the property of the United States; and that the River Mississippi, and the navigable rivers and waters leading into the same, or into the Gulf of Mexico, should be common highways and forever free, as well to the inhabitants of the said State as to other citizens of the United States, without any tax, duty, impost, or toll therefor, imposed by the said State.

The 4th Section of the Act declared that, in case the Constitution for the State to be created should not be disapproved by Congress at their next session, the said State should be admitted into the Union upon the same footing with the original States.

It was provided in the 5th and last Section, that five per cent. of the net proceeds of the sales of the lands of the United States after the first day of January, should be applied to laying out and constructing public roads and levees in the said State, as its Legislature might direct.*

The Territorial Legislature had met early in January, but had been prorogued by the Governor until the fourth Monday of the month, on account of an insurrection of negroes which had broken out in the Parish of St. John the Baptist, on the left bank of the Mississippi, about thirty-six miles above the city of New Orleans. They marched along the river toward the city, divided into companies, each under an officer, with beat of drums and flags displayed, compelling the blacks they met to join their disorderly crew, and before they could be checked, they set fire to the houses of four or five plantations.† Most of the planters, being apprised by their own slaves of the coming danger, had fled with their families. One of them, named Trepagnier, contented himself with sending to a place of safety his wife and children, but, deaf to their entreaties, remained at home for the protection of his property. Having provided himself with several fowling-pieces which he loaded with buck-shot, and having taken his stand on a high circular gallery which belted his house, and from which he could see at a distance, he awaited calmly the coming of his foes. In a short time, Bacchanalian shouts announced their approach, and they tumultuously made their appearance at the front gate which led to the planter's residence. But at the sight of the double-barreled gun which was leveled at them, and which they knew to be in the hands of a most expert shot, they wavered, lacked self-sacrific

---

* See the Act itself, in the Appendix.
† Martin's History of Louisiana, p. 300, vol. 2.

ing devotion to accomplish their end, and finally passed on, after having vented their disappointed wrath in fearful shrieks and demoniacal gesticulations. Shaking at the planter their fists, and whatever weapons they had, they swore soon to come back for the purpose of cutting his throat. They were about five hundred, and one single man, well armed, kept them at bay. This incident, among many others, shows how little that population is to be dreaded, when confronted by the superior race to whose care Providence has intrusted their protection and gradual civilization.

The misguided negroes, who had been deluded into this foolish attempt at gaining a position in society, which, for the welfare of their own race, will ever be denied to it in the Southern States of North America, as long as their white population is not annihilated or subjugated, were soon encompassed by a strong body of militia, backed by regulars under Major Milton, who had come down from Baton Rouge, and General Hampton, who had hastened up with those under his command in New Orleans. To attack was to rout the blacks; they fled in every direction with wild cries of despair, leaving sixty-six dead bodies on the field. Most of the prisoners were hung on the spot; sixteen were sent to the city for trial. The fugitives had taken shelter in the neighboring swamps, where they could be pursued but with extreme difficulty. Many of them, however, had been dangerously wounded, and every day corpses were discovered by the pursuers. The wretches sent to New Orleans were immediately tried and convicted. As it was intended to make a warning example of them, their heads were placed on high poles above and below the city, along the river,* as far as the plantation on which the revolt began. The ghastly sight spread terror far

* Martin's History of Louisiana, p. 301, vol. 2.

and wide, and further to insure tranquillity and to quiet alarm, a part of the regular forces and of the militia remained on duty in the neighborhood for a considerable time.

The Territorial Legislature, before its adjournment, had received official information of the passage of the act to enable the people of the Territory to form a Constitution and State Government, preparatory to the admission of the new State into the Union.

Congress having not as yet acted on that part of the President's proclamation which had annexed to the Territory of Orleans that portion of West Florida of which possession had been taken a few months before, its inhabitants were not authorized to elect members of the Convention for framing the Constitution.

The Legislature, without loss of time, proceeded to the apportionment of the future members of the Convention among the Parishes, and made provision for the necessary expenses of election. It then adjourned in the latter part of April, after having passed several important acts, among others, one establishing two banks, the Planters' Bank and the Bank of Orleans, which institutions were thought to be called for by the expiration of the charter of the Bank of the United States.

Another more important act was passed—more important in consequence of the discovery which had led to the passage of the act—granting to Livingston and Fulton the sole and exclusive right and privilege to build, construct, make, use, employ and navigate boats, vessels and water-crafts, urged or propelled through water by fire or steam, in all the creeks, rivers, bays and waters whatsoever, within the jurisdiction of the Territory, during eighteen years from the first of January, 1812.

On the 4th of November, the Convention met in New Orleans, and after having elected Le Breton D'Orgenois president *pro tempore*, adjourned to the 18th of the same month, when, on its meeting again, Julien Poydras was elected president, and Eligius Fromentin secretary.

On taking the chair, the President returned his thanks to the assembly for the honor it had conferred on him, and then expatiated in a somewhat dithyrambic style on the happiness which the Louisianians were to expect from a popular government and from their incorporation into the Union, as members of a sovereign State.

"Yes, gentlemen, I again repeat it," he said, "and ever with new enthusiasm, this government is the most perfect that the human mind has hitherto framed. It is that which has the most effectually, by wise and impartial laws emanating from its Constitution, secured even to the lowest of its members personal safety, the peaceable possession of his property, the free exercise of his faculties, of his talents and of his industry, the sacred rights of conscience, and above all, that right perhaps the most important of all, I mean the right of freely thinking, speaking and writing, without which liberty itself would soon prove an illusion.

"Is it not the summit of political felicity to be able to adopt the Constitution of the United States, as our birthright in our quality of Americans? Can there be anything on earth more flattering, more advantageous, than to see ourselves placed in the rank, and become the equals, of all the free and flourishing States of this astonishing Confederation, which is now the admiration of the universe, and will perhaps one day become the model of all nations? They are henceforth our friends and our brothers; they stretch forth their arms to us, and invite us to enjoy in common with them all the advantages of liberty, which they so gloriously acquired by triumphing over their enemies at the expense of their blood, of all the privations and of all the sacrifices which the love of country imperiously requires from virtuous citizens, as the indispensable pledges of their heroic devotedness to liberty.

"We are now presented with that liberty after which we have panted from the moment of our being erected into a Territory, and to obtain which we have never ceased to implore the justice of Congress, which has, at length, yielded to our entreaties, being well informed of our grievances, moved by our just complaints, and struck with the murmurs forced from us by that abject slavery into which we had been plunged by that execrable Territorial Government, that monstrosity in the annals of a free people, which it ought never to have been suffered to disfigure, and from which it ought to be forever effaced. . . . .
. . . .

"Let us hail our emancipation from that odious servitude which has cost us so dear; let us hail it, I say, with transports of gratitude, with that sensibility of soul, those emotions, those throbbings of the heart, felt by a navigator when, after having been the sport of adverse winds, tempest tost, fatigued, harassed, and on the point of perishing from want, he enters the port which is the object of his wishes and the hope of his fortune."

A less enthusiastic orator than Mr. Poydras might perhaps have discovered, on reflection, that he had permitted himself to be carried away by his imagination, and that his speech was not as compact in logic as it was florid in words. For instance: how could he in reality be so extravagantly enamored of a political system which had forced upon him and Louisiana "an abject slavery, an execrable Territorial Government, a monstrosity in the annals of a free people?" Would not a more astute statesman than Mr. Poydras have come to the conclusion that the nation, which, on the threshold of its existence, was, as it enemies pretended, intoxicated with self-love, with the incense which it burned in self-adoration on its domestic altars, and with the gorgeous prospect of its present and future prosperity, would not in the course of time, according to all probabilities, find within itself a moral or religious principle sufficiently strong to prevent popular majorities from inflicting intolerable oppressions on minorities? Would not that statesman have inferred that the nation which had perpetrated such *abominations* as are described by Mr. Poydras, could not, if these political crimes were true, be the "astonishing confederation" which he had eulogised in a preceding paragraph, and did not deserve to be the "admiration of the universe? Would he not have drawn the inevitable deduction that the nation which, in the beginning of its career, had forgotten the commandments of God, and trampled on the rights of man, if the denunciations of the epoch are to be believed, would probably improve in iniquity as it grew older in the possession and lust of irresponsible and ever-expanding power, and that it was not, therefore, destined by Providence "to become the model of nations?" Let the sentiments entertained and expressed by Louisiana, in 1861, answer these questions.

It is now to be hoped by every patriot that, taught by the dire lessons of the past, the Government of the United States, made more powerful by the late intestine war, will, by an enlightened, just and magnanimous administration, ever deserve the universal love of the people, and that no well-founded discontent will ever threaten its existence in the future, in consequence of such violations of the Federal compact as were the cause of deluging the country in blood.

On the next day, Mr. Watkins laid before the Convention a Resolution declaring it to be expedient, in the name of the people of the Territory of Orleans, that said

Territory be erected into a sovereign and independent State, under the conditions and according to the provisions of the Act of Congress to enable the people of the Territory to adopt a Constitution and State Government, as also for the admission of the said State into the Union on the same footing with the original States, and that said Convention shall proceed forthwith to form a Constitution and State Government.

In the course of the debate on this Resolution, Messrs. Guichard, Blanque, Bernard Marigny, Le Breton D'Orgenois, James Brown, Watkins, and Thomas Urquhart spoke in favor of it; and against it, Messrs. Destréhan, Alexander Porter, Morgan and Hubbard. It was finally adopted by a large majority. Those who voted in the negative were: Jean Noel Destréhan, James Dunlap, Andrew Goforth, Billy Hubbard, D. B. Morgan, Alexder Porter and James Thibodeau.*

On the 23d of November, the Convention elected by ballot a committee of seven members for the purpose of preparing and laying before the Assembly the plan of a Constitution. These members were: Magruder, Brown, Blanque, Bry, Destréhan, Johnson and Cantrelle. Destréhan having been one of those opposed to the formation of a Constitution and State Government, it is somewhat surprising that he should have been selected to be a member of this committee. In six days the committee had accomplished their work, and, on the 29th, had laid before the Convention the fruit of their labors.

1812. On the 13th of January, 1812, the Convention passed to the third reading of the Preamble of the Constitution, which defined the limits of the State. A motion was made to add to that preamble the following amendment: "That the limits of the State may be so

---

* See the Journal of the Convention on record in the office of the Secretary of State at Baton Rouge.

enlarged as to embrace that portion of the country situated south of the Mississippi Territory, and east of the Mississippi River to the Perdido, known by the name of West Florida, or any part thereof, so soon as the titles to the same may be adjusted, and it may be convenient to the Government of the United States to annex it. This motion was rejected by 24 nays to 14 yeas. The nays were: J. B. Armant, J. D. Bellechasse, J. Blanque, Placide Bossier, James Brown, Michel Cantrelle, Louis DeBlanc, J. B. LeBreton D'Orgenois, M. Guichard, S. Henderson, Sebastien Hiriart, Denis DeLaronde, W. A. Maquillé, D. B. Morgan, Bernard Marigny, Manuel Prudhomme, Louis Raynaud, Genesi Roussin, François St. Martin, S. D. Sutton, Thomas Urquhart, James Villeré, Jones Watkins, and Samuel Winter.

On the 23d of the same month, Alexander Porter, in the name of a committee appointed to draft a memorial requesting the annexation of West Florida to the new State which was to be erected, and having, on a previous occasion, reported that memorial, obtained leave to lay before the Convention certain supplemental paragraphs. A motion having been made to adopt them, together with the original report, it was carried by a vote of 25 in the affirmative to 12 in the negative. Those who voted in the negative were: J. Blanque, Michel Cantrelle, Louis DeBlanc, LeBreton D'Orgenois, M. Guichard, Denis DeLaronde, Bernard Marigny, M. Prudhomme, Louis Raynaud, Genesi Roussin, Thomas Urquhart, and J. Villeré. These members had voted on the 13th against the proposition to enlarge the limits of the State, and were, therefore, consistent on this occasion. J. B. Armant, D. Bellechasse and Placide Bossier, who had opposed the extension of the limits of the State, seem to have been absent when the question of the adoption of the memorial came before the Convention, for their votes are not recorded; and James Brown, S. Henderson, Sebastien Hiriart, W. C. Maquillé, D. B. Morgan, F. St. Martin, S. D. Sutton, Jones Watkins and Samuel Winter, who had voted with the above-named members of the Convention, changed side, and went to the opposite camp, for reasons which were no doubt satisfactory to their own minds, but which do not appear on record.

The Convention having assented to all the stipulations imposed by the Federal Government as preliminary conditions to the framing of a Constitution and State Government for the Territory of Orleans, and the Constitution having been adopted by a unanimous vote, two delegates, Messrs. E. Fromentin and A. B. Magruder, were elected to carry to Washington City, and lay before the proper authorities, the Constitution, and the other acts of the Convention, with special instructions to urge the speedy action of Congress, and with full power to give all necessary explanations. Two thousand dollars were allowed to each for their expenses.

The Convention adjourned *sine die* on the 28th of January, 1812, after having adopted all the provisions which were deemed expedient to carry the Constitution into practical effect, should it be approved and sanctioned by Congress.

Here is the Preamble of the Constitution: * "We, the representatives of the people of all that part of the Territory or country ceded under the name of Louisiana, by the treaty made at Paris, on the 30th day of April, 1803, between the United States and France, contained in the following limits, to wit: beginning at the mouth of the River Sabine, thence, by a line to be drawn along the middle of said river, including all its islands, to the thirty-second degree of latitude—thence due north to

---

* The whole document will be found in the Appendix.

the northernmost part of the thirty-third degree of north latitude—thence along the said parallel of latitude to the river Mississippi—thence down the said river to the river Iberville,* and from thence along the middle of the said river and lakes Maurepas and Pontchartrain to the Gulf of Mexico—thence bounded by the said Gulf to the place of beginning, including all islands within three leagues of the coast—in convention assembled by virtue of an act of Congress entitled: *An Act to enable the people of the Territory of Orleans to form a Constitution and State Government, and for the admission of said State into the Union on an equal footing with the original States, and for other purposes;*—in order to secure to all the citizens thereof the enjoyment of the right of life, liberty and property, do ordain and establish the following Constitution or form of government, and do mutually agree with each other to form ourselves into a free and independent State, by the name of the State of Louisiana."

* Better known as Bayou Manchac.

CHAPTER VII.

ADMINISTRATION OF GOVERNOR CLAIBORNE — ARRIVAL OF THE FIRST STEAMBOAT AT NEW ORLEANS — PART OF WEST FLORIDA ANNEXED TO LOUISIANA — DEBATES IN CONGRESS — REMARKABLE AVERSION IN LOUISIANA FOR PUBLIC LIFE — THE BARATARIANS.

1812—1813.

ON the 10th of January, an exciting event took place in New Orleans. It was the arrival from the West of the first steamboat which navigated the turbid waters of the Mississippi. Her Captain stated that he had been but two hundred and fifty-nine hours actually on the way.* This speed seemed at the time to be marvelous, and the whole population flocked to the river to examine the wonderful creation of the genius of man.

On the 19th of March, the House of Representatives at Washington resolved itself into a Committee of the Whole, on the Bill for the admission of Louisiana into the Union, and the extension of the laws of the United States thereto. An amendment was presented, giving four representatives in the State Legislature to that part of West Florida which was proposed by the Bill to be annexed to the State now formed of the Orleans Territory.

Mr. Johnson, who had offered the amendment, spoke in support of it, adverting to the memorial which had been presented from the Convention of Orleans, giving their decided assent to the annexation of that Territory

* Martin's History of Louisiana, p. 311, vol. 2.

to the State, which removed, in his opinion, the objections urged against authorizing this representation.

Mr. Calhoun opposed the amendment, on the ground of its incorporating in the law a principle of representation which was in hostility with the provisions made concerning that subject in the Constitution of the new State. He said that it came in conflict with the apportionment made by that body, which alone had the power to change or modify the principle of representation; and that body being dissolved, he advised that it should again be called together, as the only mode by which the object in contemplation could be attained.

Mr. Nelson went into an argument to show that the proposed amendment was neither incompatible with the Constitution, nor inexpedient. The error in the reasoning of gentlemen appeared to him to be, that Louisiana was considered by them as a State, which it was not until the bill now before the House should pass; and in its present inchoate situation, he contended that it was competent to Congress to annex conditions to the instrument which made it a State. He then dwelt at some length on the urgency of the claim of the population of West Florida to a representation in the Legislature of the State, of which he maintained that they could not be constitutionally deprived.

Mr. Poindexter could not conceive how a Territory could be represented in the first Legislature of a State to which it was not annexed, until the consent of the Legislature should be obtained.

Mr. Nelson replied that there was yet no such body in existence as the Legislature of Louisiana, nor would there be until this bill passed to create it a State; and in admitting the State into the Union, having already imposed certain conditions, Congress had the right to impose that further condition which the amendment proposed.

Mr. Johnson observed that his amendment was predicated on consent already given by the Convention; but, if it were not, he contended that the people to be included in the State ought to be actually represented. He went into a larger scope of argument to show that there was no difficulty in the way.

Mr. Calhoun again spoke in opposition to the amendment. He said that it proposed to annex conditions to the people of the Territory of Orleans, on its becoming a State, when there was no political body in existence competent to accept them, as the Convention which had framed the Constitution had been dissolved; that the people of West Florida would be unrepresented only until the State Government should be organized; that the interval during which they would be unrepresented was unavoidable, and, after all, that being so short, it was not very important. He further maintained that the proposed amendment would be engrafting the principle of Territorial Government on a State Government, to which it was wholly inapplicable; that it was, in fact, assuming to make a Constitution for the people of a State, whose inalienable right it was to form a Constitution for themselves.

Mr. Gholson spoke against the amendment in its present form, as he conceived it incompatible in many respects with the Constitution now offered for the consideration of Congress. "For instance," said he, "the Constitution of Louisiana provides that the Senate of the new State shall consist of fourteen members, and this amendment adds two members peremptorily, which makes the number sixteen, in defiance of that Constitution." He then read an amendment, which he said he would propose, if the one now under consideration were not agreed to. The question being on Mr. Johnson's amendment, it was negatived by a vote of 39 to 37.

Mr. Gholson then proposed his amendment, which was to add to the bill the following proviso:

"And provided, also, that the people of that portion of West Florida hereby proposed to be made a part of the State of Louisiana shall, before the election of Senators and a Representative to the Congress of the United States, be invested with and enjoy equal rights of representation, and equal privileges in every respect, with the people of the residue of the said State."

Mr. Rhea opposed the amendment, because he doubted the power of Congress to superadd conditions to those already made requisites to the admission of the State into the Union. There appeared to him but one way to remedy the evil, and that was to authorize the people of Orleans to meet again in Convention to accept the conditions required.

Mr. Clay spoke in favor of the amendment. He could see no real objection to its adoption. The Convention of Orleans had framed a Constitution for the State in conformity to the law of Congress, imposing certain conditions as preliminary. The Convention had annexed to their acceptance of these conditions another proposition, to wit: *That the Florida Territory should be incorporated in that State.* "Can we not," said Mr. Clay, "accept or reject this proposition? If we accept, may we not do it with or without qualification? We agree to give only a certain part instead of the whole Territory desired; and it is proposed to do this on certain conditions. In alienating a whole territory, an entire people (an exercise of one of the highest attributes of sovereignty), we are about to take care of their rights, and to secure to them the same political rights, privileges and immunities as are enjoyed by the people of the Territory to which it is to be annexed. If the present amendment was adopted, the question how these rights shall be invested by the Legislature, or by a new convention to be called for the purpose, is very properly left to the decision of those concerned."

Mr. Gholson's amendment was agreed to without a division.* But on the final passage of the bill, as amended, the vote stood 77 yeas to 23 nays.

The Senate disagreed to the amendment, and the bill passed in the end, through both houses, without the clause annexing West Florida, and was approved by the President on the 8th of April. The 2d section provided that, until the next general census, and apportionment of Repretentatives, the new State should be entitled to one Representative in the House of Representatives, and that all the laws of the United States, not locally inapplicable, should be extended to the said State, and should have the same force and effect within the same as elsewhere within the United States.†

The 6th section declared that the "act of admission" should commence and be in force from and after the 30th of April.

Almost simultaneously with the act for the admission of the State of Louisiana, another act had passed, "to enlarge the limits of the State," and was approved by the President on the 14th of April. It enacted, that in case the Legislature of the State of Louisiana should consent thereto, all that tract of country comprehended within the following bounds, to wit: Beginning at the junction of the Iberville River, (or Bayou Manchac,) with the Mississippi; thence along the middle of the Iberville, the river Amite, and of the Lakes Maurepas and Pontchartrain to the eastern mouth of the Pearl River; thence up the eastern branch of Pearl River to the thirty-first degree of North latitude; thence

---

* Journal of Congress, Gales & Seaton, 12th Congress, p. 1,225.
† See the Appendix, for the whole act of Congress.

along the said degree of latitude to the river Mississippi; thence down the said river to the place of beginning, shall become and form a part of the State of Louisiana, and be subject to the constitution and laws thereof, in the same manner, and for all intents and purposes, as if it had been included within the original boundaries of the said State.

It further enacted, that it should be incumbent upon the Legislature of the State of Louisiana, in case they consented to the incorporation of the Territory aforesaid within their limits, at their first session, to make provision by law for the representation of the said Territory in the Legislature of the State, upon the principles of the Constitution, and for securing to the people of said Territory equal rights, privileges, benefits and advantages with those enjoyed by the people of the other parts of the State, which law should be liable to revision, modification and amendment by Congress, and also in the manner provided for the amendment of the State Constitution, but should not be liable to change or amendment by the Legislature of the State.

On the 4th of August, the Legislature of Louisiana approved of, and consented to the enlargement of the limits of the State, in the manner provided for in the act of Congress above recited, and declared that the Territory annexed to her "should forever be and remain a part of the State of Louisiana;" and by a subsequent act of the 25th of the same month, the Legislature granted to the annexed district three Senators and six Representatives. The annual salary of the Governor was fixed at $7,500; that of the Secretary of State at $2,500. The Secretary of the Senate and the Clerk of the House of Representatives had each a regular salary of $2,000 a year.

A resolution was passed by the Legislature, and approved by the Governor on the 31st of August, declaring it to be expedient to remove the seat of government from the city of New Orleans, and directing that some place more convenient be made choice of as the permanent seat of government for the State. It further provided for the appointment of two persons on the part of the Senate and three on the part of the House of Representatives, to examine the different places designated for the seat of government, and to receive any propositions to be made, or donations to be offered of property in those different places, with instructions to report to the General Assembly at their next session.

P. B. St. Martin was the first Speaker of the House of Representatives under the State Government, and Julien Poydras the first President of the Senate.

W. C. C. Claiborne had been elected Governor of the State. It was the best proof of the satisfaction given by his administration under the territorial system of government, which, itself, had been an object of detestation to the great majority of the population. He appointed L. B. Macarty to the office of Secretary of State.

Allan B. Magruder and Jean Noel Destréhan, who had been members of the late Convention, were elected Senators of the United States; but Destréhan having resigned before taking his seat, and during the adjournment of the State Legislature, the Governor appointed in his place Thomas Posey, who was little known in Louisiana, at least to the ancient population.

Thomas Bolling Robertson, who had been Secretary of the Territory, was elected to represent the State in the House of Representatives at Washington.

Hall, Mathews and Derbigny were appointed by the Governor Judges of the Supreme Court. Each of them had a salary of five thousand dollars.

On the 18th of June, Congress had solemnly declared

to the world that war existed between the United States and Great Britain, and had empowered the President "to use the whole land and naval force of the United States to carry the same into effect."

On the 31st of July, Claiborne, in his inaugural address to the Legislature, taking into consideration the state of the country, had strenuously recommended a thorough organization of the militia, which until then had been far from effective. "A war exists," he said, "between the United Kingdoms of Great Britain and Ireland and dependencies, and the United States of America. War is not the greatest of evils—base submission to aggression would have been a greater curse. It would have entailed dishonor, cowardice, vassalage upon our posterity. The independence of America was the fruit of eight years of toil and of danger, and to maintain this inestimable advantage, the sword is again unsheathed. The wrongs of England have been long and seriously felt ; they are visible in the decline of our sea towns, in the ruin of our commerce, and the languor of agriculture. The recourse to arms may increase the pressure; but let it be recollected, that whatever sacrifice we make, is offered on the altar of our country—a consideration which will reconcile a faithful people to every privation. The President of the United States calculates on every aid which it is in the power of Louisiana to give, *as well to mitigate the evils of war to our citizens, as to make it effectual against the enemy.* In so reasonable a request, let not our chief be disappointed. For years he labored to arrest the storm, and now that it rages in all its fury, let us endeavor to carry him and our country safely through it. Union is in itself a host ; it is numbers, strength and security. Let every man put himself in armor. Age itself should be prepared to advance against an invad ing foe. Our young men should hasten to the *tented field*, and tendering their services to the Government, be in readiness to march at a moment's warning to the point of attack. In such a contest, the issue cannot be doubtful. In such a cause, every American should make bare his bosom. *Where justice is the standard, Heaven is the warrior's shield.*"

On the 14th of August, in a message which he sent to the Legislature, he said: "On turning my attention to the interior of the State, I perceive with regret that, within the Parishes of Feliciana, Baton Rouge, St. Helena, and St. Tammany, which have recently been annexed to Louisiana, the civil authority has become so weakened and relaxed, that the laws have lost much of their influence, and, in the Parish of St. Tammany in particular, are scarcely felt. I advise, therefore, that such provisions as you shall think proper to prescribe for these parishes may be passed with all convenient dispatch."

In those days there was not the same greediness for office which has since become so conspicuous, and it had frequently been difficult for the President of the United States and for Governor Claiborne to find suitable men, willing to accept political trust, or any delegation of authority from the Government. If some were tempted into it, they soon resigned, and by their very resignations increased the difficulties which beset the appointing power. The judges, in particular, were remarkable for their readiness to return to private life, and Claiborne, in a message to the Legislature, mentions one of the causes: "The collection of taxes by the Parish Judges," he said, "has at all times been considered by them as a very unpleasant duty. It has already occasioned several resignations, and in some instances prevented citizens in whom the public placed high confidence from accepting the office of judge. I much fear that a continuation of this regulation may induce some other judges to retire, and that, at the present period, when the durability of the parish court system is so very uncertain, I shall experience difficulty in filling satisfactorily the vacancies which exist, or such as may arise. With a view, therefore, to prevent embarrassments, and the better to secure a punctual collection of the revenue, I suggest for consideration the expediency of providing by law for the division of the State into four or more collection districts."*

On the 2d of September, Claiborne vetoed a bill, entitled " An Act supplementary to an act to regulate the conditions and forms of the emancipation of slaves." It must have contained very extraordinary provisions, judging from Claiborne's objections. " It puts to hazard," remarked the Governor, " the character, the peace of mind, and even the lives of unoffending citizens, by subjecting them to be denounced by slaves, to whom the bill holds out such inducement—the promise of freedom— as to expose innocence itself to accusation. In some instances, the provisions of the bill may tend to bring offenders to punishment. But, as I fear they might also operate to the injury and oppression of good men, I should regret to see them introduced into our code of laws."

The Legislature had hardly adjourned, when Claiborne thought proper, " on considerations of public interest," as expressed in his proclamation, to convene the General Assembly in extraordinary session at the seat of Government, on the 23d of November. The main object was to provide by legislation for the mode of choosing electors to give their votes for a President and Vice-President of the United States on the first Wednesday in

* Executive State Journal, p. 8, vol. 1.

December; and the Senate and House of Representatives, in joint meeting assembled on the 30th of November, chose Julien Poydras, Philemon Thomas, and Stephen A. Hopkins, as electors of a President and Vice-President of the United States.

Previous to the meeting of the Legislature, an unprecedented number of resignations had taken place among the Creole members of that body, for reasons which are not sufficiently authenticated to be historically recorded; but the fact is remarkable. Among those who thus refused to take their seats were: Joseph Landry, Senator elect for the County of Acadia; Godefroy Olivier, the Representative from the Parishes of Plaquemine and St. Bernard; P. B. St. Martin and J. C. Arnauld, Representatives from the German Coast. What is more strange is, that Alexander Labranche and René Trudeau, having been elected in the place of the two last-named gentlemen, resigned in their turn. Genesi Roussin and Le Breton Deschapelles also vacated their seats. All these gentlemen belonged to the *élite* of the ancient population, and some of them had been members of the late Convention. It must therefore be presumed that they must have had very powerful reasons for the course which they pursued. It is impossible not to suppose that there was some serious discontent and disgust at the bottom of it.

1813. On the 4th of March, commenced the second term of Mr. Madison's re-election to the Presidency. His inaugural address on that occasion sounds as a production of the present day, and, with a slight alteration in the phraseology, would be applicable to the condition of things existing in 1861, between the North and South of the disruptured Confederacy of the United States. A mere substitution of names is sufficient to suppose it delivered by Jefferson Davis. "From the weight and magnitude of the trust reposed in me," said the re-elected Chief Magistrate, " I should be compelled to shrink, if I had less reliance on the support of an enlightened and generous people, and felt less deeply a conviction that a war with a powerful nation, which forms a prominent feature in our situation, is stamped with that justice which invites the smiles of heaven on the means of conducting it to a successful termination.

" May we not cherish this sentiment without presumption, when we reflect on the characters by which this war is distinguished ?

" It was not declared on the part of the United States, until it had long been made on them in reality, though not in name; until arguments and expostulations had been exhausted; until a positive declaration had been received that the wrongs provoking it would not be discontinued; nor until this last appeal could no longer be delayed, without breaking down the spirit of the nation, destroying all confidence in itself and in its political institutions, and either perpetuating a state of disgraceful suffering, or regaining by more costly sacrifices and more severe struggles our lost rank and respect among independent Powers. . . . .

. . . .

" As the war was just in its origin, and necessary and noble in its objects, we can reflect with a proud satisfaction that, in carrying it on, no principle of justice or honor, no usage of civilized nations, no precept of courtesy or humanity, have been infringed. The war has been waged on our part with scrupulous regard to all these obligations, and in a spirit of liberality which was never surpassed.

" How little has been the effect of this example on the conduct of the enemy !

"They have retained as prisoners of war, and threatened to punish as traitors and deserters, persons emigrating without restraint to the United States; incorporated by naturalization into our political family, and fighting under the authority of their adopted country, in open and honorable warfare for the maintenance of its rights and safety. Such is the avowed purpose of a Government which is in the practice of naturalizing by thousands citizens of other countries, and not only of permitting, but compelling them to fight its battles against their native country.

"They have not, it is true, taken into their own hands the hatchet and the knife devoted to indiscriminate massacre; but they have let loose the savages, armed with these cruel instruments; have allured them into their service, and carried them to battle by their sides, eager to glut their savage thirst with the blood of the vanquished, and to finish the work of torture and death on maimed and defenceless captives . . . . .

. . . .

"And now we find them, in further contempt of the modes of honorable warfare, supplying the place of a conquering force by attempts to disorganize our political society, to dismember our Confederated Republic. Happily, like others, these will recoil on the authors; but they mark the degenerate counsels from which they emanate; and if they did not belong to a series of unexampled inconsistencies, might excite the greater wonder, as proceeding from a Government which founded the very war* in which it has been so long engaged, on a charge against the disorganizing and insurrectional policy of its adversary.

"To render the justice of the war on our part the more conspicuous, the reluctance to commence it was followed by the earliest and strongest manifestations of a

---

* Against France.

disposition to arrest its progress. The sword was scarcely out of the scabbard, before the enemy was apprised of the reasonable terms on which it would be resheathed. Still more precise advances were repeated, and have been received in a spirit forbidding every reliance not placed on the military resources of the nation.

"These resources are amply sufficient to bring the war to an honorable issue. Our nation is, in number, more than half that of the British Isles. It is composed of a brave, a free, a virtuous and an intelligent people. Our country abounds in the necessaries, the arts, and the comforts of life. A general prosperity is visible in the public countenance. The means employed by the British Cabinet to undermine it have recoiled on themselves; have given to our national faculties a more rapid development; and draining and diverting the precious metals from British circulation and British vaults, have poured them into those of the United States. It is a propitious consideration, that an unavoidable war should have found this seasonable facility for the contributions required to support it. When the public voice called for war, all knew, and still know, that without them it could not be carried on through the period which it might last; and the patriotism, the good sense, and the manly spirit of our fellow-citizens, are pledges for the cheerfulness with which they will bear each his share of the common burden. To render the war short, and its success sure, animated and systematic exertions alone are necessary; and the success of our arms now may long preserve our country from the necessity of another resort to them."

On the 15th of March, Claiborne issued the following proclamation: "Whereas, I have received information that upon, or near the shores of Lake Barataria, within the limits and jurisdiction of this State, a considerable number of banditti, composed of individuals of different nations, have armed and equipped several vessels for the avowed purpose of cruising on the high seas, and committing depredations and piracies on the vessels of nations in peace with the United States, and carrying on an illicit trade in goods, wares and merchandise with the inhabitants of this State, in opposition to the laws of the United States, and to the great injury of the fair trader and of the public revenue; and whereas there is a reasonable ground to fear that the parties thus waging lawless war will cease to respect the persons and property of the good citizens of this State, I have thought proper to issue this my proclamation, hereby commanding the persons engaged as aforesaid in such unlawful acts to cease therefrom, and forthwith to disperse and separate; and I do charge and require all officers, civil and military, in this State, each within his respective district, to be vigilant and active in apprehending and securing every individual engaged as aforesaid in the violation of the laws; and I do caution the people of this State against holding any kind of intercourse, or being in any manner concerned, with such high offenders; and I do also earnestly exhort each and every good citizen to afford help, protection and support to the officers in suppressing a combination so destructive to the interests of the United States, and of this State in particular, and to rescue Louisiana from the foul reproach which would attach to her character, should her shores afford any asylum, or her citizens countenance, to an association of individuals whose practices are so subversive of all laws, human and divine, and of whose ill-begotten treasure no man can partake, without being forever dishonored, and exposing himself to the severest punishment."

This proclamation did not prevent the individuals therein mentioned from appearing daily in the streets of

New Orleans, and from carrying on their trade with its citizens without much danger or impediment.

There were other wild guests who at that time used to pay frequent visits to New Orleans. These were numerous bands of Choctaws, who, when under the influence of intoxication, would often prove a dangerous nuisance. Several Parishes of the State, among others, those of St. Tammany, St. Helena and Baton Rouge, were exposed to Indian depredations, and the apprehensions of their inhabitants became so great, that several farms were abandoned, and the settlers fled to the interior for safety.

The belief that the British meditated an attack against Louisiana was daily gaining ground. It was sadly in want of arms and munitions of war, and yet the Government of the United States had withdrawn from the State one Regiment of infantry of the regular troops, of which measure Claiborne immediately complained to James Brown and Eligius Fromentin, who had succeeded Magruder and Posey in the Senate of the United States. He represented to them the defenceless state of the country, and also expatiated at length on the sufferings and losses of the planters on account of the overflows of the Mississippi, from the Parish of Concordia down to the Parish of Plaquemine inclusively. Even New Orleans had been partly inundated by a break in the levee at Kenner's plantation, some ten or twelve miles above the city. Fromentin had been appointed one of the Judges of the Supreme Court by Governor Claiborne, and had been rejected by the Senate. But shortly afterward he was elected by the united vote of both houses to the Federal Senate for the term of six years, which was an ample compensation for any mortification which he might have felt from his defeated aspirations to the Bench.

This overflow was not the only calamity from which New Orleans was to suffer. It was afflicted as much by fire as by water. Constant conflagrations had produced a feeling of despondency in the inhabitants, as no one was sure of a safe night's rest in his own house, which might be burned over his head before the next dawn of day. To remedy the evil, Claiborne, on the 26th of June, offered a reward of one thousand dollars to any individual who should give such information as might lead to the discovery and punishment of these lurking incendiaries. Shortly after, a female slave, thirteen years old, having been sentenced to death on conviction of arson, under circumstances which had inclined the Governor to the granting of a reprieve, with a view perhaps to a final pardon, doubts were raised as to his authority to exercise that power, on the curious ground that slaves, not being parties to the Constitution, could not derive any benefit from that instrument. The case was referred to F. X. Martin, who was then Attorney-General, and who afterward became Chief-Justice of the State. The Attorney-General replied: "That he could not find anything in the Constitution or laws of the State which authorized the Governor to commute the punishment of any person, free or slave, and did not believe that such a power was impliedly vested in the Governor by virtue of his office

"That the Governor might reprieve any person, bond or free, after conviction, till he should have an opportunity of consulting the Senate.

"The power of reprieving," said he, "is expressly given by the Constitution in cases of high treason. Hence a plausible argument might be drawn that he may in lesser offences.

"But the power of pardoning must include that of reprieving; for, during the greatest part of the year, the

Senate not being in session, if the Governor cannot reprieve alone, culprits must undergo punishment before the Senate may be consulted, unless the court will postpone the execution of their sentence till the meeting of the Senate.

"It is said that slaves are not parties to the Constitution, and therefore cannot derive any benefit from any clause in that instrument, and the Governor, deriving the power of pardoning, and consequently that of reprieving, from the Constitution, cannot exert it in favor of slaves. Neither is an alien party to our Constitution or laws, yet, when tried, he must be tried according to them, not from any right he has to their benefit, but because our judges have no other rule to go by, and are not authorized to proceed without any rule. An alien enemy, if tried here, would be tried by a jury, would have every advantage which a citizen might claim, and, no doubt, if his case called for it, would be entitled to the clemency of the State in the mode known to the Constitution and laws. If there was not a particular mode pointed out by law for the trial of slaves, no court or judge could try them in any other mode than that in which freemen are tried. If there be (one there is) no mode pointed out by which the Governor is to act toward them when they are the object of the clemency of the State, he must act toward a slave as he would toward another human being. For although, in civil cases, slaves are considered as things, in criminal cases they are considered as men."

The Constitution being a new thing, to which the people were unused, the different constructions put upon it by the public mind were manifold, and some of them, by their extraordinary nature, show how very little that document was generally understood in the first years of its existence. The Constitutional question which I have cited is one of the many which were frequently mooted.

On the 15th of July, Claiborne addressed to one of the Louisiana Senators in Congress, Eligius Fromentin, a letter, in which he depicted to him the neglected condition of the State in a military point of view. "The Third United States Regiment," he said, "commenced its ascent of the Mississippi a few days since. I much fear this regiment will be considerably reduced previous to its arrival at Cincinnati. The recent overflowings of the river have left on its margin an immense mass of vegetable matter, which, under the influence of a hot Summer's sun, will soon be in a state of putrefaction, and must render the atmosphere greatly insalubrious. The departure of the Third Regiment has diminished one half the regular forces in this quarter, and leaves us much exposed. I have issued orders for holding in a state of requisition a strong detachment of militia, to take the field in case of insurrection, invasion, or imminent danger of invasion. But the arraying of this force will necessarily be attended with delay, and to the general want of discipline will be added a scarcity of arms, unless the loans of muskets desired can be obtained from the General Department, and speedily forwarded.

"The non-payment of the bills drawn by Colonel Shaumburgh on the Secretary of War has seriously affected the credit of the War Department in this State, and will, I fear, much injure the service. Colonel Shaumburgh's bills in many cases fell into the hands of private individuals, whom their rejection submitted to serious embarrassments. I learn also that the claims of many citizens for labor done, or materials furnished at the different fortifications, remain, for the want of funds, unliquidated. It is not for me to inquire how far the moneys expended in this State under the authority of the War Department have been judiciously appropriated. But I sincerely regret that so many persons, relying on the credit and good faith of Government and its officers, should have sustained injury."

One of the Louisiana Senators, James Brown, who had also been addressed on the same subject, replied in these terms: "It is with extreme pain that I discover that the force destined for the defence of our State, instead of being augmented, is daily diminishing. I have only to assure you that no pains on my part have been wanting to induce the General Government to alter its course on that head, and to afford us something like an adequate protection. . . . .
. . . .

"So generally has our coast been menaced, so numerous have been the calls on the Department for protection at the different points immediately threatened, and so limited are the funds assigned to that object, that the complaints of our distant State, although reiterated and enforced in the best manner I could devise, have resulted in a manner in the highest degree unsatisfactory and mortifying to me. The removal of the Third Regiment, and what is more extraordinary, its removal by water, is a policy which I do not approve, and against which I have directly and repeatedly remonstrated."*

Such being the defenceless condition of Louisiana, it became necessary to compel a speedy organization of the militia, and it was presumed that a draft would be resorted to, but the mere recommendation of that measure produced much discontent in some quarters. On the 31st of July, Claiborne addressed Colonel Placide Bossier, of Natchitoches, on the subject. He informed that officer that the Adjutant-General would inclose him

* Executive State Journal, p. 123, vol. 1.

the commissions which he solicited, and that his exertions to organize his regiment were confidently relied on by the Government. "The war in which our country is involved," wrote Claiborne, "rages with unabated fury, and there appears no prospect of a speedy peace. The Creek Indians manifest an unfriendly disposition toward the United States, and seven hundred warriors of that tribe, well armed, have recently crossed the Perdido. It is probable they may be met, and, I trust, driven back by the troops of the United States on that station. As a measure of precaution, which the crisis seemed to render indispensable, I have ordered a detachment of militia to be holden in readiness for actual service, and to be obtained by draft, if the same should become necessary. A quota of this detachment has been assigned to the First Brigade, and quotas will be assigned to the several other brigades throughout the State, so soon as the regiments attached to each brigade shall be organized. I repeat, Sir, that this is only a measure of precaution, and that the citizens composing the detachment will not be called from their homes, unless in case of insurrection, or when the public safety shall require it; and, in no event, to be marched out of the limits of the State. Essential as this measure is to the public safety, it has, nevertheless, been assailed with all the bitterness of party, and is spoken of as the act of a tyrant. It consoles me, however, to know that these furious attacks are only made by a disappointed, and, I believe, unprincipled faction in this city, against whose efforts to produce disorder the good sense of the people will, I trust, be an ample barrier, and against whose calumnies as regards myself, I oppose a life exclusively devoted to honorable pursuits."

In the midst of all this war agitation, the population of New Orleans was thrown into a ferment by a decis ion of the District Court of Louisiana in the suit of Edward Livingston against Le Breton D'Orgenois, the Marshal of the United States. The decision declared "illegal" the interference of President Jefferson in the case of the Batture, and directed the claimant to be restored to the possession of the alluvial land known under that name. The Marshal refused to appeal from that decision, and the City Council of New Orleans passed a resolution whereby the Governor was invited to appeal in behalf of the city and the State, on the ground that the rights of both were infringed in the premises. In relation to this affair, Governor Claiborne wrote to the late President Jefferson: "Considering the Batture as a part of the bed of the Mississippi, and included within the port of New Orleans, I shall have recourse to our State Courts to enjoin Mr. Livingston against exercising any acts of ownership over the same, or in any manner obstructing the navigation of the Mississippi, which is declared to be a great highway, and the free use of which, as well to the inhabitants of this State, as of the other States, is one of the considerations on which Louisiana was admitted into the Union. Mr. Livingston has found means either to neutralize, or to make active partisans of, most of the lawyers in the State. The people, however, are fortunate in receiving the support of the Attorney-General, F. X. Martin, and of Messrs. Moreau Lislet and Fielding Turner, three distinguished lawyers, and I entertain strong hopes that we may yet be enabled to maintain the rights of the public."

On application of the Attorney-General, James Pitot, the Parish Judge, granted an injunction, but subsequently dissolved it, on the following grounds: That, until it was shown that Mr. Livingston had done some act to deprive the citizens of the use of the Batture, or erected some works thereon which might obstruct the navigation of the Mississippi, judicial interference would be premature and improper. "Thus the case rests for the present," wrote Claiborne to Thomas Bolling Robertson, the representative of Louisiana in the lower House at Washington; "nor has Mr. Livingston yet thought proper to prosecute the Mayor of New Orleans, or the inhabitants, who are in the habit of taking, as formerly, dirt from the Batture. I am extremely desirous to have the rights of title to the Batture finally settled, but feel some difficulty as to the best manner of bringing the question fairly before our courts."

In the month of September, the population of New Orleans was informed that the war with the Creek Indians was assuming a serious aspect, that a fort twenty-five miles from Mobile had been taken by them, and three hundred and fifty men, women and children had been cruelly massacred. It was confidently reported that many slaves had escaped from their masters to join the Indians, and it was feared also that the Choctaws would soon become hostile. Hence increased vigilance was required throughout Louisiana, and Claiborne sent a circular to all the militia colonels, pressing upon them the necessity of being ready to meet all emergencies whatever; and, on the 11th of September, he departed through Bayou St. John for the Parish of St. Tammany, to take measures for the safety of its inhabitants, who were much exposed to the depredations of the Indians.* From St. Tammany he proceeded to Baton Rouge by way of St. Helena, and then went to Lafourche, from which he journeyed to the Attakapas and Opelousas districts, actively engaged in making what preparations he could for the defence of Louisiana with the scanty materials which the State possessed at the time. He

* Executive State Journal, p. 152, vol. 1.

even went as far as Natchitoches, where a great many Spanish families had taken refuge from the neighboring province of Texas, which was then in a state of revolution. These fugitives, to the number of about twelve hundred, had crossed the Sabine in the most destitute condition, which had been generously relieved by the adjacent parishes in Louisiana.

Being at Natchitoches, Claiborne availed himself of the circumstance to send, on the 18th of October, what in Indian parlance is called " a talk," to the Great Chief of the Caddo Indians. It is preserved here as a curious specimen of the figurative style which it was universally thought proper to adopt in addressing the rude warriors and primitive denizens of the wilderness: " Friend and Brother! I arrived at this port three sleeps past, and learn from our friend, Dr. Sibley, that you had only left it last month. I should rejoice to have met you here, that we might have shaken hands in friendship, and smoked and conversed under the shade of the same tree. Seven years ago, brother, we had a conference at this place, Natchitoches, and mutually promised to keep the path between our two nations white. We have been long in authority, and know from experience the blessings of peace. We will endeavor to keep the chain bright between our two nations, and the chiefs who follow us may, I hope, so strengthen it that our children's children will live together as neighbors and friends.

" Brother, the United States are like the oak of the forest—a great body with many branches. The people of the United States are composed of eighteen families. Each family has a chief; but the great beloved man of all is your father, the President, who stands in the place of the Great Washington. Our friend, Dr. Sibley, is the agent of the President, and whatever he says in his name you must receive as his own words. I have seen, brother, and highly approve the 'talk' you gave out, when you were last in council at this point. The advice you have given to your own people, and to all Red Men with whom you have influence, is that of a father to his children. I hope they will hold it fast, and live in constant peace with the white people.

"Brother, seven years ago, you told me that your nation had but one enemy, the Osages, and I am sorry to hear that you are still at war with those people. I have often heard of the Osages. In the vast hunting-grounds where the Great Spirit has placed a sufficiency of buffalo, bear and deer for all the red men, the Osages, I hear, have already robbed the hunters of all nations, and their chiefs still wage war to acquire more skins. Among the white people, brother, there is also a nation of Osages. Beyond the sea there lives a people, called the English, who may really be considered white Osages. On the big water, which the Great Spirit made large enough for the use of all men, the English have already plundered every people, and their chiefs direct the continuance of these outrages. Many Americans, peaceably navigating the big water, had their vessels and property taken away from them, and others were compelled to serve on board of war-canoes, and made to fight against their friends and countrymen. But, brother, such injuries could not be endured; the hearts of the Americans have become cross; they have raised the tomahawk, and will not consent to bury it until the English are just toward them. The warriors of your father, the President, are marching into the country of our enemy, and the thunder of our great war-canoes is heard on every sea.

"Brother, the English, unwilling to fight us man to man, have called upon the red people to assist them. With tongues as forked and as poisonous as a snake's, they have told the Indians many lies, and made fair promises which they will not and cannot fulfill. Thus it is that many of the Red Men have been prevailed upon to throw away the peace-talks of their father, the President. But the Americans have the power and the will to punish all their enemies. The other day, the Creeks, when it was supposed they were only quarreling among themselves, surprised one of our forts, and spilled much innocent blood. A fly, you know, brother, may disturb the sleeping lion; but our warriors are now in arms against the Creeks, and it will not be in the power of their friends, the English, to shield them against our vengeance.

"I don't like many words; but there is something on my heart which I must relate to you. I hear the Creeks have sent runners with war-talks to the Couchattas and other tribes, your neighbors, but I hope all these people will look up to you as an elder brother, and hold fast your good advice. When your father was a chief, the path from your towns to Natchitoches was clean, and if an Indian struck the people of Natchitoches, it was the same as to strike him. You now, brother, stand in your father's place. I wanted, brother, to send you a token of my friendship. To a chief, a man, and a warrior, nothing could be more acceptable than a sword, but a suitable one could not be obtained at this place. I have, therefore, directed that a sword be purchased at New Orleans and forwarded to Dr. Sibley, who will very soon present it to you in my name. Farewell, brother; I pray the Great Spirit to preserve you in health and happiness."

The month of November had nearly elapsed, and the Baratarian band of smugglers against whom Claiborne had issued a proclamation on the 15th of March still continued their illegal pursuits, as if no obstacle had been intended to be thrown in their way. Wherefore, on the 24th, he issued this second proclamation:

"Whereas," he said, "the nefarious practice of running in contraband goods which has hitherto prevailed in different parts of this State, to the great injury of the fair trader, and the diminution of the revenue of the United States, has of late much increased; and whereas the violators of the law, emboldened by the impunity of past trespasses, no longer conceal themselves from the view of the honest part of the community, but, setting the Government at defiance in broad daylight, openly carry on their infamous traffic; and whereas it has been officially known to me that, on the fourteenth of the last month, a quantity of contraband goods, seized by Walter Gilbert, an officer of the revenue of the United States, were forcibly taken from him in open day at no great distance from the city of New Orleans, by a party of armed men under the orders of a certain John Lafitte, who fired upon and grievously wounded one of the assistants of the said Walter Gilbert; and although process has issued for the apprehension of him, the said John Lafitte, yet such is the countenance and protection afforded him, or the terror excited by the threats of himself and his associates, that the same remains unexecuted:

"And whereas the apathy of the good people of this State in checking practices so opposed to morality, and to the laws and interests of the United States, may impair the fair character which Louisiana maintains, and ought to preserve as a member of the American Union:

"I have thought proper to issue this my proclamation, hereby strictly charging and commanding all officers of the State, civil and military, in their respective departments, to be vigilant and active in preventing the violation of the laws in the premises, and in apprehending and securing all persons offending therein; and I do solemnly caution all and singular the citizens of the State against giving any kind of succor, support or countenance to the said John Lafitte and his associates, but to be aiding and abetting in arresting him and them, and all others in like manner offending; and do furthermore, in the name of the State, offer a reward of five hundred dollars, which will be paid out of the treasury to any person delivering the said John Lafitte to the Sheriff of the Parish of Orleans, or to any other Sheriff in the State, so that the said John Lafitte may be brought to justice."

The band of smugglers mentioned in this proclamation was composed of desperate men of all nations, chiefly under the command of two brothers, John and Pierre Lafitte, who were originally from Bordeaux, or, according to other reports, from Bayonne, but who, emigrating from their native country, had settled in New Orleans as blacksmiths. Tempted by the hope of making a speedier fortune than by continuing to hammer on the anvil, they abandoned the honest trade they were engaged in for one of a more dangerous character, but promising a life of excitement, which was probably more congenial to their temperament, and which held out to them ample compensation for the perils they were to encounter. They began with being the agents of the Baratarian buccaneers in New Orleans, and ended with being their leaders, and being proclaimed outlaws by the country where they resorted for illicit purposes.

On the coast of Louisiana, west of the mouth of the Mississippi, there is an island called Grande Terre, which is six miles in length and from two to three miles in breadth, running parallel with the coast. Behind that island, about six miles from the open sea, there is a secure harbor which is reached by the great pass of Barataria, in which there are from nine to ten feet of water. This harbor communicated with a number of lakes, lagoons, bayous, sea-outlets, and canals, leading to the Mississippi, and which, skirted by swampy forests, and forming a labyrinth of waters, offered a tempting field of operation to the Robin Hoods of the sea. These men pretended to be privateers cruising with letters of marque issued by France and the new Republic of Carthagena, to prey upon the commerce of Spain; but the world called them pirates, and accused them of capturing vessels belonging to all nations, without excepting those of the United States, within whose territory they brought their prizes in violation of law. Many horrible tales were related of them, but were stoutly denied by their friends, who were numerous and influential.

The Government of the United States had attempted several expeditions against them, but of so feeble a character as to be necessarily abortive. Whenever any attack was meditated against the buccaneers, they seemed to be mysteriously informed of the coming danger, and in time to avoid it. On such occasions, they would break up their settlement and carry it to some unknown part of the coast; should the new quarters be discovered and threatened, they were transported elsewhere; and the buccaneers would invariably return to the places formerly occupied by them, as soon as evacuated by their foes. It was even rumored, and believed by many, that the pursuers never had any serious intention of capturing the pursued. On the 23d of June, the English tried whether they would not be more successful than the Americans, and one of their sloops-of-war attacked two privateers which were at anchor off Cat Island. This time, the buccaneers, smugglers, or pirates, whatever be the name which they were entitled to, showed no inclination to avoid an armed collision, as they generally did, when threatened by the American navy, but they beat off the English, who suffered considerable loss.

Major A. Lacarriere Latour, who was then "Principal Engineer in the Seventh Military District of the United States," and who has published a valuable Historical Memoir, with maps, on the war in West Florida and Louisiana in 1814 and 1815, makes the following remarks on a state of things which he had seen, and on which, therefore, he was competent to pass judgment accurately : " Social order has indeed to regret," he said, "that those men, mostly aliens, and cruising under a foreign flag, so audaciously infringed our laws as openly to make sale of their goods on our soil; but what is much more deplorable and equally astonishing is, that the agents of Government in this country so long tolerated such violations of our laws, or at least delayed for four years to take effectual measures to put a stop to these lawless practices. It cannot be pretended that the country was destitute of the means necessary to repress these outrages. The troops stationed at New Orleans were sufficient for that purpose, and it cannot be doubted but that a well-conducted expedition would have cleared our waters of the privateers, and a proper garrison stationed at the place they made their harbor would have prevented their return. The species of impunity with which they were apparently indulged, inasmuch as no rigorous measures were resorted to against them, made the contraband trade carried on at Barataria look as if tacitly tolerated. In a word, it is a fact no less true than painful for me to assert, that, at Grande Terre, the privateers publicly made sale, by auction, of the cargoes of their prizes. From all parts of Lower Louisiana people resorted to Barataria, without being at all solicitous to conceal the object of their journey. In the streets of New Orleans it was usual for traders to give and receive orders for purchasing goods at Barataria, with as little secrecy as similar orders are given for Philadelphia or New York. The most respectable inhabitants of the State, especially those living in the country, were in the habit of purchasing smuggled goods coming from Barataria. The frequent seizures made of those goods were but an ineffectual remedy of the evil, as the great profit yielded by such parcels as escaped the vigilance of the Custom-house officers indemnified the traders for the loss of what they had paid for the goods seized—their price being always very moderate, by reason of the quantity of prizes brought in, and of the impatience of the captors to turn them into money and sail on a new cruize. This traffic was at length carried on with such scandalous notoriety, that the agents of Government incurred very general and open reprehension; many persons contending that they had interested motives for conniving at such abuses, as smuggling was a source of confiscation from which they derived considerable benefit." Such were the evils which Claiborne's last proclamation was intended to remedy.

But Claiborne had on his mind far weightier considerations than the capture of the Baratarians. The month of December had come without any of the expected assistance from the Federal Government, the year was closing with still more threatening rumors of an approaching invasion of Louisiana, and Claiborne could not lose sight of the defenceless condition of the State of which he was the Chief Magistrate. The Federal Government was either deaf to his repeated entreaties for men and munitions of war, or had not the power to grant the desired supply. General Flournoy, who was in command of the United States military forces on the Mississippi, had informed the Governor that he could not conveniently concentrate within the State more than seven hundred men; and, furthermore, he had even attempted to deprive it of a part of its own internal means of defence, by having made a requisition for one thousand militiamen to be employed in the service of the United States during six months, unless sooner discharged. The public mind in Louisiana, at the close of the year, was therefore in a considerable state of anxiety, which was somewhat relieved by the news of several victories obtained over the Indians by Generals Jackson, Floyd, and White, at the head of the Georgia and Tennessee militia.

CHAPTER VIII.

CLAIBORNE'S ADMINISTRATION—JOHN AND PIERRE LAFITTE, CHIEFS OF THE BARATARIANS—THEIR NOBLE CONDUCT—PREPARATIONS FOR WAR IN LOUISIANA.

1814.

THE Governor, in his annual message at the opening of the session of the Legislature, on the 4th of January, 1814, made on the existing war between Great Britain and the United States remarks which are not inapplicable to the conflict destined long after to originate in the systematic oppression attempted to be enforced by the Northern and Western States against the Southern members of the Confederacy, through a long series of unconstitutional aggressions inspired by an inordinate love of political power and plunder, by sectional jealousies and interests, and also by an hereditary, innate, and domineering spirit of Puritan fanaticism. "The enemy," said Claiborne, "wholly regardless of the dictates of justice and moderation, shows no disposition to arrest the desolation of war. The mediation of Russia, so readily accepted by the President of the United States, has been rejected, and the accustomed courtesy of an audience has been denied to our ambassadors. The time, however, is not distant when this repulsive deportment shall be changed, and when we shall exclaim—*How the mighty has fallen!* An overruling Providence directs the destinies of nations, and moulds their conduct to His purposes. Eight-and-thirty years ago, Great Britain manifested a spirit of injustice similar to that which at present influences her councils. A policy alike wicked and absurd was avowed, and a system of violence and tyranny toward America pursued. In every stage of oppression our fathers petitioned for redress, *but their repeated petitions were only answered by repeated injuries.* Hence it was that the war of the Revolution enlisted in its support the hand and heart of every true American. The people willed it, and they found no difficulty in conquering for themselves and posterity the rich blessings of peace and independence." The Governor does not shrink from exposing to the Representatives of the people the anticipated evils of war in all their horrid nakedness. He vividly describes the prostration of agriculture and commerce. He laments the burdens which must necessarily be inflicted on all classes of society for the support of fleets and armies, the loss of life and the general increase of human woes, but he consoles himself and those whom he addresses with the assurance that the evil of war which he so feelingly deplores has been productive of good, by unfolding the internal resources of Louisiana, and by pointing out their use.

"During a tour," he said, "which I made the past summer and fall, through the different counties of Louisiana, the loom and the wheel attracted much of my attention. I was often within view of the one and the sound of the other. Our fair countrywomen, to me always interesting, never before appeared as much so. Everywhere I saw evidences of their industry and domestic economy. The effects of such examples were obvious. Fathers of families have retrenched their expenses, and the young men are more inclined to industrious pursuits. These habits will conduce no less to the welfare of individuals than to that of the State. The times call for private and public frugality. The existing taxes, greater than at any prior period, must necessarily be continued. The surplus revenue which, for several years, had accumulated under the late Territorial Government, was all exhausted by the donations to literary institutions, the remuneration to sufferers from the late insurrection in 1810, and the expenses incurred by the Convention of Orleans. The State administration commenced at an inauspicious moment. An empty treasury was not the greatest difficulty to encounter. The war which immediately ensued depressed commercial enterprise, and discouraged agricultural exertion; nor was the hurricane in 1812 more destructive to the fruits of the farmer's industry than the subsequent overflowings of the Mississippi. Hence have arisen our final embarrassments; hence the difficulty which may in some parishes attend the payment of the public imposts."

Among the objects recommended by the Executive to the attention of the Legislature was a revision of the system of criminal jurisprudence then in vigor. "It does not answer the end of justice," observed Claiborne, "and is attended with very serious expenses to the State." He took this occasion to insist on the necessity of making provisions for the employment of convicts sentenced to hard labor in such a manner as to remunerate the State for the charges incident to their support, or of substituting for imprisonment some immediate corporal punishment. He also suggested to the Legislature, that in a government like the one which had been recently inaugurated in Louisiana, it was desirable that the people should know the laws by which they were governed. "At present," he said, "we are referred to civil, common, and statute law, and how few are there who can give a legal opinion upon any question of interest? This *glorious uncertainty* may suit those who have leisure and inclination to profit from the researches of civilians and reporters; but it illy comports with the convenience of the great mass of the citizens. The statute laws have become voluminous. *Acts amendatory and supplementary to former acts—in addition to, or repealing in whole or in part, former acts,* are so numerous as to confuse inquiry. It might probably be a work of labor to reduce into one view the remedy afforded for every wrong, and the means of pursuing redress; but it would not be an arduous undertaking to bring into one act all the statutes upon the same subject, and I recommend that provision be made for such a compilation."

These remarks of the Executive show that Louisiana, on the very threshold of its existence as a sovereign State, was already suffering from too much legislation. Then, as now, almost every member of both houses took his seat with the intention to change, modify, or abrogate some pre-existing law, or introduce some new enactment, either to promote, as he thought, the general welfare of the community, or to serve his own private purposes, if not those of designing men of whom he had become the tool. It seems also that, in those purer days of State adolescence, bribery, corruption, and other undue influences were not unknown; for Claiborne requests the Legislature to inquire into and to check this "fruitful source of evil." "It ought never to be forgotten," he said, "that a free representation forms the basis and greatest excellence of representative government, and that, whenever the freedom of opinion at elections is destroyed, the fairest principle of Republicanism is gone." He finally complimented the General Assembly on the improvements which had lately taken place in the organization of the militia. He remarked that, on the 8th of July and 6th of September last, having issued orders for holding in readiness a disposable militia force to take the field at a moment's warning, the cheerful compliance by most of the corps was a proof of the love of country by which they were animated, and of the promptitude with which they would have obeyed a further call.

On the 20th of January, the Governor was informed by the United States Collector that four hundred and fifteen negroes had lately been consigned to Pierre and John Lafitte at Barataria, and that they were to be sold at public auction. The Collector requested that a strong force be organized "to defeat the purpose of these law infractors." Four days after, the news reached New Orleans that Stout, a temporary inspector of the revenue, who had been stationed by the Collector near the place called the "Temple" at Barataria, and who had with him twelve men, had been attacked by John Lafitte and his companions. Stout had been killed, and two of his followers dangerously wounded; the rest had been made prisoners. The Collector immediately laid before the Governor all the circumstances of this outrage, with these remarks:* "It is high time that these contrabandists, dispersed throughout the State, should be taught to respect our laws, and I hold it my duty to call on your Excellency for a force adequate to the exigency of the case."

The Governor sent to the Legislature copies of the two communications which he had received from the Collector on the subject, with the recommendation that suitable provisions be made to break up the establishment of those lawless men on the coast of Louisiana. He informed them that this duty was to be performed by the State, because the General commanding the Federal troops in the district which embraced Louisiana had declared that he found it inconvenient to the service

* Executive Journal.

to withdraw at the moment any part of them from the important and exposed posts which they occupied, although he had proposed, should any militia force be employed, to afford such facilities in rations, camp equipage, munitions and other supplies, as might conveniently be issued from the public stores.

"My present powers are doubtless competent to the ordering of a detachment of militia on this service, but I owe it to myself and to the State to guard against even the probability of a miscarriage. For it would indeed be a melancholy occurrence, if the men to be detailed for this duty, encouraged to disobedience by the late conduct of some militia corps, should furnish evidence of the inability of the Executive to enforce, on this occasion, the supremacy of the laws. I therefore recommend this subject to your immediate consideration." He further added: "The evil requires a strong corrective. Force must be resorted to. These lawless men can alone be operated upon by their fears and the certainty of punishment. I have not been enabled to ascertain their numbers; by some they are estimated from one hundred to one hundred and fifty, and by others they are represented to be from three hundred to five hundred; and it is added, that their principal place of depot for their plunder, an island within the Lake Barataria, is defended by several pieces of cannon." "But," continued the Governor, "so systematic is the plan on which this daring attempt against the laws of our country is conducted— so numerous and bold are the followers of Lafitte, and, I grieve to say it, such is the countenance afforded him by some of our citizens, to me unknown, that all efforts to apprehend this high offender have hitherto been baffled." A Committee was appointed by the General Assembly to communicate with the Governor on the subject to which he had called their attention. But in the mean time, Lafitte, with the utmost unconcern as to ultimate consequences, was in the daily habit of sending his contraband goods to Donaldsonville, situated at the junction of Bayou Lafourche with the Mississippi, and to several other points of the river, under the escort of strong detachments of armed men, who put at defiance all interference with their trade.* His confidence seems to have been well founded, since the Legislature, on account of the want of funds, postponed to some more opportune moment the organization of the military expedition which Claiborne had so earnestly solicited.

Time elapsed, and the pirates of Barataria, as they were called, remained undisturbed, but Collector Dubourg and the Governor were not discouraged by the supineness of the Legislature of the State, or the indifference of the Federal Government. On the 2d of March, he sent again the following message to the General Assembly: "I lay before you a letter which was addressed to me on yesterday by Colonel Dubourg, the Collector for the District of Louisiana, from which you will perceive the great and continued violations, within this State, of the non-intercourse, the embargo, and other laws of the United States, and the necessity of affording to the officers of the revenue the support of an armed force whilst in the discharge of their duty. General Flournoy not deeming it prudent to withdraw, for the present, any of the regular troops under his command from the important and exposed posts they occupy, the Collector of the District conceives it a duty, in conformity with instructions from the General Government, to apply once more to the Chief Magistrate of Louisiana for such aid *as will enable the officers of the revenue to fulfill their obligations.*

---

* Executive Journal. The pages can no longer be referred to, as they cease to be numbered.

"I entreat you, therefore, to furnish me with the means of co-operating, on this occasion, with promptitude and effect. It is desirable to disperse those desperate men on Lake Barataria, whose piracies have rendered our shores a terror to neutral flags, and diverted from New Orleans that lucrative intercourse with Vera Cruz and other neutral ports which formerly filled our Banks with the richest deposits. It is no less an object to put an end to that system of smuggling which exists to the disgrace of the State, the injury of the fair trader, and the diminution, as I am advised, of the circulating medium of this city in so great a degree as is likely to produce serious commercial embarrassments, than it is important, above all, to prevent breaches of the embargo law, and to mar the projects of those traitors who would wish to carry supplies to the enemy. To enable me to accomplish these ends, or at least some of them, I ask for authority to raise by voluntary enlistment a force of not less than one captain, one first lieutenant, one second lieutenant, one third lieutenant, one drummer, one fifer, and one hundred privates, to serve for six months unless sooner discharged, and to be employed under the orders of the Governor in dispersing any armed association of individuals within this State, having for object the violation of the laws of the United States, and to assist the officers of the revenue in enforcing the provisions of the embargo, non-intercourse, and other acts of Congress. The officers, non-commissioned officers and privates to be entitled to the same pay, rations and emoluments as are allowed the troops of the United States, and to be subject to the rules and articles of war as prescribed by Congress. . . . .

. . . .

"As this corps will be solely employed in enforcing the laws of the United States, I am persuaded the General Government will readily defray any expense which may attend the raising and maintaining of the same. But if in this reasonable expectation we should be disappointed, I would advise that the corps be immediately discharged, for the present embarrassments of our treasury will not admit of its remaining in service at the expense of the State."

This message could not, and did not, produce on the General Assembly the stimulating effect which was desired by the Executive. Most of the members of that body were aware that their constituents thought themselves much benefited by the illicit trade which the Governor wished to suppress, and they did not care to be put to the expense and trouble of collecting revenue for a Government which could not make itself respected by a handful of depredators, whom it affected to look upon as the scum of the earth. The backwardness of the Legislature to act in this matter was extremely unpalatable to Claiborne; the more so, because he was already much annoyed by the persevering opposition of the Senate to many of his appointments, and particularly in relation to the filling up of the vacancy on the Supreme Bench occasioned by the resignation of D. Hall, who had accepted from the President a commission as District Judge of the United States in and for the State of Louisiana. The Governor had made five successive nominations to supply that vacancy, which had been rejected by the Senate. As the time for the adjournment of that body was drawing near, the Governor thought proper to submit to the Attorney-General, F. X. Martin, the following questions:

1st. "Whether, in filling up a vacancy in the Supreme Court during the session of the Senate, the Governor is not bound, according to the true intent and spirit of the Constitution, to exercise his free agency in the nominating power, and whether he ought not to resist all attempts of the Senate to influence or direct him in the nomination?

2d. "Whether, if the Senate continue to reject every individual proposed by the Governor, until the one they wish to be appointed be presented, the vacancy may be filled during the recess of the Legislature?

3d. "Whether, the Supreme Court may not be considered as competent to the dispatch of business, two judges being present, the existence of the vacancy notwithstanding?"

The Attorney-General, in his reply, expressed himself as not being able to conceive that a doubt might exist as to the obligation under which the Constitution had placed the Governor, to exert his free agency in the exercise of so important an act as the nomination of one of the chief judiciary magistrates, and absolutely to repel the slightest attempt from any man, or body of men, not excepting the Senate, to influence or direct his nomination by any other means than by affording him information or advice. The Attorney-General felt no hesitation in saying that, if it were possible that a majority of the Senate should attempt to force the Governor to nominate a person whom, in his judgment, he might consider as unfit for the office, or improper to be appointed, and should, for the purpose of insuring compliance to their wishes, determine on rejecting every other person whom the Governor might propose, then it would become the duty of the Governor to resist such an encroachment, because it would be a violation of the Constitution.

"The Constitution has provided," said the Attorney-General, "that judges of the Supreme Court shall be appointed by the joint act of the Governor and the Senate. Now, in the case put, were the Governor to yield to the Senate, the judge would be appointed by their *sole act*. The Governor could not be said to have participated in the appointment, if he were forced into compliance. Neither the Governor nor the Senate can *alone* appoint a judge. If the person chosen by the Governor be not agreeable to the Senate, it becomes his duty to look for another person it may approve. Likewise, if the Senate desire that the office may be filled by a person whom the Governor disapproves, it becomes their bounden duty to abandon him, and fairly to exercise a sound judgment on every person presented afterward, until one agreeable both to the Governor and Senate is fallen upon. For it cannot be concluded that, because the gentleman whom the Senate imagine to be most suitable does not appear in the same light to the Governor, no appointment is to take place, or that the Governor may allow the Senate to choose *alone*." . . .

. . . .

The Attorney-General further said, that if such a disagreement between the Senate and the Executive were unfortunately persisted in, and if the Senate adjourned without advising, or consenting to, a nomination, the vacancy could not be filled till the next meeting of the Senate, because the text of the Constitution is, that *the Governor shall have power to fill up vacancies that may happen during the recess of the Legislature, by granting commissions that shall expire at the end of the next session.* "If, after he has had an opportunity of consulting the Senate," argued the Attorney-General, "the Governor were to appoint a judge, he would, by his sole act, do that which the Constitution has said should be done by the *joint* act of him and the Senate. He would annihilate the right of the Senate in the same manner as they would his, if a majority of that body were to bind themselves to reject every person proposed by him, till the Governor offered the one they had determined upon."

Lastly, the Attorney-General believed that the Supreme Court was competent to transact business, when two judges were on the Bench, notwithstanding the vacancy of the third seat. He further stated that the three learned jurists who had filled the bench of the Supreme Court had always acted on that principle, as the Constitution provided that two judges should form a quorum.

The official opinion of the Attorney-General failed to bring to a concert of action the two conflicting powers, and the Senate adjourned without any appointment being made for the Supreme Court.

On the 23d of March, Claiborne, having received information that a number of individuals within the limits and jurisdiction of the State were engaged in raising troops, and preparing the means for a hostile incursion into the Spanish province of Texas, with a view of aiding in the overthrow of the Government of Spain in and over that province, and having been instructed by the Federal Government to take the necessary and proper steps to prevent any design of the kind from being carried into effect, issued a proclamation cautioning each and every good citizen of Louisiana, and all other persons within the limits and jurisdiction of the same, against being concerned in, or in any manner giving aid and countenance to, any such unauthorized expedition, and warning them of the penalties to be incurred thereby. He further strictly charged and commanded every officer, civil and military, within the State, each in his proper station, to be vigilant and active in opposing and preventing measures so contrary to the laws, and so hazardous to the peace and tranquillity of this and other States of the Union, and in securing and bringing to trial, judgment and punishment every such offender. This proclamation put an end to the intended expedition for the present, the principal leaders of which were a Doctor John H. Robinson, who had been in the service of the United States Government, General Toledo, late commander of the revolutionists in the province of Texas, and General Humbert, a Frenchman, who, having incurred the displeasure of Napoleon, had been exiled from his country, and was ready to embark in any kind of reckless adventure to better his fortune.

Seven days after the issuing of this proclamation, there came out of the Executive Office a public document, in the shape of a circular to the officers of the militia, which, to be understood, requires a short retrospect into past events. It has been stated before, that Claiborne, on the 25th of December, had issued orders to carry into execution a requisition made by the President on the State of Louisiana, for the raising of an auxiliary force to be enlisted in the service of the United States. In the interior counties of Louisiana this requisition met with no opposition. It was promptly obeyed,* and the militia of the Second Division, which included the district of Baton Rouge and the more western counties of the State, were promptly arrayed, and marched to the point of general *rendezvous*, the Magazine Barracks, opposite New Orleans. But in some of the settlements on the Mississippi, and particularly in the city of New Orleans, which were embraced within the first division of the militia, a great spirit of insubordination was manifested, if Claiborne's testimony is to be taken as entirely correct. The people were told through the medium of the public prints, that there was "no law to authorize, and no necessity to justify the requisition." The Governor was denounced as "the tyrant of the day, and resistance to his orders was advised." The public mind was greatly

* Claiborne's Letter to Gen. Thomas Flournoy, March 3d, 1814.

agitated, and the general feeling evidently much inclined against him. "With the exception," writes Claiborne, "of three or four companies of the city militia, whose conduct met my highest approbation, my orders were not only disregarded, but *resolutions* expressive of *determined disobedience* were entered into by the non-commissioned officers and privates of several separate corps, and transmitted to me. It is, however, due to the corps to add, that their resolutions conveyed assurances of the promptitude with which they would repair to arms in case of actual invasion, and some of them expressed a readiness to do duty by companies within the city and suburbs under their own officers. But all protested against entering the service of the United States, either as volunteer or drafted militia."

This was the language of Claiborne in March. It certainly expressed views and sentiments in relation to the militia very different from those contained in his message to the Legislature in the beginning of January, and recorded in the preceding pages. With regard to the Legislature itself, he wrote to General Flournoy: " I had anticipated support from the Legislature of the State, and flattered myself that their sanction of the measure would have calmed the angry passions, and invited to harmony and subordination. But the Senate of Louisiana, in their answer to my address to the two Houses, thought proper, in relation to the " requisition," to use a language which tended still more to indispose the public sentiment, and a report made by a Committee of that honorable body, which went, not only to declare the requisition illegal and unnecessary, but indirectly to question the purity of the motive which directed my conduct, was lost merely by the casting vote of the President. In the House of Representatives, an *expression of approbation* was rejected by, I believe, one vote, and although *no censure direct* was attempted, yet a refusal to approve left an impression on the public mind no less injurious to my authority than the avowed hostility of the Senate."

The arrival about this time at the Magazine Barracks of near four hundred of the militia of the Second Division, gave Claiborne some reason to hope that so patriotic an example might produce beneficial effects; and on the 21st of February, he issued a proclamation renewing the orders of the 25th of December, and directing defaulters of every rank to be proceeded against in such manner as military usage and the laws might justify. But this had no other effect than to inflame still more the public mind, and to draw down upon him an increased mass of abuse. It was again asserted in the public prints that there was no law, no necessity, no danger to justify such a measure; and the opposing of force to force, if necessary, was not only advised, but almost determined on. The officers commanding most of the city corps were assembled with the most conciliatory views on the part of Major-General Villeré, but with no satisfactory result. On the contrary, to the declaration of a positive unwillingness to obey the requisition, which, on a former occasion, had been expressed by the non-commissioned officers and privates, was now added a like determination by their several commanders, who, however, gave the most emphatic assurances of their readiness " to turn out in case of actual invasion," and who declared that, in the mean time, their men did not object to do duty by companies under the orders of *militia officers* within the city and suburbs, but to be relieved at short intervals. The secret of all this opposition was, the invincible repugnance of the Creole and French population to be enlisted in the service of the United States under officers not of their own choosing, and their apprehension of being sent out of the State, for which alone they were disposed at that time to shed their blood.

These occurrences did not pass unnoticed by the militia stationed at the Magazine Barracks, and chiefly composed of Americans. Their officers had a meeting, and sent to Claiborne an address, in which they protested for themselves and their men against being mustered into the service of the United States, until his orders of the 25th of December, 1813, and 21st of February, 1814, were obeyed by the city militia; and, being wrought to a high degree of excitement, "they made a tender of their services to enforce obedience." This circumstance, when known, produced so much irritation in the bosoms of those who were thus threatened, that it would have led to a civil war, and to the drenching of the streets of New Orleans with blood, if Claiborne had acted with less discretion and prudence. "It is unnecessary to say," he wrote to Flournoy, "that such tender of service was not accepted. Neither my judgment nor my feelings approved of the raising of the arm of one citizen against his brother. The detachment of militia at the Magazine Barracks were in consequence given to understand, that against the city corps I should alone direct the force of the *law*, which at best was feeble, but would, I fear, in the present case, prove wholly inoperative, from the unwillingness of the people to co-operate; and that, in like manner, no coercion would be used to muster the militia from the interior into the service of the United States." This determination discontented that detachment of militia to such an extent, that more than forty men deserted in a single night, and Claiborne thought it prudent to discharge the rest and send them back to their respective counties.

"I shall never cease to lament," such were Claiborne's expressions of mournful regret to Flournoy, "that this measure of the Government should have been wholly defeated, and by the very people for whose benefit it was intended, and for whose safety I believed it to have been necessary. A militia requisition is at all times unpleasant, and I had calculated on some trouble in carrying the late one into effect. But I confess that anything like a general combination against it had not entered my mind. I am happy, however, in the belief that the great body of the militia are yet sound, and, in the event of an invasion, I persuade myself that the city corps would meet the enemy with promptitude and firmness. But what I must regret is, that they will not submit *to such previous discipline* as is certainly necessary to their combating with advantage. Hence, in the moment of peril, we must place our greatest reliance on the *regular troops*, and if the State is seriously menaced, a due regard to its safety would urge their immediate augmentation. Among those who opposed your requisition for a militia military force were, doubtless, many individuals who really believed it unnecessary, illegal, and oppressive. But there were others, whose opposition was more guided by personal than public considerations. I have been too long in power in Louisiana not to have attracted the jealousy of some, the envy of others, and the ill-will of many. How far all this may have been deserved, is not for me to determine. But I am not conscious of ever having wronged an individual, or betrayed for a moment the trust reposed in me. Pending the late election for Governor of Louisiana my pretensions were resisted with great warmth and perseverance by several influential citizens of New Orleans. I nevertheless succeeded, to the great disappointment and chagrin of my opponents. In politics as in war, the vanquished party often seek an opportunity for revenge. The present was a fit occasion. The requisition was observed to be unpleasant to the cultivator, the mechanic and the merchant, and my opponents found the less difficulty in bringing the public prejudices against the measure to bear against the man. I repeat, Sir, that there were individuals among whom I had the mortification to find some of my old friends, who conscientiously believed the requisition unnecessary and oppressive. But among those who clamored most against it, are men whose views of ambition and personal aggrandizement I have opposed, and will continue to oppose, so long as I shall esteem those views inconsistent with the public weal. These men have certainly succeeded in lessening me in the confidence of a people whose approbation, next to an approving conscience, I am most solicitous to secure. But in their efforts to injure *me*, I much fear that they have also injured *a State* whose safety and prosperity constituted the first and greatest objects of my care."

These are the circumstances in which originated the "circular" to which I have already referred. In that document Claiborne vindicated the authority under which he had acted; he cited the instructions he had received, and demonstrated the necessity of obedience on his part. "The direction of the national force, of which the militia constitutes the greater portion," he observed, " belongs to the General Government. The Constitution of the United States gives to Congress power *to provide for calling forth the militia to execute the laws of the Union, suppress insurrection and repel invasion;* for organizing, arming and disciplining such part of them as may be employed in the service of the United States. In the exercise of this power, by an act passed on the 28th of February, 1795, it is declared that, whenever the United States shall be invaded, or be in imminent danger of invasion from any foreign nation, or Indian tribe, it shall be lawful for the

President of the United States to call forth such number of the militia of the State, or States, most convenient to the place of danger, or scene of action, as he may judge necessary to repel such invasion; and by another act passed on the 10th of April, 1812, one hundred thousand militia are placed at the disposition of the President for the same purposes, to be apportioned by him among the several States of the Union from the latest militia returns in the Department of War, and in cases where such returns have not been made, by such other data as he shall judge equitable. Both or either of these laws authorized the late demand on the Governor of Louisiana for a thousand militia. The authority of the first act has never been questioned, and that of the second is acknowledged by almost every State and Territory within the Union. A paper is, at this moment, before me, which announces the march of two strong detachments of the North Carolina and South Carolina militia to the Creek Nation, under the requisition of Major-General Pinckney. Is it possible that the Governors of these States, and such other Governors as have from time to time turned out their militia at the call of the President, have done right, and I alone am in error?

"In 1806, when the Spaniards had crossed the Sabine, a requisition from General Wilkinson (acting under the authority of the President) on the Executive of the then Territory of Orleans for a militia force was obeyed and, to make up the quota, a draft was ordered and enforced. Yet that requisition had no greater legal force than the late one. . . . .

. . . .

"When it was found incompatible with the protection due to the other States to add to the number of regular troops on this station, the President had reason to calcu late on the prompt and zealous co-operation of the local militia. But the result will, I suspect, be a subject of as much surprise to him as it has been of disappointment and chagrin to me. Do not the citizens of Louisiana enjoy equal privileges with citizens of other States, and have they not the same interests to defend? Are we not exposed to as great dangers? Or do we apprehend less injury from an invading foe? I could here enlarge on, and satisfactorily demonstrate, the expediency of the requisition, but prudence forbids me to be more explicit. Would it have been politic to await the actual approach of an enemy? It might have been too late to insure our safety. When clouds appear which portend a storm, does the prudent mariner delay his preparations until the blow commences? When the officer of the main-top announces danger, do those below doubt the fact? When the sentinel gives the alarm, ought not every man to repair to his post? And when the President of the United States directed measures to be taken to defend New Orleans against an attack by the enemy, did it become me to say there was no danger, no necessity? Let it not be said that the force required would have left any section of the State too weak for the maintenance of a proper internal police. Certain counties were wholly exempt; in assigning the quota to others, a due regard was paid to the local situation, and from no one Parish was a greater detachment drawn than the free population safely permitted. . . .

. . . .

" I shall say nothing, Sir, of the abuse, the invectives, with which, for the last few months, the newspapers of this city have been charged. An honest man has little to fear from paper batteries. I have been exposed to them for sixteen years, and I do not find that against the integrity of my private or public life they have made the smallest breach. It is true that, during the first two or three years of my residence in New Orleans, what with the warmth of the natural and political atmosphere, my blood was occasionally up to fever heat. But I am happily acclimated to both. The freedom of the press is justly considered the bulwark of liberty, and will, I trust, be always supported by the principles of our Government and the opinions of the people. That this freedom in Louisiana has been carried to excess is seen and regretted. Perhaps it is an inseparable evil from the good with which it is allied; perhaps it is a shoot which cannot be stripped from the stalk without injuring the plant itself. However desirable, therefore, these measures may be which might correct without enslaving the press, it would be hazardous to attempt them. The newspapers have had much agency in defeating the late requisition. But their denunciations should at all times be received with the greatest caution, for they are often directed against the wisest measures.

"I have already apprised you that General Flournoy was vested with authority to call out the militia of the 7th District, within which Louisiana is included. That this authority will be used with discretion I have no doubt. During the last winter we were indebted for our safety more to the forbearance of the enemy than to our own preparations for defence. But no blame ought to attach to the commanding general. Could his wishes have been complied with, a reinforcement of regular troops, recently arrived, would have reached him earlier, which, with a column of one thousand militia, drawn principally from the interior, would have allayed much of the anxiety so lately felt for the safety of this capital. At this season of the year, it is most probable we shall remain undisturbed, and a hope is cherished that, in the course of the summer, the sword will be sheathed. The enemy may, perhaps, incline to peace, and may accede to just and honorable terms of accommodation. That this may be the result of pending negotiations is greatly to oe desired. But I confess it is rather what I wish than what I calculate on. The rulers of Great Britain, exalted by the success of the allies, and profiting of the extensive markets opened on the Continent for English manufactures, will, I fear, be more disposed to persist than to relax in their unjust pretensions toward America. In such event, it will only remain for the United States to prosecute the war with increased energies. I entreat you, therefore, to permit no consideration to dampen your ardor in your country's cause, or to abate your exertions in organizing and disciplining the militia. Should a requisition be again made on the Executive of this State (under the orders of the President of the United States) for an auxiliary force, I have shown it to be my sacred duty to meet it, and I shall expect your zealous co-operation. What is there of novelty or oppression in requisitions of this nature? In what country, civilized or savage, have men esteemed it oppression to be called upon to resist the invader? Now that the allied armies are advancing toward the Rhine, France is said to be encircled with a forest of bayonets. When French forces were drawn to the seaboard, and an invasion of the *fast-anchored isle* menaced, no Englishman was exempt from military service. Ask the Revolutionary patriot how often, during the War of Independence, he has left the plow for the tented field? Does the spirit of our fathers sleep, or do we wish to shrink from a participation in whatever privation, trials, or dangers the safety of our common country shall render necessary? .Every true American and each faithful Louisianian will answer in the negative." This appeal, notwithstanding the earnestness of its tone, did not seem to have an immediate effect on those to whom it was addressed.

On the 14th of April, Congress repealed the embargo and non-importation laws, but it was difficult for the commerce of New Orleans, under the circumstances in which it was then placed, to recuperate from the blow which it had received under the influence of that restrictive legislation; and, in the course of that month, the Banks of the city suspended specie payment, as Banks invariably do whenever there is a political crisis of any importance.

About the same time, official accounts of the fall of the French Emperor having reached New Orleans, produced great excitement in a city where the population which was French by birth, or of French descent, was so large. Besides, it was anticipated that England, being delivered from her gigantic antagonist, would be left free to continue the war against the United States without impediment, and with all her collected energies. A report became prevalent that, as one of the conditions of peace, she would demand the retrocession of Louisiana to Spain, her faithful ally, who had protested against the cession of that province by Napoleon to the United States. This report was said to come from Spanish officers at Pensacola and Havana, who had conveyed the information to their friends in New Orleans, and also from the Spanish Minister at Washington. Folch, the late Governor of Pensacola, had recently arrived at Havana, and had expressed his belief that Spain would resort to arms, if necessary, to repossess herself of Louisiana. Referring to all the rumors which agitated the public mind in New Orleans, Claiborne thus expressed himself in a dispatch to the Secretary of State at Washington, dated on the 7th of May: "I will not undertake to say whether such be really the views of the Spanish Government, but if there be any grounds to accredit the report in circulation, the expediency of increasing the regular force on this station must be manifest. How far the militia of Louisiana in the event of a war with Spain may be relied on, remains to be proved. There is evidently a Spanish party here, but I have never thought it numerous. Should, however, an invasion ensue, I could not feel the State secure, unless there was a respectable regular force around which the well-disposed citizens might rally with confidence."

When Claiborne had felt the necessity, as previously recorded, to disband the corps of four hundred men of the Second Division who had assembled at the New Orleans Magazine Barracks in pursuance of the requisition of the United States, the Legislature, although strongly opposed to that requisition, had appropriated five thousand dollars to pay the expenses of the temporary muster, and Claiborne, on behalf of the State, had claimed the reimbursement of that sum from the United States. It was refunded, and, in acknowledging payment, Claiborne said to the Secretary of War, in a letter of the 30th of June: "This will, I trust, be received in Louisiana as a proof of the legality of such requisition. The opposition of the city corps, the indisposition of the Legislature to support the late call, have impressed the French and Creole inhabitants of the State, very generally, with an opinion that my orders on that occasion were unnecessary, illegal and oppressive. Indeed, certain influential inhabitants of New Orleans, by whose exertions, in and out of the Legislature, the requisition ultimately failed, have had the address so to manage this subject, as to bring it to bear on the State elections which are to commence on the 4th of July. The people have been told that I was guilty of high crimes and misdemeanors, and I verily believe that an impeachment was at one time contemplated."

On the 15th of July, Claiborne informed the Secretary

of the Navy that late letters from Pensacola and Havana spoke confidently of the design of Spain to repossess herself of Louisiana, and he added: "I observe with regret that many citizens of this State seem to think that their connection with the United States has become precarious. For myself, however, I have not hesitated to assert that my country will never consent to sever the Union, and that the power does not exist that can deprive the United States of the sovereignty of Louisiana."

In the mean time, the Creek Indians having sued for a cessation of hostilities, General Jackson granted it to them, and a treaty of peace was signed, on the 9th of August, by their principal chiefs on behalf of their nation, and by General Jackson in the name of the United States. It was stipulated as one of its conditions, that the Creek Nation should abandon all communication, and cease to hold any intercourse, with any British or Spanish post, garrison or town, and that they should not admit among them any agent or trader who should not have authority from the United States to hold commercial, or any other intercourse, with their tribes.

Notwithstanding this treaty, some British officers, who had landed at the bay of Apalachicola with several pieces of artillery and a few companies of regulars, had succeeded in rallying a certain number of the Creeks around the British standard. Other Indians, from almost all the tribes who dwelt to the eastward of the Choctaws, had joined this band of discontented Creeks, and those barbarians were supplied with arms, and drilled, so far as their habits and savage nature permitted the instruction. The object of the English was to gather a sufficient force to attack Fort Bowyer, at Mobille Point, which was looked upon as an important basis of operations against Louisiana.*

* Martin's History, vol. 2, p. 328.

There could be no doubt now that Louisiana was to be invaded, and, on the 6th of August, Claiborne, in obedience to instructions from the Federal Government, issued orders that one thousand men of the Louisiana militia, being the quota assigned to the State by the requisition addressed to the Executives of the several States, be organized and held in readiness for immediate service and with the least possible delay, expressing at the same time his firm reliance on the cheerful participation of Louisiana with her sister States in whatever trials or dangers the safety of their common country would demand. "If the latest reports from Europe are to be accredited," he said, "the enemy has determined on a most vigorous prosecution of the war. It is added, that this section of the Union is to be attacked with the design of wresting Louisiana from the hands of the United States and restoring it to Spain.

"A project so chimerical illy comports with that character for wisdom to which the English Government aspires, nor is it believed to be seriously contemplated. That the bare rumor, however, of such a design should awaken some anxiety, is cause of no surprise. But if there be individuals so much deceived as to suppose its accomplishment possible, they are cautioned against being instrumental in deceiving others. The principles of the American Government, no less than the interest and honor of the American people, forbid the relinquishment of one inch of the American Territory. Whilst the Western rivers flow, no foreign power can hold, or detach Louisiana from the United States. She may, indeed, be temporarily exposed to an invading foe, but, until by some convulsion of nature, that numerous, gallant, and hardy race of men inhabiting the vast tract of country watered by the tributary streams of the Mississippi shall become extinct, the political destiny of Louisiana is placed beyond the possibility of a change. Her connection, interest and government must remain American."

On the 12th of the same month, Claiborne sent to the Secretary of War a copy of the orders which he had issued on the 6th, and observed to him in relation to the requisition: "This timely measure of precaution on the part of the President will, I trust, meet the zealous support of every lover of his country. To this moment, not the slightest opposition to it has been manifested in this section of the Union, and I am happy in the belief that, on the present occasion, the force required of me will be arrayed with less difficulty than was experienced in meeting the late requisition made of me by General Flournoy, under the orders of the President. You will observe, Sir, that, in my orders, I make allusion to the report of a design on the part of the enemy *to wrest Louisiana from the hands of the United States and restore it to Spain!* A stranger to the public feeling and sentiment here might think me incorrect in noticing a rumor of the kind. But believe me, Sir, it had made a serious impression in this State. Some of the inhabitants sincerely desire a retrocession, and many seemed to consider it not only practicable, but highly probable. To caution, therefore, my fellow-citizens against harboring such a sentiment, appeared to me a duty, and more so since I was fearful they might otherwise be led to a course of conduct which would weaken their allegiance to the United States. How far this caution may produce the desired effect time will evince. But, at present, appearances are very favorable to the proudest wish of my heart, and which is, that, in any event, the Louisianians may prove faithful to themselves and to the Government of the United States."

The same day on which this communication was addressed to the Secretary of War, Claiborne wrote to

General Jackson, who was expected in New Orleans, to take command of the troops and provide for its safety, a letter in which he informed him that, in a late interview with the officers of the several militia corps of the city, he had been assured of their zealous aid in carrying into effect the orders of the 6th of August in relation to the Federal requisition. "How far their efforts," said Claiborne, "may be seconded by the body of the people, will in a short time be shown. On the native Americans and a vast majority of the Creoles of the country I place much confidence, nor do I *doubt the fidelity of many Europeans* who have long resided in the country. But there are *others* much devoted to the interest of Spain, and their partiality for the English is not less observable than their dislike for the American Government. Among the militia of New Orleans there is a battalion of chosen men of color, organized under a special act of the Legislature, of which I inclose a copy for your perusal. Under the Spanish Government the men of color of New Orleans were always relied on in times of difficulties, and on several occasions evinced in the field the greatest firmness and courage. Under the late Territorial Government, as well as under that of the State of Louisiana, much unwillingness was manifested in organizing and placing arms in the hands of free men of color. By the first it was wholly refused, but the latter has thought it advisable to recognize a battalion with limited numbers, and under certain restrictions. The command of the battalion is committed to Colonel Fortier, a respectable and rich merchant of New Orleans, and the second in command is Major Lacoste, a rich and respectable planter.

"With these gentlemen, and the officers attached to companies (these last being men of color), I had an interview on yesterday, and assured them that, in the hour of peril, I should rely on their valor and fidelity to the United States. In return, they expressed their devotion to their country and their readiness to defend it. They added their desire that all free men of color in New Orleans and its vicinity, whom they represented to be about six hundred, might be organized and received as a part of the militia, giving me to understand that such a measure would afford much satisfaction, and excite their greatest zeal in the cause of the United States.

"To this request I have for the present given no further compliance than to order that a census of the free men of color be taken and submitted to me without delay. These men, Sir, for the most part, sustain good characters. Many of them have extensive connections, and much property to defend, and all seem attached to arms. The mode of acting toward them at the present crisis is an inquiry of importance. If we give them not our confidence, the enemy will be encouraged to intrigue and corrupt them. Inured to the climate of Louisiana, and with constitutions and habits adapted to its changes, the men of color are well calculated to render service in this quarter, and in the event of invasion might be made particularly useful. I think a corps of three or four hundred might be easily raised, who would willingly enter into the service of the United States for six months, provided they be employed in Louisiana. I wish to know how far you might be authorized to receive such troops, and also your opinion as to the expediency of employing them."

On the 15th of August, General Jackson wrote a letter to Governor Claiborne, requesting that all the quota of the Louisiana militia to be furnished for the service of the United States be held in a state of preparation to march to any point required at a moment's warning. The Governor issued orders accordingly on the 5th of

September, in which he said: "The Commander-in-Chief, confiding in the patriotism of the several corps attached to the Second Division, assures himself that, at this moment of peril, they will deserve well of their country. Louisiana is openly menaced, and it is believed that the force destined to invade her is at this time assembled at Apalachicola and Pensacola. Major-General Jackson, commanding the Seventh Military District, who has often led the Western warriors to victory, invites them to lose no time in preparing for the defence of the State. This gallant commander is now at or near Mobile, watching the movements of the enemy, and making preparations to cover and defend this section of the Union. He will in due time receive reinforcements from the other States on the Mississippi. He calculates also on the zealous support of the Louisianians, and must not be disappointed. The time has come when every man must do his duty, when no faithful American will be absent from his post."

It was indeed high time to prepare for defence, for the enemy was fast approaching. Colonel Nicholls, of the British Artillery, with a body of troops which had sailed in the sloops-of-war Hermes and Caron from Bermuda, had stopped at Havana in the hope of obtaining the co-operation of the Captain-General, and the assistance of some gunboats and other small vessels to be furnished by that officer, with permission to land the British troops and artillery at Pensacola. In these expectations Colonel Nicholls was disappointed; nevertheless, he landed at Pensacola without any serious opposition from the Spanish Governor of that place, established in it his headquarters, and proceeded to enlist and drill without concealment the Indians whom he could tempt into British service, and who openly wore the British uniform in the streets, in violation of the laws of neutrality which

Spain was bound to observe.* The same officer dated from Pensacola, on the 29th of August, the following proclamation:

"Natives of Louisiana! On you the first call is made to assist in liberating from a faithless, imbecile government, your paternal soil. Spaniards, Frenchmen, Italians, and Britons, whether settled or residing for a time in Louisiana, on you also I call to aid me in this just cause. The American usurpation in this country must be abolished, and the lawful owners of the soil put in possession. I am at the head of a large body of Indians, well armed, disciplined, and commanded by British officers—a good train of artillery, with every requisite, seconded by the powerful aid of a numerous British and Spanish squadron of ships and vessels of war. Be not alarmed, inhabitants of the country, at our approach; the same good faith and disinterestedness which has distinguished the conduct of Britons in Europe, accompanies them here. You will have no fear of litigious taxes imposed upon you for the purpose of carrying on an unnatural and unjust war; your property, your laws, the peace and tranquillity of your country will be guaranteed to you by men who will suffer no infringement of theirs; rest assured that these brave Red Men only burn with an ardent desire of satisfaction for the wrongs they have suffered from the Americans, to join you in liberating these Southern Provinces from their yoke and drive them into the limits formerly prescribed by my sovereign. The Indians have pledged themselves, in the most solemn manner, not to injure, in the slightest degree, the persons or properties of any but enemies to their Spanish or English fathers; a flag over any door, whether Spanish, French, or British, will be a certain protection, nor dare any Indian put his foot on the threshold thereof, under penalty of death from his own countrymen. Not even an enemy will an Indian put to death, except resisting in arms; and, as for injuring helpless women and children, the Red Men, by their good conduct and treatment to them, will (if it be possible) make the Americans blush for their more inhuman conduct lately on the Escambia, and within a neutral territory.

Inhabitants of Kentucky, you have too long borne with grievous impositions; the whole brunt of the war has fallen on your brave sons; be imposed on no longer, but either range yourselves under the standard of your forefathers, or observe a strict neutrality. If

---

* Historical Memoir of the War in West Florida and Louisiana in 1814–15 by Major A. Lacarriere Latour, p. 11.

you comply with either of these offers, whatever provisions you send down will be paid for in dollars, and the safety of the persons bringing it, as well as the free navigation of the Mississippi, guaranteed to you.

"Men of Kentucky, let me call to your view (and I trust to your abhorrence) the conduct of those factions which hurried you into this civil, unjust and unnatural war. At a time when Great Britain was straining every nerve in defence of her own and the liberties of the world—when the bravest of her sons were fighting and bleeding in so sacred a cause—when she was spending millions of her treasure in endeavoring to pull down one of the most formidable and dangerous tyrants that ever disgraced the form of man—when groaning Europe was almost in her last gasp—when Britons alone showed an undaunted front—basely did those assassins endeavor to stab her from the rear. She has turned on them, renovated from the bloody but successful struggle; Europe is happy and free, and she now hastens justly to avenge the unprovoked insult. Show them that you are not collectively unjust; leave that contemptible few to shift for themselves; let these slaves of the tyrant send an embassy to Elba, and implore his aid; but let every honest, upright American spurn them with merited contempt. After the experience of twenty-one years, can you any longer support those brawlers for liberty, who call it freedom, when themselves are free? Be no longer their dupes; accept of my offers; everything I have promised in this paper I guarantee to you on the sacred honor of a British officer."

This document, so faulty in style, and so deficient in common sense, produced no more effect on those to whom it was addressed, than if it had forever remained locked up in the confused brains which gave it to the world. The object of this inconsiderable expedition under Colonel Nicholls, but the forerunner of the truly formidable one which was behind, seems to have been to sound the disposition of the inhabitants of the Floridas, Louisiana and Kentucky, to procure the necessary information for more important operations, and to secure pilots to conduct the main expedition to our coast and to our waters, rather than attempt anything of a decisive character. It is worthy of remark that, in the above recited proclamation issued by Colonel Nicholls it was openly declared that the Spaniards, who were called in it the lawful owners of the soil, were again to be put in possession of Louisiana, and that a Spanish squadron was expected to co-operate with the British fleet. Researches in the archives of Spain would probably demonstrate whether this assertion was true. If true, it is probable that the expected co-operation of Spain was prevented by political necessities which compelled the Government of Ferdinand VII. to turn all its attention, energies and resources to those disorders which at the time were beginning to threaten its existence at home.

Even in addressing his own troops, Colonel Nicholls had professed that the invasion of Louisiana was intended more for the benefit of its inhabitants and of Spain, than for the interest of Great Britain; for in his orders of the day to the first colonial battalion of the Royal Corps of Marines, his words were: " A cause so sacred as that which has led you to draw your swords in Europe will make you unsheath them in America, and I trust you will use them with equal credit and advantage. In Europe your arms were not employed in defence of your country only, but of all those who groaned in the chains of oppression, and in America they are to have the same direction. The people whom you are now to aid and assist have suffered robberies and murders committed on them by Americans.

" The noble Spanish nation has grieved to see her territories insulted, having been robbed and despoiled of a portion of them while she was overwhelmed with distress, and held down by the chains which a tyrant had imposed on her, gloriously struggling for the greatest of all possible blessings, true liberty. The treacherous Americans, who call themselves free, have attacked her, like assassins, while she was fallen. But the day of retribution is fast approaching. These atrocities will excite horror in the heart of a British soldier; they will stimulate you to avenge them, and you will avenge them like British soldiers. Valor, then, and humanity!"

The gathering storm, so visible on a not distant horizon, increased Claiborne's anxieties, and he wrote to General Jackson that preparations for offence and defence should rapidly progress, and that, on his part, nothing would be omitted which his means permitted, to give him (the General), whenever called upon, the most prompt support. "But," said he, "those means are at least extremely limited. With a population differing in language, customs, manners, and *sentiments*, you need not be surprised if I should not with entire certainty calculate on the support of the people."

Such communications, and they were frequent, must have produced a deep impression on Jackson's mind, and must have confirmed the worst apprehensions which he might have entertained; for, a few days before, Claiborne had informed him that the militia of the State was undisciplined, for the most part unarmed, and infected with a leaven of disobedience, *which had been encouraged by the Legislature.* "Upon the whole," said he to General Jackson, "I cannot disguise from you the fact that, if Louisiana should be attacked, we must principally depend for security upon the prompt movement of the regular troops under your command, and the militia of the Western States and Territories. At this moment we are in a very unprepared and defenceless condition. Several important points of defence remain unoccupied, and, in case of a sudden attack, this capital would, I fear, fall an easy sacrifice. I beg you, Sir, to pay us a visit as early as your public duties may permit. Your presence here is greatly desirable, for some arrangements might be made which would contribute much to our safety."

Hardly had a few days elapsed, when he again ad dressed General Jackson in these terms: "Contrary to what I had anticipated, the battalion of freemen of color have not acted *to-day* with their accustomed propriety. The great majority were absent from parade, and much discontent is said to prevail. The officers have assured me that this discontent is local, or rather of a personal nature, and not directed against the Government. I however, strongly suspect that some Spanish or English agent has made injurious impressions on the minds of the people. But the subject shall be fully probed, and the result communicated to you; for, charged as you are, Sir, with the defence of the 7th Militia District, in which Louisiana is included, I should consider myself wanting in duty not to keep you advised of every occurrence which may in any manner affect the safety of this State."

On the 26th of the same month he reverted to the subject which seemed to agitate his mind, and again communicated to General Jackson his gloomy apprehensions. "I cannot," he wrote, "disguise from you the fact that I have a difficult people to manage. At this moment, no opposition to the requisition has manifested itself; but I am not seconded with that ardent zeal which, in my opinion, the crisis demands. We look with great anxiety to your movements, and place our greatest reliance for safety on the energy and patriotism of the Western States. In Louisiana there are many faithful citizens, but I repeat that there are others in whose attachment to the United States I cannot confide. These last persuade themselves that Spain will soon repossess herself of Louisiana, and they seem to believe that a combined Spanish and English force will soon appear on our coast.   .   .   .   .
.   .   .   .

"I need not assure you of my entire confidence in you as a commander, and of the pleasure I shall experience in supporting all your measures for the common defence. But, Sir, a cause of indescribable chagrin to me is, that I am not at the head of a united and willing people. Native Americans, native Louisianians, Frenchmen and Spaniards, with some Englishmen, compose the mass of the population. Among them there exists much jealousy, and as great difference in political sentiment as in their language and habits. But, nevertheless, if Louisiana is supported by a respectable body of regular troops, or of Western militia, I trust and believe that I shall be enabled to bring to your aid a national and faithful corps of Louisiana militia; but if we are left to rely principally on our own resources, I fear existing jealousies will lead to distrust so general, that we shall be enabled to make but a feeble resistance."

Two days after, on the 29th, Claiborne, according to his constitutional habit, had oscillated from distrust to confidence, and wrote as follows to General Jackson: "The militia of Louisiana seem much better disposed than they were last year to take the field, and I hope to be enabled to array this State's quota of the requisition without difficulty." The reason for this change ought to have been apparent to his mind. The year preceding, the citizens of Louisiana did not believe in the rumors of danger with which they were threatened, and were, therefore, loath to turn away from their ordinary pursuits and the comforts of home. But when the invasion with which they had been menaced became a demonstrated calamity against which they had to guard their country, they, to one man, sprang to such arms as were within their reach.

In the beginning of September, Claiborne addressed to Girod, the Mayor of New Orleans, a communication enjoining the utmost vigilance and the strictest police with respect to the admission and residence of strangers in the city. "The attention of the Mayor and City Council to this interesting subject is," he said, "respectfully invited. It is confidently reported that a British officer, coming from the Balize, passed whole weeks in this city, and unless some efficient measures by the city authorities are promptly resorted to, I fear that their visits may be repeated, and without detection."

On the 8th, he issued general orders for the militia, in which he stimulated their zeal in these words: "The Commander-in-Chief persuades himself that no efforts which have been, or may be made, to divide us, will prove successful. The intrigues, the means of corruption by which in other countries our enemy has so much profited, will doubtless be attempted here. But his character is well understood, and it is hoped that his arts will not avail him. In defence of our homes and families there surely will be but one opinion—one sentiment. The American citizen, on contrasting his situation with that of the citizen or subject of any other country on earth, will see abundant cause to be content with his destiny. He must be aware how little he can gain, and how much he must lose, by a revolution or change of government.

"If there be any citizen who believes that his rights and property would be respected by an invading foe, the weakness of his head would excite pity. If there be an individual who supposes the kind of force with which we are menaced could be restrained from acts of violence, he knows little of the character of those allies of Great Britain who committed the massacre at Fort Mimms.

"In these evil days, small indeed is the portion of affliction which has hitherto befallen Louisiana. When a hostile army breaks into the territory of a nation, its course is marked with scenes of desolation which centuries of industry cannot repair. With what union, with what zeal, should all our energies be exerted to defend our country against like misfortunes!"

The same day on which he issued these general orders for the militia of Louisiana, he wrote to Governor Shelby, of Kentucky, to impress him with the urgency of forwarding to the defence of New Orleans all the troops which were expected from that State. "I do not know," he said, "how far I shall be supported by the militia of my own State. It grieves me to say that, to this moment, there has not been manifested all that union and zeal which the crisis demands, and which is so essential to our safety. There is despondency among the Louisianians which palsies all my preparations for defence. They see no strong regular force around which to rally, and they seem to think themselves not within the reach of seasonable succor from the Western States. But were a strong detachment of the militia of your State to descend the Mississippi, it would, I am persuaded, inspire my fellow-citizens here with confidence, and call forth their zealous and united effort in the defence of the country and Government."

On the 15th, a very numerous and respectable meeting of the citizens of New Orleans and its vicinity was held, pursuant to public notice, at Tremoulet's Coffee House, to consider the propriety of naming a committee to cooperate with the constituted authorities of the State and General Government in suggesting measures of defence, and calling out the force of the country in the present emergency. Edward Livingston was called to the chair, and Richard Relf was appointed Secretary. Livingston, after an eloquent speech, proposed the following Resolutions:

" *Resolved*, That on all important national questions it is proper, and in urgent emergencies it is necessary, for the citizens of a free government to aid their magistrates and officers by a proffer of their support in the performance of their functions.

" *Resolved*, That in this State such an expression of public opinion is peculiarly proper, because the enemy has dared to allege that we are disaffected to our government, and ready to assist him in his attempts on our independence—an allegation which we declare to be false and insidious, tending to create doubts of our fidelity to the Union of which we are a member, and which we repel with the indignation they are calculated to inspire.

" *Resolved*, That a union with the other States is necessary to the prosperity of this, and that while we rely upon them for assistance and protection, we will not be wanting in every exertion proportionate to our strength, in order to maintain internal tranquillity, repel invasion, and preserve to the United States this important accession to its commerce and security.

" *Resolved*, as the sense of this assembly, that the good people of this State are attached to the Government of the United States, and that they will repel with indignation every attempt to create disaffection and weaken the force of the country, by exciting dissensions and jealousies at a moment when union is most necessary.

" *Resolved*, That we consider the present as a crisis serious, but not alarming—that our country is capable of defence—that we do not despair of the Republic, and that we will, at the risk of our lives and fortunes, defend it.

"*Resolved*, That a committee of nine members be appointed to co-operate with the constituted civil and military authorities in suggesting means of defence, and calling forth the energies of the country to repel invasion and preserve domestic tranquillity."

Edward Livingston, Pierre Foucher, Dusuau de La Croix, B. Morgan, G. M. Ogden, D. Bouligny, J. N. Destréhan, J. Blanque and A. Macarty were appointed on the Committee.

They immediately issued the following address:

" Fellow-citizens:—Named by a numerous assembly of the citizens of New Orleans to aid the constituted authorities in devising the most certain means of guarding against the dangers which threaten you, our first duty is to apprise you of the extent of those dangers. Your open enemy is preparing to attack you from without, and, by means of his vile agents dispersed through the country, endeavors to excite to insurrection a more cruel and dangerous one in the midst of you.

"Fellow-citizens, the most perfect union is necessary among all the individuals who compose our community; all have an equal interest in yielding a free and full obedience to their magistrates and officers, and in forwarding their views for the public good; all have not only their property, but their very existence, at stake. You have, through your representatives in the Convention, contracted the solemn obligation of becoming an integral part of the United States of America; by this measure you secured your own sovereignty, and acquired the invaluable blessing of independence. God forbid that we should believe there are any among us disposed to fail in the sacred duties required by fidelity and honor. A just idea of the geographical situation of your country will convince you that your safety, and in a greater degree your prosperity, depends on your being irrevocably and faithfully attached to a union with the other States. But if there exist among you men base or mad enough to undervalue their duties and their true interest, let them tremble on considering the dreadful evils they will bring down upon themselves and upon us, if by their criminal indifference they favor the enterprises of the enemy against our beloved country.

"Fellow-citizens, the navigation of the Mississippi is as necessary to two millions of our Western brethren, as the blood is to the pulsation of the heart. Those brave men, closely attached to the Union, will never suffer, whatever seducing offers may be made to them, the State of Louisiana to be subject to a foreign power; and should the events of war enable the enemy to occupy it, they will make every sacrifice to recover a country so necessary to their existence. A war ruinous to you would be the consequence; the enemy, to whom you would have had the weakness to yield, would subject you to a military despotism, of all others the most dreadful; your estates, your slaves, your persons would be put in requisition, and you would be forced, at the point of the bayonet, to fight against those very men whom you have voluntarily chosen for fellow-citizens and brethren. Beloved countrymen, listen to the men honored by your confidence, and who will endeavor to merit it. Listen to the voice of honor, of duty, and of nature. Unite! Form but one body, one soul, and defend to the last extremity your sovereignty, your property; defend your own lives, and the dearer existence of your wives and children."

It is not known why Blanque, who was one of the

Committee and one of the leading members of the Legislature, did not sign this address, which it is impossible to read without inferring from its tone that its authors had some secret misgivings as to the existence of that unity of feeling and action which they so pathetically recommended, and of which they affected to have no doubts.

On the 17th, Claiborne sent to Girod, the Mayor of the City, a communication, in which he informed that magistrate that New Orleans had been of late visited by a number of persons of suspicious conduct and character, and among them, as he had reasons to believe, by agents of the enemy, who had been busily engaged in exciting the negroes to insurrection. He said he knew that the powers of the City Council were merely local, and that its means of action were circumscribed, but nevertheless he invited the city authorities to co-operate with him as far as they could, and he invited them also to a careful revision of the several ordinances relative to the admission and residence of strangers, and to the police of slaves. "Regulations the most rigid on these points," he said, "are highly desirable. Such as are now in force were made in the calm of peace, and may not be suited to the evil times on which we have fallen. We must not scruple, at the present moment, about the exercise of authority; we must proceed direct to our object, and do whatever may depend upon us for the general security."

In the mean time, the British were carrying on with activity their plan of invasion. Their first effort was directed against Fort Bowyer, which, commanding the entrance of Mobile Bay, and consequently the navigation of the rivers which empty into it, was a point of considerable military importance, particularly in contributing to the success of the intended operations against

Louisiana.* It also commands that species of Archipelago which extends in a parallel direction to Pass Marianne and Pass Christianne, affording to its possessors an exclusive control over the navigation of the coast of West Florida. This important strategical point was defended by Fort Bowyer, which was but a very incomplete fortification. It was destitute of casemates even for the sick, the ammunition and provisions. Moreover, it was badly situated, as it was commanded by several mounds of sand at the distance of two to three hundred yards. The garrison, under Major Lawrence, consisted of one hundred and thirty men, including officers, with twenty pieces of cannon, but indifferently mounted. Some of them were on temporary platforms, and the men were exposed from their knees upward.

On the morning of the 12th, the enemy landed six hundred Indians and one hundred and thirty marines. In the evening, two English sloops-of-war and two brigs anchored within six miles east of the fort.

On the 13th and 14th, the forces of the enemy which were to operate on land were engaged in reconnoitering the back part of the fort, and in fortifying their own position. A few cannon-balls and shells were exchanged between the belligerents, without much effect on either side. Early on the morning of the 15th, the movements of the enemy gave clear indications of his intention to attack, and a very active communication was perceived between the ships and the troops on shore. The conflict was to be an unequal one; for, as I have said, the Americans numbered only one hundred and thirty men with twenty pieces of artillery, whilst the British forces amounted to thirteen hundred and thirty men, with ninety-two guns, ninety of which were thirty-two-pound

* Lacarriere Latour's Historical Memoir, p. 31.

carronades. Their fleet consisted of the sloops Hermes and Caron, and of the brigs Sophia and Anaconda, under the command of Captain Percy.

Major Lawrence, at this critical moment, called a council of all his officers. They unanimously agreed to make the most obstinate and vigorous defence, and adopted the following resolution :

"That in case of being, by imperious necessity, compelled to surrender (which could only happen in the last extremity, on the ramparts being entirely battered down, and the garrison almost wholly destroyed, so that any further resistance would be evidently useless), no capitulation should be agreed on, unless it had for its fundamental article that the officers and privates should retain their arms and their private property, and that on no pretext should the Indians be suffered to commit any outrage on their persons or property; and unless full assurance were given them that they would be treated as prisoners of war, according to the custom established among civilized nations." All the officers of this Spartan band unanimously swore that in no case, nor on any pretext, would they recede from the above conditions; and they pledged themselves to each other that, in case of the death of any of them, the survivors would still consider themselves bound to adhere to what had been resolved on."

Late in the afternoon, at half-past four, the Hermes came to anchor within musket-shot of the fort's batteries, and the other three ships took their line of battle behind her. Soon the engagement became general, and a land battery, which had been established by the enemy at seven hundred yards from the fort, opened fire against it with a twelve-pounder and a six-inch howitzer. It was soon silenced, however, but the firing between the ships and the fort was kept up with great fury until half-past five, when the English commander's flag was carried away by a cannon-ball.

On observing this occurrence, Major Lawrence instantly ordered the fire to cease, thus chivalrously pausing for a further manifestation of the intention of the enemy, who also discontinued firing for about five minutes, at the expiration of which all doubts were removed by a broadside from one of the ships, and the hoisting up of a new flag on board of the Hermes. The fort replied with all its guns, and the battle continued for some time without any abatement, when the Hermes, having had her cable cut, was carried away by the current, and presented her prow to the fort, whose well-directed fire swept her deck for fifteen or twenty minutes. At the moment when the fire was most intense, the flag-staff of the fort was shot away; but the Hermes, instead of following the example so recently set by Major Lawrence, redoubled her fire instead of suspending it, and each one of the other ships poured her broadside against the fort. When the American flag thus accidentally disappeared, the land forces, thinking that the fort was to surrender, hastily advanced toward it, with loud shrieks on the part of the Indians, but a few discharges of grape-shot sent them away to seek shelter behind their sand mounds, and the star-spangled banner soon rose up again on the edge of the parapet in a still more defiant position. During this interval, the Hermes, having not been able to repair the loss of her cable, had drifted away with the current about a mile, when she got aground, and was set on fire and abandoned by the British. Soon after, the other ships, which had been much damaged, retired gradually beyond the reach of our guns, and finally disappeared seaward. At 11 o'clock the Hermes blew up, suddenly illumining with her explosion the late scene of that fierce contest, on which now had settled the darkness and the repose of night.

The Americans were justly proud of this victory, for its results were remarkable, considering the disparity of the forces engaged and of the implements of war used on the occasion. They had only twelve guns which could be brought to bear on the enemy, and these guns were worked by inexperienced men, who knew nothing of artillery service, with which even some of their officers were far from being familiar. Yet they succeeded, with very little loss, in signally defeating an enemy whose superiority has been shown to be so striking. Only two of their guns had been silenced; their killed did not exceed four, which was also the number of their wounded, whilst the British had one hundred and sixty-two men killed and seventy wounded, losing one 28-gun ship, and having the other three badly damaged. The humiliation of the enemy was complete, and made keener from the fact that Captain Percy, relying with too much pride on the number of troops and guns with which he was to attack Fort Bowyer, had openly boasted that he would take it in twenty minutes.

This victory produced great elation, and was looked upon as the welcome harbinger of future triumphs. On the 21st, General Jackson issued from his headquarters at Mobile the two following proclamations—one addressed to the white population of Louisiana, and the other to its free colored inhabitants:

"Louisianians, the base, the perfidious Britons have attempted to invade your country; they had the temerity to attack Fort Bowyer with their incongruous horde of Indians and negro assassins; they seemed to have forgotten that this fort was defended by freemen; they were not long indulged in their error; the gallant Lawrence, with his little Spartan band, has given them a lesson that will last for ages; he has taught them what men can do, when fighting for their liberty and contending against slaves. He has convinced Sir W. H. Percy that his companions-in-arms are not to be conquered by proclamations, and that the strongest British bark is not invulnerable to the force of American artillery, directed by the steady, nervous arm of a freeman.

"Louisianians, the proud Briton, the natural and sworn enemy of all Frenchmen, has called upon you, by proclamation, to aid him in his tyranny, and to prostrate the holy temple of our liberty. Can Louisianians, can Frenchmen, can Americans, ever stoop to be the slaves or allies of Britain?

"The proud, vain-glorious boaster, Colonel Nicholls, when he addressed you, Louisianians and Kentuckians, had forgotten that you were the votaries of freedom, or he never would have pledged the honor of a British officer for the faithful performance of his promise to lure you from your fidelity to the government of your choice. I ask you, Louisianians, can we place any confidence in the honor of men who have courted an alliance with pirates and robbers? Have not these noble Britons, these honorable men, Colonel Nicholls and the Honorable Captain W. H. Percy, the true representatives of their royal master, done this? Have they not made offers to the pirates of Barataria to join them and their holy cause? And have they not dared to insult you by calling on you to associate, as brethren, with them and these hellish banditti?

"Louisianians, the government of your choice is engaged in a just and honorable contest for the security of your individual and national rights. On you, a part of America, the only country on earth where every man enjoys freedom, where its blessings are alike extended to the poor and the rich, she calls to protect these rights from the invading usurpation of Britain, and she calls not in vain. I well know that every man whose soul beats high at the proud title of freeman; that every Louisianian, either by birth or adoption, will promptly obey the voice of his country, will rally round the eagle of Columbia, secure it from the pending danger, or nobly die in the last ditch in its defence.

"The individual who refuses to defend his rights when called upon by his government deserves to be a slave, and must be punished as an enemy to his country, and a friend to her foe.

"The undersigned has been intrusted with the defence of your country. On you he relies to aid in this important duty; in this reliance he hopes not to be mistaken. He trusts in the justice of his cause and the patriotism of his countrymen. Confident that any future attempt to invade our soil will be repelled as the last, he calls not upon either pirates or robbers to join him in the glorious cause."

This document did not escape criticism. It was thought by some to be written in an undignified tone of anger, which had betrayed its author into the use of epithets both unbecoming and untrue in their application. Britons were not "slaves," and it was hardly possible to proclaim them to be in this degraded condition, without ranking still lower the rest of mankind, with the exception of the Americans. The Louisianians were very unwilling thus to admit constructively that they had been slaves, even when living under Governments by which the liberties and rights of subjects were far more restricted, than by the one which has been the boast and the glory of Great Britain since the overthrow of the Stuarts. The word "slave" applied to Englishmen grated harshly, notwithstanding national antipathies, on the ears of Frenchmen, Spaniards and other Europeans, who constituted a numerous body in New Orleans, and who felt instinctively that this contemptuous expression could not strike England without glancing from her breast to their own. It might be inferred that they were at best but emancipated slaves among the free-born Americans. Hence this address was looked upon by the discontented as a poor specimen of tact and policy; and there were others who took pleasure in railing at the assertion, so complacently repeated, that the Louisianians were bound in honor to defend the Government of the United States, as "the Government of their choice," when it was so well known how little they had been consulted on the subject, and how harshly they had been treated on their first contact with their new brethren—with that great national family into whose bosom it had been expressly stipulated that they should be admitted on a footing of equality with the other members. These censorious remarks, however, did not produce much effect on the mass of the population. But his second proclamation was considered more objectionable even by the well-affected. It was addressed to the free colored men, and ran as follows:

"Through a mistaken policy you have heretofore been deprived of a participation in the glorious struggle for national rights in which our country is engaged. This no longer shall exist.

"As sons of freedom, you are now called upon to defend our most inestimable blessing. As Americans, your country looks with confidence to her adopted children for a valorous support, as a faithful return for the advantages enjoyed under her mild and equitable government. As fathers, husbands, and brothers, you are summoned to rally round the standard of the eagle, to defend all which is dear in existence.

"Your country, although calling for your exertions, does not wish you to engage in her cause without amply remunerating you for the services rendered. Your intelligent minds are not to be led away by false representations. Your love of honor would cause you to despise the man who should attempt to deceive you. In the sincerity of a soldier and the language of truth I address you.

"To every noble-hearted, generous freeman—men of color, volunteering to serve during the present contest with Great Britain, and no longer, there will be paid the same bounty in money and lands now received by the white soldiers of the United States, viz: one hundred and twenty-four dollars in money, and one hundred and sixty acres of land. The non-commissioned officers and privates will also be entitled to the same monthly pay and daily rations, and clothes, furnished to any American soldier.

"On enrolling yourselves in companies, the Major-General commanding will select officers for your government from your white fellow-citizens. Your non-commissioned officers will be appointed from among yourselves.

"Due regard will be paid to the feelings of freemen and soldiers. You will not, by being associated with white men in the same corps, be exposed to improper comparisons, or unjust sarcasm. As a distinct, independent battalion, or regiment, pursuing the path of glory, you will, undivided, receive the applause and gratitude of your countrymen.

"To assure you of the sincerity of my intentions and my anxiety to engage your invaluable services to our country, I have communicated my wishes to the Governor of Louisiana, who is fully informed as to the manner of enrollment, and will give you every necessary information on the subject of this address."

This proclamation was looked upon by many as exceedingly objectionable, on the ground of its putting the colored men too much on a footing of equality with the whites. It was denied that the native mulattoes of Louisiana were entitled to the appellation of "sons of freedom," and that the colored refugees from St. Domingo had any claim to being called the "adopted children" of the State. It was still more strenuously denied that they could, whether "natives" or "adopted children," be properly designated as "Americans,"—a question which was judicially raised years afterward, and which was decided in the negative by the Supreme Court of the United States. Even those who were the best disposed toward that peculiar class of the population objected to their being raised to the dignity of being denominated as the "fellow-citizens" and the "countrymen" of the white race. Claiborne had foreseen, as will be seen hereafter, the bad effect to be produced by this last proclamation, and had in vain sought to avert it by sending gentle hints on the subject to General Jackson.

Whilst planning against Fort Bowyer the attack which has been described, and which was so signally defeated, the English had not been unmindful of another point from which, as alluded to in one of General Jackson's proclamations, they had hoped to derive assistance in their contemplated invasion of Louisiana. This was the Bay of Barataria, which was known by them to be the asylum of a large number of desperate outlaws, who were supposed to be inimical to the Government of the United States, by which they were proscribed. On the 3d of September, an English brig had anchored six miles from the Barataria Pass, and had sent ashore a flag of truce with Captain McWilliams and Captain Lockyer, of the

British Navy, as special messengers to John Lafitte and his associates. They delivered to that individual a letter from Colonel Nicholls, who addressed Lafitte as " The Commandant at Barataria," and in the following style:

"I have arrived in the Floridas for the purpose of annoying the only enemy Great Britain has in the world, as France and England are now friends. I call on you, with your brave followers, to enter into the service of Great Britain, in which you shall have the rank of a captain. Lands will be given to you all, in proportion to your respective ranks, on a peace taking place, and I invite you on the following terms: Your property shall be guaranteed to you, and your persons protected--in return for which I ask you to cease all hostilities against Spain, or the allies of Great Britain—your ships and vessels to be placed under the orders of the commanding officer on this station, until the commander-in-chief's pleasure is known; but I guarantee their full value, at all events. I herewith Inclose you a copy of my proclamation to the inhabitants of Louisiana, which will, I trust, point out to you the honorable intentions of my Government. You may be a useful assistant to me in forwarding them; therefore, if you determine, lose no time. The bearer of this, Captain McWilliams, will satisfy you on any other point you may be anxious to learn, as will Captain Lockyer, of the Sophia, who brings him to you. We have a powerful reinforcement on its way here, and I hope to cut out some other work for the Americans than oppressing the inhabitants of Louisiana. Be expeditious in your resolves, and rely on the *verity of your very humble servant.*"

It is certainly not possible to suppose from the tone of this letter, and the offers which it contains, that Colonel Nicholls, of the British Army, would ever have dared, under any circumstances, to address such a communication to any one whom he considered as justly bearing the character of a " captain of pirates," which imputation John Lafitte had always protested against, and indignantly repelled as a calumnious aspersion.

To this letter of Colonel Nicholls were annexed the instructions given by Sir W. H. Percy, Captain of His Britannic Majesty's ship Hermes, and senior officer in the Gulf of Mexico, to Captain Lockyer, of his Majesty's sloop Sophia. In that document he applies the softest and most guarded language to Lafitte and his companions, in relation to their status, and designates them as the "inhabitants of Barataria." It ran as follows:

"Having understood that some British merchantmen have been detained, taken into, and sold by the inhabitants of, Barataria, I have directed Captain Lockyer to proceed to that place and inquire into the circumstances, with positive orders to demand instant restitution, and, in case of refusal, to destroy to his utmost every vessel there, as well as to carry destruction over the whole place; and, at the same time, I have assured him of the co-operation of all his Majesty's naval forces on this station. I trust, at the same time, that the inhabitants of Barataria, consulting their own interest, will not make it necessary to proceed to such extremities. I hold out at the same time a war instantly destructive to them, and, on the other hand, should they be inclined to assist Great Britain in her just and unprovoked war against the United States, the security of their property, the blessings of the British Constitution; and should they be inclined to settle on this continent, lands will, at the conclusion of the war, be allotted to them in his Majesty's colonies in America. In return for all these concessions on the part of Great Britain, I expect that the directions of their armed vessels will be put into my hands (for which they will be remunerated)—the instant cessation of hostilities against the Spanish Government, and the restitution of any undisposed property of that nation.

"Should any inhabitants be inclined to volunteer their services into his Majesty's forces, either naval or military, for limited service, they will be received; and if any British subject, being at Barataria, wishes to return to his native country, he will, on joining his Majesty's service, receive free pardon."

It is evident that Sir W. H. Percy, in concert with Colonel Nicholls, did not choose to consider "the inhabitants of Barataria" in any other light than belligerents against Spain. It certainly did not suit his purpose to acknowledge them as "pirates, or bandits."

The British officers, on landing, met with considerable hostility from those whom they had come to visit, but were protected by John Lafitte. What passed between that chief of outlaws and the British emissaries is thus related by Major La Carriere Latour, who knew Lafitte personally, who served with him under the orders of General Jackson, when Lafitte's proffered assistance was accepted, and who may have heard from his own lips all the details of that interesting interview. "When Mr. Lafitte," says Latour, "had perused these papers, Captain Lockyer enlarged on the subject of them, and proposed to him to enter into the service of his Britannic Majesty with all those who were under his command, or over whom he had sufficient influence; and likewise to lay at the disposal of the officers of his Britannic Majesty the armed vessels he had at Barataria, to aid in the intended attack of the fort of Mobile. He insisted much on the great advantages that would thence result to himself and his crews; offered him the rank of Captain in the British service, and the sum of thirty thousand dollars, payable at his option, in Pensacola or New Orleans, and urged him not to let slip this opportunity of acquiring fortune and consideration. On Mr. Lafitte's requiring a few days to reflect upon these offers, Captain Lockyer observed to him that no reflection would be necessary respecting proposals that obviously precluded hesitation, as he was a Frenchman, and of course now a friend to Great Britain, proscribed by the American Government, exposed to infamy, and had a brother, at that very time, loaded with irons in the jail of New Orleans. He added that, in the British service, he would have a fair prospect of promotion; that having such a knowledge of the country, his services would be of the greatest importance in carrying on the operations which the British Government had planned against Lower Louisiana; that, as soon as possession was obtained, the army would penetrate into the upper country, and act in concert with the forces in Canada; that everything was already prepared for carrying on the war against the American Government in that quarter with unusual vigor; that they were nearly sure of success, expecting to find little or no opposition from the French and Spanish population of Louisiana, whose interests, manners and customs were more congenial with theirs than with those of the Americans; that, finally, the insurrection of the negroes, to whom they would offer freedom, was one of the chief means they intended to employ, being confident of its success.

"To all these splendid promises, all these ensnaring insinuations, Mr. Lafitte replied that, in a few days, he would give a final answer; his object in this procrastination being to gain time to inform the State officers of this nefarious project. Having occasion to go to some distance for a short time, the persons who had proposed to send the British officers prisoners to New Orleans went and seized them in his absence, and confined both them and the crew of their pinnace in a secure place, leaving a guard at the door. The British officers sent for Mr. Lafitte; but he, fearing an insurrection of the crews of the privateers, thought it advisable not to see them, until he had persuaded their captains and other officers to desist from the measures on which they seemed bent. With this view, he represented to the latter that, besides the infamy that would attach to them, if they treated as prisoners persons who had come with a flag of truce, they would lose the opportunity of discovering the extent of the projects of the British against Louisiana, and learning the names of their agents in the country. While Mr. Lafitte was thus endeavoring to bring over his people to his sentiments, the British remained prisoners the whole night, the sloop-of-war continuing at anchor before the Pass, waiting for the return of the officers. Early the next morning, Mr. Lafitte caused them to be released from their confinement, and saw them safe aboard their pinnace, apologizing for the disagreeable treatment they had received, and which it had not been in his power to prevent."

Immediately after the departure of the British officers, John Lafitte addressed, on the 4th of September, to John Blanque, a leading member of the Legislature, a letter, in which he began with saying: "Though proscribed by my adopted country, I will never let slip any occasion of serving her, or of proving that she has never ceased to be dear to me. Of this you will see here a convincing proof." He then related to Blanque what had happened, and forwarded to him the papers which had been left in his hands by Captains Lockyer and McWilliams. "You will see from their contents," continued Lafitte, "the advantages which I might have derived from that kind of association." Three days later, on the 7th, he addressed to Blanque this second letter: "Sir, you will always find me eager to evince my devotedness to the good of the country, of which I endeavored to give some proof in my letter of the 4th, which I make no doubt you received. Amongst other papers that have fallen into my hands, I send you a scrap which appears to me of sufficient importance to merit your attention.* Since the departure of the officer who came with the flag of truce, his ship, with two other ships of war, have remained on the coast within sight. Doubtless this point is considered as important. We have hitherto kept on a respectable defensive; if, however, the British attach to the possession of this place the importance they give us room to suspect they do, they may employ means above our strength. I know

---

* It was an anonymous communication from Havana, giving information of the intended operations of the enemy.

not whether, in that case, proposals of intelligence with the Government would be out of season. It is always from my high opinion of your enlightened mind that I request you to advise me in this affair."

Within this letter was inclosed another, which was addressed, and to be delivered, to Claiborne. "In the firm persuasion," wrote the outlaw to the Chief Magistrate of the State, who had repeatedly made every exertion to have him captured and punished as a bandit, "that the choice made of you to fill the office of First Magistrate of this State was dictated by the esteem of your fellow-citizens and was conferred on merit, I confidently address you on an affair on which may depend the safety of the country.

"I offer to you to restore to this State several citizens, who, perhaps in your eyes, have lost that sacred title. I offer you them, however, such as you would wish to find them, ready to exert their utmost efforts in defence of the country. This point of Louisiana which I occupy is of great importance in the present crisis. I tender my services to defend it; and the only reward I ask is that a stop be put to the proscription against me and my adherents, by an act of oblivion for all that has been done hitherto. I am the stray sheep wishing to return to the sheepfold. If you were thoroughly acquainted with the nature of my offences, I should appear to you much less guilty, and still worthy to discharge the duties of a good citizen. I have never sailed under any flag but that of the Republic of Carthagena, and my vessels are perfectly regular in that respect. If I could have brought my lawful prizes into the ports of this State, I should not have employed the illicit means which caused me to be proscribed. I decline saying more on the subject until I have the honor of your Excellency's answer, which I am persuaded can be dictated only by wisdom. Should your answer not be favorable to my ardent desires, I declare to you that I will instantly leave the country, to avoid the imputation of having co-operated toward an invasion on this point, which cannot fail to take place, and to rest secure in the acquittal of my own conscience."

These two letters of John Lafitte the younger were forwarded to their destination by Pierre Lafitte, the elder, who had found the means not to remain long in the jail where he was incarcerated in New Orleans, and who added to the package this note to Blanque: "On my arrival here, I was informed of all the occurrences that have taken place. I think I may justly commend my brother's conduct under such difficult circumstances. I am persuaded he could not have made a better choice than in making you the depositary of the papers that were sent to us, and which may be of great importance to the State. Being fully determined to follow the plan that may reconcile us with the Government, I herewith send you a letter directed to his Excellency the Governor, which I submit to your discretion to deliver, or not, as you may think proper. I have not yet been honored with an answer from you. The moments are precious; pray, send me an answer that may serve to direct my measures in the circumstances in which I find myself." It is certainly difficult to imagine, in presence of the noble attitude taken by these two men, that, culpable as they undoubtedly were in many respects, they could be guilty of the atrocious crimes attributed to them, and deserved the appellation of "pirates."

Claiborne, to whom Blanque delivered the letters of the Baratarian chiefs, with the papers which accompanied them, submitted the whole to a council of the principal officers of the army, militia and navy, which he had convened to deliberate on the subject. They recommended that there be no intercourse or correspondence whatever with any of "those people." Major General Villeré was the only one who expressed a different opinion. Governor Claiborne agreed with him, but acquiesced in the decision of the majority.*

Whilst the two outlawed brothers were thus generously sacrificing their own private interest and the most advantageous offers, to the desire of protecting Louisiana against invasion, there was in preparation for their destruction an expedition which was carried through, notwithstanding a full knowledge of the patriotic course they were pursuing. That expedition had been got up at the earnest instigation of Claiborne, and organized under the command of Commodore Patterson, and of Colonel Ross of the U. S. Army. It succeeded in completely breaking up the establishment of the Baratarians, and in capturing many of them. Some made their escape, and among them the two Lafittes, who fled to the German Coast, where they found friendly aid and efficient shelter. Commodore Patterson and Colonel Ross returned to New Orleans with the vessels of the Baratarians and a very rich booty, which they claimed as lawful prize.

On the 19th of September, Claiborne wrote to General Jackson, informing him of the success of the expedition, and of the seizure of the "ill-begotten treasures of the pirates," as they were called. He further said : "The only difficulty I have hitherto experienced in meeting the requisition has been in the city, and exclusively from some European Frenchmen, who, after giving in their adherence to Louis XVIII. have, through the French Consul, claimed exemption from the draft as French subjects. The question of exemption, however, is now under discussion before a special court of inquiry,

---

* Martin's History of Louisiana, p. 329, vol. 2.

and I am not without hopes that these ungrateful men may yet be brought to a discharge of their duties. The body of city militia begin to manifest a proper feeling and conduct, and perform with cheerfulness patrol duty.

. . . .

"I have taken means to acquire information daily from the Pass of Chef Menteur, as also from the various Passes in the vicinity of Terre aux Bœufs. But I am vastly solicitous about the Pass of Barataria. Excuse me for suggesting the expediency of your directing immediate possession to be taken of Grande Terre, the spot from which the pirates were recently expelled, and of occupying the place called the 'Temple.'"

The next day, he resumed the pen, to inform General Jackson that Louisiana had much to apprehend from domestic insurrection, and that he had every reason to believe that the enemy had been intriguing with the slaves. "In my letter of yesterday," he said, "I mentioned that many of the fugitives from Barataria had reached the city. Among them are some St. Domingo negroes of the most desperate character, and no worse than most of their white associates." He added, that he had called the attention of the Mayor and City Council to these facts; that he had strongly urged the necessity of adopting stringent measures; and that the city authorities "seemed fully impressed with the importance of the crisis."

In relation to the address of General Jackson to the free people of color, dated on the 21st of September, which I have recited in the preceding pages, Governor Claiborne sent him the following observations, on the 17th of October: "The publication of your address to the free people of color is delayed a few days. An unfortunate misunderstanding between the officers of the battalion of color, which excites much interest, is the subject of investigation before a court of inquiry now sitting. The difficulty will, I hope, soon be arranged. In the mean time, I have deemed it best to postpone giving publicity to your address. I cannot disguise from you the fact that many excellent citizens will disapprove the policy you wish to observe toward the free people of color. The battalion already organized, limited as it is, excites much distrust, and I should not be surprised if, at the ensuing Legislature, an attempt should be made to put it down. I must confess that, for myself, I have no cause to lament the confidence which the Local Government has placed in these men. Their general deportment has been correct, and they have done nothing to create in my mind any doubt as to their fidelity. It does appear to me that, at the present crisis, these men ought to be attended to; that it is not probable they will remain careless and disinterested spectators of the present contest, and more particularly if the war should be brought into the bosom of Louisiana; but, on the contrary, that their feelings and best wishes would be enlisted in some way, and that if we distrusted their fidelity, the enemy might the more acquire their confidence. But this mode of reasoning makes no impression upon some respectable citizens here. They think that, in putting arms in the hands of men of color, we only add to the force of the enemy, and that nothing short of placing them in every respect upon a footing of equality with white citizens (which our Constitution forbids) could conciliate their affections. To two gentlemen of influence, members of the Committee of Defence, with whom I conversed on last evening, your policy of raising a regiment of free men of color was suggested, with the observation that, by removing it from the State, the jealousy and distrust of the citizens would surely cease. They, however, seemed to think that the measure was advisable, provided there would be a guarantee against the return of the regiment; but that if, at the close of the war, the individuals were to settle in Louisiana with the knowledge of the use of arms, and that pride of destination which a soldier's pursuits so naturally inspire, they would prove dangerous. Such are the sentiments of men well informed and well disposed, and I transmit them for your perusal. My impression is, that several companies composed of men of color may be raised upon the plan you suggest; but I cannot say to what number. Such as are natives of Louisiana are much attached to their families and homes, and I am inclined to think would not enlist during the war; but such as have emigrated from St. Domingo and Cuba may probably be desirous to join the army."

Referring to the general condition of the public mind, he added: " A patriotic spirit pervades this State, and I observe with sincere pleasure that you possess the entire confidence of the people." As to Lafitte and his companions, the attitude of hostility which they had taken toward the British, the valuable information which they had imparted to Claiborne, and the offer of their services, do not seem to have softened his disposition toward them, and changed his views of their demerits; for he thus expressed himself when mentioning them to General Jackson : 'Since the pirates of Barataria have been dislodged from Grande Terre, they have taken post at Last Island, near the mouth of the Lafourche.'"

On the 24th of October, Claiborne wrote to Fromentin, one of the Senators for Louisiana in Congress: "I have made and am still making every possible exertion to defend Louisiana against all attacks from within and without. I am zealously supported by Major-Generals Villeré and Thomas, and have reason to be content with the patriotic spirit which pervades the State. There are, indeed, individuals on whose friendly disposition toward the American Government I cannot depend, but I calculate with certainty on the fidelity of the great mass of the population. There has unquestionably been of late a change in the public opinion, and I see with pleasure that the best informed citizens are perfectly convinced that the safety and welfare of Louisiana can alone be secured by an indissoluble union with the American States." He addressed the Secretary of State, Mr. Monroe, in the same spirit, and gave him the same encouraging information, but added: "I must not, however, disguise from you the fact that Louisiana must look for permanent safety to the support of our gallant Western States."

It is gratifying to see that, as time progressed, Claiborne's confidence in the people of Louisiana became better rooted in his mind, for, in a communication by him to General Jackson, dated October 24, the following passage is to be found: "Your address to the Louisianians is well received, and will make a favorable impression. A feeble attempt has been made in a paper called the *Louisiana Gazette* to take exception to its style and manner, but I do not learn that a single worthy citizen unites in opinion with this newspaper scribbler. The natives of Louisiana are for the most part a gallant and virtuous people, and I am proud in the belief that, in any event, they will prove faithful to the United States."

As to the address of the General to the free people of color, I have already said that Claiborne had been somewhat startled by its tone; that he had mildly insinuated to its author that it would be unpalatable to the white population, and that the publication of it "had been suspended for the present." The well-known temper of General Jackson must, however, have precluded the hope that he would change or modify his course on the subject.

It does not seem that he proved more pliant on this occasion than on any other, for, on the 24th of October, Claiborne wrote to him: "Your address to the chosen men of color will be printed on this day. I will use my best efforts to promote your wishes, but I do not know with what success. I have already apprised you of the distrust which exists here against this class of people. I believe it to be ill-founded; but its existence may, and I fear has, in some degree, indisposed them toward us. The difficulty among the officers of the battalion of color of which I informed you is nearly arranged, and I continue to think that, in the hour of trial, they will prove a meritorious corps. Fort St. Philip, at Plaquemine, is in need, I learn, of a reinforcement. If it meets your approbation, I will detach to that post a lieutenant and forty men of color." Certainly nothing could better prove than this proposition the real confidence which Claiborne professed to repose in the men of color.

The best way to narrate events faithfully, and to convey impressively a correct idea of the moral tone and of the manners of society at any particular epoch, is, in my opinion, to borrow the very language of those who have described them as witnesses, and frequently as participators in what they recorded. Under this impression, I give in full the following letter addressed by Claiborne, on the 30th of October, to Mr. Rush, the Attorney-General of the United States at Washington:

"You no doubt have heard that the late expedition to Barataria had eventuated in the entire dispersion of the pirates and smugglers, and capture of nearly all their cruisers. It is greatly to be regretted that neither the General nor State Government had not sooner been enabled to put down these banditti. The length of time they were permitted to continue their evil practices added much to their strength, and led the people here to view their course as less vicious. Measures tending to the prevention of crimes can alone relieve us from the distress of punishing them. Had such measures in relation to the offenders in question been earlier taken, we should not have to lament the frequency of their commission. I have been at great pains to convince the people of this State that smuggling was a moral offence. But in this I have only partially succeeded. There are individuals here who, in every other respect, fulfill with exemplary integrity all the duties devolving upon them as fathers of families and as citizens; but as regards smuggling, although they may not be personally concerned, they attach no censure to those who are. It is the influence of education, of habit, of bad example. Formerly, under the Government of Spain, smuggling in Louisiana was universally practiced from the highest to the lowest member of society. To show you the light in which it was then viewed, I will only observe that, occasionally in conversation with ladies, I have denounced smuggling as dishonest, and very generally a reply, in substance as follows, would be returned: *That is impossible, for my grandfather, or my father, or my husband was, under the Spanish Government, a great smuggler, and he was always esteemed an honest man.* It takes time to remove the influence of prejudice, of example, of former habits. Much has already been done to reconcile the Louisianians to the Government, laws and usages of the United States, and more must yet be done to do away all traces of those improper feelings and sentiments which originated with, and were fostered under, the corrupt Government of Spain. Prosecutions are now pending in the District Court against several of the Barataria offenders, and, in the course of the investigation, it is probable that the number implicated will be very considerable. Justice demands that the most culpable be punished with severity. But I see no good end to be attained by making the penalties of the law to fall extensively and heavily. The example is not the less imposing, by circumscribing the number of its victims; and the mercy which should dictate it seldom fails to make a salutary and lasting impression. Should the President think proper to instruct the Attorney for the District of Louisiana to select a few of the most hardened offenders of Barataria for trial, and to forbear to prosecute all others concerned, I think such an act of clemency would be well received, and be attended, at the present moment, with the best effects. A sympathy for these offenders is certainly more or less felt *by many of the Louisianians.* With some it arises from national attachment, but with most from their late trade and intercourse with them. Should the Attorney for the District be instructed not to prosecute the case of minor offenders, it is desirable that such instructions be accompanied with the opinion of the Executive as to the offence of smuggling, and that publicity be given to the same. Such a document would, I am persuaded, be productive of great good. It may be I am in error. Some of my countrymen of talents and virtue think differently. But, for myself, I have always thought that as much may be done with the Louisianians by a mild policy as with any people I ever knew. Such impression has always influenced my public conduct. It is true I have often failed in my objects, but a chief magistrate, with more talents and discretion than I possess, who should pursue such a course of policy, could not fail to succeed." These are noble sentiments, and they are expressed with a simplicity of manner and a modesty of feeling which reflects much honor on the memory of Claiborne, whose benevolence and kindness of heart have already been fully established in the pages of this History.

A treaty of peace had been signed between the Creek Nation and the United States in the month of August, as previously recorded in this narrative, but some of the tribes constituting that nation had refused their assent to the treaty, and continued their hostilities. They used to procure clothing, ammunition and arms from the Spaniards, and sell in Pensacola the fruits of their depredations on American property. Generel Jackson had demanded satisfaction from the Governor of Pensacola, but it had been refused. To make matters worse, the British force which, allied with six hundred Creek warriors, had lately attacked Fort Bowyer on Mobile Point, had departed from Pensacola, and, after being defeated, had returned to that town, whose forts were suffered to be garrisoned by the British. Moreover, the Spanish authorities had even arrested and imprisoned some American citizens who were suspected of being unfriendly to the British Government.

Jackson, thinking that these facts constituted a breach of neutrality and a violation of the laws of nations, concluded that he was authorized to dispossess the British and their Indian allies of the shelter which they had found in Pensacola, and which they used as a base of operations. He, therefore, assembled near Fort Montgomery, on the River Alabama, an army of about four thousand men, composed of a detachment of regulars, of militia of Tennessee, and of a battalion of volunteer dragoons of Mississippi. On the 6th of November, this army encamped within three miles of Pensacola. General Jackson sent Major Peire* to demand that an American garrison be received in the fort St. Michael and Barrancas, until the Spanish Government could procure a sufficient force to enable it to maintain its neutrality against the British, who had possessed them-

* Lacarriere Latour's Historical Memoir, p. 46.

selves of these fortresses, notwithstanding the remonstrances and protest of the Spanish Governor, with the assurance on the part of the American General that his forces should be withdrawn as soon as a Spanish force sufficiently numerous to make itself respected should arrive. On these propositions having been refused, Major Peire declared that recourse would be had to arms.

On the next day, the 7th of November, the attack was made. The Spaniards were too feeble in numbers to make any effective resistance to the four thousand men who were under the control of General Jackson, and the small town of Pensacola was taken without much difficulty. It had no fortified walls, and the American column easily penetrated without any opposition into the principal street, where it met a Spanish battery of two pieces, which, having fired once, was carried at the point of the bayonet. Then all further resistance ceased. The loss of the Americans was eleven killed and wounded; that of the Spaniards still less. Shortly after, Fort Michael surrendered, and Fort Barrancas was evacuated, after having been partially blown up by the Spanish commandant, who, with his men, took refuge on board of the British ships in the Bay, which departed unmolested. The object of the expedition having been obtained, Jackson hastened to return to Mobile.

Bonaparte, whose fall from the imperial throne I have already mentioned, had many enthusiastic admirers in Louisiana, particularly among the French population, by whom the Bourbons were proportionately hated. When the French Consul, the Chevalier de Tousard, who had been appointed to that office in New Orleans by the recently established Government of Louis XVIII., arrived at his post, he found that he had to overcome strong prejudices, and even decided hostility His person was insulted, and violence was offered to his house, from which the arms of the King of France, appended to its front, were taken down and carried away. Some of the rioters were apprehended, and bound to good behavior; but the outrage having been renewed, Claiborne, on the 2d of November, issued a proclamation, in which he announced that, whereas it was essential to the preservation of order, and especially due to the good understanding which happily existed between the government of the United States and that of France, that such indecorous and unprovoked attacks and indignities should not be continued, or remain unpunished, he thought it his duty to notify the good citizens and the inhabitants of the State, that the Chevalier de Tousard was to be respected as the accredited Consul of the King of France in Louisiana, and to recommend to the civil officers of the State to be active and vigilant in suppressing any attempt that might be made to ill-treat or to insult the said Consul, or to offer any violence or indignity to his dwelling. He furthermore offered a reward of two hundred dollars for the discovery and apprehension of the person or persons who had forcibly taken and carried away the arms of the sovereign of France, which the Consul, according to custom, had placed on the door of his dwelling.

On the 5th, Claiborne thus wrote to General Jackson: "In this city there are several uniform militia corps of much promise, and my impression is, that on *these*, with other companies of the militia, much confidence may be reposed in the moment of trial. There are individuals who believe otherwise; it may be I am in error, but there certainly has been a sensible change in the public mind. There is not displayed by the people at large that enthusiastic ardor which is to be found in the Western States, but there is no symptom of opposition to the Government and laws. A strong hatred is manifested toward the enemy, and a determination expressed to unite in the defence of the State. You will observe, Sir, that I speak of the people at large. I know there are some disaffected characters, and in this city there are many vagabonds, who, if the occasion served, would be disposed for mischief. The Legislature of the State will be in session on the 10th instant, and their zealous support, at this moment of danger, will confirm the Louisianians in their present good disposition. But if, unfortunately, a spirit anything like that which led the Legislature, the last winter, to oppose a militia requisition, should again prevail, I shall encounter great embarrassment. But, as I have already observed, a great change in the public mind has apparently taken place; many members of the Legislature have always had American feelings and sentiments; others, whom I have lately seen, profess the most patriotic intentions, and all will, I hope, act a part which the crisis advises, and the surety of the country demands."

On the 10th, as Claiborne had informed General Jackson, the Legislature met in extra session at the request of the Governor, who, the next day, sent them a message, in which he said: " An English commander has dared to make his first call on the *Louisianians*, and to invite them to outrage the very ashes of their fathers, and welcome an English army on their *paternal soil!* He has added insult to injury, by first inviting us to the desertion of our country, and then by supposing us capable of cowardly displaying at our dwellings a foreign flag as a passport to his protection. I am, however, fully apprised of the *profound contempt* with which this base address has everywhere been received; and in the patriotic ardor which pervades the State, I behold a pledge of its fidelity and devotion to the American Union. This ardor, this American spirit, has been tested by the facility with which the late requisition for an auxiliary force of militia infantry has been carried into effect."

He added: "In addition to the forces now in the field, and those expected from Tennessee and Kentucky, I shall, if the danger of invasion increases, order out the whole, or such part of the militia as may be deemed expedient; but, to do so with effect, the Executive arm must be strengthened, and such funds provided as may be requisite to procure all necessary supplies. In times of public danger no able-bodied citizen, when ordered into the field, should be excused from serving, either in person, or by substitute. When our homes and families are menaced, we should not commute the personal services of a citizen for a sum in money. The expenses incident to all movements of militia under the immediate authority of the State must be defrayed by the State. As these movements, on the *present occasion*, will have for object the *common defence*, the expenses will probably hereafter be reimbursed by the General Government, but the State must make the advance."

The object of Claiborne in convening the Legislature was "to strengthen the arm of the Executive, and provide such funds as might be requisite to procure all necessary supplies." Beyond that, their services were not needed, in his opinion. Claiborne, whose views had frequently been thwarted by both Chambers, and who was not on the best of terms with either, particularly with the Senate, felt a nervous anxiety to get rid of them as soon as possible. He therefore, in his Message, gave them the following hints: "To all the subjects which may come under your deliberation I recommend the most unwearied attention. The Treasury is illy calculated to meet the expenditures incident to a protracted session, and I sincerely hope you may be enabled speedily to dispatch all necessary business. The times are eventful, and your early return to your respective parishes may become desirable. We are exposed to many perils. The enemy is disposed to do us every ill, and will use all his means. We know not how soon we may be called upon to defend everything dear to us as citizens and fathers of families. I have exacted from the military officers throughout the State a faithful discharge of duty, and endeavored to awaken all the vigilance which the crisis demands. Your *counsel* and example in your respective parishes will tend greatly to the support of measures for the public good. They will particularly invite to that harmony, mutual confidence and mutual exertion, so promotive of tranquillity within, and so essential to our security from without."

Five days later, he laid before the General Assembly an extract of a letter from Jackson, which gave positive assurance of the danger with which Louisiana was threatened. " Recent information from the most correct sources," said the General to Claiborne, " has been received of an expedition of twelve or fifteen thousand men, sailing from Ireland early in September last, intended to attempt the conquest of Louisiana. You will therefore see the necessity of preparing for service, at an hour's notice, the whole body of the Louisiana militia. I rely on your patriotism and activity, and hope not to be disappointed."

On the 17th of November, Claiborne wrote to General Jackson : " It is certainly true that the Louisianians have of late manifested the most patriotic disposition, and that, if the spirit which exists be cherished and encouraged, we have everything to hope from the majority of this population. The Legislature have not as yet done anything to damp the public ardor. But I hope this body will be justly impressed with the dangers to which we are exposed, and will warmly second all my efforts. But I fear, I much fear, they will not act with the promptitude and the energy which the crisis demands." Such language from a man who had been, without any interruption, the Executive of Louisiana since 1803, and who was supposed to be thoroughly acquainted with its population, could not but produce a deep impression, and will explain subsequent events.

About this same time, he expressed the same apprehensions to Governor Blount of Tennessee: "But," said he, "we shall, in any event, be made secure by those brave and determined men who are hastening from Tennessee and Kentucky. I await their arrival with much anxiety."

Such was the condition of Louisiana as described in the preceding pages, when Jackson departed by land from Mobile for New Orleans, on the 21st of November.

CHAPTER IX.

GOVERNOR CLAIBORNE'S ADMINISTRATION — NAVAL ENGAGEMENT ON LAKE BORGNE — REFUSAL OF THE LEGISLATURE TO SUSPEND THE WRIT OF HABEAS CORPUS AND TO ADJOURN — ARRIVAL OF GENERAL JACKSON — BATTLE OF THE 23D OF DECEMBER.

1814.

GENERAL JACKSON arrived in New Orleans on the 1st of December.* He was emphatically the man for the occasion; for not only did he possess military talents of the highest order, but his love of country was intense, his energy of character unsurpassed, his decision as prompt as his comprehension of exigencies was clear and rapid. He was, above all, pre-eminently gifted with that precious faculty which Nature imparts to some of her favorites among the predestinated rulers of men—the faculty of subjecting the minds of others to his own by that kind of magnetism which seems to emanate from an iron will. Where that man was as a chief, there could be, within the legitimate sphere of his action, but one controlling and directing power. All responsibility would be unhesitatingly assumed and made to rest entirely on that unity of volition which he represented. Such qualifications were eminently needed for the protection of a city containing a motley population, which was without any natural elements of cohesion, and in which abounded distraction of counsel, conflicting opinions, wishes and

---

* Claiborne's Dispatch to Monroe, December 9, 1814.

feelings, and much diffidence as to the possibility of warding off the attack with which it was threatened by a powerful enemy. Various measures had been discussed, but none effectively executed. Governor Claiborne, Commodore Patterson, the Military Commandant of New Orleans, and a Joint Committee of both Houses of the Legislature, had frequently met on the subject, but their deliberations had led to no practical results. There was a multitude of advice and schemes, but nothing was done, whilst the population was becoming daily more excited and alarmed on hearing of the nearer approach of the enemy. "There was wanting," says Major Lacarriere Latour,* in his very interesting memoir, page 53, "that concentration of power so necessary for the success of military operations. The citizens, having very little confidence in their civil or military authorities for the defence of the country, were filled with distrust and gloomy apprehensions. Miserable disputes on account of two different Committees of Defence, unfortunately countenanced by the presence and influence of several public officers, had driven the people to despondency; they complained, and not without cause, that the Legislature wasted time, and consumed the money of the State in idle discussions on empty formalities of election, while all their time and all the wealth which they squandered might be profitably employed in the defence of the country. Credit was annihilated; already for several months had the Banks suspended the payment of their notes; to supply the want of specie one and three dollar notes had been issued, and dollars had been cut as a substitute for small change. On the Banks refusing specie, the moneyed men had drawn in their funds, which

---

* Major Lacarriere Latour was a Frenchman, and a very able officer. He was employed as Principal Engineer in the Seventh Military District of the U. S. Army.

they no longer lent out without a usurious interest of three or four per cent. per month. Every one was distressed, confidence had ceased, and with it almost every species of business. Our situation seemed desperate."

It was in these circumstances that General Jackson made his appearance. His very physiognomy prognosticated what soul was incased within the spare but well ribbed form which had that "lean and hungry look" described by England's greatest bard as bespeaking little sleep of nights, but much of ambition, self-reliance, and impatience of control. His lip and eye denoted the man of unyielding temper, and his very hair, slightly silvered, stood erect like quills round his wrinkled brow, as if they scorned to bend. Some sneered, it is true, at what they called a military tyro, at the impromptu general who had sprung out of the uncouth lawyer and the unlearned judge, who in arms had only the experience of a few months, acquired in a desultory war against wild Indians, and who was, not only without any previous training to his new profession, but also without the first rudiments of a liberal education, for he did not even know the orthography of his own native language. Such was the man who, with a handful of raw militia, was to stand in the way of the veteran troops of England, whose boast it was to have triumphed over one of the greatest captains known in history. But those who entertained such distrust had hardly come in contact with General Jackson, when they felt that they had to deal with a master-spirit. True, he was rough hewn from the rock, but rock he was, and of that kind of rock which Providence chooses to select as a fit material to use in its structures of human greatness. True, he had not the education of a lieutenant in a European army; but what lieutenant, educated or not, who had the will and the remarkable military adaptation so evident in General

Jackson's intellectual and physical organization, ever remained a subaltern? Much less could General Jackson fail to rise to his proper place in a country where there was so much more elbow-room, and fewer artificial obstacles than in less favored lands. But, whatever those obstacles might have been, General Jackson would have overcome them all. His will was of such an extraordinary nature that, like Christian faith, it could almost have accomplished prodigies and removed mountains. It is impossible to study the life of General Jackson without being convinced that this is the most remarkable feature of his character. His will had, as it were, the force and the fixity of fate; that will carried him triumphantly through his military and civil career, and through the difficulties of private life. So intense and incessantly active this peculiar faculty was in him, that one would suppose that his mind was nothing but will—a will so lofty that it towered into sublimity. In him it supplied the place of genius—or, rather, it was almost genius. On many occasions, in the course of his long, eventful life, when his shattered constitution made his physicians despair of preserving him, he seemed to continue to live merely because it was his will; and when his unconquerable spirit departed from his enfeebled and worn-out body, those who knew him well might almost have been tempted to suppose that he had not been vanquished by death, but had at last consented to repose. This man, when he took the command at New Orleans, had made up his mind to beat the English; and, as that mind was so constituted that it was not susceptible of entertaining much doubt as to the results of any of its resolves, he went to work with an innate confidence which transfused itself into the population he had been sent to protect.

General Jackson arrived in New Orleans after a fatiguing journey of eleven days through a barren and thinly settled country, and yet, without allowing himself any time for repose, on that very day he reviewed the battalion of the uniform companies of the New Orleans militia, commanded by Major Daquin. These companies were composed of natives of Louisiana of French descent and of Frenchmen. They were completely equipped, well drilled, and manœuvred with admirable precision. The General was highly pleased, and expressed his satisfaction to the officers. The next day, true to the natural activity of his disposition and to his constant practice of seeing everything himself as far as practicable, he went to visit Fort St. Philip, in the Parish of Plaquemine, and to determine what other parts of the River Mississippi, below New Orleans, it might be expedient to fortify. Fort St. Philip was but an indifferent fortification, which had been constructed as far down the river as the nature of the ground had permitted. On that visit to Fort St. Philip, General Jackson ordered its wooden barracks to be demolished, and several additional pieces of artillery to be mounted on its ramparts. He also ordered a thirty-two-pounder and a mortar to be put in its covered way, and two batteries to be constructed—the first, on the right bank opposite Fort St. Philip, and on the site of a former fort now entirely in ruins, called Fort Bourbon. The second battery was to be half a mile above the fort, and on the same bank. These were to be mounted with twenty-two-pounders. The latter, in particular, was in a situation extremely advantageous for commanding the river, and could join its fire with that of Fort St. Philip.*

On his return to New Orleans General Jackson proceeded to visit that part of the country which is back of

---

* Latour's Historical Memoir, p. 55.

the city, and which forms a kind of peninsula bordering on Lake Pontchartrain. At the confluence of Bayou Chef Menteur and Bayou Sauvage, or Gentilly, he ordered a battery to be erected. At the same time he had sent orders to Governor Claiborne to cause all the bayous leading from the Gulf of Mexico and from the adjacent lakes into the interior of the country to be obstructed. In obedience to these instructions, Bayou Manchac, a well-known and much used outlet from the Mississippi to Lake Pontchartrain, was closed, where it meets the Mississippi a few miles below the town of Baton Rouge, and has remained closed ever since.

General Jackson found that the country he had come to defend was in the most defenceless condition. It had a considerable extent of coast connecting with the interior through many water communications; and having hardly any fortified points, it was open on all sides. It had, besides, in its neighborhood the Spanish harbor of Pensacola, which, until General Jackson put an end to it, had freely admitted the enemy's ships, and the greater part of whose population was hostile to the United States. For the defence of its extensive shores it had six gun-boats and a sloop-of-war, with Fort St. Philip on the Mississippi, and Fort Petites Coquilles on the Rigolets between Lake Borgne and Lake Pontchartrain, on the present site of Fort Pike. Both were thought incapable of standing a regular siege. The supply of arms of all sorts and of ammunition was very deficient, particularly in artillery. As to mortars, there were but two; they had been landed from bomb-ketches which had been condemned, and there were not a hundred bombs of the calibre required by these mortars. Besides, from the construction of their carriages, they were only fit to be mounted on board of vessels, and by no means adapted to land-batteries. The Fort of Petites Coquilles was not finished, nor was it in a condition to make an ordinary resistance.*

"Such was the inconsiderable defence," says Major Latour, "that protected the shores of Louisiana and covered a country that has an extent of coast of upward of six hundred miles, and of which even a temporary possession by an enemy might be attended with consequences baneful to the future prosperity of the Western States. The General Government might and ought to have been well informed of the vulnerable points of Louisiana. Accurate maps of the country on a large scale had been made by the engineer, B. Lafon and myself, and delivered to General Wilkinson, who, it is presumable, did not fail to forward them to the Secretary of War. That part of the State in particular by which the enemy penetrated was there laid down, and, in 1813, Brigadier-General Flournoy ordered Major Lafon, the Chief Engineer of the District, to draw up an exact account of all the points to be fortified for the general defence of Louisiana. The draughts, which were numerous and formed an atlas, were accompanied with very particular explanatory notes. That work, which reflects great credit on its author, pointed out in the most precise and clear manner what was expedient to be done, in order to put the country in a state of security against all surprise. I have always understood that those drafts were ordered and executed for the purpose of being sent to the then Secretary of War, to enable the Government to determine in their wisdom the points proper to be fortified. To what fatality then was it owing that Louisiana, whose means of defence were so inadequate, which had but a scanty white population composed in a great

* Latour's Memoir, p. 7.

proportion of foreigners speaking various languages, and which was so remote from any succors, though one of the keys of the Union, was so long left without the means of resisting the enemy? I shall be told that to fortify the coast in time of peace were to incur an unnecessary expense. This position I by no means admit; but I further observe that the war had already existed two years; and we ought to have presumed, had positive proof been wanting, that the British, having numerous fleets, and every means of transporting troops to all points of the coast of the United States, would not fail to make an attempt against Louisiana—a country which already, by its prodigious and unexampled progress in the culture of the sugar-cane, had become a dangerous rival to the British Colonies. The City of New Orleans contained produce to a vast amount. The cotton crops of the State of Louisiana and the Mississippi Territory, accumulated during several years, were stored in that city which was surrounded with considerable plantations having numerous gangs of slaves. It was, in a word, the emporium of the produce of a great portion of the Western States. The Mississippi, on which it lies, receives the streams that water upward of a million of square miles, and wafts to New Orleans the annually increasing productions of their fertile banks. It is by the Mississippi and the rivers emptying into it, that the communication is kept up between the Western and Northern States; and by the Mississippi and the Missouri there will, at no distant period, be carried on without difficulty, or with very little obstruction, the most extensive inland navigation on the globe.

"All these advantages were calculated to excite the cupidity of the British, and inspire them with the desire of getting possession of a country which, besides its territorial wealth, insured to whoever might hold it, an immediate control over the Western States. In possessing themselves of Louisiana, the least favorable prospect of the enemy was the plunder of a very considerable quantity of produce, the destruction of a city destined to become commercial and opulent in the highest degree, and the ruin of numerous plantations which must one day rival in their productions those of the finest colonies of European nations. Their other prospects, less certain indeed, but in which they were not a little sanguine, were the separation of the Western States from the rest of the Union; the possibility of transferring the theatre of war to the westward by the possession of the Mississippi, and effecting a junction with their army in Canada; and lastly, being masters of Louisiana, to import by the river their various manufactures, and secure to themselves the monopoly of the fur trade."

These strictures of Major Lacarriere Latour, who was an able engineer, and an eye-witness to all that happened in Louisiana on that critical occasion, show that the United States which, in time of peace, had treated the inhabitants of Louisiana, from the cession of that province by France in 1803, until its admission into the Union in 1812, with harshness and injustice, and with very little regard for their feelings, as I have shown in the preceding pages, had been very negligent in providing for their defence in time of war. It must be remembered that several of the States, and particularly the New England States, had seen its incorporation into the Union with such aversion as to threaten, in consequence of it, a dissolution of the fundamental compact; and some of their most distinguished Representatives in Congress had even declared that they would forever consider it as foreign territory. One is almost tempted to suppose that the General Government had at last adopted the same views, from the defenceless condition in which it had left an acquisition which had proved so objectionable to a powerful minority—a minority whose delegates were now assembled in Convention at Hartford in the State of Connecticut, and threatening, if not to side with England in the present war, at least to throw every obstacle in the way of its successful prosecution. Fortunately the man who was sent for the defence of Southern Territory was southern born. He was a native of South Carolina, and had grown to hardy manhood on the forest-clad hills of Tennessee. It is still more fortunate that he was equal to the occasion. He did not deplore, in helpless despair, the scarcity of his resources; he did not write to his Government that he could not defend New Orleans with his limited means; he never thought of retreating, or abandoning one inch of territory; he saw that he had to create everything for defence, and everything he did create. In reply to timid insinuations he swore his favorite oath—that well-known oath which always escaped from his lips when he was excited or indignant—an oath which sprang from a religious and not profane heart—he swore "by the Eternal" that not one foot of the soil of Louisiana should be permanently held by the English, and he kept that oath to the letter.

Governor Claiborne seems to have fully appreciated the merits of General Jackson, and to have been disposed from the beginning to co-operate zealously with him, for, on the 9th of December, a few days after General Jackson's arrival, he wrote to the Secretary of State, Mr. Monroe, that the nomination of no officer to the command of the District could have been more generally approved, " nor do I know one," said he, " under whose orders in the field I would more cheerfully place myself." But, added he: " in the event of General Jackson's death, or absence from the district, it is not improbable

that some contest may arise as to the right of command."
His reasons for apprehending the possibility of such a conflict between State and Federal authority he expressed as follows:

"At the last Session of the Legislature of the State, by a Resolution of the two Houses I have been requested, whenever the militia of Louisiana was ordered into the field, to command in person. In consequence it has been and is still my determination, whenever the danger of invasion becomes imminent, to order out the whole, or such portion of the militia of the State as circumstances shall render necessary, and to place myself at the head. It, however, is far from my wish to interfere with the command of General Jackson. On the contrary, I have assured him that, on all occasions, I would obey his orders. I, however, should be unwilling to acknowledge any other officer, either of the regular army, or of the militia, *on duty in this State*, as my military superior. I do not know how far General Jackson may be inclined, should I take the field, to consider me as his second, nor do I design at present to press a decision. It is not improbable but the General would rather the President should determine the rank to which a Governor of a State, taking the field, was entitled, and I would myself prefer that course. I observe that, if the newspapers are to be accredited, Governor Tompkins of New York has been vested by the President with the command of all the forces within the State. I do not ask *for a like command* within Louisiana. It has been committed to much abler hands, and I should regret a change. But, diffident as I am of my military talents, I must confess, Sir, I should, with extreme reluctance, within my own State, submit to the control of any one of the militia Generals in the service of the United States who had no greater military experience than myself, and less knowledge of the country. I solicit, therefore, that whenever, in case of invasion, or imminent danger of invasion, I should in my character as Governor of Louisiana order out any portion of the militia and place myself at their head, General Jackson may be instructed to consider me as second in command of the forces to be employed within this State." It is not known what reply the General Government made to this communication.

Whilst the city of New Orleans was resounding with the clash of arms and full of military preparations, the Governor was in vain endeavoring to fill up the seat which had been so long vacant on the bench of the Supreme Court, and to make nominations which continued to be rejected by the Senate. On the 6th, he sent in the name of the Attorney-General, Xavier Martin, but on the 9th he wrote to Senator Fromentin in Washington: "I do not at present know an individual who would unite a majority of the Senate. Seven members have voted for Martin, and will, I believe, be satisfied with no other person." Thus the Governor found the Senate as refractory at this session as at the preceding one; and he did not seem to be better satisfied with the Lower House, for in the same letter he said: "The House of Representatives consumes much time in debate, and as yet the Legislature have answered no one of the objects for which they were called. I trust and hope, however, that they will unite in some measures which the interest and safety of the State imperiously demand."

I write these lines when the State of Louisiana has been invaded by Northern troops, when a general from New England is a military dictator in New Orleans, when Louisianians are called traitors and rebels, when their property is confiscated, and all sorts of outrages are heaped upon them by the sons of sires who sat in the Hartford Convention, where treason was meditated, but found not hearts bold enough to carry it into execution. It may not be here out of place to record what a Governor of Louisiana then thought of the purposes of that Convention. In the communication of the 9th of December to Monroe, which I have already quoted, Claiborne said : "What is likely to result from the New England Convention? For myself, I view this proceeding with much anxiety and inquietude. It surely presents an alarming aspect to the friends of the Union, and will not fail to encourage the enemy to attempt the overthrow of our Government." Whilst treason was thus lurking in more than one Northern breast, Louisiana was preparing to show that such a crime was not of Southern growth.

It is, however, mortifying to a Louisianian to know that a Governor of Louisiana, on the same day on which he expressed these patriotic anxieties about the fidelity of New England, felt himself justified, perhaps with too much reason, to write the following lines to one David M'Gee : " As regards the literary work you contemplate, I am assured of its usefulness, and desire its completion. I fear, however, that in this city and State, useful as the work would be to its inhabitants, it would not meet with liberal encouragement. A love of letters has not yet gained an ascendency in Louisiana, and I would advise you to seek for your production the patronage of some one of the Northern cities." How bitter is the thought that this is true! How hard it is for the veracity of the Southern historian to admit that, even in 1864, a judicious and frank adviser would be compelled to say to a man of letters in the language used by Claiborne in 1814: "I would advise you to seek for your production the patronage of some one of the Northern cities."

On the 14th of December, Governor Claiborne laid

before the Legislature a communication from Commodore Patterson, which informed him of the approach of the enemy in considerable force, and another communication from General Jackson which requested him to hold in readiness to take the field the whole militia of the State. Accompanying these two communications was a message in which he said: "Among the measures which our safety requires, permit me to recommend the suspension for a limited time of the Writ of Habeas Corpus. This will, as the Commodore suggests, enable him to press hands for manning the vessels of the United States under his orders; nor is there any doubt also, in case of the landing of the enemy, but it will be found expedient to enable the commander of the troops of the United States and of the militia of the State to apprehend and secure disaffected persons."

This message gave rise to warm debates in both houses of the Legislature. A State, it was admitted, could suspend the Writ of Habeas Corpus in its own courts, but could its authority extend to the Federal courts? Besides, many entertained great doubts on the question, whether any person arrested by any of the commanding officers of the land or naval forces of the United States could be relieved on Writs of Habeas Corpus issued by a State court. All knew that Judge Hall, who presided in the District Court of the United States, was of opinion that Congress alone had authority to withdraw the protection of that writ by which the Constitution of the United States intends that the humblest citizen shall be made as secure in his person as if covered with a shield of divine manufacture. All knew that, in 1806, General Wilkinson had treated with contempt the writs of territorial judges, but had not dared to disobey those of Hall. The firmness of that magistrate, and his inflexibility in the discharge of what he thought his duty, made it a matter of certainty that he would disregard the State legislation in relation to the suspension of the Writ of Habeas Corpus. Why, therefore, should the State place itself in the undignified position of legislating in vain, and of assuming an authority which would be set at naught? Such was the language of those who were adverse to the measure.

General Jackson, Governor Claiborne, and many of the military, they further said, are incessantly talking of sedition, disaffection, and treason. But we are better acquainted with the people of Louisiana than those who are vociferating against them. We have come from the bosom of that people; we have come from every part of the State; we have witnessed the universal alacrity with which General Jackson's requisition for a quota of the militia has been complied with; we know that our constituents can be depended on; we know that no State is more free from treason, and if we suspended the Writ of Habeas Corpus, we would admit that there are grounds for the vain and injurious apprehensions entertained by those who do so much injustice to Louisiana. We remember but too well the days when General Wilkinson, arresting and transporting whom he pleased, filled New Orleans with so much terror. Did not, in those days, the President of the United States, the illustrious Jefferson, make application to Congress for a suspension of the Writ of Habeas Corpus, on the ground that the safety of the country was endangered by Burr's conspiracy? Did not Congress refuse to grant what the President desired? It is a safe precedent; and General Jackson has no right to complain, if we refuse to him what was refused to the President by Congress. These arguments prevailed, and both houses voted against the measure desired by General Jackson, and recommended by Governor Claiborne.

Louaillier, whose name will figure somewhat conspicuously in the sequel of this History, in consequence of his arrest by order of General Jackson, and who, at this time, acted as chairman of a " Committee to whom was referred the consideration of suspending the Writ of Habeas Corpus, in order to enable Patterson to impress seamen, reported* the recommended measure as inexpedient. The Committee thought the country would be ill defended by men forced into service ; and that it was better to induce sailors, by the offer of ample bounties, to repair on board of the ships of the United States, than forcibly to drag them on board. A sum of six thousand dollars was therefore placed by the Legislature at the disposal of the Commander, to be expended in bounties, and, with a view to remove from seamen the opportunity to decline entering the service of the United States by the hope of a more profitable employment on board of merchant vessels, an embargo law was passed.† It is difficult to conceive how the same Legislature which had refused to suspend the Writ of Habeas Corpus, on the ground that it could not legislate on that matter for the Federal courts, did not doubt its authority to arrest the commerce of the United States by an embargo law.

The adverse report made by Louaillier to Commodore Patterson's application cannot be looked upon as having been dictated by a want of patriotism, because the same member of the Legislature had, as chairman of the Committee of Ways and Means, made the most spirited and earnest report on the necessity of taxing all the resources of the State for defensive preparations. " Who has not admired," he said in that document, " the patriotic ardor which was displayed in the execution of the works, deemed by the principal cities of the Union and our sis-

---

* Martin's History of Louisiana, p. 346, vol. 2.
† Do., p. 346, vol. 2.

ter States necessary for the protection of such as could be assailed by the enemy? The magistrates, the citizens, the officers of the General Government, manifested the utmost zeal to obtain the desired object; their safety and the ignominious retreat of the enemy were the glorious result of their efforts. How does it happen that such a noble example has not been followed in this part of the Union? Are we so situated as to have no dangers to dread? Is our population of such a description as to secure our tranquillity? Shall we always confine ourselves to addresses and proclamations? Are we always to witness the several Departments intrusted with our defence, languishing in a state of inactivity hardly to be excused even in the most peaceable times? No other evidence of patriotism is to be found than a disposition to avoid every expense, every fatigue; nothing as yet has been performed. It is the duty of the Legislature to give the necessary impulse, but it is only by adopting a course entirely opposite to that which has been hitherto pursued that we can hope for success. If the Legislature adds its own indolence to that which generally prevails, we can easily foresee that, ere long, a capitulation, similar to that obtained by the city of Alexandria, will be the consequence of a conduct so highly culpable.

"A considerable force is now assembled under the orders of General Jackson, which will speedily receive large reinforcements from the militia of the Western States, but it is nevertheless true that the principal avenues to our capital are not in a situation to insure its preservation; and that, unless we are determined to provide for its safety ourselves, unless we act with a promptness and energy equal to the torpor which seems to have invaded the principal branches of our Government, that force will only be employed in retaking this territory, which must fall an easy prey to the first efforts of an in vading foe. The Legislature has been convened for the purpose of supplying a fund adequate to the expenses necessary to ward off the dangers by which we are threatened. This is the object which we must accomplish. Little does it matter whether this or that expenditure ought to be furnished by the Federal administration, or by the State Government; let us not hesitate in making such as safety may require. When this shall have been secured, then our claims to a reimbursement will be listened to."

This document demonstrates the zeal which actuated this distinguished member of the Legislature, but, at the same time, considering the source from which it came, it is a singular bill of indictment against the Federal Government, against the Legislature itself and all the State authorities, as well as against the whole population. It proclaimed "that the noble example given by the principal cities of the Union and our sister States had not been followed by this part of the Union; that our population was not of such a description as to secure tranquillity; that we had confined ourselves to addresses and proclamations; that the several Departments intrusted with our defence had been languishing in a state of inactivity hardly to be excused even in the most peaceable times; that no other evidence of patriotism was to be found than a disposition to avoid every expense, every fatigue; that nothing as yet had been performed when the enemy was already on the threshold of the country; and that if the Legislature added its own indolence to that which generally prevailed, it was easy to foresee that, ere long, a capitulation, similar to that obtained by the city of Alexandria, would be the consequence of a conduct so highly culpable." This censorious report was adopted without any denial of the facts which had elicited such harsh comments. It was speedily followed by action; the Legislature sanctioned the loan of twenty thousand dollars which the Governor had effected during its recess, to provide for the defence of the State. The sum of seventeen thousand dollars* which remained in the Treasury out of that loan was directed to be applied, under the orders of General Jackson, to procuring materials and workmen for the completion of such batteries and other fortifications as he had directed; and a further sum of eleven thousand dollars was appropriated to the same subject.

Such was the condition of the country as described in Louaillier's report on the 22d of November, before the arrival of General Jackson, which took place on the 1st of December, as I have already stated. It is probable that General Jackson had heard of this state of things. It is known that, from various sources, he had been informed that the country was full of spies and traitors.† It is known that he had written to that effect to Claiborne, and that Claiborne had replied: "I think with you that the country is full of spies and traitors." To this must be added what Judge Martin, who was an eye-witness to all that happened at that epoch, says in his valuable work on Louisiana: "The Governor, who was not unwilling to increase his own merit by magnifying the obstacles he had to surmount, stated in his correspondence with Jackson every opposition he met with, and did not fail to represent every one who did not think as he did, as inimical to the country. Those who immediately surrounded Jackson on his arrival, with a view to enhance his reliance on them, availed themselves of every opportunity to increase his sense of danger." Is it then to be wondered at if General Jackson, who was an utter stranger to the population of New Orleans, came

---

* Martin's History of Louisiana, p. 344, vol. 2.
† Martin's History of Louisiana, p. 340, vol. 2.

to that city with a mind somewhat unfavorably prejudiced, and that he should have acted as he did hereafter, on the occasion which is to be recorded in the pages of this History?

But the state of things described in Louaillier's report had changed as soon as General Jackson had set his foot on the soil of Louisiana. Indolence had given way to zeal and activity, distrust to confidence, confusion to order, diversity of counsel and action to the sole direction of one controlling mind which made itself felt everywhere, and which gave an impulse to everything. Throughout the State, in obedience to the call of the General, the whole militia was organizing and preparing to march to any threatened point. In New Orleans and in its environs every man capable of bearing arms was already in the field, and the planters of the neighboring parishes of Plaquemine, St. Bernard, St. Charles and St. John the Baptist, had sent more negroes than the General needed to erect his intended fortifications.

In the mean time, the enemy was approaching and preparing to land. The naval armament which protected Lakes Borgne and Pontchartrain consisted of five gun-boats, with 23 guns and 182 men. To this force must be added the schooner Seahorse with one six-pounder and fourteen men, and the sloop Alligator, armed with one four-pounder and manned by a crew of eight men. This sloop acted as tender to the little fleet. On the 12th of December, the commander of this flotilla, Thomas A. C. Jones, observing that the enemy's fleet off Ship Island had increased to such a force as to render it no longer safe or prudent for him to continue on that part of the Lakes, determined to gain, as soon as possible, a station near Ile Malheureuse, because it would enable him to oppose a further penetration of the enemy up the Lakes, and at the same time afford to the American gun-boats the opportunity of retreating to the Fort of Petites Coquilles, if necessary.

On the 13th, at 10 A. M., a large number of barges left the English fleet, and moved toward Pass Christianne. At first, it was supposed that they intended to disembark troops at that place, but, as they continued their course to the westward, Commander Jones became convinced that they meditated an attack on his gun-boats. These gun-boats were aground on account of a strong westerly wind which had prevailed for several days, and which had made the water in the lakes uncommonly low. They were got afloat by throwing overboard all articles of weight that could be dispensed with. At last, at 3.30 P. M., the flood-tide commenced, the fleet got under way, and began to fall back toward the Rigolets; but unfortunately, early on the morning of the 14th, the wind having died away entirely, the vessels were compelled to anchor in the channel which exists at the west end of Ile Malheureuse. At daylight, the barges of the enemy were ascertained to be at anchor about nine miles from the Americans; but they soon got in motion and rapidly advanced. This flotilla consisted of forty-five launches and barges with forty-three cannon and twelve hundred men, including officers, under the command of Captain Lockyer. They had already cut off the schooner Seahorse, which had been sent to Bay St. Louis to assist in the removal of the public stores. The captain of the schooner, after having bravely and successfully repulsed seven of the enemy's boats, which had attacked him, and after having done them much damage, had blown up his ship and destroyed the public stores. The Alligator (tender), which had been separated from the gun-boats, had also been captured while endeavoring to rejoin them.

At the time when the British were pressing forward

with the utmost power of their well-managed oars, there continued to be a dead calm, and a strong ebb-tide was setting through the pass, or channel—which circumstances were unfavorable for manœuvring the gun-boats. The American commander had but one alternative, which was, to put himself in the most advantageous position he could take and give the enemy as warm a reception as possible. With this view he formed a close line abreast across the channel, anchoring each vessel by the stern with springs on the cable, and having boarding nettings triced up. Unfortunately, that line was soon broken up by the force of the current, which drove two of the gun-boats about one hundred yards in advance. At ten minutes before eleven, the enemy opened fire from the whole of his line, when the action became general and destructive on both sides. Jones was on board of one of the gun-boats which had been driven forward by the current. Three boats attempted to board his ship, but were repulsed with the loss of nearly every officer killed or wounded, and two boats sunk. A second attempt was made by four other boats, which shared almost a similar fate. At that moment Captain Jones received a severe wound which compelled him to quit his deck, leaving it in charge of George Parker, master's mate, who gallantly defended it until he also was disabled by a wound, when the enemy by his superior number overcame all resistance. The guns of the prize were immediately turned against the other gun-boats, and the action continued with unabating severity until all the gun-boats fell into the hands of the assailants.* The engagement lasted an hour and a half, and does infinite credit to the American arms, considering the disparity of forces. The loss on board of the gun-boats was forty-five killed and

---

* { Jones's Report to Commodore Patterson.
  { Lockyer's to Admiral Cochrane.

wounded. On the side of the British it was not less than three hundred. The destruction of these gun-boats left Louisiana entirely defenceless on its waters, and permitted the enemy to land whenever and wherever he pleased. This was almost all the naval defence which had been prepared for the protection of Louisiana by the Federal Government. Major Latour, whose testimony as a skillful officer and an actor in most of the scenes which he describes I always quote with confidence and respect, says:

"Commodore Patterson, who had served several years on the New Orleans Station, which he had commanded from nearly the commencement of the war, was perfectly acquainted with our coast, and consequently knew what means were necessary to defend it. On this subject he had written at an early period, and several times since, to the Secretary of the Navy. At Tchifonctee, on the eastern shore of Lake Pontchartrain, a flat-bottomed frigate had begun to be built two years before, calculated for the navigation of the lakes and our coasts. She was to carry forty-two pieces of cannon, twenty-six of which were to be thirty-two-pounders. The building of this frigate was suspended, in consequence, I believe, of the representations of Brigadier-General Flournoy, then commanding this District. From his first taking command of the Station, Commodore Patterson had not ceased to solicit the Government to authorize him to have that frigate finished. Governor Claiborne's correspondence with the heads of the different Departments was also to the same effect; but though much was promised, nothing was performed. It might have been thought, from the little regard that was paid to the representations of the superior officers of the District and of our representatives in Congress, that Louisiana was considered as a bastard child of the American family or that to attack her was looked upon as an impossibility. Yet the attack made on us was within a hair's breadth of succeeding; for had the enemy appeared a few weeks sooner, before General Jackson arrived in New Orleans, he might have entered the city with little or no opposition, there being no means of resisting him; and however well-inclined the citizens were to defend themselves, it would have been impossible to prevent the taking of the city."

On the 15th, Claiborne informed the Legislature of the disaster which had befallen our fleet. This information was accompanied with these observations: "The length of the combat is a proof of the valor and firmness with which our gallant tars maintained the unequal contest, and leaves no doubt that, although compelled ultimately to strike, their conduct has been such as to reflect honor upon the American name and navy. The ascendency which the enemy has now acquired on the coast of the lakes increases the necessity of enlarging and completing our measures of defence."

On the next day, Claiborne sent to the Legislature the following short and pithy message: "The moment is certainly inauspicious for that cool and mature deliberation which is essential to the formation of laws. The enemy menaces this capital, and we know not how soon he may effect a landing. Every hand must be raised to repel him, and all our time should be occupied in arranging and completing our measures of defence. Permit me, therefore, to suggest the propriety of adjourning the two Houses for fifteen or twenty days." This message was referred to a Committee, who reported that an adjournment at the present crisis was inexpedient; that it might be highly dangerous; that accidents might happen, and unforeseen cases might occur, when the interference of the Legislature might be necessary; that, should they adjourn, and the State should thereby be endangered, they would incur the just reproaches of their constituents; besides, that few members would have time to leave the city during so short an adjournment as the one urged upon them, and if they did, their mileage in going and returning would be such as to increase the expenses of the State, much more than if they remained in session, wherefore the Committee recommended that the members should stay at their post, ready on an emergency to contribute, as far as in them lay, to the defence of the country. These views of the Committee were adopted by the Legislature, but produced an unfavorable impression on General Jackson. He immediately proclaimed martial law, and issued with his characteristic energy the following iron-clad address to the citizens of New Orleans:

"The Major-General commanding has, with astonishment and regret, learned that great consternation and alarm pervade your city. It is true the enemy is on our coast and threatens an invasion of our Territory; but it is equally true, with union, energy, and the approbation of Heaven, we will beat him at every point his temerity may induce him to set foot upon our soil. The General, with still greater astonishment, has heard that British emissaries have been permitted to propagate seditious reports among you that the threatened invasion is with a view of restoring the country to Spain, from a supposition that some of you would be willing to return to your ancient government. Believe not such incredible tales; your government is at peace with Spain. It is the vital enemy of your country, the common enemy of mankind, the highway robber of the world that threatens you, and has sent his hirelings among you with this false report, to put you off your guard, that you may fall an easy prey to him. Then look to your liberties, your property, the chastity of your wives and daughters; take a retrospect of the conduct of the British army at Hampton and other places, where it has entered our country; and every bosom which glows with patriotism and virtue will be inspired with indignation, and pant for the arrival of the hour when we shall meet and revenge those outrages against the laws of civilization and humanity.

"The General calls upon the inhabitants of the city to trace this unfounded report to its source, and bring the propagators to condign punishment. The rules and articles of war annex the punishment of death to any person holding secret correspondence with the enemy, creating false alarm, or supplying him with provisions; and the General announces his unalterable determination rigidly to execute the martial law in all cases which may come within his province.

"The safety of the District intrusted to the protection of the General must and will be maintained with the best blood of the country; and he is confident all good citizens will be found at their posts, with their arms in their hands, determined to dispute every inch of ground with the enemy; and that unanimity will pervade the country generally; but should the General be disappointed in this expectation, he will separate our enemies from our friends. Those who are not for us are against us, and will be dealt with accordingly."

This address was signed by Thomas L. Butler, aid-de-camp to the General.

Fully aware of the importance of the advantage which the enemy had gained on the lakes, General Jackson lost no time in protecting every assailable point. He immediately ordered the battalion of men of color commanded by Major Lacoste, who must not be supposed to be of African descent, but who was an influential planter of Caucasian blood, to take post with the dragoons of Feliciana and two pieces of artillery, at the confluence of Bayou Sauvage or Gentilly and Bayou Chef Menteur, in order to cover the road to the city on that side, and watch the enemy's movements. Major Lacoste was also instructed to erect a close redoubt surrounded with a fosse, according to a plan drawn by Major Latour in compliance with General Jackson's orders. To Captain Newman, who commanded the fort of Petites Coquilles on the Rigolets, he sent these instructions: "Defend your post to the last extremity, and in case you should not be able to hold out, spike your guns, blow up the fort, and evacuate on Post Chef Menteur." Neglecting no means of assistance, however apparently unimportant, he authorized Captain Juzan to form into companies all the Choctaw Indians he could collect in the environs of the city, and on the other side of Lake Pontchartrain. He sent expresses to Generals Coffee, Carroll and Thomas, who were on their way, to accelerate their march. He earnestly charged General Winchester, who commanded at Mobile, to use the greatest vigilance in protecting that locality, as the enemy might endeavor to make an attack in that quarter.* He wrote to the Secretary of War, complaining of the neglect of the Federal Government in providing him with proper means of defence, but it was in no dejected mood, and not as a prepared excuse for anticipated disaster. "Should the enemy," he wrote, " effect a landing, I will, with the help of God, do all I can to repel him." He also acquainted the Secretary of War with the destruction of the gun-boats and with the taking of the Post of the Balize, including all the pilots, and a detachment of troops that was there stationed. He further informed him that the troops from Tennessee and Kentucky, although expected, had not yet arrived. "But," said he, " the country shall be defended, if in the power of the physical force it contains, with the auxiliary force ordered. We have no arms here. Will the Government order a supply? Without arms a defence cannot be made." Major Latour relates that during the summer, General Jackson, while yet among the Creeks, had made a requisition of a quantity of arms, ammunition, heavy cannon, balls, bombs, &c., to be sent to New Orleans; " but such was the fatality," observes the Major, " which happened to be attached to all the measures adopted for our defence,

---

* Latour's Historical Memoir, p. 65.

that it was not till the middle of January, 1815 (after the decisive battle of the 8th had been fought), that a very small proportion of what had been ordered arrived at New Orleans."

General Jackson had been so well pleased with the battalion of colored men under Major Lacoste, that it was thought proper to levy a new battalion of the same description. A colored man named Savary, who had distinguished himself in the wars of St. Domingo, by fighting ably and valiantly against those of his own race, undertook to form a battalion of refugees from that island, who had cast their lot with the whites when they had fled to Louisiana on being overpowered by their enemies. They had thus given a remarkable proof of attachment to the superior race for which it might have been supposed that they entertained feelings of hatred and envy. Savary obtained the grade of Captain, and was remarkably successful in his efforts to raise a company. The new battalion was soon formed, and its command was intrusted to Major Daquin, of the Second Regiment of Militia, who was one of the white refugees from St. Domingo. Michel Fortier, a native of New Orleans, and one of the wealthiest merchants of the city, was appointed Colonel, and took command of the whole corps of colored men, who, it must be understood, were all free. None had been taken from the slaves. Many of them had received a certain degree of education, and some possessed considerable property.

On the 18th of December, General Jackson reviewed such of his forces as were in New Orleans, and, on their being drawn up on their respective parades, the following eloquent address was read to them by Edward Livingston, one of his aids:

"To the Embodied Militia."

"*Fellow-Citizens and Soldiers:*

"The General commanding in-chief would not do justice to the noble ardor that has animated you in the hour of danger; he would not do justice to his own feelings, if he suffered the example you have shown to pass without public notice. Inhabitants of an opulent and commercial town, you have, by a spontaneous effort, shaken off the habits which are created by wealth, and shown that you are resolved to deserve the blessings of fortune by bravely defending them. Long strangers to the perils of war, you have embodied yourselves to face them with the cool countenance of veterans; and, with motives of disunion that might operate on weak minds, you have forgotten the difference of language and the prejudices of national pride, and united with a cordiality that does honor to your understandings as well as to your patriotism. Natives of the United States! They are the oppressors of your infant political existence, with whom you are to contend; they are the men your fathers conquered, whom you are to oppose. Descendants of Frenchmen! Natives of France! They are English, the hereditary, the eternal enemies of your ancient country, the invaders of that you have adopted, who are your foes. Spaniards! remember the conduct of your allies at St. Sebastian, and recently at Pensacola, and rejoice that you have an opportunity of avenging the brutal injuries inflicted by men who dishonor the human race.

"Fellow-citizens of every description, remember for what and against whom you contend—for all that can render life desirable—for a country blessed with every gift of nature—for property, for life—for those dearer than either, your wives and children—and for liberty, without which country, life, property, are no longer worth possessing—as even the embraces of wives and children become a reproach to the wretch who would deprive them by his cowardice of those invaluable blessings. You are to contend for all this against an enemy whose continued effort is to deprive you of the least of these blessings—who avows a war of vengeance and desolation, carried on and marked by cruelty, lust, and horrors unknown to civilized nations.

"Citizens of Louisiana! The General commanding-in-chief rejoices to see the spirit that animates you, not only for your honor, but for your safety; for whatever had been your conduct or wishes, his duty would have led, and will now lead him, to confound the citizen unmindful of his rights with the enemy he ceases to oppose.

Now leading men who know their rights, who are determined to defend them, he salutes you, brave Louisianians, as brethren in arms, and has now a new motive to exert all his faculties, which shall be strained to the utmost in your defence. Continue with the energy you have begun, and he promises you not only safety, but victory over the insolent enemy who insulted you by an affected doubt of your attachment to the Constitution of your country.

"To the Battalion of Uniform Companies.

"When I first looked at you on the day of my arrival, I was satisfied with your appearance, and every day's inspection since has confirmed the opinion I then formed. Your numbers have increased with the increase of danger, and your ardor has augmented since it was known that your post would be one of peril and honor. This is the true love of country! You have added to it an exact discipline, and a skill in evolutions rarely attained by veterans. The state of your corps does equal honor to the skill of the officers and the attention of the men. With such defenders our country has nothing to fear. Everything I have said to the body of militia applies equally to you—you have the same sacrifices to make—you have the same country to defend, the same motive for exertion—but I should have been unjust, had I not noticed, as it deserved, the excellence of your discipline and the martial appearance of your corps.

"To the Men of Color.

"Soldiers! From the shores of Mobile I collected you to arms; I invited you to share in the perils and to divide the glory of your white countrymen. I expected much from you, for I was not uninformed of those qualities which must render you so formidable to an invading foe. I knew that you would endure hunger and thirst and all the hardships of war. I knew that you loved the land of your nativity, and that, like ourselves, you had to defend all that is most dear to man; but you surpass my hopes. I have found in you, united to those qualities, that noble enthusiasm which impels to great deeds.

"Soldiers! The President of the United States shall be informed of your conduct on the present occasion, and the voice of the Representatives of the American Nation shall applaud your valor, as your General now praises your ardor. The enemy is near; his sails cover the lakes; but the brave are united; and if he finds us contending among ourselves, it will be for the prize of valor, and fame its noblest reward."

This exceedingly complimentary address to the men of color was expressed in language which, like that of the one he had sent from Mobile, did not meet with general approbation. True, the assistance of those men was of great importance, as it was thought that six hundred of them could be brought under arms, which was no despicable number, when the force we had to oppose to the enemy was so scant. But still it was deemed bad policy by many to address them in terms which were not in accordance with the inferiority of their social position, and which might tend to raise hopes that could never be gratified. There were some who predicted that it was a precedent of a dangerous nature. These apprehensions, in the course of time, have been strangely realized; for these two addresses of General Jackson to the men of color, and the use which he made of their services, were afterward seized upon by a far more barbarous foe than the English, as a pretext for putting in Louisiana the Blacks on a footing of equality with the Whites, and were even quoted as a justification for arming the slaves against their masters.

There was a small fort at the mouth of Bayou St. John on Lake Pontchartrain, whose garrison had lately been reinforced by a volunteer company of light artillery. On the 18th, immediately after the review, General Jackson ordered Major Plauché, with his battalion, to take command at that post. To all officers commanding detachments, outposts and pickets, he gave the following instructions: " On the approach of the enemy, remove out of his reach every kind of stock, horses, provisions, etc.; oppose the invaders at every point; harass them by all possible means." To the people at large he said: " The Major-General, expecting that the enemy will penetrate into this district in a few days, requests of the people of Louisiana to do their duty cheerfully, and bear the fatigues incident to a state of war as becomes a great people." The guard of the city was committed to a corps of veterans and fire-enginemen under the command of General Labatut. They were to occupy the barracks, hospitals and other posts, as soon as the troops of the line and the militia should be ordered into the field, and the following military regulations were established for New Orleans and its environs:

1. Every individual entering the city shall report himself to the Adjutant-General's office, and on failure shall be arrested and held for examination.

2. None shall be permitted to leave the city, or Bayou St. John, without a passport from the General or his staff.

3. No vessel, boat or other craft shall leave the city or Bayou St. John without such passport, or that of the Commodore.

4. The lamps of the city shall be extinguished at nine o'clock, after which, every person found in the streets, or out of his usual place of residence, without a pass, or the countersign, shall be apprehended as a spy and held for examination.

Captain W. B. Carrol, the officer who had the command of the navy-yard at Chefuncte, was ordered by Commodore Patterson to cause the brig Etna to ascend the bayou, and take a station opposite the unfinished frigate which I have already mentioned, in order to protect her in case of the approach of the enemy. Captain Carrol was further ordered not to suffer any boat to leave Chefuncte for Bayou St. John without a passport, and in the event of the enemy's entering Lake Pontchartrain, not to let the mail-boat pass.*

Certain offenders against the law, who were in prison, having begged to be released and to be permitted to

* Latour's Historical Memoir, p. 74.

meet the invaders of their country, their request was granted. In relation to individuals of this description, I have already recorded in the course of this History, that John Lafitte, his brother and his companions, had offered their services against the British before the arrival of General Jackson, and had been refused. He now waited in person on the General to renew his patriotic offers, and this time they were accepted. It must have been a highly interesting sight to witness the interview between the outlaw and the stern chief whom it was so difficult to move from any of his resolves. General Jackson had determined to have nothing to do with those he called "pirates and infamous bandits," unless it was to have them speedily hung, as he thought they richly deserved to be. He had said in an official proclamation, which was on record, "that no confidence was to be placed in the honor of men who courted an alliance with pirates and robbers." He had designated the Baratarians as "hellish bandits." He had emphatically declared that, unlike "the hateful and despicable Englishmen, he would not call upon either pirates or robbers to join him in the glorious cause he had to defend." Notwithstanding all this, the two men met—Jackson and Lafitte—and General Jackson, fettered as he was by his own words and acts, revised his decision, changed his mind, and henceforth trusted to the utmost Lafitte and his "bandits." Some of them he sent to assist in the defence of forts Petites Coquilles, St. Philip and Bayou St. John. The rest formed a corps under two of their leaders, Dominique and Beluche, and they were so far trusted by General Jackson as to be put in command of a portion of his artillery. They subsequently proved by their skill and bravery that General Jackson had been a correct judge of human nature on that memorable occasion. In the mean time, all judicial proceedings on the part of the

United States were, of course, suspended against those for whose heads rewards had been offered, and who, whatever their guilt might be, were anxious to endeavor to atone for it by dying, if necessary, on the field of honor.

At this time the Legislature, considering* that the present crisis would oblige a great number of citizens to take up arms in defence of the State and compel them to quit their homes, and thus "leave their private affairs in a state of abandonment, which might expose them to great distress," if the Legislature should not, by measures adapted to the circumstances, come to their relief, enacted :

"That no protest on any note, or bill of exchange, payable to order or bearer, or on any note, bill of exchange, or obligation for the payment of money, should or could be legally made, until one hundred and twenty days after the promulgation of the act.

"That, during the same space of time, no property, either movable or immovable, belonging to successions or bankrupts, or any property seized by virtue of any execution issued by the courts of justice, or justices of the peace of the State, should be sold; provided that this delay should not prejudice the holders or proprietors of the said notes, bills, obligations, or judgments, from demanding the interest which they would or might have legally demanded, if the said delay had not been granted.

"That, from and after the promulgation of this act, no civil suit or action should be commenced before any court of record or other tribunal of the State, nor should any execution issue or be proceeded upon; and that all proceedings in civil suits or actions, now pending before any such court or tribunal, should henceforth cease, and be suspended until the first of May, 1815.

"That no sale of lands or slaves which might be passed during the time this act was to remain in force, should have any effect to the prejudice of the rights of the creditors of the person making such sale; provided that such creditor or creditors who might have no existing lien on such property, should, before the first day of

---

* Preamble of the Act to grant delays in the cases therein mentioned, approved December 18, 1814.

June, make known to the person possessing the same the claim or demand they might have against the seller.

"That, for the purpose of preserving the securities of creditors under the suspension of judicial proceedings, the several judges and justices of the peace of the State, having original jurisdiction, should have the power of granting writs of sequestration, in case debtors, during such suspension, should attempt to remove their personal estate and slaves out of the jurisdiction of the courts, which property might be detained under sequestration on petition filed by the creditor whose allegations should be supported by his oath, or that of his agent or attorney, provided that the debtor might replevy his estate so sequestrated, on giving bond and security for the payment of any judgment against him, or any debt to be liquidated by judgment or otherwise."

On the motion of Louaillier, whose energy and patriotism seemed not disposed to slumber, the Legislature appointed a Committee,* at whose disposal they placed a sum of two thousand dollars for the relief of the militia of the State, seafaring men and persons of color in the service of the United States. The Committee were instructed to invite their fellow-citizens to make donations of woolen clothes, blankets, and such other articles as, in case of an attack, might be useful to the wounded.

On the 19th, General Carroll arrived with a Tennessee Brigade of two thousand five hundred men, and on the next day, General Coffee, with twelve hundred riflemen from the same State. This addition to the forces then existing in New Orleans diffused general confidence. Besides, all the measures already taken by the Commander-in-Chief, and the wonderful activity, energy and skill which he displayed, had produced such a change that the alarm which he had reprobated in a recent proclamation, and the gloom, despondency, distrust and apathy which have been described by Louaillier and others, had entirely disappeared. As a proof of this change, I can do no better than quote the language of

* Martin's History of Louisiana, p. 351, vol. 2.

Judge Martin, then acting as Attorney-General, and who afterward occupied with so much distinction, for more than a quarter of a century, a seat on the bench of the Supreme Court.

"At this period," says this highly respectable witness, whose testimony is entitled to so much weight, "the forces at New Orleans amounted to between six and seven thousand men. Every individual exempted from militia duty, on account of age, had joined one of the companies of veterans which had been formed for the preservation of order. Every class of society was animated with the most ardent zeal; the young, the old, women, children, all breathed defiance to the enemy, firmly disposed to oppose to the utmost the threatened invasion. There were in the city a very great number of French subjects, who, from their national character, could not have been compelled to perform military duty; these men, however, with hardly any exception, volunteered their services. The Chevalier de Tousard, Consul of France, who had distinguished himself and had lost an arm in the service of the United States during the Revolutionary War, lamenting that the neutrality of his nation did not allow him to lead his countrymen in New Orleans to the field, encouraged them to flock to Jackson's standard. The people were preparing for battle as cheerfully as if for a party of pleasure; the streets resounded with martial airs; the several corps of militia were constantly exercising from morning to night; every bosom glowed with the feeling of national honor; everything showed that nothing was to be apprehended from disaffection, disloyalty or treason."

Such is the description left us by this distinguished civilian, who himself was a participator in these scenes. Another, given by *the graphic pen of a military witness, is no less emphatic:*

"General Jackson had electrified all hearts," wrote Major Latour: "all were sensible of the approaching danger; but they waited for its presence undismayed. They knew that, in a few days, they must come to action with the enemy; yet, calm and unalarmed, they pursued their usual avocations, interrupted only when they tranquilly left their homes to perform military duty at the posts assigned them. It was known that the enemy was on our coast, within a few hours' sail of the city, with a presumed force of between nine and ten thousand men; whilst all the forces we had yet to oppose him amounted to no more than one thousand regulars, and from four to five thousand militia.

"These circumstances were publicly known, nor could any one disguise to himself, or to others, the dangers with which we were threatened. Yet, such was the universal confidence inspired by the activity and decision of the commander-in-chief, added to the detestation in which the enemy was held, and the desire to punish his audacity should he presume to land, that not a single warehouse or shop was shut, nor were any goods or valuable effects removed from the city. At that period, New Orleans presented a very affecting picture to the eyes of the patriot, and of all those whose bosoms glow with the feelings of national honor, which raise the mind far above the vulgar apprehension of personal danger. The citizens were preparing for battle as cheerfully as if it had been for a party of pleasure, each in his vernacular tongue singing songs of victory. The streets resounded with Yankee Doodle, La Marseillaise, Le chant du Départ, and other martial airs, while those who had been long unaccustomed to military duty were furbishing their arms and accoutrements. Beauty applauded valor, and promised with her smiles to reward the toils of the brave. Though inhabiting an open town, not above ten leagues from the enemy, and never till now exposed to war's alarms, the fair sex of New Orleans were animated with the ardor of their defenders, and with cheerful serenity, at the sound of the drum, presented themselves at the windows and balconies, to applaud the troops going through their evolutions, and to encourage their husbands, sons, fathers and brothers to protect them from the insults of their ferocious enemies, and prevent a repetition of the horrors of Hampton. The several corps of militia were constantly exercising from morning till evening, and at all hours was heard the sound of drums and of military bands of music. New Orleans wore the appearance of a camp; and the greatest cheerfulness and concord prevailed among all ranks and conditions of people. All countenances expressed a wish to come to an engagement with the enemy, and announced a foretaste of victory."

This was a transformation indeed, and it was all due to General Jackson! On the 20th, Governor Claiborne in a communication addressed to our Senator in Congress, Fromentin, in which he spoke of the approaching force of the enemy, remarked : " We, however, feel ourselves secure; there is but one sentiment, one mind; and old and young are alike prepared to meet and repel the foe."

The expedition against Louisiana was composed of 14,450 men, forming three divisions. Sir Edward M. Packenham was Commander-in-Chief. Major-General Samuel Gibbs commanded the First Division, General Lambert the Second, and General Keane the Third. The fleet which had transported these large forces, and which was to aid them with its co-operation, was of proportionate strength, under the command of Admirals Cochrane, Codrington and Malcolm. These three divisions of British troops were composed of regiments which had covered themselves with glory on many a battle-field, and which were again, on the banks of the Mississippi, to behave with their usual gallantry, but not with such success as they had met with elsewhere. The water-course through which they penetrated into Louisiana, and which is put down in old French maps as the River St. Francis, was also called by the people of the neighborhood " Bayou des Pëcheurs." By Admiral Cochrane and the other British officers it is designated in their dispatches under the name of Bayou Catalan, but it is more generally known as Bayou Bienvenu. It requires a short description, which I cannot give in more accurate words than in those which I shall borrow from *Major Lacarriere Latour, who says:*

"Through this bayou run all the waters of a large basin of a triangular form, eighty miles square in surface, bounded on the south by the Mississippi, on the west by New Orleans, on the northwest by Bayou Sauvage or Chef Menteur, and on the east by Lake Borgne, into which it empties. It receives the waters of several other bayous formed by those of the surrounding cypress swamps, and of innumerable little streams from the low grounds along the river. It commences behind the suburb Marigny at New Orleans, divides the triangle nearly into two equal parts from its summit to the lake which forms its basis, and runs in a southeasterly direction. It is navigable for vessels of one hundred tons as far as the forks of the canal of Piernas' plantation, twelve miles from its mouth. Its breadth is from one hundred and ten to one hundred and fifty yards, and it has six feet water on the bar at common tides, and nine feet at spring tides. Within the bar there is, for a considerable extent, sufficient water for vessels of from two to three hundred tons. Its principal branch is that which is called Bayou Mazant, which runs toward the southwest, and receives the waters of the canals of the plantations of Villeré, Lacoste and La Ronde, on which the enemy established his principal encampment. It was at the forks of the Canal Villeré and Bayou Mazant that the British ascended in their pinnaces, and effected a landing."

On the left bank of this Bayou Bienvenu, a mile and a half from its entrance into Lake Borgne, there was a village of Spanish and Italian fishermen, who used, through the canals which I have mentioned, to bring fish in their boats for the market of New Orleans. General Jackson, having given a general order for the obstruction of all the bayous below Manchac, was under the impression that the navigation of Bayou Bienvenu had been stopped. "This important service," says Jackson to the Secretary of War, in his Report of the 27th of December, 1814, "was committed, in the first instance, to a detachment from the Seventh Regiment, afterward to Colonel de La Ronde of the Louisiana Militia, and lastly, to make all sure, to Major-General Villeré, commanding the district between the river and the lakes, and who, being a native of the country, was presumed to be best acquainted with all those passes." But, from some unknown cause, General Jackson's intentions were defeated, and be it from the want of time, or of materials, or from neglect or oversight, it was very near producing the fall of New Orleans into the hands of the enemy. Major Villeré, however, the son of the major-general of that name, who was stationed at his father's plantation with a small force, knowing that the British were hovering on Lake Borgne, sent in a boat, on the 21st, a squad of nine white men, two mulattoes and one negro, to the village of the fishermen, for the purpose of ascertaining the movements of the enemy. Unfortunately these fishermen had been bribed by the British, to whom they used to carry all the information they could pick up in New Orleans, where they were permitted to come daily and without suspicion to sell their fish. Three of them had even piloted, on the 20th of December, a British captain disguised like one of them, as far as the bank of the river, whose water he boasted of having tasted with impunity on that occasion. He had thus the opportunity of making a full survey of that part of the country, and, on his report, the commander-in-chief determined to penetrate into Louisiana by Villeré's canal, the banks of which were found, at the time, to afford a firm footing for a landing-place in the prairie which skirts the lake, and a practicable highway to the river.

The village of the fishermen was inhabited by about thirty men. When the detachment sent by Major Villeré arrived there on the 21st, they found only one fisherman, who was lying in bed from sickness. The rest were said to have gone away the day before, in pursuit of their usual avocation, but in reality it was to serve as pilots to the British. The commander of the detachment immediately ordered a few men to proceed to some distance into the lake, and ascertain whether they could see anything of the enemy. They reported that they had ob served nothing of a suspicious nature. A sentinel, however, was posted at some distance in advance of the last cabin toward the lake for the rest of the night, which was already partly spent. The same vigilance was exercised during the whole day of the 22d; at regular intervals, men were sent as far as two miles into the lake, and they saw nothing. Toward evening, three men arrived in a pirogue from Chef Menteur. They had traversed a considerable portion of the lake, and their report was that no enemy was to be seen. That night a sentinel was again posted near the mouth of the bayou in advance of the cabins. During the preceding night, the numerous dogs that were in the village kept up an incessant barking from some unknown cause, but during the next night not a bark was heard. The reason was, as discovered subsequently, that the fisherman who pretended to be sick had got up and locked all the dogs in one of the cabins. Some time after midnight the sentinel heard a noise in the direction of the lake; he gave the alarm, and the detachment ran to their arms. At that moment, the moon was disappearing behind the horizon, but by its last gleams they saw five barges rapidly advancing up the bayou with glittering bayonets and some light pieces of artillery. The disproportion of numbers was so great that they feared to fire, and retreated for concealment behind one of the cabins. As soon as the five barges had shot ahead of this cabin,* seven men of the detachment jumped into a boat, to escape by the lake, but they were cut off before they could push the boat from the shore. Then they attempted with the rest of their companions to escape in different other ways, but they were, some at the time, and others in a few hours afterward, all made prisoners, with the exception of only

* Lacarriere Latour's Historical Memoir, p. 82.

one, named Rey, who, after three days of uncommon fatigue, hardships and perils over trembling prairies, bayous, lagoons and canebrakes, arrived at the post of La Bertonniere on the road leading from Gentilly to Chef Menteur, too late to give timely information; for the battle of the 23d had already been fought.

Among the prisoners was the son of a respectable planter, called Ducros. He was interrogated as to the number of troops in New Orleans and its environs. His reply was, that there were from twelve to fifteen thousand men in New Orleans, and from three to four thousand at the English Turn. The other prisoners agreed in the same statement, which seems to have been the result of a preconcerted understanding among them on the subject. The fishermen had represented the forces in New Orleans as being insignificant, but as they were men of low character, very little weight was attached to their declarations, particularly when contradicted by more reliable testimony, according, besides, with the conjectures of the British, which were founded on what they thought strong probabilities. If this picket had been established on the shore of the lake itself, instead of its being permitted to take more comfortable quarters at the fishermen's village on the bayou, our men would not probably have been surprised, as they would have commanded a full view of the lake. It is also to be regretted that Major Villeré had not posted several intermediate pickets between the lake and his own quarters on the river. This omission was rendered more fatal by the unforeseen treachery of the fishermen and by the failure to obstruct the bayou according to orders. As it was, it seems that a sort of fatality was attached to the spot, and militated in favor of the invaders. It is due to the memory of that high-minded and patriotic gentleman, Major Villeré, to state that a court-martial held on the 15th of March, 1815, acquitted him of all blame, although he did not choose to introduce any testimony in his favor.

At four o'clock in the morning of the 23d, the first division of the British troops under General Keane had arrived at the mouth of Villeré's Canal, where they rested some hours. The forces which were destined for the attack of New Orleans had been collecting at Ile Aux Poix, or Pea Island, at the entrance of Pearl River, since the 17th. General Keane's division, which had thus reached the mouth of Villeré's Canal on the morning of the 23d, had sailed the day before, at 10 A. M., from Ile Aux Poix. From the head of this canal to the skirts of the woods which lined the rear of Major-General Villeré's plantation, there was about a mile, and from the skirts of the woods to the river about two miles. At about half-past eleven in the morning, the British troops had emerged from the woods, and a detachment headed by Colonel Thornton had surrounded the house of General Villeré, in which was stationed a company of militia, who were all captured, with Major Villeré and another of the General's sons; but, a short time after his capture, the Major, with great presence of mind and cool intrepidity, availed himself of an opportunity to escape, and, jumping through a window, was soon out of the reach of the enemy, who fired at him many shots as he fled, and pursued him hotly for a considerable distance. It was during this pursuit that he is reported to have sheltered himself in the dense foliage of one of those magnificent live oaks so common in Louisiana, and an affecting anecdote is told of his having been compelled, with tears in his eyes, to kill at the foot of the protecting tree a favorite dog who had followed him in his flight, and who might have involuntarily betrayed his master.

At about 2 o'clock P. M. General Jackson was informed of the close proximity of the enemy and of the position he had taken. With his characteristic energy and clearness of perception he instantly decided to attack what he considered the vanguard of the invaders and give them no breathing-time. In half an hour after he had received the information, he had thrown forward, as far as Montreuil's plantation, one detachment of artillery with two field-pieces, one regiment, the 7th of the line, commanded by Major Peire, and a detachment of marines. Subsequently, General Coffee, who was in command of the Tennessee mounted riflemen encamped four miles above the city, the volunteer dragoons of Mississippi under Colonel Hinds, and a company of New Orleans riflemen under Captain Beale, were hurried forward in the direction of the enemy, and at 4 oclock P. M. they had taken a position on the Rodriguez Canal. At 5 o'clock, the battalion of men of color under Major Daquin, the 44th Regiment of the line under Colonel Ross, and Plauché's battalion of uniform companies, composed of the *élite* of the native population of the city, of French origin, and of Frenchmen who had made it their home, came from Bayou St. John at a running pace, and traversed the city with the utmost expedition, while the windows and balconies were lined with women, children and old men, who waved handkerchiefs, bestowed cheerful tokens of encouragement with tears in their eyes, and warmed the hearts of the citizen soldiers with all the demonstrations which anxious affection can suggest. Governor Claiborne was ordered, with the First, Second, and Fourth Regiments of Louisiana Militia, and a volunteer company of horse, with Carroll's Brigade of Tennesseeans, to take a position between the Colson and Darcantel plantations, in the plain of Gentilly, in order to cover the city in case of an attack on the side of Chef Menteur.

In the mean time the British had been leisurely establishing their camp on the bank of the Mississippi. Outposts and pickets were set out; toward the city a strong detachment was thrown out on which might fall back, in case of need, the advanced posts which had been stationed behind fences and ditches; and the Commanding General, having established his headquarters in General Villeré's house, before which he placed in battery the three small cannons he had brought with his division, determined to wait for his expected reinforcements, with his left resting on the river, and his right on the swamp and forest from which he had just emerged. About four o'clock, a picket of five mounted riflemen, belonging to the dragoons of Feliciana, who had been sent to reconnoitre, having approached the enemy with too rash daring, received a well-directed fire of musketry from a British outpost concealed behind a fence on the boundary of Lacoste's and Laronde's plantations, by which they had one horse killed and two men wounded. Colonel Haynes, with Hinds' Mississippi troop of horse, composed of one hundred and seven men, next made his appearance; but, not being able to proceed beyond the strong advance which the British had thrown forward on the road to the city, he could not make a correct estimate of the strength of the forces which had landed. It was then that a negro was arrested, who had been sent by the British with printed copies of a proclamation in French and Spanish, nearly in the following lines: "Louisianians, remain quiet in your homes; your slaves shall be preserved to you, and your property respected. We make war only against Americans." This was signed by Admiral Cochrane and Major-General Keane. The same proclamation had been stuck up on the fences all along the road below Laronde's plantation.* In confirma-

* Lacarriere Latour's Historical Memoir, p. 91.

tion of their benevolent intentions for the native population, they had begun to make it known by every means in their power that they had on board of their fleet, as a sort of friends, guests, or spectators accompanying the expedition, three natives of Louisiana, then officers in the Spanish army, and whose names were Reggio, Guillemard and Grandpré.

At about seven o'clock P. M., night having completely set in, a part of the British troops, exhausted by fatigue, had lain down in their bivouacs in perfect confidence and security; others in the camp, and some pickets of the outposts, had lighted up large fires, at which they were cooking their suppers. At that moment a vessel made her appearance, gliding down the river with the current. She was frequently hailed by the British sentinels, but no answer was returned. It was the United States armed schooner Carolina, commanded by Captain Henley, and having on board Commodore Patterson, who, in obedience to the orders of General Jackson, had hurried from Bayou St. John, where he had been examining the batteries erecting by the navy, under Capt. Henley. His instructions were to anchor abreast of the enemy's camp and open fire upon them, whilst General Jackson should attack them on land. With the aid of sweeps and a strong scope of cable the ship sheered close ashore at the designated spot, and anchored quietly and silently, whilst her manœuvres were examined with wondering curiosity by about a hundred of unsuspecting Englishmen who had taken her for a common boat plying on the Mississippi. Suddenly the stern and measured voice of command was heard, uttering distinctly these words: "Now, boys, give it to them for the honor of America." Then the vesssel poured a heavy fire from her starboard batteries and small-arms, which was returned most spiritedly by the enemy with Congreve rockets and musketry from their whole force, when, after about forty minutes of most incessant fire, the enemy was silenced; but although it was too dark to see anything on shore,* the fire from the ship was continued until nine o'clock, on what was supposed to be the enemy's left flank, whilst engaged with our troops, as I shall presently describe. No injury was done to the schooner, nor to any of her crew, whilst it is believed that the British suffered a loss of about a hundred men from her fire. It is strange that Major-General Keane, in his report to Major-General Packenham, should have stated that "he was attacked by a large schooner and two gun-vessels, which had anchored abreast of the fires of his camp." There could be no possibility of mistaking one ship for three, particularly by so cool and so brave a man as Colonel Thornton, who, "in the most prompt and judicious manner, placed his brigade under the inward slope of the bank of the river," and by so experienced an officer as Lieutenant-Colonel Brooke, who, "with the 4th Regiment, took shelter behind some buildings which were near at hand." General Keane adds: "This movement was so rapid that the troops suffered no more than one casualty." It is fair to presume that this statement was as erroneous as that which he made concerning the number of the attacking vessels.

Whilst this engagement was going on between the Carolina and the British, the land attack began as it had been preconcerted, it having been understood that the fire from the Carolina was to be the signal. At five o'clock, General Jackson had put himself at the head of all his available forces, which, he says in a dispatch to the Secretary of War, "did not exceed fifteen hundred men, with an artillery composed of only two six-pounders," although it appears that he had in reality two

* Commodore Patterson's dispatch to the Secretary of the Navy.

thousand one hundred and thirty-one men, of whom about eighteen hundred were engaged.* At seven o'clock, General Jackson had arrived near the enemy's encampment, which he estimated at three thousand strong, drawn up in *échelons* half a mile on the river bank, and extending their right wing nearly to the woods. The American General immediately made his dispositions to attack. He ordered General Coffee, who had about six hundred men under his command, to turn the British right, whilst with the residue of his force he would attack his left near the river, which was his strongest position. Colonel De Laronde, the owner of the plantation on which our troops were formed, and who therefore knew every inch of the ground, was ordered by General Jackson to accompany General Coffee as a guide. Colonel Piatt, quartermaster-general, with a company of the Seventh Regiment, commanded by Lieutenant McKlelland, was the first to drive the enemy's outposts on the high road near the river; but the British having received reinforcements, and being now about three hundred strong, resumed their former position, and kept up a brisk fire of musketry against our detachment, who as briskly returned it. Colonel Piatt received a wound in the leg, Lieutenant McKlelland and a sergeant were killed, and a few privates wounded. In the mean time, the Seventh Regiment of the line, coming to the support of the corps thus engaged, had advanced by heads of companies, parallel to the right resting on the high road near the river, until within one hundred and fifty yards, where it formed in battalion before the enemy, with whom it instantly exchanged a very brisk and close fire.† The Forty-fourth came up at the same time, formed on the left of the Seventh, which had begun the

---

* Latour's Historical Memoir, p. 106.
† Latour's Historical Memoir, p. 96.

action, and, on the right of the artillery, the marines were drawn up on the river bank. The engagement now became general on both sides.

The enemy, seeing that he could not make our troops give way, attempted to flank us on our left about three hundred yards from the river, and the Forty-fourth, commanded by Captain Baker, had already begun to oblique to meet the flanking column of the enemy, when Major Plauché's battalion, with Major Daquin's battalion of colored men, and a small number of Indians under Captain Juzan, advanced to meet the movement of the British, with their right a little in the rear of the Forty-fourth, and their left resting on the angle of Laronde's garden. The enemy's column, which had advanced silently in the dark to flank the Forty-fourth, almost stumbled within pistol-shot on the extremity of Daquin's battalion, and instantly a well-sustained fire began, and was warmly kept up on both sides. Plauchè's battalion, which was now between the Forty-fourth and Daquin's colored men, and therefore forming the centre, advanced in close column and deployed under the enemy's fire, which extended along our whole front from the bank of the river to Laronde's garden, where it formed a kind of angle or curve, on account of the attempted flanking movement. At this moment some confusion occurred, because some of the men of Plauché's battalion mistook the Forty-fourth for the English, and fired into them, but the disorder was soon repaired and already were our troops, carried away by their martial enthusiasm, clamoring from rank to rank to charge with the bayonet, and already was Plauché giving the desired order, when it was countermanded by Colonel Ross, who had the superior command of the two battalions, and who inopportunely came up in time to check this able and judicious manœuvre. Had it been made; had Plauché's battalion advanced to the charge, observes a competent military critic,* the enemy's retreat would have been cut off on his right, and he would have been completely surrounded by General Coffee's brigade, which was advancing in his rear, by Plauché's battalion on his left, Daquin's in front, and Laronde's great hedge of orange-trees on the right; so that most of that column would have been compelled to lay down their arms. As it was, the enemy gradually gave way, and retired in safety, favored by the darkness which was increased by a rising fog, and the smoke which a light breeze blew full in the face of our men. The British must have retreated with the conviction that their hopes of neutrality on the part of the French and of the natives of Louisiana were entirely frustrated, for they heard everywhere, during the engagement, the French words of command with which they had become so familiar on the European battle-fields. Whilst this was going on, our two six-pounders had been playing successfully upon the British, who attempted to seize them; but the marines rushed to the rescue on the right, and a close and rapid fire from the Seventh of the line, on the left, effectually kept them off. It was, however, a critical moment, for the British attacked with their usual impetuous gallantry. But General Jackson in person, in advance of all who were near him, within pistol-shot of the enemy, in the midst of a shower of bullets, was spiriting and urging on the marines and the men of the Seventh. Animated by such a voice, and with such an example before their eyes, our men could not but act heroically, and the enemy's charge on the artillery was repulsed with a heavy loss on his side.

While such were the operations on our right, General Coffee's Division on our left had attempted to execute

* Latour's Memoir, p. 110.

the movement of flanking the enemy's right near the woods and swamp. Arriving at a ditch and a fence separating Laronde's plantation from Lacoste's, on his way to Villeré's plantation on which Keane had established his camp, and which was next to Laronde's, General Coffee ordered his riflemen to dismount, and left one hundred of them to take care of the horses and have them ready when wanted. He then with the rest of his troops pushed forward, followed by Capt. Beale's Orleans Riflemen, and by the Mississippi dragoons under Hinds, numbering one hundred and seven men. But this detachment of cavalry, finding that it was impossible for them to manœuvre in fields cut up with ditches at very close intervals, remained drawn up on the edge of a ditch in the middle of Lacoste's plantation. Coffee moved on rapidly after having ordered his men to advance in profound silence, and to fire without order, taking deliberate aim with their utmost skill. He knew from experience what that skill was, and what destruction it would produce. He briskly drove the enemy's outposts before him until he met the Eighty-fifth drawn up on Lacoste's plantation, but on the first fire of the Tennesseeans, that regiment fell back toward their camp behind an old levee near the river. About that time General Coffee discovered that several parties of the enemy were posted among Lacoste's negro huts, and ordered his men to drive them out, which was soon effected. These negro huts long exhibited evident proofs of the unerring aim of the gallant Tennesseeans. In one spot particularly were seen half a dozen marks of their balls in a diameter of four inches, which were probably all fired at the same object. Some British soldiers were killed or taken prisoners in endeavoring to escape toward the woods, in a direction opposite to their camp; "so true was it," as observed by Major

Latour, "that the British troops were struck with consternation on being attacked in so vigorous, judicious and unexpected a manner." Captain Beale's Riflemen, having become separated from Coffee's Division, advanced within Villeré's plantation, penetrated into the very camp of the enemy, and after having made several prisoners, were attempting to rejoin General Coffee, whose movement had been steady from our left to our right, when unfortunately, through a mistake owing to the darkness of the night, some of these intrepid men fell among a strong body of British troops who were just arriving from the Lake, and moving rapidly from the woods toward their camp. They took those troops for Coffee's Division, and were captured. The rest of the company had succeeded in retreating to our lines with several prisoners.*

General Coffee's Division was now maintaining its position in front of the old levee on Lacoste's plantation, where it continued to keep up a galling and well-directed fire on the troops it had driven toward the river, and which it thus exposed to the fire of the Carolina. It was half after nine o'clock, and the enemy, who certainly had got the worst of the battle, finding his position, if not untenable, at least dangerous, fell back to his camp on Villeré's plantation, where he passed the night under arms and without fire. General Coffee, aware of the retreat of the enemy, and thinking it prudent not to remain in a position which exposed him to the broadsides of the Carolina, when, owing to the darkness, friends could not be distinguished from foes, fell back also, and took a position for the night in front of Laronde's garden, on the left of the other troops. When this engagement began on the plain extending from the river to the swamp, the second division of British troops

* Latour's Memoirs, p. 99.

were arriving at the fishermen's village. They were disembarking, when they heard the firing which announced to them that their first division was engaged. Admirals Cochrane and Malcolm, who were present, hurried the disembarkation of the troops, and pushed them forward with such rapidity that, in less than an hour, a considerable portion of them had reached the scene of action, in which they were enabled to take an active part. Although thus reinforced, the enemy, after retreating to their camp, were very much alarmed at the prospect of being cut off from the only communication they had through Villeré's canal with their fleet, and took every precaution to prevent such a disaster. Such were their apprehensions,* that they posted double lines of sentries, so that, in walking in a contrary direction, they met and crossed each other.

In this battle the British artillery consisted only of two three-pounders. They went into it with about eighteen hundred men, but with the reinforcements which they received before it was over, the British force engaged may be estimated at two thousand five hundred men. There was little method or system observed in the course of this action, on account of the obscurity of the night and the nature of the ground, which was intersected with ditches and fences. The difficulty on the part of the combatants to ascertain their respective positions naturally produced a good deal of confusion. There could not be any concert of action; detachments and small bodies of men, being accidentally separated from the larger corps they belonged to, acted for themselves according to circumstances. It was a series of duels between regiments, battalions, companies, squads, and even single men. There was a great deal of hand-to-

* Latour's Memoir, p, 100.

hand fighting, and much individual prowess was displayed. In such a *mêlée* many a lamentable mistake was made, and friends fired at friends on repeated occasions. Major-General Keane, in his report of the 26th December to the Commander-in-Chief, Sir Edward Packenham, says, particularly in relation to the conflict between his troops and Coffee's Tennesseeans and Beale's Orleans Riflemen: "A more extraordinary conflict has perhaps never occurred; absolutely hand-to-hand, both officers and men." He erroneously estimates General Jackson's forces in the battle at five thousand men, which may be accounted for on the ground that the British took every uniform company of the Louisiana militia for a battalion, as each of them wore a different uniform. But another error which cannot be so easily explained is, that he claimed to have remained master of the battle-field; which is not the truth. General Jackson, with much more correctness, says in his report to the Secretary of War dated on the 27th of December: "There can be but little doubt that we should have succeeded, on that occasion, with our inferior force, in destroying or capturing the enemy, had not a thick fog which rose about eight o'clock occasioned some confusion among the different corps. Fearing the consequences, under this circumstance, of the further prosecution of the night attack with troops then acting together for the first time, I contented myself with lying on the field that night." The fact is that General Keane's report is written with remarkable inaccuracy, for he states that the battle began at eight and ended at twelve, whilst it is beyond doubt that it began at seven and was entirely over at half-past nine. The time of its duration, according to his statement, is as apocryphal as the victory he claims. The loss of the enemy in this affair was about four hundred Ours was 24 killed,

115 wounded, officers included, and 74 prisoners—in all 213. The death of Colonel Lauderdale, of General Coffee's brigade of mounted riflemen, was particularly regretted. He fell at the post of honor, leaving the reputation of a brave and accomplished officer. In his official report on this battle, General Jackson uses the following language:

"In this affair the whole corps under my command deserve the greatest credit. The best compliment I can pay to General Coffee and his brigade, is to say, they behaved as they have always done while under my command. The 7th, led by Major Peire, and the 44th, commanded by Colonel Ross, distinguished themselves. The battalion of city militia, commanded by Major Plauché, realized my anticipations, and behaved like veterans; Savary's volunteers manifested great bravery; and the company of city riflemen, having penetrated into the midst of the enemy's camp, were surrounded, and fought their way out with the greatest heroism, bringing with them a number of prisoners. The two field-pieces were well served by the officer commanding them.

"All my officers in the line did their duty, and I have every reason to be satisfied with the whole of my field and staff. Colonels Butler and Piatt, and Major Chotard, by their intrepidity, saved the artillery. Colonel Haynes was everywhere that duty or danger called. I was deprived of the services of one of my aids, Captain Butler, whom I was obliged to station, to his great regret, in town. Captain Reid, my other aid, and Messrs. Livingston, Duplessis and Davezac, who had volunteered their services, faced danger wherever it was to be met, and carried my orders with the utmost promptitude. Colonel De Laronde, Major Villeré of the Louisiana militia, Major Latour of Engineers, having no command, volunteered their services, as did Drs. Kerr and Flood, and were of great assistance to me."

A detachment of the Louisiana drafted militia, three hundred and fifty men strong, under the command of Brigadier-General David Morgan, was posted at the English Turn, below Villeré's plantation. It was about one o'clock in the afternoon when they became aware of the appearance of the British on the bank of the river, one hour sooner than the news reached General Jackson. The men ran to their arms, and both privates and officers were clamorous to be led to meet the foe. But General Morgan, in the absence of orders from headquarters, and acting under the impression that it would be better to wait for some indication of what General Jackson intended to do, refused to gratify the importunities of his subordinates, whose impatience at their inactivity increased every hour. But when they heard the roar of the artillery and the discharges of the musketry, it became impossible to restrain their ardor any longer, and the consent of General Morgan to their marching instantly was hailed with universal acclamation. Full of enthusiasm, they pushed forward so rapidly, that the action was at the hottest when they arrived at the spot where the road which leads to Terre aux Bœufs diverges from the one which runs along the bank of the river, and they continued to advance, preceded by two pickets, the one on the high road, and the other in the fields near the woods. On reaching Jumonville's plantation, which preceded Villeré's plantation, our pickets which were coming up on the high road fired at a party of the enemy posted at a bridge thrown over a canal running perpendicularly to the road. The British, after having returned the fire, retired behind the canal. It was now half-past eleven, and the battle between Jackson's forces and Keane's had ceased for two hours. Vain efforts were made to reconnoitre, and to ascertain the strength of the enemy. The obscurity of the night was such, and the danger of falling into some ambuscade was so probable, that General Morgan ordered his battalion to take a position in a neighboring field, where it remained until about three the next morning, when General Morgan held a council of war, in which it was deemed expedient by the officers, on account of their ignorance of what had become of our main forces under General Jackson, to retreat to their former position at the English Turn, where they arrived early on the morning of the 24th, after fatiguing marches through mud and darkness. Several soldiers belonging to this battalion, who had just left the hospital to march against the enemy, had been obliged to remain behind from exhaustion, when the battalion retreated. At daybreak they could reconnoitre to some extent, and on their return they reported that in the same field in which the battalion had formed in the night, there was, within a short distance, a British corps of six hundred men,* who, probably thinking the Americans stronger than they were, had not dared to attack them.

The discharges of artillery and musketry were as distinctly heard in New Orleans, whilst the battle was going on, as if the event had taken place in its suburbs. Describing the condition of the city during this period of suspense and anxiety, Judge Martin, who witnessed all that occurred, who, in his History of Louisiana, does full justice to the patriotism displayed by the State during the invasion, and who treats with much asperity the attitude which, five days after the battle of the 23d, General Jackson assumed toward the Legislature, says:

"A report was spread that Jackson, before his departure, had taken measures and given positive orders for blowing up the magazine and setting fire to various parts of the city, in case the British succeeded in forcing his ranks. His conduct in this respect was considered by some as an evidence of his deeming his defeat a probable event. The old inhabitants, who had great confidence in the natural obstacles which the situation of the capital presents to an invading foe, and which they thought insurmountable if proper attention was bestowed, concluded that it had been neglected. They lamented that the protection of the city had been confided to an utter stranger to the topography of its environs,

* Latour's Memoir, p. 102.

and while frequent explosions of musketry and artillery reminded them that their sons were facing warlike soldiers, they grieved that the commander was an officer who, in the beginning of the year, had hardly ever met any but an Indian enemy, and whose inexperience appeared demonstrated by the rash step attributed to him. The truth or falsity of the report was sought to be ascertained by an application to the officer left in command at the city, who declined to admit or deny that the steps had been taken, or the order given.

"A circumstance tended to present the conflagration of New Orleans as a more distressing event than that of Moscow. The burning of the houses of several planters above the city, in 1811, was remembered, and apprehensions had been entertained that British emissaries would be ready, a short time before the main attack, to induce the slaves toward Baton Rouge, or Donaldsonville, to begin the conflagration of their owners' houses, and march toward the city, spreading terror, dismay, fire and slaughter; and a dread prevailed that Jackson's firing of the city would be taken by them for the signal at which they were to begin the havoc, even in case their apprehensions from British emissaries were groundless. The idea of thus finding themselves with their wives, children, and old men driven by the flames of their houses toward a black enemy bringing down destruction, harrowed up the minds of the inhabitants. Persons, however, who hourly came up from the field of battle, brought from time to time such information as gradually dispelled these alarms, and in the morning a sense of present safety inspired quite different sensations, and the accounts which were received of Jackson's cool, intrepid, and soldierlike behavior excited universal admiration."

If this is the truth; if General Jackson was informed, as he must have been by those who were thought to be interested in prejudicing his mind, that while he was confronting the enemy, and doing his best to save New Orleans from the direful calamity with which it was threatened, his conduct was considered by "some" in the city "as an evidence of his deeming his defeat a probable event;" and that the old inhabitants had come to the conclusion "that he did not know how to avail himself of the naturally insurmountable obstacles which the capital offered to an invading foe;" if they lamented that the protection of the city "had been confided to an utter stranger to the topography of its environs;" if, while frequent explosions of musketry and artillery reminded them that their sons were facing warlike soldiers, "they grieved that their commander was an officer who, in the beginning of the year, had hardly met any but an Indian enemy, and whose inexperience appeared demonstrated by the rash step attributed to him," in ordering the burning of the city, is it not to be supposed that, in this convulsive state of terror and distrust, those who thus suffered in mind may have used imprudent expressions, and been betrayed into the uttering of sentiments liable to misconstructions, which, being reported to General Jackson with the usual exaggerations in such cases, may have produced an impression that explains what he did subsequently, much to the mortification and resentment of those for whom it was perhaps but too natural that they should not be able to take a dispassionate view of the whole question?

We must also bear in mind that an application was made to the officer left in command of the city, at the time when the issue of the battle was doubtful, to ascertain what orders the commander-in-chief had given him. That officer very properly refused to reply to such inquiries. Who took such an extraordinary step? Could they be others than citizens of note and influence? Were they members of the Legislature, although acting in an unofficial capacity? Judge Martin does not say. What could be the object, when the battle was going on, in thus attempting to ferret out the orders left by General Jackson with the commanding officer in the city? Was it to facilitate those orders? Was it to obstruct them? However patriotic or guiltless the intention was, the act itself was highly injudicious; it was probably the mere consequence of extreme fear. If these facts were reported to General Jackson, they certainly must have produced an unpleasant impression, and may have revived some of those suspicions which he had unfortunately entertained, and which seemed lately to have entirely died away, although he must have made a large allowance for the thoughtlessness and imprudence of minds " harrowed up by the recollection of the burning of Moscow," by the apprehensions of a worse fate in consequence of a negro insurrection, or by the prospect of a Saragoza conflict from street to street in New Orleans, and of the horrors which might be perpetrated by an infuriated foe. All these circumstances we shall have to take into consideration, when we shall relate and appreciate, like an honest and truthful historian, an event which has produced so deep a feeling of resentment that, to the present day, a tone of anger frequently pervades the pages of history when treating of the subject. We shall endeavor to divest ourself of all passion and to do sober justice to all parties.

Well, however, might the citizens of New Orleans on the next morning feel their alarms of the preceding night "gradually dispelled;" well might, when rose the sun of the 24th, " a sense of safety have inspired them with quite different sensations;" well might " the accounts which they received of Jackson's cool, intrepid and soldierlike behavior have excited universal admiration;" for the battle of the 23d had saved Louisiana. Jackson had accomplished all that he wanted; he had successfully opposed his raw troops to far-famed veterans, and gloriously administered to his undisciplined and new-fledged soldiers the baptism of fire. The result was that they now had confidence in him and in themselves. He had stunned the enemy by giving him a sudden and unexpected blow which made him reel back. He gained time by it—the time which he needed to fortify, and receive reinforcements. He made the enemy believe that he was stronger than he was, caused him to hesitate, and inspired him with doubts and apprehensions which he did not entertain before. The British now felt that there were no despicable obstacles before them. If General Jackson had wavered, if he had not marched to attack the foe with such well-devised impetuosity, it is not improbable that at daybreak, on the 24th, the two divisions of the British troops, having operated their junction and being five thousand strong, would have marched against New Orleans, which was situated in an open plain without the shadow of any fortification. General Jackson could at best have brought into the field no more than an equal number of men to those of the British, who, in broad daylight, would at a glance have seen the small number of badly-armed militia they had to contend with. Most of the militia were unprovided with bayonets, that terrible weapon which the highly disciplined troops of Great Britain would have used with its usual efficacy. It is not, therefore, too much to say that, according to all human probabilities, the British would have won the day, and the consequences of such a disaster can easily be appreciated.

Fortunately, General Jackson gave them no such chance. He fought the battle of the 23d under circumstances which permitted him to hope for the victory which he gained. After that victory he acted with consummate prudence. Aware of the necessity of immediately assuming a position where he might throw up intrenchments, at 4 o'clock in the morning, after having passed the night on the battle-field, he fell back about two miles nearer to the city, where he determined to remain encamped behind a canal known as the Rodriguez Canal, and wait there for the arrival of the expected

Kentucky militia and other reinforcements. "As the safety of the city," wrote Jackson to the Secretary of War, " will depend on the fate of this army, it must not be incautiously exposed."

Governor Claiborne, in the relation* which he sent of this affair to Governor Blount of Tennessee, rendered full justice to the Louisianians and to the patriotic concord which existed among all the troops: "The enemy," he said, "suffered considerably, and, but for the darkness of the night which caused some little confusion in our ranks, the affair would have been decisive. The Tennessee troops equal the high expectations which were formed of them. It is impossible for men to display more patriotism, firmness in battle, or composure under fatigue and privations. The Louisianians also deserve and will receive the highest approbation. We are united as one man, and a spirit prevails which insures our safety."

* Claiborne to Gov. B ount of Nashville, Dec. 30, 1814.

CHAPTER X.

GOVERNOR CLAIBORNE'S ADMINISTRATION — BLOWING UP OF THE CAROLINA — BATTLE OF THE 28TH OF DECEMBER — BATTLES OF THE 1ST AND 8TH OF JANUARY — DEFEAT AND RETREAT OF THE ENEMY — PUBLIC REJOICINGS IN NEW ORLEANS.

1814—1815.

GENERAL JACKSON, on falling back two miles toward the city, left the Mississippi mounted riflemen, the Feliciana dragoons and the Seventh Regiment of the line near Laronde's plantation, in order to watch the enemy's movements. Early on the morning after the battle, the enemy was seen to be drawn up and to have thrown forward strong detachments, as if he had expected a renewal of the late attack; but, about eight o'clock, the British, discovering no probability of such an event, broke their line and returned to their encampment, after having taken, however, all the precautions which military foresight suggested. A strong body of British troops were posted behind the principal ditch on Lacoste's plantation, and their advanced pickets covered their whole front, extending from the high road near the river to the woods and swamps.

In the mean time the American troops were actively engaged in widening and deepening the Rodriguez Canal. The two four-pounders which had already done such good service in the late battle were mounted, in order to command the high road, behind the embankment thrown up; and the levee which confined the waters of the river to their channel was cut for the purpose of overflowing the ground in front. A sufficient quantity of water was let in to render the road impracticable for troops,* but unfortunately this measure proved of very little efficiency, for the river suddenly subsided, and the water retired from the inundated road. The enemy, however, showed no disposition to advance, and although Major Hinds, with his cavalry, frequently deployed in his sight, and although many reconnoitering parties were sent forward and close to his lines, he could not be tempted out of his position. But, apparently inactive, the British were not wasting their time, or enjoying any unseasonable repose; they were landing more troops, artillery, stores and provisions.

On the 25th, the commander-in-chief, Sir Edward Packenham, Wellington's brother-in-law, who had acquired some military renown, and who, it was said, had been promised an Earl's coronet as the future reward of his expected conquest of Louisiana, arrived and took command of the army of invasion. On the next day, the 26th, the enemy was employed day and night in erecting a battery near the upper line of Villeré's plantation, for the purpose of firing at the schooner Carolina, which, immediately after the battle of the 23d, had moved to the other side of the river, where she had been joined by the Louisiana. It was evidently of extreme importance for the British to destroy these two vessels, which otherwise, by firing at their left flank, would so effectually interfere with their operations against Jackson's lines, and which would be so serious an obstacle, if they deemed it expedient to cross the river; in prevision of which event, General Jackson had ordered a great quantity of powder stored on the right bank opposite the city to be put on board of a vessel, with

* Latour's Memoir, p. 113.

a view to its transportation to Baton Rouge in case of necessity.

Whilst General Jackson was giving all his attention to the strengthening of his position in front of the enemy, there came an alarming report that some British troops had landed at Chef Menteur. The report was credited at first, because the prairies of that locality were at that time very dry, and some British sailors had been seen and pursued in them by our soldiers. Probably to facilitate their escape, these sailors had set those prairies on fire, and given rise to this report of the landing of the enemy in that direction. Some excitement and some movements of troops were produced by this false alarm, but the truth being soon discovered, all apprehensions were dispelled.

Thinking that the forces of General Morgan were no longer necessary at the English Turn, General Jackson ordered him to evacuate that post, to cross the river with his artillery, and to take a position opposite our lines. He also caused the levee to be cut at Jumonville's plantation, below the British camp, as near as possible to it, and within musket-shot of the advanced sentries. If the river had continued to rise, as it promised to do, this operation would have made an island of the enemy's encampment, because trenches from the river had been opened in its front, as already stated, and the British would have been compelled to resort to their boats, and evacuate without being able to attack the American lines. But the river not rising as expected, this measure had the reverse of the desired result, for instead of introducing a sufficient quantity of water to injure the British, it let in barely the volume of water which was necessary to fill up the canals and bayous leading to Lake Borgne, and to facilitate the enemy in bringing up his heavy artillery.

Captain Henley, the Commander of the Carolina, had not suffered to pass unnoticed the preparations made to destroy his vessel, and had made every effort to move her higher up the river and near General Jackson's camp. The wind was adverse, and the current was too rapid to propel the ship by warping, although the attempt was made. At daylight on the morning of the 27th, the enemy* concentrated on the Carolina the fire of a battery of five guns, from which they threw shells and hot-shot. The vessel returned the fire with a long twelve-pounder, which was the only one on board that could reach across the river, the remainder of her battery being light twelve-pound carronades. The wind, being very light, rendered it impossible for her to get under way. The engagement was very short, hardly more than fifteen minutes, the British firing with extraordinary accuracy. Their second shot lodged in the schooner's main-hold, under her cables, and set her on fire. Finding that red-shot were passing through her cabin and store-room, which contained a considerable quantity of powder, that her bulwarks were all knocked down, that the fire was increasing, that the vessel was in a sinking condition, and expecting at every moment that she would blow up, Captain Henley, a little after sunrise, reluctantly gave orders for the crew to abandon her, which was effected with the loss of one killed and six wounded. So rapid was the progress of the fire, that every article of clothing belonging to the officers and crew was lost, and the men had hardly got on shore when she blew up, to their extreme mortification. The British, having accomplished this success, now directed their fire against the Louisiana, which it was so important for us to preserve, as she was the only remaining armed vessel on the river, but her preservation was rendered

---

* Henley to Commodore Patterson, Dec. 28.

more difficult from the fact of her having her powder magazine above water. Fortunately her commander succeeded in having her safely towed up beyond the range of the enemy's guns.

Notwithstanding our falling back to the Rodriguez Canal, our outposts had still continued to occupy Laronde's plantation, and every day saw our reconnoitering parties extending as far as the British lines. Major Hinds, with his cavalry, was constantly in the field molesting the enemy, with whose pickets and outposts ours exchanged shots almost without intermission, and the 7th Regiment of the line, which had been thrown forward to support our pickets, lost no opportunity to harass the foe. But in the evening of the 27th, the British came forward with such a superiority of force, that we had to fall back. They occupied Bienvenu's and Chalmette's plantations, and, during the night, it was discovered that they were engaged in erecting several batteries on the bank of the river. There was therefore every indication of an action for the next day, and our troops prepared for it with martial alacrity. Early in the morning, on the 28th, the enemy commenced hostilities, as was anticipated, and advanced in serried columns on the high road, driving in our advanced posts.* He was preceded by several pieces of artillery, some of which played on the Louisiana, and the others on our lines, which had only five pieces in battery. The Louisiana suffered the enemy's columns to advance a considerable distance without attempting to check them, but as soon as they had come as near as her captain desired, she opened on them a tremendous fire, which was briskly returned, but their guns were silenced by the combined fire of the Louisiana and of our lines, which soon dismounted one of the field-pieces they had put in battery

* Latour's Historical Memoir, p. 119.

on the high road. So destructive was the fire of our artillery from the ship and from our intrenchments, that the British columns broke, dispersed, and fell back to Bienvenu's plantation, where they took shelter under some buildings, after having abandoned the several batteries they had established on the bank of the river in the preceding night, and suffered a loss of two to three hundred men. The casualties in Jackson's lines consisted of seven men killed and ten wounded. The Louisiana had but one man slightly wounded, and she was struck under her bowsprit by a red-shot, but without much damage. The lives of the few men whom we lost would have been saved, if Colonel Henderson, of the Tennessee Division under Carroll, had not, in executing a manœuvre, committed an error which proved fatal to himself. He had been ordered by General Carroll to take a detachment of two hundred men, and with that force to dislodge some of the light British troops who were posted behind a fence and a ditch, and whose fire was beginning to be a serious annoyance. His order was to file along the woods, and turn the British by moving to the left between the woods and the fence; but instead of moving to the left, he moved to the right, leaving the fence between him and the woods. Thus covered by the fence, the enemy opened on our detachment a well-directed fire, which killed Colonel Henderson and some of his men, forcing the rest to fall back. In an account given of this affair to the Secretary of War, General Jackson said: "I lament that I have not the means of carrying on more offensive operations. The Kentucky troops have not arrived, and my effective force at this point does not exceed three thousand. Theirs must be at least double; both prisoners and deserters agree in the statement that seven thousand landed from their boats."

The British pretend to have intended merely a demonstration on that day, or a sort of feigned attack, to test our spirit and strength. If such was their intention, they must have been satisfied by their experiment that we were determined to defend our homes to the utmost, that our artillery was served with remarkable skill, promptitude and precision, and that their marching, deploying and forming in order of battle, far from eliciting on our part the slightest evidence of wavering, hesitation or intimidation, brought out the proof that our military organization was excellent, and that they had to expect the most obstinate resistance from the valor, patriotism and ability which defended the avenue to New Orleans. They were also much disappointed as to the effect of their Congreve rockets, which they used largely on that day. They thought that the very noise which accompanies the course of those rockets through the air would strike terror into the Americans, who had never before seen that kind of missile. But they discovered that we had very soon grown accustomed to its harmless explosions, for we were not long in ascertaining that it was more formidable in sound than in anything else. The fact is that these rockets, although used with the utmost profusion, only wounded ten men and blew up two caissons during the whole campaign.

General Jackson does not appear to have been of opinion that this affair of the 28th was a mere demonstration, as English writers affirm, for in his dispatch of the 29th to the Secretary of War he said: " Emboldened by the blowing up of the Carolina, the enemy marched his whole force the next day up the levee, in the hope of driving us from our position, and, with this view, opened upon us, at the distance of about half a mile, his bombs and rockets. He was repulsed, however, with considerable loss. Commodore Patterson, in his dispatch to the Secretary of the Navy, endorses General Jackson's opinion, for his words are: "The enemy drew up his whole force, evidently with an intention of assaulting Genersl Jackson's lines, under cover of his heavy cannon; but his cannonading being so warmly returned from the lines and ship Louisiana, caused him, I presume, to abandon his project, as he retired without making the attempt." He added that, "although the crew of the Louisiana was composed of men of all nations (English excepted), taken from the streets of New Orleans not a fortnight before the battle, yet he had never known guns better served, or a more animated fire than was supported from her." But whatever it was, a feint, a demonstration, or an intended attack which had miscarried, the affair of the 28th turned out to be a mere artillery duel, which lasted seven hours, and which terminated gloriously for the Americans.

It was on this day, the 28th of December, toward noon, that members of the Legislature were prevented by an armed force from meeting as usual in the State House in the city, and although that interference was but momentary, and the result of error and misconstruction, it nevertheless produced the deepest sensation, and an excitement which, for a long time, it was found impossible to allay, whenever this event became a subject of discussion, or even reference. We shall postpone its consideration, in order not to interrupt the thread of military operations.

Encouraged by the results of the fire kept up by the Louisiana, on the 28th, against the flank of the enemy, Commodore Patterson, during the night of the 29th, had brought down from the New Orleans Navy Yard, and mounted in silence a twenty-four-pounder on the right bank of the river, in a position where it could most annoy the enemy when throwing up works on the levee or in the fields. On the 30th, he opened upon the British with this twenty-four-pounder, which drove them from their works, whilst the ship Louisiana was firing at the same time upon their advanced guard, who retired from the levee, and sheltered themselves behind buildings and some epaulments which had been raised for their protection.

Some other works of defence were erected by us on the right bank of the Mississippi; among which was the conversion of a brick-kiln, opposite the city, on the very margin of the river, into a redoubt, of which Captain Henley, of the late Carolina, took command. A fosse twenty-five feet wide was dug all around it, and the earth from it was used to form a very steep glacis from the summit of the wall, serving as a parapet to the brink of the fosse. A palisade extended along its whole length on the inside. This redoubt was furnished with a small powder magazine, and was mounted with two twenty-four-pounders. Its battery commanded at once the high road and the river.*

Back of Jackson's lines on the Rodriguez Canal, there was another canal on the Piernas plantation, which communicated with Bayou Bienvenu. As it was possible for the enemy to ascend this bayou up to the mouth of the canal, and by that canal to penetrate to his rear, General Jackson had an advanced post stationed at the spot where the canal empties into the bayou, and ordered the First Regiment of Louisiana Militia, under Colonel Déjean, to take a position in the wood on the bank of the canal, with intermediate posts to its connection with Bayou Bienvenu.

Every day, the Louisiana dropped down to the station which she had occupied during the engagement of the

---

* Latour's Historical Memoir, p. 125.

28th, annoyed the enemy greatly by her fire, and returned every night to a safe position up the river.

Every precaution was taken to guard against any attempt which the enemy might make to turn our left, which rested on the wood and swamp. Colonel Haynes, Inspector-General, accompanied by intrepid hunters and pioneers, was kept actively engaged in reconnoitering in that direction, and in looking to the safety of our lines.

On the 30th, in the morning, some reinforcements came from the Acadian coast, whither Major-General Villeré, commanding the First Division of Louisiana Militia, had been sent to forward their arrival. He made his appearance at the head of three hundred men, who encamped back of our lines, and he subsequently took the command of the troops stationed on the Piernas Canal. On that day, Major Hinds was sent reconnoitering toward the advanced posts of the enemy. He performed that duty with much intrepidity, and returned with several of his dragoons wounded. In the mean time, we were strengthening our lines with the utmost expedition, and a patriotic rivalry prevailed among the several corps as to which of them would make the greatest show of work done, and done skillfully and efficiently, although they were composed of men very few of whom were used to manual labor. Our batteries were increasing rapidly on the left, right and centre, and the centre batteries particularly, which were of heavy metal, galled the enemy without discontinuance. It being discovered that he was throwing up a redoubt toward the woods, a thirty-two-pounder commanded by Lieutenant Crawley, and a twenty-four-pounder under Captain Dominique, one of the Baratarians, were directed against it with splendid effect. Notwithstanding the great distance, most of the balls struck the parapet, demolishing the works and killing many men. Meanwhile, the marine battery established by Commodore Patterson on the right side of the river was playing with efficacy on the camp and outposts of the enemy. To meet our galling fire, the British attempted, without much success, an innovation in the art of war, which was the erection on the levee of a battery with hogsheads of sugar, in front of Bienvenu's house. It was evident, besides, that they were engaged in many other preparations, and deserters reported that considerable reinforcements were expected shortly, and that heavy artillery was on the way to batter down our breastworks.

From all accounts* it appears that, at that time, the British troops of the line amounted to between nine and ten thousand men. Their hospitals were established in the buildings of Jumonville's plantation, where some black troops which they had, and which like all black troops proved of no account, were stationed; the headquarters of the Commander-in-Chief were in General Villeré's house. All the horses of the neighboring plantations had been swept into the British camp, and the best appropriated to the use of the officers of the staff. The rest served to mount a squadron of dragoons, or draw the artillery. The British extended their reconnoitering parties down the river as far as Philippon's plantation, where they established a post of black troops, which remained there in a kind of frozen torpidity until the final evacuation of the country. It follows, of course, that all the cattle of the planters within the reach of the beef-loving and beef-eating Englishmen were entirely destroyed. These predatory excursions of the enemy were pushed with lamentable effect as far as the English Turn, and the farthest end of that section of the country known under the appellation of Terre aux Bœufs, "land of oxen," in the present parish of St. Bernard.

* Latour's Memoir, p. 125.

As there was a strong apprehension of an attempt on the part of the enemy to turn our lines on the left, great efforts were made to prolong them as rapidly as possible into the wood, to the most impassable part of the swamp; but fortunately the enemy seems to have entertained a kind of salutary terror of that very wood and swamp, and had for it a very good reason. He apprehended that every tree, bush, or other place of concealment might hide from his view the unerring Tennesseean rifle, which already had scattered death and dismay among the British sentinels and advanced posts. Even while confining himself to open fields, he had experienced that it was with much difficulty that he could keep sentries at some distance from his camp, without exposing them to certain death from the unsparing Tennesseean bullet, which never missed its aim. The dress of those riflemen consisted chiefly of a kind of brown homespun tunic, which the British called in derision a "dirty shirt," and the color of which prevented the wearer from being distinguished from the bushes and tall dry grass through which he crept like a snake, now in ditches, now behind fences, toward the British outposts. The Tennesseeans were fond of indulging in these expeditions, which they called "hunting parties," and it is related that one of them, on such an occasion, made himself famous by killing successively three sentinels who had been posted one after the other at the same spot, carrying away, every time, the arms and accoutrements of these unfortunate victims, as proofs of his exploits. The British at last gave up the idea of keeping a sentinel at that fatal spot. By such daily occurrences in the open fields they were admonished not to hazard themselves into the woods and swamps, on the skirts of which they never even ventured to post a single picket throughout the whole campaign; such was the dread which they entertained of the "dirty shirts!"

They bitterly complained of this mode of warfare as being contrary to the usages of civilized nations, and as no better than assassination; but we shall reply to this accusation in the words of one of their most distinguished historians, who thinks that, in a war of invasion, when every man among the invaded is a soldier, and a soldier fighting for his nearest interests, when his own trees have been cut down, his own corn has been burnt, his own house has been pillaged, his own relations have been killed, he cannot entertain toward the enemies of his country the same feelings with one who has suffered nothing from them, except perhaps the addition of a small sum to the taxes which he pays.*

"In such circumstances," says Macaulay, "men cannot be generous. They have too much at stake. It is when they are, if I may so express myself, playing for love, it is when war is a mere game at chess, it is when they are contending for a remote colony, a frontier town, the honors of a flag, a salute, or a title, that they can make fine speeches, and do good offices to their enemies. The Black Prince waited behind the chair of his captive; Villars interchanged repartees with Eugene; George II. sent congratulations to Louis XV., during a war, upon occasion of his escape from the attempt of Damien; and these things are fine and generous, and very gratifying to the author of the Broad Stone of Honor, and all the other wise men, like him, who think that God made the world only for the use of gentlemen. But they spring in general from utter heartlessness. No war ought ever to be undertaken but under circumstances which render all interchange of courtesy between the combatants impossible. It is a bad thing that men should hate each other, but it is far worse that they should contract the habit of cutting one another's throat without hatred. War is never lenient but where it is wanton; when men are compelled to fight in self-defence, they must hate and avenge; this may be bad, but it is human nature, it is the clay as it came from the hand of the potter."

The Tennesseeans were the clay as it came from the hand

---

* Macaulay's Essays, Milford's Greece, vol. 3, p. 373.

of the potter. They knew nothing about the code of chivalry and the customary rules of conducting war according to the artificial standard of European courtesy. They only knew that their country was invaded, and that their sacred duty was to kill the invader by day or by night, as long as the foe had arms in his hands and did not sue for mercy, whether they shot at him from an ambuscade, from behind a tree, a bush, or a parapet, or whether they met him, face to face and hand to hand, in the open field. Those untutored, rough-hewn and uncouth patriots were right, and may " war to the knife and the knife to the hilt " be forever the motto of every Louisianian whenever his native State shall be invaded!

The British, however, were industriously preparing to put an effectual stop to this shooting down of their sentinels, by making a bold effort to drive Jackson out of his intrenchments, and, on the 31st, having succeeded, notwithstanding the fatal effects of our batteries, in completing the redoubt which they had begun on our left near the woods, and which had been demolished once or twice, they opened a fire on our advanced posts which had been skirmishing with their own; in consequence of which, a spirited cannonade was kept up on both sides for the greater part of the day. The Louisiana, as usual, joined her fire to that of our lines and again drove the enemy to shelter. We suffered very little from this artillery encounter, whilst we inflicted several casualties on the enemy, among which he had to regret the loss of an officer of engineers, who was reconnoitering and was killed by our advanced posts.

The year was closing with plain indications from the movements of the enemy that he meditated an immediate attack. When night came and when he could labor with comparative security, noises were heard which manifested to us that he was working at platforms and mounting pieces of cannon, and it was subsequently discovered that he had, during that night, constructed two batteries behind a ditch on Chalmette's plantation, at the distance of about six hundred yards from our lines, and about three hundred yards apart. The one nearer to the river was about three hundred and fifty yards from its bank.

On the morning of the first of January there was one of those dense fogs which are so common in that season on the banks of the Mississippi, but, at 10 o'clock, when it cleared off, the enemy opened upon us a heavy cannonade proceeding from three batteries. The one which was mounted on the road near the river, and which played upon our right, consisted of two twelve-pounders; the next, acting against our centre, had eight eighteen-pounders and twenty-four pound carronades; and the last, on our left, eight pieces of cannon and carronades—in all twenty-eight guns. The missiles which they sent were accompanied with innumerable Congreve rockets. The first discharges of the battery on the road were directed against a house in which it was known that General Jackson had established his headquarters, and where he happened to be at that moment with his staff and other officers. In less than ten minutes, upward of one hundred balls, rockets and shells struck the house, and drove everybody out of so dangerous and exposed a situation. It is strange that, notwithstanding this sudden gush of fire and iron which swept over the house in an instant and surprised its tenants, notwithstanding bricks, splinters of wood and fragments of furniture were flying in every direction, not a death, not a wound was inflicted. Our reply was as fierce as the enemy's attack, although we had only ten guns to oppose his twenty-eight, and for an hour a hot cannonade was steadily continued on both sides; at the expiration of that time it became perceptible that the enemy's fire was slackening. It was, however, still vigorously kept up; but it was evident that ours was more precise and effective. "Yet," says the engineer, Major Latour, "every advantage was on the side of the enemy; his batteries presented but a narrow front and very little elevation on a spacious plain, the soil of which was from four to six feet below the level of our platforms; his gunners had for a target a line about one thousand yards long, the top of whose parapet was eight or nine feet higher than his platforms, whilst our guns might be said to have only points to aim at; and our balls could not rebound on so soft a soil. Our batteries were the principal object against which the enemy's fire was directed; but we were no less intent on demolishing his; for in about an hour's time our balls dismounted several of his guns, and when the firing ceased, the greater part of his artillery was unfit for service." It must also be kept in mind that his artillery was more than twice ours in number; it was, besides, well served, and was not without doing some damage by breaking the carriages of a twenty-four and a thirty-two pounder, with the foretrain of a twelve-pounder, and blowing up two artillery caissons. Some bales of cotton had been used to form the cheeks of the embrasures of our batteries, and, notwithstanding the popular tradition that our breastworks were lined with it, this was the only use which, on that occasion, was made of that great staple of our country. The enemy's balls struck those bales, scattered them in all directions and set them on fire.

The enemy's object seems to have been, on that day, to silence our artillery, make a breach in our lines and carry them by storm. His troops were observed to be in readiness, drawn up in several parallel lines between the batteries, prudently taking shelter in ditches, and waiting for the favorable moment to rush to the contemplated assault. When our cotton bales were knocked down in a blaze, when our two caissons with a hundred rounds in them blew up, a certain degree of confusion ensued. The enemy thought that the breach was made, and that the expected moment had come. He suspended his fire at once, and the troops ranged in the ditches, with those at the batteries, gave three loud cheers; but a simultaneous and well-directed discharge from the whole artillery of our lines dampened their enthusiasm, and informed them of the frustration of their hopes. From that moment the animation of the enemy's fire went on decreasing. In the mean time he had sent some platoons of sharp-shooters into the woods to ascertain if our left could be turned, but they were no match for the "hunters" of Coffee's brigade, and they soon fell back with a full conviction that nothing could be done in that direction. At noon his fire had become languid, and at one he abandoned his two batteries on our left and centre. There was but one remaining, that on the road, which, with feeble and expiring efforts, continued to throw a few balls and rockets until three in the afternoon, when it fell into an ominous silence. Then the British troops were seen retiring slowly and in apparent dejection to their camp.

Whilst this artillery engagement was going on with our lines, Commodore Patterson did not drop down the river as usual with the Louisiana, to fire at the flank of the British. He was now apprehensive of coming within range of their shot, having learnt from deserters that a furnace of hot-shot was kept in constant readiness at each of their batteries to burn her;[*] and the guns of two marine batteries on shore being of much greater effect than those of the Louisiana, the crew of the ship was

[*] Patterson to the Secretary of the Navy, January 2d, 1815.

withdrawn to man them. The Commodore was particularly desirous to preserve her from the hot-shot, as he deemed her of incalculable value to cover the army in case General Jackson should retire from his present line to those which he had thrown up in his rear. With his guns on shore he kept up, however, an intense fire upon the enemy, and although the balls from the British batteries went through his breastworks, and the shells fell in great numbers in and about his batteries, he had the good luck not to lose a single man, nor did his fire slacken a moment. Toward the evening the enemy called in all his outposts, as he had done after the engagement of the 28th; during the night his batteries were dismantled, and with much difficulty and fatigue his guns were removed by being dragged through mud and darkness, with the exception of five which had to be abandoned. On the next day, early in the morning, several parties of our men visited the deserted batteries, and witnessed the damage which had been done by our artillery. They saw pell-mell broken gun-carriages belonging to the navy, shattered carronades, barrels of powder, and a large quantity of cannon-balls and implements of artillery. The enemy's loss was estimated to have been heavy; ours was trifling in comparison, for it did not exceed thirty-four in killed and wounded, eleven of the former being persons who were going to or returning from the camp, and who were struck on the high road behind our lines.

On the day of this engagement, Major-General Thomas, commanding the Second Division of Louisiana Militia, arrived with five hundred men from Baton Rouge. As many of our men were destitute of arms, General Jackson ordered the Mayor of New Orleans to make domiciliary visits in that city, in order to ascertain what arms were in the possession of individuals.

The enemy, although defeated in his purpose, did not abandon the redoubt which he had erected near the woods, with the intention, probably, of guarding against an attack in that direction and protecting his pickets. On the contrary, he went zealously to work to increase its strength. That redoubt was of a quadrilateral form; two embrasures were made on the small front opposite our lines, but forming an angle with them. Each of the lateral fronts had likewise an embrasure in the middle, and that on the back had an opening twelve feet wide, serving as an entrance and covered by a traverse within the fort. Along the intervals between the embrasures above the ground ran banquettes raised three feet for the musketry.* The parapet, which was fourteen feet thick at the base, and nine at the summit, had battlements for the musketry on three aspects. A fosse from twelve to fifteen feet wide and three in depth surrounded this redoubt. Not only did the enemy retain possession of this fortification, but he soon began to erect another smaller redoubt in advance of this one, with an embrasure in each of its angles toward our lines. The British suffered considerably in constructing these works under the galling fire of our heavy guns which mowed down their men. At last the officer commanding the working parties bravely stood up on the parapet, and as soon as he perceived the flash of our guns he gave a signal to his men, who put themselves under cover.

On the 3d of January, during the night, General Jackson was informed that the enemy had ascended Bayou Bienvenu as far as the Piernas Canal, where he was landing in considerable force. This, if true, would have been a serious movement in our rear. General Jackson immediately dispatched two hundred men of General Coffee's Brigade, with the pithy order to attack the

* Latour's Memoir, p. 187.

enemy boldly and drive him into the bayou. With great promptitude, these men, although it was raining heavily at the time, and although they sank knee-deep into the mud, pushed on to the point indicated, where they found nothing but a dreary solitude whose silence was disturbed only by the croaking of frogs.

General Jackson, however, thought it prudent to ascertain whether there was any probability that the enemy would penetrate in that direction. In conformity with his orders, a score of active and intrepid woodsmen went down the Piernas Canal into Bayou Bienvenu as far as its junction with Bayou Mazant, occasionally climbing up trees on their banks to see if they could discover any enemy. When they approached* the junction of the two bayous they perceived that the British had established at that spot a fortified inclosure, or kind of breastwork, within which they had built magazines for stores, which were guarded by a strong detachment, and that they kept an advanced sentinel posted in a tree which commanded a view of the whole prairie and of the bayou. One man also discovered five small vessels ascending Bayou Bienvenu, with sailors looking out from the mast-head. These vessels, it seems, were on a scouting expedition, and, as they advanced, parties would come out of them and set on fire the tall prairie grass, in order to drive away any human being to whom it might offer a place of concealment. These precautions taken by the enemy were looked upon as indications that he was fearful of an attack in that direction, instead of meditating one against us—which would not have been an unfounded apprehension on his part, if we had been better supplied with boats and stronger in troops. In that case, we might have surprised his post at the

---

* Latour's Memoir, p. 140.

mouth of Villeré's Canal and endangered his communication with his fleet.

On the 4th of January we were highly elated at the arrival of two thousand two hundred and fifty Kentuckians, under the command of Major-General John Thomas and Brigadier-General John Adair, but, unfortunately, only five hundred and fifty of those men were properly armed. "Hardly," wrote Jackson to the Secretary of War, "one-third of the Kentucky troops so long expected have arrived, and the arms they have are not fit for use." It was more apparent than ever that the Federal Government had done nothing for the defence of Louisiana, and that so much imbecility, or neglect, was to be remedied by the genius of the Commander-in-Chief and by the patriotism of the invaded State. Both were certainly left, in a great degree, to their own resources. Not only were many of the militiamen totally unprovided with arms, but they were also destitute even of clothing, and yet the season was inclement, and the exposure and hardships to be incurred were of a nature to try the most robust constitution. The indefatigable Louaillier immediately obtained from the Legislature the appropriation of a sum of money which was put at the disposal of a Committee for their relief, and a considerable additional sum was procured by private subscription, making, with the amount voted by the Legislature, more than sixteen thousand dollars, with which blankets and woolens were purchased and distributed among the ladies of New Orleans, to be made into clothes. Within one week, twelve hundred blanket cloaks, two hundred and seventy-five waistcoats, eleven hundred and twenty-seven pairs of pantaloons, eight hundred shirts, four hundred and ten pairs of shoes, and a great number of mattresses, were made up, or purchased ready made, and distributed among those of our brethren in arms who stood most in need of them. On that occasion, as during the whole war, the women of Louisiana pre-eminently showed that patriotism and complete devotion which, on such emergencies, their sex so frequently exhibited in all ages of the world. An old widow and rich inhabitant of Attakapas, named Devins Bienvenu, after sending her four sons to the defence of New Orleans, wrote to Governor Claiborne that she sincerely regretted having no other sons to offer to her country, but that, if her own services in the duty of taking care of the wounded should be thought useful, notwithstanding her advanced age she would hasten to New Orleans for that purpose.* No less enthusiastic was a Miss Sauvé, then in the bloom of youthful beauty, when she replied to a British officer, made prisoner, who permitted himself to sneer at the admiration she expressed for the Tennesseeans: "Major, I had rather be the wife† of one of those hardy and coarsely clad, but brave and honest men, who have marched through a wilderness of two thousand miles to fight for the honor of their country, than wear an English coronet." These anecdotes are related as manifestations of feelings which were common to all the mothers, wives and daughters of Louisianians in the day of danger, and which, no doubt, have been bequeathed unimpaired to their present posterity.

Thus far the enemy had been completely foiled, and we gave him no repose in the intervals of his attacks. The boom of our artillery was constantly sounding in his ears, day and night, and our balls continued to carry destruction into his ranks. Wherever a group of four or five red-coats showed themselves, thither flew missiles of death. By this incessant cannonade we gained a double advantage: we exercised our gunners, and at the

---

* Latour's Memoir, p. 229.
† Alex. Walker's Life of General Jackson, p. 185.

same time interrupted the works of the enemy during the day, and his rest at night. His deserters were numerous, and by them we learned that Major-General Lambert had arrived with an expected reinforcement of troops, and that a general attack would shortly be made. For some days we had also observed that between the fleet and Bayou Bienvenu there was an unusually active communication. We, therefore, prepared to meet the coming conflict, which probably would be the one that would decide the fate of Louisiana. Reinforcements were sent to General Morgan on the other side of the river, and, at the confluence of the Piernas Canal and Bayou Bienvenu, a post of cavalry was established, to give prompt information of any occurrence in that direction.

On the 6th, we learned from prisoners that the enemy was digging out Canal Villeré and extending it to the river, in order to get a passage for his boats. On that day, and on the following one, there was more stir and bustle in the British camp than usual. Canal Villeré swarmed with soldiers and sailors, who, thick as bees, seemed to be dragging boats; bodies of troops were kept in motion, exercising or reviewing; and other preparations were on foot, which, even to an unmilitary eye, announced an approaching attack. To resist it, what was the condition of our lines, which were drawn within only five miles of New Orleans? On their extremity near the river, we had an unfinished redoubt with two six-pounders, and a shallow fosse without water in consequence of the fall of the river. The Rodriguez Canal, which had rather the appearance of a draining ditch than a canal, had been excavated, and the earth thrown on the left side, where had been laid that which had been originally dug out. A parapet running along that canal had been hastily constructed, and the other side of the canal, being but little elevated above the soil, formed a kind of glacis. To prevent the earth of the parapet from falling into the canal, it was lined with all the rails of the fences in the neighborhood. These works were done under unfavorable circumstances, by different hands, which were frequently changing in consequence of frequent mutations in the disposition of our troops, and during incessant rain. Much regularity and system could not therefore prevail, although there had been much good will to do right, and earnest exertions to accomplish all that could be done. Hence the parapet was in some places thicker and higher than at others, and sometimes twenty feet thick at the top, when it was only five feet high, whilst in other places the base was so narrow that it was easily perforated by the enemy's balls, although this defect was subsequently remedied. It is, therefore, wonderful that the heavy cannonade of the 1st of January, carried on by twenty-eight pieces, did not produce a disastrous effect.

The site of these lines, however, had been judiciously selected. They were established at a point where the cypress swamp which follows laterally the course of the river projected toward its bank, and left the least intervening space between the two, from Villeré's plantation up to New Orleans. The length of these lines was about half a mile, and after penetrating some distance into the swamp, they turned at right angle toward the city. The breastwork of that part of the lines which extended through the wood and swamp was not thicker than necessary to resist musketry. It was formed of a double row of logs,* laid one over the other, leaving a space of two feet which was filled up with earth. Along one part of the lines ran a banquette; in some parts the height of the breastwork above the soil was hardly sufficient to cover the men. These fortifications.

* Latour's Memoir, p. 147.

if they deserve such a name, were armed with only twelve pieces of artillery of various calibre, and were to resist the attack of an army of fourteen thousand regulars, belonging to the wealthiest nation of the world, and equipped with all the completeness which was to be expected from her resources. At the left extremity of the lines near and in the swamp were the hardy Tennesseeans of Carroll's and Coffee's Brigades, and a part of the Kentucky troops. It was there that they gave, without being conscious of it, a memorable example of those virtues which ought to characterize the soldier, and showed powers of endurance which surpassed their bravery, great as that was. There they waded in mud, knee-deep, during the day, and they slept on it at night in the best way they could. To make their quarters still more uncomfortable, it rained most of the time; the cold was pinching, and they were but indifferently provided with tents. But, although their hardships were extreme in these domains of the alligator; although the dreary sights around them were sufficient to produce some feeling of despondency; although the melancholy-looking cypress, hoary with the long gray moss of our Southern latitude, reared its gaunt, funereal form over their heads; although far distant from their home and all that was left there dear to the heart, yet not a word of wail, not a syllable of discontent did they utter. They showed heroic resignation, and even that strange kind of alacrity with which a noble heart braces up its energies to encounter uncommon dangers or sufferings. What is here said of the Tennesseeans is applicable to all our troops. They all exhibited the same qualifications; they were equal to the emergency; they more than met the exacting expectations of such a man as General Jackson; they were a unit; they felt, thought, and acted as men should, when the fire of an enemy's camp has been lighted in sight of those paternal roofs where throb with anxiety the hearts of old men, women and children. Hence it was that our lines, although weak in appearance, were strong in reality.

General Jackson was fully aware that, on the 6th, the enemy was preparing, as stated before, for a more serious attack than any he had yet made. But against what point was that attack to be directed? Was it against our lines on the left side of the river, or against General Morgan on the right side? All doubts vanished on the evening of the 7th, it having become evident that the enemy had made up his mind to storm our breastworks. With the aid of telescopes we discovered a number of soldiers making fascines and scaling-ladders · officers of the staff were riding about, and stopping at the different posts, as if they carried orders; the artillery was in motion; troops were marching to and fro; the pickets had been increased and stationed near each other; at sunset, the enemy's guards were reinforced, probably to cover his movements. When night came sounds were heard, the import of which it was not difficult to understand. Numbers of men were evidently at work in all the batteries; the strokes of the hammer were loud and distinct; and the reports of our outposts confirmed our conjectures. In our camp there was that composure which generally is the harbinger of victory, and which in our troops was the result of their confidence in their chief and in themselves. Officers and men were ready to spring to action at the first signal, and during the night, from time to time, fresh troops relieved those which had remained under arms. Our lines were defended by three thousand two hundred men, General Jackson having detached from the four thousand he had on hand eight hundred, to guard our camp, to protect the Piernas Canal, and for other purposes. In front of this small body of militia, and of a line of defence which would have elicited a smile of contempt from a European military man, were drawn up from twelve to fourteen thousand of the best troops of England, supported by a powerful artillery. There could hardly be a more unequal contest; but it was with no other feeling than a sort of stern cheerfulness that our troops surveyed this disproportion of forces.

A little before daybreak on the 8th the enemy began moving toward our lines, and our outposts came in without noise, reporting his advance. As soon as there was sufficient light for observation, his position was clearly ascertained, and he was seen to occupy about two-thirds of the space extending between the wood and the river. Immediately a Congreve rocket went up from the skirt of the wood. It was the signal for the attack. One of our batteries responded by a shot, and at the same moment the British, giving three cheers, formed into a close column of about sixty men in front, and advanced in splendid order, but with too slow and measured steps, chiefly upon the battery commanded by Garrigues Flaugeac, which consisted of a brass twelve-pounder, and was supported on its left by an insignificant battery with a small brass carronade, which could render but very little service on account of the ill condition of its carriage. These two batteries were the nearest to the wood, and against them the main attack was evidently directed. Flaugeac's battery opened upon the advancing column an incessant fire, indifferently supported by the small carronade on its left, and more powerfully on its right, by a long brass eighteen-pound culverine and a six-pounder, commanded by Lieutenants Spotts and Chauveau, and served by gunners of the United States artillery. A shower of rockets preceded the storming column, which was provided with fascines and ladders. That part of our intrenchments was defended by the Tennesseeans and Kentuckians, who shot at will with such rapidity, that their whole line seemed to be but one sheet of fire. So effective were the incessant discharges of the artillery and musketry, which rolled like uninterrupted peals of thunder, that the British, before they had gained much ground, gave signs of confusion. The officers were seen animating their men, and urging them onward when they wavered. An oblique movement was made to avoid the terrible fire of the Flaugeac battery, from which every discharge seemed to tear open the column and sweep away whole files. But new men would, each time, rush to fill up those fearful gaps, and the column still advanced steadily and heavily. A few platoons had even succeeded in reaching the edge of the ditch in front of our lines, when the main column of attack, staggering under the irresistible fire of our batteries, broke at last after an ineffectual struggle of twenty-five minutes—some of the men dispersing, and running to take shelter among the bushes on their right, and the rest retiring to a ditch where they had been stationed when first perceived, at a distance of about four hundred yards from our lines. There the officers rallied their troops, ordered them to lay aside the heavy knapsack with which they were encumbered, and, being reinforced by troops which had been kept in reserve, led back their battalions to renew the attack. This time, having experienced the nature of the fire which expected them in front, the British advanced more rapidly, without pretending to observe the slow parade, precision and regularity which had been already so fatal to them. They came very near our lines, irregularly, with some confusion, but with exemplary courage. They met, however, the same overwhelming hail-storm of grape and bullets from our artillery and musketry. Sir Edward Packen ham, commander-in-chief, lost his life whilst gallantly leading his troops to the assault; soon after, Major-General Gibbs was carried away from the field, mortally wounded; then fell Major-General Keane, also severely wounded, with a great number of officers of rank, who had assumed the most dangerous positions to encourage their subordinates. The ground was literally strewed with the dead and wounded. Further to advance seemed to be courting destruction for every man. A feeling of consternation pervaded the ranks, which broke for the second time in the utmost confusion. In vain did the officers throw themselves in the way of the fugitives; vain were their appeals to the sense of honor and the love of country; vain were their threats and reproaches; vain were the blows which they were seen to give with the flat of their swords; the men were demoralized; and all that remained to be done was to lead them back to the ditch from which they had come in an evil hour, and which they could not be prevailed upon to leave for a third attack. In that safe cover they remained drawn up for the rest of the day.

Whilst this was occurring on the edge of the wood, a false attack had been made in the wood itself, chiefly by some black troops; but it was faint and languid, and easily repulsed by Coffee's Brigade. On our right near the river there had also been another false attack, conducted with far more vigor by Colonel Rennie. This column had pushed on so precipitately, and had followed so closely our outposts, that they reached our unfinished redoubt before we could fire more than two discharges. To leap into the ditch, to get through the embrasures into the redoubt, to climb over the parapet, to overpower our men by superior numbers, was but the affair of an instant. Colonel Rennie, although severely wounded in the leg, attempted next, at the head of his men, to clear the breastwork of the intrenchments in the rear of the redoubt, but now he had to meet the intrepid Orleans Riflemen, under Captain Beale, who had so much distinguished themselves in the battle of the 23d. Colonel Rennie, however, had the honor to scale those breast works with two other officers, and already waving his sword, he was shouting: "Hurra, boys, the day is ours," when he fell back a corpse into the ditch below with his two companions, who shared his noble fate; and soon after, the redoubt was retaken from their disheartened followers. It is fortunate that the two other attacks, particularly the main one, had not been conducted with the same impetuosity.

During this attack two British batteries had kept up a warm engagement with some of our centre batteries, by which they were at last demolished. As on the 1st of January, the first discharges of the enemy's artillery had been concentrated upon the house occupied as headquarters by General Jackson. But this time he was not in it, and the only mischief done, at a prodigious expense of balls and shells, was the knocking down of four or five pillars of the house, and the inflicting of a contusion on the shoulder of Major Chotard, Assistant Adjutant-General. Commodore Patterson, on the other side of the river, had, simultaneously with our lines, opened a heavy fire on the enemy from his marine battery, until he was stopped by the landing of the British troops which had been sent to dislodge General Morgan. His fire proved very destructive, " as the British columns, in their advance and retreat," says the Commodore in his report to the Secretary of the Navy, " afforded a most advantageous opportunity for the use of grape and canister." The battle did not last more than one hour. At half-past nine it was all over, although the cannonade between the batteries continued until two o'clock. The loss of the enemy was enormous, amounting to near three thousand, which was about one-half of the number of his men supposed to be engaged. This loss will appear still more extraordinary, when it is considered that the enemy had encountered only half of our troops, as he was out of the range of the musketry of our centre, which was not even threatened during the whole engagement. Our loss was incredibly small, not exceeding thirteen. "After his retreat, the enemy," says Major Latour, "appeared to apprehend that we should make a sortie and attack him in his camp. The soldiers were drawn up in the ditches in several parallel lines, and all those who had been slightly wounded, as soon as their wounds were dressed, were sent to join their corps, in order to make their number of effective men appear the greater, and show a firm countenance."

The same author, whose Historical Memoir on the War in West Florida and Louisiana in 1814–15 is so accurate and valuable a narrative, makes in that work the following critical commentaries on the battle of the 8th of January:

"I deem it my indispensable duty to do justice to the intrepid bravery displayed in that attack by the British troops, especially by the officers. If anything was wanted toward the attack's being conducted with judgment (speaking in a general and military point of view), it was, in my opinion, that they did not in the onset sacrifice the regularity of their movements to promptitude and celerity. The column marched on with the ordinary step, animating their courage with huzzas, instead of pushing on with *fixed* bayonets *au pas de charge*. But it is well known that agility is not the distinctive quality of British troops. Their movement is in general sluggish and difficult, steady but too precise, or at least more suitable for a pitched battle, or behind intrenchments, than for an assault. The British soldiers showed, on this occasion, that it is not without reason they are said to be deficient in agility. The enormous load they had to carry contributed, indeed, not a little to the difficulty of their movement. Besides their knapsacks, usually weighing nearly thirty pounds, and their musket too heavy by at least one-third, almost all of them had to carry a fascine from nine to ten inches in diameter and four feet long, made of sugar-canes perfectly ripe, and consequently very heavy, or a ladder from ten to twelve feet long.

"The duty of impartiality, incumbent on him who relates military events, obliges me to observe that the attack made on Jackson's lines by the British, on the 8th of January, must have been determined on by their Generals, without any consideration of the ground, the weather, or the difficulties to be surmounted, before they could storm lines defended by militia indeed, but by militia whose valor they had already witnessed, with soldiers bending under the weight of their load, when a man, unencumbered and unopposed, would, that day, have found it difficult to mount our breastwork at leisure and with circumspection, so extremely slippery was the soil. Yet those officers had had time and abundant opportunity to observe the ground on which the troops were to act. Since their arrival on the banks of the Mississippi, they had sufficiently seen the effects of rainy weather, to form a just idea of the difficulty their troops must have experienced in climbing up our intrenchments, even had the column been suffered to advance without opposition as far as the ditch. But they were blinded by their pride. The vain presumption of their superiority, and their belief that the raw militia of Kentucky and Tennessee, who now for the first time had issued from their fields, could not stand before the very sight of so numerous a body of regular troops advancing to attack them, made them disregard the admonition of sober reason. Had they at all calculated on the possibility of resistance, they would have adopted a different plan of attack, which, however, I am far from thinking would have been ultimately successful.

"It has been reported that divisions prevailed in a council of war, and that Admiral Cochrane combating the opinion of General Packenham, who, with more judgment, was for making the main attack on the right bank, boasted that he would undertake to storm our lines with two thousand sailors armed only with swords and pistols. I know not how far this report may deserve credit, but if the British commander-in-chief was so unmindful of what he owed his country, who had committed to his prudence the lives and honors of several thousands of his soldiers, as to yield to the ill-judged and rash advice of the Admiral, his memory will be loaded with the heavy charge of having sacrificed reason in a moment of irritation, though he atoned with his life for having acted contrary to his own judgment."

It may not be uninteresting to know what so competent a judge as Marshal Soult thought of that battle. Major Davezac, who had acted on that occasion as a volunteer aid to General Jackson, and who, many years afterward, when Jackson was President of the United States, represented our government in Holland, having obtained a furlough, went to Paris, where he met Marshal Soult, who was then acting as Secretary of War. The old veteran expressed, in relation to the battle of the 8th of January, the keenest desire to obtain such information as might enable him to form a correct appreciation of what he called "a most unaccountable event." Major Davezac happened to have in his possession the maps and other materials which were desired, and which he accompanied with his own explanations. The Marshal's eye was soon riveted to the map, and his finger running over its surface rested on the wood. "Sir," said he, "this mode of attack is incomprehensible. The British should have gone through that wood and flanked you.—But that was an impassable swamp.—You may think so; I do not.—You do not know the nature of our swamps.—I may know more of them than you are aware of; besides, I have learned enough from your own lips to be satisfied that a horse could have gone through that swamp; and where a horse passes a man can. Sir, there is no excuse for General Packenham."—Davezac maintained the contrary opinion; a discussion ensued; the Marshal grew warm, and at last, shaking his fist, angrily exclaimed: "Sir, I would have shot that blunderer for the destruction of that fine army, had he survived and been under my command. The English would have done the same, if he had returned home. They are not in the habit of forgiving such things. It is well for him that he died on the battle-field."

Marshal Soult was right as to the nature of the swamp.

It was not impassable, although the rifles of the Tennesseeans might have made it so for any body of troops who might have attempted to penetrate in that direction. Alexander Walker, who, in his "Life of General Jackson," has put on record the most minute details concerning the invasion of Louisiana by the British, after having, with indefatigable industry and scrupulous zeal, consulted many of those who had been actors or eyewitnesses on that occasion, says: "The British made another discovery, which ingenious and quick-witted people would have turned to better use. They found the horrible swamp, of which they stood in such dread that their outposts would not approach within a hundred yards of its edge, and of which such marvelous stories are related of men who sunk into it and disappeared forever from sight, quite practicable and passable for light troops." This seems, however, not to be admitted by the British; for General Lambert, in his report of the 10th of January to Lord Bathurst, says "that the wood had been made impracticable for any body of troops to pass." But if the swamp or wood was "practicable and passable" for light troops, and we have no doubt of it from the information which we have received from men well acquainted with that locality, Marshal Soult's sagacity stands fully confirmed, and his harsh military comment upon the mode of attack was founded on what he considered an unjustifiable piece of folly, stupidity or temerity. The fact is, that the British advanced against the American lines with the same splendid, but brainless, fool-hardy temerity which, lately in the Crimea, drove them like madmen upon the Russian batteries, to be slaughtered and defeated. "This is magnificent," exclaimed their judicious French allies, when witnessing that Quixotic exhibition, " but this is not war." The same exclamation might have been uttered at the sight of the assault of Jackson's lines by the British, in 1815. The more inexcusable were they from the fact that they had their own time to make their preparations for the attack on both sides of the river, and could bring all their resources into action without impediment. Speaking of their preliminary operations, General Jackson, in a communication to the Secretary of War, observes: "It had not been in my power to impede these operations by a general attack. Added to other reasons, the nature of the troops under my command, mostly militia, rendered it too hazardous to attempt extensive offensive movements in an open country against a numerous and well-disciplined army."

In his official report of the battle, dated on the 9th of January, the General rendered full justice to the troops to which he was indebted for his success. He said: "I cannot speak sufficiently in praise of the firmness and deliberation with which my whole line received the approach of the enemy. More could not have been expected from veterans inured to war." It seems that General Jackson would have ventured out of his intrenchments in pursuit of the enemy, if he had not been checked by the disaster which befell our arms on the other side of the river, and which we shall presently relate, for he added: "The entire destruction of the enemy was now inevitable, had it not been for an unfortunate occurrence which, at this moment, took place on the other side of the river." The wisdom of such a movement on his part must, however, appear questionable. The British, although defeated and probably demoralized, were still very superior in numbers to our troops, and the fortune of the day might have been hazarded if we had come out of our intrenchments. As to our casualties in the battle, amounting only to thirteen killed and wounded, a number which seems almost fabulous when compared to the well-ascertained loss of at least two thousand six hundred sustained by the enemy, General Jackson, in the same communication to the Secretary of War, remarked: "Such a disproportion, when we consider the number and the kind of troops engaged, must, I know, excite astonishment, and may not everywhere be fully credited; yet I am perfectly satisfied that the account is not exaggerated on the one part, nor underrated on the other."

Our troops had acted with intrepidity during the combat. When it was over, they manifested commendable dignity and magnanimity. We quote, with pleasure, on this subject the testimony of Major Latour, who was a foreigner, although in the service of the United States, and who may fairly be supposed to be more impartial than a native could be. He says:

"At the time of the preceding attacks, those of the 28th December and 1st of January, after our artillery had silenced that of the enemy, and forced his troops to retire, repeated huzzas from the whole of our line rent the air; the most lively demonstrations of joy were everywhere exhibited by our soldiers—a presage of the fate of the enemy in a general attack. On the 8th of January, on the contrary, no sooner was the battle over, than the roar of artillery and musketry gave place to the most profound silence. Flushed with victory, having just repulsed an enemy who had advanced to scatter death in their ranks, our soldiers saw, in the numerous corpses that strewed the plain, only the unfortunate victims of war, in the wounded and prisoners whom they hastened to attend, only suffering and unhappy men, and in their vanquished enemies brave men worthy a better cause. Elated with their success, but overpowered by the feelings of a generous sympathy for those miserable victims of the ambition of their masters, they disdained to insult the unfortunate by an untimely exultation, and cautiously avoided any expression of joy, lest they should wound the feelings of those whom the chance of battle had placed in their hands. In the midst of the horrors of war, humanity dwells with delightful complacency on the recital of such noble traits; they soothe the heart under the pressure of adversity, and divert the mind from the contemplation of ills which we can neither avoid nor entirely remedy."

This chivalrous delicacy was not the only honorable feeling exhibited in our ranks. As soon as the wrecks of the retreating British columns had disappeared, as soon as the fire of our musketry had ceased, and whilst our artillery was still firing at intervals at the enemy's batteries, or at scattered platoons that lingered in the woods, some of our men, touched with pity at the sight of so many of the wounded British soldiers who strewed the field, and whose groans of agony and cry for water made so strong an appeal to their humanity, rushed out of our intrenchments to offer them all the assistance in their power. In those bleeding bodies, stretched helpless on the ground, they no longer saw enemies, but fellow-beings in distress, toward whom their hearts melted with compassion. Warm expressions of applause came from our ranks, when we saw our soldiers staggering under the weight of the wounded whom they were endeavoring to carry on their backs within our lines. At that moment, to our intense indignation, the British troops who were in the ditch in front of our lines fired at these generous men, killing and wounding some of them. They fell, but, regardless of that inexplicable outrage and of the danger to which they were exposed, the rest continued to fulfill their mission of charity.

In the evening of the 8th the inhabitants of New Orleans witnessed the arrival of a long train of wounded prisoners, whose number amounted to about four hundred. Immediately a large quantity of lint and old linen for dressing their wounds, of mattresses and pillows and other articles for their comfort, were furnished by private contributions. All kinds of refreshments and every attendance which their situation required were liberally provided by the spontaneous action of our citizens. The colored women of New Orleans have acquired an honorable reputation for the skillful nurses they supply during those fatal epidemics which have so often desolated that city. On this occasion, several of them tendered their services gratuitously, and deserved the lasting gratitude of the numerous wounded whom they attended with the most humane disinterestedness.

But our triumph was not without its alloy, and we were soon reminded that there is but one step from exultation to humiliation. In the midst of the pæans sung in his honor, the Roman triumpher was compelled to listen to words of censure, reproach, or admonition, in order that he should not forget his human fragility. Without the apprehension or the recollection of blame, praise would lose its attraction or its value. The one sets off the other, and both have an equally useful mission to perform. We must, therefore, resign ourself with a good grace to the painful necessity of admitting and recording the sad truth, that a shameful panic took place on the right side of the river, when Colonel Thornton attacked General Morgan's lines, almost at the same time when General Packenham, with the main body of his troops, was assaulting Jackson's intrenchments. We shall console ourself with the reflection that more than once two armies, inured to perils and used to glorious deeds, have been known suddenly to run away from each other, as if obeying, by a sort of tacit understanding, the same reciprocal impulse of the most intense and unaccountable fear. The ancients attributed it to some supernatural cause—to the influence of some god or other. This excuse, however, we shall not plead, but we shall give others which may be received in extenuation of what cannot be justified. The Spaniards shrewdly say: "Such a man was brave on such a day," thereby admitting that on another day, or on another occasion, the same man may appear in a different light. This is human nature. The lion himself is known at times to

put his tail between his legs and run like a whipped cur
After this preamble, and after having taken delight in
showing how very brave we were on the left side of the
Mississippi, we shall, with candor, proceed to relate how
it was that we were not equally so on the other side of
that river.

We have said before that General Morgan had, according to orders, after the battle of the 23d of December, crossed the river and taken a position almost opposite Jackson's lines. He was a worthy man in his private character, brave personally, but an incompetent officer. He showed his incapacity at once by the very choice of the spot which he selected to make a stand against the enemy. It was behind a canal, it is true, but there were other canals; and this one was at a point where the cypress swamp recedes from the Mississippi more than at any other for miles, and leaves the largest space between itself and the river. Jackson had done the very reverse on the other side, but his example was not followed. It was therefore the most injudicious ground that could be selected. Behind that old canal, however, Morgan established his line of defence, two hundred yards in length, leaving more than eighteen hundred yards unprotected, and offering no other obstacle to the enemy than this canal or ditch. On his two hundred yards of breastwork were mounted three pieces of artillery. The weakness of this position was evident, for it might easily have been foreseen that the enemy, coming up the high road near the river, and finding these fortifications in his front, would not butt his head against them, when he could avoid them by obliquing to the left toward the wood. The Second Regiment of Louisiana Militia, under the command of Colonel Zenon Cavelier, presenting an effective force of one hundred and seventy-six men, had been sent, on the 4th of Janu ary, to reinforce Morgan. On their arrival they received unfavorable impressions from the nature of the means of resistance which were in the course of preparation. In the evening of the 6th, the First Regiment of Militia under Colonel Déjean quitted the position it occupied on the Piernas Canal and crossed the river. Although a detachment of the Sixth Militia Regiment was added to it, the whole force did not exceed one hundred and ten. Those who were armed were ill-armed, and the rest had no arms at all.* The arrival of these men, in such a condition, could not have the effect of giving much relief to the well-founded apprehensions already entertained by the regiment of Zenon Cavelier. These two skeletons of regiments, when looking at each other's meagre proportions, did not feel much encouraged. Anybody who is acquainted in the slightest degree with the population of Louisiana will not doubt that those men were brave and patriotic, but was it not natural that they should have felt somewhat despondent, when brought into contact with those who were already under the command of General Morgan, and whom they found either lamenting the incapacity of their leader, or making it a subject of joke or ridicule? Is it to be wondered at if they fraternized in grumbling, in railing, and in vague apprehensions of some approaching catastrophe? It was a bad preparation for meeting the enemy. Three miles in advance of Morgan's lines, Major Arnaud had been stationed with one hundred men to prevent the British from landing; fifteen of them had no arms at all, and the rest only fowling-pieces. These men thought that they were required to do what was impossible, that they could accomplish no good; that they would be uselessly sacrificed; and that this was another proof

---

* Latour's Historical Memoir, p. 16⁶

of a want of common sense in their General. They became demoralized.

In the evening of the 7th, both General Jackson and General Morgan were informed that the enemy would cross on the next morning. There was therefore no surprise produced by that movement, as stated in some of the British accounts written by officers who did not know that their intention had been detected by the Americans. On receiving this information, General Jackson ordered five hundred Kentuckians under Colonel Davis to join General Morgan. When at four o'clock in the morning they arrived at the place of their destination, after having undergone much fatigue on their march, and some vexatious delay on account of the difficulty of procuring suitable means of transportation across the river, they were reduced to one-half. What had become of the other half? Is it possible, as alleged in their favor, that they had remained behind because spent with fatigue and faint from the want of food? But, on the whole day of the 7th, they were in a camp full of provisions. How is it possible, therefore, to suppose that they did not receive their usual rations? This supposition being rejected as not probable, and there being no proof to the contrary, it remains that they were without food only from the evening of the 7th to the morning of the 8th. Was that enough to make them "physically faint?" Granting that they marched eight or ten miles in darkness, and on muddy roads, and that the crossing of the river was attended with difficulties, was that enough to justify robust men inured to hardships of all kinds in pretending that they were "spent with fatigue?" Granting that many of them were without arms, was this circumstance sufficient to induce them to leave their ranks, without waiting to the last for the arms to which they were entitled, and without which they could not be expected to meet the enemy? The inference must be that these men, for some cause or other which we do not know, were not animated with a proper spirit when they left their camp, and experience has proved that nothing is more contagious in armies than moral infirmities. The one-half who continued their march to Morgan's lines must have arrived there greatly demoralized by the desertion of their companions. They probably were discontented and moody; it is reported that they looked ragged, jaded, dirty, unsoldierlike, and very much like men disposed to run away on the first favorable opportunity. Unfortunately, and to make matters worse, they were to co-operate chiefly with troops whose language they did not understand, and with whom they could not sympathize. A mutual distrust ensued. It must be admitted that there could hardly be a more heterogeneous crowd than this badly-armed mob, assembled on that occasion under the command of General Morgan. If General Jackson had been there, his strong will might have welded into a compact, solid and harmonious mass these discordant and jarring elements. He would, at least, have inspired a confidence which did not exist, and that would have gone a great way toward insuring success.

As if these had not been sufficient causes to produce demoralization, General Morgan continued to order movements which increased the distrust of his troops as to his capacity. For instance, as soon as the Kentuckians arrived, after the heavy and fatiguing night's march of which they complained so much, he ordered them, in the state of exhaustion and inanition in which they pretended to be, to move beyond his lines and join Arnaud's command in advance. They obeyed, it is said, without murmur, but much doubting, probably, the propriety of such an order. They soon met Arnaud's one hundred men, who, not deeming themselves strong enough to prevent the British from landing, were hastily retreating. This detachment, and the Kentuckians who numbered about two hundred effective men, were made to draw up in a line between the river and the swamp—the Kentuckians near the river, and the Louisiana Militia on their right, in the direction of the swamp. If these three hundred men had been posted behind the levee, at the spot where the British landed, they might have been of good service. But what could be the object in thus posting them a short distance in advance of our fortified lines, not as outposts, it seems, but as a presumed effective obstacle in the way of the enemy? As outposts, they were too many, for they constituted half of Morgan's force, and as a resisting body they were too weak. These badly equipped, badly organized, and badly disciplined militiamen could not reasonably be thought capable of coping effectively, in an open field, with the much superior force of veteran regulars who were expected. Why this division of our little army—one-half behind the breastworks, and the other half about a mile in front? Why expose them to further demoralization by subjecting them to certain defeat, and then trust to the chance of rallying them, when under hot pursuit, behind our fortifications in their rear? These thoughts probably occurred to them, and were not of a nature to allay those instinctive apprehensions which they seem to have entertained before. As to Arnaud's men, who had thought themselves unnecessarily placed in a very perilous position, they did not draw much comfort from the reinforcement which had been sent them. "Surely," they may be presumed to have said to each other, "if these are the ragamuffins who are to help us in beating the British in an open plain, we had better take care of ourselves." "Verily," probably said the Kentuckians, "if this handful of frightened Creoles is our only assistance, we are in a bad way."

What was the consequence? Colonel Thornton, who had landed at the head of* six hundred men, soon made his appearance, accompanied by several gun-boats which hugged the bank of the river as they ascended. The enemy attacked briskly our extended line established behind an unfortified canal, whilst his gun-boats poured grape-shot into our flank. The Kentuckians, although thrown into some confusion, answered with two or three well-directed volleys. Just at this critical moment, when some hesitation or wavering had begun to manifest itself, General Morgan had the unlucky inspiration to order a retreat. The order was communicated in English by one of Morgan's aids: "What is it?" said in French one in Arnaud's command, who did not understand the language used. A voice replied: "The General says, '*sauve qui peut*,'" which may be translated thus: *the Devil take the hindmost*. Upon this, Arnaud's detachment broke and fled to the wood, and the Kentuckians, seeing themselves abandoned, fell back in much disorder to our breastworks, where they were posted to the right of the Louisiana regiments. Certainly it can be no injustice to the commander-in-chief, General Morgan, to hold him responsible for the manner in which his troops were again stationed, to meet the advancing column of the enemy. Davis' Kentuckians were placed alongside of that part of the canal which was not fortified, and at such a distance from each other that they looked like a long line of sentinels. Besides, a large space was left unoccupied between them and the Louisiana militia on their left.

On the high road, in front of our breastworks, soon appeared the British, advancing rapidly to profit by the

* Colonel Thornton's Official Report, 8th of January, 1815.

advantage which they had already obtained. Our artillery played upon them with effect, and our musketry had begun to open its fire, when Colonel Thornton saw at one glance the weakness of our position. He fell back, and making an oblique movement to the left, he sent a column to penetrate through the gap in our centre, and another toward the wood to turn and envelop the sparsely scattered Kentuckians. At the sight of this manœuvre the Kentuckians broke, and no exertions on the part of their officers and of General Morgan could rally them. "Confidence had vanished," says Major Latour, "and with it all spirit of resistance." Well might confidence have vanished, if it had ever existed, for the most robust faith would not have been proof against the perpetration of such a series of blunders! Our right was turned, and between it and our Louisiana militia and artillery, in a few minutes, there was nothing but a broad space left vacant by the flight of the Kentuckians. The Louisianians and the artillery continued to fire as long as possible. At last the cannon was spiked, and the First and Second Regiments of Louisiana Militia retreated in tolerable order on the high road. Commodore Patterson, finding himself deserted by the force he had relied upon to protect his marine battery, was compelled, "most reluctantly and with inexpressible pain," to abandon it, having only thirty men under his command, including officers. He took time, however, to destroy his ammunition and spike his cannon. In his report to the Secretary of the Navy he is very severe on the Kentuckians. When the attack had begun, he had ordered his guns to be turned in their embrasures, and so pointed as to protect General Morgan's right wing:

"Whose lines," says he, "not extending to the swamp, and being weakly manned, I apprehended the enemy's outflanking him on that wing; which order was promptly executed, under a heavy and well-directed fire of shot and shells from the enemy on the opposite bank of the river. At this time, the enemy's force had approached General Morgan's lines under the cover of a shower of rockets, and charged in spite of the fire from the twelve-pounder and field-pieces mounted on the lines, as before stated; when, in a few minutes, I had the extreme mortification and chagrin to observe General Morgan's right wing, composed of the Kentucky militia, commanded by Major Davis, abandon their breastwork and flying in a most shameful and dastardly manner, almost without a shot; which disgraceful example, after firing a few rounds, was soon followed by the whole of General Morgan's command, notwithstanding every exertion was made by him, his staff and several officers of the city militia, to keep them to their posts. By the great exertions of those officers a short stand was effected on the field, when a discharge of rockets from the enemy caused them again to retreat, in such a manner that no efforts could stop them."

We deem it an act of justice to correct an error committed by Commodore Patterson, who must have been blinded by his indignation. The Kentuckians were not behind any "breastworks;" they were, on the contrary, totally unprotected by any kind of fortifications, unless that name be given to the canal behind which they stood. General Jackson in his report to the Secretary of War, dated on the 9th of January, also censures the conduct of the Kentuckians: "What is strange and difficult to account for," he says, "at the very moment when the entire discomfiture of the enemy was looked for with a confidence amounting to certainty, the Kentucky reinforcements, in whom so much reliance had been placed, ingloriously fled, drawing after them, by their example, the remainder of the forces, and thus yielding to the enemy that most formidable position."

Whatever was the guilt of the Kentuckians, it must be admitted that General Jackson was not correct in his statement "that they occupied a most formidable position." We have shown that it was anything but that. He must also have been under some extraordinary delusion when he asserted that the Kentuckians fled at the moment "when the entire discomfiture of the enemy was looked upon with a confidence approaching to certainty." The British on the right side of the river, and in their attack on Morgan's lines, never were, for a moment, threatened with the slightest discomfiture. The State of Kentucky never forgave the charge which General Jackson had thus officially recorded against her sons, and she subsequently never failed to oppose him with the bitterest hostility throughout his political career. In extenuation of that charge, the Kentuckians had replied:

"We were ill-armed; we had been on our feet for twenty-four hours, during which time we had hardly tasted food; the cartridges we had were too large for our pieces; on our arrival before day, after a hard march of several miles, partly through the mud, without being allowed a moment's rest, we were ordered to advance a mile further. Having obeyed without a murmur, we found ourselves within view of the enemy, on whom we fired several volleys, maintaining that position, which was none of the best, until, being outflanked on our right, and cannonaded with grape-shot from the barges on our left, we were forced to retreat on Morgan's line, where we were ordered to take a position along a canal, uncovered and extended on a front of three hundred yards, our left separated from the other troops by an unguarded space of ground, and our right covered by a paltry detachment of sixteen men, stationed two hundred yards from us; a vast plain, offering no manner of shelter, lying in our rear. We were turned on the right and cut off on the left. In so precarious a situation, how could we avoid giving way?"

This is the manner in which they attempted to explain what General Jackson had said was "strange and difficult to account for."

Admitting as true these allegations, and giving to the plea of the Kentuckians in their own defence all the force which they might have desired, it is impossible to free them altogether from the shame of having fled in the wildest affright, without even attempting anything like an orderly retreat. So extreme was their panic that some of them ran eleven miles without stopping, and with the most extraordinary speed, to a spot up the river, where they found some means of crossing it. When safely on the other side, at the distance of six miles above New Orleans, they ran pell-mell into the court-yard of the planter whose lands fronted the river, clamoring for food, and vociferating that the American army was annihilated. They still seemed as if they were under the influence of terror, and became composed only after having obtained the food they desired.

Considering the feebleness and short duration of our defence, the loss of the enemy was very remarkable. It amounted to one hundred and twenty men killed and wounded—more than one-sixth of his whole force—which shows the extraordinary accuracy of our fire, and what might have been done under an abler leader than General Morgan. Our loss was one man killed and five wounded.

For the expedition intrusted to Colonel Thornton the British had needed boats. Those boats had to be dragged through Canal Villeré, which had been lately extended to the river with so much labor. It was an operation of much difficulty; some of the boats stuck fast in the muddy bed of the canal, and those which reached the Mississippi were not sufficient to carry the whole force which it was intended to throw on the other side of that river. Hence it was curtailed down to one-third of its original number, and, on account of the delays experienced, it could not proceed until eight hours after the time appointed.* This destroyed the *ensemble* of the plan of attack. The current was strong, and the difficulty of keeping the boats together was so great, that

---

* Colonel Thornton's Report, 8th January.

Colonel Thornton only reached his destination by daybreak instead of the early part of the night as expected, and by the time his troops had disembarked on the right side of the river, he perceived that the attack had begun on the left side. He did not, therefore, arrive in time to prevent our batteries from pouring, in the beginning of the battle, a destructive enfilading fire on the British columns who were advancing against Jackson's lines, and when he became master of Morgan's position, we were completely victorious in the plains of Chalmette. It was the only success obtained by the invaders on the soil of Louisiana. Colonel Thornton claimed to have captured a great abundance of provisions, a large store of all sorts of ammunition, sixteen pieces of ordnance, and the colors of a regiment. "Our prisoners," about thirty in number, he says in his report, "agree in stating that the force under General Morgan was from fifteen hundred to two thousand men." If the prisoners agreed in such a statement, they agreed in a misrepresentation; General Morgan's force was not much greater than six hundred men.

"This unfortunate rout," wrote Jackson to the Secretary of War, "had totally changed the aspect of affairs. The enemy now occupied a position from which they might annoy us without hazard, and by means of which they might have been able to defeat, in a great measure, the effects of our success on this side of the river. It became, therefore, an object of the first consequence to dislodge him as soon as possible." He immediately issued this stirring and appropriate address to the troops stationed on the right bank of the Mississippi:

"While by the blessing of Heaven directing the valor of the troops under my command, one of the most brilliant victories in the annals of the war was obtained by my immediate command, no words can express the mortification I feel at witnessing the scene exhibited on the opposite bank. I will spare your feelings and my own by entering into no detail on the subject; to all who reflect, it must be a source of eternal regret that a few moments' exertion of that courage you certainly possess, was alone wanting to have rendered your success more complete than that of your fellow-citizens in this camp, by the defeat of the detachment which was rash enough to cross the river to attack you."

This passage is in accordance with the impression under which he was, and which we have shown to have been erroneous, when he wrote to the Secretary of War that the Kentuckians had fled at the time that the entire discomfiture of the enemy was looked for with a confidence amounting to certainty.

"To what cause," proceeds the General to ask, "was the abandonment of your lines owing? To fear? No! You are the countrymen, the friends, the brothers of those who have secured to themselves by their courage the gratitude of their country, who have been prodigal of their blood in its defence, and who are strangers to any other fear than that of disgrace. To disaffection to our glorious cause? No! my countrymen; your General does justice to the pure sentiments by which you are inspired. How then could brave men, firm in the cause in which they were enrolled, neglect their first duty, and abandon the post committed to their care?"

The answer which the General gives to his own interrogatories confirms the view which we took of the causes of that disaster, and which he attributes " to the want of discipline, the want of order, a total disregard to obedience, and a spirit of insubordination, not less destructive than cowardice itself." Whilst thus upbraiding the troops for their want of discipline and order, for their disregard to obedience, and their spirit of insubordination, he could scarcely, in the same breath, comment on the deficiencies of their officers, and particularly on the incapacity exhibited by General Morgan. This would have weakened the effect he intended to produce; but we shall show that he was not unaware of the existence of that evil, although he probably did not think it proper to take notice of it in his address. He sternly tells our men, however, that the causes which led to their late disaster must be eradicated, or that he must cease to command:

"I desire to be distinctly understood," he says, "that every breach of orders, all want of discipline, every inattention to duty will be seriously and promptly punished, in order that the attentive officers and good soldiers may not be exposed to the disgrace and danger which the negligence of a few may produce. Soldiers! you want only the will, in order to emulate the glory of your fellow-citizens on this bank of the river. You have the same motives for action, the same interest, the same country to protect, and you have an additional interest from past events, to wipe off the stain on your honor, and show what, no doubt, is the fact, that you will not be inferior in the day of trial to any of your countrymen."

After having animated them by this powerful appeal to their manhood, he gives them this salutary lesson, which we hope will be forever remembered in our Southern armies: "But remember that, without obedience, without order, without discipline, all your efforts are vain, and the brave man, inattentive to his duty, is worth little more to his country than the coward who deserts her in the hour of danger." This sententious truth, so tersely expressed, and coming from such a source, should be inscribed on the flag of every regiment. "Private opinions," he continues, "as to the competency of officers must not be indulged, and still less expressed. It is impossible that the measures of those who command should satisfy all who are bound to obey, and one of the most dangerous faults in a soldier is a disposition to criticise and blame the orders and characters of his superiors." This may be sound doctrine, but how will it work in its practical application? Was there ever a body of intelligent soldiers, particularly if they were veterans and had the experience of war, who ever refrained from indulging in having their "private opinion" as to the competency of their officers? Can it be otherwise? We think not. It is impossible for a general at the head of an army not to reveal his capacity or incapacity in a few days. Men in front of danger have a keen instinct. No captain ever could handle an army with credit to himself, without possessing the confidence of that army, and that confidence will ever be the result of "opinion." There had been no "insubordination, no want of order and discipline" in our camp on the left side of the Mississippi. General Jackson had had nothing to apprehend on the battle-field from the criticism of his soldiers. Why? Because they believed in him, and they believed in him because they had seen him at work, and they had *judged* the workman accordingly. It is, probably, because every soldier under General Morgan and General Jackson had entertained a "private opinion" as to the competency of his commander, that one army fought gloriously, and the other fled precipitately.

The General wound up his address with much military tact, and with a kind of tender consideration for the feelings of those for whom it was intended:

"Soldiers," he said, "I know that many of you have done your duty, and I trust, in my next address, I shall have no reason to make any exceptions. Officers, I have the fullest confidence that you will enforce obedience to your commands, and, above all, that by subordination in your different grades, you will set the example of it to your men; and that, hereafter, the army of the right will yield to none in the essential qualities which characterize good soldiers; and that they will earn their share of those honors and rewards which their country will prepare for its deliverers.'

After having issued this address, General Jackson deemed it expedient to put an able officer at the head of the defeated troops on the right side of the Mississippi. He ordered Humbert, a French General who had been exiled from his country on account of his extreme republican ideas, and who had tendered his services against the invaders of Louisiana, to cross the river and recover the ground which we had lost. "I," said Jackson, "expect you, General, to repulse the enemy, cost what it may." "I will; you may rely on it," replied Humbert, delighted with an order which suited exactly the well-known temerity of his natural disposition. The occasion was so urgent, and Humbert was in such haste to drive the British into the river, that he neglected or forgot to ask General Jackson for his written authority. On his arrival, this led to unpleasant discussions, which produced delay. General Morgan appeared inclined, at first, to receive as sufficient evidence the word of General Humbert, and ready to accept his assistance, if not to serve under him in a subordinate capacity, but finally demurred to it by the advice and on the representations of some of his officers. "General Humbert," they remarked, "may be a very able man, but he is an unnaturalized foreigner. We think that none but an American should command Americans. Are we to admit that we have no native military talent among us to lead us to victory in the defence of our country? This foreigner claims to have the right to ask of you four hundred men. It is derogatory to our national character, and a personal affront to you. It implies that you are believed to be incapable of repairing the disaster which has lately befallen your arms, and there is a great want of generosity, to say the least of it, in not allowing you the opportunity, by striking another blow at the enemy, to regain what you may have lost in military reputation. It is hardly possible that General Jackson intended thus to lacerate your feelings. Such an order should have been in writing. General Humbert may have misconstrued his mission." Others were indignant at General Humbert's word being doubted: "General Jackson could not have supposed such a thing, and therefore had not, in the hurry of the moment, taken time to reduce his order to writing. The mere fact of General Jackson's telling Humbert to demand 400 men was a proof of his being intended as Commander-in-Chief. Was such a man, who had risen to his grade, step by step, from the lowest ranks, by the valor he had displayed in so many battles, to be under the command of a raw militia general? The appointment of Humbert was no doubt intended by General Jackson, not only as a compliment to that distinguished foreigner, who had shown such zeal in our cause, but also as an act of kindly consideration for the feelings of General Morgan, who ought to be proud to serve under such a leader. General Morgan might have complained with some reason, if his command had been transferred to some other militia dignitary like himself, of no higher rank and of no greater distinction. General Jackson had probably viewed it in that light, and had therefore shown his usual delicate tact, when sending to General Morgan a veteran known in history as the hero of Castlebar. To such a man, coming to his assistance, General Morgan should feel that he ought to tender the command, even if it had not been given by General Jackson. French, English, Spanish, and other troops had more than once been commanded by foreigners. Why should Americans be more sensitive?" Thus reasoned those who favored General Humbert.

But General Humbert was "displeased and went off," writes Colonel Shaumburgh to Governor Claiborne. There seems, indeed, to have been some cause for confusion as to who was to command on that day on the right side of the river, for General Jackson had sent the following note to Claiborne: "I have sent you all the reinforcement that I can spare, or that I have arms for. The enemy on the other side is not more than five hundred strong. *They must be destroyed!*" This reinforcement was but feeble in number, and not in a condition to do much service. The men had passed the preceding night under arms, had fought the whole morning, and then marched four miles from Jackson's camp to New Orleans in the rain and shivering from cold. Some had no arms at all, and the arms and ammunition of the rest were wet. In this condition they were to be hurriedly transported on the other side of the river, and to march four other miles before meeting the enemy. "In fact," says Colonel Shaumburgh, the Governor's aid, "they were not fit for a new combat for that day." The Governor took it for granted that he was to cross the river and take the command immediately over Morgan. In the mean time he ordered Shaumburgh to proceed to Morgan's lines, consult with him, and "see what could be done." Shaumburgh found Morgan's command "greatly scattered, disheartened and discontented." He spoke to several of the men, and, on his reprobating their conduct, they replied: "Give us officers and we will fight better."* General Morgan, on being shown Jackson's characteristic note to Claiborne, in which it was emphatically said, *the enemy must be destroyed*, thought that it could not be executed, and, "indeed, by the looks of things, I thought so too," observes Shaumburgh. Governor Claiborne arrived, noticed the "unpleasant situation of the troops," and, after consulting with Morgan and his subordinate officers, came to the same conclusions. Under these circumstances, he determined to make a "true statement" to General Jackson on the subject, and recrossed the river for that purpose.

---

* Executive Journal, Shaumburgh's communication to Claiborne.

Fortunately the British retired, and returned to their camp on the other side, thus saving us from the necessity of an attack. Immediately after the retreat of the enemy our troops reoccupied their former position, and went to work with such zeal, that Commodore Patterson, on the 13th of January, wrote to the Secretary of the Navy: "Our present situation is now so strong, that there is nothing to apprehend should the enemy make another attempt on this side."

On the morning of the 9th, General Jackson granted a suspension of arms to bury the dead, at the request of General Lambert, who had assumed the command of the British army. A touching scene occurred when we delivered the bodies of the three officers who had been killed on our breastworks. Colonel Rennie, in particular, must have been an object of love and admiration to his men; for those brave soldiers shed tears when taking possession of his lifeless form. Some knelt and kissed his corpse; they called the dead "father," and showed all the depth of filial grief. Those of our men who witnessed this honorable exhibition of feeling were so moved, that they deplored the dire necessity of the loss they had inflicted on an enemy. When this mournful duty of giving sepulture to the dead had been performed, our artillery resumed its fire, and gave no rest to the British camp, into which the balls of our heavy pieces fell with great accuracy. Commodore Patterson sent to Lake Borgne, through Bayou St. John and the Rigolets, six armed boats, which captured several transports, made a good many prisoners, and annoyed the enemy. On the 15th, several of our most experienced officers thought they saw in the British camp unmistakable indications of a contemplated retreat, and on that same day their conjectures were confirmed by the report of a deserter. On the 17th, General Lambert proposed to draw up a cartel of prisoners, which was accepted, and on the next day we delivered to the British sixty-three of their prisoners in return for the same number of our men, leaving in our hands an excess of several hundred.

The British had intended to send into the Mississippi some armed vessels, to co-operate with their land forces in the subjugation of Louisiana. But this object it was impossible to accomplish without first taking possession of Fort St. Philip, which prohibited their entrance into the river. Early on the morning of the 8th, Major Overton, who had the command of the fort, was advised of the approach of the enemy, and on the 9th there hove in sight two bomb-vessels, one sloop, one brig, and one schooner. They anchored two and a quarter miles below the fort, and two barges were sent apparently for the purpose of sounding within a mile and a half of the fort. At this moment our water battery opened upon them, and its well-directed shot caused a precipitate retreat. Shortly after, the enemy opened their fire from four sea-mortars, at a distance which was beyond the reach of any of our pieces, and it continued with little interruption until the 17th. Occasionally our batteries replied with great vivacity, particularly when the vessels showed any disposition to change their position, and make a forward movement. On the evening of the 17th, we succeeded in having a heavy mortar in readiness, which opened upon them with so much effect, that they evidently became disordered from that moment, and at daylight on the 18th they commenced their retreat. Our loss was uncommonly small, although the shot of the enemy had scarcely left ten feet of the fort untouched; it amounted to two killed and seven wounded. "The officers and soldiers," says Major Overton in his report to Commodore Patterson, " although nine days and nights under arms in the different batteries, and notwithstanding the consequent fatigue and loss of sleep, have manifested the greatest firmness and the most zealous warmth to be at the enemy." This failure to pass the fort, or to take it, probably contributed to strengthen General Lambert's determination to evacuate.

On the morning of the 19th an unusual quietness was observed to prevail in the British camp. Was it evacuated? But how could it be? There, as before, were the huts standing, the flags streaming to the breeze, the sentinels posted as usual. Telescopes were put in requisition, but those who used them differed in their conclusions. The majority thought that the enemy was still in possession of his camp. The veteran Humbert was consulted. His reply was positive: the enemy had evacuated. "How can you be so certain, General?" said Jackson. Humbert pointed at a crow which was in a state of unnatural proximity to one of the sentries. Evidently there could be no life in those pretended custodians of the approaches to the British camp, notwithstanding their British uniforms and their glittering muskets. They were mere images; the hunted and wounded lion had fled during the night. Fearful of some stratagem, General Jackson, in order to ascertain the real state of things, was ordering out a reconnoitering party, when a flag of truce came with a letter from General Lambert, informing General Jackson that the British army had evacuated its position on the Mississippi, and had, for the present, relinquished all undertaking against New Orleans and its vicinity. He further recommended to the humanity and generosity of General Jackson some wounded men whom he had been compelled to leave. There was no attempt made on our part to harass the enemy, "because such was the situation of the ground which he abandoned," said Jackson in his dispatch of the 19th of January to the Secretary of War, " and that through which he retired, protected by canals, redoubts and intrenchments on his right, and the river on his left, that I could not, without encountering a risk which true policy did not seem to require or authorize, annoy him much on his retreat. We took only eight prisoners."

General Lambert, in his dispatch of the 28th of January to Earl Bathurst, says " that he effected his retreat without molestation; that all the sick and wounded, with the exception of eighty whom it was considered dangerous to remove, with all the field artillery, ammunition, hospital and other stores of every description, which had been landed on a very large scale, were all brought away; and that nothing fell into the hands of the Americans, excepting six iron eighteen-pounders mounted on sea-carriages, and two carronades." We say fourteen instead of eight pieces of artillery, but we admit, as General Lambert avers, " that they were rendered perfectly unserviceable." General Lambert further informs his Lordship that only four men were reported absent on the next morning after his retreat; " and these," he adds, " must have been left behind, and must have fallen into the hands of the enemy; but when it is considered that the troops were in perfect ignorance of the movement until a fixed hour during the night; that the pickets did not move off till half-past three o'clock in the morning, and that the whole had to retire through the most difficult new-made road, wet, marshy ground, impassable for a horse, and where, in many places, the men could only go in single files, and that the absence of men might be accounted for in so many ways, it would be rather a matter of surprise that the number was so few." The General declares in the same communication " that he has every reason to believe that the treatment of the prisoners and the wounded by the Americans had been kind and humane."

On the day on which the evacuation of the British camp was ascertained, General Jackson wrote to the Secretary of War :

"Whether it is the purpose of the enemy to abandon the expedition altogether, or renew his efforts at some other point, I shall not pretend to decide with positiveness. In my own mind, however, there is very little doubt but his last exertions have been made in this quarter, at any rate for the present season; and by the next, if he shall choose to revisit us, I hope we shall be fully prepared for him. In this belief I am strengthened, not only by the prodigious loss he sustained at the position he has just quitted, but by the failure of his fleet to pass Fort St. Philip."

Glorious as had been this campaign for the United States, General Jackson thought that it might have been still more glorious, for he added:

"I am more and more satisfied in the belief that, had the arms reached us which were destined for us, the whole British army in this quarter would, before this time, have been captured or destroyed. We succeeded, however, on that day (8th of January) in getting from the enemy about one thousand stand of arms of various descriptions, my artillery from both sides of the river being constantly employed till the night and the hour of their retreat in annoying them. It was time to quit a position in which so little rest could be enjoyed."

The retreating army, having reached the bleak and swampy shores of Lake Borgne, remained encamped for several days in that uncomfortable position, and it was not until the 27th that it was entirely removed.

In the mean time, General Jackson, accompanied by his staff, had visited the camp lately occupied by the formidable foe against whom he had preserved Louisiana, and had assured the wounded whom he found in it that they would promptly receive all the assistance and attention which their situation required. It must have been a proud day for General Jackson, but in his exultation, the warrior did not forget Him who is the Great Dispenser of all human triumphs and humiliations, and hastened to pay his debt of gratitude by writing the following appropriate letter to the Abbé Dubourg, who was then at the head of the Catholic Diocese of New Orleans:

"Reverend Sir: The signal interposition of Heaven, in giving success to our arms against the enemy who so lately landed on our shores—an enemy as powerful as inveterate in his hatred—while it must excite in every bosom attached to the happy government under which we live emotions of the liveliest gratitude, requires at the same time some external manifestation of those feelings. Permit me, therefore, to entreat that you will cause the service of public thanksgiving to be performed in the Cathedral, in token of the great assistance we have received from the Ruler of all events, and our humble sense of it."

On this same day of patriotic rejoicing—the day which marked the evacuation of Louisiana by the British—Claiborne, in a communication to the President of the United States, said, with little foresight of the future: " The opponents of the American Union will no longer, I hope, think it easy to make an impression on its distant sections, and the friends of our common country may hereafter look with calmness on any attempt which may be made to sever any of its members from the original stock." The " American Union" has been dissolved, temporarily at least; its members have been severed from what the Governor calls the " original stock," but the tempestuous wind which caused the wreck blew from another quarter than the one which was then looked to as the source of danger.

Thus the enemy had gone away, crippled but still powerful—baffled at one point, it is true, but might not he return at another? General Jackson, to provide against this contingency, took the most active and well-devised measures in strengthening all his defensive positions. He left a regiment of Louisiana Militia on Villeré's plantation, a detachment of Kentucky troops on Lacoste's, the 7th Regiment of regulars in the lines which he had occupied, and returned to New Orleans on the 21st with the rest of his troops, after having sent numerous parties to reconnoitre the enemy on the shore of Lake Borgne, in order to be kept advised of his movements.

Before breaking his lines, General Jackson had an eloquent address read at the head of each corps, in which he said :

"The enemy has retreated, and your General has now leisure to proclaim to the world what he has noticed with admiration and pride—your undaunted courage, your patriotism, and your patience under hardships and fatigues. Natives of different States, acting together for the first time in this camp, differing in habits and language, instead of viewing in these circumstances the germ of distrust and division, you have made them the source of an honorable emulation, and from the seeds of discord itself have reaped the fruits of an honorable union."

Alluding to the alacrity and promptitude with which the troops, from their scattered encampments, had gathered to meet the enemy on the 23d of December, he made use of these expressions :

"The gay rapidity of the march, the cheerful countenances of the officers and men, would have induced a belief that some festive entertainment, not the strife of battle, was the object to which they hastened with so much eagerness and hilarity. In the conflict that ensued the same spirit was supported."

In this rapid and masterly review of the achievements of the army, the General, coming to the great battle of the 8th of January, observed :

"The final effort was made. At the dawn of day the batteries opened, and the columns advanced. Knowing that volunteers from

Tennessee and the militia from Kentucky were stationed on your left, it was there they directed their attack. Reasoning always from false principles, they expected little opposition from men whose officers even were not in uniform, who were ignorant of the rules of war, and who had never been caned into discipline. Fatal mistake! A fire incessantly kept up, directed with calmness and unerring aim, strewed the field with the bravest officers and men of the column, which slowly advanced according to the most approved rules of European tactics, and was cut down by the untutored courage of American militia."

In conclusion, he summed up in these few lines the results obtained, as being incalculably important:

"The pride of an arrogant enemy humbled, his forces broken, his leaders killed, his insolent hopes of our disunion frustrated, his expectations of rioting in our spoils and wasting our country changed into ignominious defeat, shameful flight, and a reluctant acknowledgment of the humanity and kindness of those whom he had doomed to all the horrors and humiliation of a conquered State. On the other side, unanimity established, disaffection crushed, confidence restored, your country saved from conquest, your property from pillage, your wives and daughters from insult and violation, the Union preserved from dismemberment, and perhaps a period put by this decisive stroke to a bloody and savage war. These, my brave friends, are the consequences of the efforts you have made and the success with which they have been crowned by Heaven."

In the general orders which were appended to this address, the Commander in-Chief publicly noticed the conduct of the different corps which composed the army, and paid a just and well-merited tribute of praise to the officers and men who had particularly distinguished themselves. In speaking of the Mississippi cavalry, under Hinds, he said: "The daring manner in which they reconnoitered the enemy on his lines excited the admiration of one army, and the astonishment of the other." If he had severely reprobated as dastardly the conduct of the Kentuckians on the right side of the river, he warmly commended their behavior on the left.

"General Adair," he said, "who, owing to the indisposition of General Thomas, brought up the Kentucky militia, has shown that troops will always be valiant when their leaders are so. No men ever displayed a more gallant spirit than these under that most valuable officer. His country is under obligation to him." The plain inference from this paragraph is, that if the Kentuckians and other troops under General Morgan had shown timidity, it was *because they had not been under valiant leaders.* This explains why General Jackson sent General Humbert to supersede General Morgan. He thus noticed the Baratarians—those whom he had so lately called "hellish banditti:" "Captains Dominique and Beluche, lately commanding privateers at Barataria, with part of their former crew and many brave citizens of New Orleans, were stationed at batteries Nos. 3 and 4. The General cannot avoid giving his warm approbation of the manner in which these gentlemen have uniformly conducted themselves while under his command, and of the gallantry with which they have redeemed the pledge they gave at the opening of the campaign to defend the country. The brothers Lafitte have exhibited the same courage and fidelity; and the General promises that the Government shall be duly apprised of their conduct." It is impossible to refrain from a smile when observing in how short a time General Jackson had modified his views and expressions concerning these men. On the 21st of September they were "pirates and hellish banditti;" on the 21st of January they were "privateers and gentlemen."

It has been related in the course of this History that Governor Claiborne and General Jackson had been very anxious for the adjournment of the Legislature during the invasion, and that the Governor had in vain invited both Houses to cease their labors until a more opportune time. In the following paragraph of an order of the day, Jackson indirectly censures the members who had preferred legislating instead of rushing to arms, when the enemy was almost at the door of the State House:

"The General takes the greatest pleasure in noticing the conduct of General Garrigue de Flaugeac, commanding one of the brigades of militia of this State, and *member of the Senate*. His brigade not being in the field, as soon as the invasion was known he repaired to the camp, and offered himself as a volunteer for the service of a piece of artillery, which he directed with the skill which was to be expected from an experienced artillery officer. *Disdaining the exemption afforded by his seat in the Senate*, he continued in this subordinate but honorable station, and by his example as well as his exertion, has rendered essential services to his country. Mr. Sebastian Hiriart, of the *same body*, set *the same example*, served a considerable time in the ranks of the volunteer battalion, and afterward as adjutant of the colored troops."

In relation to these colored troops, the formation of which had produced some feeling of discontent, he said: "The two corps of colored volunteers have not disappointed the hopes that were formed of their courage and perseverance in the performance of their duty. Majors Lacoste and Daquin, who commanded them, have deserved well of their country." He thus complacently noticed the conduct of two distinguished foreigners: "General Humbert, who offered his services as a volunteer, has continually exposed himself to the greatest dangers with his characteristic bravery, as has also the Mexican field marshal, Don Juan de Anaya, who acted in the same capacity." Of Major Lacarriere Latour, from whose Historical Memoir on this campaign we have so often quoted, he said: "The Chief Engineer, Major Lacarriere Latour, has been useful to the army by his talents and bravery."

With regard to the humiliating event which had occurred on the right bank of the Mississippi, a court of inquiry was subsequently held, and was presided over by Major-General Carroll. The court decided that the conduct of Colonels Davis, Déjean and Cavelier had not been "reprehensible;" that the causes of the disaster were to be attributed to the "shameful flight of the command of Major Arnaud"—to the retreat of the Kentucky militia, which, considering their position, the deficiency of their arms and other causes, "might be excusable"— and to the panic and confusion introduced in every part of the line, thereby occasioning the retreat and confusion of the Orleans and Louisiana drafted militia.

With regard to General Morgan, the court held the following language:

"Whilst the court find much to applaud in the zeal and gallantry of the officer immediately commanding, they believe that a further reason for the retreat may be found in the manner in which the force was posted on the line, *which they consider exceptionable*. The commands of Colonels Déjean, Cavelier and Declouet, composing five hundred men, supported by three pieces of artillery, having in front a strong breastwork, occupying only a space of two hundred yards, whilst the Kentucky militia, only one hundred and seventy men strong, without artillery, occupied more than three hundred yards, covered by a small ditch only."

Certainly, General Morgan had no right to complain of the mildness of this censure, the word "exceptionable" being as soft an adjective as could be applied to his military dispositions on that day.

It is needless to attempt to describe the ovation which attended the return of the victorious army to New Orleans. It can be more easily imagined. The whole population was in the streets, at the balconies, at the windows, and even on the tops of the houses. There was joy in every breast, joy in every face; there were such greetings as the heart alone can give; it was a feast of the soul for those who received, and those who tendered, the welcome. The 23d had been appointed for the celebration of a Solemn Thanksgiving in the Cathedral, with all the gorgeous ceremonies of the Catholic Church. All the citizens, whatever their religious creed was, joined their exertions to make that festival as impressive as it was in their power. In front of the Cathedral, in the middle of that square which is now known as Jackson Square, and where the equestrian statue of the hero commemorates his fame and the gratitude of Louisiana, a triumphal arch was temporarily erected. It was supported by six columns. On the right was a young woman with the attributes of Justice which she represented, and another, on the left, personated the Goddess of Liberty. Under the arch two beautiful boys, looking as if they were angels dropped from heaven on the pedestals on which they stood, held, each in his tiny hand, a crown of laurels. From the arch to the Church, at proper intervals, were ranged young ladies representing the different States and Territories of the American Union. They were all dressed in white, and covered with transparent veils. A silver star glittered on their foreheads. Each one held in her right hand a flag on which was inscribed the name of the State she represented, and in her left a basket of flowers trimmed with blue ribbons. Behind each was a shield appended to a lance stuck in the ground, and inscribed with the name of a State or Territory. These shields were linked together with verdant festoons, and formed a kind of lane from the triumphal arch to the gray towers of the time-honored Cathedral. In the rear on both sides, and extending from the entrance of the Square which faced the river to the Church, was a glittering avenue of bayonets formed by the uniform companies of Plauché's Battalion, and back of them, in every direction, surged and undulated like a sea of human beings the immense multitude assembled to witness the pageantry of the day. The boom of artillery and a burst of military music announced the approach of the hero. The air was rent with acclamations, and the hands of beauty waved handkerchiefs and flags from the adjacent buildings, which were crowded with eager spectators. As General Jackson passed under the triumphal arch he was crowned by the two youthful genii who expected him on their pedestals, and was congratulated in an address delivered by the girl who personated the State of Louisiana. Then, as he proceeded to the Church, the other States and Territories gracefully bowed their heads to him, each waving her flag, and strewing his path with flowers. At the door of the Cathedral he met Abbé Dubourg with all his clergy. That venerable personage thus addressed him in terms well suited to the occasion and to the sacred character of the orator:

"GENERAL:"

"Whilst the State of Louisiana, in the joyful transports of her gratitude, hails you as her deliverer and the asserter of her menaced liberties; whilst grateful America, so lately wrapped up in anxious suspense on the fate of this important city, the emporium of the wealth of one-half of her territory, and the true bulwark of her independence, is now re-echoing from shore to shore your splendid achievements, and preparing to inscribe your name on her immortal rolls among those of her Washingtons; whilst history, poetry, and the monumental arts will vie in consigning to the admiration of the latest posterity a triumph perhaps unparalleled in their records; whilst thus raised by universal acclamation to the very pinnacle of fame, and surrounded with ascending clouds of incense; how easy it had been for you, General, to forget the Prime Mover of your wonderful success, and to assume to yourself a praise which must essentially return to that exalted source whence every sort of merit is derived! But, better acquainted with the nature of true glory, and justly placing the summit of your ambition in approving yourself the worthy instrument of Heaven's merciful designs, the first impulse of your religious heart was to acknowledge the signal interposition of Providence; your first step is a solemn display of your humble sense of His favors.

"Still agitated at the remembrance of those dreadful agonies from which we have been so miraculously rescued, it is our duty also to acknowledge that the Almighty has truly had the principal hand in our deliverance, and to follow you, General, in attributing to His infinite goodness the homage of our unfeigned gratitude. Let the infatuated votary of a blind chance deride our credulous simplicity; let the cold-hearted atheist look up for the explanation of such important events to the mere concatenation of human causes; to us, the whole universe is loud in proclaiming a Supreme Ruler, who, as he holds the hearts of man in his hands, holds also the thread of all contingent occurrences. 'Whatever be His intermediate agents,' says an illustrious prelate, 'still on the secret orders of His all-ruling providence depend the rise and prosperity, as well as the decline and downfall of empires. From His lofty throne above He moves every scene below, now curbing, now letting loose the passions of men; now infusing His own wisdom into the leaders of nations; now confounding their boasted prudence, and spreading upon their councils a spirit of intoxication, and thus executing his uncontrollable judgments on the sons of men according to the dictates of His own unerring justice.'

"To Him, therefore, our most fervent thanks are due for our late unexpected rescue, and it is Him we chiefly intend to praise, when considering you, General, as *the man of his right hand*, whom he has taken pains to fit out for the important commission of our defence. We extol that fecundity of genius by which, in circumstances of the most discouraging distress, you created unforeseen resources, raised as it were from the ground hosts of intrepid warriors, and provided every vulnerable point with ample means of defence. To Him we trace that instinctive superiority of your mind, which alone rallied around you universal confidence, impressed one irresistible movement to all the jarring elements of which this political machine is composed, aroused their slumbering spirits, and diffused through every rank that noble ardor which glowed in your own bosom. To Him, in fine, we address our acknowledgments for that consummate prudence which defeated all the combinations of a sagacious enemy, entangled him in the very snares which he had spread before us, and succeeded in effecting his utter destruction, without hardly exposing the lives of our citizens. Immortal thanks be to His Supreme Majesty, for sending us such an instrument of His bountiful designs! A gift of that value is the best token of the continuance of His protection—the most solid encouragement to us to sue for new favors. The first which it emboldens us humbly to supplicate, as it is the nearer to our throbbing hearts, is that you may long enjoy, General, the honors of your grateful country, of which you will permit us to present you a pledge in this wreath of laurel, the prize of victory, the symbol of immortality. The next is a speedy and honorable termination of the bloody contest in which we are engaged. No one has so efficaciously labored as you, General, for the acceleration of that blissful period. May we soon reap that sweetest fruit of your splendid and uninterrupted victories!"

In this address a just tribute was paid to the merits of General Jackson and to the leading traits of his character, which, in a few phrases, were accurately delineated. Having received the wreath of laurel presented by the apostolic hands of the speaker, the General made this modest and felicitous reply:

"Reverend Sir, I receive with gratitude and pleasure the symbolical crown which piety has prepared. I receive it in the name of the brave men who have so effectually seconded my exertions for the preservation of their country. They well deserve the laurels which their country will bestow.

"For myself, to have been instrumental in the deliverance of such a country, is the greatest blessing that Heaven could confer. That it has been effected with so little loss—that so few tears should cloud the smiles of our triumph, and not a cypress leaf be interwoven in the wreath which you present, is a source of the most exquisite enjoyment.

"I thank you, Reverend Sir, most sincerely, for the prayers which you offer up for my happiness. May those your patriotism dictates for our beloved country be first heard! and may mine for your individual prosperity, as well as that of the congregation committed to your care, be favorably received! The prosperity, the wealth, the happiness of this city will then be commensurate with the courage and other qualities of its inhabitants."

It is painful to record that, amidst all these rejoicings, there were hearts which still remained deeply ulcerated by that military interference with the Legislature of Louisiana on the 28th of December, which many attributed to General Jackson.

CHAPTER XI.

GOVERNOR CLAIBORNE'S ADMINISTRATION—TREATY OF PEACE BE-
TWEEN THE UNITED STATES AND GREAT BRITAIN—NEGOTIATIONS
WITH THE BRITISH ABOUT THE SURRENDER OF SLAVES—CONFLICT
BETWEEN THE LEGISLATURE AND GENERAL JACKSON.

1815.

GENERAL JACKSON, having now established his camp and headquarters at New Orleans, extending to a distance of about four miles all round, was actively engaged in providing to meet any renewal of the attack lately made, and in strengthening every point where it was possible that the enemy might undertake to penetrate a second time into Louisiana. So effective were his measures, that toward the end of January, the State was in a condition to defy double the force that had at first attacked her.*

The British army had finally withdrawn from Louisiana on the 27th of January, carrying away one hundred and ninety-nine negroes. General Jackson had already taken steps to claim them as private property, and to demand their restoration to their legitimate owners, when, on the 31st, Claiborne addressed him on the subject, and inquired if anything further had been heard from the British commander-in-chief respecting those slaves. "You will excuse my solicitude," he said, "on a subject so immediately interesting to many good citizens of the State, and in whose behalf, in my charac

---

* Latour's Historical Memoir, p. 204.

ter as civil Governor, I would wish to address a letter to the British commander, and to convey it by three distinguished citizens, if you should not already have effected the restoration of their property." This seems to have been looked upon by General Jackson as an officious kind of intermeddling, which excited his displeasure. Was his zeal doubted on the subject? If not, why not leave it in his hands altogether? Could the remonstrances of an obscure Governor of a feeble State which had just sprung into existence, have more influence over the British authorities than those of a victorious General representing the United States, and acting on their behalf? General Jackson did not reply himself, but his Adjutant-General and Aid, R. Butler, writing in the name of the General, informed Claiborne in a few stiff words, that Captain Henley had been appointed to receive the slaves who might be delivered, but that from information obtained, although not official, "it appeared that the restoration of those slaves was not to be hoped for." Claiborne laid this correspondence before the Legislature with a special message, and, on the 2d of February, that body adopted "Resolutions" approving the course pursued by the Governor, and requesting him to take all other steps "which, in his wisdom, might be thought expedient to attain the object he had in view." This was evidently an attempt to give more weight to an interference which was already deemed exceptionable. It certainly had no tendency to remove some bad feelings which, for some time past, had produced a coolness between Jackson and Claiborne. The former had not been remiss, however, in his exertions to obtain the abducted negroes, but they had been without success. General Lambert pretended that the negroes had not been *taken away*, but had *come* of their own accord to the British camp. "I did all I could," he said, "to persuade them to return at the time, but not one was willing, as will be testified by Mr. Célestin, a proprietor whom I had detained until the British forces had evacuated their last position. This gentleman saw the slaves that were present, and did all he could to urge them to go back."

On the 12th of February, Lieutenant-Colonel Lawrence, who had so bravely and successfully defended Fort Bowyer, at Mobile Point, on a former occasion, informed General Jackson that "imperious necessity" had compelled him to enter into articles of capitulation with Major-General Lambert," feeling confident, he said, " and it being the unanimous opinion of the officers, that we could not retain the post, and that the lives of many valuable officers and soldiers would have been uselessly sacrificed, I thought it most desirable to adopt this plan." General Jackson felt keenly this insignificant discomfiture; he grudged his adversaries this small success, and he thought that the resistance of Lawrence had not been sufficient. His mind was so peculiarly constituted, that it never permitted him to entertain the idea of defeat, much less of capitulation and surrender, either in his military or political career. A surrender could not but strike him as something unnatural and monstrous. It is not, therefore, to be wondered at if he wrote to the Secretary of War: "This is an event which I little expected to happen but after the most gallant resistance. That it should have taken place without even a fire from the enemy's batteries is as astonishing as it is mortifying." But General Jackson's mortification made him unjust on this occasion. Fort Bowyer had been attacked by such overwhelming forces, by land and water, that the surrender followed of course, and there was in it nothing "unexpected, astonishing, or mortifying." According to General Lambert's opinion, expressed to Lord Bathurst, "the fort was formidable only against an assault, and batteries being once established, it was bound to fall speedily," which event took place as soon as the enemy had succeeded in erecting powerful batteries, on which were mounted sixteen guns, within one hundred yards of our parapets. Major Latour relates with professional minuteness all the details of this siege, and concludes with these observations:

"From this circumstantial account of the taking of Fort Bowyer, the impartial reader will see that the brave garrison who defended it, being left to their own resources, deprived of all communication, and cut off from all hope of receiving relief, exerted all the means in their power to defend the fort intrusted to them; never failing to annoy the enemy, when he came within the range of their guns. What could they do more? What useful purpose could it have answered to expose themselves to a bombardment in a fort entirely constructed of timber, so combustible that a single shell falling within the parapet would have sufficed to set the whole fort on fire? Attacked on the land side, what defence could they make against sixteen pieces of artillery, within so short a distance and behind strong intrenchments? Those pieces in less than half an hour would have battered down the parapet of the fort, which, on that side, was not more than three feet thick above the platforms."

A court of inquiry held at the request of Lieutenant-Colonel Lawrence, and assembled at New Orleans, acquitted him of all blame for the surrender of Fort Bowyer. The conduct of Major Overton and his men in Fort St. Philip, when attacked as we have before related, was more in accordance with General Jackson's own temper, and therefore more gratifying to him. "They nailed their own colors to the standard," he wrote to the Secretary of War, "and placed those of the enemy underneath them, determined never to surrender the post."

The correspondence between General Jackson and General Lambert was conducted with the most high-bred courtesy, and with feelings which do honor to both; but the one which took place between Commodore Patterson and Admiral Cochrane seems to have been rather of a rugged nature. On the 12th of February, Admiral Cochrane complained to General Jackson of the style adopted by Commodore Patterson, and said that he would hold no further correspondence with that officer in relation to the exchange of prisoners. General Jackson replied: "The Naval and Military Departments in our service being totally independent, I am not permitted to defend, still less to censure, the conduct or correspondence of the officer at the head of the former. His distinguished merit and general correctness of conduct make it presumable that he will be able to justify his proceedings to the Government, to whom alone he is accountable." On the 13th, Admiral Cochrane wrote to General Jackson: "I have exceeding satisfaction in sending to you a copy of a bulletin that I have this moment received from Jamaica, proclaiming that a treaty of peace was signed between our respective Plenipotentiaries at Ghent, on the 24th of December, 1814, upon which I beg leave to offer you my sincere congratulations." On the 19th, General Jackson was also congratulated on the prospect of peace by General Lambert, who said: "I hope I shall soon have to communicate to you the notice of the ratification being exchanged." On the 20th, General Jackson addressed, as follows, Admiral Cochrane, in relation to the slaves belonging to several inhabitants of Louisiana, and now on board the British fleet: "I had written to General Lambert on this head two successive letters, in consequence of his informing me that these persons would be delivered to their masters on their application. To the first I received no answer; to the last, I am informed that General Lambert *has nothing to do with it.* Mr. White, to whom an order was given to receive such as were willing to return to their masters, having reported to me that he found several who were ready to accompany him, but that he was not permitted to take them, I am now obliged, Sir, explicitly to ask whether the property thus taken is intended to be restored, and if it be, that a time and place may be appointed for its delivery." He further inquired of Admiral Cochrane how far he considered the news of peace, *communicated by him*, authorized and required a cessation of hostilities between the military and naval forces of Great Britain and those of the United States in the district in which they had been lately carried on with such activity.

Whilst the hopes of peace were thus entertained by both parties, a chivalrous incident took place, which is not unworthy of being recorded. Major-General Keane, who had been severely wounded on the 8th of January, had lost his sword on the battle-field. It was in the possession of General Jackson, who, on such a desire being expressed by General Keane, sent it back through his Aid, Colonel Livingston, with courteous inquiries after the health of his defeated enemy. The British General acknowledged the compliment in these words: "Major-General Keane presents his best respects to General Jackson, and feels particularly thankful for the kindness he has experienced from him through the medium of Colonel Livingston. He is still further obliged for General Jackson's kind wishes for his recovery." Jackson rendered an account of this incident to the Secretary of War in these simple and noble words: "Major-General Keane having lost his sword in the action of the 8th of January, and having expressed a great desire to regain it, valuing it as the present of an esteemed friend, I thought proper to have it restored to him; thinking it more honorable to the American character to return it, after the expression of those wishes, than to retain it as a trophy of victory. I believe, however, it is a singular instance of a British General soliciting the restoration of his sword fairly lost in battle."

He further stated that some entire Congreve rockets had been found, which, with a rest from which they are fired, would be sent to the seat of Government, together with the instruments of the British band of music and their quarter-flag. "General Keane's trumpet," he wrote, "as well as that which was used on the right column of the enemy, were taken in the action of the 8th January. These instruments are in the possession of General Coffee's Brigade, where I hope they will be permitted to remain."

General Jackson continued to press upon General Lambert the question of the restoration of the negroes to their masters; and the magnanimous courtesy which he had lately shown to Major-General Keane ought to have disposed the British authorities to be accommodating at least in their transactions with him. To these continued solicitations General Lambert replied on the 27th of February, from Dauphine Island: "With regard to the negroes that have left their masters and are with this force, any proprietor, or person deputed, that chooses to present himself to me will be received, and every facility afforded him to communicate with those people, and I shall be very happy if they can be persuaded all to return, but to compel them is what I cannot do." It is worthy of remark that, in 1815, the Commander-in-Chief of a British army was not afraid to say in an official document, that *he would be happy if slaves could be persuaded to return to their masters.* In 1864, the year in which we record this fact, any Englishman, placed in the same position with General Lambert, would probably utter some popular sentimental cant about the blessings of liberty for the poor injured sons of Africa.

In the same communication General Lambert gives a singular proof of the infatuation which had possessed the minds of the invaders as to the disposition of the Creoles toward them. With bull-dog tenacity they seem to have clung to the last to the idea, that what they considered as the French element of the population of Louisiana was still inclined to hail them as friends, notwithstanding the manifest demonstration to the contrary given on the battle-field and in every other possible way. It appears that Major-General Villeré had written to General Lambert, after the retreat of the British army, to claim payment for a considerable number of cattle which had been swept from his plantation. General Lambert appears to have been astonished at this call for full indemnity, and at what he considered the unfriendly tone of the communication, as if he could have expected anything else. He forwarded it to General Jackson with these remarks: "I should have been glad to have known the Major-General's sentiments previous, as I certainly should not have troubled myself about his concerns, or endeavored to render as little painful as I was able, not living in his house, the unavoidable circumstances attending the immediate theatre of war toward his son, whom he had left unprotected."*

On the 6th of March, General Jackson informed General Lambert of his having just received intelligence from Washington, which left little doubt in his mind that the treaty signed at Ghent between the United States and Great Britain had been ratified by the Presi-

---

* In that passage General Lambert alludes to General Villeré's youngest son who had remained in the hands of the British, when his brother, Major Villeré, made his escape on the 23d of December, 1814.

dent and Senate of the United States, but that, by some unaccountable accident, a dispatch on another subject had been substituted for the one intended to give him official information of that event:

"The one I have received, however," he continued, "is accompanied by an order from the Postmaster-General directing his deputies to forward the express carrying intelligence of the recent peace. Of this order I inclose a copy, and from other sources to which I give credit, I learn that the same express brought official notice of the treaty to the Governor of Tennessee. I have deemed it a duty, without loss of time, to communicate the exact state of those circumstances, that you might determine whether they would not justify you in agreeing, by a cessation of hostilities, to anticipate the happy return of peace between our two nations, which the first direct intelligence must bring to us in an official form. * * I pray you, with the assurance of high respect, to receive that of the satisfaction I feel in reflecting that our correspondence, begun as commanders of hostile armies, should terminate as officers of nations in amity."

On the next day, the 7th of March, he informed General Lambert that, in consequence of the intimation contained in his former letters that every facility would be given to the proprietors of slaves now with the British forces to induce them to return, he had given permission to certain individuals to pass under a flag of truce to the fleet for the purpose of seeing and reclaiming their slaves, and "he prayed that those slaves might be returned to them."

On the 17th, General Jackson communicated to General Lambert that official information had reached him of the ratification of the treaty of peace, whereupon he proposed to make such arrangements as might be necessary to receive such forts, garrisons, artillery, munitions, or other property as might be embraced in the first article of that treaty. General Jackson further claimed under the treaty such slaves as might be within the control of the British commander, belonging to any inhabitant or citizen of the United States, to the end "that their owners might again obtain possession of them." On the 18th, General Lambert informed General Jackson that he and Admiral Malcolm had issued orders for the cessation of hostilities, and for all detached posts and ships to be withdrawn in their respective commands. He added that Fort Bowyer would be restored in every respect as when it fell into his hands, with the exception only of a brass mortar, cast in George the Second's reign, which had been sent away the day after the surrender. With regard to his construction of the treaty in relation to the restoration of property, he said, with bad logic and equally bad phraseology:

> "In the fulfilling the first article of the treaty, I cannot consider the meaning of ' not causing any destruction, or carrying away any artillery, or other public property, *originally* captured in the said forts or places, and *which* shall *remain therein* upon the exchange of the ratification of this treaty, or any slave, or other property,' as having reference to any antecedent period to the 18th of February, the day of the exchange of ratifications; because it is only from that time that the article could be fulfilled in a long war. If those negroes (the matter now in question) belonged to the *territory*, or *city*, we were actually *in occupation of*, I should conceive we had no right to take them away; but by their coming away, they are virtually the same as deserters, or property taken away at any time of the war. I am obliged to say so much in justification of the right; but I have from the first done all I could to prevent, and subsequently, together with Admiral Malcolm, have given every facility, and used every persuasion that they should return to their masters, and many have done so; but I could not reconcile it to myself to abandon any, who, from false reasoning perhaps, joined us during the period of hostilities, and have thus acted in violation of the laws of their country, and, besides, become obnoxious to their masters. Had it been an object to take the negroes away, they could have been embarked in the first instance; but they have been permitted to remain in the hope that they might return."

On the next day, the 19th of March, General Lambert,

in another communication written from Dauphine Island, said to General Jackson: "The preparations for a long voyage may detain the troops here a few days longer, out no exertion will be wanting to embark the whole as soon as possible." He concluded his letter with such expressions of high-toned courtesy as it is pleasant to see exchanged between men who had lately met as foes on the battle-field. "As I may not have another opportunity of addressing you," said Lambert to Jackson, "permit me to avail myself of the present to wish you health and happiness, and to express my regret that circumstances will not allow me to assure you personally of the same."

Major Woodruff had been appointed by General Jackson to receive the negroes to be delivered by the British under the treaty of peace. But, on the 20th, all hope that the treaty would be executed on that point was put at an end by the following note addressed by General Lambert to that gentleman: "I answer to that part of your letter which touches upon the negroes who have come into the British force previous to the ratification of the peace, that is, on the 18th of February last, that I do not feel myself authorized to deliver them up under the treaty, without their consent." On the 23d, Major Woodruff communicated to General Jackson the strange interpretation put on the treaty by General Lambert: "He informed me," said Woodruff, "that he would be prepared to execute, on the part of his Government, every article of said treaty, except that part relating to *slaves*, as it was totally incompatible with the spirit and constitution of his Government to recognize *slavery* at all; that he would use his influence in persuading them to return to their masters, by every argument in his power; but that he would not use force in compelling their obedience, or permit it to be used within the British lines."

Governor Claiborne, who, thus far, had delayed acting in conformity with the "Resolutions" passed by the Legislature on the 2d of February, approving his intention to intervene in the negotiation carried on in relation to the slaves between Jackson and Lambert, and who, on reflection, had probably seen the propriety of waiting until it was concluded, now determined, on the 25th of March, apparently with a sort of ingenuous belief in his own importance or that of the Legislature, to send Commissioners to General Lambert, in order to obtain that in which General Jackson, acting in the name of the United States, had failed to succeed. "These gentlemen," he said to Lambert, "at the solicitation and in behalf of the owners of the negro slaves who are understood to have followed the English army to Dauphine Island, have repaired to your headquarters for the purpose of receiving, and providing the means of sending back to their masters, such of the negro slaves aforesaid as, in conformity to the first article of the treaty of peace, your Excellency shall deem proper to decline *carrying away*." Major-General Power, who had been left in command during the absence of General Lambert, replied:

"I should feel happy in rendering any assistance to those gentlemen, to enable them to execute the object of their mission, but agreeably to the determination of Major-General Lambert before he went away, all those slaves who were not willing, and who objected to return to their former masters, have been embarked for the Island of Bermuda, to be sent from there to Trinidad. The Major-General did everything in his power to induce the whole of the slaves who deserted from New Orleans to return; but he did not feel himself authorized to resort to force to oblige them to do so, as they threw themselves on his protection, which they were entitled to, having served with the British army, and which they did voluntarily and without compulsion."

That part of the first article of the treaty which is

referred to in this correspondence as embracing the question of the restoration of slaves to their masters ran as follows:

"All territories, places and possessions whatsoever, taken from either party by the other during the war, or which may be taken after the signing of this treaty, excepting only the islands hereinafter mentioned, shall be restored without delay, and without causing any destruction, or carrying away any of the artillery or other public property, originally captured in the said forts or places, and which shall remain therein, upon the exchange of the ratification of this treaty, or any slaves or other private property."

It seems to us clear that, in this document, the Government of Great Britain acknowledges slaves as property, and yet, in the face of it, a British General is seen assuming the responsibility of declaring that he would not execute that part of the treaty relating to slaves, because "it was totally incompatible with the spirit and Constitution of his Government to recognize slavery at all." To elude what to him is an obnoxious stipulation, he further resorts gravely to a miserable quibble, unworthy even of a pettifogger. He alleges that the slaves *were not carried away*, according to the expressions used in the treaty, but that *they carried themselves away*, and were therefore to be looked upon in the light of deserters, forgetting that they could not be deserters, and treated as such, if they were property, as expressly acknowledged in the treaty, the words being "slaves or other property." He further takes the extraordinary ground that he is only bound to restore what property belonged to the *city or territory the British were actually in possession of on the 18th of February*, the day of the exchange of ratifications, so that the treaty being signed on the 24th of December, and the British officers having had ample time to know its contents before it was ratified and the ratifications exchanged, had only to remove beyond their actual lines every sort of private property they had taken in order to escape the obligation of restoring it, on the exchange of the ratifications. Thus General Lambert, according to his interpretation, was not bound to restore any private property which he might have carried away from the Parishes of St. Bernard and Plaquemine, antecedent to the 18th February, but only such as he might have taken on Dauphine Island, of which he was still in possession at that time. This concession, however, restricted as it was, he refused to apply to slaves, because they could not, as he maintained, be property according to the Constitution of England. For instance, on or after the 18th of February, he would have considered himself bound not to *carry away* any slaves *belonging* to Dauphine Island, which was still in British hands, but had a slave and a cow *come* to his camp pitched on that island, he would have restored the cow and not the slave, although in the text of the treaty a cow and a slave were placed on the same footing as property. As this same forced construction was put on the treaty by all British officers, from the shores of Maryland to those of Louisiana, without the possibility of previous consultation and agreement, it is fair to suppose that during the time which elapsed between the 24th of December and the 18th of February, the British Government, alarmed at the consequences of the concession which it had made in the treaty, and which probably threatened to provoke the resentment of Exeter Hall and other congregations of negro worshipers, had sent secret instructions for the non-execution of that part of the treaty. The Government of the United States remonstrated with uncompromising firmness and unanswerable logic, but the British Government adopted, if it had not dictated, the construction put upon the treaty by its agents. John Quincy Adams, then the Minister Plenipotentiary of the United

States at the Court of St. James, although himself an abolitionist of the deepest dye, and supposed to be hostile to the South, demonstrated victoriously, in his correspondence with Lords Bathurst and Castlereagh, how erroneous were the views of the British Government on the subject.

According to grammar and to the common understanding of language, it would seem that there could be no doubt but that the terms of the "First Article" had established in a most guarded manner a distinction between public and private property. All territories, places and possessions (with a particular exception) were to be restored, without destroying or carrying away any of the artillery, or other public property, originally captured in the said forts or places, and which remained there upon the exchange of ratifications. Had it been intended to put slaves and other private property on the same ground with artillery and other public property, the terms *originally captured in the said forts and places, and which shall remain therein on the exchange of the ratifications of this treaty*, instead of being inserted after "artillery and other public property," would have been put at the end of the sentence after "slaves and other private property." In that case both interests, the public and the private, would have been subject to the same restraint. But, by separating them from each other, and putting the restrictive words immediately after "artillery and other public property," it showed that it was intended to confine their operation to these subjects only, excluding from it "slaves and other private property."

This is amply demonstrated by a reference to the *procès verbal* of the conferences between the British and American Plenipotentiaries. The first project of the Treaty of Ghent was offered by the American Plenipotentiaries, and that part of the first article relating to slaves was therein expressed in the following manner:

"All territories, places and possessions, without exception, taken by either party from the other during the war, or which may be taken after the signing of the treaty, shall be restored without delay, and without causing any destruction, or carrying away any other public property, or any slaves or other private property."

The British Plenipotentiaries proposed the following alterations:

"All territory, places and possessions, without exception, belonging to either party, and taken by the other during the war, or which may be taken after the signing of this treaty, shall be restored without delay, and without causing any destruction, or carrying away any of the artillery or other public property, or any slaves or other private property, originally captured in the said forts or places, and which shall remain therein upon the exchange of the ratifications of this treaty."

It will be observed that, in this proposal,* the words, "originally captured in the said forts or places, and which shall remain therein upon the ratifications of this treaty," operated as a modification of the article as originally proposed in the American project. Instead of stipulating that no property, public or private, artillery or slaves, should be carried away, they limited the prohibition of removal to all such property as had been originally captured in the forts and places, and remained there at the exchange of the ratifications. They included within the limitation private as well as public property; and had the article been assented to in this form by the American Plenipotentiaries and ratified by their Government, it would have warranted the construction which the British Commanders gave to the article as it was ultimately agreed to, and which it cannot admit. But the American Plenipotentiaries proposed to

* John Quincy Adams to Lord Castlereagh, August 9th, 1815.

transpose the words, "originally captured in the said forts or places, and which shall remain therein upon the exchange of the ratifications of this treaty," and to insert them *before* the words "slaves or other property," instead of *after*, as they stood. This was agreed to by the British Plenipotentiaries. It is as evident as anything can be, that it was intended by this transposition of words to admit, with regard to artillery and public property, the limitation proposed by the British project, but not to assent to it with regard to slaves and private property. On the contrary, we asked such a transposition of the words of limitation as would leave them applicable only to artillery and public property, and would except slaves and private property from their operation altogether. The British Plenipotentiaries could not but understand the meaning of this transposition, and could not plead ignorance of the views of the other party in persisting in the general prohibition to carry away slaves and private property, while acquiescing in the limitation with respect to artillery and public property. With this implied, if not expressed, understanding, the British Government agreed to the transposition of the words; and, accordingly, that part of the "First Article" of the treaty stood and was ratified as it reads now. Had its grammatical construction been in any degree equivocal, this statement of the manner in which it was drawn up would have sufficed to solve every doubt of its meaning. Therefore, John Quincy Adams contended with great force that the article, as originally drawn by the American Plenipotentiaries, was plain and clear; that it admitted of no other construction than that for which the American Government now contended; that it avowedly and openly contained a stipulation that, in the evacuation of all the territories, places and possessions to be restored, no slave should be carried away; that an alteration was proposed by the British Plenipotentiaries, which was accepted only in part; that in this partial acceptance the British Government acquiesced; that when Great Britain proposed an alteration to the American project, of the meaning of which there could be no doubt, when her alteration was accepted conditionally, and under a modification to which she agreed, she was bound to perceive that the modification thus insisted upon by the other party was not a mere verbal change in the phraseology of her proposal, but, so far as it extended, a substantial adherence to the original draught of the article.

"That the British Government gave it then another construction," added Mr. Adams, "was not only never communicated to the Government of the United States, but was impossible to be foreseen by them. When Great Britain had solemnly agreed, without hinting an objection, to the principle of restoring captured slaves, it could not have been foreseen that the engagement could be narrowed down to nothing by the strained extension of a condition, limited by the words of the treaty to another species of property. It was impossible to anticipate a construction of an important stipulation which should annihilate its operation. It was impossible to anticipate that a stipulation not to carry away any slaves would by the British Government be considered as faithfully executed by British officers in carrying away all the slaves in their possession. The only foundation which these naval commanders have alleged for this procedure was a construction of the paragraph containing this stipulation so contrary to its grammatical sense and obvious purport, that the undersigned is well assured, if the same phrase had occurred in any municipal contract between individuals, no judicial tribunal in this Kingdom would entertain for a moment a question upon it—a construction under which the whole operation of the words 'slaves or other private property' was annihilated, by extending to them the limitation confined by the words of the treaty to artillery and private property."

Notwithstanding these unanswerable arguments, the British Government still contended that the limitation not to carry away slaves applied only to such of them as had been originally captured in certain forts or places, and still remaining therein upon the exchange of the ratifications of the treaty, well knowing that there was not perhaps one single slave to carry away in all those which were occupied by the British troops when the treaty was concluded. In his desperate attempts to escape from Mr. Adams' inexorable logic in relation to the manner in which the "First Article" of the treaty was drawn, Lord Bathurst, a member of the British Ministry, made use of this extraordinary language: "It is certainly possible that one party may propose an alteration, with a mental reservation of some construction of his own, and that he may assent to it on the firm persuasion that the construction continues to be the same, and that, therefore, he may conciliate, and yet concede nothing by his assent." Mr. Adams witheringly observed, in relation to this passage, that "he trusted that some error of a copyist had left its meaning imperfectly expressed."

Considering some of the features assumed by the war carried on between the Confederate States and the United States of America, after the lapse of about half a century since that correspondence, it is curious to notice several of the grounds taken by John Quincy Adams in his discussion with the British Ministry in relation to the Treaty of Ghent. For instance, he maintained that, according to the usages of war among civilized nations, no private property, including slaves, ought to be taken; that all private property on shore partook of that sacred character; that it was entitled by the laws of war to exemption from capture; that "slaves were private property." Lord Liverpool* said that he thought they could not be considered precisely under the general denomination of private property; a table or a chair, for instance, might be taken and restored without changing its condition

---
* John Quincy Adams to the Secretary of State, August 22d, 1815.

but a living and huma being was entitled to other considerations.

"I replied," wrote Mr. Adams to the Secretary of State at Washington, "that the treaty had marked no such distinction: the words implicitly recognized slaves as private property in the articles alluded to: 'slaves or other private property.' Not that I meant to deny the principle assumed by him: most certainly a living, sentient being, and still more a human being, was to be regarded in a different light from the inanimate matter of which other private property might consist. And if, on the ground of that difference, the British Plenipotentiaries had objected to restore the one while consenting to restore the other, we should readily have discussed the subject; we might have accepted or objected to the proposal they would have made. But, *what could that proposal have been? Upon what ground could Great Britain have refused to restore them?* Was it because they had been seduced away from their masters by the promises of British officers? But had they taken New Orleans, or any other Southern city, would not all the slaves in it have had as much claim to the benefit of such promises as the fugitives from their masters elsewhere? How then could the place, if it had been taken, have been evacuated according to the treaty, without carrying away slaves, if the pledge of such promises was to protect them from being restored to their owners? It was true, proclamations inviting slaves to desert from their masters had been issued by British officers. We considered them as deviations from the usages of war. We believed that the British Government itself, when the hostile passions arising from the state of war should subside, would consider them in the same light; that Great Britain would then be willing to restore the property, or to indemnify the sufferers by its loss. If she felt bound to make good the promises of her officers to the slaves, she might still be willing to do an act of justice by compensating the owners of the slaves for the property which had been irregularly taken from them. Lord Liverpool manifested no dissatisfaction at these remarks, nor did he attempt to justify the proclamation to which I particularly alluded."

The British Government, however, would not recede from the position it had taken, and, after several years of negotiation, the decision of the question was referred to the arbitration of Russia, who declared in favor of the American construction of the treaty, and Great Britain finally paid a certain sum of money for the slaves she had carried away.

Verily is history full of strange contrasts. We now see the United States denying what they compelled Great Britain to acknowledge, by the treaty of Ghent: *that negroes are property.* We see them asserting at one time, through Mr. John Quincy Adams, their Minister Plenipotentiary in London, that private property on shore, according to the usages of modern warfare, cannot be captured by belligerents; that proclamations to induce slaves to desert from their masters are unjustifiable; and that such practices are deviations from the usages of war. We see them now informing that same Government of Great Britain, through Mr. Adams, their Minister Plenipotentiary, and a son of the former minister, that it is right for them to capture private property on land, to destroy it in every possible way, to cut down crops, to break all agricultural implements, to produce a general famine in the land they invade, to remove even clothing, food and medicine from the desolated homes of the widow and the infant; we hear their loud proclamation, reverberating throughout the world, that not only is it right to seduce away slaves from their masters, but that it is in conformity with the usages of civilized war, and one of its necessities, to arm slaves against their masters. Mr. John Quincy Adams charitably expressed the hope that when the hostile passions arising from a state of war should have subsided, the Government of Great Britain would consider the impropriety of its conduct in its proper light. We entertain the same hope in relation to the Government and people of the United States, notwithstanding the variety of the monstrous national crimes which have been perpetrated, notwithstanding the Congressional denial that eight millions of their fellow-beings had "any rights whatever."

There was one man, however, who, it is said, succeeded in getting back most of his negroes, if not all of them. It was Major Lacoste, afterward major-general in the militia of the State. He was a man of commanding presence, having a striking military air, and really looked superb in full uniform. There was a great deal of dry humor and practical shrewdness concealed under his somewhat exaggerated loftiness of manner, and, as he was a man of real worth, the occasional ebullitions of a temperament inclining to pomposity were sources of amusement even to those who liked and appreciated him the most. He had been one of the planters authorized by General Jackson to repair to the British camp at Dauphine Island, with a view to regain their slaves, and was told, with the rest, that he could have his negroes only with their consent. He did not lose his time, however, in remonstrating with the British officers against their shameful construction of the treaty, but seemed to assent with cheerful philosophy to this manifestation of their Punic faith. This apparent acquiescence, and a stately urbanity which could not be ruffled, predisposed the British in his favor. He did not speak one word of English, but several of the British officers spoke French perfectly. They and the Major soon became friendly; his dignified conviviality won their hearts and commanded their respect. "Surely," said the Major to them, "you will spare me the humiliation of coaxing, in the presence of anybody, my runaway slaves to return to me. British officers cannot but be gentlemen, and must appreciate the feelings of one in my position. I doubt not, therefore, that you will permit me to remain alone with my slaves, and use with them what arguments I can find, without being overheard by any evil-disposed witnesses who may laugh at my vain efforts. What I am compelled to do is sufficiently vexatious without unnecessarily making it more painful to me." The British officers, whom he had put in good-humor, and whose vanity he had gently patted on the shoulder, assented to his desire. "But," said they, "there must be no force used, Major; the slaves must express clearly their consent to return." "Force!" exclaimed the Major; "you speak in derision. What force can I use in the circumstances in which I am, unless you allude to the force of persuasion?" "Oh! no," replied the British officers, laughing; "that kind of force is legitimate. You have our consent to that." With this understanding, the Major was taken to the quarters of his negroes, who behaved with some degree of civility when they saw him, and who were particularly struck with the military honors paid to their master as he approached the guards who watched over them. This did not escape the keen eye of the Major, and, taking advantage of this circumstance, he bowed with great majesty and condescension to the officers who had accompanied him, and who retired according to their promise. As soon as he was left alone with his slaves, he drew himself up to his full height and assumed a menacing attitude and tone. "Ah! my darkies, here you are!" he said. "You thought you could escape me, you fools! You never knew before what a great man I am; you never dreamed that the British respect me so much that they are willing to be commanded by me and have your master for their chief. But you see it with your own eyes; nobody tells you that. I flogged the British well, as you know; and I will flog you well too, if you continue to misbehave as they once did. But now I am their friend, because they have repented,—so much have they repented that they want to kill you for having left me as you did, you ungrateful rascals! 'Major Lacoste,' they said to me, 'is it true that these dirty, stinking fellows used to steal your chickens and your pigs?' 'Yes,' said I; 'it is but too true.' 'Well, what did you do with them on such occasions?'—'I shook my fists at them, and threatened to cut their throats, but never did it, as you see, because I loved them like children.'—' Ha, ha, Major Lacoste,' they said, 'that is not the way to treat niggers. Now that we are friends, if you say the word, we will make an example of them for having left so kind a master. We will shoot every one of them, and bring you better niggers from Africa for ten dollars apiece.' I see that you look terrified, brigands; but you know I am good—too good. I pardon you all, unfortunate wretches." He seemed so powerful, he looked so grand, so imposing, that the negroes fell on their knees and thanked him for his mercy. "Rise, hypocritical scamps!" he continued, with an expression in his face of Olympian benignity, which still retained something of the awful and the terrible, "rise; I will save your lives; not because I believe in your repentance, not because I am your dupe (Major Lacoste cannot be duped by anybody); but because I am used to you, and we may as well grow old together. I will take you home safely without loss of time. The British may soon get drunk like Choctaws; it is their habit; and then perhaps I could not save you. Form a line, two by two, keep behind me, close on my heels— no straggling—and I will carry you safe through the British lines to the boat which awaits us." The trembling negroes did as he commanded. Putting himself at their head, he marched toward a company of British soldiers who had been commanded to watch him, and to ascertain if the slaves followed him willingly. As he approached in the full dress of his grade, the soldiers were courteously ordered to present arms. " Don't fire," exclaimed the Major, in French, waving his hand in a manner which might be taken for a sign of command, or an acknowledgment for the honors paid to him. "Don't fire, they follow me willingly;" then turning to the negroes, he said, in their corrupt French idiom, which they alone could understand: "You see! they wanted to shoot you and I prevented them. Now, speak your mind. Do you want to come with me? Yes or no." "We want to go with master; we want to go home," shrieked the negroes, huddling round the Major, and almost hugging him in their arms. There was no denying such a manifestation of consent. The Major bowed superbly to the bewildered Britons and marched off. He met on his way several other corps of British troops, and the same scene was reacted with equal success, until he reached his boat and departed in triumph. It is reported that the Major was fond of relating this exploit, of which he was very proud, and would say, on such occasions, with ineffable self-complacency and a dash of contempt: "I taught those thick-witted Englishmen how to interpret a treaty."

The happy effects of peace were soon felt in Louisiana. On the 16th of March, Governor Claiborne wrote to Mr. Monroe, Secretary of War: "Great is the change which the return of peace has already made in this capital (New Orleans). Our harbor is again whitening with canvas; the levee is crowded with cotton, tobacco, and other articles for exportation. The merchant seems delighted with the prospect before him, and the agriculturist finds in the high price for his products new incitements to industry." This war had been conducted on the part of the British with an inhumanity and with a contempt of the usages of civilization which it is the duty of the historian to censure; they had armed negroes and Indians, and had showed a love for devastation and plunder which could be expected only from barbarians. In many letters written at the time by British officers, and which fell into the hands of the Americans, that love for plunder is openly developed, and proved beyond contradiction. Colonel Malcolm, in a letter to the Rear-Admiral of that name, expresses his chagrin that his share of the prize-money at St. Mary's "did not exceed five hundred pounds." In another communication of a similar tone from the same to the same, the hope is entertained "that New Orleans will repay the troops for all their trouble and fatigues." Sir Thomas Cochrane laments that St. Mary's was taken two days before his arrival, which, of course, "cut him out of what had been captured." He adds in the same mercenary strain: "It was at first supposed, as is usual on these occasions, that a great deal of money would be made, but if they do clear *thirty thousand pounds, it will be as much* as they will do." Condoling with Captain Evans on the defeat of the British army at New Orleans, Admiral Cockburn said: "We have been more fortunate here *in our small way*. We have taken St. Mary's, *a tolerably rich place.*" Another individual writes to Lieutenant Douglas, of the brig Sophia, off New Orleans: "We have had *some fine fun and plenty of plunder* at St. Mary's. How are you off for *tables* and *chests of drawers*, etc."? Here are the words of J. Gallon to J. O'Reilly, of the ship Tonnant, off New Orleans: "We have had fine fun since I saw you. What with the Rappahannock, and various other places, we have contrived *to pick up* a few trifling things, such as mahogany tables, chests of drawers, etc. One J. R. Glover writes from Cumberland Island, on the 1st of February, to Captain Westful of the Anaconda: "We have established our headquarters here, after ransacking St. Mary's, from which we brought away property to the amount of *fifty thousand pounds;* and had we two thousand troops, we might collect *a good harvest* before peace takes place." Captain Napier informs Captain Gordon that he has " petitioned the Prince Regent for *a good slice* of prize-money, and hopes to succeed."

From these specimens of the greedy disposition of the British officers at the time, we can easily imagine what " fine fun" they would have had if they had taken possession of New Orleans, and what would have been the fate of the " chests of drawers," and other valuables of the inhabitants of that city, ·if they had come in contact with the hands of these *gentlemen.* It is generally believed in the United States that, on the memorable day of the 8th of January, the parole and countersign of the enemy's army were " booty and beauty." That belief, which contains a most heinous and almost incredible charge against so civilized a nation as Great Britain, is founded partly on the rapacity exhibited, and the brutish depredations committed by the British army wherever it landed in America, and partly on the concurrent report of a great number of the British prisoners and deserters. It is hardly probable that they should have agreed in such an invention. Was it a calumny? In that case, why was not the infamous report contradicted? Why was not the proof of the genuine parole and countersign on that day furnished by the British Government? They must have been easily obtained, for they must have been consigned on the orderly-books of every corps in the army. It was correctly observed at the time, " that the fame of General Packenham and his officers, the moral character of the British military, strongly implicated by a charge of this nature, and the honor of the British Government, all imperiously demanded that it be refuted, if capable of refutation;" and yet no such attempt was made, although so grave an accusation was blazoned forth in every newspaper and periodical publication in the United States, and thus assumed the authority and importance, as it were, of a national act. Was it beneath the dignity of Great Britain to notice it in the same way through her public press? Could it have been derogatory to a great nation to have disproved an allegation which left a stain on her character, and which was made by her peer in power, in rank, in civilization, and in morality? She has chosen, however, to remain silent; and her silence, when her sensitiveness as to her national honor is so well known, must, under the circumstances we have mentioned, be received as an implied confession of the truth of what was universally believed in America. She has, therefore, no right to complain if American historians record that "booty and beauty" were the parole and countersign given by General Packenham on the 8th of January, when he led his troops to the assault of General Jackson's lines. It is from the fate which such words imply that General Jackson saved New Orleans; and so horrible are the scenes which they must conjure up in the imagination of every one, that it is really to be wondered at that the Legislature of Louisiana refused to vote him a sabre, as proposed, and to include him in those thanks which they lavished on every human being who had participated in the defence of New Orleans. Not only had Louisiana been protected against an army of fifteen thousand men, but this large army of veterans had been driven away with a loss of more than four thousand men, whilst our casualties consisted in 55 killed, 185 wounded, 93 missing—grand total, 333. This is an historic fact, as well authenticated as any one of those which are accepted without a doubt:

and yet it must be confessed that it presents itself in the shape of fiction, although sober truth claims it as belonging to her domain.

So certain of success had the British been when they attacked Louisiana, that they had come ready prepared with all the officers necessary for her civil administration —which shows what we must think of their assertions that they had come to restore to their allies, the Spaniards, a province which they had lost. On the subject of that "certainty" which had possessed itself of the British mind, Colonel Malcolm wrote to Admiral Malcolm: "From all accounts New Orleans is very strong. . . . . . What a disappointment it will be in England, should you fail! The chance of failure has not been calculated on, and from the force employed it has been made too sure at first."

Having dismissed the British, loaded with humiliation instead of that plunder and glory which they had expected, we shall now proceed to record and examine some of the events which had taken place in New Orleans during the invasion, and which we had purposely passed over, with the intention of returning to them after we had done relating in a connected manner the military operations against Louisiana and their conclusion by the treaty of peace.

We have already mentioned in the preceding pages that, on the 28th of December, 1814, in the morning, the halls of the Legislative Assembly had been closed by military authority, and the members prevented from meeting as usual. This order was enforced until the next day, when it was revoked early in the morning, and both Houses permitted to resume their functions. Their first act was to appoint a Joint Committee to inquire into the cause of this extraordinary proceeding, and to ascertain the source from which it had emanated. General

Jackson was immediately addressed on the subject, and his reply was as follows :

"CAMP AT MACARTY'S, 4 MILES BELOW NEW ORLEANS,
" *Headquarters, December* 31, 1814.

" The Major-General commanding has the honor to acknowledge the receipt of the joint resolution of both Houses of the Hon. the Legislature of the State of Louisiana, now in session, dated the 30th inst., and communicated to him by a Joint Committee of both Houses, to which the General gives the following answer:

"That just after the engagement between the British and American armies had commenced on the 28th inst., when the enemy was advancing, and it was every moment expected they would storm our lines; as the General was riding rapidly from right to left of his line, he was accosted by Mr. Duncan, one of his volunteer Aids, who had just returned from New Orleans. Observing him to be apparently agitated, the General stopped, and, supposing him the bearer of some information of the enemy's movements, asked what was the matter. He replied that he was the bearer of a message from Governor Claiborne that the Assembly were about to give up the country to the enemy. Being asked if he had any letter from the Governor, he answered in the negative. He was then interrogated as to the person from whom he received the intelligence; he said it was from a militia Colonel. The General inquired where this Colonel was; that he ought to be apprehended, and if the information was not true, he ought to be shot, but that the General did not believe it. To this Mr. Duncan replied that the Colonel had returned to New Orleans, and had requested him, Mr. Duncan, to deliver the above message.

" The General was in the act of pushing forward along the line, when Mr. Duncan called after him and said: 'The Governor expects orders what to do.' The General replied that he did not believe the intelligence, but to desire the Governor to make strict inquiry into the subject; and if true, to blow them up. The General pursued his way, and Mr. Duncan returned to the city. After the action, Mr. Duncan returned, and on the General's stating to him the impropriety of delivering such a message—publicly, in the presence of the troops, as well as the improbability of the fact—he excused himself by the great importance of the intelligence; and then, for the first time, the General heard the name of Colonel Declouet as Mr. Duncan's author. . . . .

" The above statement the General gives as a substantial one of the matter referred to in the Resolutions of the Senate and House of Representatives; and to this he adds, that he gave no order to the Governor to interfere with the Legislature, except as above stated."

The next application for information, on the part of the Committee, was to Governor Claiborne. He replied that he had never sent any message to General Jackson on such a subject, either through Colonel Declouet, or anybody else. On the morning of the 28th, on hearing the discharges of the artillery and musketry, which announced to him that an engagement had begun, the Governor was advancing toward General Jackson's camp with an escort of cavalry, when he met his Aid, Colonel Fortier, who said to him: " Major-General Jackson has received the information that the Legislature is on the point of assembling to give up the country. His orders are that the Governor should immediately close the doors of the State House, surround it with guards, and fire on the members should they persist in assembling." Colonel Fortier said that these orders had been delivered to him by Abner Duncan, one of General Jackson's volunteer Aids. The Governor immediately returned to the city and executed what he believed to be instructions from the Commander-in-Chief. The Governor expressed his regrets that there should have been an error, or misunderstanding, and that it should have given rise to so grave a measure as a military interference with the functions of the Legislature, but added that, with regard to the part he had taken in it, he confidently believed that, with the information which had been given him, and in the extraordinary circumstances in which the State was placed, he had pursued the course which prudence and duty required;* for, admitting that the in-

* Not having the original English text, I regret that I cannot give the very words of the Governor. I am compelled to retranslate from a French transla-

formation was without real foundation, it was not the less evident that suspicions very injurious to the Legislature had been spread among the public, and that the mere fact of the meeting of the Legislature on that day might, and probably would, have caused some popular commotion, the repression of which would have been difficult. On the other hand, supposing the information to have been well founded, the momentary suspension of the services of the Legislature had then become essential to the safety of the State. Such was the substance of the Governor's declaration made on the 4th of January, and transmitted to the Legislature.

Colonel Fortier related that, on the morning of the 28th, being on his way to our lines, he met Mr. Duncan coming to New Orleans, who said to him: "Have you seen Colonel Declouet?—Yes.—What did he say to you?—Nothing, except that our affairs were going on well at Camp Jackson, and that the British were retiring.—Has he not told you something else?—No.—Do you know if the Legislature is in session?—No.—Do you think that they are to meet to-day?—I do not know, but I do not believe it; for I saw, not long ago, several members, and among others, Mr. Harper, who was on his way to the camp with his gun." After this Colonel Fortier, as he alleges, received the message which he transmitted to Governor Claiborne.

General Jackson's volunteer Aid, Abner Duncan, seems to have been the cause of the regrettable occurrence which had taken place. He had misapprehended the orders given him, and he had not even carried and reported them as he had understood them to be. According to his own declarations before the Committee, he had met Colonel Declouet, who was coming from the city in

tion, which is, however, official and sanctioned by the Legislature, as it is published in the French side of their Journal.

great haste and in a great state of agitation, and who begged him to inform General Jackson that there was a plan among several members of the Legislature to surrender the country to the enemy, and named the individuals who were engaged in the plot. He admits that Colonel Declouet never told him that he was sent by the Governor, and he avers that he never told General Jackson that the message came from the Governor, "although," he says, "the General seems to have been under that impression at the time." As to General Jackson's orders, he believed them to have been, *as far as the agitation in which he was permitted him to understand and remember them:* "Tell the Governor to prevent it, and if they attempt it, to blow them up." Even this message he did not transmit faithfully, and he assumed the responsibility of prescribing to Claiborne the measure which was to be taken, instead of leaving what was to be done to the wisdom of that magistrate. If there is any excuse for Mr. Duncan, it must be looked for in the perturbed state of mind in which he confesses to have been. To this cause it must be safe also to attribute the discrepancy existing between General Jackson's circumstantial account and Duncan's declarations.

Colonel Declouet certainly found himself in a very critical situation. According to Duncan's and Davezac's testimony, which is given at length in the report of the Committee of Investigation, he had accused the Legislature of treason; he had accused Guichard, the Speaker of the House, Blanque, Marigny and others who always voted with Blanque, a very influential member of the House, of being at the head of the movement. He had asserted that Guichard had attempted to obtain his cooperation by telling him that General Jackson made war after the Russian fashion, which was to destroy everything rather than give up the possession of the country to the British, whilst the enemy would respect property. Major Tully Robinson and Major Tessier also swore that Declouet had mentioned to them Blanque, Guichard and Marigny as using their influence in the Legislature to dispose that body to a capitulation, in order to prevent the destruction of property, "which should not be sacrificed to military pride."

Davezac, one of the voluntary Aids to General Jackson, being at headquarters, conversing with the General a short time after the meeting of Duncan and Declouet which we have related, the latter, accompanied by the former, as Davezac believes, entered the room in which he, Davezac, and the General stood. Declouet, who seemed to labor under some degree of embarrassment, having told the General that he wished to speak with him in private, Davezac was preparing to withdraw, when the General desired him to remain and to serve as interpreter, because he did not understand the French language, which was the only one used by the Colonel. Declouet spoke slowly, and Davezac interpreted each phrase as it came out. The purport of Declouet's communication was as follows: "That since the invasion of the country he had had with one of his friends, a member of the Legislature, a conversation which he considered of the utmost importance." He refused at first to name the individual, but on being assured of secrecy, he declared that it was Mr. Guichard, Speaker of the House of Representatives. After some vague observations relating to the pending hostilities, Mr. Guichard had said with much warmth, "that war, such as it was carried on by General Jackson, was horrible; it was a Russian war; Jackson would destroy everything after the Russian fashion, and was worse than the British." Having observed to Guichard that he did not understand why the Legislature continued in session in such times as these,

Guichard replied that "it was to save the country, and take proper measures to preserve it from ruin." To this he answered not, but made many reflections which he imparted to a friend, who advised him to discover to General Jackson what he knew. Being still in a state of indecision, during the late attack of the 28th, he had met Duncan, whom he had desired to communicate these facts to General Jackson. What had induced him to take that step was the apprehension that should our army meet with a disaster, the Legislature would treat with the enemy. He stated his private opinion to be, that the feelings and dispositions of the majority of the Legislature agreed with those of Guichard. By the majority, he explained that he meant such members as always voted with Blanque, and composed the French side of the House, with the exception of Rouffignac and Louaillier, who sometimes dissented. He believed that the men he named had sufficient influence to control and lead the Legislature as they wished. Such was, in substance, Davezac's testimony.

On examining all the proceedings of the investigation carried on by the Committee of the Legislature and all the documents annexed to their Report, it seems evident to us that Colonel Declouet had only intended to put secretly General Jackson on his guard against the danger which he apprehended, and had never anticipated his being brought out publicly to confront the Legislature with hostile denunciations against any of its members. Great, therefore, was his embarrassment; he shrank from the dangerous position he was made to take so unwillingly and unexpectedly, and he looked round for some shelter against the storm which he had raised. He denied having accused anybody, either Blanque, Guichard or Marigny; he knew nothing positive; he had no facts to allege; he knew of no plot or well-ascertained design to capitulate; no treasonable proposition had been made to him, or, with his knowledge, to any other human being; the consternation he had seen in the city had alarmed him; the tone and tenor of his conversation with his friend Guichard had confirmed and even increased that alarm. He had conceived apprehensions, and those apprehensions he had communicated to General Jackson. But, said the Committee to him, "Since you knew nothing treasonable, on what grounds were your apprehensions founded?" His reply was: "I always apprehended, from the very beginning of the war, a considerable diversity of opinions, a want of unanimity in the Legislature." "Are these sufficient reasons to believe the Legislature composed of traitors capable of surrendering the country to the enemy?" "I believed that division would prevail among the Legislature as in all deliberative assemblies; and, as I have a right to my apprehensions,[*] I feared that the Legislature would capitulate rather than see the city destroyed and sacked; and as by that capitulation I did not see that the war would be terminated, because more troops would come from the upper country to recover the State, I was terrified at the consequences. But I never told anybody that there were traitors in the Legislature." "If the Legislature had put the British in possession of the country, according to those apprehensions which you wished to communicate to General Jackson, would you not have considered the members of the Legislature as traitors?" "If the British had beaten us, I should have feared, as I did fear, a capitulation on the part of the Legislature, for the reasons which I have already given." This was, to use an inelegant but expressive word, *dodging* the question. But the Colonel was probably anxious not to commit himself any further; the ground on which he stood was sufficiently full of

---

[*] Et comme je suis maître de mes appréhensions.

perils and enmities. Hence the discrepancies of his statements, as related by himself and by those to whom he had made them; hence the vague nature, the clumsiness of his answers, and the "inconsistencies and absurdities" with which he is taxed in the Report of the Committee. The only individual who was somewhat implicated by anything positive, which Declouet did not deny or retract, was Magloire Guichard, whose conversation, as related by Declouet, was translated by Davezac to Jackson. Guichard was, therefore, interrogated by the Committee as to what had passed between him and Declouet on the day preceding the 28th, when Declouet's apprehensions, after that interview, had become so pressing as to induce him to communicate them to General Jackson.

But before giving the narrative of Guichard, which is of a very striking nature, it is proper to ascertain who this Colonel Declouet was, who had thus been made to assume the attitude of an accuser, face to face with so formidable a body as the Legislature of the State. It is not a little singular that he seems to have been a favorite with that same Legislature, who, a short time before, had voted a stand of colors to his regiment, a favor which, so far as we know, had been granted to no other. In delivering that stand of colors, the Governor had addressed the Colonel in these words:

"In the name and by the authority of the General Assembly, I have the honor to present to your regiment a stand of colors. They will be borne to you by the Adjutant-General, and you will be pleased to receive them as evidence of the highest confidence in the patriotism and valor of yourself and your companions-in-arms. The regiment under your command is particularly distinguished. It composes the first corps of militia which Louisiana furnished for the service of the great family, to which she is united by the indissoluble ties of interest, affection and gratitude. The occasion which called you to the field was of the greatest importance to your country, nor could the zeal and promptitude with which the call was met escape the notice and approbation of your Government. With these sentiments I commit this standard to the protection of your regiment."

This is, certainly, a flattering testimonial by the Legislature and by the Governor of the State to the worth and importance of Colonel Declouet. It will be sufficient to add, that he belonged to one of the oldest and most distinguished families of Louisiana, and that the Committee of Investigation, although censuring him with severity for his groundless and extravagant apprehensions, acknowledged his high social position and his unblemished reputation as a man of honor and integrity.

Let us now see how Magloire Guichard treated such a man, if Guichard's testimony is to be received without full allowance for the ill-concealed irritation which he seems to have felt against Declouet for his disclosures—which irritation may have produced a distempered recollection of what had passed between himself and that individual.

On the 27th of December, in the evening, Guichard was visited by Declouet. "The conversation was entirely carried on by him," says Guichard. "I took very little part in it, if any, and I should be much embarrassed to tell what it was about. About eight o'clock I entered by bed-chamber, with the intention of going to bed. He followed me, and said: "Wy do you go to bed so early?" I replied that, being fatigued, I needed rest, and that when he should be ready to follow my example, he would find his bed ready prepared." There certainly are very few men who, on receiving such an intimation, would not have retired and left Guichard to himself. Colonel Declouet remained, however, observing "that it was early yet, and that they might still continue to talk a little while." "Very well," replies

Guichard; "don't mind what I do, and talk as much as you please." Upon this, he unceremoniously undresses himself and goes to bed. Did Declouet cease the monologue with which he is represented as having bored his friend since the beginning of the evening? No. "He seated himself by the fireside," says Guichard, "and began to talk—on what—I cannot recollect. What I perfectly recollect is that, as I did not answer, he said to me once or twice: '*You sleep, I believe.*' 'No,' I replied, 'go on'—but the fact is that I went to sleep, whilst he was speaking, without my being able to say what he talked about, and when he stopped." This time Declouet retires, not, however, to quit the house in which he was treated with so little consideration, but to accept that bed which Guichard had so pointedly invited him to seek.

On the next morning, at nine o'clock, he is called to breakfast—during which, he asks Guichard why the Legislature had not adjourned. The answer was: "I do not know. After all, there is nothing which I should like better; for my private affairs suffer in consequence of the Legislature continuing to sit." It is strange that the Speaker of the House of Representatives should not have remembered that the Legislature had refused to adjourn for reasons which had been made public and recorded in their journal*—and of which one was: "That accidents might happen, and unforeseen cases might occur, when the interference of the Legislature might be necessary." To these reasons he might have referred his inquisitive visitor.

The conversation then fell on the invaders of the country and on the attack of the 23d. "I recollect perfectly," continues Guichard, (and it will be observed that he always recollects perfectly what has a

* See pp. 402, 403.

tendency to make Declouet an object of ridicule or enmity,) " that I expressed to him my surprise that he had not attacked them in the rear.* I remarked to him that, if he had struck a blow at the British with his five hundred men at the time when our forces from the city were pressing them in the opposite direction, the campaign would have been closed that evening, as they would have surrendered." This reproach must have been keenly felt, for Declouet, to use Guichard's words, pretended to become so desperate as to make a show to pull off his hair, and expressed great regret at not having been master of his own movements on that occasion. He had desired to attack, but General Morgan had not consented; he, however, and the General had, about midnight, made up their minds to reconnoitre a picket of twelve men who fired at them twelve shots, to which they replied with precisely the same number of shots. After this exploit they had retired, and in their retreat, General Morgan, in order to conduct it with more security and celerity, had ordered his men to vault clear over the fences which might be in their way. In so doing, the militia came tumbling upon each other and in such disorder that they could all have been routed or taken, if they had been pursued by a handful of British soldiers who were at a short distance. " Many and deep were his lamentations," says Guichard, " and they provoked my laughter." All these circumstances, Guichard, who had not noticed what Declouet had been talking about for hours, distinctly remembers, for their bearing was to excite the displeasure of General Morgan and of his saltatory militia, and to bring Colonel Declouet before the public in the light of a buffoon who tugged at his

---

* Colonel Declouet was under General Morgan at the English Turn, and that body of militia had made, but too late, an effort to operate a division in favor of General Jackson, who was attacking the enemy in front.

hair in mimic rage. The personage who had been so burdensome to Guichard had now become amusing; "but," observes Guichard, sarcastically, "as one grows weary of everything,* I left the table to retire to my chamber and write. I had opened my desk and taken a cigar which I was lighting, when he entered, took a chair, sat by the fire, and, taking hold of my arm, said to me in a friendly and mysterious tone: 'Tell me, my friend, do you believe that the British wish to keep the country for themselves, and that it is in their power to do so? For my part, I do not believe it.' 'Nor I,' replied Guichard. 'It is impossible.' 'How is it reported that they treat the inhabitants below?' added he. 'Do they commit depredations?' 'It is said that they do not,' answered Guichard. 'Besides, they are too politic not to use moderation. It has always been a part of their tactics to present themselves as friends and protectors wherever they go.'"

Guichard's memory, which had been oblivious of so much of Declouet's insignificant and tiresome conversation, now revives, and he is put in mind that his insupportable guest had said: "I do not believe that the British will do any harm. We do worse than they do; for our militia will plunder; they steal all the cows; the planters complain of it." If Declouet held such language, it is impossible to reconcile it with those extreme apprehensions which drove him into the imprudent position which he took the next day, and which had induced him to be so nervously inquisitive, on his visit to Guichard, about the supposed intention of the Legislature to capitulate. Be it as it may, Guichard's mind again loses suddenly its retentive faculties and forgets the rest of Declouet's remarks. Probably they were not of a nature to expose that gentleman to any resentment. "But I

---

* Mais comme on s'ennuie de tout.

remember," swears Guichard, "his concluding observation to be that, should the British take the country, and should the Americans retake it, he would be crushed." These scraps of recollection which rise up, by fits and starts, from Guichard's vast fount of oblivion, are so evidently impregnated with venom, that we cannot but receive them with some degree of caution. We almost yield to the suspicion that their object was to turn the tables upon Declouet. "Tell me frankly," continues Declouet, "what you think would happen, if the British succeed?" "I think," replied Guichard, "that the country would be ruined." "He believes," he added, "that he had good reasons to know them, as they had once been the cause of his losing all he had."*

Here Guichard attempts again to get rid of Colonel Declouet, as he had attempted more than once before, and betakes himself to his desk. The imperturbable Declouet, nothing abashed, takes his stand before the fireplace, and for the second time asks Guichard why the Legislature does not adjourn? "I have already told you," replies Guichard, "that I do not know, and that I could not know the opinion of all the members who compose it. Why, and always why! And *why* (since you are so fond of why) did you not co-operate in repulsing the enemy on the evening of the first attack? You would have added to the glory of the American arms; instead of which, you have left the inhabitants of the country exposed to be sacrificed." Why such a question should have been so unpalatable to Guichard, why it should have produced such an ebullition of temper, remains to be explained. "At this point of the interview there was a pause," observes Guichard; and well might there be a pause; for it is incredible that Guichard's de-

* Guichard was a native of France, or of St. Domingo, where he is said to have been ruined by the effects of British influence on the negroes.

portment had not compelled Declouet, to put an end to his visit long before. But it seems that there was merely a "pause," during which Declouet, who may be supposed to have been stunned, probably took breath. "The *why* came back again," says Guichard:" "Why those nocturnal meetings? Why those secret sessions?" Guichard does not answer, but shrugs up his shoulders. " Why, when the Governor wished you to adjourn, did you not comply with his request? Tell me what it means. There must be something in it. Why did you give no answer to his message?" "You are insane, I believe," exclaims Guichard, with what he takes care to call "*an air of contemptuous commiseration.*" * "Is the Legislature the creation of the Governor, and to obey his whims? Finally, all these whys weary and displease me." Colonel Declouet, whose openly professed friendship for Guichard must be supposed to be the cause which prevented him from taking offence at these repeated acts of rudeness, meets this unkind retort with these deprecating words : " What I say does not apply to you; for nobody renders more justice to your character, and loves you more than I do. But there are in that Legislature so many intriguers, who would like to usurp authority, or set the country topsy-turvy, that I have my misgivings. The Legislature can have no reason for not adjourning, and cannot but have suspicious intentions when refusing to do so. It is I who tell you so." " On hearing this remark," relates Guichard, "I left my desk abruptly,† and said with bad-humor to Declouet: "You will always be the same ; you never will part with your suspicions ;" and borrowing his own manner and tone when making his last remark, I said that the Legislature

---

* D'un air de pitié.
† A ce propos, je quittai mon bureau avec vivàcité, et dis avec humeur à M. Declouet, etc.

was to be the people's sentinel, and should be ready in these critical times to take such measures as the calamities of the war and other circumstances might render necessary. But, I added, to cut the matter short, let us break off here." Not contenting himself with thus closing the door to further conversation, Guichard went back to his desk, as he declares, took his hat, and left his bed-chamber to the sole possession of Declouet.

It results from this circumstantial narrative made by Guichard, that he denies the language attributed to him by Declouet. Which spoke the truth? Without deciding this question, it is evident that the interview, even admitting it to have been as Guichard represents it in all its details, increased instead of allaying Declouet's apprehensions, and induced him to communicate them to General Jackson. The testimony of Guichard closed the evidence which was laid before the Joint Committee of Investigation, who, in their Report, declared, as the conclusions they had come to, that there had not existed the slightest cause for the measure which had been taken against the Legislature; that military orders had been issued to close their doors without the faintest proof establishing any guilt on their part; finally, that so violent a proceeding had been resorted to with little foundation; that Abner Duncan had perverted the orders he had received, and had been the sole cause of the incredible and unprecedented outrage which had been committed; that, as to the message sent by Jackson to Claiborne, " it had been dictated by prudence itself; that a Republican, a military man, who finds himself at the head of an army, in the midst of a battle on which depends perhaps the fate of the country whose defences had been intrusted to him, and who receives such information as was conveyed to him by Mr. Duncan, could not have held a language more discreet, nor more characteristic of his love for his country; that the conduct of Declouet had been extravagant, and his declarations full of inconsistencies, contradictions and absurdities; that he had yielded to chimerical apprehensions, and to that miserable mania which some people have of seeking to make themselves important near those who are in power, of pretending to penetrate into the minds of men and envenoming their words; that Governor Claiborne had sent no message to General Jackson in relation to any intended capitulation on the part of the Legislature; that, if the order he had received had emanated from the General, nothing ought to have induced him to execute them; that the Committee had seen with extreme surprise the course pursued by him; that his paramount duties were those he had assumed toward the State and her Constitution; and that it was evident that he could not obey those orders without violating the oath he had taken to support that Constitution. This Report was presented and unanimously adopted on the 6th of February.

On the same day, Governor Claiborne transmitted to the Legislature the following letter, which he had received from General Jackson :*

"SIR: The Legislature of your State being on the eve of closing their labors, it is necessary, as much for the honor of the members of that body, as for the interest of those whose defence is intrusted to me, that I should take cognizance of the different testimonies and other documents which have been collected by the Committee instructed to investigate the causes of proceedings, which, on the 28th of December, had a tendency to produce an accusation of treason against that body. If so grave an accusation has been *unjustly* brought by any one of the officers of my army, he must be immediately prosecuted, and the innocence of every member of the Assembly whom he has so shamefully calumniated must be

* Having failed to procure the original in English I am again compelled to retranslate from a French translation.

made public. On the other hand, if this denunciation can be *justified by proofs* against such of the members as it may concern, it is equally necessary that they should be prosecuted without delay, in order that the guilty may be punished and the innocent sheltered against any suspicion. Were it possible for me to obtain all that part of the proceedings of the General Assembly which relates to this matter, I might perhaps cease to find myself under the necessity of making an inquest which now seems to me exceedingly important."

The Legislature immediately voted that a copy of this Report, and of the documents annexed to it be transmitted to General Jackson by the Secretary of the Senate, and adjourned *sine die*. It does not appear that, after receiving that copy, General Jackson thought it advisable to take further action in the matter.

That adjournment had not taken place without voting thanks to all those who had in the slightest degree contributed to the defence of the State, except General Jackson. A Resolution to present him with a sabre of the value of $800, as a testimonial of gratitude on the part of the State, had passed the House of Representatives, but had been rejected by the Senate. Yet that very same Legislature had, on the 1st of December, 1814, voted thanks to General Jackson for the "great and important services" which he had rendered *out* of the State! His subsequent services *in* the State, which were incomparably greater and more important, they chose to pass over in silence! We had adopted the popular impression that this remarkable silence had been observed by the Legislature in consequence of the offensive orders issued against that body on the 28th of December, but on examination we soon discovered our error; for instead of being blamed, he was, as we have shown, unanimously praised and approved for the message which he had sent to Claiborne on that occasion.*

* See page 554.

Why, therefore, was the name of the savior of Louisiana so strikingly omitted in those resolutions of thanks which embraced the names of Generals Coffee, Carroll, Thomas, Adair, and others much less conspicuous than the Commander-in-Chief? We cannot but feel that it is a curious subject of inquiry. General Coffee, in his reply, took notice of that glaring omission:

"To know," he said, "that we have contributed in any degree to the preservation of our country, is to myself and the brave men under my immediate command a source of the most pleasing reflection. To have received so flattering and distinguished a testimonial of our services adds to the pleasure which that consciousness alone would have afforded.

"While we indulge the pleasing emotions that are thus produced, we should be guilty of great injustice, as well to merit as to our own feelings, if we withheld from the Commander-in-Chief, to whose wisdom and exertions we are so much indebted for our success, the expression of our highest admiration and applause. To his firmness, his skill, his gallantry, to that confidence and unanimity among all ranks produced by those qualities, we must chiefly ascribe the splendid victories in which we esteem it a happiness and an honor to have borne a part."

This was an indirect but keen rebuke. We cannot but think that it would have better comported with the dignity of the Legislature to have shown a proper sense of the services of General Jackson, and, at the same time, expressed the censure or disapprobation which they might have thought that any of his acts deserved. As it is, we are left to our conjectures. Can it be permitted to suppose that, whilst they solemnly acquitted him of all blame, and even lauded him for the propriety of his message to Claiborne on the 28th, they secretly nourished feelings of resentment? Was it because they believed that the General had not sufficiently appreciated the zeal of the Louisianians in the defence of their country? The pages of this History establish that his heart was full of gratitude for their patriotic co-opera tion in every possible way, and that he had expressed it in energetic and beautiful language in more than one official document. Even a few days before the adjournment of the Legislature he had written, on the 27th of January, to Nicolas Girod, the Mayor of New Orleans, the following letter, which ought to have removed any such impression, if it had ever existed in the mind of anybody:

"SIR: Deeply impressed since my arrival with the unanimity and patriotic zeal displayed by the citizens over whom you so worthily preside, I should be inexcusable if any other occupation than that of providing for their defence had prevented my public acknowledgments of their merits. I pray you now to communicate to the inhabitants of your respectable city the exalted sense I entertain of their patriotism, love of order, and attachment to the principles of our excellent Constitution. The courage they have shown in a period of no common danger, and the fortitude with which they have rejected all the apprehensions which the vicinity of the enemy was calculated to produce, were not more to be admired than their humane attention to our own sick and wounded, as well as those of that description among the prisoners. The liberality with which their representatives in the City Council provided for the families of those who were in the field evinced an enlightened humanity, and was productive of the most beneficial effects. Seldom in any community has so much cause been given for deserved praise; while the young were in the field and arrested the progress of the foe, the aged watched over the city, and maintained its internal peace; and even the softer sex encouraged their husbands and brothers to remain at the post of danger and duty. Not content with exerting for the noblest purpose that powerful influence which is given them by nature (and which in your country women is rendered irresistible by accomplishments and beauty), they showed themselves capable of higher efforts, and, actuated by humanity and patriotism, they clothed by their own labor, and protected from the inclemency of the season, the men who had marched from a distant State to guard them from insults. In the name of those brave men, I beg you, Sir, to convey to them the tribute of our admiration and thanks; assure them that the distant wives and daughters of those whom they have succored will remember them in their prayers, and that, for myself, no circumstance of this important campaign touches me with more exquisite pleasure than that I have been enabled to lead back to them, with so few exceptions, the husbands, brothers, and other relatives of whom such women only are worthy.

"I anticipate, Sir, with great satisfaction, the period when the final departure of the enemy will enable you to resume the ordinary functions of your office, and restore the citizens to their usual occupations—they have merited the blessings of peace by bravely facing the dangers of war.

"I should be ungrateful or insensible, if I did not acknowledge the marks of confidence and affectionate attachment with which I have personally been honored by your citizens; a confidence which has enabled me with greater success to direct the measures for their defence; an attachment which I sincerely reciprocate, and which I shall carry with me to the grave.

"For yourself, Mr. Mayor, I pray you to accept my thanks for the very great zeal, integrity, and diligence with which you have conducted the arduous department of the police committed to your care, and the promptitude with which every requisition for the public service has been carried into effect.

"Connected with the United States, your city must become the greatest emporium of commerce that the world has known. In the hands of any other power it can be nothing but a wretched colony. May your citizens always be as sensible of this great truth as they have shown themselves at present; may they always make equal efforts to preserve this important connection, and may you, Sir, long live to witness the prosperity, wealth and happiness that will then inevitably characterize the great sea-port of the Western world."

Certainly, this eloquent tribute to the merits of the citizens of New Orleans must have more than surpassed the expectations of the most exacting. To some other cause, therefore, than the want of a just appreciation of the Louisianians on the part of General Jackson, must the feelings of the Legislature against him be attributed. Can such deep resentment have been produced by so trifling a cause as General Jackson's answer to a communication by Claiborne in relation to the discharge of some of the militia from military duty? "Applications being hourly addressed to me," wrote Claiborne to Jackson on the 31st of January, " by the militia officers of the State to learn the disposition to be made of the various detachments now at this place, and finding a wish very general on the part of the citizens to return to their respective homes, I take the liberty to ask whether, in your judgment, the services of the whole, or what part of the militia of the State now in the service of the United States, can be dispensed with, and at what period." Major Butler answered in the name of Jackson : " The* Major-General requests me to announce to you that, as long as the enemy shall be within six hours' sail of New Orleans, no part of the militia shall be dismissed ; and that they should not apply for it under such circumstances." This correspondence was, on the same day, laid before the Legislature by Claiborne, but we do not feel justified in looking to this refusal for the explanation which we desire, as the effect would be too disproportionate to the cause ; and yet we do not find anything else on record to which we might turn for a solution of the difficulty. In the absence of any positive evidence, we shall resort, as we have already said, to conjectures founded on what we believe to be logical and impartial deductions.

We have seen, in the course of this History, that there had been no harmonious concert of action between the Governor and the Legislature, and that this officer, even before Jackson had set his foot on the soil of Louisiana, had, in his correspondence with him, used language which showed his apprehensions that the Legislature would do more harm than good during the impending crisis. For this reason, perhaps, if not for others, Jackson and Claiborne, as soon as Louisiana had been actually invaded, had desired the adjournment of that body.

* A retranslation from a French translation.

Besides, it was thought both by Jackson and Claiborne that the enemy being within six miles of the capital, the presence of the members of the General Assembly would be more useful in the field in front of the invaders than in the halls of legislation. Such had been the opinion of several of the members themselves, who had left their seats and had repaired to the camp of General Jackson. The majority, however, had decided otherwise, and soon discovered that their decision had been disapproved, not only by the Chief Magistrate of the State, not only by the Federal Commander-in-Chief, to whom their defence had been intrusted, but also by a considerable portion of the public and of the army. It is not in the nature of man to feel amiably toward those by whom he suspects that he is censured. Hence a degree of restive sensitiveness on the part of some of them, as strikingly evinced in the interview between Guichard and Declouet, when the propriety of their motives for not adjourning seemed to be questioned. It must be recollected that one of their reasons[*] for continuing in session was, " that contingencies might happen and unforeseen cases might occur, when the interference of the Legislature might be necessary." Could it be a matter of astonishment, had those who were dissatisfied with the refusal of the Legislature to adjourn, whispered that there was some definite and dark purpose concealed under the vague meaning of these words? Martial law had been proclaimed; the guns of the enemy were thundering at the gates of the besieged city. What could be those "contingencies," what could be those "unforeseen cases" which might require the "interference" of the Legislature? Interference in what? interference with whom in such critical times? Was not everything in the hands of the Commander-in-Chief? Hence unfounded suspicions may have arisen;

See page 402.

they may have been expressed, or guessed at; and the consequence was some soreness on the part of the Legislature, who thought themselves unjustly treated. Such was the state of things when, on the 23d, during the battle, or shortly before, it was reported that General Jackson, if defeated, would destroy the city. It created great consternation;* the lamentations were loud; the censure of General Jackson's defensive measures was unsparing; the doubts as to his capacity for command were not concealed; and the cry that he was conducting war after the Russian or Barbarian fashion was raised. Application was made to Major Butler, who had been left in command of the city, to know the truth of the report; he refused to admit or to deny it; this increased the alarm. It is not unnatural to imagine that some of the members of the Legislature, witnessing the terror of many of their constituents, and perhaps trembling for the safety of their families and property in the midst of a general conflagration, may have blamed the supposed determination of General Jackson, and that their expressions of censure or dissent may have been spread among the public in a distorted sense, and reported with exaggerations to General Jackson, engendering feelings of an unpleasant nature. We fancy that we can trace up to the refusal to adjourn and to the report that the city was to be destroyed in case of a disaster to the American arms, the origin of the mutual distrust and estrangement which sprang up between General Jackson and the Legislature.

In a letter written nine years after, on the 22d of March, 1824, General Jackson said :

"When I left the city and marched against the enemy on the night of the 23d of December, 1814, I was obliged to leave one of my aids in command, having no other confidential officer that could

* See pp. 435, 436.

be spared from command. A few days after, Mr. Skipwith, in person, applied to my Aid to be informed what would be my conduct, if driven from my lines of defence, and compelled to retreat through New Orleans—whether I would leave the supplies for the enemy or destroy them? As reported by my Aid to me, he wanted this information for the Assembly, that, in case my intention was to destroy them, they might make terms with the enemy. Obtaining no satisfaction from my Aid, a Committee of three waited on me for satisfaction on this subject. To them I replied: 'If I thought the hair of my head knew my thoughts, I would cut it off or burn it'—to return to their honorable body, and to say to them from me, that if I was to be so unfortunate as to be driven from the lines I then occupied, and compelled to retreat through New Orleans, they would have a warm session of it."

Skipwith, who was President of the Senate in 1815, noticed these charges by publishing the following address to General Jackson:

"It was on one of the nights about the time alluded to by Major Butler, that, returning from patrol duty from the grand round of the city, in passing, and seeing lights in the house of Mrs. F——, an old and much respected acquaintance of mine, and a great admirer of yours, I called in to pay her my respects, and found with her another very interesting lady, Mrs. E——, who, in the course of her conversation, mentioned a report, as circulated in the city, and I think she said, by some Kentuckians just from your lines of defence, that, if forced, you would destroy rather than see the city fall into the hands of the enemy. A day or two after, at the request of the military council of the City Guard, of which I was a member, I waited on Major Butler concerning a citizen under arrest, and not directly or indirectly charged with anything concerning that report; and being asked by him, 'if there was anything new in the city,' I remember replying that such was the report 'among women.' Conscious, General, of having, through life, treated the names and characters of married ladies with the most scrupulous caution and respect, I cannot believe that I mentioned the names of the two ladies, between whom I heard the report; and never having, at any time, attached to it myself either belief or importance, I could not have made it a subject of serious communication to the Senate, to the Military Council, or to any member of them, individually. I am willing, therefore, to rest the truth of my assertions, in repelling this most slanderous and bolstered charge of yours, and consequently its utter falsehood, as far as it criminates my conduct and views, on the testimony not only of the remaining individuals who composed the Senate and the Military Council, but on the testimony of any two or three remaining individuals in society, who were eye-witnesses of my conduct at the invasion of New Orleans, and whose oaths would be respected by a well-composed jury of their vicinity.

"I may well, then, Sir, pronounce this last charge of yours to be false, utterly false, as applying to me individually, or to the Senate over which I presided, or to the Military Council of which I was a member, and deny that the most distant hint, or wish, was ever expressed in any of their deliberations, or in private, by any one of their members with my knowledge, or within my hearing, 'to make terms with the enemy.' And more false, if possible, is it still, that the Legislature should, with my consent or connivance, depute a Committee to wait on you on that subject, or on any other during the invasion, in which I had any agency, that was not founded, in my humble estimation at least, on principles of patriotism and honor. I may, therefore, hope to find indulgence in every honest breast for having expressed, in some degree, the profound contempt which this charge so justly merits, and which it is impossible for me, with life, to cease to feel."

On reading Skipwith's letter to General Jackson, Thibodaux, who was a member of the Senate at the time, and a man of great political influence, addressed to Skipwith a communication, in which he said that the notoriously ungenerous and unmerited accusation which had been cast upon the whole Legislature of Louisiana, and particularly upon the Senate, by General Jackson, was, in his humble opinion, such as ought to be taken up and repelled with the indignation it really deserves.

"This charge," he added, "was not laid upon you alone, but it embraces the whole Senate. Could you not, Sir, as being then the President of that honorable body, could you not, with propriety, call upon the members who were sitting with you, and prevail upon them to join in clearing, through the same medium that was made use of, those shameful stains with which that body was stigmatized? And would it not be but fair if this infamous calumny recoiled toward its source and against its very author? A supine silence appears to operate on the part of the members of the General Assembly as a conviction of the truth of the accusation; and this opinion, as you may know yourself, is circulating in the public by the exertions of the General's friends. I beg leave to be excused for attempting to suggest the right course you have to follow. These are the dictates of a heart indignantly offended at the rash attack of the General, and, although it does not fall upon me directly (for you will recollect I was on active service), it rebounds upon me very heavily, and wounds me to the very heart's core."

Without attempting to reconcile the conflicting assertions of Major Butler and General Jackson, with the denegations of Skipwith and Thibodeau, we think that we have now sufficient light before us to review understandingly the extraordinary proceedings which took place on the 28th of December, and to discover the cause of the secret feeling of hostility existing between the Legislature and General Jackson. After much reflection and patient examination we have come to the gratifying conclusion that the Legislature of the State, including all its members, and, among others, those influential leaders, Blanque, Marigny and Guichard, whose names are mentioned in the testimony of Declouet and other witnesses before the Committee of Investigation, acted with undeviating patriotism, and that, after the arrival of General Jackson, they had, as a body and individually, done all that could be expected of them to secure the defence of the State. Blanque, in particular, had, on the 15th of December, introduced into the House of Representatives this short spirited address to the citizens of the State of Louisiana, which had been enthusiastically adopted:

"Your country is in danger; the enemy is at your doors; the frontiers of the State are invaded. Your country expects of you the greatest efforts to repulse the bold enemy who threatens to penetrate, in a few days, to the very hearth-stones of your homes, the safety of your own persons, that of your property, of your wives and children, yet depends on you. Rush to arms, fellow-citizens, enlist promptly under the banner of General Jackson, of that brave chief who is to command you; give him all your confidence; the successes he has already obtained assure you that to march under his standards is to march to victory. There is no longer any alternative; dear fellow-citizens, we must defend ourselves; we must conquer, or we must be trampled under the feet of a cruel and implacable enemy, whose known excesses will be as nothing when compared with those which he will perpetrate in our unfortunate country. To arms! Let us precipitate ourselves upon the enemy; let us save from his cruelty, from his barbarous outrages all that is dear to us, all that can bind us to life. Your Representatives have supplied the Executive with all the pecuniary means which he required of them for the defence of the State, and they will give you the example of the devotion which they expect of you."

It was to Blanque that Lafitte had appealed when he wished to offer his services and those of his companions to the State, and it was because he knew the undoubted devotion of that gentleman to the cause which he, Lafitte, desired to be permitted to embrace.

We say with a feeling of legitimate pride, that after having made the most minute researches, we have not been able to discover the slightest proof that the Legislature ever entertained treasonable purposes, or that any member of that body ever thought of "making terms with the enemy," as long as all the means of the most obstinate defence should not have been exhausted. But, at the same time, it is not equally demonstrated to us that there were not many members of the Legislature in favor of capitulating, when capitulation could have been honorably made, rather than destroying New Orleans and exposing its numerous population to all the horrors which would have been the consequences of such an act. They may have thought that the destruction of that city would not have answered the same purpose which had been obtained by the conflagration of Moscow, because it would have been done under different circumstances. It is probable that, entertaining such views, and whilst in a state of excitement which was but too natural, on witnessing the agonies of terror which prevailed in New Orleans when the uncontradicted report spread that the city was to be set on fire in case of a defeat, some of them, by words or actions which were misconstrued, gave rise to those suspicions which we have found existing against them to an extraordinary extent, as we shall show. That one man, that Declouet should have been visionary and should have taken as realities the dreams of his own over heated imagination, we admit to be possible; but it seems to us totally inexplicable that the same delusion should have been shared by so many others, if there had not been some grounds for its existence. If the refusal to adjourn had not been interpreted in a manner as injurious to the Legislature as represented by Declouet, if those suspicious nocturnal meetings, those secret sessions with which he taxed them when addressing the very head of one of the Houses, had never been held, how comes this dreamer to have obtained such credit with Duncan, a distinguished member of the New Orleans Bar and an Aid to General Jackson, when he was understood to accuse the Legislature of treason? Would Duncan have been thrown into a violent state of agitation? Would he have given faith to such a charge, would he have admitted the possibility of such an event, had he not been disposed to it by something antecedent? In a matter of this importance, would General Jackson have acted on a mere verbal message delivered to his Aid by a militia Colonel whose name he, Jackson, did not even know at the time? Would he not have scouted at so startling an intelligence brought to him in this loose manner, if he had had full confidence in the Legislature? Would he have ordered to make strict inquiry into a fact which he would have thought impossible, and which he did not believe ? Would he have empowered the Governor, whom he understood to be the accuser of the Legislature, to become also their judge, to pass sentence on their guilt, and to "blow them up," if he had not been laboring under a degree of indignant excitement which blinded his reason, and which shows that he did not altogether discredit, as he pretended, the probability of the event? Are we not warranted in believing that we interpret correctly the state of his mind on that occasion when we take into consideration his letter of the 22d March, 1824, which informs us of what occurred between the President of the Senate and Butler, and between a Committee of the Legislature and himself in relation to their "making terms with the enemy ?"

Colonel Fortier, Governor Claiborne's Aid, a native of the State, a man of extensive family connections, who had friends and relations in that Legislature, does not show any astonishment at the wonderful message of which Duncan is the bearer. He transmits it without doubts, remarks or comments of any kind, as far as we know. The Governor is startled, it is true, as we are informed, but consents to execute, in clear violation of his official oath, and against those whom it was his duty to protect, the mere verbal order of a Federal officer, which might have been altered or modified in passing through the lips of two different persons—and what an order! to prevent by force the meeting of the Representatives of that sovereign State of which he was the Chief Magistrate! Could anything so monstrous have happened without foundation; and, if that foundation was laid in error, was there not something plausible, or having the color of truth, for that error or delusion to stand upon? General Labatut, a State officer, who commanded the corps of veterans to whom the guard of the city had been intrusted, receives the Governor's mandate to close the doors of the State House, and to fire at the members of the Legislature if they attempt to meet notwithstanding his prohibition, and he obeys with as little hesitation as if he had been commanded to pass a review according to law; he obeys it as readily as Harrison and Worsley, when, at the beck of Cromwell, they caused the British Parliament to be thrust out of doors by a file of musketeers. If there had not been something in the public mind against that guiltless but unfortunate Legislature, would Labatut, the kindest and mildest of men, a respectable and peaceful merchant of the city, have accepted the responsibility of a measure, for which there were then but two precedents in history? Would he have shown the unreasoning obedience of a janissary? Would the Governor himself, who did not leave behind him the reputation of a rash man, and whose desire for popularity was said to be the weak part of his character, have dared to justify that measure in a special message to the Legislature—in which he said "he had pursued the course which prudence and duty required?"[*] Would he, whom his very friends accused of shrinking too much from taking responsibilities, have assumed one of this frightful magnitude without feeling sure that there was a condition of things existing which would shelter him from all consequences? Would he have boldly told the Legislature themselves, "that so much suspected were their intentions by the public, that had they met on the 28th there might have been a popular commotion which he could not have repressed?" If these facts had not been true, or had been even doubtful, would he have ventured to assert them in an official document destined for publication? Would not the Legislature, between

[*] See page 541.

whom and him there never had existed any very good understanding, have turned upon him and crushed him for inventions of so calumnious a nature? Would they not have arraigned the Governor at their bar? Would they not have insisted upon a retractation? Would they have permitted his communication to have remained unexplained, unanswered, on their records, as an eternal proof of their tacit assent to the truth of his declarations? Can we admit that mere slanderous denunciations, without at least some superficial appearances of fact to rest upon, would have produced among the people such a state of distrust of the Legislature as is described by the Governor—a Legislature composed, almost without an exception, of men of high social positions, and whose personal influence throughout the State must have been greater than that of their calumniators? It is commonly said, in familiar parlance, that there never is smoke without fire. On this occasion, as there was no little smoke, there must have been some sparks of fire.

The truth was, we suspect, as we have already said, that there were some members of the Legislature who, after having exhausted all means of defence, and after having made all the necessary efforts to repulse the enemy from New Orleans, were in favor of a capitulation, if it could be made honorably, rather than of destroying the city, because they considered that destruction would have no practical and advantageous results, and would would be a " mere sacrifice to military pride." We are confirmed in coming to this conclusion by the following language which we find in the Report of the Committee of Inquest: " It is glorious, no doubt, for citizens to bury themselves under the ruins of their city rather than surrender it to the enemy; but that man never was reputed a traitor who, no longer able to resist a barbarous and triumphant enemy, has sought, by an honorable capitulation, to preserve for his children the roof under which they were born." Such may have been the dominant idea in the mind of more than one of the members of the Legislature. Accordingly, those whose views agreed on the subject may have met to consult together and attempt to devise some means, legal in their opinion, by which they might prevent the calamity they dreaded. They might have considered it as one of those "contingencies and unforeseen cases which they said might arise and might require the interference of the Legislature," and to meet which they had refused to adjourn, when desired to do so by Claiborne and Jackson. Those members may, in an informal way, have sent a Committee to wait on General Jackson, to know his real intentions, as he mentions in his letter of the 22d of May, 1824; and as this may not have been done in any of their regular sessions, either public or secret, according to official forms, but in one of those irregular meetings which are frequently preparatory to legislative action, it is not astonishing if no record was kept of such proceedings in their journals. Their object may have been to capitulate *after* a disaster, and the public, alarmed at what may have appeared to be indications or symptoms of disaffection, agitated by the reports of secret sessions, misconstruing ambiguous expressions, exaggerating the import of hasty words of passion or vague threats, may have supposed that the intention of the suspected members was to capitulate *before* a disaster—which was very materially different. Hence the public excitement; hence the strange declaration of Claiborne to the Legislature: "If you had met on the 28th of December, there probably would have been a popular commotion which it might have been impossible to repress."

Although there might have existed, and, according to Claiborne's positive and official declarations, there did exist, among the public considerable apprehensions that the Legislature entertained some mischievous purposes of capitulation, whilst our forces were still confronting defiantly the enemy, and although these apprehensions can be easily conceived, because in days of great and imminent danger the masses seldom reason and are carried away by impulses, yet we do not believe that General Jackson anticipated any such action on the part of the Legislature, because something like absolute impossibility would have stood in their way. It was evident that as long as his army remained intact between New Orleans and the enemy, the Legislature, if unpatriotic and ill-disposed, could not treat with the enemy without his consent, even if they had possessed the competent authority. But he probably knew that he was bitterly censured for his supposed intention to destroy the city, rather than allow the British to take possession of it; he may have believed in a disposition, on the part of certain members of the Legislature, to attempt to frustrate that design in case of a disaster to his army; and he may have looked upon it in a very different light from what they did. They thought, as expressed in the Report of the Committee of Inquest, that it was no treason. He may have thought it was. He may have thought that, as Commander-in-Chief of the forces of the United States, he was the sole authority to decide whether or not the destruction of New Orleans was a military necessity; that he was in duty bound to assume that responsibility; and that actual resistance to any of his military measures would be treason. Although the members of the Legislature who may have been opposed to what was called making war " after the Russian fashion," may not have been able to agree to any feasible plan to prevent Jackson from carrying into execution his supposed determination to imitate in New Orleans the conflagration of Moscow, yet their intention may have been known at headquarters, and they may have been looked upon as contingent traitors. Otherwise, how came Jackson to send them this stern message: "Tell them that if I am so unfortunate as to be driven from the lines I now occupy, and compelled to retreat through New Orleans, they will have a warm session of it?" Certainly, this was not the friendly language of confidence and esteem; it rather sounded like the warning threat of angry distrust. If such a message was sent and carried to its destination, it explains that secret state of feeling which prevented any vote of thanks to General Jackson, although he was publicly acquitted of all improper interference with the Legislature on the 28th of December, and even praised by that body for the discretion and patriotism which he exhibited on that occasion. If the deductions which we have drawn from the facts we have stated are not correct, we do not see how it is possible to account, in any rational way, for the mysterious historical anomaly which we have recorded.

We regret that the Legislature, at the time, did not act with a foresight, a firmness and a dignity which would have redounded to their credit, and would have freed them from unworthy suspicions. We think that, if they had attached any importance to the report that General Jackson intended to reduce New Orleans to ashes in case he retreated through that city, they might with propriety, in one of their public sessions, have appointed a Committee to ascertain what truth there was in it, in order, not to "make terms with the enemy," but to provide for the removal of the numerous women, children, and old men whom New Orleans contained, and to make arrangements to procure for them food and shelter in the interior of the country; they might have represented that such had been the precautions taken ir

Russia, and that Moscow had been deserted by its population before it was burned. We believe that this would have been a legitimate interference, and would not have been looked upon by Jackson as exceeding their proper sphere of action. We are under the impression that, whilst assuring the General that they were still disposed to co-operate with him as they had previously done, to the full extent of the resources of the State, and ready to make every sacrifice which patriotism might require, and whilst disclaiming all idea of entering into any conflict with the exercise of his military authority, and leaving with him all the unrestrained responsibilities of his acts as Commander-in-Chief, they might have remonstrated with him on his determination to destroy New Orleans, as not being in their opinion an imperious necessity of defence, and as a measure which would have inflicted on the community incalculable losses and sufferings without adequate results. Such a course, which would have threatened no resistance to what he might ultimately decide, would have entitled them to his respect and confidence, to the commendation of the world, and might have strengthened their rights to claim afterward from the United States a full compensation for the wanton destruction of their property. Such proceedings, held openly, in broad daylight, conducted with moderation and with the deference due to him who was intrusted with the defence of the State, might, if it could not have prevented the dreaded calamity, have put it beyond the power of their enemies to misrepresent their intentions.

Much as we admire General Jackson, we cannot coincide with the Legislature in commending him for the " prudence, patriotism and propriety " of his message to Claiborne on the 28th of December—a message which he sent on the mere information of a militia colonel

whose name he did not even know at the time. The
General understood the Governor to accuse the Legislature of treason, and what was his order? "Tell the
Governor to make strict inquiry into the subject; and,
if true, to blow them up,"—which meant: tell the Governor that I empower him to decide if his own accusation is well founded, and in that case to apply the penalty
which I decree—"blow them up." We suspect that
Duncan, who was a lawyer, and understood the rights
of the accused, was struck with the monstrosity of the
order of which he was the bearer. He well knew that
if the members of the Legislature were guilty of treason,
if they had committed any overt act, they might be
arrested, but that they were entitled to trial, and that
the Governor of the State was not the competent tribunal before which that trial could take place. He knew
very well that if, on the other hand, they had not committed any overt act, but merely meditated treason, they
might be prevented from carrying their purposes into
execution, but that they could not be punished for a
mere intention. Hence his changing of the order, according to all probabilities, and his merely "requesting
the Governor to prevent the Legislature from meeting
in order to ward off the anticipated evil."*

We cannot but remember that General Jackson, when
he gave his celebrated order, had received the information which provoked it, within the hearing of his troops
and in the midst of a battle, and we are willing, therefore, to make ample allowances for the circumstances in
which he was placed. Nevertheless, we think that the
Legislature ought to have protested in suitable terms
against his message to Claiborne, as being wrong in
itself and as establishing a dangerous precedent, and
that, at the same time, they ought to have had the mag-

* See Duncan's Testimony, Journal of the Legislature.

nanimity and justice to vote him thanks and the proper testimonials of gratitude he was entitled to for his military services. We think that, on receiving communication of Jackson's letter to Claiborne, on the 6th of February, in which he expressed the opinion that it was "as much for the honor of the members of the Legislature as for the interest of those whose defence was intrusted to him," that he should proceed to an investigation of the causes which had led to an accusation of treason against their body, they ought to have shown their gratification at his determination, and instead of contenting themselves with coldly sending to him a copy of the proceedings of their Committee, they ought to have expressed the wish that he should go on with his own investigation, in order, as he said, "that if any officer of his army had unjustly brought such an accusation, he should be punished as he deserved, and the innocence of the calumniated be made manifest; and on the other hand, if the charges were well founded against some members of the Legislature, that they should be prosecuted, and the rest sheltered against further suspicion." They might have made their position still stronger by appointing a Committee to join and assist him in his investigation. If such an attitude had been taken by them, they would not have made themselves liable to Thibodeau's reproach in his letter to Skipwith: "that a supine silence appears to operate on the part of the members of the General Assembly as a conviction of the truth of the accusation."

We think that the mild censure which the Legislature passed on Governor Claiborne for his blind and unconstitutional obedience to Jackson on the 28th was not sufficient. We think that they ought to have demanded of him full and satisfactory explanations about the contents of his communication to them, of the 4th of January; we think that they ought to have appointed a Committee to inquire into the causes of the suspicions which, according to the Governor's assertions, had taken such root in the public mind as to work injuriously to their character and their usefulness as Representatives of the people, and which had prevailed to such an extent that, "had they met on the 28th, a popular commotion might have taken place." It would also have been necessary to have had it explained why they had been made more obnoxious on that day than on any other. If the Legislature had pursued such a course, they could not have been exposed to any painful suspicions; or those suspicions, if they had existed, would have been instantly removed; and we should have been spared the mortification, after the lapse of half a century, of defending their memory against unfounded charges of guilt, whilst at the same time admitting, with what we believe to be a becoming impartiality, that those charges seem to have originated in their want of prudence, firmness and dignity on an occasion which required a judicious exercise of those qualities.

CHAPTER XII.

CLAIBORNE'S ADMINISTRATION.

JACKSON'S QUARREL WITH THE FRENCH IN NEW ORLEANS — HE ORDERS THEM OUT OF THE CITY WITH THEIR CONSUL — PAMPHLET OF LOUAILLIER — HIS ARREST — JUDGE HALL, HOLLANDER AND DICK ALSO ARRESTED — CONFLICT BETWEEN JACKSON AND CLAIBORNE — LOUAILLIER'S TRIAL — HIS ACQUITTAL — RELEASE OF JUDGE HALL — TRIAL OF GENERAL JACKSON — HIS DEPARTURE.

1815.

THE Legislature had adjourned on the 6th of February, with full confidence that Louisiana was free from danger; this impression was shared in by the people, and particularly by the militia, who, unused to the hardships and irksome discipline of camp life, were anxious to resume those industrious and profitable pursuits from which they derived their support, and the comforts with which they surrounded their families. The fall of Fort Bowyer they considered as of no importance, and as the last expiring effort of the enemy. Rumors that a treaty of peace had been signed between the United States and Great Britain were also rife and generally credited. This circumstance increased the impatience of the militia to be relieved from military duty. So excited the public became on the subject, that Jackson thought proper, on the 19th of February, to issue the following address:

" FELLOW-CITIZENS AND SOLDIERS:

"The flag-vessel which was sent to the enemy's fleet has returned, and brings with it intelligence, extracted from a London paper, that, on the 24th of December, articles of peace were signed at Ghent, by the American Commissioners and those of her Britannic Majesty.

"We must not be thrown into false security by hopes that may be delusive. It is by holding out such that an artful and insidious enemy too often seeks to accomplish what the utmost exertion of his strength will not enable him to effect. To put you off your guard and attack you by surprise, is the natural expedient of one who, having experienced the superiority of your arms, still hopes to overcome you by stratagem. Though young in the *trade* of war, it is not by such artifices that he will deceive us.

"Peace, whenever it shall be re-established on fair and honorable terms, is an event in which both nations ought to rejoice; but whether the Articles which are said to have been signed for its restoration will be approved by those whose province it is to give to them their final confirmation, is yet uncertain. Until they shall be ratified by the Prince Regent and the President of the United States, peace, though so much desired, may be still distant. When that shall be done, the happy intelligence will be publicly and speedily announced. In the mean time, every motive that can operate on men who love their country, and are determined not to lose it, calls upon us for increased vigilance and exertion.

"If peace be near at hand, the days of our watchfulness, of our toils, and our privations, will be proportionably few; if it be distant, we shall at any rate hasten its arrival by being constantly and everywhere prepared for war.

"Whatever be the designs of the enemy, we must be ready to meet them. Should he have the temerity to assail us again, we will once more drive him ignominiously from our shore; if he places his hopes of success on stratagem, our watchfulness will disappoint him; if on an exertion of his strength, we have proved how successfully that can be resisted.

"It is true Fort Bowyer has fallen, but it must and will be speedily regained. We will expel the invader from every spot of our soil, and teach him, if he hopes for conquest, how vain it is to seek it in a land of freedom."

These admonitions, although very proper and presented in an impressive manner, failed to produce the intended effect. The tide was ebbing fast in another direction from the one in which General Jackson wished it to run. The militia, as long as they thought that there was a necessity for their being in arms, were all enthusiasm and patriotism; they had been heroes when the country required it; now they wanted to be, as speedily as possible, farmers, merchants, brokers, mechanics, lawyers, doctors, anything else than a soldier. They were burning to be at home with their wives and children, far away from the tap of the drum, luxuriating, however, in the recollection of past perils and the consciousness of having done their duty. On the 22d, a Gazette of Charleston was received in New Orleans, announcing that the Treaty of Peace had been ratified by the British Government. This intelligence swelled to overflowing the joy which was filling up every heart, and the clamor for the disbanding of the militia, or the greater number of them, became louder and louder. The French, who, with the approbation of their consul, Tousard, for they had not needed his instigation, had flocked to one man around the standard of the country they resided in, and had contributed so effectually to its defence, now that they thought their services no longer a matter of absolute necessity, now that they had enjoyed the satisfaction of seeing their hereditary foe fly utterly discomfited before them, were anxious to resume their independence. In the presence of the hated British flag they had forgotten that their own Government had become friendly to that of Great Britain; they had ceased to be Frenchmen; they had scorned to claim themselves aliens in order to avoid bearing arms; they had become Americans to fight the veterans of Wellington; but this object being once accomplished, they were Frenchmen again, and as such, they asserted their right to leave our ranks as freely as they had entered them. A number of them obtained certificates from Tousard as to their national character, which they presented to General Jackson by whom they were countersigned and the bearers permitted to be discharged. But, in a few days, so many of these certificates were issued, that Jackson suspected them of being improperly granted by Tousard. Remonstrances were made to the Consul, his replies or explanations were not deemed satisfactory, and, on the last day of February, General Jackson published a General Order, commanding all the French subjects to retire into the interior, to a distance not nearer than Baton Rouge. This measure was stated in the Order to have become indispensable by the frequent applications for discharges. The time allowed to leave the city was short; it did not exceed three days, after which, the French remaining in the city were to be registered and remain subject to his further orders. Tousard immediately applied to the Governor for the protection of the French subjects. His answer was, that the Executive of Louisiana had no control over the acts of the federal officer commanding the military district within which it was inclosed. "Whether or not," he said, "the rights secured by treaties and the laws of nations to the subjects of His Christian Majesty residing within this State are violated by the General Order of which you complain, is a question not for me to determine. It properly belongs to the judicial power, and there can be no doubt but, on proper application, it will interpose its authority in such manner as justice and the laws shall prescribe." Tousard was, perhaps, preparing to act according to Claiborne's advice, when Jackson, considering that the French Consul was interfering with his authority as Military Commander, ordered him out of the city, which order was instantly obeyed. The French, who were already exasperated, thinking that such a treatment offered to their Consul was a national insult, were fired with indignation, and they talked and acted as people who are in such a state of feeling usually do. Was this the return for all their services tendered spontaneously and greedily accepted? Those who were blinded by passion even asserted that Jackson could have done nothing without the French, and that he had been guided entirely by French officers in all his measures of defence. Were not the fortifications planned by Lafon, Latour and others? Was not Captain St. Geme of the dismounted dragoons, always at his elbow, and suggesting all his military movements? Had not Flaugeac, Beluche, Dominique and Lafitte won the battle of the 8th of January with their artillery? General Jackson, if they were to be believed, could not command a company; he was even ignorant of the very terms used in military science. The saving of New Orleans, if not due to the French, was certainly not due to the capacity of General Jackson, but to the arrant stupidity of the British, who, if they had acted as they should, ought, on the 23d, to have caught the Commander-in-Chief of the American forces in his bed. Language of this disparaging nature was but too freely used. "Let him treat his Kentuckians and Tennesseeans with his accustomed arrogance," said others, "but we shall teach him that we are not his subjects." These murmurs and threats could not but reach the ears of General Jackson. He was not slow in picking up the gauntlet which had been flung at his feet as soon as he could lay his hands on some responsible individual.

This measure of expulsion adopted against the French was considered by many as harsh and impolitic. It was harsh, because "the people against whom it was directed," says Judge Martin, in his History of Louisiana, " were loyal; many of them had bled, all had toiled and suffered in the defence of the State. Need in many instances, improvidence in several, had induced the families of these people to part with the furniture of their houses to supply those immediate wants which the absence of the head of the family occasioned. No distinction, no exception was made. The sympathetic feelings of every class of inhabitants were enlisted in favor of these men; they lacked the means of sustaining themselves on the way, and must have been compelled on their arrival at Baton Rouge, then a very insignificant village, to throw themselves on the charity of the inhabitants." It was impolitic, because if the British returned, as General Jackson seemed to apprehend, he would discover that he had imprudently dismissed and alienated men whom he had found so useful as artillerists, engineers and soldiers. Thus reasoned those who blamed the General. On the other hand, those who supported him maintained that the French sounded and trumpeted their services too high. True, they were entitled to much gratitude, but, at the same time, they seemed to forget that many of them, although foreigners, had fought to protect their own property; that those who were domiciliated were bound, although aliens, to defend in case of invasion the country where they resided and which protected their persons, whether they had property or not; that those who were not residents, but mere transient persons, could not be permitted to remain within the lines, if they refused to serve; that New Orleans was a camp; and that in a camp all capable of bearing arms must be subject to military duty; that those who complained of the "order" and might suffer from it, had provoked it by their own impatience and want of subordination. It was their own fault. As foreigners, they might perhaps have claimed exemption from enlisting; they might not have volunteered their services; but, as they had, they were, after their services had been accepted, on the same footing with the natives and naturalized, and were bound to abide with them the decision of the Commander-in-Chief as to the proper time for their discharge. What great hardship was it to wait a few days for the ratification of the treaty of peace? It could not possibly be delayed more than two or three weeks. To be retained in the ranks for so short a time, in a large city where they were among their friends and provided with many comforts, where they had the opportunity of seeing every day their families, who, although suffering privations, were assisted by the City Council, by Legislative appropriations, and by private liberality, and therefore far from starving, was not after all so intolerable a condition. But granting that they suffered as much as they represented, it was for the general good. Their sufferings were but a partial evil; better that, than the country should be endangered. Admitting that there was no necessity for so much caution on the part of General Jackson, could they not appreciate his motives; and if he erred, could they not have some indulgence for the chief who had led them to victory? What object of personal advantage could he obtain by insisting upon detaining them under arms for a few more days? The obvious reason was that he could not permit such a large number of men to leave the army; the rest would be disorganized and could not be kept together. It was further alleged that these manifestations of discontent would not have taken place, if the incident of the 28th of December had not occurred; and that the "French Party" in the Legislature, who had prevailed upon that body to abstain from voting thanks to General Jackson on account of the secret resentment which they felt against him for suspecting them of being traitors, had stirred up the French in the army to desert it. Such were the criminations and recriminations by which the public mind was still more inflamed.

Several respectable citizens called on General Jackson in the hope of inducing him to reconsider his determina tion to expel the French; but they found him inflexible. This intercession having failed, the French were advised to stay quietly at home. "Let us see," said their leaders, "what the tyrant will do. Let him arrest and drag from the bosom of their families, one by one, those who so lately exposed their lives for him and his country. Let him transport them by brute force where he pleases; let him assume that responsibility; but no expressed or implied assent must be given to this usurpation of authority. The French must protest in a body; they must apply to the judicial tribunals for protection and for the punishment of the man who, in his military arrogance, tramples on the laws of his country and the laws of nations." In the meanwhile, the Northern mail brought the news that the treaty of peace had arrived at Washington on the 14th of February. This grateful intelligence excited a general hope that Jackson would declare martial law at an end, but he was immovable, and remained determined to keep everything on the war footing until he received official notice of the ratification of the treaty by the President and the Senate of the United States. The discontent increased, the murmurs waxed louder and fiercer, and from headquarters there came a rumor that Jackson, far from being intimidated, was preparing to arrest some of the ring-leaders. Then the cry rose that Jackson hated the French; that he had never treated them with proper consideration; that he had always kept himself aloof from the Creole and French population, whose language he did not understand; that he had, notwithstanding his compliments and honeyed words dictated by policy, entertained against them the most insulting suspicions; that, on his arrival, he had systematically surrounded himself with the "new-comers" in the State, and taken as his confidential advisers men who were notorious for their prejudices against the old population.

To understand the force of this accusation, it must be known that, since the United States had taken possession of Louisiana in 1803, there had always been in it two parties, designated as the "French," and "American" party, which were bitterly opposed to each other, and invariably pitted in hostile array, particularly in the Legislature. The French party had opposed with violence the annexation to the State of what was called the "Florida Parishes,"* because it increased the American population and consequently the American influence; and the American party, for the very same reason, hailed it with enthusiasm. It is difficult, at the present time, to convey an adequate idea of the virulence of feeling then entertained by these two parties, and of the jealousies, injustices, and collisions to which it gave rise. It embittered social intercourse, made a perpetual storm of political life, and, at one time, almost threatened the State with civil war.† It was lamentable, and a sad specimen of human infirmities, to see New Orleans, in the hour of triumph, suddenly transformed into an arena of strife and angry passions, where the citizens seemed ready to fly at each other's throats. In this state of excitement, Louaillier, a native of France, but a naturalized citizen, whom we have mentioned several times as one of the leading and most active members of the House of Representatives, and who, although residing in the county of Oppelousas, had remained in town since the adjournment of the Legislature, gave vent to his imprudent indignation in the following publication which appeared

---

* See page 273.

† See the testimony given before the Committee to investigate the causes which gave rise to a military interference with the Legislature on the 28th of December, 1814.

in one of the journals of New Orleans, on the 3d of March:

"Mr. Editor,—To remain silent on the last General Orders, directing all the Frenchmen who now reside in New Orleans, to leave within three days, and to keep at a distance of 120 miles from it, would be an act of cowardice which ought not to be expected from a citizen of a free country; and when every one laments such an abuse of authority, the press ought to denounce it to the people.

"In order to encourage a communication between both countries, the 7th and 8th articles of the treaty of cession secure to the French who shall come to Louisiana, certain commercial advantages which they are to enjoy during a term of twelve years, which are not yet expired. At the expiration of that time, they shall be treated in the same manner as the most favored nation. A peace, which nothing is likely to disturb, uniting both nations, the French have until this moment been treated in the United States with that regard which a great people deserves and requires, even in its reverses, and with that good will which so eminently distinguishes the American Government in its relations with foreign nations. In such circumstances, what can be the motives which have induced the Commander-in-Chief of the 7th district, to issue general orders of so vexatious a nature? When the foreigners of every nation, when the Spaniards, and even the English, are permitted to remain unmolested among us, shall the French alone be condemned to ostracism, because they rendered too great services? Had they remained idle spectators of the last events, could their sentiments toward us be doubted, then we might merely be surprised at the course now followed with regard to them. But now, are we to restrain our indignation when we remember that these very Frenchmen who are now exiled, have so powerfully contributed to the preservation of Louisiana? Without speaking of the corps who so eminently distinguished themselves, and in which we see a number of Frenchmen rank either as officers or privates, how can we forget that they were French artillerists, who directed and served a part of those pieces of cannon which so greatly annoyed the British forces? Can any one flatter himself that such important services could have so soon been forgotten? No, they are engraved in everlasting characters on the hearts of all the inhabitants of Louisiana, and they shall form a brilliant part in the history of their country; and when those brave men ask no other reward than to be permitted peaceably to enjoy among us the rights secured to them by treaties and the laws of America, far from sharing in the sentiments which have dictated the General Order, we avail ourselves of this opportunity to give them a public testimony of our gratitude.

"Far from us be the idea, that there is a single Frenchman so pusillanimous as to forsake his country merely to please the military commander of this district, and in order to avoid the proscription to which he has condemned them. We may therefore expect to see them repair to the Consul of their nation, there to renew the act which binds them to their country. But supposing that, yielding to a sentiment of fear, they should consent to cease to be French citizens, would they by such an abjuration become American citizens? No, certainly they would not; the man who would be powerful enough to denationalize them, would not be powerful enough to give them a country. It is better, therefore, for a man to remain a faithful Frenchman, than to suffer himself to be scared even by the *martial law*, a law useless, when the presence of the foe and honor call us to arms, but which becomes degrading, when their shameful flight suffers us to enjoy a glorious rest, which fear and terror ought not to disturb.

"But could it be possible that the Constitution and laws of our country should have left it in the power of the several commanders of military districts, to dissolve all at once the ties of friendship which unite America and the nations of Europe? Would it be possible that peace or war would depend upon their caprice, and the friendship or enmity they might entertain for any nation. We do not hesitate in declaring, that nothing of the kind exists. The President alone has, by law, the right to adopt against *alien enemies* such measures as a state of war may render necessary, and for that purpose he must issue a proclamation; but this is a power he cannot delegate. It is by virtue of that law and a proclamation that the subjects of Great Britain were removed from our seaports and and sea shores. We do not know any law authorizing General Jackson to apply to *alien friends* a measure which the President himself has only the right to adopt against *alien enemies*.

"Our laws protect strangers who come to settle or reside among us. To the Sovereign alone belongs the right of depriving them of that protection; and all those who know how to appreciate the title of an American citizen, and who are acquainted with their prerogatives, will easily understand that, by the Sovereign, I do by no means intend to designate a Major-General, or any other military commander, to whom I willingly grant the power of issuing general orders like the one in question, but to whom I deny that of having them executed.

"If the last General Order has no object but to inspire us with a salutary fear; if it is only destined to be read; if it is not to be followed by any act of violence; if it is only to be obeyed by those who may choose to leave the city in order to enjoy the pure air of the country, we shall forget that extraordinary order; but should any thing else happen, we are of opinion that the tribunals will, sooner or later, do justice to the victims of that illegal order.

"Every alien friend, who shall continue to respect the laws which rule our country, shall continue to be entitled to their protection. Could that General Order be applied to us, we should calmly wait until we were forced by violence to execute it, well convinced of the firmness of the magistrates who are the organs of the law in this part of the Union, and the guardians of public order.

"Let us conclude by saying, that it is high time the laws should resume their empire; that the citizens of the State should return to the full enjoyment of their rights; that, in acknowledging that we are indebted to General Jackson for the preservation of our city and the defeat of the British, we do not feel much inclined, through gratitude, to sacrifice any of our privileges, and less than any other, that of expressing our opinion about the acts of his administration; that it is time the citizens accused of any crime should be rendered to their natural judges, and cease to be dealt with before special or military tribunals—a kind of institutions held in abhorrence even in absolute governments; and that having done enough for glory, the time for moderation has arrived; and finally, that the acts of authority which the invasion of our country and our safety may have rendered necessary, are, since the evacuation of it by the enemy, no longer compatible with our dignity and our oath of making the Constitution respected."

The very next day, the 4th, Jackson ordered the arrest of Louaillier, and, in explanation or in support of his order, the publication of the Second Section of the Act of Congress for establishing Rules and Articles of War, which reads as follows: "In time of war, all persons, not citizens of, or owing allegiance to, the United States, who shall be found lurking as spies in or about the fortifications or encampments of the armies of the United

States, or any of them, shall suffer death, according to the laws and usages of nations, by sentence of a general court-martial." On Sunday, the 5th, at noon, near the Exchange Coffee House which was then a place of much resort, Louaillier was arrested. He instantly desired Morel, a member of the bar and a man of great energy, who happened to be near him, to adopt legal means for his relief. Morel immediately applied for a writ of Habeas Corpus to Martin, who had, at last, been recently appointed with the consent of the Senate, to occupy the seat so long vacant on the bench of the Supreme Court on account of the persevering rejection by the Senate of all the nominations made by the Governor. But Martin refused to interfere on the ground that, in a previous case, the Court had already decided that, having only appellate jurisdiction, it could not issue the writ of Habeas Corpus, especially as it was alleged that the prisoner was arrested and confined for trial before a court-martial, under the authority of the United States.* Morel's next step was to apply to Hall, the District Judge of the United States, for a writ of prohibition, to stay proceedings against his client in the court-martial. As it was Sunday, the court was not in session; Judge Hall expressed a doubt of his authority to order such a writ in Chambers, and said he would take time to consider. Morel withdrew, but soon after returned with a petition for a writ of Habeas Corpus, which Hall ordered to be issued after exacting of Morel the promise that he would, before the serving of the writ, have the courtesy to give General Jackson information of his application for it, and of the order of the Court. Morel's communication produced one of those terrific explosions of anger to which, unfortunately, the General was but too much inclined. He immediately wrote to Colonel Arbuckle

* Martin's History, p. 394, vol. 2, Do. p. 395.

ARREST OF JUDGE HALL.

that, having received proof that Dominic A. Hall had been *aiding, abetting* and *exciting mutiny* in his camp, he desired that a detachment should be sent forthwith to arrest and confine him, and that a speedy report be made of the execution of the order. "You will," said the General, "be vigilant, as the agents of our enemy are more numerous than we expected. You will be guarded against escape." Hall was an Englishman by birth, and this circumstance perhaps contributed to inflame the wrath of General Jackson.

The judge was arrested in his own house, at nine o'clock in the evening, on Sunday, and taken to the Barracks where he was confined in the same room with Louaillier. As soon at this was ascertained, an officer was sent to demand from the clerk of the District Court of the United States the surrender of Louaillier's petition, on the back of which Hall had written the order for issuing the writ of Habeas Corpus.* The clerk replied, that according to the rules of the court, he could not part with any original paper filed in his office, and that he was ignorant of any right in the Commander-in-Chief to interfere with judicial records. After much solicitation, however, he was prevailed upon to accompany Jackson's emissary to headquarters, and carry with him the document for the inspection of the General. On his arrival, he was asked by Jackson whether it was his intention to issue the writ ordered by the imprisoned judge. The clerk firmly answered that, "it was his sworn duty to do so, and that he, most assuredly, would not fail to perform it." He was threatened with being treated like the judge, but he boldly persisted in his determination, and, on retiring, asked for the return of the petition which he had handed to Jackson for perusal. He met with a peremptory refusal; he was told that

* Martin's History of Louisiana, p. 397.

the paper was retained to convict the judge of *forgery*, because he had altered the date from the 5th, which was originally that of his order, to that of the 6th. This had been done on his reflecting that the fifth was Sunday. At this juncture, an express arrived from Washington, bringing intelligence that the treaty of peace had been ratified, and that the exchange of the ratifications had taken place on the 17th of February, but, " by some unaccountable accident, a dispatch on another subject had been substituted for the one intended to give an official notice of the event," as stated by General Jackson in a communication which he had addressed, some time since, to General Lambert, as already recorded in this History."

The exciting news of the arrival of the courier and of the arrest of Louaillier and Judge Hall had attracted a great crowd to headquarters. It was drawing late in the night. At 12 o'clock, Duplessis, the Marshal of the District Court of the United States, who, during the invasion, had acted as a volunteer Aid to General Jackson, made his appearance in the saloon of his Chief. On seeing him approach, Jackson walked to him hastily, saying: " I have shopped the Judge." Duplessis looked very grave, and uttered no words of approbation; this struck the General. " Is it possible," he said, "that you would have served the writ?" " Certainly," replied Duplessis; " I am the ministerial officer of the Court, and, as such, bound to execute any writ which it may direct to me. I have ever done my duty, and will continue to do so;" and, casting a stern look at the General,* whose frowning brows showed his displeasure, he added: " I will, without hesitation, serve the Court's writ on *any man*." Jackson pointed to a copy of the proclamation of mar-

---

* Martin's History of Louisiana, p. 398, vol. 2.

tial law which was lying on a table, and said with emphasis: "I also will do my duty."

Having taken these energetic measures to give assurance to the public that he would permit no interference with what he thought his legitimate authority, Jackson was becoming more self-possessed, and his judgment was recovering the mastery over the natural heat of his temper, when an orderly-sergeant sent by Colonel Arbuckle, who had Judge Hall in custody, arrived and informed the General that the Judge wished to be permitted to make an affidavit before a magistrate, in order to resort to legal measures for his release, and that Colonel Arbuckle desired to know if the prisoner's application was to be granted. Jackson immediately fired up again at this attempt to resist him; he refused to permit the access of a magistrate to Hall, and ordered the arrest of Hollander, one of the principal merchants of New Orleans, for some reason which has never transpired, but soon after released him. Dick, the District Attorney of the United States, came to the assistance of Hall, and applied to Lewis, one of the District Judges of the State for a writ of Habeas Corpus on behalf of the Judge. Lewis was then acting as a subaltern officer in the Orleans Rifle-company, whose conduct during the invasion had received the special commendation of General Jackson. Lewis did not hesitate, he laid down his soldier's rifle, resumed his functions as Judge, and issued the writ. Jackson instantly ordered the arrest of Dick and Lewis; but Colonel Arbuckle to whom the writ issued by Lewis had been directed, having refused to surrender his prisoner on the ground that he had been committed by the Commander-in-Chief, under the authority of the United States, Jackson countermanded his orders as to Lewis who had not yet been arrested. But Dick* was confined at the Barracks with Hall and Louaillier.

On the 8th, perhaps as a set-off to the rigor of these proceedings, and as an act of conciliation, Jackson issued the following " general order," disbanding the militia of the State:

"Although the commanding General has not received official advice that the state of war has ceased by the ratification of the treaty of peace between the United States and Great Britain, he has persuasive evidence of the fact, and credits it, at the risk of being misguided by his wishes. Under this impression, his first act is to release from actual service the body of the militia of the State, who have taken the field in obedience to the orders for a levy *en masse*. In discharging them from the noble duty which they were called to perform, the General does justice to the alacrity with which they have in general obeyed the call, to the enthusiasm which animated them on the first invasion of the enemy, and the unanimity and patriotism which disappointed his insolent hopes. He thanks them, in the name of their common country, for the noble defence they have made, and he congratulates them in his own, on the consequences it has produced. Louisiana, though not called on for any exertion in assuming her independence, has shown, by her courage in its support, that she knows how to prize the inestimable blessing; her sons have not only insured safety, but have acquired even a greater good—national reputation."

This was again another full tribute paid to the patriotism of the Louisianians and a complete vindication, if they had needed any, against all those rumors of disaffection and treason which had been circulated against them:

"Preserve this national reputation," continued Jackson, "as the best reward of your exertions, and hand it down untarnished, together with your example, to your posterity. Let no designing men induce you to destroy it, by exciting jealousies of your best

* Claiborne's Letter to the Secretary of State, March 10, 1815. Executive Journal.

friends, or divisions among yourselves, by preaching party spirit in peace, insubordination in war, injustice to your brave companions in arms, blindness to your own interests and to the true character of those enemies of your peace. Guard against these evils as you hope to enjoy the blessings you have so bravely won; and before you yield to such perfidious counsels, examine scrupulously whether those from whom they proceed, deserve your confidence by any exertion they have made in your defence."

This was a plain allusion to those against whom he was contending. He then asseverated that a zealous wish for the prosperity of the interesting country in whose defence he had been instrumental by the blessing of Heaven, had induced him " to give this admonitory caution, which those who court popularity might represent to the people as being unnecessary." He, however, valued no popularity but that which arises from a faithful discharge of duty. He assured the Louisianians that, in performing that duty, his sole object had been to secure their happiness, and that he would always consider it as one of the most fortunate incidents of his life, to have contributed by his exertions to the prosperity of their country.

This was very soothing language, and, as he seemed to be now in a relenting mood, he suspended, until his pleasure should be further signified, the order of expulsion he had issued against the French, who, regardless of it, had all remained quietly at home. He stated that he granted that favor at the solicitation of the principal militia companies of the city, who had pledged themselves for the future good conduct of the French subjects. This was pouring some oil on the stormy waves which were every moment lashing themselves into greater fury. But it was too late, and it was not enough. The excitement was too intense, and nothing would have appeased it but the immediate release of the prisoners and the revocation of the proclamation of martial law, and Jackson was not disposed to yield to that extent, if disposed to yield at all. Those who were most indignant against the General, and were the loudest in the expression of their feelings, were encouraged by the knowledge that Claiborne, who had been accused of timidity and of bending too much under the federal rod, was now disposed to show more energy, and to use what authority he had for the protection of the citizens. The Executive of the State had long been on bad terms with General Jackson, by whom he thought that he had been treated with studied neglect.

When the appointment of the volunteer Aids-de-Camp to General Jackson, and that of the Judge Advocate, appeared in the "general order" of the 17th December, 1814, Claiborne had observed to his Aid, Colonel Shaumburgh : " These men will do me much harm, if the General suffers himself to be imposed upon."* It seems that Claiborne's apprehensions were soon verified. " From that moment," wrote Shaumburgh to Claiborne, " the intercourse between you and the General became less frequent, and I know also that the General often found fault with you ; but whether it proceeded from the intrigues of those gentlemen, I am not able to determine. I am, however, aware that they were *every one* your enemy." On the 23d of December, when the troops were marching from the city to meet the British on Villeré's plantation, Claiborne, at the head of three regiments of militia was moving rapidly in that direction, when he received the order from General Jackson to turn back and occupy the Gentilly road. This order dampened the enthusiasm of the men, as all of them were anxious to meet the enemy, and produced for a moment among them a feeling of discontent, which broke out into murmurs. On that occasion, Claiborne

* Executive Journal, Correspondence between Claiborne and Shaumburgh.

turned to Shaumburgh and said: "Do you see that, sir? This is the beginning of a plan devised to keep me in the background." Shaumburgh disagreed with the Governor, and expressed the opinion that it was highly necessary that the Gentilly road should be strongly guarded, as the landing of the enemy below the city might be merely a false attack. Claiborne retained his first impression, however, and the coolness between him and Jackson sunk every day to a lower degree of refrigeration. On the 24th of February, he had ventured to send to Jackson the following communication:

"The undersigned, the Governor of the State of Louisiana, presents his respects to Major-General Jackson, and informs him how important it is that such part of the militia of this State whose services can safely be dispensed with, be early disbanded and permitted to return to their respective homes. Independent of the convenience to fathers of families, on whose personal labor, this present year, will depend the cultivation of their little farms, the undersigned brings to the view of the General the neglected state of the levees on the Mississippi; which, if not soon attended to, there will be no security, on the rise of the Mississippi, against the inundation of the lower part of the State. The undersigned persuades himself that the several detachments on duty in the interior of the State may now be relieved without endangering the public safety, it being understood that they be held in readiness to take the field, whenever danger menaces. The militia of the city, whose private affairs do not so immediately suffer, will enable the Government to dispense with the services of the whole until official notice of the ratification of the treaty of peace."

Claiborne does not appear to have had any reason to congratulate himself on the manner in which his suggestions were received, and, on the same day, addressed this communication to Mazureau, who had succeeded Martin as Attorney-General for the State:

"I find that the Martial Law which was proclaimed in the City of New Orleans by the "General Orders" of the officer commanding the forces of the United States, in the Seventh Military District of which this State makes a part, continues to be enforced to the injury of our fellow-citizens. If the liability of an American citizen, not in the military service of the United States, to have his conduct tested by the arbitrary principle of Martial Law can ever exist, it cannot certainly be expected to be endured at another moment than that of the actual invasion of that part of the country in which it is proclaimed. Yet, although the enemy does not at this time occupy an inch of ground within this State, the capital of Louisiana, the City of New Orleans and its environs, continue to be the theatre of military dominion. The *plea of necessity* under which alone this measure is said to be grounded ceasing to give it any justification, I can no longer remain a silent spectator of the prostration of the laws. I therefore request you, without loss of time, to repair to this city and resume your official duties, in order to give your aid to the civil magistrates, particularly the inferior ones; and, on receiving information of any attempt of the military to seize the person of any private citizen not actually in the military service of the United States, you are specially instructed to take for his protection, and for avenging the injured laws of this State, such measures as your knowledge of those laws will point out."

Claiborne also took the rather extraordinary step of sending to Governor Shelby of Tennessee and other persons in authority, a *circular*,* in which he said:

"You will learn with regret that an unfortunate misunderstanding exists between Major-General Jackson and the Legislative and Executive authorities of Louisiana, against the *latter* of which I have every reason to believe his resentment is more immediately directed. With a favorite and victorious chief, whose gallantry and exploits have attracted *so much admiration*, I am well aware I can enter into no contest upon equal grounds. There, however, is a shield which a kind Providence furnishes the cause of justice and truth, which resists present attacks and grows stronger with time. On former trials I have experienced the strength of this shield, nor on the present can it fail to extend to me the most ample security. I acknowledge that General Jackson has rendered important service, nor do I deny him the possession of some great qualities; but the violence of his temper casts a shade upon them all, and in this

* Executive Journal.

capital he has observed a course which cannot easily be excused, much less justified, by those who feel a proper regard for the rights of others."

All these proceedings seemed to indicate preparations to resist the federal authority exercised by Jackson. The public mind was, therefore, much agitated at the prospect of such a conflict. Claiborne* had been heard to declare in words of mysterious import: "That serious difficulties would be shortly witnessed in New Orleans." Large meetings of citizens were held; some suggested that a formal request should be addressed to the Governor, to put himself at the head of the militia of the State, and that Duplessis, the Marshal of the United States District Court, be invited to call out the *posse comitatus* of the district, to support the authority of the judiciary. Fortunately, the counsels of moderation prevailed, and no other act of violence was perpetrated than the destruction of a transparent portrait of General Jackson, which had been displayed in the main hall of the Exchange Coffee House. A number of officers immediately assembled, and compelled the proprietor of the Coffee House to exhibit a new transparent like the preceding one, and illuminate the hall in more than the usual manner.* They took their stand near the obnoxious painting, with the obvious intention of resisting by force any attempt to pull it down. It is even said that troops were in readiness to march to the Coffee House on the first summons. New Orleans had become like a magazine of gunpowder; the least spark might have produced an explosion.

Livingston, the great jurist, who was one of the Aids, the confidential adviser, and the bosom friend of General Jackson, was suspected of not disapproving, if he had not sanctioned or suggested the proceedings to which

* Martin's History, p. 405, vol. 2.

Jackson had resorted. He had become an object of execration to many; he truckles now, they said, to that very tyranny which he so courageously opposed in 1806, when he confronted General Wilkinson. Are we not now in the very same circumstances which he described "as so new in the history of our country, that they will not easily gain belief at a distance, and can scarcely be realized by those who beheld them? A dictatorial power assumed by the Commander of the American army—the military arrest of citizens charged with a civil offence—the violation of the sanctuary of justice! An attempt to overawe, by denunciations, those who dared professionally to assert the authority of the laws—the unblushing avowal of the employment of military force to punish a civil offence, and the hardy menace of persevering in the same course, were circumstances that must command attention, and excite corresponding sentiments of great indignation and contempt." Such was his language in former days. He then said:

"We must suffer the evils to which we are exposed. Let us, however, do it with fortitude, and never be tempted to any act which may enlist us on the side of those who trample on our Constitution, sport with our liberties, and violate our laws. Let us remember that the day of retribution will arrive, and is not far distant, when a strict account will be taken as well of the wanton abuses as of the shameful dereliction which permits them. But let us strive, by our zeal in the support of our country, by our submission to lawful authority, by our opposition to every foreign or domestic foe, to show that there is no pretext for the dictatorial power that is assumed over us."

What more appropriate in the present state of things than the emphatic expressions used by him in identical circumstances:

"I have said that we *must suffer*. Never were two words more applicable to our situation. It is one of the most dreadful to an independent mind, of any that can be imagined—subject to the uncontrolled will of a single man, to whom the hearsay tales of slander are proofs; and who, on his own evidence, arraigns, condemns, and punishes the accused, and insults the tribunals of justice! What state of things can be worse? No caution can protect! No consciousness of innocence secure! The evidence is taken in private; malicious, cowardly informers skulk around the proconsul's office; their tales give food to pre-existing enmity, and they avenge their own quarrels by secret denunciations of guilt. The objects of official suspicion are confined!"

How comes the same man, it was asked, to act so differently from his antecedents? How comes he now to be found in the proconsul's office? Is it because General Wilkinson was then thwarting his views, and General Jackson is now favoring them? But if he does not continue true to the liberties of the people, said those who denounced him, we shall profit by his former advice, and "give no pretext" to General Jackson for indulging in his favorite acts of violence.

The multitude were therefore advised to be satisfied with giving vent to their indignation in words, but to abstain carefully from any outbreak or riot, and whilst waiting a few days longer for the official news of the restoration of peace, to repeat to General Jackson and his advisers what the eloquent Workman had said to Wilkinson in similar circumstances:

"The law is not dead, but sleepeth; the Constitution is eclipsed, indeed, but the dark bodies of hideous and ill-omened forms which have intercepted its light, and deprived us of its genial influence, will soon pass away, and we shall again behold the glorious luminary shining forth in all its original splendor."

Meanwhile the Court-Martial had met, and, presided by General Gaines, was proceeding with the trial of Louaillier. There were seven charges against him:— 1. mutiny; 2. exciting mutiny; 3. general misconduct; 4. being a spy; 5. illegal and improper conduct and disobedience to orders; 6. writing a willful and corrupt libel; 7. unsoldierlike behavior and violations of the proclamation of martial law. All these charges rested on one single fact—the publication of the 3d of March—and show what varieties of guilt could be extracted from it. The prisoner, when brought to the bar and arraigned, refused to answer, and the plea of not guilty was ordered to be entered. His counsel pleaded to the jurisdiction of the Court, on the ground that the accused was a member of the Legislature, and, as such, exempt from militia duty; that the rules and articles of war were expressly established for the government of the Army and Navy of the United States, and were not binding on any individual out of it; that his client was neither of the army or militia, although, during the invasion, he had performed military duty in one of the volunteer companies embodied for the maintenance of order in the city;* that the proclamation of martial law made no one a soldier who was not so before; that it vested no right in the General, nor imposed on any one any obligation which did not exist before; that the proclamation of martial law was a mere warning that it would be enforced as it previously existed, and not the creation or introduction of something new. What was martial law in the United States? It was no more than that code of regulations by which their martial affairs were to be governed. By what authority was that code to be established? By the Legislative power alone, and by that power accordingly it had been framed and made binding upon the land. Congress had prescribed rules and articles of war, and the President of the United States himself, as Commander-in-Chief, could not add anything to their provisions nor modify them in the slightest degree. He could no more make *martial law*, than he could *fiscal, commercial*, or *criminal law*. It is the province of the Legislature to enact a law; it is the

---

* Martin's History, p. 404, vol. 2.

exclusive right of the Executive to proclaim and to enforce it. In the establishment of the rules and articles of war as prescribed by Congress and in their legal application there was nothing, it was alleged, incompatible with the rights of the citizen, and the independence and ordinary authority of the Judiciary. On the other hand, it was maintained that, by universal usage, when martial law is proclaimed in a place, all the citizens are subjected like the soldiers to the severity of military regulations, and that Louaillier could not therefore claim any exemption from them; that he was in Jackson's camp, and as long as he remained there, and the proclamation of martial law was not revoked, all his acts were liable to be tried by a court-martial in conformity with the rules and articles of war existing in the United States. The Court sustained Louaillier's plea to its jurisdiction as to all the charges, except that of being a spy. The ground of this decision was, that Louaillier, not being in the service of the United States, could not be tried by a court-martial in relation to the other charges submitted to their consideration; but they declared themselves competent to take cognizance of the accusation brought against him of being a spy.

The decision of the Court was manifestly wrong as to the last part of it; they had no authority, under the 2d section of the rules and articles of war, to try Louaillier as a spy, because he was a *citizen* of the United States, to which he *owed allegiance.* In the case of Elijah Clark, condemned, in 1812, to be hung as a spy at Buffalo, in the State of New York, by sentence of a court-martial, the execution being suspended by General Hull until the pleasure of the President of the United States should be known, the Secretary of War wrote to the General, "that Clark, being considered a citizen of the United States, and not liable to be tried by a court-martial as a spy, the President directed that, unless he should be arraigned by the Civil Court for treason, or a minor crime, under the laws of the State of New York, he must be discharged." In the case of Smith, a naturalized Scotchman, claiming damages for false imprisonment, the Supreme Court of the United States decided, that, "as he was an American citizen, he could not be chargeable with such an offence as that of being *a spy;* that he might be amenable to the civil authority for *treason*, but could not be prosecuted under *martial law*, as *a spy*." The Court, however, although maintaining that they had jurisdiction to try Louaillier as a spy, acquitted him of the offence, on the ground that there was no evidence before them of his being found "*lurking about any fortification or encampment of the Army of the United States.*" Whatever may be said of the other charges brought against Louaillier, it must be admitted that the one which placed him before the Court-Martial as a spy was most extraordinary, for it was a matter of public notoriety that he was a member of the Legislature, in which he had acted a conspicuous part; therefore a citizen of the United States; and not only was he not *found lurking* about any fortification or encampment, but he had openly taken an attitude of defiance against the Commander-in-Chief, whom he had attacked by a publication which was destined to meet that commander's eye immediately after its appearance. But, setting aside the rules and articles of war as established in the United States, what is a spy in the common acceptation of the word? "It is a person* *sent* into an enemy's camp to inspect their works, ascertain their strength and their intentions, to watch their movements, and *secretly* communicate intelligence to the proper officer." Certainly, it is difficult to imagine how General Jackson, even when laboring under the greatest

* Webster's Dictionary.

excitement, could persuade himself that this definition of a spy could apply to Louaillier's character and position. On his being informed of the decision of the Court, which was given on the 9th, he had another of his explosions of wrath. He refused to release the prisoner, and, on the next day, issued the following General Order:

"The Commanding General disapproves of the sentence of the Court-Martial, of which Major-General Gaines is President, on the several charges and specifications exhibited against Mr. Louaillier; and is induced, by the novelty and importance of the matters submitted to the decision of that Court, to assign the reasons of this disapproval.

"The charges against the prisoner were mutiny, exciting mutiny, general misconduct, for being a spy, illegal and improper conduct, and disobedience of orders, writing a willful and corrupt libel against the Commanding General, unsoldierly conduct, and conduct in violation of a General Order; all which charges are, on the face of them, proper to be inquired into by a court-martial. The defendant pleaded to the jurisdiction of the Court, and founded his exceptions on matters of fact, which exceptions, as to all the charges and specifications but one, the Court sustained, without inquiring into the truths of the facts (which not otherwise could have appeared to them), upon which those exceptions were bottomed.

"The Commanding General is not disposed, however, to rest his objections upon any informality in the mode of proceeding adopted by the Court; but presuming that the Court really believed the truth of the facts set forth in the exceptions, deems it his duty to meet the doubts as he supposes them to have existed. The character of the prisoner (a citizen not enrolled in any corps, and a member of the State Legislature, though that Legislature was not in session), probably, in the opinion of the Court, placed him without their reach upon the several charges on which they declined acting.

"The enemy having invaded the country, and threatening an attack on New Orleans, many considerations growing out of this contingency, and connected with the defence of the city, rendered the adoption of the most energetic and decisive measures necessary. Martial law, as the most comprehensive and effectual, was therefore proclaimed by the Commanding General—a state of things which made it the duty of every inhabitant, indiscriminately, to contribute to the defence of his country—a duty, in the opinion of the Commanding General, more positive and more urgent than any resulting from the common and usual transactions of private, or even public life. The occasion that calls it forth involves, at once, the very existence of the Government, and the liberty, property, and lives of the citizens.

"Martial law, being established, applies, as the Commanding General believes, to all persons who remain within the sphere of its operation, and claims exclusive jurisdiction of all offences which aim at the disorganization of the army over which it extends. To a certain extent, it is believed to make every man a soldier to defend the spot where chance or choice has placed him; and to make him *liable* for any misconduct calculated to weaken its defence.

"If martial law, when necessity shall have justified a resort to it, does not operate to this extent, it is not easy to perceive the reason, or the utility of it. If a man who shall, from choice, remain within the limits of its operation, and whose house is without these limits, and who shall there labor by means in his power to stir up sedition and mutiny among the soldiery, inspire them with distrust toward the commanding officer, and communicate to the enemy intelligence of the disaffection and discontent which he himself has created, may safely avail himself of what he may please to call his constitutional rights, and continue his dangerous machinations with impunity, the Commanding General believes that it can easily be conceived how a man, thus influenced and thus acting, might render the enemy more important services, and do his country more injury than he possibly could by entering the ranks of the enemy, and aiding him in open battle. Why is martial law ever declared? Is it to make the enlisted or drafted soldier subject to it? He was subject to it before. It is, that the whole resources of a country, or of that district over which it is proclaimed, may be successfully applied for its preservation. Every man, therefore, within the limits to which it extends, is subject to its influence. If it has not this operation, it is surely a perfect nullity. Apply this view of the subject to the case before the Court, and how is it? After the adjournment of the Legislature, of which the defendant claims to be a member, he remained within the camp of the American army, and within the limits which are declared to be embraced by martial law. How does he then deport himself? Instead of contributing to the defence of his country, instead of seeking to promote that unanimity which a love of country, and the important trust which had been reposed in him might have led us to expect, we behold him endeavoring to stir up discord, sedition, mutiny; laboring to disorganize and destroy an army which had so lately defended his country, and might so soon again be necessary for its defence—not only inviting the enemy to renew his attempt, but contributing his utmost to enable him to succeed, if he should obey the invitation. Is there no power to restrain the efforts, or to punish the wickedness of such a man? If he aids and comforts the enemy by communicating to him information of the mutinous and seditious spirit, of the distraction and confusion which he himself has created—why—this is treason, and he cannot be punished by a court-martial. If he excites mutiny, disobedience to orders, and rebellion among the soldiery, he is not attached to the army, and cannot be restrained. Why is he not attached to the army? Why, at such a moment, when he remains within it, is he not subject to its rules and regulations? If the enemy comes, may he fold his arms and walk unconcernedly along the lines, or remain inactive in his room? Can he not be called upon for his exertions? May he not only refuse to render any assistance himself, but, without fear or reproach, do all in his power to render ineffectual the exertions of others, of that army which, in the most threatening crisis, is fighting for the liberty and safety of that country whose liberty and safety he professes to have so much at heart? May he, at such a moment, proclaim to the enemy that we are dissatisfied with our General, tired of the war, determined no longer to bear the restrictions which it imposes, in a word, disaffected and disunited, and ready to yield to him on his first approach? May this man, a foreigner, retaining the predilections for the country which gave him birth, and boasting of those predilections, may such a man, under such circumstances, excite sedition and mutiny, division and disorganization in our army; and when he is called before the court-martial to answer for his crimes, say: *Gentlemen, you have no right to take cognizance of the offences of which I am charged?* Decide with the accused, no army can be safe, no general can command; disaffection and disobedience, anarchy and confusion must take place of order and subordination, defeat and shame, of victory and triumph. But the Commanding General is persuaded that this is a state of things which no Government can, or does, tolerate. The Constitution of the United States secures to the citizen the most valuable privileges; yet that Constitution contemplates the necessity of suspending the exercise of the same, in order to secure the continuance of all. If it authorizes the suspension of the Writ of Habeas Corpus in certain cases, it thereby implicitly admits the operation of martial law, when, in the event of rebellion or invasion, public safety may require it. To whom does the declaration of this law belong? To the guardian of the public safety, to him who is to conduct the operations against the enemy, whose vigilance is to destroy danger, and whose arms are to repel it. He is the only authority present to witness and determine the emergency which makes such a resort necessary, and possessed of the means to make suitable provision for it. For the correctness of his conduct, under the circumstances which influenced him, he stands responsible to his government."

It seems, from the language and conduct of General Jackson, that his understanding of martial law was very different from the one entertained by jurists; that he had concluded that the proclamation of martial law carried within itself, as a necessary consequence, the suspension of the Habeas Corpus, of all civil laws and constitutional privileges within the sphere of its action; that it vested absolute authority in the Commander-in-Chief, and was a thing so plastic and comprehensive that it embraced and meant whatever the "*sole guardian of the public safety*" deemed expedient—an opinion which is generally favored by military men in such circumstances.

After the decision of the Court-Martial in the case of Louaillier, the General foresaw that he had nothing to hope from the trial of Hall for *aiding, abetting* and *exciting mutiny* in his camp. The sentence of the Court would, of course, have been a foregone conclusion. Therefore he gave up the idea of a criminal prosecution, and, putting the prisoner under a strong guard, ordered him, on the 11th of March, to be led several miles beyond the limits of the city, where he was left, with a prohibition to return "before the ratification of the treaty of peace should have been *regularly* announced, or the British should have departed from the Southern coast."

On the 13th, early in the morning, the inhabitants of New Orleans were awakened by the firing of cannon, repeated at measured intervals. They rushed into the streets for inquiry, and in gladsome expectation of hearing the official news of the ratification of the treaty of peace. They were not disappointed; a courier had arrived, at the dawn of light, with the important document which had been so long desired, and with instructions from the President, directing General Jackson to issue a proclamation for the pardon of all military offences. There could be no longer any excuse for retaining Louaillier in custody; the doors of his prison were thrown open; the proclamation of martial law was revoked; the French Consul came back to resume his functions, and Judge Hall returned to town amidst the acclamations of the citizens. He was greatly and universally esteemed, and was described* "as a magistrate of pure heart, clean hands, and a mind susceptible of no fear but that of God."

General Jackson communicated " with satisfaction " to the troops under his command the testimonials which had been sent him of the "just sense which the President of the United States entertained of their patriotism, valor and good conduct," and congratulated them particularly on "their being able to receive this applause with the consciousness of having deserved it." In the communication which James Monroe, Secretary of State, had addressed on the subject to Jackson in the name of the President, were the following lines, which were received with pleasure, as making amends for suspicions which ought never to have been entertained: "To our newly adopted fellow-citizens of Louisiana you will give assurance of his great sensibility to the decided and honorable proof which they have given of their attach

---

* Martin's History of Louisiana, p. 416, vol. 2.

ment and devotion to the Union, and of their manly support of the rights of their country."

On the 14th, General Jackson began to take the necessary measures to disband the troops, and to restore to their usual peaceful avocations, and to their respective States, Tennessee, Kentucky, Louisiana, and to the Territory of Mississippi, the brave men who had acted such a distinguished part in the war which had just terminated. Those who could not be removed without imminent danger of their lives were to be well accommodated, and supplied with hospital stores, and a sufficient number of surgeons were retained to attend them. Contractors were to furnish provisions to the troops on their return march, on the requisition of their respective commanding officers, who were instructed to use every care and attention to prevent depredations on private property, and who were admonished that they would be held personally responsible to indemnify the sufferers, agreeably to the regulations of the War Department, for all damages done or property injured or destroyed by their commands. His farewell address to his late companions-in-arms was dignified in tone, tender and affectionate in sentiment:

"In parting," he said, "with those brave men whose destinies had been long united with his own, and in whose labors and glories it was his happiness and his boast to have participated, he could neither suppress his feelings, nor give utterance to them as he ought. In what terms could he bestow suitable praise on merit so extraordinary, so unparalleled? Let him in one burst of joy, gratitude and exultation, exclaim: These are the saviors of their country—these the patriot soldiers who triumphed over the invincibles of Wellington, and conquered the conquerors of Europe." With what patience did you submit to privations! With what fortitude did you endure fatigue! What valor did you display in the day of battle! You have secured to America a proud name among the nations of the earth, a glory which will never perish!

"Possessing those dispositions which equally adorn the citizen and the soldier, the expectations of your country will be met in peace as her wishes have been gratified in war. Go, then, my brave companions, to your homes, to those tender connections and those blissful scenes which render life so dear—full of honor, and crowned with laurels which will never fade. With what happiness will you not, when participating, in the bosoms of your families, in the enjoyment of peaceful life, look back to the toils you have borne, to the dangers you have encountered! How will all your past exposures be converted into sources of inexpressible delight! Who, that never experienced your sufferings, will be able to appreciate your joys? The man who slumbered ingloriously at home during your painful marches, your nights of watchfulness and your days of toil, will envy you the happiness which these recollections will afford—still more will he envy the gratitude of that country which you have so eminently contributed to save. Continue, fellow-soldiers, on your passage to your several destinations, to preserve that subordination, that dignified and manly deportment which have so ennobled your character.

. . . .

"What happiness it is to the commanding General, that while danger was before us, he was, on no occasion, compelled to use toward his companions-in-arms either severity or rebuke! If, after the enemy had retired, improper passions began to show their empire in a few unworthy bosoms, and rendered a resort to energetic measures necessary for their suppression, the commanding General has not confounded the innocent with the guilty, the seduced with the seducers. Toward you, fellow-soldiers, the most cheering recollections exist, blended, alas, with regret, that disease and war should have ravished from us so many worthy companions. But the memory of the cause in which they perished, and of the virtues which animated them while living, must occupy the place where sorrow would claim to dwell.

"Farewell, fellow-soldiers. The expression of your General's thanks is feeble; but the gratitude of a country of freemen is yours; yours the applause of an admiring world!"

Two days after, on the 16th, the "City Battalion of Uniform Companies" presented to General Jackson an address glowing with a warmth of feeling which seemed to attest its sincerity. This address was signed by seventeen officers, all of whom, with the exception of two, were French, or of French origin,* which shows that the whole of that population was not alienated from General Jackson by the course which he had lately pursued against those with whom they were connected by language and the pride, communion, and endearments of race :

"We have delayed," they said, "until this moment, the expression of our feelings toward you, lest the honest emotions of our hearts should be ascribed to a desire of propitiating the favor of our Commander. At this moment, when neither hope nor fear can be supposed to have influenced us, we pray you to receive the sincere tribute of our thanks : as soldiers, for the confidence you have reposed in us, for the paternal care with which you have watched over our comforts, and above all for that justice you have done to our zeal in assigning us on every occasion a post of *danger* and of *honor*—as citizens, for the wisdom of the measures you devised to protect our country, for the skill and bravery with which they were executed, and that indispensable energy to which we owe our safety. Leaving to others the task of declaiming about *privileges* and *constitutional rights*, we are content with having fought in support of them ; we have understanding enough to know when they are wantonly violated; and no false reasoning shall make us ungrateful to the man whose wisdom and valor have secured them to us and to our posterity. We do not deal in professions ; we pray you, General, to be assured, that in the officers and men of this battalion you have *soldiers*, who have been and are always ready to confront every danger under your command—*fellow-citizens*, grateful for your services—*friends*, personally attached to your fortunes, and ready to promote your happiness at the risk of their own. You have allowed us the endearing title of your *brothers-in-arms ;* it was given to us on the field, then strewed with the bodies of our enemies; and we feel a noble pride in the consciousness which allows us to accept it. That fraternity, cemented in hostile blood, shall be the pride of our lives ; and in after times will secure to our children the respect of posterity. General, common phrases cannot express the emotions which agitate us at the moment of our separation ; but we pray Heaven to watch over your safety ; and we trust to a

---

* Their names were : J. B. Plauché, St. Geme, M. White, A. Guibert, Hudry, P. Roche, St. Jean, Cœur de Roy, De St. Romes, N. Thompson, C. Fremont, Duhulquod, L. Pilié, Benetaud, Bertel, Huet, Lemounier.

grateful country for the honors and advancement which your services have merited."

We shall give in full the reply of General Jackson, because it is evidently written with great care, and intended as a vindication of those energetic measures which he had lately adopted, and which had produced such a commotion in the city of New Orleans:

"*Fellow-Soldiers:*

"Although born and bred in a land of freedom, popular favor has always been with me a secondary object. My first wish, in political life, has been to be useful to my country. Yet I am not insensible to the good opinion of my fellow-citizens. I would do much to obtain it; but I cannot, for this purpose, sacrifice my own conscience, or what I conceive to be the interests of my country.

"These principles have prepared me to receive, with just satisfaction, the address you have presented. The first wish of my heart, the safety of our country, has been accomplished; and it affords me the greatest happiness to know that the means taken to secure this object have met the approbation of those who have had the best opportunities of judging of their propriety, and who, from their various relations, might be supposed the most ready to censure any which had been improperly resorted to. The distinction you draw, gentlemen, between those who only declaim about civil rights and those who fight to maintain them, shows how just and practical a knowledge you have of the true principles of liberty. Without such knowledge all theory is useless or mischievous.

"Whenever the invaluable rights which we enjoy under our happy Constitution are threatened by invasion, privileges the most dear, and which in ordinary times ought to be regarded as the most sacred, may be required to be infringed for their security. At such a crisis, we have only to determine whether we will suspend, for a time, the exercise of the latter, that we may secure the permanent enjoyment of the former. Is it wise, in such a moment, to sacrifice the spirit of the laws to the letter, and, by adhering too strictly to the letter, lose the *substance* forever, in order that we may, for an instant, preserve the *shadow?* It is not to be imagined that the express provisions of any written law can fully embrace emergencies which suppose and occasion the suspension of all law, but the highest and the last, that of self-preservation. No right is more precious to a freeman than that of suffrage; but had your election taken place on the 8th of January, would your declaimers have advised you to abandon the defence of your country, in order to exercise this inestimable privilege at the polls? Is it to be supposed that your General, if he regarded the important trust committed to his charge, would have permitted you to preserve the Constitution by an act which would have involved Constitution, country and honor in one undistinguished ruin?

"What is more justly important than personal liberty? Yet, how can the civil enjoyment of this privilege be made to consist with the order, subordination and discipline of a camp? Let the sentinel be removed by *subpœna* from his post, let writs of *habeas corpus* carry away the officers from the lines, and the enemy may conquer your country by only employing lawyers to defend your Constitution.

"Private property is held sacred in all good Governments, and particularly in your own. Yet, shall the fear of invading it prevent a General from marching his army over a corn-field, or burning a house which protects the enemy?

"These and a thousand other instances might be cited to show that laws must sometimes be silent when necessity speaks. The only question with the friend of his country will be, have these laws been made silent wantonly and unnecessarily? If necessity dictated the measure, if a resort to it was important for the preservation of those rights which we esteem so dear, and in defence of which we had so willingly taken up arms, surely it would not have been becoming in the Commander-in-Chief to have shrunk from the responsibility which it involved. He did not shrink from it. In declaring martial law, his object, and his only object, was to embody the whole resources of the country for its defence. That law, while it existed, necessarily suspended all rights and privileges inconsistent with its provisions. It is matter of surprise that they who boast themselves the champions of those rights and privileges, should not, when they were first put in danger by the proclamation of martial law, have manifested that lively sensibility of which they have since made so ostentatious a display. So far, however, was this from being the case, that this measure not only met, then, the open support of those who, when their country was invaded, thought resistance a virtue, and the silent approbation of *all*, but even received the particular recommendation and encouragement of many who now inveigh the most bitterly against it. It was not until a victory, secured by that very measure, had lessened the danger which occasioned a resort to it, that the present *feeling guardians of our rights* discovered, that the Commanding General ought to have suffered his posts to be abandoned through the interference of a foreign agent, his ranks to be thinned by desertion, and his whole army to be broken to pieces by mutiny, while yet a powerful force of the enemy remained on your coast, and within a few hours' sail of your city.

"I thought and acted differently. It was not until I discovered that the civil power stood no longer in need of the military for its support, that I restored it to its usual functions; and the restoration was not delayed a moment after that period had arrived.

"Under these circumstances, fellow-soldiers, your resolution to *let others declaim about privileges and constitutional rights* will never draw upon you the charge of being indifferent to those inestimable blessings. Your attachment to them has been proved by a stronger title—that of having fought nobly to preserve them. You, who have thus supported them against the open pretensions of a powerful enemy, will never, I trust, surrender them to the underhand machinations of men who stood aloof in the hour of peril, and who, when the danger is gone, claim to be the *defenders of your Constitution*.

"An honorable peace has dissolved our military connection; and, in a few days, I shall quit a country endeared to me by the most pleasing recollections. Among the most prominent of these, gentlemen, are those I shall ever entertain of the distinguished bravery, the exact discipline, the ardent zeal, and the important services of your corps. The offered friendship of each individual composing it I receive with pleasure, and with sincerity reciprocate. I shall always pride myself on a fraternity with such men, created in such a cause."

It appears by this document that General Jackson unequivocally admitted that he had violated the Constitution and the laws, but alleged in his justification that it had been done as a matter of necessity for the protection and safety of the country. There were many who were convinced that this necessity had never existed, that a dangerous precedent had been established, and who were determined that the prestige of victory should not shield against punishment the man who, in their opinion, had wantonly trampled on the dearest rights and privileges of his fellow-citizens. With these views, Dick, the District Attorney for the United States, immediately after the return of Hall, lost no time in calling the attention of the Court to those proceedings which had culminated in closing by violence one of the tribunals of the United States. The Judge, however, refused to entertain any such proposition for the present, stating that the laws would assert their majesty and supremacy in due time, but that, to celebrate the restoration of peace, a few days of public rejoicings should be allowed to pass by without any interruption of an unpleasant nature. But, on the 21st of March, Dick was permitted to proceed against General Jackson. He represented to the Court that, more than six weeks after the enemy had evacuated Louisiana, there had been a publication animadverting on the official conduct of the Commander-in-Chief; that the author of it had been arrested as a spy and for other crimes, and a court-martial assembled to pass sentence on him; that the prisoner, thinking that his arrest was illegal, that the Court had no jurisdiction over him, being deprived of liberty and threatened with death in case of conviction, had applied to that tribunal which, under the Federal Constitution, had specially been established to prevent such abuses, and give him the protection to which he was entitled; that the Judge presiding in that tribunal, on taking the proper steps, according to the petition of the plaintiff, to investigate the matter, was himself arrested by order of the defendant, and thereby the course of justice obstructed; that the clerk of the Court had been compelled to carry a record of the Court to headquarters, where it was taken and withheld from him; that the said clerk and the marshal of the Court had been threatened also with arrest if they performed their duty; that these transactions had taken place when there was not the least prospect of the renewal of hostilities, or the least appearance of danger from any quarter, but, on the contrary, after "*persuasive*" information had been received from various sources as to the existence of a lately signed treaty of peace between Great Britain and the United States; whereupon, the District Attorney, having laid before the Court the necessary affidavits, moved for a rule to show cause why process of attachment should not issue against General Jackson for contempt of Court. The motion was granted, and on its return day, Reid, one of the General's Aids, accompanied him to the court-house, and presented a paper sworn to by the General, as his answer to the rule. It was a solemn protest against the unconstitutionality and illegality of the proceedings; a denial of the authority of the District Attorney to institute it, as well as that of the Court to punish him for the alleged contempt. General Jackson further maintained that, if he was accused of any statutory offence, the prosecution should be carried on by presentment or indictment; and that in such a case he could not be deprived of a trial by jury. As to the charge of contempt, his counsel urged that it had not been committed in Court; and several other technical objections were also presented.

In the concluding part of this document, the proclamation of martial law, says Martin in his History, was justified on the report which the General had received of the disaffection and seditious disposition of the French portion of the population of Louisiana; and various extracts were given from letters of the Governor on the difficulties he had to encounter, the opposition he met with from the Legislature, and the little dependence there was for success, except on a regular force to be sent by the United States. The interference with the records in the clerk's office was justified on the belief the defendant entertained, that it was within his authority.

The proclamation of martial law was held to have made the publisher of the libel a soldier, and his offence cognizable by a court-martial, and the imprisonment of the Judge was said to have been a matter of necessity.

"The Attorney of the United States opposed the reading of this paper. He said that, in no case, the defendant was permitted to make evidence for himself, and justify himself by swearing he was innocent, although, on a process of attachment, the defendant's answers to interrogatories put by the officer who conducted the prosecution were conclusive evidence.

"In the present stage of the cause, the inquiry was confined to the sufficiency of the facts sworn to—whether they did constitute an offence—and one which did support a prosecution by process of attachment. When the hearings would be on the merits, the defendant might avail himself of his answers to interrogatories, to show that the facts in the affidavits on which the rule was obtained were not true. The Judge took time to deliberate."

On the next day he said : "The Court has taken time to consider the propriety of admitting the answer offered yesterday. It was proper to do so, because it is the first proceeding of any importance instituted in a matter like the present, since the establishment of the Court, and because by the constitution of the Court it is composed of one Judge only; and it so happens that one of the charges of contempt is his imprisonment, and the consequent obstruction of the course of justice. This is no reason why the proceedings should not have been instituted, and be persevered in; but it is a good one for deliberation. No personal consideration ought, for a moment, to allow the abandonment of the defence of the laws, the support of the dignity of the tribunal, and of the rights of the citizens.

"I have considered the case, and I think I see a clear course.

"On a rule to show cause, the party called on may take all *legal* grounds to show that the attachment ought not to issue. He may take exceptions to the *mode* of proceedings, and prove, from the affidavits on which the rule was obtained, that the facts do not amount to a contempt.

"If the Court be convinced that the attachment may legally issue, it goes to bring the party into court; the interrogatories are propounded; he may object to any of them as improper, or deny the facts charged, and purge himself of the contempt on oath. His single testimony counteracts all other that may have been adduced.

"I will hear any of the exceptions taken in the answer, or any question of law that may be urged."

Arguments of counsel were therefore patiently listened to on all the "exceptions taken, and on all the questions of law" which incidentally arose; after which the rule was made absolute, and the case ordered to be tried on its merits on a particular day. On that day the excitement was intense in the city; the timid expected bloodshed, and, being haunted by imaginary terrors, confined themselves to their houses; the greater part of the population, however, was not of this disposition, and an immense crowd assembled at an early hour round the court-house. Many were moved by curiosity; others by feelings of sympathy for the General, or resentment and indignation against the Judge. Among the most ardent against the latter were remarked the Baratarians, who were said to nourish toward him the bitterest hostility, on account of his having been very strict on several occasions, when prosecutions had been instituted against some of their leaders. They were represented as panting for an opportunity to wreak their vengeance on the magistrate whose inflexible rigor they had experienced to their cost. Distinct threats would occasionally burst from the impatient crowd; and one voice was heard to exclaim, "Let the General say but one word, and we will pitch into the river the Judge, the lawyers, and the court-house itself." This sentiment was greeted with fierce shouts of applause. At last, the long-expected hour had arrived. The General, followed by a numerous escort of officers, entered the hall of judgment, which was crowded to suffocation. The dense multitude had opened before him as he advanced and then closed again in deep silence; but when he reached the bar where he was to stand as a culprit, and confronted the Judge on his seat, one wild yell of defiance, which was echoed by the multitude outside, swept over the building and seemed to shake the roof and walls against which it reverberated. Jackson looked round with an expression of calm and august majesty, which was long remembered by those who saw his commanding features on that occasion; he only waved his hand in rebuke, and instantly order and silence were re-established. Then turning to the Judge, he slightly bowed his head, as if he meant to say: I am here in obedience to your command. The Judge looked as serene and impassible as if nothing unusual had happened. There was a grandeur in the scene which struck all the bystanders. Presently the clear voice of the Judge was heard: "Mr. Clerk, proceed with the business of the Court." The Clerk called the case: "The United States *vs.* Andrew Jackson." The General rose, and, with much dignity, signified to the Court his intention to decline answering interrogatories—a determination to which he said he had come, on account of the Court having refused his answer to the rule to be read. The Court replied, that it was for him to decide on the proper course to be pursued in his own defence, and that every indulgence had been extended to him which the law authorized. The District Attorney of the United States now rose to address the Court;* we give a synopsis of his remarks:

"My task," he said, "is much simplified by the course which the defendant has taken. The defendant is charged with having obstructed the course of justice, and prevented, by violence the interference of the District Court of the United States, in order that an illegal prosecution for a capital offence should be carried on before a military tribunal, against a citizen absolutely disconnected with the army or militia. The greatest part of the paper which he produced on his first coming into Court is filled with extracts of letters and with arguments, to justify his issuing a proclamation of martial law. He might have spared himself so much unnecessary labor; no one ever pretended that there was any degree of guilt in his proclamation of martial law. In the beginning of an invasion, it was very proper for the commander of the army raised to oppose it, to warn, by a solemn appeal, his men and his fellow-citizens around him, that circumstances required the exertion of the faculties of *all* to repel the enemy, and that the martial law of the United States, which means the system of rules established by the acts of Congress, and the laws and usages of civilized nations with regard to martial matters, would be strictly enforced. The question 's not whether the General was wrong in proclaiming martial law, but whether, in his acts, he did not go *beyond martial law*, and beyond what circumstances required, in the exercise of the authority which he had assumed. The defendant seems to have been under the impression that martial law vested in him absolute powers. Where does he find a precedent for it in the annals of jurisprudence? Is it in England? We have the authority of Sir Matthew Hale to say: 'That martial law is no law there, but something indulged as a law'; and Lord Loughborough maintains that martial law, even as described by Sir Matthew Hale, 'does not exist at all.' There is a contradiction in the very terms. If law regulates the actions of delegated power, how can uncontrolled, unbounded power be consistent with the existence of law? What is commonly understood as law cannot have life where despotism

* Martin's History of Louisiana, p. 422, vol. 2.

rules supreme. Despotism is not martial law, nor any other law; 't is the absence of all laws. Judge Bay, of the Supreme Court of South Carolina, in the case of Lamb, says correctly: 'If by martial law is to be understood that dreadful system, *the law of arms*, which in former times was exercised by the King of England and his lieutenants, when his *word was the law*, and *his will the power* by which it was exercised, I have no hesitation in saying, that such a monster could not exist in this land of liberty and legality. The political atmosphere of America would destroy it in embryo. It was against such a tyrannical monster that we triumphed in our Revolutionary conflict; our fathers sealed the conquest with their blood, and their posterity will never permit it to tarnish our soil by its unhallowed feet, or harrow up the feelings of our gallant sons by its ghastly appearance. All our civil institutions forbid it; and the manly hearts of our countrymen are steeled against it. But if by this military code are meant to be understood the rules and regulations for the government of our men in arms, when marshaled in defence of our country's rights and honor, then I am bound to say there is nothing unconstitutional in such a system.' Therefore, we candidly admit that, although the acts of the defendant cannot, by any means, be justified by his proclamation of martial law, they can certainly be so on the plea of necessity—that necessity which justifies any act it commands for good purposes; and we grant that the defendant is entitled to any benefit he can derive from this plea, if it can be proved to have any foundation to rest upon; and we say, on the part of the United States, that success in this prosecution is neither expected nor desired, if that necessity can be shown, which the General invokes in his behalf.

"The defendant, in several documents, and particularly in his printed reply to the 'address of the uniform companies of the City of New Orleans,' admits without reserve or equivocation that he has violated the Constitution and laws of his country, but rests his defence on the law of necessity. We agree with him on this point; we allow that this is the proper ground for him to take; and we shall now proceed to demonstrate that there never was any necessity for his arbitrary acts.

"On the 29th of January there was not a British soldier left in arms on the soil of Louisiana, nor within a shorter distance than six hours' sail from its shores. True, the enemy was still in its neighborhood, and still powerful, but his force consisted of a defeated, demoralized army, much reduced from its original numbers, while our powers of resistance had been greatly increased by reinforcements, by better preparations, and by the confidence resulting from the successes already obtained. On the 13th of February, Admiral Cochrane sends to General Jackson a copy of a bulletin received from Jamaica, proclaiming that a Treaty of Peace was signed, on the 24th of December, between Great Britain and the United States, and 'begs leave to offer his sincere congratulations.' On the 19th, General Lambert, the Commander-in-Chief of the British forces, confirms the information, compliments the defendant on the prospect of peace, and 'hopes soon to communicate the notice of the ratification being exchanged.' On the 21st, General Jackson so far believes in the near prospect, if not the actual existence of peace, as to write to Admiral Cochrane about the restoration of private property taken from our citizens, and the propriety of the cessation of hostilities. At this juncture, Louaillier, a member of the Legislature of the State, one of our most respectable citizens, and in noway connected with the army and militia of the United States, published in one of the journals of the city a communication censuring some of the official acts of the defendant. He is arrested on the 5th of March as a spy, and brought before a court-martial to be sentenced to death in case of conviction. This was clearly an act of illegality. Was the danger of his remaining at liberty so great as to justify this illegality? On the very same day, the magistrate whose protection is sought by Louaillier is also arrested by the defendant. What pressing danger required such a step? Would the safety of the country have been put in peril if the District Court of the United States had been permitted to decide on the legality of the arrest of Louaillier? A few hours after this extraordinary proceeding and this monstrous exercise of brute force, on the 6th of March, the defendant informs General Lambert that he, General Jackson, had received intelligence from Washington that the treaty had been ratified by the President and Senate of the United States, but that, by some unaccountable accident, a dispatch on another subject had been substituted for the one intended to give him official notice of this event. He has, however, before him the courier's declarations; he has the order of the Postmaster-General directing his deputies to forward the express carrying intelligence of the recent peace. 'From other sources, to which he gives credit,' he has also learned that the same express has brought *official notice* of the treaty to the Governor of Tennessee. Therefore, he tells Lambert that 'very little doubt is left in his mind' about the restoration of peace. He proposes a cessation of hostilities in anticipation of the expected communication in an official form; he assures the British General of the satisfaction he feels in reflecting, 'that their correspondence, begun as commanders of hostile armies, terminates as officers of nations in amity.' Where was the *necessity*, under such circumstances, to keep in prison a member of the Legislature of the State of Louisiana and a Judge of the United States, in open and admitted violation of the Constitution and laws of the land? Nay—'so little doubt' had the defendant in his mind of the restoration of peace, so 'persuasive' of the fact, to use his own expression, was the evidence he had received, that, on the 8th, he disbanded and dismissed to their homes the whole militia of the State, and consented that the French subjects residing in New Orleans should be free from military duty and exempted from the decree of expulsion he had issued against them. If, on that occasion, he did not believe in the suspension of the state of war, he acted in a manner which would have subjected him, as a military man, to disgrace and severe penalties before a court-martial. If, on the contrary, he was satisfied, as everybody was, that a treaty of peace had been signed and ratified, where was the necessity of still retaining Louaillier and Judge Hall in durance? The defendant is placed in a dilemma of his own making, and whichever alternative he takes, it works to his injury. It seems to us we may be permitted to say in conclusion, that credulity itself could not admit the proposition that persuasive evidence of the cessation of war, and belief in the necessity of such a violent measure as the prevention of the exercise of judicial power by a legitimate tribunal, could exist at the same time in the defendant's mind. We are compelled, therefore, to attribute the arbitrary proceedings of the defendant, not to his conviction of their necessity, but to the indulged infirmity of an obstinate and morbidly irascible temperament, and to the unyielding pride of a man naturally impatient of the least show of opposition to his will."

We regret to record, that General Jackson so far forgot what was due to his personal dignity and to his national reputation, as to allow himself to be persuaded to resort to a petty quibble, in order to avert the judgment of the Court. He was made to asseverate that his intention had been to imprison Dominick A. Hall, and *not the Judge*. Dick coolly referred him to the affidavit of his own Aid, Duplessis, the Marshal of the Court, who swore to his having used these words: "I have shopped the Judge."

The case was closed, and sentence remained to be passed. The Court said that it was becoming to manifest moderation in the punishment of the defendant for the want of it; and that, in consideration of the services the General had rendered to his country, imprisonment should make no part of the sentence, which was limited to a fine of one thousand dollars and costs. It was instantly discharged, and the General, on his coming out of the court-house, entered his carriage; the horses were removed, and the people enthusiastically dragged it to the Exchange Coffee House, where he addressed a large crowd in a manner worthy of himself. "I have," he said, " during the invasion, exerted every one of my faculties for the defence and preservation of the Constitution and the laws. On this day, I have been called on to submit to their operation under circumstances which many persons might have thought sufficient to justify resistance. Considering obedience to the laws, even when we think them unjustly applied, as the first duty of the citizen, I did not hesitate to comply with the sentence you have heard pronounced, and I entreat you to remember the example I have given you of respectful submission to the administration of justice." The citizens insisted on refunding to him the amount of the fine he had paid, on the ground that they considered it their own debt; but he peremptorily refused.

A reaction had taken place in favor of General Jackson, even among his most violent opponents, on account of the propriety and nobility of his late deportment. It would have been well for him to have permitted things to remain as they stood; but, either guided by some malignant adviser, or goaded by the rashness of his own temper, he published, a few days after, in one of the journals of New Orleans, the answer he had offered to the District Court, preceded by an exordium,* in which he complained that the Court had refused to hear it. He added, that the Judge " had indulged himself, on his route to Bayou Sara when driven out of the city, in manifesting apprehensions as to the fate of the country, equally disgraceful to himself, and injurious to the interest and safety of the State," and concluded : " Should Judge Hall deny this statement, the General is prepared to prove it fully and satisfactorily."

This provocation and this reopening of the conflict did not remain long unnoticed, and the following piece appeared in answer :

"It is stated in the introductory remarks of General Jackson, that, on the Judge's route to Bayou Sara, he manifested apprehensions as to the safety of the country, disgraceful to himself and injurious to the State. Judge Hall knows full well how easy it is for one with the influence and patronage of General Jackson to procure certificates and affidavits. He knows that men, usurping authority, have their delators and spies ; and that, in the sunshine of imperial or dictatorial power, swarms of miserable creatures are easily generated from the surrounding corruption, and rapidly changed into the shape of buzzing informers. Notwithstanding which, Judge Hall declares, that on his route to Bayou Sara, he uttered no sentiment disgraceful to himself, or injurious to the State. He calls upon General Jackson to furnish that full and satisfactory evidence of his assertion which he says he is enabled to do."

The General probably discovered, but too late for his honor, that he had imprudently taken a position which he could not sustain; for he remained silent, and thus left all the advantage with his adversary. It must have been to him a source of deep humiliation to retire from the conflict which he had invited, without redeeming the word which he had pledged with such solemnity. It

* Martin's History of Louisiana, p. 425, vol. 2.

gratified the malice of his enemies, and it mortified his friends. He soon after departed from the theatre of his glory. We now dismiss him from the pages of this History, after having represented his acts and character with those lights and shades which appertain to them, and observed that strict impartiality of truth which we have considered as our sacred duty. He lived to be twice elected President of the United States, and to exercise over the destinies of his country an influence which was still felt long after he had descended into the grave. He would have saved himself from many difficulties and painful struggles, if the iron bar, to which his indomitable will was compared, had been lined with silk or velvet, and if he had not neglected those arts of conciliation which are not incompatible with the utmost firmness of purpose and rectitude of conscience. But he always preferred to break through, than to go round, any obstacle. Such as he was, however, he commanded more than any other man ever did the instinctive sympathies of that vigorous, restless, thoroughly democratic commonwealth among which his lot had been cast, and whatever his faults were, his country remembers only his virtues, his patriotism and his glory.

The following Resolutions, complimentary to the people of Louisiana, and of New Orleans in particular, were unanimously adopted by Congress:

"*Resolved*, That Congress entertain a high sense of the patriotism, fidelity, zeal, and courage with which the people of the State of Louisiana promptly and unanimously stepped forth, under circumstances of imminent danger from a powerful invading army, in defence of all the individual, social, and political rights held dear to man. Congress declare and proclaim that the brave Louisianians deserve well of the whole people of the United States.

"*Resolved*, That Congress entertain a high sense of the generosity, benevolence, and humanity displayed by the people of New

Orleans, in voluntarily offering the best accommodations in their power, and giving the kindest attention to the wounded, not only of our own army, but also to the wounded prisoners of the vanquished foe."

The President of the United States issued a proclamation declaring "a free and full pardon" of all offences committed in violation of any act or acts of Congress touching the revenue, trade and navigation of the United States, or touching the intercourse and commerce of the United States with foreign nations, at any time before the 8th of January, in the year eighteen hundred and fifteen, by any person or persons whatsoever, being inhabitants of New Orleans and the adjacent country, or being inhabitants of the Island of Barataria and the places adjacent, in the State of Louisiana.

"It had been long ascertained," said the President, "that many foreigners, flying from the dangers of their own home, and that some citizens, forgetful of their duty, had co-operated in forming an establishment on the Island of Barataria, near the mouth of the river Mississippi, for the purpose of a clandestine and lawless trade. The Government of the United States caused the establishment to be broken up and destroyed; and, having obtained the means of designating the offenders of every description, it only remained to answer the demands of justice by inflicting an exemplary punishment.

"But it has since been represented that the offenders have manifested a sincere repentance, that they have abandoned the prosecution of the worst cause for the support of the best, and, particularly, that they have exhibited in the defence of New Orleans unequivocal traits of courage and fidelity. Offenders, who have refused to become the associates of the enemy in war, upon the most seducing terms of invitation, and who have aided to repel his hostile invasion of the territory of the United States, can no longer be considered as objects of punishment, but as objects of a generous forgiveness."

Before the end of the Spring, Louisiana, which had been so recently in a condition of tumultuous agitation, had returned to the unruffled calmness of a state of profound peace. There were hardly any traces left of the late invasion, save angry discussions which would occasionally arise in relation to those misunderstandings which had existed between General Jackson, the Legislature, the Governor, Judge Hall and other prominent individuals. It was the remaining, but subsiding turbulence of the waters, after the storm had swept away. Claiborne had been severely blamed by some for having put the whole militia of the State under the command of a Federal officer, and for having thereby made of her Executive a nullity for the protection of her citizens. At the next session of the Legislature, he noticed this charge in these terms, in his annual message:

"It is known to you, gentlemen, that, on the requisition of Major-General Jackson, acting under the authority of the President, I did, in the late great emergency, order into the service of the Union the militia of this State, and that, during the continuance of such service, the whole remained out of my control. I am aware that my conduct in this respect, together with subsequent events, in which I either had, or was supposed to have had, an agency, has become the subject of much severe animadversion. It is not easy to limit the influence of calumny and misrepresentation, and, therefore, it is very probable that impressions to my injury may have been effected. But, if there is an honest man in this State, or elsewhere, who supposes that I would shrink from the investigation of any charge which could be exhibited, or apprehend aught from the result of such investigation, *he little knows how strongly I am fortified in conscious rectitude.* As regards our militia, the total number was no more than equal, with the succor received in time from the sister States, to repel the invasion. This militia were badly armed, and destitute of camp equipage and munitions of war. Funds to procure these necessary supplies were not at my disposal, much less had I the means of providing for their transportation, subsistence and pay. To have retained the command, I must have declined obedience to the call, and, in that case, all the expenditures on account of our militia must have been defrayed by the State, conformably to the principles established by the War Department, as I then, and do still, understand them.

But, by meeting the requisition, these expenditures devolved upon the United States. Hence a part of the militia have been paid off, and I shall be disappointed if the claims of the rest are not soon discharged with all the good faith which characterizes the General Government. A call on an individual State for its quota of any number of a required force, apportioned under the orders of the President among the several States, is a common occurrence. An obedience *to it* would always be considered by me as a duty imposed by the Constitution and laws. A demand on a State for its whole force can seldom happen. It perhaps never will be made on a State strong in population and rich in resources. Should it occur, the Governor, finding himself enabled, *in any emergency, to move his militia with dispatch and effect*, may be permitted to deliberate, before he gives up the whole of that force intrusted to him for the maintenance, within his own State, of good order and the supremacy of the law. But I was without any ground for hesitation; and the more readily placed our whole militia in the service of the United States, under a conviction that they would, in consequence, be brought to the field with more promptitude and efficacy. For such individual distress of feeling as may have resulted, I find an ample recompense in the triumphs of my country, to which the people of the State where I have long presided so greatly aided."

Availing himself of this opportunity to express his views in relation to the perturbation in New Orleans that had been produced by the course which General Jackson had deemed proper to pursue, after the retreat of the invaders, the Governor further said:

" Great as is the cause for patriotic exultation, on the glorious defence of the country, grateful as we must all feel for the rescue of this capital from capture, rapine, and perhaps conflagration, I shall never cease to regret that it was accompanied and succeeded by the prostration of a part of our laws and civil authorities. I know this is justified on the plea of necessity, and apparently to the satisfaction of the nation. I cannot suppose that any opinions of mine will in the least affect the public sentiment. They would probably have no other tendency than to raise the angry passions of the intolerant of the prevailing faith. But I shall not hesitate to say, that if, at any time, I listened to the doctrine of *doing evil, that good might come out of it,* and that *the end justifies the means*, I am now convinced that the admission of this principle into affairs of State must prove invasive of the rights and destructive to the happiness of a free people. Yes, gentlemen, my experience in Louisiana has taught me how to reverence the sage advice of the great Washington, when he urges his countrymen to respect the authority of the laws, and cautions them *to resist the spirit of innovation, however specious the pretext, and to permit no change by usurpation ; for although this,* says this illustrious patriot, *may in one instance be the instrument of good, it is the customary weapon by which free governments are destroyed. The precedent must always greatly counterbalance in permanent evil any partial or transient benefit which the use can at any time yield.*"

The annual messages of our Governors, for some time after the formation of the State, used to be responded to, as the speech from the throne, on the opening of the sessions of the British Parliament, calls for an address from that body. This usage has since been discontinued. On this occasion, in reply to that part of the Governor's message in which he alluded to the violent measures pursued by General Jackson, the House of Representatives said : " Great indeed is the cause for patriotic exultation in the glorious defence of this country, and the rescue of this capital from the manifold dangers with which it was menaced. To Heaven, to the hero who led our forces, and to the brave men composing them, we owe the greatest gratitude; and where there is so much to admire, we are not disposed *to dwell upon some deeds which we cannot approve.*"

SUPPLEMENTAL CHAPTER.

1816—1861.

1816. With the preceding Chapter closes the detailed histo y of Louisiana. From that time until the epoch when she, in company with several of her sister States of the South, declared the Federal Union at an end, and resumed, as an independent Sovereign, the powers which she had delegated, her annals ceased to be marked by any of those striking events which commonly give attraction to the pages of history. Her life, as a Commonwealth, was on the whole but a quiet, ever-swelling stream of uninterrupted prosperity, save occasionally by those epidemics to which her climate is subject, by the overflowing of her grand river, by the imprudence of commercial speculations, the abuse of credit, the too great emission of paper money, and the unwise expansion and contraction of banking operations, which always result in a fatal crisis that is invariably felt in all the arteries and sinews of the social body. But Louisiana hardly halted in her march to wealth and power, notwithstanding these temporary calamities and these agricultural, commercial and financial reverses, which were soon forgotten, and hardly left any traces of their passage under the luxuriant development of her unbounded resources, which speedily covered these ruins with the rich mantle of their tropical vegetation. Notwithstanding Federal injustices or neglects and sectional jealousies, her magnificent city of New Orleans, the emporium of a mighty trade, was annually visited by a thousand ships; her broad fields, teeming with exuberant fertility, continued to be the scenes of Arcadian felicity, and the homes of all her inhabitants the ever remembered seats of cordial and refined hospitality. Disdaining too long to resent, in her generous imprudence, the constant attacks of her enemies against one of her internal institutions, she concentrated her attention and her energies on the amelioration of her Legislation, on the building of railroads, the excavating of canals, the erection of charitable and educational institutions, the establishment of a system of public schools, and the complete development of her vast resources by State action, or by assisting the individual enterprise of her citizens. A minute record of those domestic events and industrial efforts would hardly be of sufficient interest to most readers, and would compel us to exceed the limits which we have prescribed to this work. We shall, therefore, content ourself with taking only a general view of the progressive condition of the State from the end of Governor Claiborne's administration to the time when she withdrew from the Federal Union.

The administration of Governor Claiborne drew to a close with the year 1816. When the Legislature met in November, Claiborne complimented them on the fortunate results of the restoration of peace. He said "that its auspicious influence on agriculture, commerce, and indeed all the pursuits of civil life, was sensibly felt." He warmed up at the prospect of uninterrupted prosperity which he saw looming up for the State. "The press of migration to our peaceful shores," he observed, "the preference shown by the unhappy exile to this favored land, assure me that, elsewhere, man cannot find as great a share of safety and felicity. How fortunate is our lot! Amidst the afflictions of nations, small is the portion fallen to the United States! Whilst with pious humility we bow in gratitude to God for such signal proofs of His favor, let us with zeal and assiduity persevere in every measure which promises to strengthen and perpetuate the great principles of civil and religious freedom." He concluded this valedictory address with the sincerest acknowledgments for the many proofs of personal confidence for which he was indebted to the people of Louisiana, and which, as he assured them, "would remain deeply engraved on a grateful heart." He was succeeded in December, 1816, by Major-General Villeré, after having been thirteen years Governor of Louisiana. He did not remain long in private life; for, a few days after, on the 13th of January, 1817, he was elected to the Senate of the United States for a full term. He died on the 23d of November, in the same year, leaving a respected memory in the State of which he had been so long the Chief Magistrate. He was succeeded in the Senate by Henry Johnson, who, subsequently, became Governor of the State.

1818. Governor Villeré, in his annual message of the 17th January, 1818, is as enthusiastic as his predecessor on the prosperity of Louisiana, and on the advantages which she is to derive from her admission into the great family of the United States. Alluding to the late invasion, he said: " Providence, after having protected us in battle, deigned to yield peace to our desires. Our political and commercial relations with foreign countries were immediately re-established; and it is this day a just subject of congratulation to observe with what rapidity the continually increasing prosperity of our affairs has in a manner, as it were, effaced even the recollection of our sufferings. The most abundant crops have, especially during the last year, rewarded the labors of agriculture, and commerce finds every day, in profits continually renewed, the just price of its indefatigable activity. What other people can flatter themselves, fellow-citizens, to enjoy, under the sole government of laws, an extent of liberty and happiness comparable to ours? The Louisianian who retraces the condition of his country under the government of Kings, can never cease to bless the day when the great American Confederation received him in its bosom." The worthy Governor, evidently, was no prophet, and did not foresee that, before half a century had elapsed, his own grandsons would have to *curse the day* when they became politically united under the same General Government with their new "fellow-citizens" of the North and West, and would probably think that the worst tyranny of *Kings* was amiable, when compared with the treatment they were destined to undergo from the fierce, fanatical and unrelenting majority of their *Republican* associates and *loving* brothers. It seems, however, that whatever were his Utopian hopes, "the press of migration to our peaceful shores" which Claiborne had seen with so much satisfaction, was not unattended with evils, for he states that "the multitude of strangers who crowd here daily necessarily occasion a multiplicity of offences." He recommends the adoption of a more stringent judicial organization to prevent the repetition of "those scandalous practices which are, almost at every instant, taking place in New Orleans and its suburbs." On the 5th of March of the same year, "the preference shown by the unhappy exile to our favored land," as exultingly expressed by Claiborne, had become so threatening to the safety of our capital, that Governor Villeré made it the subject of a special message to the Legislature. "A melancholy experience has convinced me," he said, "that if our institutions tend, in general, to insure the happiness of a people no less generous than worthy of liberty, we still have occasion to adopt some new measures for the purpose of protecting ourselves against the flagitious outrages to which the peace and security of our citizens are exposed through the great lenity of our laws.

"I will not attempt to describe to you the disorders and crimes of which, during nearly all last month, this city has been the theatre; public report has probably informed you of them; nor do I doubt but you will agree with me in ascribing their cause to the prodigious increase of our population. It is natural to think that a great number of those men who lately, under the false pretext of serving the cause of the Spanish patriots, scoured the Gulf of Mexico, making its waves groan under the direful weight of their vessels fraught with depredation, have come to take refuge among us; and we daily see arriving in our hospitable land a multitude of foreigners, whom the calamities, the revolutions and the peace of Europe compel or induce to emigrate.

"Among those of the latter description, there are doubtless many individuals respectable for their virtues, their talents, morals, industry, and especially for their misfortunes; but it were madness, I think, not to be aware that, among the emigrants, as well as among the maritime freebooters, there must be an infinite number who, if not wholly unprincipled and void of honor, are little estimable and little worthy of our confidence. If those are to be received with kindness, these have little or no claim to our protection, and indeed we should be cautious in receiving all foreigners." The Governor then recommended that, in imitation of the State of New York and others, "some provisions wisely rigorous" should be adopted, "for the purpose of obliging foreigners, of whom there was so great an influx hither from all parts, to give us some reasonable assurance of their good conduct, before they should be entitled to enjoy the protection of our laws, and participate with our citizens in the advantages afforded by our happy country." In conclusion, he observed: "By these additional means we shall be able to keep from our land ill-disposed persons, and to secure ourselves from the dangers to which we are exposed from those who are already among us. It is thus, and only thus, that Louisiana, while she continues to be the sacred asylum of the worthy and virtuous, will cease to be looked upon as the resort of those profligate wretches, whose existence is everywhere a burden."

1819. On the 6th of January, 1819, Governor Villeré, in addressing the Legislature, congratulated himself on not having, as at the period of the last session, to lay before the General Assembly a frightful picture of disorders and enormities." He attributed it "to the creation of the Criminal Court of the City of New Orleans, and to the indefatigable zeal with which the judges who composed it had discharged their duties." He added: "Owing also to the just firmness of juries, the violators of our laws, the malefactors of every description have suffered, or are undergoing the punishment due to their crimes. Hence it is that the City is now in the enjoyment of the most perfect security." According to the same authority, the ever-growing prosperity of the State left hardly anything to be desired. "The mild and powerful influence of the lately restored peace had been felt throughout all classes of the community. Party spirit had almost entirely disappeared, and hardly did any remembrance remain of those dangerous distinctions which had been created by idle prejudices between citizens of foreign origin. Our population had been considerably augmented; agriculture, industry and commerce were in the most flourishing condition. If commerce, indeed, had for some time experienced, and still continued to experience pecuniary embarrassments, the careful observer could easily discover the cause of it in its very prosperity, or, at least, in the great extension which the speculating and enterprising spirit that animated and marked the character of our citizens had given it in all parts of the Union. Hence, far from being uneasy, he conceived the most brilliant hopes for the future." Such is the glowing description given by the Governor. Well might he exclaim: "May we always by our conduct render ourselves deserving of such blessings!"

1820. In January, when the Legislature met, Louisiana was still luxuriating in the smiles of Heaven, with the exception of the infliction of yellow fever, which, as usual, had visited New Orleans during the preceding autumn. But a great portion of her inhabitants had almost become reconciled to its ravages from the frequency of their return. For them it had no more terrors than had for the ancients the skull which used to figure among the roses and other luxuries that adorned their banqueting tables. There were even some who felt friendly to the scourge, as, in their opinion, it checked that tide of immigration which, otherwise, would have speedily rolled its waves over the old population, and swept away all those landmarks in legislation, customs, language and social habits to which they were fondly attached. "Among the opulent States which compose this immense and powerful Republic," said the Governor, "the State of Louisiana is not the least remarkable. The observer no longer recognizes the feeble and languid colony, which, yielding to a foreign impulse, seemed ever ignorant of the vast resources it possessed in the astonishing fertility of its inexhaustible soil, and unconscious of the high destinies to which it was called by its felicitous topography. The progress of its agriculture, the increase of its commerce, and its population now trebled under the auspicious influence of its wise and beneficent institutions, all attest that the people were worthy of the emancipation so essential to their prosperity." On the 22d of November, 1820, when he delivered his last message, no cloud had arisen to darken the Elysian fields of Louisiana. Peace and contentment dwelt alike in the rich man's luxurious house and in the humble cabin of the pioneer. In that message we remark the following passage: " Wherever we turn an inquiring eye, it is impossible among the civilized nations of the earth to discover one whose situation we can reasonably envy. The most powerful are certainly much less free, the most free are less tranquil, the most tranquil less independent, and the most independent less sheltered from foreign influence than the great American family." It will be the painful task of the future historian to discover and relate the causes which led to the rapid decay, fall and destruction of this social and political paradise.

Thomas Bolling Robertson, who had for several years represented the State with distinguished talents in the Lower House of Congress, succeeded Villeré as Governor, in 1820. In his inaugural address he was as enthusiastic as his predecessor, when reviewing the resources, the merits and the future of the State of which he had become the Chief Magistrate. " When we contemplate the destinies of our State, confided in an especial manner to your care," he observed, " what irresistible inducements to exertions present themselves ! Blessed with a fertile and everlasting soil, yielding products of inestimable price; a river the most useful and magnificent in the universe, passing through regions rich with the labors of a numerous and increasing population; a city unrivaled in its commercial advantages, a natural internal navigation, requiring but little improvement to pervade every part of the State; forests of timber universally sought after as best adapted to purposes of civil and naval architecture; a community peaceful, industrious, flourishing and submissive to the laws ;—these are some of the proud boasts of Louisiana. Let us unite, then, to improve and develop them, and where the God of nature has done so much, do something ourselves, that we may not seem insensible of the bounties He has bestowed." As to the General Government, he declared that, "compared with the other Governments of the earth, it towered high above them in the wisdom, economy and virtue of its measures. Respected by the Monarchs of Europe for its power, and feared for its purity, it receives," he said, " as it merits, an almost undivided portion of the affection of its citizens at home."

He admitted, however, that this best of Governments had not been just to the State in relation to her public lands: "The public domain in Louisiana," he said, "before the change of Government, was parceled out and given to those who would emigrate and settle in the country; now it is neither given away nor sold, and extensive tracts which, if inhabited, would add to the strength and wealth of the State, still remain waste and uncultivated. This has not been the case in other parts of the United States; and although it is admitted that, with respect to us, there are great and peculiar difficulties, it is hoped that we shall soon be placed in a situation as eligible as the other frontier States of the Union." The Governor soon discovered that this hope was not to be realized. Louisiana, notwithstanding her merits, and perhaps on account of her merits, never ceased to play the part of Cinderella in the "glorious American family," into which she had been introduced amidst jeers and gibes, and despite the irate opposition of some of its members who dwelt in the inhospitable regions of the North.

The Governor also complained of the defenceless condition in which our maritime coast was left, leaving it accessible to invasion at any time; of the repeated attempts to force upon the country an "unconstitutional and unjust tariff for the benefit of manufactures to the detriment of agriculture; and of the restrictions which were sought to be imposed on the people of Missouri, about now to exercise their right of throwing off a worse than colonial dependence and taking their equal stand among the States of the Union." If the people of Missouri, who were then living under a form of Territorial Government established by Congress, were in a worse condition than "colonial dependence," it is difficult to imagine how such a state of things could exist under a Government which "towered far above the other Governments of the earth for its wisdom and virtue." The fact is, that it had been the settled policy of that pre-eminently "virtuous" Government to grind Missouri and Louisiana to the dust, and to make them pant to throw off the "yoke" which had been put upon their necks, in order to compel them to renounce rights which had been secured to them by treaty, in the hope of escaping from their oppressive bondage. The Federal Shylock exacted from them the "pound of flesh nearest to the heart," when he had no bond for it, and when, on the contrary, he had given his own bond not to pull off one single hair from the sacred heads of the minors whom France, in her confiding credulity, had intrusted to his paternal care. In relation to the discussions in Congress about the admission of Missouri, he added:

'Fortunately for us, the newly invented sympathy for a certain portion of our population had not been discovered at the time of our introduction into the Union, or it is probable a state of things would have been attempted as insulting to the independence as ruinous to the best interests of the State. . . . . . On the subject of slavery all we have to ask is this, that our Eastern and Northern brethren would forgive us the vice, or immorality, or misfortune, as they indifferently term it, of holding slaves, as we forgive them the disingenuousness that would convert the circumstance into purposes of unholy ambition." These were specks on the horizon, at which, however, the Governor took no alarm, for he considered these questions as of " little importance in themselves, but unfortunate from their mischievous tendency and from the unfriendly feelings which they generated."

1822. In January, Governor Robertson represented to the Legislature that health had spread its blessings over us; that agriculture well repaid the labor bestowed on it ; that commerce added its accustomed wealth and embellishment; that crimes and offences had decreased, whilst the laws had been rendered less sanguinary, and that we had escaped the difficulties and embarrassments so keenly felt in other parts of the world, arising from a want of value in their products, or in their circulating medium; but " he could not persuade himself that the United States had performed the duties which they owed to this interesting section of our interesting country." Its defences were still neglected, while large sums had been expended " on distant and comparatively insignificant positions." The topography of the State was not understood at Washington, and, to be understood, required to be seen ; but " ours is unfortunately the only portion of the Republic," he observed, " not only always unrepresented in what is termed the Cabinet, but unknown by personal observation, as well to all its members as, with few exceptions indeed, to the legislators of the nation." This was not the only oversight which he laid at the door of the Federal Government. " He had not been able to perceive the wisdom of that policy which had sent our naval force to Africa, whilst our own coasts, particularly those of the Gulf of Mexico, had been permitted for years to exhibit scenes of blood and rapine unequaled in atrocity in the annals of the world." As to the public lands, the Governor said in a special message to the Legislature, on the 21st of January : " This State, so far from having been favored, as seems to be generally supposed, will be found, after examination, to stand almost alone in the injustice which it has experienced; for, whether we compare our situation with that of the Atlantic or the Western States, it will be perceived that we have not enjoyed the advantages of either. The Atlantic States reserved to themselves all the vacant lands within their limits; some of them large tracts without. Let it not be supposed that this arrangement is considered by me as objectionable. At the time of effecting their independence and changing their political situation, they were separate existing communities, and could not be expected to act otherwise; so Connecticut, Georgia, Kentucky, and others, enjoyed, and still enjoy their extensive domains. But the country now forming this State was, at the time of the change of its political character, an existing community, a colony of France as they were colonies of Britain, and although I will not assert that Louisiana, as a Government, possessed the vacant territory, yet, as a society, it enjoyed customs and usages of which it ought not to have been deprived. Among these was the gratuitous concession of public lands to all natives and emigrants. When we take a view of this subject connected with the donations bestowed on the Western States by the General Government, we are still more forcibly struck with the little attention which our interests appear to have received.

"It is estimated that already 7,909,903 acres on the East side of the Mississippi have been appropriated for the purposes of education, and that the quantity of lands on the West of the same, yet to be disposed of in a similar manner, will give to the whole appropriation a value amounting in money to nearly $30,000,000. I now ask, of all this how much have we received? How much can we ever hope to receive? The reservation of the 16th section, and the donation of two townships of land, are too inconsiderable in point of value to deserve consideration. From circumstances peculiar to our country, the 16th section, in a general survey, will, most commonly, be found to fall to the West in swamps, or barren prairies; to the East, in the pine woods; whilst from the delay of the Federal Government to adjust and settle land claims in this country, no portion of the domain of value, now belonging to the public, will furnish a sufficient extent on which to locate the townships intended in their munificence to be bestowed upon us." Thus the fat oysters had all been given to the favorite members of the family, and a few shells thrown in mockery to Louisiana. From the Governor's own representations, it seems that *the best of Governments* was not free from prejudices and undue partialities, and that it had ever been guilty of neglect, injustice, oppression and exaction, to our detriment. It is no wonder that he began to speak ironically of the munificence of Federal donations to the noble and generous State of which he was the Executive.

1823. This year, the Governor became still more explicit in his comments on the same subject, and more severe in his strictures on the General Government. "It has been too often," he said, "the painful duty of the Executive to complain of the injustice and neglect of the United States. Were not our grievances heavy and flagrant, a very sincere respect which I feel for the General Government would induce me to remain silent, in the indulgence of a hope that time might bring about changes favorable to our rights and interests; but there is no ground for such expectation. We have too few votes in the council of the nation; we are too far from the centre of power to be regarded at Washington. Distance seems to operate upon them like time; and events which are a thousand miles off, are like those which happened a thousand years ago. Yet duty to ourselves compels us to inquire if we are now to become sovereign and independent. Are we forever to be deprived of rights enjoyed by the original States of the Union? Are we to see our State, as far as territory constitutes it such, in the possession of another government? Does not the fact carry on the face of it contradiction and absurdity? If large portions of Louisiana remain waste and unsettled, there is no difficulty in pointing out the cause. If internal improvements languish, what prospect have we of their assuming a more favorable aspect, when we are told that, for such purposes, the United States cannot interfere, and when we know that the land is without our jurisdiction? The lands within a State without its jurisdiction! Our necessities require taxation, and the natural subject of it throughout the world is denied us. Even when their property is reluctantly disposed of, it is still protected for years against all burdens and impositions. Roads, levees and bridges are servitudes which attach to the lands of individuals; but the United States, our great landholder, make none, and leave us the alternative of non-intercourse with the different parts of the State, or of giving value to their lands by cutting roads, and raising embankments on them at our own expense.

"The sovereignty of the United States over the territory within our limits, if not utterly incompatible with the sovereignty of the State, is in the highest degree vexatious and inconvenient. No other part of our common country has suffered to the same extent. Millions of acres in other States, and even in the Territories, have been promptly brought into market, whilst here, at this late day, after eighteen years' delay, the public domain remains undisposed of, unsurveyed, impeding our progress, encumbering our operations, and proving, however anomalous the idea, a curse instead of a blessing to the community. Even the wood of their swamps, useless for every other purpose, and necessary for that, is refused to the wants of the numerous steamboats which navigate our magnificent rivers; and the humble and laborious wood-cutter is harassed with prosecutions in regions which will never be cultivated.

"The Constitution of the United States authorizes Congress to hold and exercise legislation over places purchased by the consent of the State Legislature in which the same shall be, for the erection of forts, magazines, arsenals, dock-yards, and other useful buildings. The places held and legislated over within this State have not been purchased by the consent of the Legislature, and are rather more extensive and numerous than the purposes enumerated require. Congress has power also "to dispose of and make all needful rules and regulations respecting the territory or other property belonging to the United States." May we not consider the territory as *disposed* of, when the territory becomes a State, when it is placed on the same footing with the original States of the Union, when its sovereignty is acknowledged? Is not territory that transcendental property, that eminent domain, without which sovereignty cannot exist? Is it not everywhere considered as inseparable from it? Virginia, New Hampshire, and other States support these principles. The President of the United States declares that, after the most liberal construction of the enumerated powers of the General Government, the territory within the limits of the respective States belongs to them; that the United States have no right, with the exception specified in section 8, article 1 of the Constitution, to any the smallest portion of territory within a State.

"Property in lands is but of two sorts—general and particular. The first is the right of the whole society, exclusive of the rest of mankind—the second is the right of individuals. It would be strange to contend that any other than the individuals who possess the particular rights could form that society to which *belongs* the general right. The United States derive their powers from the States or the people, whilst Louisiana is in the situation of a colony, a province, holding such rights as that Government has chosen to bestow. This is an inversion of the station which properly be longs to the United States and the States respectively. But it may be said that it was under the conditions complained of, and some others, I will add, highly disgraceful—such, for instance, as requiring our records to be kept in the English language, that we were permitted to rid ourselves of the oppression of territorial vassalage. For this is but too true, and I am disposed to yield up the question, if it shall be established that the General Government possesses other rights than those conferred on it by the Constitution. But to that instrument it must look alone, nor can a State, with safety to others, be allowed to divest itself of powers, or to bestow them at will. Some might allow the United States to hold the whole or half of the land within their limits, as we have done; others might give them their navigable rivers, as I believe we have not done; although, at the negotiation of Ghent, it was a question of giving them to the British. It is useless to go further into detail; permit the States to give, and the United States to receive, and the whole character of our governments is changed.

"It is probable that no Power, until Congress adopted the expedient, ever conferred that kind and degree of sovereignty which belongs to the States of this Union, retaining at the same time the vacant lands. When North Carolina agreed to the independence of Tennessee, and Virginia to that of Kentucky, surely nothing so preposterous was pretended, as the retention of the unappropriated territory within their limits. But it is unnecessary at present to press this subject further; it is not the swamps, the prairies, the pine-barrens, nor their value, which Louisiana needs; it is that sovereignty, that equality, that exemption from interference and annoyance in her domestic concerns, enjoyed by her sister States, which she respectfully asks; and to this end, she contents herself with insisting again, as she has before done, that Congress would, in obedience to the Constitution, *dispose* of the territory within her boundary."

This is a true and graphic description of the wrongs sustained by Louisiana from the United States, in flagrant violation of the faith of a public treaty and of the Federal Constitution. But there is nothing more conspicuous in the history of the United States than the repeated and shameless violations of that solemn compact, whenever this was found to be the interest of a hungry majority, until it became such a convenient instrument of oppression against a down-trodden and plundered minority, that it wore out at last, and broke to pieces from its being used too unsparingly.

It is not perhaps astonishing that the Federal Government should, at that time, have hardly condescended to treat Louisiana as a State, when we see that her Legislature, with the approbation of her Executive, proclaimed that her capital and largest city would be in a condition of great insecurity, without the presence of Federal troops. None but the powerful command respect among communities, and the following communication from her high-spirited Governor to President Monroe, on the 12th of April, 1823, showed but too clearly her weakness and her dependence on the ruling powers at Washington. It accompanied "Resolutions" adopted by the Legislature and forwarded by the Governor to the President : "I respectfully," he said, "ask your attention to the inclosed Resolutions. The situation of New Orleans cannot be considered as secure—surrounded by a numerous black population, in its nature always hostile, filled up with emigrants, and free negroes and mulattoes from all parts of the world. It is wonderful that we have escaped for so long a time from serious internal commotion. We cannot conclude that this fortunate state of things is to continue always. I add, then, my wishes to those of the Legislature, and earnestly request that the already feeble support which we may receive from the troops of the United States may not be diminished, but rather that its efficiency should be increased. My own opinion is, that our situation requires that there should be at all times a few companies of infantry, and at least one of artillery, conveniently posted, and at all times prepared to defend and protect this city."

1824. In the beginning of this year, in a message to the Legislature, the Governor resumed the subject of the public lands in the same mournful strain. "We have a larger portion of fertile soil than any other State in the Union ; our products are of a greater value ; but when compared with these advantages, our strength and resources are extremely insignificant. When I took my seat in the House of Representatives—your only member—Ohio had but one, Illinois, Missouri, Mississippi, Alabama, none. Since that time, millions of acres of land within their respective limits have been offered for sale ; immigration has been thus permitted, and a change in their situation commensurate with this great impulse has taken place. Contemplate for a moment their growing prosperity, their imposing representation, their numerous and formidable militia ; then look at home, and behold a scattered population, unsettled and interminable forests, unadjusted titles, extensive domains in endless dispute between the United States and its own citizens—indeed, the State itself, after years of connection with the Union, a mere debatable land. When we read of the honorable exertions of our sister States, their canals and roads and bridges, often surpassing in excellence works of a similar nature in the Old World, we feel, as Americans, proud of their enterprise—as Louisianians, unavailable regret that we cannot imitate their example and rival their success. We cannot, because of their unjust conduct toward us. In the nicest point, in the honor of our State, in denying to us an essential attribute of sovereignty, they have done us wrong. Ireland may complain that her wealthy satraps abscond from a country where they hold their possessions; our sister States of the West may experience inconvenience from their class of non-residents; but in both these instances the property, perhaps of more value than its owners, is left behind, subject to the ordinary or extraordinary demands of the public. Here our great landlord is not only an absentee, a non-resident, but turns his key as well as his back on his possessions, exempts them from all taxation, declares them *tabooed*, sacred as the ark of the covenant, and denounces heavy pains and penalties on all by whom their sanctity is not sufficiently respected, whilst they stand a nuisance in our way, poisoning the sources of our prosperity, and impeding our every step toward that greatness to which we are invited by our otherwise enviable and unequaled advantages. The day on which the disputed land claims shall be adjusted, and the domain of the United States, as it is, I apprehend, unconstitutionally considered, finally disposed of, will be hailed by me, if I live to see it, as the commencement of the real independence of the State; for I repeat that our present situation shocks all the ideas I entertain of the nature of that sovereignty which we are entitled to enjoy." The Governor might have added, that those who thus "turned the key" on the public domain and prevented our population from increasing by immigration, tauntingly asserted that, if our resources remained undeveloped, it was through our fault, because we persevered in keeping up among us the sinful institution of slavery. He contented himself with saying that, "notwithstanding those obstacles, Louisiana would become, as far as affluence could make her so, splendid to a degree that must eclipse the rival pretensions of any other section of the Union, and that she was approaching with rapid strides the great destinies which awaited her, as her own Mississippi rolled on its waters, though impeded by casual obstructions, to the goal to which it necessarily tended." At the end of his administration, in November, 1824, he congratulated the Legislature " on the happy effect of that policy which had heretofore been perseveringly pursued. Exempt from the effects of stop-laws, relief-laws, and other similar quackery, resorting to industry and economy, and aided by better crops than had for some years past been enjoyed, the people would probably find themselves enabled to contribute whatever funds might be necessary for purposes of general improvement." He commented in proper terms on the malignant audacity with which a member of the Federal House of Representatives had lately said in an address to his constituents, " that the best way to secure New Orleans to the United States was to reduce its consequence."

A few weeks before the expiration of his term of office, Governor Robertson having been appointed by the President Judge of the United States Court for the District of Louisiana, H. S. Thibodaux, who was then President of the Senate, became, by virtue of the Constitution, Acting Governor, until the Governor elect, Henry Johnson, was inaugurated in December, 1824. The new Governor had been for several years a member of the Federal Senate, and may, therefore, be supposed to have possessed a good deal of political experience. He found, on his being installed into office, that the finances of the State had been administered with singular economy, for at the end of Governor Villeré's administration she was without a cent of debt, and she now owed only forty thousand dollars. In his inaugural address, delivered on the 13th of December, 1824, he recommended to the heterogeneous population of Louisiana the observance of a spirit of concord and reciprocal good-will, which could hardly be supposed to prevail, without interruption, among the discordant elements which composed it. " All invidious attempts," he said, " to foment discord, by exciting jealousies and party spirit, with reference to the accidental circumstances of language or birth-place, will be strongly reprobated by every man who loves his country and respects himself. We are all united by one common bond. We neither have, nor can have, any separate or distinct interests; we are all protected by the same laws, and no measure of policy can be adopted injurious to one portion of the community, without affecting every other in the same ratio."

1826. In January, when the Legislature met, the Governor informed them that the hitherto flattering condition of the State was still in the way of further improvement. He had, during their recess, traveled over the whole State on a tour of inspection, and the result of his observations had been most satisfactory. " I have been highly gratified," he observed, "in witnessing in every parish the utmost harmony and good-will. Those symptoms of discord which, to the mortification of every friend to his country, manifest themselves on some occasions in this our favored city of New Orleans, are nowhere perceptible in the circumjacent country; and even in the city they are circumscribed, and confined chiefly to the columns of gazettes, and perhaps to a few persons of intemperate feelings, or whose views do not extend beyond the mere surface of things. A reader assuming the statements of some of our city journals as a criterion, would be apt to deem it a singular anomaly that an assemblage of persons united by the bond of common interest, living under the same laws, possessing equal devotion to the institutions of their choice, and who, in a trying hour, have stepped forth with one accord to defend them with their blood, should take occasion, from mere imaginary distinctions, to express an asperity of feeling toward each other, calculated to derogate from our character and consideration abroad. Let us unite in pursuing a course, and in setting an example, that may tend to unite the hearts of all our fellow-citizens."

According to the Governor's statements, "our proximity to the province of Texas, and the peculiar situation of that country, had given rise to disorders and depredations along our frontier on the Sabine, which had become truly alarming, and required the utmost vigilance on the part of the public authorities. A number of slaves and horses of our citizens had been stolen, and carried into that province by a lawless band of men associated for that purpose. It also had proved a place of refuge for dishonest debtors, who fled from the justice of their own country, taking with them, in some instances, property mortgaged for the payment of their debts. The Government of the United States, at the request of the Louisiana delegation in Congress, had stationed a detachment of troops near the Sabine, with a view to prevent these abuses; but their efforts on that exposed and extensive frontier had proved inadequate to the end proposed." This state of things shows clearly, without mentioning other considerations, how extremely important it was for Louisiana that Texas should become a part of the United States.

Like his predecessor, Governor Johnson felt himself compelled to advert to the evils resulting from the condition of our landed interests: "The large claims, embracing several millions of acres, to which the attention of the Legislature had been called on several occasions, still remained unadjusted. Upward of twenty years had elapsed since we had become a part of the American Confederacy, and had looked to the Congress of the United States for the redress of our grievances in this respect. Nothing effectual, however, had been done. All attempts which had been made in Congress to refer our claims to the United States District Court, subject to an appeal to the Supreme Court of the United States, and which was perhaps the most expedient method of settlement that could be devised, had entirely failed of success. If these claims were good, they should have been confirmed; if invalid, they should have been expressly rejected. It was not only the parties interested who suffered by keeping these in suspense; the great and increasing injury inflicted on the State called loudly for redress." Such was the Governor's language, and he recommended a memorial to Congress from the Legislature, " couched in strong but respectful terms." It was like a petition to the lion to relinquish the sheep on which he was feeding, and proved equally ineffective.

The question of slavery, gathering impetus and strength as it rolled on, was no longer to be permitted to rest, for it had become a settled policy to keep it constantly before the public. The Governor laid before the Legislature "Resolutions" of the States of Connecticut, Delaware, New Jersey, Indiana, Illinois, Georgia and Mississippi, the five former approving, the two latter disapproving a "Resolution" of the State of Ohio, recommending to Congress and to the States the abolition of slavery. "That Resolution," said the Governor, " was presented to your consideration by my predecessor. The high source from whence these Resolutions emanate entitle them to respectful consideration." The impudent, intermeddling, and unconstitutional "Resolution" of the State of Ohio, recommending to Congress and Louisiana to abolish slavery, entitled to respectful consideration! It is by such timid language, by such knee-bending attitude, that the abolitionists were encouraged in their aggressions from the beginning. "But however pure," continues the Governor, " the intention in which that of Ohio may have originated, I cannot withhold the expression of my regret that it should have been proposed; nor can I help considering such attempts as unconstitutional in their character and dangerous in their tendency. They are justly regarded as tending to impair the validity of the right to a species of property which is as much guaranteed by the Constitution as any other, and even as an infringement of the sovereignty of the States concerned. Nor do they subserve the interests of an enlightened philanthropy inasmuch as they may awake in the minds of those who are otherwise quiet, and as happy as their condition will admit, a desire and hope of change extremely hazardous, and prompting to acts which would necessarily bring down upon them calamities far greater than any which now exist. The evil in question has been entailed upon us by the mother country; an evil which the progress of things is tending to mitigate, and finally to remove. Being called upon to act on this delicate question, we should be unjust to ourselves were we not to express our opinion temperately, but decisively."

Thus the State of Ohio dares openly to pursue a course of action toward the State of Louisiana which is "unconstitutional in its character, and dangerous in its tendency," which "impairs the validity of property" to an immense amount within her limits, which is an "infringement of her sovereignty," in the opinion of her Executive, and that effete Executive is only roused to the expression of a "regret" that such should be the purposes of Ohio, and does not even permit that regret to be expressed without qualifying it with a compliment to the probable "purity of the intention" of the offender. Nay, he admits, much to the gratification, no doubt, of the State of Ohio, that the internal institution of Louisiana which she had attacked, and with which she had no more to do than with the laws of Japan, is an "evil!" He seems to apologize for its existence by giving it to be understood that it is through no fault of ours, and that it has been "entailed upon us by the mother country;" and, making his deference stoop as low as the bows of Eastern veneration, he appears to seek to deprecate the displeasure of Ohio, by informing her that "the progress of things," whereby he means, we suppose, the christianizing public opinion radiating from that enlightened land, and other effective agencies of the like nature, is "tending to mitigate, and finally to remove the evil," which, with a sisterly affection, she wished to eradicate from the bosom of Louisiana. The Governor was a very worthy gentleman in private life, anxious to please everybody and offend none; but, it is by such men as he, thus deplorably deficient in statesmanlike energy, in elevation of views and sentiments, and in official self-respect; it is by such men who, in their public and political capacity, turned the other cheek, whenever slapped in the face even by the hand of Thersites, that the Northern and Eastern States were induced to come to the conclusion that the Southern States "could not be kicked out of the Union." These expressions have become famous, and were the offspring of a convic tion which, leading to the perpetration of incessant outrages, produced at last one of the greatest struggles of modern times.

1827. The Legislature, being officially informed by the Governor of the death of Thomas Jefferson, and of his having left to his family no other inheritance than that of his illustrious name, voted the sum of ten thousand dollars to his heirs, which were delicately tendered as "a tribute of gratitude" from the State to the representatives of the man by whom "she had been acquired to the Union," and to whom she was indebted for the "blessings of political and civil liberty."

The plea which had been put forth in justification of the Federal Government for stripping the new States of the vacant lands within their respective territories, was based on the necessities of that Government. "But the period seems now to have arrived," said the Governor in his annual message of 1827, "when the fiscal situation of the National Government is so flourishing, that sound policy would dictate the propriety of putting the new States on an equality with the old in regard to the subject of the vacant lands. Should this be done, they would emulate the example of their elder sisters, and like them build up useful institutions, and essentially ameliorate their condition. Without these lands, the new States have no resources but direct taxation, which is inadequate to their wants and necessities. It is now believed that an appeal on this subject will not be made in vain to the justice of the older States." Such "justice" as Louisiana obtained from the "older States," from the date of her cession by France to 1861, when she attempted to become really and effectually independent, is recorded in the pages of history.

1828. It is impossible, at this time, to read without a sigh the following dithyrambic effusion sent by the Governor to the Legislature, in 1828: " Our form of government was once regarded as an experiment; its success is now the proudest triumph of reason and philosophy. Here all political power emanates from the people; the laws are made and administered by men of their choice, and to them the public agents are directly responsible. *Talents and virtue form the greatest distinction in society.* Untrammeled by the prejudices which elsewhere paralyze the efforts of genius, every individual, however humble his birth or fortune, may freely aspire to the highest honors of the Government. Those inestimable privileges of freemen, the trial by jury, the Writ of Habeas Corpus, *the purity of elections,* the freedom of the press, are enjoyed by no other people in an equal degree." With a depth of faith

which must have been based on the consciousness of his own recti
tude, and which he must since have lost, for he still lives a mournful patriarch in a devastated land, he thus continued: " But if the
temple of the Constitution should ever, indeed, be assaulted, the
safeguards, provided by its founders, defended with the vigilance
and courage of the people, will, we trust, prove adequate for its
preservation." The Governor forgot that, if we are taught by religion to put our "trust" in God, we are equally taught by history
not to put any in political constitutions, and are informed that the
day comes, sooner or later, when "the vigilance and courage" of
a people are no longer to be relied on for the preservation of their
liberties.

The Legislature had passed a bill " more effectually to prohibit free
negroes and persons of color from entering into this State." It was
vetoed by the Governor on three grounds: The first was, that by the
8th section of the 2d article of the Federal Constitution, the power
is reserved to Congress "to regulate commerce with foreign nations, and among the several States." " Yet," observed the Governor, " several of the sections of this bill relate to ships and to
their masters and owners, laying restrictions and imposing penalties of a nature that have always been considered as appertaining
to commercial regulations." The second objection was, that a free
negro, or person of color, excluded from the State by the operations
of this bill, might be a Frenchman, or an Englishman, or a subject
of some other power, and that to seize, fine and imprison black
seamen for the offence of coming into our port, and captains of
vessels for introducing them, " would be to exercise a power paramount to the treaty-making power of the United States, and would
be a positive infraction of existing compacts with foreign nations,
to whose subjects the right of free ingress and egress for the purpose of commerce is guaranteed. Those nations have subjects
of the class of people embraced in this bill. Might not the enforcement of such restrictions lead to retaliation and war?" According to these views, a French or English negro, for instance, being
entitled to enjoy all the rights of Frenchmen and Englishmen
among us, could not be prevented from establishing a commercial
house in one of the principal streets of New Orleans, from driving
his gay equipage, with white footmen, on a parallel line with that
of the Governor, and from figuring in all places of public resort
such as theatres, and other houses of entertainment, on the same
footing with our white population, because his English or French
countrymen had such privileges secured to them by treaties!

The third, and last, constitutional objection to this bill, the Governor considered as "equally strong." He remarked that the 2d section of the 3d article of the Constitution secures to the citizens of each State all the privileges and immunities of citizens of the several States. "In the consideration of this bill," said the Governor, "it is only necessary to ascertain whether the persons who are its objects are citizens of any of the States of the Union. In this inquiry, the fact presses itself upon us, that, in some of the States, they are citizens to the full extent of the term. If we can exclude one portion of the citizens of those States, we can exclude the whole. If we are free to refuse ingress to them, they are equally at liberty to deny access to us; and thus the most fatal animosities and collisions might arise between the States, a calamity which it was the object of the Federal Constitution to obviate." These were unexpected admissions from the Executive of a slaveholding State; and it was with feelings of mortification that many remembered, ever since, that there was a Governor of Louisiana who openly declared to her Legislature,* that a negro was as much a citizen of Massachusetts as John Quincy Adams or Daniel Webster, and, as such, entitled in our State to all the rights guaranteed by the Constitution to these two distinguished men, or any other white man, whilst the Federal Government and Daniel Webster himself, as Secretary of State, refused to consider persons of that class as citizens of the United States, and the Supreme Court of the United States subsequently confirmed this view of the question. But the negro has much advanced since, and there is no telling where he will stop.

On the 18th November, 1828, Governor Johnson, whose term of office was near expiring, sent his last annual message to the Chambers. Nothing had happened to check or mar the happiness of the people of the State, and to impede her growth in wealth, population and power. Reverting to the sore question of the public lands, the Governor asserted that "although twenty-five years had elapsed since the transfer of Louisiana to the American Government, and although we had abundant reason to rejoice at our happy condition, and to acknowledge in other respects the wisdom and justice of the Government of the United States toward us, yet it was certain that the prosperity of the State had been greatly retarded by the national jurisdiction exercised over the public lands." The Governor thus admits that, in one respect, the prosperity of Louisiana had been retarded by the policy pursued by the United States.

* Executive Journal, p. 525.

In such policy there certainly was neither "wisdom" nor "justice." It is to be regretted that the Governor did not point out in what other respects Louisiana had to acknowledge, in relation to her own individual prosperity and interests, as a distinct unit from the general welfare, the "wisdom" and "justice" of the Federal Government. Cinderella had thriven with the rest of her family, but not in consequence of any particular attention paid to her.

It seems that some of our sister States had also no cause to congratulate themselves on the "wisdom" and "justice" of that same Government, so far as their own individual interests were concerned; for the Governor informs the Legislature, that in certain quarters of the Union, "an opposition to certain acts of Congress had been recently manifested, even indicating a threat of separation." But he winds up with saying: "However oppressive those acts may be in their operation upon the Southern States, the character and extent of the opposition is deeply to be regretted. The charter of our liberty is too sacred thus to be sported with. Separate the Union, and our free institutions may be forever destroyed. But these symptoms of partial discontent afford no just ground of alarm. The character of the American people, the devotion they have displayed to the principles of true liberty, and to the Constitution, which is its palladium, afford a sufficient pledge for its preservation. We have enjoyed too much happiness as a nation, and can indulge too many proud recollections, to doubt the durability of our Federal Government. All attempts at disunion or consolidation will be met by the frowns, and, if necessary, resisted by the arms of an indignant public." Those politicians who, with the Governor, affected to look upon a confederacy of independent and sovereign States as a "nation," in the sense in which the word is applied to France or England, always advocated measures tending to "consolidation," and it was to avoid this dreaded consolidation, so fraught with sectional oppression, and the direful consequences of it, that "opposition was made to certain acts of Congress," which went so far as to "indicate a threat of separation" in those days. Governor Johnson has lived to see a proclamation from a President of the United States declaring, with the approbation of a slavish Congress, that the State of Louisiana was nothing but a "county" in the Union. His term of office expired with the end of the year 1828, and he was succeeded by P. Derbigny.

This year, 1828, was marked by the visit to New Orleans of General Jackson, who had been invited by the Legislature to participate in the celebration of the anniversary of the victory of the 8th of January, 1815. Ten thousand dollars had been appropriated for his reception as a guest of the State, and it was such as became that illustrious personage and the community who remembered his services. Three years before, in 1825, Louisiana had also received, with the utmost enthusiasm, General Lafayette as her guest, and had exhibited in her hospitality, as usual, that refined taste and liberality for which she is distinguished.

1829. Governor Derbigny had previously occupied conspicuous positions in the State, such as Judge of the Supreme Court, and had been also Secretary of State. His administration was short, for he was killed on the 7th of October, 1829, by being thrown out of his carriage. The Constitution devolved the office on the President of the Senate until a Governor should be elected by the people and be duly qualified. A. Beauvais and J. Dupré successively officiated in that capacity from the Governor's death until the 31st of January, 1831, when A. B. Roman was sworn into office. That gentleman had been a District Judge, and had fulfilled with talent and dignity the duties of Speaker of the House of Representatives. In his inaugural address the Governor informed the Legislature "that all Europe was shaken by the endeavors which nations were making to obtain institutions more or less like our own, and that our Government was pointed out by all high-minded men as the model of that perfection to which they hoped one day to bring the institutions of their own country, and that the United States would know how to preserve the exalted station which they held in the estimation of the other nations of the earth." These much envied United States were, however, threatened at the time with internal convulsions, and, in relation to this fact, the Governor remarked : " Demagogues may speak of disunion, and threaten to assemble Conventions for the purpose of resisting the laws of the United States; they cannot succeed in their attempt. But even should they contrive to convoke those assemblies, no serious danger would result to the Union ; the Constitution of the United States has already withstood, without being impaired, shocks much more violent than these. In the history of a notorious Convention, to which, since many years, no man can be found willing to acknowledge that he ever belonged, the nullifiers of South Carolina ought plainly to read their impending fate."

The question of the public lands, so vital to the State, pressed itself upon the Governor's mind as it had upon that of his predecessors, but he observed that the session of Congress was so far advanced, that any claims or representations which the Legislature might make on the subject would reach the seat of Government but on the eve of their adjournment. "It is for this reason," he said, "that I abstain, at this time, from submitting to your consideration various representations which we ought to address to the General Government, in order to insure the maintenance of rights that they seem disposed to forget, but which they must acknowledge as sacred, if it be admitted that they have not the privilege of violating treaties." If, according to the uniform statements, as we have seen, of all the Governors of Louisiana, the United States had fallen into the chronic habit of "forgetting the rights" which had been secured to her by treaties, she might well, we think, have been forgiven if she had not thought their Government as "perfect" as it was held by the "other nations of the earth."

1833. On the 9th of December, when the Legislature met, the State was just recovering from the terrors of the ravages produced during the preceding autumn by the yellow fever and the cholera. The Governor, however, informed them that now "health prevailed throughout the whole of the State, and that the resources which her geographical position and the inexhaustible fertility of her soil afforded were so great, that, after all those calamities, her situation was at present very prosperous." He estimated the exports of New Orleans at $36,700,000, twenty millions of which were the produce of Louisiana. He saw no reason why there should not be a rapid progression of her resources; the policy of the emancipation of the blacks which England had adopted in relation to her colonies, "however disastrous it might be to those intended to be benefited by it," could produce among us no other than a favorable effect on that branch of agriculture which consisted in the cultivation of the sugar-cane. "We are, fortunately," he said, "too far removed from the theatre in which those visionary improvements are to be attempted, for the reaction which they may produce to be felt among us. Our position and divers other causes, too well known to you to be recapitulated, put us at least beyond the reach of danger. London and Paris have more to fear from their populace than we have to apprehend from our negroes." Time proved, however, in less than twenty years, that we were not beyond the "reach of danger," and whatever is the degradation of the populace of London and Paris, no one believes that they could ever be tempted to take arms against their countrymen by the blandishments of any invader of their native soil. We have been taught the use which an unprincipled enemy can make of our negroes.

1835. The administration of Governor Roman, during which many internal improvements of all sorts had been completed or begun, closed on the 2d of February, 1835. He was succeeded by E. D. White, who had been for several years a member of Congress. The new Governor, in his short inaugural address, complained of the " vacillating legislation" of Congress in relation to one of the principal agricultural interests of the State. The duty on foreign sugars had been lowered in conjunction with the reduction of the whole tariff of the United States—a conciliatory measure, which had been adopted to put an end to the " acrimonious conflict" between those who desired a protective tariff, and those who thought that a tariff for revenue was the only one which the Constitution permitted. "The Union," he said, "had been shaken to its very foundations" by the violence of the storm, and the celebrated Compromise Bill of Henry Clay had been adopted as a sheet-anchor of safety. Louisiana would be the sufferer by it; but he trusted in the inherent energy and industry of her inhabitants, to make them " independent of this precarious decision of Congress." With regard to our land claims, the Senate of the United States had lately passed a bill by which they were referred to the ordinary tribunals of the country; but the House of Representatives had not "condescended" even to look into it. He had been a witness to the " indifference or levity" with which this important subject, on which depended the prosperity of the State, had always been treated in Congress, and he recommended to the Legislature the experiment of trying if an expression of their views on this matter would not draw to it a " more serious attention " from the Federal Legislators.

1836. On the 4th of January, the Governor informed the Legislature that, since the invasion of Louisiana by the British, she had not been placed in circumstances which required so much wisdom, prudence and patriotism from the Representatives of the people. In the midst of profound peace and uninterrupted prosperity, the " most alarming excitement " prevailed in the whole country, and in more than one circumstance, there had been manifested "dispositions fatal to the social order, and tending to substitute tumultuous violence to the power and majesty of the laws." The clash of arms, produced in the vicinity of our Western frontier by the collision which had taken place between Texas and Mexico, had reverberated throughout Louisiana, and thrown her into a state of warlike commotion. Many of her people were disposed to rush to arms and march to the assistance of those whom they considered as their countrymen in Texas. The Governor had been compelled to issue a proclamation threatening with condign punishment all those who should violate those laws of neutrality which they were bound to observe. The Louisianians had been presented, this year, with a more legitimate opportunity of showing their martial spirit. The United States were then at war with the Seminoles of Florida, and a requisition having been made on Louisiana for troops, her quota was furnished with great alacrity in ten days.

Governor White warned the Legislature against the designs and schemes of the pretended friends of the Blacks at the North and in the West, who covered their wicked designs with the mask of hypocrisy, and whose efforts tended to plunge those they affected to love, honor and protect, into an abyss of misery and ruin. He predicted that, should they ever succeed in their nefarious purposes, they would " inundate the land with human blood," and would be the criminal cause of the extermination of the unfortunate victims of their deceitful doctrines." He informed the Legislature that those demons, in order to carry into execution their infernal plans, had formed affiliated societies in divers parts of the Union; that considerable sums had been furnished by private contributions; and that the press itself had become their auxiliary. They printed and scattered " collections of horrors and atrocities" which had no other reality than what was given to them by the heated brains of their inventors. Every day, books, pamphlets and all sorts of publications, calculated to operate on both sexes from childhood to senility, and full of fantastic images, engravings and emblems destined to act on the imagination, were belched forth upon the public; and the mail, which had been established for the common benefit, had become an agent of destruction and hostility to the Southern States, and was freely used for the propagation of those incendiary compositions. " I congratulate myself," said the Governor, " on my being able to lay before you a collection, although very incomplete, of the edifying works to which I have alluded. They will suffice, however, to give you a just idea of the kind of war which is prepared in the bosom of our own country, against our peace, our fortunes, our lives and those of our children. These productions, these engines of destruction, are openly sold, and distributed with impunity in cities which are united to us by the bonds of commerce, of consanguinity and nationality." He advised the adoption of precautionary measures and the better organ ization of our militia, who had never been in a satisfactory condition since the formation of the State.

As to the public lands within the State, he said that, when she had renounced all the titles and rights which she might have had to them in order to be admitted into the Union—a renunciation whose validity she might well have questioned since—she had thus stripped herself, under the belief that the United States and Louisiana could have but one common interest in the public domain, which would be disposed of equitably by the Federal Government for the benefit of all, and with an eye to the individual necessities of the States. "But, the experience of more than twenty years," continues the Governor, "is very far from having confirmed these first impressions. Congress has been less liberal to Louisiana than to any other section of the country. Either by accident or by design, the policy pursued toward us has been a system of exclusion. Immense concessions of lands have been made to all the new States, whilst Louisiana has only been able to obtain the petty donation of two townships; and, although the grant was made so far back as 1827, it has been impossible to locate the townships, on account of the captious difficulties raised by the Land Office.

1837. This year was marked by an extraordinary financial crisis throughout the United States. All the Banks suspended specie payment, including those of Louisiana. The paper currency became greatly depreciated; the metallic one disappeared, as is always the case in such circumstances; ruin and desolation seemed to have overspread the land; every kind of industry was paralyzed; produce of every sort fell so low that it hardly paid for the cost of transportation; the value of real estate fell to nothing; credit, which is the life of commerce, died away; and agriculture languished from the want of stimulation. One would have supposed that it would have taken years to recover from such a shock, and yet, on the 7th of January, 1839, Governor White informed the Legislature with great satisfaction that the Banks had resumed specie payment, and that the State was beginning to emerge from her difficulties. It was consoling to him to leave her in the enjoyment of her usual prosperity, at the end of his administration, which terminated on the 4th of February. On that day, A. B. Roman, who had been elected Governor a second time, was inaugurated. On being sworn, he stated to the Legislature that, for several years, a tendency to disorder and license had made itself felt in society; that violence and brutal force had but too often usurped the place of the law from one extremity of the Union to the other; and that he relied on their co-operation to check in Louisiana any transgressions of a similar nature. "The invasion of her territory," he said, "by a troop of armed men, who, under the orders of an officer of the Republic of Texas, marched as far as the town of Shreveport, in the Parish of Caddo, is too extraordinary an event not to be noticed by the authorities of this State." He assured the Legislature that he would call on the Federal Government to prevent the repetition of such an outrage.

With regard to the increasing agitation of the question of slavery, he considered that the incendiary doctrines on which it was based had come to America from the other side of the Atlantic, and were propagated among us by a foreign influence, with a view to bring about a dissolution of the Union. "It becomes us," he said, "to act on this subject with much reserve and prudence, and always to show a spirit of conciliation; but our moderation must not be taken as a proof of apprehension or weakness. I do not fear* to be disavowed by my fellow-citizens when I declare in their name, that they shall always be found ready to maintain their rights by peaceful means, if those means are sufficient, but also by force, if force should become necessary." Thus were beginning to be heard the distant mutterings of the coming storm.

1840. The resumption of specie payment by our Banks in 1838 did not last long, and those institutions again forfeited their charters—a penalty from which they had been released by the Legislature. In consequence of this suspension, unprecedented distress and embarrassment pervaded every class of society. The Governor, in a message delivered on the 7th of January, 1840, attributed this general crisis to the destruction of the Bank of the United States. "The State Banks," he said, "from that time, no more restrained, and freed from the control that prevented their increase when wanting the basis of solid capital, began to multiply in every part of the Union. They extended their discounts beyond measure, and have since inundated the Union with an unprotected paper currency. Extravagant speculations were the necessary result of this new order of things; all classes of society were hurried along; no project was too vast or too chimerical not to be attempted by individuals, corporations, and even legislatures. The facility with which new loans were negotiated stimulated the spirit of commercial enterprise, and caused a startling difference between exportations

* This passage is re-translated into English from a French translation, the original English text not being at hand.

and importations—a difference which, in the two years of 1835 and 1836, amounted to eighty-nine millions five hundred and nineteen thousand one hundred and sixty dollars. This immense debt, due to foreign countries, occasioned a constant demand for the precious metals piled in the vaults of our Banks. England, whose interests were the most connected with our own, and who, until then, had been lavish of her loans to different States of the Union, or for individual commerce, found it necessary, for her own safety, to oppose the further extension of American credit; and the Bank of England, in order to accelerate the importation of gold and silver, proscribed the paper of the strongest American houses. This hostility between the Bankers of the two most commercial nations of the world was followed by disasters to both. The first suspension of our Banks was one of the results."

1841. In January, when the Legislature met, the Banks of New Orleans had not yet resumed specie payment, but their situation was considered as so satisfactory, their solvency so well established, that their notes were hardly at a discount of two per cent., and were in demand throughout the West, whilst they formed very nearly the only circulation of a neighboring State.* In connection with these institutions, it is curious to observe the rapid increase of the debts due to them by the State. At the beginning of the year 1839 the State owed to the Banks $75,000; at the beginning of 1841 the debt amounted to $850,000; and it was generally believed at the time, on the authority of persons who had made the calculation, that the members of the Legislature, in their private capacity, owed to those institutions about one million of dollars. This simple statement suffices to show the danger of increasing too much the facilities of borrowing.

The incessant complaints of Louisiana, and the demonstrations of the injustice with which she had always been treated, had at last wrested from Congress the grant of 784,320 acres for the support of her primary schools, but of that amount 187,584 acres were to be deducted, as being of no value, or not available.* "Louisiana," observes the Governor, "seems destined to derive less advantages from the bounties of Congress toward public schools than any other of the new States."

1842. At the beginning of this year, the Banks of New Orleans became divided as to the propriety of resuming specie payments, and some of them acknowledged that they were not in a situation

* Governor Roman's Message, 4th January, 1841.

to resume without assistance. Two of them were paying specie; the others wished to continue the suspension until November of that year. Shortly after the meeting of the Legislature in January, the first signal for the depreciation of the paper money of the Banks was given by the refusal of some of these institutions to receive, either in payment or deposit, the notes of those whose solvency was suspected.* Besides, the Legislature having passed a law for the liquidation of such Banks as might be insolvent, and created a "Board of Currency" to control the operations of all those institutions, and to examine and publish their real situation, the failure of all those whose credit had no other foundation than the confidence inspired by the fact that their paper was received at par by other Banks of undoubted solvency, became inevitable when that paper was rejected. There was a crash; Bank after Bank went down, like trees under the strokes of a sturdy woodman; the financial crisis which had given signs of abating returned with more violence, and the distress became universal, "in the midst of unusually large returns which a bountiful Providence had that year bestowed upon the labors of the husbandman."* Fortunately, the immense resources of our agriculture, and the incalculable advantages of the commercial position of New Orleans, enabled us soon to overcome the numberless difficulties and obstacles with which we had to struggle. Seven of the Banks were prostrated, never to rise any more; but nine weathered the storm, and in the beginning of 1843 were paying specie. The actual circulation of the solvent Banks had been reduced to $1,261,514, whilst they had in their vaults $4,565,925. Notwithstanding this accumulation of strength, which would, in ordinary times, have permitted them to afford every facility to business, the want of confidence and credit was such, that they were compelled to be very restricted in their operations, and could not work in a manner beneficial to the public and profitable to themselves. Such was the pressure throughout the whole community from the absence of a sufficiency of sound currency to meet the general wants, that even the taxes could hardly be collected, and the revenue of the State had diminished to the amount of near two hundred thousand dollars in the year 1842. Unfortunately, at that time, her finances were not in a proper condition, as her expenses had long since exceeded her receipts. In a late message the Governor had said to the Legislature: "Our debts are annually met by new loans, the interest on

* Governor Roman's Message, January 3d, 1843.

which, added to the capital, and the appropriations of each session of the Legislature, present every year a heavier deficit." In these untoward circumstances, the State found herself exposed to be called upon to pay for bonds to a very large amount, which she had given for some of these Banks, in order to supply them with a capital which could only be procured from Europe. The difficulty to collect in time the funds which these institutions had so imprudently loaned as to place them beyond their immediate control, would, in the course of the year 1843, render it impossible for them to fulfill punctually their obligations to the holders of the bonds. It remained for the State to provide for this contingency, and save herself from the disgrace of a protest. On this subject Governor Roman addressed the Legislature in these terms: "Louisiana will not shrink from the call that will be made on her to keep the faith which she has pledged. You know she would disclaim those who represent her if they could think of not fulfilling the promises she has made, and I feel that I express her opinions and yours in stating that the purity of her honor must be maintained, and that she will never furnish the enemies of popular governments with a new cause to charge them with dishonesty. Your predecessors and mine concurred in this belief, for they have rendered the system of repudiation as impossible among us as it is unjust, the negotiation of the State bonds having been directly or indirectly sanctioned by every succeeding Legislature since their emission." These were the proper sentiments to be expressed on such an occasion, and may Louisiana never entertain any other in similar circumstances! The Legislature responded to the appeal of the Governor, and the credit of the State was saved. The Governor concluded his last message in these words: "I leave the office with which I have been honored, with the painful conviction of having done very little for the good of the State, and of having often failed in preventing what was injurious. It affords me some relief, however, to be able to say, that I have refused my signature to various bills which, but for my disapproval, would have added to the debts of the State the sum of $7,185,000, and that the act which binds us to pay, without any consideration, $500,000 for the Clinton and Port Hudson Railroad, does not bear my name. My true consolation is in the certainty that distress, in a country so endowed with every element of prosperity and wealth, cannot be durable. The greatness of our resources has, for some years past, tended to lead us astray. We thought them without limit, and abandoned ourselves to undertakings and speculations far beyond our real strength. The errors of the past will not be without their benefit, if they serve as beacons to warn us from similar mistakes in future. The country has not changed; the wide career offered to our agricultural and commercial industry is not closed; no convulsions of nature have destroyed the fertility of our soil, or turned away from our capital the stream of the Mississippi. We are now aware of our real situation; we enjoy the advantages of self-government, and our destinies are in our own hands. Louisiana might yet be properous and happy, if the means which we still retain are administered with that prudence and economy which should have been always observed." He was succeeded by Alexander Mouton, who began his administration on the 30th of January, 1843. The new Governor had been known before as Speaker of the House of Representatives of the State, and as a member for several years of the United States Senate. He was, like his predecessor, a native of the State, and, like him, a man of much good sense and firmness, although they differed in their political creed, Roman being a Whig, and Mouton a Democrat.

1843. On assuming the reins of government, Governor Mouton told the Legislature "that we could justly attribute the evils we suffered to no other cause than ourselves. Louisiana, under a good Government, and poised on her own resources, would leave nothing to be wished for by her sons. It was but too common to look abroad for causes which were to be found immediately among ourselves. It was too customary to look to the General Government for relief in distress, whilst that relief should have been sought at home. By the manly exercise of our own faculties, availing ourselves of our natural advantages, and calling to our aid the sovereign power of the State, we could overcome all our difficulties." During his long residence at Washington, as a Senator, the Governor seems to have become well acquainted with the spirit of the Federal Government, and to have mistrusted its tendencies. He knew that it was a friend to whom it was dangerous to appeal, and whose services might be too dearly bought. "It is our duty," he said, "to watch closely the action of the General Government, so far as it can affect, for good or for evil, the great interests for which its powers were delegated; and we should never suffer those powers to be enlarged by construction, so as to interfere with the powers vested in the States of the Union."

In relation to the public lands, he described in a perspicuous manner the extraordinary injustice with which Louisiana had always been treated: "Near forty years had now elapsed since the district of country composing the State of Louisiana became a part of the United States, and more than thirty years since she was admitted into the Union as a sovereign State; and yet large portions of her territory are covered with unadjusted claims of land, derived from the former Government of the country; and a much less portion of the public domain has been disposed of within her bounds than in other parts of the Union, possessing, to say the least of it, no greater advantages. Louisiana was the first State, formed from territory derived from foreign countries, admitted into the Union, and there are several Territories not yet admitted. For every other State or Territory thus situated, provision has long since been made by Congress for the adjustment of all disputed land claims in the Federal Courts, and they have long since been decided; while for our State no such provision has yet been made, *though a bill for that purpose has frequently passed that branch of Congress in which the representation of all the States is equal.*" This simple statement alone proves more clearly than a volume of arguments could, the state of systematic oppression in which Louisiana had always been held by an envious, prejudiced, and fanatical majority. "At this time," continued the Governor, "large districts of country in other States and Territories are offered for sale, while none has been offered in Louisiana, at public sale, for years. The State has not even yet been authorized to make any disposition of the school lands in each township. These are objects of just complaint."

Governor Mouton found the finances of the State in a fearful condition. "I learn," he said, "with deep mortification and regret, from the Treasurer's reports and otherwise, that there is now due by the State to our Banks, in round numbers, one million two hundred thousand dollars; that there is due for salaries, interest and other ordinary expenses, about two hundred thousand dollars; that there are State bonds, for the payment of which the State has no guarantee, to the amount of one million two hundred and seventy-three thousand dollars, on which the interest is unpaid; that there are State bonds to a large amount, for which the State has the guarantee of the stockholders of the Citizens' Bank, and of the consolidated Association of Planters, now in liquidation, on which the interest will probably not be paid; that the ordinary expenses of the Government exceed, and have for several years exceeded its ordinary income by more than two hundred thousand dollars; **that there is nothing in our exhausted treasury; that the State can no** longer draw a dollar from her own Banks, and that the people are taxed as heavily as they can bear. This is indeed a deplorable situation of our affairs. Having within our limits the greatest commercial metropolis in the Union, a luxuriant climate, and the richest and most inexhaustible soil in the world, we are forced to ask what has produced this disastrous result." The Governor answered the question by attributing our misfortunes to the inordinate inflation of our paper currency and to the mushroom multiplicity of our Banks, which had tempted our whole population and the State itself into such extravagance, that the State was almost bankrupt, and that there were few of our citizens who were not heavily in debt to those institutions. "The evils under which we suffer," he said, "are to be ascribed to the ascendency, the supremacy this interest attained in our State. Had Banks been held to the responsibilities of individuals; had they at all times been kept in a sphere subordinate to the Government itself; had the supremacy of the laws been asserted and maintained, things would not have come to the present stage of discredit and disaster. What citizen who feels for the honor of his State would wish to see the late condition of things renewed? Our policy, our duty, then, is obvious. We must prevent, by all possible means, all tendency in our legislation to a revival of the Banking system as heretofore organized."

1844. So recuperative is Louisiana in her energies and resources, that, on the 1st day of January, 1844, the sad condition of which we have seen the description had much improved, notwithstanding she had been afflicted, in an unusual degree, with the diseases incident to the climate and to local circumstances, and notwithstanding the rich productions of her prolific soil had been curtailed by an unpropitious season. "We have," said the Governor to the Legislature, "evidently passed the deplorable crisis of immorality and distress, in which idleness, extravagance and reckless speculation, engendered by improvident legislation, the credit system and paper money had involved the whole country. Industry now animates all classes of society, and economy surrounds every fireside. But lately the pervading spirit of our citizens was to transcend each other in luxury and splendid extravagance; now their patriotic emulation is to surpass each other in useful productions, and thereby to secure the comfort and independence of families, and add to the wealth and prosperity of the State. The planter, mechanic, and professional man has each returned to his peculiar occupation and proper pursuits; and none are now seduced by the bright, but fallacious, prospects of fortune without labor. Our Banks, by their intolerable abuses, had brought the State, our public corporations and individuals, to the brink of moral degradation and pecuniary bankruptcy; but an entire revolution in public opinion and the passage of salutary laws have effectually restrained them within their proper sphere; and, while these opinions and laws are maintained, they will no longer have power to ruin themselves by ruining the community; they will cease to mingle in political strife, and be, as they should always have been, harmless handmaids to commerce."

1845. In January, a great excitement was produced in New Orleans by the arrival of an individual from Massachusetts, named Hubbard. It seems that Massachusetts had heard that some of her citizens of African descent were put in jail in New Orleans for visiting that city in contravention of laws which prohibited all persons of that class from coming to the State. That Commonwealth, always so intensely hostile to the Southern States, had authorized her Governor to employ an agent in New Orleans, for a term of time not to exceed one year, for the purpose of collecting and transmitting accurate information respecting the number and the names of citizens of Massachusetts who had heretofore been, or might be, during the period of the agent's engagement, imprisoned without the allegation of any crime. The same agent was also to bring and prosecute, with the aid of counsel, one or more suits in behalf of any citizen that might be so imprisoned, at the expense of Massachusetts, for the purpose of having the legality of such imprisonment tried and determined upon in the Supreme Court of the United States. Hubbard had been the agent selected. He soon found out, however, that he would not be permitted to do all the mischief that was intended; and, shortly after his arrival, he wrote to the Governor that, not from intimidation, but from the conviction that his mission would be fruitless, he was ready to depart and to return his commission to the source from which it had originated. It is gratifying to record his admission that he "did easily see the high moral influence which must pervade and prevail in the City of New Orleans, in the courteous, bland and humane manner in which her citizens of the first respectability conveyed to him their sentiments respecting his agency and the excitement it occasioned." These are his very words.

Texas had for some time achieved her independence from Mexico, and become a Republic acknowledged by France, Great Britain and the United States. She was called the " Lone Star." It was extremely desirable for Louisiana that she should be admitted as soon as possible into the firmament of the United States. She had applied for it and Governor Mouton, considering the great interest which this subject had excited throughout the State, and the important bearing that it must have upon her future prosperity, had suggested, in his annual message on the 6th of January, 1845, the propriety of such action on the part of the Legislature as would be expressive of the wishes and feelings of the people of the State concerning this measure. This part of the Governor's message was referred to a special committee, the majority of which reported adversely. We made a minority report in favor of expressing by the Legislature the desire of the people for the immediate annexation of Texas by all lawful and constitutional means. But this measure, in support of which it would have been natural to expect a unanimous vote, was only carried through after much discussion and considerable opposition, and with a proviso tacked to it, which was not free from objections.

The State had been a large stockholder in several of the Banks, and as such used to appoint a certain number of directors in those institutions. It was found that this connection between the State and the Banks worked injuriously to all the parties concerned, and it was deemed expedient to put an end to this unwise and unnatural partnership. An act had passed to that effect in the session of 1844, but it had not been accepted by the Banks, which had objected to some of its provisions. The Governor, at the session of 1845, recommended that the subject should be resumed, and that amendments should be made which might be acceptable to those institutions. We moved in the House of Representatives that this part of the Governor's message be referred to a special committee, and, as chairman, we reported a bill which passed, after having undergone some modifications, and to which the Banks gave their adhesion. The result was the discharge of more than three millions of the debts proper of the State, leaving only a balance of $1,600,000, maturing between 1845 and 1872, which, by an annual surplus revenue, she could discharge gradually, or which could be mostly absorbed by the sale of such portion of the public domain as she had at last, after years of repeated efforts, wrested from the avaricious grasp of the Federal Government.

During the same session, we introduced "Resolutions," which were adopted, requesting our Senators and Representatives in Congress to lay before that body and the President of the United States the remonstrances of the State in relation to the want of

Mail facilities throughout the State, and to use their utmost efforts to obtain the redress of the grievances which she suffered in this respect. To show in the most glaring manner the injustice with which Louisiana was treated, we stated in the preamble of those "Resolutions" that, during the year ending June 30, 1843, Louisiana had paid to the Post-Office Department $104,261, whilst only $37,976 had been expended in the State for Mail transportation, when $218,055 were spent in Alabama, whose net postage was only $89,441; and $95,530 were spent in Mississippi, whose net postage was only $49,734; and $58,825 were spent in Arkansas, whose net postage was only $12,819—the same favors being extended in the same ratio to sixteen other States.

On the 14th day of May, 1845, there was adopted a new Constitution for the State, which had been framed by a Convention assembled on the 5th of August, 1844. The Convention had first met at Jackson, in the Parish of East Feliciana, but had subsequently adjourned to New Orleans. The collective wisdom and talent of the State had certainly deliberated long enough to have produced something durable and satisfactory to the people. We shall see, however, that but a few years had elapsed, when another Convention had to be convened to amend the one which had been so elaborately discussed and framed. This Constitution of 1845 was much more democratic than that of 1812. It proclaimed the right of general suffrage, by granting the privilege to vote to every free white male who had been two years a citizen of the United States, who had attained the age of twenty-one years, and who had resided in the State two consecutive years next preceding the election in which he desired to participate; it limited to a short term the tenure of judicial offices, which, hitherto, had been during good behavior. A peculiar oath about not having been engaged in a duel, directly or indirectly, since the adoption of the Constitution, was exacted from all the members of the General Assembly and from all State officers, before they could enter upon the duties of their offices. A special provision was inserted in the Constitution to remove the Seat of Government from New Orleans and its vicinity. The aggregate amount of debts hereafter to be contracted by the Legislature was never to exceed one hundred thousand dollars, except in particular cases, distinctly specified. The State was prohibited from ever becoming subscriber to the stock of any corporation or joint-stock company, and no corporate body should be hereafter created, renewed, or extended, with banking or discounting privileges. These last restrictions show that the

Convention, warned by the bitter experience of the past, intended to guard against the return of those evils from the consequences of which the State had not yet liberated itself completely. No corporations, hereafter to be created, should ever endure for a longer term than twenty-five years, except those which were political or municipal. No exclusive privilege or monopoly was to be granted for a longer period than twenty years. The Constitution was to be submitted to the people for their ratification or rejection, and, in case of its being ratified, it became the duty of the Governor forthwith to issue his proclamation declaring the Legislature elected under the old Constitution to be dissolved, and directing elections to be held for Governor, Lieutenant-Governor, Members of the General Assembly, and all other officers whose election was provided for. The Constitution was ratified by the people, and the new Legislature, elected according to its provisions, met on the 9th of February, 1846. The retiring Governor, Alexander Mouton, complimented the Legislature on the wonderful change which, in three years, since his inaugural address, had taken place in the condition of the State, under a wise legislation and a proper system of economy and retrenchment. He informed them that he had caused to be canceled bonds and coupons of interest of the debt proper of the State to the amount of more than three millions and a half of dollars, which had been paid or settled by the Treasury, under the Act providing for the adjustment and liquidation of the debts proper of the State, approved the 28d of March, 1844.

"The Banks are extinguishing," he said, "as rapidly as could be expected, the bonds unfortunately issued by the State to enable them to raise their capital. The Municipalities of the City have withdrawn their depreciated circulation, and our State and City are now blessed with a sound constitutional currency, amply adequate to all domestic or commercial purposes.

"On taking charge of the Executive office of the State, I formed the deliberate opinion that it was for the interest of the people and the duty of the Government to disconnect itself with all companies and corporations; to avoid embarking in improvements which, either on account of their national character, should properly be made by the General Government, or in those which could be effected by the local authorities or individual efforts; to pay off the whole State debt and reduce the taxes; to direct the efforts of the State Government mainly to the adoption and administration of wise laws for the protection of persons and property, and the promotion of education and morality, and limit the offices and expenses of the State to those which were absolutely necessary for these purposes; and to encourage among the people a disposition to prosper, not by speculative schemes, but by industry in productive occupation, and economy in their mode of living." These were judicious views, and the Governor had been remarkably successful in carrying them in to execution, for " the public credit," he said, " has been entirely restored, and our treasury is in a most prosperous condition. On the 31st of December last, there was a surplus in cash of two hundred and twenty-five thousand dollars in the Treasury, after having paid the extraordinary expenses incurred for the State Convention, amounting to nearly ninety thousand dollars. The State debt, in round numbers, may be stated at one million three hundred thousand dollars, payable from 1848 to 1872. The cash and other assets in the Treasury, and the land fund of the State, would at once extinguish the debt; and, in my opinion, the appropriation of these means to this end would be the most advisable course to pursue at present, and ever hereafter to rely upon the yearly income for all purposes of yearly expenditure." This tableau presented by the Governor shows what wonders can be worked in such a country as Louisiana under a wise and economical administration. Like Antæus, she can be prostrated only to rise up with more vigor and elasticity.

1846. The Governor-elect under the new Constitution, Isaac Johnson, was installed into office on the 12th February, 1846. He had been a member of the State Legislature and a District Judge. Shortly after his inauguration, hostilities began on the Rio Grande, between the United States and Mexico, and the greatest excitement prevailed in New Orleans, when it was heard that General Taylor, who commanded a small Federal army in that District, was threatened to be overwhelmed by immensely superior forces which the enemy had brought rapidly against him. Taylor made à requisition on Louisiana for reinforcements, and the manner in which it was answered is aptly described by Governor Johnson in a letter to Marcy, the Secretary of War, dated June 12, 1846 : " The call upon the patriotism of Louisiana presented a startling view of the critical and perilous situation of the army and of Point Isabel, and left no time for calculating reflection, and none for delay. An absorbing, energetic sentiment of duty to the country possessed the minds and hearts of this entire community. The Judge deserted the Bench, the lawyer his clients, the physician his patients, the merchant his counting-house, the mechanic his workshop, and the minister of the Gospel his pulpit, to respond to the proclamation for volunteers; and, though we had severe difficulties to encounter, by union and decision of action they were speedily overcome. In an incredible short space of time several thousand brave and devoted men were forwarded to the seat of war, where they happily arrived in time to enable General Taylor more confidently to assume an offensive attitude against the enemy, and to crown the brilliant victories of the 8th and 9th, already achieved, with the conquest of Matamoros." The State had equipped a large force at a cost of very near three hundred thousand dollars, which were subsequently reimbursed by the General Government, not, however, without treating our volunteers with some illiberality, and rejecting some of their just claims on the plea of the absence of certain formalities, which had not been observed, either from ignorance, or from the want of time, when circumstances were so pressing and delays so full of danger.*

After years of hesitation, the State had at last established a Penitentiary, at the high cost of $400,000. Besides this original cost, the keeping up of that establishment turned out to be a very expensive affair for the State, for it amounted yearly to $20,000. The policy of farming it out was suggested, and the suggestion was adopted. The Penitentiary was leased out for five years, during which it not only ceased to be an expense to the State, but yielded large profits to the lessee, who realized more than $19,000 a year. In subsequent leases the State even derived a handsome revenue from the Penitentiary. It is a striking illustration of the manner in which certain institutions are administered in the name and on behalf of the State. She will become bankrupt where individuals will become rich.

1848. In his message of the 18th of January, the Governor had the satisfaction to inform the Legislature that, with regard to the banking institutions of the City of New Orleans which were not in a state of liquidation, "there was nothing hazarded in expressing the opinion that, at no period of their history, were they in a sounder and more healthy condition than at this time." Although the Legislature had yearly appropriated large sums for public works and improvements throughout the State, yet the results had always been far from meeting the expectations entertained on the subject. Hence the Governor, in 1848, had felt authorized to inform the General Assembly " that the Civil Engineer of the State had been indefatigable in his Department, and that his Report would

* Governor Johnson's Message, January 11, 1847.

announce the startling and unprecedented fact that he had performed all the duties imposed on him by the last Legislature." In relation to some neglect which our volunteers were suffering from the General Government during the Mexican War which was still progressing, he said: "The proud and sensitive soldier may brood over his wrongs in silence, and find solace in a manly fortitude which may reconcile him to obedience as a paramount duty; but the State, whose flag he bears, cannot be thus reconciled, but should assert his rights in a fearless and proper manner, and redress his wrongs if possible."

It was foreseen that the invasion of Mexico by the armies of the United States would lead to the acquisition of territory, and, in prevision of this event, a member of Congress from Pennsylvania, named Wilmot, intending to guard against the extension of the area of slavery, had proposed a legislative enactment which would confine it to its present limits. It was called the "Wilmot Proviso," and revived the excitement which the discussion of such a subject always produced. In relation to it the Governor observed: "The issue has been forced upon us, and it should be met respectfully and temperately; but at the same time with a firm and uncompromising resistance. Let us, at least, take care that they who have sowed the speck of storm shall not force us to reap the whirlwind."

The Legislature having adjourned on the 16th of March, 1848, without adequately providing, as required by the Constitution, for the establishment, organization and support of public schools throughout the State, were convened by the Governor in extradinary session, and met on the 4th of December in the same year, when they repaired the omissions of the last session. Already were biennial sessions, limited to sixty days, found to be an evil. The object of this constitutional change had been to guard against too much legislation, but it seems to have been a leap from Scylla into Charybdis.

1850. On the 21st of January the Legislature met for the first time, under the new Constitution, at the new seat of Government, the town of Baton Rouge, where a State House, in the Gothic style of architecture, had been constructed.

On the 2d of March, 1849, Congress had passed a law granting to the State all the swamp and overflowed lands within her limits, on the condition of her constructing such levees and drains as would render those lands cultivable. On the recommendation of the Governor, this conditional grant was accepted. The area of the swamp lands thus ceded by the Federal Government was estimated at about two millions two hundred and sixty-six thousand acres.

In relation to the slavery question, which was still agitated in and out of Congress with greater violence than ever, and which, henceforth, was never to be permitted to slumber until it culminated to one of the grandest catastrophes of modern times, Governor Isaac Johnson said: "Non-interference by Congress with the slavery question is the surest means of preserving the Union, and that doctrine should be insisted on with an unflinching resolution never to surrender it. To any proposition, therefore, to compromise that doctrine, the South, with the bitter and humiliating experience of the past before her, will turn a deaf ear. Submission to incipient oppression prepares men for the yoke, and compromises on this question are nothing else than anti-slavery victories. The repeated, galling and unprovoked aggressions of anti-slavery leave no room to anticipate a cessation of hostilities, and the South has been sufficiently warned that, if it is wise to hope for the best, it is equally prudent to prepare for the worst. It is far better to be lawless than to live under lawless rule."

On the 23d of January, 1850, we, as Secretary of State, and P. E. D. Livaudais, State Treasurer, who constituted the Board of Currency, laid before the Legislature our Report, which concluded in these words: "From the examination of the annexed documents, we hope that your Honorable Body will come to the conclusion that we have exercised with due vigilance that supervision which was intrusted to us by the Act of 1842; that the institution of the Board of Currency has been a measure productive of salutary influence over our banking system; that it has prevented the recurrence of the same errors from which this community has suffered so much; that our Banks continue to be in a flourishing condition, and that the currency of the State of Louisiana is now as sound as could be desired."

On the 28th of January, 1850, Joseph Walker, the successor of Isaac Johnson, was inaugurated. He had long been in public life as a member of the Senate, as State Treasurer, and as President of the late Convention who had framed the new Constitution. He expressed, in the following terms, his views on the slavery question: "Situated as we are, I think we owe it to ourselves, to our sister States of the South, and to our Northern brethren, to declare that if, unhappily, the anti-slavery agitation which has so long been allowed to insult our feelings should be carried to the point of aggression upon our rights; if the equality between all the members of the Confederacy, established and guaranteed by the Constitution, should be destroyed or trenched on by the action of the General Government, then we are prepared to make common cause with our neighbors of the slaveholding States, and pronounce the Union at an end. For myself, I do not hesitate to say, that I should look upon a dissolution of the Union as the greatest calamity that could befall us; but that, great as this calamity would be, I am certain there is not one of our citizens who would be willing, for a moment, to weigh it in the balance against the dishonor of submission."

1852. When the Legislature met in January, there was a general impression that they would call a Convention to amend the Constitution so lately adopted in 1845. The people seemed to be already dissatisfied with it, and, in relation to the supposed disposition entertained by their Representatives, the Governor, who was opposed to the contemplated measure, stated in his address on the opening of their session, "that he did not see any good ground in what had passed, or was passing in State affairs, for another change in our organic law." He recommended to their attention the principle enunciated by Jefferson, "that forms of government should not be changed for light, trivial causes." He observed, that "nothing contributes more to a sound state of things than stable laws, faithfully executed, and a conviction in the public mind that they will not be changed until such change is demanded by reasons of an irresistible character." He judiciously remarked, that a new Convention probably would not, upon trial, "meet every expectation of the people more satisfactorily than the one which framed the present Constitution." The Governor did not seem to be aware that perpetual change is the essential characteristic of democracy, and that one might with as much reason expect steadiness from the wind, as stability in legislation under a popular government. Thus, notwithstanding his arguments, an Act was passed "to take the sense of the people on the expediency of calling a Convention to change the Constitution, and to provide for the election of delegates, and the holding of the Convention." The sense of the people, as a matter of course, was for calling a Convention, which assembled on the 5th of July, 1852. The result of their labors was the framing of as radical a Constitution as could be devised. Every office, even that of the judiciary, was made elective, and for a very short tenure. Constant elections and "rotation in office" were for the future to be the order of the day. The sessions of the Legislature were again to be annual, as under the Constitution of 1812, but still limited to sixty days. The restriction against running the State into debt and against creating banks being found inconvenient, was left out in the new Constitution, under which an election having taken place for Governor, P. O. Hebert, who had been President of the late Convention, and who had filled the office of State Engineer, was raised to the dignity of Chief Magistrate of the State, and sworn as such in January, 1853.

1853. On the 17th of the same month, Joseph Walker, who was retiring into private life, had sent to the Legislature his last message, in which he congratulated them on the present peaceful, flourishing and happy condition of the State, and on her prospective prosperity. In relation to the new Constitution, the Governor observed: "The authority granted to the Legislature by this instrument, to pledge the faith of the State, and contract debts for other purposes than to prosecute war and subdue insurrections, is a power that should be guarded with sleepless vigilance, and exercised with extreme caution. The experience of a long life, no small portion of which has been spent in the public service, has convinced me that the best policy, both for individuals and governments, is to avoid debt as far as practicable."

With regard to the removal of the prohibition to create banking institutions, Governor Walker said: "There never was probably a time when it was less necessary to extend this class of facilities than the present. A long period of comparative economy and successful industry has relieved the great mass of the community from harassing debts, money is abundant and cheap, the community is solvent, enterprise is active without wild speculation, and the precious metals are constantly and abundantly increasing. Why should we then flood the country with bank issues? Why afford the means of hasty speculation? Why run the risk of former painful evils? The influx of precious metals from California, Australia, and other sources, is unparalleled in the monetary history of the world, and bids fair to change even of itself, without artificial aid, the healthy relations of capital and labor." The Governor's views were correct, but he seemed to forget, when indulging in these interrogations, that the recent Convention had been called by the influence of stockjobbers and politicians, precisely to remove *these restrictions*, which they had found to be unpleasant fetters to their designs. As to the Banks then existing, whatever might be the future condition of those to be created, they were stronger than similar institutions ever were, for according to the statement of the Board of Currency, dated December 30, 1852, the amount of circulation of the Banks was $5,400,946, while the specie in their vaults was $8,207,042.

During the administrations of Johnson and Walker, New Orleans had been the centre of an organization to revolutionize the Island of Cuba, and procure her annexation to the United States. It ended in the failure of the ill-advised Lopez expedition, which brought the leader of that name to the scaffold, caused the death of many of his rash companions, and produced a riot against the Spanish flag and Consul in New Orleans, for which the Federal Government had to give redress to Spain. A large number of Coolies had been permitted to be introduced at that time into the Island of Cuba, and it was supposed, at least in Louisiana, that Spain, under the pressure of Great Britain, was taking initiatory steps to abolish slavery in that colony. Acting under the influence of these apprehensions, Governor Hebert, in his annual message of 1854, said: "Will the Federal Government, charged with the international interests of States, anticipate the threatened peril, or patiently and quietly await the occurrence of it? The evil would then be irremediable. Confiding, as we may justly do, in the firmness, patriotism, and truly national spirit of the Chief Magistrate of the Union, the deliberate expression of the sentiments of the people of Louisiana upon this all-important subject would at once sustain the watchfulness of the Administration, and strengthen their hands in executing any measure for our protection which they might deem necessary to adopt." The Chief Magistrate of the Union was then Franklin Pierce, and the "measure" which was expected for our protection was the acquisition of the Island of Cuba. We know that the negotiation which was attempted on this subject failed as miserably, if not as tragically, as the Lopez expedition. Danger came to us from a very different source from the one alluded to by Governor Hebert; for slavery is still protected by Spain in her West India colonies, whilst all the Southern States are in arms, at the time when we write these lines, to defend this institution against the Federal Government.

1854. When the Legislature met on the 16th of January, the gloom and desolation produced by the extraordinary and fatal fever which had prevailed throughout the State during the summer and autumnal months of the preceding year were not yet dissipated, and well might the State grieve, for she had been deprived of thousands of her sons by the most frightful epidemic

which she had ever witnessed. It had not confined its ravages to
New Orleans, but had spread to distant parishes in the country.
Notwithstanding this heavy blow, she was otherwise prosperous,
and energetically engaged in the construction of railroads, and in
carrying on other works of internal improvement. She had made
large appropriations to organize and support her new system of
Public Schools, and to survey and reclaim the swamp lands granted
to her by Congress. She had therefore increased her debt proper
to $3,281,809, but there was not in this amount of indebtedness
any disproportion with the extent of her resources. It must be
admitted, however, that she had been remarkably unfortunate in
the choice of her collectors of taxes; for it appears from a list published in 1854, by the State Auditor, agreeably to law, that there
had been from 1830 to 1848 inclusive, sixty defaulters for public
moneys, and that the sums of which she had been thus defrauded
amounted to $271,655 95.

1855. On the 15th of February the Legislature met at Baton
Rouge, a few months after the yellow fever had, for a second time,
desolated the State. "The general prevalence of that disease,"
said the Governor in his annual message, "during two successive
years, in the most malignant form, seems to authorize the conclusion that, supposing it to have been at any time of foreign origin,
it has now assumed a fixed habitation within our borders." He
called the attention of the General Assembly to the Report of the
Swamp Land Board, which showed that at least six hundred and
fifty thousand acres of overflowed lands had been reclaimed, at a
cost of one hundred and fifty-six thousand dollars. A most gratifying result, if strictly accurate. An intelligence which was less
gratifying was, that the Report of the Superintendent of Public Education exhibited an unsatisfactory condition of our educational
system. "Indeed," said the Governor, "the system may be considered almost a failure, or rather it is not a system. It is the bewildering confusion of chaos." The Governor also complained of
the disorganized state of the militia—a steady complaint from all
our Governors ever since 1804. All had remonstrated against
that evil with indefatigable pertinacity, but their remonstrances
had been but seeds cast on the rock, or on such light soil as not to
germinate and bear fruit. "It is the duty of Louisiana," observed
Governor Hebert, "a duty which she owes to her own self-preservation and to her sister States of the South, to cultivate the martial
spirit of her people. Her position exposes her to the first assault
of the enemy. She should be ready at all times to contribute her

full share to defence. She must be prepared to meet the responsibilities which the spirit of fanaticism at home may impose upon her, and which an attitude of firmness, with all the preparation to maintain it, may alone avert.

1855. This year was marked by what may be called the demolition of the "Know Nothing" party in Louisiana. It was a secret Order which had been imported into the State from New England, and into which numbers were introduced under the sanctity of an oath. They recognized each other by certain signs and grips, and could not penetrate into the halls where the society met without exchanging pass-words, and without other formalities. There were several grades, and those who belonged to the highest knew more of the real designs of the society than those who were on the inferior steps of the ladder. The Know Nothing party had no other ostensible object than that of excluding foreigners from participating in the administration of the affairs of the country, of securing the purity of elections, and establishing firmly the practical operation of the golden rule, "that office must seek the proper man, and not be sought by him." Partly seduced by this standard, partly by the attractions of novelty, and perhaps also from other motives, almost the whole of Louisiana may be said, with truth, to have rushed with enthusiastic precipitation into the arms of this mysterious Order. Thus far it was a mere State organization, but it soon was found indispensable to connect it with the other Lodges of the same Order in the other States, with a view to establish upon the original association a national party. To this effect, there was to be a grand meeting of all the Lodges in Philadelphia in the month of May. It was to be an imposing Convention, in which means were to be devised to strengthen the association, and to enable it to elect a President of the United States and secure the reins of the Government. But it began to be rumored at this time in Louisiana that the main object of this wide-spread organization was the proscription of Catholics. It produced great excitement, and it was determined to test the question. Six delegates, of which five were Protestants and one Catholic, were elected to the Philadelphia Convention. On their presenting themselves to that body, the five Protestants were told that they could come in, but the Catholic was rejected unless he consented to make certain concessions, to which he was not in the least disposed to assent. His Protestant colleagues remonstrated in vain against such a distinction, and the result was that they retired with their Catholic associate. On the report of this fact made in an immense meeting which took place in New Orleans, the Know Nothing party of Louisiana emphatically refused affiliation with the party of that name in the other States, and from that time this celebrated Order, which seemed at first to be gifted with such exuberant vitality, rapidly decreased in numbers and influence in Louisiana, because many hurried to withdraw their names and co-operation. It had the same fate from Maine to Florida, when the truth was known. The religious persecution which it carried in its bosom, and which it wished to hatch, tainted its blood as if with leprosy, and it withered away as rapidly as it had sprung up into gigantic proportions. To Louisiana belongs the merit of having spurned and repudiated the poisonous cup which Northern fanaticism had so successfully sweetened with honey.

1856. In January, the official relations of Governor Hebert with the State terminated. In his valedictory message he referred with deep mortification to the scenes of intimidation, violence and bloodshed which had marked the late general elections in New Orleans. He said that the repetition of such outrages would tarnish our national character, and sink us to the level of the anarchical Governments of Spanish America; that before the occurrence of those "great public crimes," the hideous deformity of which he could not describe, and which were committed with impunity in mid-day light and in the presence of hundreds of persons, no one could have admitted even the possibility that a bloodthirsty mob could have contemplated to overawe any portion of the people of this State in the exercise of their most valuable rights, "but that what would then have been denied, even as a possibility, is now an historical fact." He committed to the wisdom and patriotism of the Legislature the entire subject, as perhaps the most important in its nature and general bearings which could engage their attention.

During the preceding summer of 1854, Louisiana had again been submitted to the desolating ordeal of the Yellow Fever. It originated in New Orleans, from which it spread to the most remote parts of the State. It had always been a dark spot among those elements of prosperity which had continued to develop themselves in a country so richly favored by nature, and by those free institutions which, though so frequently abused, are yet so conducive to human happiness. Great works of internal improvement had been steadily advancing to completion, and had already realized some of the advantages which were expected from them. The New Orleans, Jackson, and Great Northern Railroad had been pushed beyond the limits of the State, and the New Orleans, Opelousas and Great

Western Railroad was in successful operation over a distance of sixty-six miles. The finances of the State were in a sound and healthy condition, there being a balance in the Treasury of $632,395 on the 31st of December, 1855.*

The Governor concluded his message in these words: "The wild spirit of fanaticism which has, for so many years, disturbed the peace of the country, has steadily increased in power and influence. It controls the councils of several States, nullifies the laws of Congress enacted for the protection of our property, and resists the execution of them, even to the shedding of blood. It has grown so powerful that it now aspires to control the Federal Legislature. The fact can no longer be concealed, however much it may be regretted. The slaveholding States are warned in time. They should be prepared for the issue. *If it must come, the sooner the better.* The time for concessions on our part and compromises has past. If the Union cannot be maintained upon the just and wholesome principles of the Constitution, concessions and compromises will only retard its dissolution, not save it. They have had thus far no other result than to encourage attack and increase the numbers of abolitionists. It would, however, be premature to suggest practical measures of resistance or retaliation. The present session of Congress will develop fully the plans of that party. Your own action must depend, in a great measure, upon the course which they shall pursue. The responsibility will be upon those who have forced us, in defence of our most sacred rights, of our honor, and of our very existence, to resort to extreme remedies."

Governor Hebert was succeeded by Robert C. Wickliffe, a Kentuckian by birth, whose family had obtained great political distinction in that State. Robert C. Wickliffe had settled in the Parish of West Feliciana, had practiced law and become a leading Democrat in that section of the country. After having served in the Senate of the State for several years, he was raised to the Executive chair. In his inaugural address he said: "It is deeply to be regretted that the overshadowing power of the Federal Government, in its actual administration, should so much divert the attention of the people from a proper consideration of the local wants of their respective States. In the struggle, on the one hand, to enlarge, and, on the other, to limit the power of Congress to those positively delegated, parties are organized with reference to Fed-

---

* Governor Hebert's Message, 1856.

eral issues alone. Our domestic interests are forgotten, neglected, or absorbed in the contest for Federal power.

"This practical working of our double systems was not anticipated by the framers of the Constitution of these United States. Had Congress confined itself to the execution of the few grants of power delegated to it by the several sovereignties that compose the Union, the result would have been different, and would not have deviated from that anticipated by our fathers. But Congress has proceeded step by step to extend by implication its power, and to control, develop, or modify interests which were left by the Constitution to the operation of natural causes, the sharp rivalry of individual enterprise and the wisdom of State legislation.

"It is not my purpose to review the history of what has been justly regarded as the usurpations of Congress, nor to trace out the manner in which its limited powers have been extended to subjects not properly within its control, and made to bear on the highest interests, which ought to have been, and were reserved as exclusively appertaining to the State Governments. But I am compelled to say, that the steady encroachments made by Congress on the reserved rights of the States have not only sanctioned but encouraged outrages, that, if not checked, will undoubtedly result in a dissolution of the Union.

"I do not wish to speak lightly of the Union. Next to the liberty of the citizen and the sovereignty of the States, I regard it as 'the primary object of patriotic desire.' It should be dear to us as a sentiment, and dearer to us for its real value. But it cannot have escaped observation, that the hold which the Union once had upon the affection of the South has been materially weakened, and that its dissolution is now frequently spoken of, if not with absolute levity, yet with positive indifference, and, occasionally, as desirable.

"It should always be remembered that every interpretation of the Constitution, not sanctioned by its letter and spirit, forms the *basis* for future unwarranted construction, and so we shall go on, until, in the end, the States become mere dependencies, and life, liberty and property shall lie at the mercy of naked majorities of Congress. Such has been and such is the tendency of Federal legislation; nor is this all. Disregarding the rights of the States, Congress seems to have looked mainly to the interests of a section of the country, until that favored section has begun to consider the Constitution, not only made for its advantage alone, but actually as a means of aggression upon the rights, the interests and the honor of the Slave States; so that, at this time, a party has been formed, and is in a relative ascendency in the lower branch of Congress, with no other bond of union than a settled purpose to make war on the institutions of the South, not that these institutions are hurtful to the North, but because they are in conflict with one of the forms of fanaticism, which the misguided people of the North have adopted through the designs of artful men, covetous only of their own political advancement.

"Unless the progress of this insanity is checked, the Union will soon be a matter of history. Unity of action on the part of the South, a determination calmly made and fearlessly executed, to permit no further encroachments, can alone perpetuate the Union of these States; and that Union is not worth preservation, if we of the South are to be incessantly engaged, in and out of Congress, in defending ourselves from the attacks of those who use the Union as a means of assault upon us.

"It has, therefore, become the painful duty of every slave State distinctly to declare that no further aggression will be permitted, and to invite the co-operation of every State in vindicating, *to the last extreme*, the rights secured by the Constitution, and *which are immeasurably of more value than the Constitution itself.*" The Governor went on in the same strain sounding the tocsin of alarm. There was unfortunately but too much cause for apprehension, for the dullest eye could see the danger as it came onward on the wings of the lightning which announced the storm.

Referring to the internal condition of the State, Governor Wickliffe said : "Bountiful as nature has been to Louisiana, the skill of the engineer is still essential to her full development. With twenty-five millions of acres of fertile lands, hardly a tenth is in cultivation ; with a sea-coast a third in length of the State, we have a tonnage almost in its infancy. With capacity to produce all the cotton needed for the British Empire, and all the sugar required for this great Confederation, we are as yet but laggards in their growth. With thousands of miles of internal navigation, our productions frequently can find no market, and North and South Louisiana are strangers to each other. Toward the cultivation of these millions of acres, toward the improvement of these miles of navigation, toward cementing together these sections, discreet and timely legislation can do much. As yet nothing, absolutely nothing, has been accomplished. A fund for internal improvements has existed for years. Large amounts of it have been expended. Yet it would be difficult for even a curious inquirer to discover any benefit that has resulted from it." These were sad truths from the lips of the Chief Magistrate. He further said: "It is passing strange that, in a popular Government, without privileged classes, without stipendiaries on the bounty of the State, mismanagement and recklessness should be tolerated." If the Governor had reflected a little on the nature of man and looked into the pages of history, he would not have thought it "passing strange" that popular Government should be liable to mismanagement and recklessness. "May," continued the Governor, "the future redeem the errors of the past, and, striking boldly and freely at all maladministration, vindicate the purity and wisdom of republican institutions, while we promote and enlarge our material interests." Thus far this patriotic hope has not been realized.

1857. At the opening of the annual session of the Legislature in 1857, the Governor complimented them on the result of the late Presidential election, which had secured the success of the Democratic Party represented by James Buchanan and John C. Breckenridge over Frémont and Dayton, who were the exponents of the subversive doctrines of Black Republicanism. He expressed the conviction that their wise and conservative rule would give peace and quiet to our country, and would bring back that fraternal love which existed during the earliest days of our Republic, and which gave such bright hopes to our forefathers throughout the darkest hour of our struggle for independence. "Should, however," he continued to say, "those bright and cheering anticipations, which we now so fondly indulge, not be realized, when freedom and equality in the Union are denied us of the South by the people of the North, then Louisiana will take her position, and maintain her rights by the strong arms and bold hearts of her brave sons."

He also informed the Legislature that the immigration of free negroes from other States of the Union into Louisiana had been steadily increasing for years, that it was a source of great evil, and demanded legislative action: "Public policy dictates," he observed, "the interests of the people require, that immediate steps should be taken at this time to remove all free negroes who are now in the State, when such removal can be effected without violation of law. Their example and association have a most pernicious effect upon our slave population. At the same time, the law forbidding the master to allow the slave to hire his own time should be made more stringent, and more vigorously enforced — these examples being scarcely less injurious to the slave than that of the free negro."

Although the late Presidential election to which Governor Wickliffe refers had been considered as determining whether the Southern States should continue, or not, to remain in the Union, and although it had been, for this reason, the most important which had been held since the foundation of the Federal Government, yet, out of 11,817 votes registered in the City of New Orleans, only 8,333 were cast, showing, apparently at least, an inexplicable apathy on the part of 3,484 citizens. The Governor commented on this regrettable fact in the following language: "It demonstrates that some extraordinary cause was at work to prevent a large proportion of lawful voters from enjoying the sacred franchise of the Constitution. It is well known that, at the two last general elections, many of the streets and approaches to the polls were completely in the hands of organized ruffians, who committed acts of violence on multitudes of our naturalized fellow-citizens who dared venture to exercise the right of suffrage. Thus nearly one-third of the registered voters of New Orleans have been deterred from exercising their highest and most sacred prerogative. The expression of such elections is an open and palpable fraud on the people, and I recommend you to adopt such measures as shall effectually prevent the true will of the majority from being totally silenced." The evil pointed out by the Governor was of the utmost magnitude, but there was one still more dangerous than any which resulted from open violence. It was that corruption which enabled foreigners just landing on our shores to vote, and which put two or three thousand illegal voters at the disposal of whatever party had the means of buying them. This was the main cause which, by producing intense disgust, went much farther than the fear of assassination to prevent honest citizens from resorting to the ballot-box. They knew all our elections to have become so hopelessly fraudulent, that it was disgraceful to participate in them. They had retired from the political arena in sullen despair.

1858. In the beginning of this year the Governor made known to the Legislature that the total receipts for the year, less the unexpended balance from the accounts of the various special and trust funds, were estimated at twelve hundred and twenty-two thousand five hundred and six dollars, and that the most rigid economy was demanded of the Government, not less by a consideration of peculiar exigencies, than by the depressed prices of all the great staples of our agriculture and the pecuniary distress which prevailed amongst the commercial and industrial classes. "It will be readily perceived," he said, "that the current general resources of the State are gradually sinking below the general and extraordinary expenditures; and, each year, the State has been forced to borrow a larger sum from the Special and Trust Funds of the Treasury, to make good this continually swelling deficit. It is time this vicious practice be corrected, and the expenditures of the Government confined within the limits of its own proper revenues." This advice was wise and opportune, for Louisiana had been suffering from one of those periodical financial crises which are so frequent in the United States. It had originated toward the close of the month of August, 1857, in New York, and in October began to be severely felt in New Orleans. Three of the Free Banks were forced to succumb to the storm, and one of the chartered Banks had practically suspended. There was a deficiency of specie in the vaults of those institutions, to the amount of about eight hundred thousand dollars."* But, fortunately, a few weeks sufficed to reinstate them in the position which they ought to have maintained. The temporary shock which they had received showed after all their real strength, and increased the confidence deservedly reposed in them, not only in the State, but also in other parts of the Union, where they stood higher in reputation than any other institutions of the like nature.

For years past the Governors of Louisiana, whenever they referred to our Federal relations, had never had any satisfactory communications to make. Again Governor Wickliffe, like his predecessors, informed the Legislature "that the affairs of the Federal Government had been by evil-disposed persons seriously disturbed." He called their attention to Mormonism in Utah, whither United States troops had been ordered to quell an anticipated rebellion, and to the Territory of Kansas, where events were occurring which seemed to render civil war and bloodshed inevitable.

1859. The Governor took in his annual message a more hopeful view of our Federal relations. "It has become apparent," he said, "that the entire South is with the Democratic party, and recent events have shown that a portion of the Northwest is also with us. This state of affairs tends to give us some assurance that we may, for the present at least, hope to defeat the purposes of that strong party at the North which is animated by a firm hostility to our social and industrial system. These two parties, only, now occupy the field. The Democratic is based upon the idea that each separate State is sovereign, and that the Government at Washington

---

* Monthly Statements of the Board of Currency.

only intended to be the agent of the combined States for certain special purposes. The Republican appears to foster the idea that State lines are mere boundaries for convenience in local jurisdiction, and that the majority of voices in the whole United States, considered as one nation, ought to rule. This last idea would be so fatal to the South, if carried out, that nearly all Southern men are now with the Democratic party. The position of the Northwestern States of the Mississippi Valley, on this question, is of special interest to us. These States are, by geographical position, commercially our allies, whether slave or free, while many of the States on the Atlantic side of the Alleghanies are necessarily hostile in commercial interest. Our principal city is the metropolis of the Mississippi Valley, and does much of the importation and most of the exportation. The Atlantic cities are rivals of New Orleans in both of these trades. It is cheering to find our commercial allies of the Northwest sustaining your Southern policy."

1860. In his annual message of 1860, Governor Wickliffe conveyed to the General Assembly the grateful intelligence that the receipts into the State Treasury, for the present year, on account of the General Fund, were estimated at $1,205,000, which, with a balance of $133,696 remaining on the 31st of December, 1859, would make a sum-total of $1,338,696; that the estimated expenditures for the same period, including the unexpended balances, would amount to $1,174,553; showing a balance in favor of the State on the 31st of March, 1861, of $164,142, and exhibiting a far more prosperous condition of the finances of the State than had been presented for eight years. "It will therefore be seen," said the Governor, "that without increasing the rate of taxation, the annually increasing revenues of the State will enable her to meet promptly all the wants of the Government."

Returning to the absorbing topic of our Federal relations, which was daily becoming more exciting, he said: "The times that are upon us are rapidly precipitating a crisis which must be met manfully. In any event, I know that the people of Louisiana will not be found wanting in a practical vindication of their assailed rights and in a proper defence of their honor. The times and the crisis to which I have alluded will bring into requisition, I apprehend, all the qualities indispensable to the vindication of the one and the defence of the other. The character of Louisiana has not yet been stained with servility or dishonor, and I know her people in the present, like her people in the past, would gladly accept any alternative which carries with it honor and insures self-respect, rather than take a position which might secure temporary profit at the sacrifice of every principle of manhood, every element of independence, every attribute of that lofty sovereignty upon which we have so justly prided ourselves. And when it is taken into consideration that submission will hardly insure temporary security—for compacts with cravens are invariably broken by the stronger party the very instant they have answered their purposes—that aggression aftei aggression *invariably* succeeds each compromise of constitutional right and submission to wrong—it is not possible that Louisiana will abate one jot or tittle of her inalienable prerogatives, or swerve in the least from the true, just and patriotic position she has ever nobly occupied."

Governor Wickliffe went on recapitulating the grievances which the South had against the North: "For more than a quarter of a century a sectional warfare, based upon hatred of the institution of slavery, has been waged by the North upon the South. At the outset, the members of this despicable organization were contemptible in number and intellect, and their fanatical, treasonable and atrocious promulgations were deemed fit subjects for mirth in both sections of the Confederacy. At that time each State respected its constitutional obligations, the comity of the respective Sovereignties was maintained, brotherhood and good feeling prevailed well-nigh universally. All the South requires now, or wanted then, was the simple observance of the organic compact, which was cheerfully rendered on all sides; the most beneficent system of government the earth ever knew, when rightfully administered—a nation of sovereignties under a confederated head, armed with expressly delegated powers—worked so beautifully and harmoniously, that it was the wonder and admiration of the world. It grieves me to say that this happy picture has been changed; that the small band of fanatics, once only deemed fit subjects for laughter, have grown into a powerful organization; that the cloud, once a mere speck upon the horizon, has attained such dimensions that it blackens the skies of the majority section of the Confederacy; that sovereign States, through their Legislatures and Governors, have passed laws which set at defiance the Constitution of the United States, which nullify the laws of Congress, which trample under foot the decisions of the Federal Courts of last resort, and which openly contemn the executive authority of the Government when exercised in strict conformity to the demands of the Constitution. All this is done too without cause, provocation, or warrant of any kind. The slaveholding States have not wronged, nor attempted to wrong, their Northern brethren in any manner, and in all controversies they have been the first to yield. They have compromised, and compromised for the sake of peace, when they had rights and interests at stake, and the North none. But every yielding and each compromise has been followed by fresh demands and renewed aggression, until fanaticism, grown bold by our yielding and compromises, as well as by the wondrous growth of its power in the North, now says in the Federal Senate, in the Hall of the House of Representatives, and from the Legislatures of most of the non-slaveholding States, backed by an overwhelming preponderance of the masses almost sufficient to elect a President, that not another slave State shall ever be admitted into the Union—no matter what the circumstances of the case, no matter what the obligations imposed by one common organic law."

The Governor then referred to the attempt made at Harper's Ferry by John Brown, with a band of fanatics from the North, to produce an insurrection of negroes in Virginia. "The number actively engaged in it," he said, "were insignificant; but when we take into consideration that they committed the crimes of treason and murder, and were provided to equip with arms, for the work of death, several thousand slaves or other confederates; that the general press and people of the extreme North, on various grounds, sympathized with the traitors and murderers, and solicited their pardon, we cannot close our eyes to the inauspicious condition of affairs."

Thomas O. Moore, of the Parish of Rapides, succeeded Governor Wickliffe. He was a wealthy sugar-planter, and had been for many years a member of the Senate of the State. He was in his inaugural address as denunciatory of the dangerous purposes of the abolition party as his predecessor had been in his valedictory. "So bitter," he said, "is this hostility felt toward the slavery which these fifteen States regard as a great social and political blessing, that it exhibits itself in legislation for the avowed purpose of destroying the rights of slaveholders guaranteed by the Constitution, and protected by acts of Congress. Popular addresses, Legislative resolutions, Executive communications, the press and the pulpit, all inculcate hatred against us and war upon the institution of slavery—an institution interwoven with the very elements of our existence. The fanaticism engendered in the popular mind by the doctrines taught and the enmity excited, manifested itself very recently by an irruption of armed men in the State of

Virginia, whose object was to excite insurrection, and whose means were treason and murder. The abrupt end to which the conspiracy was brought, and the sharp, just, and quick punishment of the conspirators, proved that the South had not over-estimated the stability of her institutions. But the apologies and eulogiums which developed at the North a wide-spread sympathy with felons, have deepened the distrust in the permanency of our Federal Government, and awakened sentiments favorable to a separation of the States."

In the fall of 1860, it was ascertained that the Abolition party, who had been so long rampant in the United States, and who had always been so explicit in their desire to become the Government, in order to use all its power for the destruction of slavery, had at last succeeded in electing Abraham Lincoln, of Illinois, President of the great American Republic. The President-elect represented the doctrine, that there was an irrepressible conflict between the free labor of the North and the slave labor of the South, that the South must become free, or the North slaveholding, and that, as the North could not adopt slavery, that institution must inevitably be abolished at the South, and that the Government should resort to such means as would gradually lead to that desired result—among which means was the reorganization of the Supreme Court, which had hitherto protected the South in the enjoyment of its rights under the Constitution. An immense excitement pervaded the Southern States, public assemblies were held everywhere, in every city and village, and the sentiment of the great majority of their population from Virginia to Texas was, that the Union should be dissolved before the President-elect should have in his hands all the powers of the Government. The Legislature of Louisiana having met in extraordinary session at the call of Governor Moore, he informed them, on the 10th of December, of the election of Abraham Lincoln, as President, and Hannibal Hamlin, as Vice-President, "by a purely sectional vote, and in contempt of the earnest protest of the other section." He argued that the election, made under such circumstances, " was to be considered as evidence of a deliberate design to pervert the powers of the Government to the immediate injury and ultimate destruction of the peculiar institution of the South." The Governor advised the Legislature to issue a call for a Convention, "to meet *at once*, and determine *at once*, before the day arrived for the inauguration of the Black Republican President."

" I do not think, " said the Governor," it comports with the honor and self-respect of Louisiana, as a slaveholding State, to live under the government of a Black Republican President. I will not dispute the fact that Mr. Lincoln is elected according to the forms of the Constitution, but the greatest outrages, both upon public and private rights, have been perpetrated under the forms of law. This question rises high above ordinary political considerations. It involves our present honor and our future existence as a free and independent people. It may be said that, when this Union was formed, it was intended to be perpetual. So it was, as far as such a term can be applied to anything human; but it was also intended to be administered in the same spirit in which it was made, with a scrupulous regard to the equality of the sovereignties composing it. We certainly are not placed in the position of subjects of a European despotism, *whose only door of escape from tyranny is the right of revolution.* I maintain the right of each State to secede from the Union, and, therefore, whatever course Louisiana may pursue now, if any attempt should be made by the Federal Government to coerce a sovereign State, and compel her to submission to an authority which she has ceased to recognize, I should unhesitatingly recommend that Louisiana assist her sister States with the same alacrity and courage with which the colonies assisted each other in their struggle against the despotism of the Old World."

1861. The Convention called by the Legislature to take into consideration the state of the country, assembled at Baton Rouge, on the 23d of January, 1861, and Alexander Mouton, a sugar-planter in the Parish of Lafayette, who had been Speaker of the House of Representatives, Governor of the State, and Senator in Congress, was elected President of that body. The Legislature had met on the same day, and Governor Moore transmitted to the Convention a copy of the message which he had caused to be delivered to the General Assembly. He stated to them that the people, by their recent vote in relation to the Convention, " had confirmed the faith of their Representatives in the Legislative and Executive station that the undivided sentiment of the State was for immediate and effective resistance; and that there was not found within her limits any difference of sentiment, except as to minor points of expediency, in regard to the manner and time of making such resistance, so as to give it the most imposing form for dignity and success." " Our enemies," he said, " who have driven on their conflict with the slaveholding States to this extremity, will have found that, throughout the borders of Louisiana, we are one people—a people with one heart and one mind—who will not be cajoled into an abandonment of their rights, and who cannot be subdued." The Governor expressed the conviction that the Southern States would not be permitted to depart from the old Union peaceably, and that there would be an attempt to coerce them to remain within the Federal compact, and to make it binding upon them, when it was set at naught by the majority of the members of that great national copartnership. "I have therefore determined," he said, "that the State of Louisiana should not be left unprepared for the emergency. She has a long and exposed frontier, on which the Federal Government possesses fortresses capable of being used for the subjugation of the country, and to annul the declared will of the people. Near this capital, where the delegates of the sovereign people are about to assemble, was a military depot, capable, in unscrupulous hands, of being employed for the purpose of overawing and restraining the deliberations of a free people. On these grounds, respecting the manifest will of the people, and to the end that their deliberations shall be free, and their action supported by the full possession of the whole territory of the State, I decided to take possession of the military posts and munitions of war within the State, as soon as the necessity of such action should be developed to my mind. Upon information which did not leave me in doubt as to my public duty, and which convinced me, moreover, that prompt action was the more necessary in order to prevent a collision between the Federal troops and the people of the State, I authorized these steps to be taken, and they were accomplished without opposition or difficulty. In so doing, I was careful to confine myself to such acts as were necessary to effect the object with the greatest certainty and the least risk of violence.

"In accordance with an arrangement entered into with the commanding officer, in the presence of a force too large to be resisted, Baton Rouge barracks and arsenal, with all the Federal property therein, were turned over to me on the 11th and 12th instant, and on the 13th the Federal troops departed. About the same time State troops occupied Fort Pike on the Rigolets, and Forts Jackson and St. Philip on the Mississippi River; and such other dispositions were made as seemed necessary for the public safety. Receipts were given in all instances for the property found, in order to protect the officers who were dispossessed and to facilitate the future settlement." On the 26th of the same month, the Convention passed an Ordinance to dissolve the union between the State of Louisiana and the other States bound together by the compact entitled "The Constitution of the United States." South Carolina, Mississippi, Florida, Alabama and Georgia had already taken that formidable step. The Ordinance of Secession was conceived in these terms:

"We, the people of the State of Louisiana, in Convention assembled, do declare and ordain, and it is hereby declared and ordained, that the ordinance passed by us in Convention on the 22d day of November, in the year eighteen hundred and eleven, whereby the Constitution of the United States of America, and the amendments of said Constitution, were adopted, and all laws and ordinances by which the State of Louisiana became a member of the Federal Union, be and the same are hereby repealed and abrogated, and that the union now subsisting beween Louisiana and other States, under the name of 'The United States of America,' is hereby dissolved.

"That the State of Louisiana hereby resumes all rights and powers heretofore delegated to the Government of the United States of America; that her citizens are absolved from all allegiance to said Government, and that she is in full possession and exercise of all those rights of sovereignty which appertain to a free and independent State.

"That all rights acquired and vested under the Constitution of the United States, or any act of Congress or treaty, or under any law of this State, and not incompatible with this Ordinance, shall remain in force, and shall have the same effect as if this Ordinance had not been passed."

The financial condition of the State, when she seceded, may be easily seen from the Auditor's account, presented in January, 1861. The receipts into the State Treasury, from all sources, for the year ending on the 31st of December, 1860, were $2,378,793 44, out of which the taxes on real estate amounted to $680,705 75, and the taxes on trades, professions, occupations, and auction sales to $309,475. The expenditure was $2,224,702, and the liabilities amounted to $10,099,074. The population, according to the late decennial census of the United States, was 709,433; of which 332,523 were slaves.

Louisiana was then in as high a state of prosperity as ever any land was blessed with, but with sublime imprudence she did not hesitate to stake the whole of it on the cast of a die, at what she conceived to be the call of honor and duty. Four years have since elapsed; she is now the seat of desolation—the footstool of subjugation; the hoof of the conqueror's horse has withered her opulent fields in the land which was once a fit residence for her brave and free population of the Caucasian race, and an Elysium for her African bondsmen. Another pen than mine will relate her sufferings, her sacrifices, her heroism in battle, her fortitude and resignation in defeat and humiliation, after prodigies of resistance against overwhelming numbers on land and water. Farewell, O sainted and martyred mother! My task as historian is done, but my love, as thy son, shall cling to thee in poverty and sorrow, and nestle in thy scarred bosom with more rapturous constancy than when thy face was beaming with joy and hope, when wealth was thy handmaid, and the eye of God not averted in anger from that noble brow where once rested the pride of sovereignty.*

* This was written whilst Louisiana was under Federal military authority in 1865.

THE END.

INDEX.

d'Abbadie, II 94, 95, 97, 100, 101, 103, 106, 107, 108, 112, 115, 130, 168, 172, 269, 330; III 2.
Abrado, Marchioness of, Wife of Ulloa, II 177, 220.
Acadia, II 93; IV 117.
Acadian Coast, III 32, 125, 126; IV 451.
Acadians, II 115, 116, 117, 119, 121, 122, 166, 189, 236, 373; III 131, 170, 171, 185, 186, 223.
Acapulco, III 133, 137.
Acakia, I 474; II 109.
d'Acosta, Captain of Frigate, II 185, 277, 279.
Adair, John, General, IV 174, 461, 504, 557.
Adais, IV 87.
Adams, John, Prest., III 399.
Adams, John Quincy, IV 524, 526, 527, 528, 529, 530, 531, 549, 555, 557.
Addington, Henry, III 500, 501.
Adet, III 384, 465.
Africa, III 314, 325, 433.
Agriculture, II 65.
de Aguiar, Antonio Joseph, III 43.
Aiguillon, I 494.
d'Aix, Chateau, I 370.
Alabama, I 17; IV 644.
Alabama River, IV 372.
Alabamas, Indians, III 160, 316.
de Alcoran, Don Martin, I 238, 257, 258.
Alatamaha, III 150.
Alba, Duke of, II 249, 330.
Alcaldes, III 3, 4, 5, 11.
Alexandre I, 520.
Alexis, I 263, 272.
Alibamon, Mengo, I 432, 483; II 26.
Alibamons, I 450; II 75, 88, 104, 105; III 174, 329, 419, 422.
Alibamos, (dist.), I 273.
Alicant, III 44.
Allard, III 605.
Allyator, Sloop, IV 398, 399.
Alsatia, I 354, 489.

Almonaster, Don Andres, III 35, 205, 271, 336, 583.
Altariva, Michel &, II 231.
Alvarado, I 1, 15, 19.
Alvarez, Don Julian, III 125, 129.
Amiens, III 459, 463, 501.
Amite River, I 235; III 127; IV 280.
d'Amon, I 493.
Amsterdam, Bank of, I 196.
Anaconda, Brig, IV 350.
Anastase, Father, I 36.
Anaya, Don Gaspardo, I 169, 171.
de Anaya, Don Juan, IV 505.
d'Ancenis, Marquis, I 241, 354.
Anderson, Council at Havana, IV 219.
Andry, Sub-engineer, II 121, 122, 245.
Andry, Manuel, III 588.
Anemiche, I 520.
Anilco, I 20.
Antoine, Father, IV 154, 155.
Apalache, II 263.
Apalaches, III 174.
Apalachicola R., III 157; IV 332, 337.
Appalachian, Mts., III 213, 230.
Aragon, Pedro, III 204.
Aranda, Count, II 249, 255, 393, 394.
Aranjuez, IV 99.
Arbuckle, Col., IV 590, 593.
de Arcas, R., III 190.
d'Arensbourg, Chevalier, I 279, 435; II 46, 127, 131, 189, 234, 255.
d'Argenson, Minister of Police, I 198.
d'Arges, Pierre Wower, III 197, 198, 199, 200, 201, 238.
Arkansas, River, I 18, 22, 240, 354.
Arkansas, Terr., I 273, 449, 488; II 241, 355; III 22, 101, 170, 176, 215, 379, 380, 418.
Armant, J. B., IV. 273.
de Armesto, Andreas Lopez, III 204, 593.
Armstrong. General, IV 95.

INDEX

Arnaud, Major, IV 480, 482, 483, 484, 506.
Arnauld, J. C., IV 286.
Arriaga, Juliande, II 249, 250, 253.
Arroyo, Don Francisco, Comptroller, III 373.
d'Artagnac, I 241, 354.
d'Artagnette, Diron, I 99, 233, 236, 241, 354, 404, 434, 435, 449, 450, 455, 457, 461, 462, 463, 466, 470, 471, 473, 485, 486, 487, 488, 500, 525, 526.
Artus, Negro, II 344.
Ascension Island, III 319.
Assinais, Indians, I 277.
Atlantic States, III 229, 230, 231, 242, 248; 249, 252, 360, 416, 422.
Attakapas, Dist., II 355; III 32, 320, 126, 171, 180, 181, 215, 408, 418, 434, 436, 596; IV 12, 122, 134, 150, 157, 228, 298, 462.
d'Aubant, Chevalier, I 266, 272.
Aubert, Adjutant Major, II 309; III 625.
d'Auberville, Intendant Commissary, II 76, 82.
d'Auberville, Demoiselle, III 311.
Aubry, II 101, 122, 123, 132, 161, 164, 165-71, 185, 203, 205, 206, 207, 210, 211, 225, 227, 232, 243, 244, 246, 248, 272, 273, 276, 278, 281, 285, 289, 290, 291, 292, 295, 296, 312, 319, 322, 327, 328, 340, 344, 348, 349; III 44, 625, 630.
Audubon, Jean Jacques, III 626.
Augliakabee, III 362.
d'Auleck, Marquis, I 240.
D'Aunoy, III 626.
d'Aunoy, Mme., II 235.
Austria, III 448.
Avoyelles, Indians, I 428.
Avoyelles, Parish, II 355; III 170, 215.

Baby, Dancing Master, II 44.
Bagot, I 127.
Bahamas,, I 492; III 316.
Bailleul, III 448.
Baker, Capt., IV 427.
Balize, I 39, 358, 361, 436, 500, 501, 502, 516, 578, 579; II 173, 174-7, 186, 245, 284, 289, 292, 356; III 30, 31, 47, 121, 135, 170, 177, 236, 373, 417, 585; IV 344, 405.
Baltimore, IV 228.
Banbaras (Negro Tribe), I 440.

Bando, de bien Gubierno, III 313.
Banks, IV 15, 268, 658, 661, 667, 685.
Bar, English Captain, I 60.
Barataria, I 388; III 215; IV 33, 228, 289, 303, 305, 312, 313, 314, 356, 358, 359, 365, 369, 370, 371, 628; IV 290, 304, 305, 307, 364, 410, 504, 619.
Barcelona, III 44.
Barrancas, IV 372, 373.
Barracks, I 470.
Bastille, I 494.
Bastrop, Baron de, III 353, 456.
Bathurst, Lord, IV 474, 499, 514, 525, 529.
Baton Rouge, I 241, 354; II 94, 115, 125, 126, 131; III 45, 113, 116, 127, 128, 129, 131, 132, 135, 143, 149, 170, 171, 177, 181, 215, 223, 608; IV 18, 69, 71, 73, 76, 77, 87, 226, 230, 284, 298, 320, 384, 436, 443, 458, 581, 583, 672, 677, 690, 691.
Battle of New Orleans, 8th of January, IV 467, 472, 534.
Batture, The, IV 185, 190, 192, 297.
Baudrot, II 75, 76.
Baudry de Lozieres, I 496.
Bay, St. Bernard, I 250; IV 76, 111.
Bay St. Louis, I 50, 57, 241; IV 399.
Bay, Santo Spiritu, I 14.
Bayagoulas, I 39, 59, 443, 444.
Bayamo, III 455.
Baynton, III 243, 266.
Bayonne, I 493.
Bayou Bienvenu, IV 416, 417, 449, 459, 460, 463.
Bayou Catalan, IV 416.
Bayou Chetimaches, I 60.
Bayou Lafourche, I 354; II 104; III 116; IV 314.
Bayou Manchac, I 40, 234, 241, 354; III 116, 130, 132, 591; IV 275, 280, 384, 417.
Bayou Mazant, IV 417, 460.
Bayou des Pecheurs, IV 416.
Bayou Pierre, IV 150.
Bayou Savage, IV 384, 404, 417.
Bayou Teche, IV 229.
Beale, Captain, IV 422, 429, 430, 432, 470.
Bealk, Benjamin, III 369.
Bearn, I 426.
Beauchamp, I 450, 451, 452, 488, 514.
Beaudoin, Pere, I 463.
Beaujeu I 28, 39.
Beaujolais, Count of, III 389, 390.

INDEX

Beaulieu, I 236, 237, 444; II 234.
Beauregard, Bartholomew, III 103.
Beaurand, interpreter, II 101.
Beauvais, A., IV 654.
Bellagues, I 508.
Bellechasse, Deville de Goutin, III 605, 609, 615; IV 19, 68, 189, 273.
Bellehot, II 87.
Belleville, Count de, I 240.
Bellevue, II 183.
Belot, II 85.
Beluche, IV 411, 504, 582.
Benac, I 443.
Bernard de la Harpe, I 221, 242, 257, 366, 368.
Beneteaud, IV 612.
Berard, II 241.
Bermuda, IV 337, 522.
Bernadotte, III 461, 465, 503, 504.
Bertel, IV 612.
de Berthel, Commr. of the Illinois, I 484; II 42.
Bienvenu, Antoine, III 31.
Bienvenue, Devins, IV 462.
Bienvenu's Plantation, IV 444, 445, 446, 447.
Bienville, Jr. (Nozan), II 127, 187. 211, 232, 233; III 118, 119.
Bienville, Jean Baptiste Le Moyne de, I 36, 38, 40, 58, 59, 60, 69, 71, 80, 81, 85, 87, 88, 95, 98, 99, 100, 234, 235, 242, 243, 245, 246, 248, 250, 253, 259, 260, 262, 263, 272, 278, 279, 285, 338, 353, 360, 361, 362, 363, 364, 367, 368, 451, 456, 458, 460, 462, 463, 468, 469, 470, 471-4, 483, 484, 485, 487, 490, 497, 498, 500, 501, 503, 504, 505, 507, 508, 509, 511, 514, 517, 518, 519, 520, 521, 522, 524.
Big Miami, III 235, 236.
Billets de Caisse. bonds of the India Company, I 453.
Biloxi, I 57, 69, 72, 254, 255, 272, 273, 278, 356, 375; IV 243.
Biloxi Indians, I 37, 38, 60.
Biloxi (dist.), I 273.
Bizoton, I 574.
Blache, F., III 589.
Black Code, I 362, 364; II 311; III 37, 606.
Black River, I 435, 439, 448, 449.
deBlanc, III 596.
de Blanc, Louis, IV 273.

Blanque, J., III 618; IV 272, 273, 346, 347, 361, 363, 543, 544, 545, 565, 566.
Blennerhasset, IV 179, 180, 181.
Blount, Gov. Tennessee, IV 378, 440.
Bobadilla, Isabella de, wife of de Soto, R. I, 14.
Bobé, Descloseaux, Intendent Commissary Intendant, II 82, 192, 309, 311.
Bocca, de Leon, I 237.
Boileau, I 41.
Boisblanc, Perre Hardy, II 187, 192, 202, 303, 337, 339, 343.
Boisbriant, Major, I 88, 252, 280, 362, 369, 371.
Bolchoz, Capt. Alexander, III 373.
Bollman, Dr. Eric, IV 170, 171, 191.
Bonaparte, Joseph, III 469, 472, 503.
Bonaparte and Louisiana, III 410, 466, 470, 471, 486, 487, 496, 497, 498, 522, 525, 526; IV 44.
Bonnet Carré Levee, III 223.
Booty and Beauty, IV 537.
Bordeaux, I 493; II 344; III 596, 599.
Bordenave, II 295.
Boré, Etienne, III 347, 348, 349. 385, 389, 589, 605, 606, 609, 610; IV 91.
Boré, Robert, III 347.
Bossier, Placide, IV 273, 295.
Bossu, II 306.
Boston, III 100.
Boucher, Pierre, Canadian, II 54.
Bouchereau, II 44.
Boudousquié, Antoine, King's printer, III 151.
Bouguer, I 46.
Bouligny, D., IV 68, 346.
Bouligny, Francisco, II 289, 290, 292, 293, 295, 350; III 120, 311, 405.
Boundaries, II 92; III 356, 361; IV 274, 277, 281.
Bouvines, I 61.
Bowles, William Augustus, III 315, 316, 317, 318, 319, 320, 325.
Bradford, IV 174, 175.
Braquier, Syndic, II 239.
"Bras Pique," putting the French on guard, I 410, sold as slave 444.
Braud, II 109, 127, 308, 313.
Breckenridge, John C., III 492, 553, 555; IV 683.
British Colonists, R. I, 59.
British Invasion feared, II 78, 81, 82.

INDEX

British, III 177, 181, 186, 196.
—— Colonies, III 393.
Brooke, Lieut. Col., IV 425.
Brossard, I 242.
Broutin, II 90.
Broutin, N., III 589.
Brown, James, attorney, IV 19, 183, 186, 195.
Brown, John, III 222, 241, 243, 272, 273, 291, 295.
Bruin, Col. Peter, III 215.
Brussels, III 509.
Bru, I 455.
Bruslé, I 455.
Buchanan, James, Prest., IV 683.
Buildings, Public, Surrendered to U. S., IV 119.
De la Buissoniere, I 507.
Bullit, Col. Alexander Leatt, III 209, 224.
Burr, Aaron, IV 19, 80, 82, 167, 171, 174, 179, 180, 184.
Burthe, Adjutant General, III 597, 598.
Butler, History of Kentucky, III 195.
Butler, Wm., III 268.
Butler, Major R., Adj. Genl., IV 404, 433, 512, 561, 562, 563, 565.
De Buys, IV 19.

Cabildo, III 9, 10, 12, 13, 31, 32, 34, 301—305, 314, 350, 353, 355, 455, 613.
Caddos, IV 299.
Caddo Parish, IV 659.
Cadillac, administration, I 259, 376, 392.
Cadis, Mde., II 380.
Cadix, II 265, 268; III 37, 102, 270.
Cahokia, III 243.
Cahokias, Indians, I 485.
Calderon, Pedro, I 15.
Calhoun, J. C., IV 277, 278.
Cambrai, Treaty of, IV 111.
Calhoun, J. C., IV 277, 278.
Cantrelle, Michel, IV 19, 273.
Camel, Ship, II 38.
Camp Jackson, IV 542.
Campbell, H. R. 47.
Campbell, General, III 136, 143, 144, 145, 316.
Campeachy, III 106, 437, 442, 443.
Campo, Alanga, Count of, III 305.

Canada, I 24, 507; III 196, 234, 236, 306, 345, 366, 449, 490, 497, 502, 512, 533, 569; IV 360, 387.
Canadians, I 39.
Canary Islands, III 115, 120, 595.
Cannes Brulées, I 241, 354.
Canterelle, I 41˥: II 235.
Cantrelle, Michel, IV 19, 273.
Caouis, I 169, 171, 177, 178.
Cape, Francis St. Domingo, II 242. III 309.
Cape, Capt., III 274, 276.
Cape Girardeau, dist., III 406.
Capuchins, I 357; II 71, 79, 99, 189; III 36, 49, 57, 62, 63, 64, 73, 79, 82, 87, 89, 90, 92, 95, 97, 270.
Caraccas, II 167; III 45, 104.
Caresse, Pierre, II 180, 187, 239, 303, 337, 338, 342.
Carignan, II 20.
Carmelites, Jurisdiction from the Alibamos to Mobile, I 357.
Carnot, III 448.
Carolina, (ship), attack by the, IV 424, 442, 444, 447.
Carolina, State, I 515, 523.
Caron, IV 337, 350.
Carondelet Canal, I 382; III 351, 352.
Carondelet, dist, III 406.
Carondelet, Hector Francois, Louis, III 312, 313, 314, 315, 317, 318, 325, 326, 328, 329, 330, 331, 332, 333, 335, 336, 340, 341, 345, 346, 351, 358, 359, 360, 364, 365, 367, 383, 384, 385, 392, 395, 404, 456, 582.
Carriere, II 57, 127.
Carrol, Capt. W. A., IV 410.
Carthagena, III 44: IV 304; 362.
Casa Calvo, Marquis de, III 406, 407, 447, 545, 590, 593, 594, 598, 599, 612, 614, 616; IV 19, 31, 76, 77, 80, 81, 84, 85, 86, 89, 99, 132, 133.
Casa Irujo, III 536, 540, 541, 544, 576; IV 69, 70, 71, 72.
Casket Girls, Arrival of, I 390.
Cassagne, Auguet Ramond & Co., III 407.
Castaignes, I 233.
Cat Island, I 37: II 74, 78; III 48.
Catahoula, I 445.
Cathedral in New Orleans, III 271, IV 507.
Cavalier, Jr., III 509.
Cavalier, Petit, III 605.
Cavalier, Zenon, IV 479, 480, 506.
Celeron, I 507, 509, 510, 511.
Celestin, M., IV 513.

INDEX

Census, Louisiana, II 28, 133, 355; III 170, 215; IV 212.
Census, Upper Louisiana, III 406.
Cevallos, III 540; IV 84, 93.
Chaise, De la. August, III 31, 341, 342, 344, 350.
Chaise, De la, King's Commissary, I 283, 370, 372, 373, 374, 392, 393, 437; II 127, 183.
Chalmette's Plantation, IV 445, 455, 489.
Chamard, II, 241, 242.
Chamilly, Phillippe de, I 342, 343.
Champagne, III 46, 72.
Champmeslin, M, I 247.
Chandeleur Islands, I 36.
Chaonanons, II 78.
Chaptal, III 585.
Chapultepec, III 165.
Charity Hospital, I 337, 437 499; II 46; III 36.
Charles III, History of, II 133, 141; III 269.
Charles IV, III 269.
Charleston, S. C., I 356; III 272.
Charlevoix, Father, I 90.
Charlotte, Princess of Brunswick, I 263, 272.
Chassin, I 280.
Chateaugue, I 84, 87, 88, 243, 280, 368, 369.
Chaterpé Line, III 412.
Chattahouchie, R. III 316.
Chaumont, Mme. de, lands granted to, I 241, 261.
Chauvean, Lieut., IV 467.
Chauvin, I 354; II 234.
Chef Menteur, I 351; III 47, IV 365, 384, 404, 405, 417, 419, 422, 442.
Cherokees, I 520; III 296, 329, 421.
Chester, Gov. West Florida, III 143, 144.
Cherval, settler on German coast, II 44.
Chicago, III 382.
Chickasaw Bluffs, III 362, 367.
Chickasaws, I 17, 59, 94, 260, 286, 351, 360, 361, 434, 439, 449, 450, 459, 462, 464, 465, 470, 471, 485, 504, 505, 509, 511, 513, 519, 523, 524; II 20, 27, 64; III 111, 106, 174, 191, 219, 272, 282, 296, 323, 362, 367, 412, 419.
Choctaw Indians, I 286, 350, 352, 360, 369, 382, 424, 428, 429, 431, 433, 442, 456, 460, 465, 472-3, 482, 483, 498, 503, 505, 506, 517, 519, 523; II 39, 40, 43, 88; III 111, 160, 174, 191, 272, 273, 275, 277, 282, 412, 419, 422; IV 133, 291, 405.
Choiseul, duc de, I 494; II 91, 128, 268, 274.
Chopart, I 396, 397, 410, 411, 412, 414, 415, 437.
Chotard, Major, IV 433, 470.
Chouchas, I 423.
Chowriac, Comm. at Illinois, I 241, 243, 244.
Cirilo, Father, his accounts of religion in Louisiana, III 55, 56, 57, 65, 71, 78, 84, 85, 95, 156.
Citizenship, IV 139.
Citizens' Bank, New Orleans, I 197.
Civil Law, Digest of, IV 195.
Claiborne, W. C. C., III 608, 018, 619, 620; IV 2, 23, 25, 31, 35, 38, 69, 74, 79, 90, 100, 104, 116, 127, 135, 140, 143, 147, 151, 152, 159, 165, 168, 175, 181, 185, 193, 205, 210, 211, 238, 299, 324, 328, 331, 337, 342, 343, 346, 348, 362, 365, 368, 369, 376, 405, 511, 541, 597, 632.
Claiborne, Major Richard, IV 193.
Clairaut, I 46.
Clark, Daniel, Jr., III 211, 267, 341, 342, 397, 471, 472, 584, 607, 613; IV 19, 80, 144, 161.
Clark, Col., III 112.
Clark, Eliiah IV 603.
Clay, William, III 287.
Clay, Henry, IV 279.
Clenton, M., in the Senate, III 401.
Clinton & Fort Hudson Railroad, IV 662.
De Clouet, III 596.
de Clouet Bronier, III 626.
Clouet, Chevalier de, III 181.
De Clouet, Don Jose, IV 69, 541, 542, 543, 544, 547, 548, 549, 550, 551, 552, 553, 554, 555, 561, 565, 567.
Cochart, I 444.
Cochrane, Admiral, IV 416, 423, 431, 472, 415, 516, 536, 623.
Cockburn, Admiral, IV 536.
Cocke, Mr., in the Senate, III 489, 490, 530.
Codrington, Admiral, IV 416.
Cofachiqui, Choctaw princess, R. I 16.
Coffee, General, IV 405, 422, 426, 428, 429, 430, 432, 433, 457, 459, 465, 469, 517, 557.
Colapissas, I 59; II 64.
Cold Weather, III 163, 223.

Cole's Creek, III 294.
Colleges in Louisiana, I 522; II 125.
Collins, Judge, IV 153.
Collot, Victor, III 379, 385, 453, 465.
Colonial Perfect, powers, III 579.
Colorado, IV 97, 98.
Colson Plantation, III 422.
Comanches, III 176.
Commercial Regulations, II 167, 169, III 155, 173.
Commerce in Louisiana, I 259; II 370; III 115, 326, 406.
Committee of Public Safety, III 369, 370, 390, 391.
Company of the Indies, I 192-3, 207, 357, 372, 375, 391, 395, 453, 454, 501, 502.
Conception, Ship, III 253.
Concordia, IV 118, 158, 291.
Conflagrations in New Orleans, III 200, 203, 335; IV 292.
Congress, U. S. Louisiana in, III 266, 285, 290, 291, 475, 479, 494, 548, 575; IV 39-57, 64, 244-264, 276-281, 627.
Connecticut, IV 640, 648.
Connelly, III 235, 236, 256.
Conspiracy against Ulloa, II 187, 209.
Constitution, Conventions, IV 264, 269-275, 668, 674.
Constitution, Martin on the, IV 293.
Conti, Prince de, R. I, 25.
Prince of Courtship, I 444.
Contre Coeur, Chevalier de, account of his death, I 474.
Cordova, Gonzalor de, R. I, 15, F. 8.
Cour, V. Maj., I 425, 447.
Corunna, I 493; III 43.
Cotton, III 437.
Le Coulanges, I 444, 463, 464, 486.
Couillard, I, 415.
Council of State, I 282, 376, 518.
Council of Indies, III 5, 184; IV 4.
De Courtigny, I 417.
Crowley, Lieut., IV 450.
Creeks, III 111, 315, 316, 317, 319, 320, 324, 329, 341, 342, 421, 461, 550, IV 298, 326, 332, 372, 405.
De la Croix, Dusiean, IV 346.
Croizet, S., IV 145.
Cuba, II 265; III 5, 19, 27, 90, 94, 103, 106, 137, 156, 164, 309, 330, 439, 440, 489, 545, 584, 594; IV 456, 214, 216, 219, 220, 226, 227, 367, 676.
Cresnay, Baron de, I 435, 443, 445.
Crozat, his charter, I 191, 192, 205.

Cumberland R, III 197, 213, 214, 258.
Dist., 259 260, 261, 262, 421.
Cumberland Island, IV 536.
Cunningham, William, III 318.
Cupidon, Negro, II 344.
Curnell, Joseph, III 321.
Currency, I 365, 377, 453, 468; II 21, 36, 51, 53, 159; III 523.
Cushing, Col., IV 151, 152.
Cushing, Major, III 403.

Dagobert, Pere, II 80; III 36, 50, 53, 54, 60, 65, 68, 87, 156.
Dana, Mr., in the House, II 568, 571.
Daquin, Major, IV 383, 406, 422, 427, 428, 505.
Danville, III 225, 226.
Darcantel Plantation, IV 422.
Dartigo, III 19, 20.
Date Tree, legend of, I 386, 389.
Dauphine Island,, I 81, 245, 255, 375, 491, 575;IV 69, 517, 521, 522, 524, 532.
Davezac, Major, IV 433, 473, 543, 544, 547.
Davion, Father R., I 61, 64, 65, 67.
Davion's Bluff, I 68; II 102.
Davis, Col., IV 481, 484, 486, 506.
Dayton, General, IV 191.
Dearborn, Sec. of War, IV 89.
Debates in Congress, IV 40, 54.
Debuys, G., III 589.
Decres, III 518-521, 582, 592.
Defensive Resources of the Colony 1176, III 100.
Dejean, Col., IV 449, 480, 506.
De Lara, Mannuel Diaz, III 204.
De la Celena, Francisco, III 204.
De la Germardiere, I 445.
de la Groue. Jacques, III 588.
de la Houpe, II 241.
de la Houssaye, Scouvion, I 241, 242.
de la Pedrera, Jose Martinez, assessor, III 445.
Delassus, IV 230.
de la Torré, Marquis, III 90, 91.
de la Touche, I 444.
De Laye, I 446.
Delery, I 236, 237.
Delino, Ensign Comm. at the Arkansas, II 59.
De Lisle, put in command of Pensacola, I 249.
De l'Orme, I 282.
Deposit. III 478, 585.
Depuyabre, letter from, II 344.

INDEX   vii

Derbigny, Pierre, III 589, 605; IV 17, 58, 65, 67, 68, 282, 653, 654.
Deruisseau, receives concession of trading on Missouri River, II 23.
Deschapelles, Le Breton, IV 286.
Desclozeaux, Bolé, III 37.
Des Essarts, I 487.
Desforges, French Consul, IV 137, 143, 144.
Desmarets, I 199.
Desnoyers, I 426.
Dessales, II 127.
Destrehan, Comptroller, II 85, 375; III 348.
Destrehan, Jean Noel, III 605; IV 17, 58, 65, 67, 68, 272, 282, 346.
Detroit, III 235, 237.
Deverges, I 506, 508, 514.
Dick, U. S. Dist. Atty., IV 593, 594, 616.
Dickens, Mahlon, District Attorney, IV 19.
Dickson, Lt. Col., III 131, 143, 145.
Digest of Civil Laws, IV 195, 198, 199.
Donaldson, III 605.
Donaldsonville, IV 314, 436.
Dorchester, Lord, III 234, 236, 345.
Dorciére, IV 21.
Dormenon, Parish Judge, IV 209.
Dow, IV 19.
Dorsey, III 246.
Dorville, II 87.
Doucet, Julien Jerome, II 187, 192, 303, 337, 339, 343.
Doutreleau, Father, I 424.
Doyle, Lieutenant, IV 102.
Drake, Admiral, IV 170.
Drama, refugees from Cape Francois open a theatre in 1741, III 309.
Dreux, II 183.
Dubayet, Aubert, III 625.
Dubois, Sergeant, I 394, 395.
Dubourg, Abbé, IV 101, 508, 510.
Dubourg, Colonel, IV 314.
Dubreiul, I 518; II 86.
Duché, I 233.
Duclos, King's Commissary, I 392.
Du Coder, I 418, 464.
Ducros, Joseph, III 31.
Ducros, R., III 589.
Ducros, II 192.
Ducros, IV 420.
Duhulquod, IV 612.
Dumont, I 415; II 341.
Dunbar, IV 83.

Duncan, Abner, Aide de Camp, IV 540, 541, 542, 543, 545, 554, 567, 575.
Dunlap, James.
Dunmore, Lord, III 316.
Dunn, Major Isaac, III 208, 211, 212, 221, 223, 224, 225, 226, 234, 240, 242, 243, 245, 250, 260.
Du Parc, I 430; II 123.
Duplessv, Ensign, II 57.
Duplessis, IV 433, 592, 599.
Duponceau, IV 19.
Dupré, J., IV 654.
Duralde, III 507.
Durand, III 20.
Duras, Duke de, III 118.
Durel, B, III, 589.
Du Saunoy, I 369.
Dutch, III 297.
Duties of Public Officers, III 9, 14.
Duty, Exemption of all Goods Exported and Imported, II 62.
Duvergier, I 280.
Duvivier, III, 20.

East Baton Rouge, IV 243.
Ecclesiastical Districts of Louisiana Divided Among the Capuchins, Carmelites and Jesuits, I 357.
Ecores a Margot, II 241; III 380.
Ecores a Prudhomme, I 485.
Eden, William, III 234.
Education, Public, IV 225.
Elephant, Ship, brings flour, II 24.
Ellicot, Andrew, III 366, 368, 369, 370, 371, 397.
Elliot, H. R., IV 39.
Embargo Law, IV 173, 394.
Emigrants, I 259; III 353; IV 214.
England, III 121, 134, 153, 157, 412, 451, 453, 454, 463-7, 487, 508, 572, 573, 574, 578; IV 76.
English, The, I 434, 437, 486, 503, 523; II 78, 97, 100, 113, 114, 125, 250, 256, 258, 261, 280; III 21, 24, 26, 28, 101, 113, 114, 125; III 45, 46, 106, 107, 111, 113, 117, 122, 125, 127, 128, 131, 133, 146, 149, 315, 333, 345, 430; IV 386, 540.
English, Proclamation, IV 338.
English Traders, II 40, 41, 47, 75.
English Turn, I 61; II 33; IV 196, 420, 433, 435, 443, 451.
D'Ennemoser, IV 68.
Epidemics, I 86; III 190; IV 221.
Escambia, IV 338.

INDEX

Espeleta, Joseph de, III 140, 142, 145, 146.
Estecheria, Don J., III 30, 47, 100, 156.
d'Estrées, I 494.
Etna, Brig, IV 410.
Etruria, IV 446, 468, 571, 537, 545.
Ette Actal, Natchez Indian, I 357, 432.
Eustis, III 262.
Expenses of Colony, I 514, 518, 523; II 39, 47, 65, 70, 78; III 28, 171, 371, 332, 401; IV 692.
Exports, II 355.

Faget, Commissary, I 282, 284.
Fagot, III 262.
Farmer, R., II 96, 100.
Faurié, III 605.
Favre d'Aunoy, II 167, III 106, 107, 114, 117.
Favrot, II 87, 109.
Fazende, I 371, 455.
Feliciana, III 191, 215, 253; IV 18, 243, 284, 404, 423, 441.
Flemish, III 375.
Ferdinand VII, IV 203, 204.
Ferrand Commissary, I 282, 284.
Flaugeac, Genl. Garrigues, IV 467, 468, 505, 582.
Fleurian, C. J. B., Attorney General, I 371; II 61. 192; III 31.
Flint River, III 157.
Flood Dr., William, III 607; IV 21 433.
Florida, I 14, 15; III 27, 93, 608.
Florida, East, III 342, 531.
Florida, Parishes, IV 586.
Florida, West, III 143, 147, 154, 156, 178, 181, 185, 197, 292, 313, 359, 361, 362, 412, 413, 447, 531, 591; IV 29, 69, 71, 76, 78, 82, 89, 226, 231-233, 236, 239-245, 279, 280, 531.
Floridas, The, 109, 117, 134, 157, 158, 164, 175, 234, 251, 306, 319, 329, 448, 449, 458, 460-468, 470, 480, 486, 496, 498, 501, 507, 526, 529-534, 554.
Florida Blanca, Count of, III 217, 218, 234.
Floridians, Address to the, 239, 240.
Flournoy, General, IV 306, 314, 323, 328, 334, 385, 401.
Floyd, General, IV 307.
Folch, Governor, IV 19, 29, 31, 32, 68, 72, 78, 89, 137, 330.
Fontainebleau, I 59.
Fonteneau, F., IV 145.

Ford, T., II 97.
Forstall, Nicholas, III 170.
Fort Adams, I 68; II 102; III 392, 608, 618; IV 15, 82, 221.
Fort Bourbon, IV 383.
Fort Bowyer, IV 332, 348, 349, 352, 356, 372, 513, 514, 517, 520, 579.
Fort Burgundy, III 381.
Fort Bute, III 132.
Fort Charlotte, III 136.
Fort Chartres, I 464, 507.
Fort Claiborne, IV 129.
Fort Concord, III 398.
Fort Condé, Mobile, I 279; II 94.
Fort Duqusne, II 83.
Fort George, Pensacola, III 144, 145.
Fort Jackson, IV 691.
Fort Louis, at Mobile, I 278.
Fort Manchac, III 126, 127, 135.
Fort Massac, III 361.
Fort Mimms, IV 344.
Fort Montgomery, IV 372.
Fort Necessity, II 99.
Fort Panmure, III 129, 132, 133, 147, 148, 149, 368, 391, 398.
Fort Petites Coquilles on Rigolets, IV 384, 385, 399, 404, 411.
Fort Pike, IV 384, 691.
Fort Pitt, III 109, 265, 267, 423.
Fort Plaquemine, III 382, IV 196.
Fort Rosalie, I 70, 329, 342.
Fort St. Charles, III 381, 382; IV 117.
Fort St. Claude, I 418.
Fort St. Francis, I 508.
Fort St. Ferdinand, III 381.
Fort St. Joseph, III 381.
Fort St. Louis, III 381, 383; IV 117. 194.
Fort St. Michael, IV 372, 373.
Fort St. Philip, IV 196, 221, 369, 383, 384, 411, 497, 500, 514, 691.
Fort Stoddard, Alabama, IV 182.
Fort Toulouse, I 281; II 94.
Fortier, Michel, III 589, 605; IV 335, 406, 541, 542, 568.
Fortifications of New Orleans, II 33, 87; III 328, 329, 330, 380, 382, 582, 583; IV 117, 195.
Foucault, II 90, 92, 122, 161, 166, 187, 192, 195, 196, 197, 199, 201, 203, 205, 222, 233, 236, 238, 243, 246, 275, 276, 278, 308, 309, 312, 313; III 625.
Foucher, Louis, III 588.
Foucher, Pierre, III 268; IV 346.
Fourmont, I 46.

INDEX

Fox, Indians, I 343.
Foxes, I 443.
France, I 24, 27, 30, 41, 50, 51, 54, 57, 61, 63, 69, 73, 74, 81, 82, 86, 90, 99, 102, 108, 110, 113, 117, 192, 193, 201, 204, 208, 231-233, 241, 243, 251, 274, 280-282, 285, 338, 355, 367, 372, 387, 391, 438, 454, 455, 457, 458, 492, 493, 496, 518, 524.
France, II 227, 229, 247, 251, 252, 254, 255, 257, 262, 263, 281, 349; III 448, 449, 451, 454, 458, 460, 461, 462-3, 464-5-7, 481, 484, 491, 498, 508, 512, 513, 517, 518, 519, 520, 522, 523, 524, 525, 528, 537, 540, 541, 542, 543, 553, 556, 557, 559, 560, 562, 567, 570, 574, 576, 583, 587, 598, 599, 600, 601, 604, 605, 617, 620, 621.
France, III 121, 157, 171, 193, 201, 238, 327, 329, 340, 366, 393, 408, 413, 421, 424, 426, 427, 428, 429, 430, 431, 434, 437, 439, 442, 443, 444, 446; IV 1, 4, 7, 8, 12, 214, 407.
Frankfort, Ky., III 293; IV 179.
Frankland, State, III 257, 258, 259, 260, 261, 263.
Franklin, Dr., III 246, 420.
Free Men of Colour, III 131; IV 227, 335, 355. 367.
Freeman, Colonel U. S. A., IV 117, 120, 129.
Fremont, C., IV 612.
French Spoliations, IV 98.
French I, 33-35, 40, 57, 58, 59, 60, 62, 77, 78, 83, 91, 95, 141, 142, 145, 148, 150, 154, 155, 158, 203, 204, 206, 207, 237, 244, 249, 258-261, 278, 279, 283, 313-315, 317, 331, 333, 335, 336-342, 348, 349, 352, 357, 358, 360-362, 364, 368, 376, 392, 394, 396, 400, 401, 404, 405, 407, 409-421, 423-436 439-452, 456, 459, 460-465, 468, 470, 473-481, 483, 485-487, 498, 499, 500, 505, 506, 508-510, 512, 513, 516, 517, 521, 523.
French II, 18, 20, 24-30, 38-44, 49-52, 54, 68, 72, 75, 78, 79-85, 99-103, 110, 113, 115-117, 122-125, 145, 163, 166-9, 171, 174, 175, 198, 203, 204, 207, 211, 225-227, 230, 241, 251, 260-262, 272, 275, 280, 295, 300, 302, 309, 319, 330, 333, 341, 373.
French, III 106, 108, 164, 186, 297, 314, 345, 366, 330, 333, 335, 353, 607, 613.
French IV. 1, 3, 6, 8, 9-11, 13, 15, 17, 25, 26-28, 216, 218, 219, 354, 581.
French Islands, III 314, 329.
French King, II 172; III 393.
French Language, in Judicial and Notarial Acts, III 7, 206.
Fromentin, E., IV 269, 274, 291, 294, 367, 390, 416.
Frontenac, Count, R. 1, 24, 25.
Frontigny I 486.
Fuentes, Count of, II 251, 264, 345; III 624.
Fulton, IV 268.

Gage, General, II 228.
Gaines, General, IV 182, 601.
Galatin, Albert, IV, 100, 119, 133.
Garcia, IV 29, 30.
Garcillasso, Historian, R. 1, 16.
Garderat, H., interpreter, II 343.
Galvez, Bernardo de, III 100, 105, 106, 115, 120, 129, 133, 135, 146, 149, 156, 164, 167, 216, 310, 314, 436, 439.
Galveston, III 116, 130, 170, 215.
Galvezton, Brig. III 140, 141.
Gardoqui, A., III 185, 193, 197, 198, 204, 206, 213, 217, 220, 241, 242, 243, 245, 246, 247, 253, 257, 258, 259, 261, 264, 265, 279, 291.
Garic, Jean Baptiste, II 127, 343, 383; III 31.
Garidel, A., III, 589.
Garland, Administrator General, III 605.
Gayarre, Carlos Anastasio, III 373, 306.
Gayarré, C. A., Sec. of State, IV 673.
Gayarre, Estevan, Comptroller, II 132, 152-5, 185, 190, 201, 203, 272, 279, 283, 289, 290, 313, 340; III 36, 42.
Gayarre, Juan Antonio, III 43, 122, 125, 132·136, 311.
Gayoso, de Lemos, Gov. of Natchez, III 203, 311, 329, 358, 359, 362, 366, 367, 368, 370, 386, 389, 390, 394, 399, 405, 501.
Gazette de France, II 269.
Genet, III 340, 341, 342.
Genoveaux, Hilaire de, III 49, 50, 54, 55, 72, 84, 86.
Gentilly, I 351; II 355; IV 384, 420, 422, 597.
George I, I 230.
George III, III 112.

Georgia, III 149, 150, 175, 181, 272, 282, 288, 289, 291, 298, 342, 412, 420, 482; IV 307, 640, 648, 692.
Gerel, Horatio, IV 131.
German Coast, The, I 354, 355; II 28, 42, 44, 131, 234, 278, 353; III 125, 126; IV 364.
Germans, I 241; II 236, 257; III 291.
Sisters Gertrude, Louise, Bergere, I 261.
Ghent, Treaty signed at, IV 518, 579.
Gholson, IV 278, 279, 280.
Gibbs, Major General Samuel, IV 416.
Gibraltar, III 234.
Gibson, III 100.
Gilbert, Walter, IV 302.
Girod, Mayor, N. O., IV 343, 348, 558.
Gironde, Ship, I 484.
Gobierno, Bando de Buen, III 178, 312.
Godin, I 46.
Goforth, Andrew, IV 272.
Gold, IV 263.
Gonzales, Col. Manuel, III 125, 133.
Graham, Secretary of Terry., IV 68, 122, 127, 120.
Grandchamp, II 87, 90.
Grandmaison, de Major, II 127, 183, 309, 311.
Grandpré, his share in the attack on the Chickasaws, I 485, 489; II 41, 53, 89, 183.
Grandpre, Carlos de, III 127, 132, 201, 203, 390, 483; IV 69, 86, 424.
Grandpré, Constance, III 311.
Grandpré, Louis, IV 230.
Grande Terre, IV 303, 305, 365, 367.
Grands Osages R., III 379.
Gravier, John, IV 188.
De la Graviere, I 486.
Great Britain acknowledges Independence of the U. S., III 157, 232, 235, 236, 237, 251, 282, 367, 527, 531, 542, 545.
Great Sun, I 426, 447, 448.
Great Temple, I 430.
Gregg, H. R., IV 39.
Grieux, Chevalier de, in the Expedition against Pensacola, I 249.
Grimaldi, Marquis of, II 91, 179, 229, 231, 264. 313, 347; III 43, 46, 624.
Griswold, Gaylord, III 493, 494, 558, 560, 564, 567, 571, 572.

Grondel, John Philip, I 475, 489, 491, 499; II 90.
Guadeloupe, IV 220.
Guatemala, III 45, 201, 312.
De Guiche, I 241, 259.
Guichard, Magloire, IV 272, 273, 543, 544, 545, 546, 547, 548, 549, 550, 551, 552, 553, 554, 561, 565.
Guibert, A., IV 612.
Guzman, Juan de, R. I., 15; F. 12.
Guienne, I 493.
Guillaume, II 45.
Guillemard, IV 424.
Guion, Captain, III 391.
Gulf of Mexico, III 115, 154, 307, 319, 394, 397, 411, 423, 439, 441, 442, 444, 457, 487. 489, 513; IV 384, 639.
Gurley, IV 68.
Habeas Corpus, IV 182, 392, 393.
Hall, Judge, IV 19, 121, 172, 282, 316, 392, 590, 591, 593, 594, 608, 626, 629.
Hallwill, I 494.
Hamilton, A., IV 80.
Hampton, Gen. Wade, IV 222, 226, 267.
Harper, IV 542.
Hartford Convention, IV 388, 390, 391.
d'Hauterive, I 475; II 90.
Havana, II 130, 162, 229, 230, 240, 248, 262, 296, 343, 345, 347; III 27, 28, 37, 57, 66, 70, 71, 90, 96, 122, 133, 137, 142, 143, 147, 201, 300, 318, 320, 328, 334, 385, 439, 440, 591; IV 76, 221, 330, 332, 337.
Havre, I 251; III 577.
Hawkesbury, Lord, III 499, 458, 464, 528.
Haynes, Col., IV 423, 433, 450.
Hebert, Gov., IV 676, 677, 679, 680.
Hechevarria, Don Santiago, Bishop of Cuba, III 56.
Helene, I 90.
Henderson, S., IV 273, 274, 446.
Henley, Capt., IV 424, 444, 449, 512.
Hermes, Sloop, IV 337, 350.
d'Herneuville, II 87.
Hero, IV 29.
Herrera, IV 150, 151.
Hickory Ground, III 324.
Hillhouse, James, Senator, III 549, 557.
Hinds, Colonel, IV 422, 423, 429, 442, 445, 503.

INDEX

Hiriart, Sebastian, III 589; IV 273, 274, 505.
Hispaniola, II 356; III 453.
Hoa. Don Manuel, III 374.
Holder, Col., III 272, 287.
Holland, III 426, 427, 471, 496.
Holland, H. R., IV 54.
Hollander, IV 593.
Holmes Governor, IV 239.
Deiston, III 112.
 ᶐ well and Seneca, III 282, 419.
Hop ins, Col. S. A., IV 120, 286.
Hol Houssaye, Comm. at New Orleans, II 89.
Hurard Capt. Charles, III 291.
Hudard, Col., IV 156.
Hubbard, Billy, IV 272, 666.
Huert, I 241, 252, 361.
Hury, IV 612.
Huger, H. R., IV 53, 54, 55.
Huet, IV 612.
Huger, Isaac, III 272, 274, 276.
Huling, III 397.
Hull, General, IV 603.
Humbert, General, IV 320, 493, 494, 498, 524.
Hurricane (1723), I 356, 514; (1746) II 35.
Hutchins, Thos., III 267.
d'Iberville, Pierre, Lemoyne, I 34-36, 40, 50-57, 58, 60, 69, 70, 71, 79-82, 87, 90-93, 367.

Iberville, La., II 227, 245, 355; III 32, 170, 215.
Ildephonso St., Treaty of, III 445.
Ile aux Poix, IV 421.
Ile Malheureuse, IV 398, 399.
Illinois (dist.), I 273, 394, 395, 424, 443, 450, 464, 503, 507, 523; II 98, 115, 239, 241, 355; III 23, 101, 112, 176, 223, 347, 383; IV 644, 648.
Illinois Indians Visit France, I 394-5.
—— River, III 196, 358.
India Co., I 369, 375, 391, 395, 455, 409, 502; II 20, 108, 357.
Indian Slaves, New Orleans, Emancipation of, III 334.
Indians, I 18, 19, 27, 39, 245, 247, 286, 352, 383; II 25, 44, 45, 73, 82, 94, 98, 101, 103, 104; III 20, 22, 23, 26, 126, 132, 133, 161, 162, 173, 175, 184, 186, 191, 192, 219, 243, 294, 300, 315, 316, 331, 332, 335, 338, 345, 362, 408. 425, 461, 550; IV 79, 89, 201, 307, 337, 350, 352.
Indigo, III 346.

Innis, Harry, III 209, 224, 226, 24, 278, 279, 346, 358, 360.
Inquisition, Holy, III 269, 270.
Inundations, II 20, 111, 306; III 22, IV 292.
Insurrection against Spaniards, I 187, 211, 213, 228; arrest of leader 304; trial of, 315.
Insurrection of negroes, IV 267.
Iphigenia, Brig, III 384.
Irazabal, Jose Cabro de, III 138, 139 141.
Irish, III 178, 181, 291.
Jackson, Andrew, General and President, IV 182, 307, 332, 336, 33; 341, 343, 352, 356, 364, 365, 36 372, 384, 388, 389, 393, 398, 40 409, 411, 416, 417, 422, 425, 42 433, 439, 490, 492, 511, 512, 58 586, 605, 609, 610, 615, 616, 62, 625, 626, 628, 653.
Jackson, Mr., in the Senate, III 48; 488, 492; IV 53, 54.
Jacobinism in Louisiana, III 327.
Jallot, I 167, 168, 177, 178.
Jamaica, I 466; III 171, 236, 309, 31, 315; IV 220.
Jeannot, negro, II 341, 342.
Jefferson, Thos., President, III 476 IV 11, 56, 57, 221, 297, 650.
Jennings, III 255.
Jesuits, I 357, 377, 380, 417, 521; I 63, 79, 81, 90; III 68.
Jews, Expelled, I 362.
Johns, III 605.
Johnson, Henry, IV supplementa chapter, 633, 646, 653.
Johnson, Isaac, IV 670, 672, 676.
Johnson, H. R., IV 277.
Johnston, G., Gov. West Florida, I 94.
Joliet, I 21, 22, 23.
Jones, Evan, First U. S. Consul, N O., III 397; IV 17, 19, 68, 142.
Jones, Thomas Catesby, IV 398, 39 400.
Jousset, Claude, the first Creole bor in the Colony, I 458, 459.
Judicial Proceedings, III 583; IV 20
Judice, Capt., II 236.
Judiciary, III 579; IV 3, 190, 31; 321.
Juez, de Residencia, III 169, 404.
Jumonville, de Villiers, II 99.
Jumonville's Plantation, IV 434, 44. 451.

Jussieu, I 46.
de Juzan, I 475.
Juzan, Capt., IV 405, 427.
Karbonary, II 295.

Karrer, Regiment de, I 489.
Kaskaskia, I 485; III 112, 135, 243, 382.
Keane, General, IV 416, 421, 423, 425, 432, 434, 469, 516, 517.
Kely, Juan, II 343.
Kemper, Col. Reuben, III 607; IV 19.
Kenner, IV 19, 219.
Kentucky, III 181, 193, 194, 197, 199, 200, 201, 206, 212, 214, 218, 224, 226, 228, 229, 238, 240, 244, 247, 248, 254, 258, 261, 262, 265, 267, 275, 279, 283, 286, 287, 296, 339, 341, 343, 345, 358, 359, 365, 396, 403, 413, 415, 423, 429, 473, 482, 618; IV 167, 338, 339, 376, 378, 405, 440, 446, 461, 465, 468, 472, 481, 483, 486, 487, 490, 502, 503, 506, 582, 610, 640.
Kerlerec, I 491, 494,; II 65, 68, 72, 73, 78, 82, 80, 95, 107, 108, 165, 232, 238.
Kernion, Huchet de, II 127, 192, 203, 205, 375.
Kerr, Louis, IV 29, 174, 433.
King, George, III 617.
King, Rufus, United States Minister at London, III 448, 449, 450, 451, 452, 458, 463, 464, 466, 500.
Kingsbury, St. Col., IV 174.
Kirby, IV 19.
Know Nothing Party, IV 678, 679.
Knox, III 420.
Kolly, I 283, 499.

Labarre, I 499; II 192.
Labatut, General, III 589, 605; IV 410, 568, 569.
Labranche, Alexander, IV 286.
La Bertonniere, IV 420.
La Condamine, I 46.
Lacoste, Major, IV 335, 404, 406, 417, 423, 429, 430, 441, 502, 505, 532, 535.
Lafayette Gen., Visit to N. O., IV 170, 654.
Lafitte, John, IV 357, 358, 359, 360, 361, 363, 367.
Lafitte, John and Pierre, IV 302, 304, 312, 314, 411, 504, 566, 582.
Lafitte, Pierre, IV 363.
Lafon, B., Map by, IV 385, 582.

Lafourche, dist., II 355; III 170, 215, 436; IV 228, 229, 298 367.
Lafreniere, I 236, 237, 455; II 91, 10 127, 157, 190, 192, 204, 206, 20; 232, 234, 235, 236, 237, 238, 24 278, 282, 291, 292, 303, 320, 321, 32 328, 337, 338, 341, 344, 348, 350, III 31, 109, 119, 149.
de Laire, I 242.
Lake Borgne, I 49; II 232; III 4 48; IV 384, 398, 400, 417, 442, 4 5, 500, 502.
Lake Erie, III 236.   51,
Lake Maurepas, III 130; IV 2 280.
Lake Pontchartrain, I 49, 59, 373, 381; III 47, 130, 352; IV 280, 384, 401, 405, 409, 410.
Lalande d'Apremont, I 487; II 205.
La Loire des Ursins, I 414.
Lamazeliere, Capt., II 309, 311.
Lambert, General, IV 416, 463, 474, 496, 498, 499, 512, 513, 517, 518, 519, 520, 521, 522, 524, 592, 625.
Land, Grants of, I 391; III 32, 387, 398, 456; IV 71.
Land Titles, II 101.
Lands, Power of Granting and where Vested, III 101.
Landais, III 608.
Landry, Joseph, IV 145, 286.
Langlois, I 417.
La Lanterne Magique, IV 209.
Lanusse, Paul, IV 165.
De Lapeyriere, II 211.
La Place, II 192.
De Lamarnage, Marquis de, I 173.
De Laronde, IV 273, 417, 423, 426, 428, 430, 433, 441, 445.
La Salle, Robert Cavalier de, I 23, 24, 25, 26, 27, 28, 30, 36, 39, 40, 61, 258, 285.
de Lassus, Charles Dehault, III 406.
de Lassus de St. Vrain, Jacques Ceran, III 353.
Lassus, Engineer sent to survey Louisiana, I 364, 424.
La Sonora, Marquis de, III 184, 186.
Last Isand, IV 365.
Latour, Major L. Lacarriere, IV 305, 350, 380, 385, 387, 401, 405, 415, 416, 433, 471, 476, 485, 505, 514, 582.
——— Historical Memoir, IV 470, 571.
Lauderdale, Col., IV 433.

INDEX　　　　　　　　　　　　　　　xiii

Laussat, Colonial Prefect, III 580, 582-588, 592, 594, 605, 608-616, 620; IV 7, 9, 12, 15.
Lavillebeuvre, II 242.
Law, John, I 191, 193, 210, 231, 232, 262, 279, 454.
Lawrence, Major, IV 349, 350, 351, 573.
De Laye, I 435.
Lead Mines, II 24.
Lebas (Controller), I 127.
Lebeau, I 415.
Le Blanc, Sec. of State, I 240.
Leblanc, M. de, II 380.
Leblanc de Villeneuve, Tragedy by, II 65.
Le Blond, I 240.
Le Breton, II 239.
Leclerc, III 512.
Lefebvre, III 589.
Legislative Council, IV 16, 19, 36, 66, 121, 134.
Legislature, IV 113, 139, 145, 211, 308, 375, 392-398, 448, 539-556.
Leib, H. R., IV 39.
Lemonnier, I 46.
Lemonnier, IV 602.
Lenormant, King's Commissary, II 29.
Le Page du Pratz, I 313, 331, 425, 427, 437.
Lepers' Bluff, located between St. John and New Orleans, I 381.
Lepers' Land, La terre des Lepreux, III 167, 168.
Leprosy, III 167.
Léry, II 234, 235.
Lesassier, II 127, 211.
Lespinasse, Abbé, IV 209.
Le Sueur, commands the Choctaws against the Natchez, I 424, 429, 463, 464.
Lettres de Cachet, II 55.
Levees, I 382, 469.
Levieux, I 487.
Levin, 46.
Lewis, Micajah J., IV 104, 105, 593.
Lewisburg, I 59.
Lexing n, Ky., III 223, 276, 342, 344.
de Lima, Jaime Masones, II 249, 250, 253.
Linares, Duke of, I 175, 238.
Lislet, IV 195, 297.
Little Meadows, III 406.
Little Sun, I 447, 448.

Livaudais, his service as pilot; in employ of the India Company, I 501, 502.
Livaudais, Harbor Master, II 361.
Livaudais, E. A., IV 673.
Livaudais, J., III 589, 605.
Liverpool, Lord, IV 529.
Livingston, Robert R., Minister to France, III 450, 452; III 459, 460, 461, 463, 465, 466, 467-8, 469, 470, 474, 475, 495, 498, 501, 503, 521, 523, 524, 525, 527, 528, 529, 531, 536; IV 17.
Livingston, Edward, IV 103, 171, 185, 186, 187, 188, 192, 268, 297, 298, 345, 346, 406, 516, 599, 600, 601.
Lockyer, Capt., IV 356, 357, 358, 359, 361, 399.
Loftus, Mapor, II 94, 101, 103.
Loftus Heights, III 181, 392.
London, III 184, 448, 458, 500, 507, 523, 527, 529, 536, 545.
De Longueil, Governor of Montreal, I 368.
de La Longueville, I 247.
(Angullo Ramon), Lopez Z. Intendent, III 407, 409, 454.
Lopez, IV 676.
Larient, I 395, 495.
Loubois, I 423, 424, 427, 434, 435, 455, 516, 517; II 27.
Louailler, IV 394, 397, 398, 413, 461, 545, 586, 589, 590, 591, 594, 601, 602-5, 608, 600, 623.
Loubois, Chevalier de, I 440.
Louette, I 415.
Louis, Jean, I 499.
Louis IX, I 50.
Louis XIII, III 389.
Louis XIV, I 42, 199.
Louis XV, I 45, 47; II 112; III 237.
Louis XVI, III 327.
Louise, Sister, I 261.
Louisiana Bank, IV 15.
Louisiana, District, IV 4.
Louisiana, Gazette, IV 368.
Louisiana, Regiment of, III 30.
Louisiana, Sloop, IV 422, 444, 446, 448, 449, 454, 457.
Louisville, III 235, 238, 423.
Loyola, M. de, II 131, 151, 152, 185, 190, 201, 272, 279, 283, 289, 290, 340; 387.
Loyola, Don Jean Joseph de, III 36, 43, 629.

Lucas, Rep., IV 39, 44.
De Lusser, I 445, 474.
Lyceum, Peoples' Lectures Delivered at, R., I 1.
Lyman, General, III 147.
Lyon, Rep., IV 43.
Lyons, III 453.

Macarty, Col., IV 157, 346.
McDowell, Samuel, III 225. 278.
McGee, David, IV 391.
McGillivray, Alexander, III 157, 158, 160, 175, 213, 214, 300, 316, 320, 325, 421.
McGillivray, Lachlan, III 321.
McIntosh, III 149.
McKlelland, Lieut., IV 426.
McWilliams, Capt., IV 356, 357, 361.
Macarty, III 311.
Macarty L. B., IV 68, 189, 190, 282.
Macé, I 411.
Machinet, I 282, 284.
Macon, H., Rep., IV 46.
Madison, James, President, III 450, 452, 454, 458, 460, 463, 465-8, 470, 472, 473, 474, 494, 495, 496, 497, 535, 536, 543, 545; IV 24, 25, 26, 67, 81, 191, 221, 237, 287-9.
Madrid, II 343; III 108, 110, 121, 124, 134, 156, 158, 166, 171, 195, 217, 234, 249, 264, 270-300, 308, 315, 330, 392, 407, 443, 450, 472, 529, 538, 584, 593.
Madrid Gazette, III 123, 126, 131.
Madrid Treaty of, 1795, 350-7, 367, 396, 398.
Magazine Barracks; Arrival of Militia, IV 322; insubordination of militia, IV 323.
Magruder, A. B., IV 272, 274, 282, 291.
Maison Rouge, Marquis de, III 353.
Malaga, III 44, 164.
Malcolm, Admiral, IV 416, 431, 520, 538.
Malcolm, Colonel, IV 536.
Manchac, II 115, 123, 124, 239, 305; III 45, 101, 113, 170, 215, 223; IV 18.
Mandeville, I 59.
Manilla, III 319.
Manon, Lescaut, and the story of Chevalier des Grieux, I 249, 252.
Mansolia, Iroquois Chief, I 26.
Maquille, W. C., IV 273, 274.
Marais des Liards. dist., III 406.
Maramec, dist., III 406.

Barbe Marbois, III 238, 457, 509, 505, 507, 511, 514, 570, 571, 573, 523, 524, 528, 530, 534, 581.
Marchand, Capt., I 281.
Marel de la Tour, II 87.
Marey, Sec. of War, IV 670.
Margot River, I 488, 506, 513.
Marigny de Mandeville, I 127, 279, 364.
Marigny de Mandeville, Philippe, II 10 101.
Marigny, Bernard, IV 273, 543, 544, 545, 565.
Marquette, Father, journey towards the Gulf, return to Quebec, I 21, 22, 23.
Marquis, Pierre, II 127, 187, 189, 200, 236, 239, 284, 291, 292, 337, 338, 342, 350.
Marseilles, I 456; III 443.
Marshall, Colonel, III 225, 228, 229, 239, 254, 256, 278.
Martial Law, IV 403, 605-8, 621.
Martin, F. N., IV 292, 297, 316, 390, 397, 414, 435, 437, 590, 597.
Martin's History of Louisiana, III 109, 112, 114, 143, 145, 148, 153, 171, 178, 193, 312, 326, 327, 350, 404, 577, 586, 618, 619, 620; IV 3, 200, 589, 592, 602, 617, 621, 626.
Martin, George, III 605.
Martinique, I 498, 519; III 222; IV 7.
Maryland, III 315.
Masan, Balthasar, II 127, 187, 188, 303, 337, 338, 343.
Masanfils, II 232, 233.
Masderall, Dr., M. D., III 375.
Massachusetts, IV 40, 44, 50, 666.
Massacre Island, afterward called Dauphine, I 81.
Massange, II 127.
Matamoras, IV 671.
Mather, IV 21.
Mather, James, III 162, 184, 185.
Mathews, Judge of Supreme Court, IV, 68, 282.
Maupertuis, I 46.
Maurepas, Count Jean Frederick Phelyppeaux, I 40, 43, 44, 45, 47, 48, 49; II 47.
Mayeux, I 415.
Mayronne, Francois, III 335.
St. Masent, II 127, 183, 188, 189, 235, 236.
Mazureau, IV 597, 598.

Meade, Cowles, Gov. Mississippi Terry., IV 150, 152.
Méchin, I 243.
Medea, Ship, II 90.
Memorial of the Planters of Louisiana burned, II 301, 308, 343.
Memphis, I 18, 506.
Mendez, III 349.
Mendoza, Don Francis de R., I 21.
Mercier "l' an 2004," III 117.
Mesplais, Mesplet, I 426.
de Meuse, I 241, 354.
Mexico, I 20, 24, 29, 166, 172, 174, 176, 182; II 254, 255, 256, 257, 259, 261, 262; III 107, 137, 164, 166, 183, 189, 308, 319, 372, 379, 393, 394, 431, 432, 440, 533; IV 56, 76, 80, 241, 656, 670, 672.
Mezieres, Mme. de, I 241, 354.
de Mezieres, III 19, 20, 21.
Michilimakinac, III 176.
Mifflin, Gov., III 246.
Milhet, Jean, II 128, 129, 180, 187, 192, 211, 291, 292, 303, 337, 339.
Milhet, Joseph, II 121, 187, 192, 337, 338, 342.
Military Barracks, IV 119.
Military, I 260, 364, 470; forces increased 1748; II 35, 52; stations 56; force decreased 86; French soldiers refuse to serve Spain, 161; IV 123.
Military resources of New Orleans, III 341-2.
Miitia, III 131, 613; IV 91, 196, 202, 321-326, 377, 406, 483.
Miller, H. R., IV 247.
Milton, Major, IV 267.
Mines, Iron, I 26.
Minor, Capt., III 370, 390, 391.
Miro, Estevan, III 125, 133, 142, 145, 157, 160, 167, 168,, 170, 172, 178, 180, 184, 185, 191, 201, 204, 208, 211, 219, 221, 223, 247, 250, 256, 259, 267, 270, 271, 274, 276, 282, 284, 287, 293, 294, 299, 300, 305, 308, 310, 314, 318, 334, 342, 346, 395.
Miro dist., III 261, 262.
Mississippi Company, I 202, 205, 206, 230, 251, 262.
Mississippi Dragoons, IV 422, 429, 441, 503.
Mississippi River, I 17, 22-23, 26, 36-39, 60, 69-72, 234, 235, 297, 357-360, 378, 381-385, 394, 416, 424, 460, 469, 471, 501-523; II 20, 30, 31, 77, 104, 123, 250, 255, 263, 356; III 21, 24, 32, 35, 45, 107-113, 117, 123, 130-135, 147-154, 157, 159, 167, 171, 174, 176, 181-185, 193-196, 203, 211, 213, 218, 219, 228-233, 236, 242-244, 248, 254, 255, 258, 272, 279, 280, 294, 295, 307, 332, 340-344, 348, 361-364, 367, 389, 402, 408, 411, 419, 422, 436, 439, 449, 451, 457, 459, 460, 463, 464, 470, 476, 485, 489, 494, 497, 567, 512, 514, 519, 525, 527, 533, 548, 550, 554, 569, 576, 591, 603; IV 18, 77-88, 98, 127, 184, 383, 416, 424, 449, 455, 597, 640, 663, 686, 692.
Mississippi Territory, III 392, 482; IV 10, 46, 47, 52, 88, 152, 180, 182, 197, 386, 608, 610, 641.
Missouri, II 23, III 23, 525. 531; IV 357, 638, 644.
Missouri, census 1745, II 28.
Mitchigamias, I 485.
Mobile, I 236, 237, 255, 273, 369, 384, 424, 450, 457, 463, 466, 471, 490, 514; II 26, 28, 30, 42, 96, 124, 228; III 48, 109, 111, 137, 160, 162, 170, 174, 185, 215, 331, 332, 412, 413, 422, 440, 529, 530; IV 69, 76, 87, 89, 137, 245, 298, 332, 337, 348, 352, 359, 373, 378, 405, 409.
Mobilians, R., I 16, 60; F. 9.
Moelobites, I 60.
Monbazon, Prince of, Governor of St. Domingo, II 369.
Monette's History of Mississippi Valley, III 351, 357, 567, 395, 606.
Monongahela, III 417.
Monroe, President, II 476, 496, 497, 503, 504; III 505, 506, 509, 510, 521, 523, 527, 528, 530, 531; IV 78, 84, 94, 368, 388, 391, 535, 609, 644.
Montbrun, I 475.
Montcherval, I 485, 488, 489.
Montereau, I 496.
Montfort, I 490.
Montigny, Galon de, I 63.
Montigny, Father, R., I 61, 62, 63.
Montpensier, Duke of, visits New Orleans in 1798, III 389.
Montreal, I 507.
Montreuil's Plantation, IV 422.
Moore, T. O., Gov. Louisiana, IV 688.
Moorhouse, III 456.
Morales, Don Juan Venturo, intendant, III 373, 375, 398, 406, 454,

INDEX

457, 472, 576, 577, 585, 632, 649; IV 69, 70, 73, 131.
Moreau, General, IV 191.
Moreau, I 233.
Morel, IV 590.
Morgan, David, Brig. Gen., IV 433, 434, 443, 463, 466, 470, 478, 479, 480, 481, 482, 483, 484, 485, 486, 487, 488, 490, 492, 494, 495, 504, 506, 550.
Morgan, D. B., IV 272, 273.
Morgan, B., III 607; IV 19, 29, 346.
Morgan, Charles, IV 201.
Morgan, Col. George, III 109, 110, 197, 220, 221, 235, 243, 244, 245, 264, 265, 266, 268.
Morier, IV 241.
Moro, Fort (Havana), II 343.
Mouchard of La Rochelle, I 233.
Moultrie, Alexander, III 272, 274, 276, 281.
de Moustier, C., III 238.
Mouton, Alexander, IV 663, 669, 690.
Muniain, Juan Gregorio, II 249, 262.
Municipal Council, III 605.
Murray, III 358, 359, 360.
Muter, Colonel, III 223, 228, 229, 240, 254, 256.
Muzquiz, Miguel de, II 249, 250, 260.
de Muys, I 241.

Nacogdoches, IV 90, 203.
Nante, III 433.
Napoleon, IV 330.
Natchez (town), I 70, 157, 241, 253, 454, 523; II 94, 227, 239, 245; III 45, 114, 122, 127, 129, 132, 133, 135, 147, 148, 170, 177, 178, 181, 201, 208, 215, 243, 265, 294, 298, 329, 331, 332, 366, 367, 369, 390, 391, 396-8, 402, 412, 413, 416, 419, 437, 471, 569, 572; IV 164, 179.
Natchez Indians, I 12, 71, 139, 142, 147, 148, 155, 158, 259, 273, 283, 286, 349, 361, 369, 374, 397, 398, 399, 409, 410, 411, 416, 420, 425, 427, 428, 429, 435, 437, 439, 442, 445, 447, 448, 450, 516, 519, 522.
Natchez (war song), I 151, 154.
Natchitoches, I 28, 70, 166, 167, 236, 241, 257, 273, 418, 459, 471, 508; II 133, 355; III 19, 21, 32, 101, 170, 215, 373, 408, 418, 431, 434, 437; IV 15, 79, 80, 83, 87, 90, 138, 150, 152, 154, 166, 203, 295, 299, 301; III 19, 21, 408, 418, 431, 434, 437;

IV 15, 79, 80, 83, 87, 96, 138, 150, 152, 154, 203, 295, 299, 301.
Navailles, Treasurer, III 605.
Navarre, I 415, 425.
Navarro, Martin, Treasurer, II 132, 155, 185, 190, 201, 203, 272, 279, 283, 289, 290; III 125, 151, 152, 162, 176, 177, 182, 185, 186, 190, 192, 206, 208, 212, 216, 224, 228, 230, 241, 250.
Negroes, I 273, 277, 278, 357, 415, 439, 446; IV 203, 208, 266, 267, 335, 336, 517, 531.
Nelson, IV 277, 278.
Nemours, I 495.
Nericourt, I 90.
New Bourbon, dist., III 406.
New Hampshire, IV 642.
New Iberia, III 120, 170, 215.
New Jersey, III 220, 243, 267, 296.
New Madrid, III 198, 244, 266, 267, 268, 279, 281, 354, 406, 418, 426.
New Mexico, I 166, 523; II 256, 257, 260, 262, 263; III 122, 190, 408.
New Orleans, I 49, 60; foundation 234, 235, 284; becomes seat of Gov., 353, 354, 359, 361, 369, 377, 380, 381, 395, 396, 398, 415, 420, 435, 443, 448, 464, 469, 470, 490; II 18, 27, 28, 31, 32, 33, 35, 38, 40, 42, 44, 46, 48, 64, 75, 79, 80, 86, 87, 89, 92, 94, 95, 101, 103, 106, 110, 114, 115, 121, 128, 131, 168, 169, 189, 231, 242, 256, 259, 262, 263, 277, 281, 284, 289, 295, 327, 331, 332, 355, 356, 373, 377; III 1, 3, 7, 12, 22, 28, 29, 34, 36, 37, 44, 45, 46, 47, 49, 57, 99, 100, 101, 103, 106, 109, 110, 113, 114, 116, 122, 123, 124, 125, 126, 130, 133, 134, 136, 140, 153, 163, 164, 170, 174, 176, 181, 191, 193, 194, 195, 196, 198, 203, 217, 218, 225, 234, 246, 247, 249, 251, 256, 260, 262, 264, 267, 269, 271, 274, 275, 277, 278, 281, 283, 288, 292, 297, 306, 309, 310, 314, 317, 321, 325, 326, 327, 328, 329, 330, 331, 332, 334, 336, 342, 347, 352, 354, 355, 357, 359, 366, 373, 374, 375, 380, 381, 383, 389, 396-399, 402, 405, 409, 415-417, 431, 439, 443, 458, 463, 467-8, 471, 472, 476, 478, 480, 481, 485, 486, 489, 493, 495, 496, 497, 498, 499, 500, 501, 502, 506-507, 513, 514, 519, 527, 538, 546, 547, 549, 550, 570, 576, 580, 581, 583, 585, 589, 596, 598, 599.

INDEX   xvii

New Orleans—(*Continued*)—
606, 616, 622, 623, 624.; IV 3, 8, 15, 19, 23, 24, 36, 68, 69, 80, 81, 82, 85, 86, 88, 90, 110, 112, 119, 120, 128, 129, 133, 137, 146, 149, 150, 154, 157, 159, 160, 161, 162, 165, 174, 175, 184, 185, 194, 197, 204, 205, 206, 208, 209, 215, 219, 220, 221, 222, 227, 228, 253, 258, 267, 282, 291, 297, 298, 302, 303, 305, 320, 324, 327, 330, 331, 335, 345, 359, 375, 378, 382, 383, 386, 388, 390, 403, 406, 410, 413, 414, 415, 417, 420, 421, 435, 438, 461, 462, 463, 464, 477, 488, 498, 502, 504, 511, 514, 535-539, 542, 558-560, 567, 572, 573, 580, 586, 587, 597, 599, 622, 626 628, 644, 655, 671, 677.
N. O. Fort Jackson & Gt. Northern R. R., IV 679.
New Orleans, District Limits, I 273; II 38, 56.
New Orleans, Navy Yard, IV 448.
N. O. Opelousas & Gt. Western R. R., IV 680.
New Providence, III 316, 317.
New Spain, I 176; III 183, 189, 199, 298, 401, 447, 458.
New York, III 100, 207, 242, 245, 261, 278, 300, 316, 402; IV 14, 306.
Newman, Captain, IV 404.
Newman, George, III 607.
Newspaper, first regular newspaper appeared in 1794, called "Le Moniteur de la Louisiane," III 336.
Nicaragua, IV 56.
Nicholas, George, III 278, 358, 359, 360.
Nicholls, Colonel, IV 337, 338, 339, 340, 353, 357.
Nicholson, III 571.
de Noailles d'Aime, I 503, 506, 508, 513, 514.
Nogales (Walnut Hills), III 392.
Nolan, Philip, III 447.
Nootka Sound, III 306.
North Carolina, III 112, 257, 258, 263; IV 326, 643.
de Noyan, Chevalier, I 368, 369, 471, 475, 483, 505, 507; II 42, 187. 205, 237, 337, 338, 341.
Nunez, Vincente Jose, III 203.
Nuno, Tobar, I 15.
Nyon de Villiers, Comm. of Illinois, II 98, 109, 114.
Oath opposed to Emigrants, III 202.

Ocona, Juan, Alcalde, IV 19.
Odoardo, Cecilio, III 36, 37, 311.
O'Fallon, James, III 281, 288, 291, 292.
Officials of Louisiana, III 578.
Ogden, IV 170, 171, 346.
Ohio, III 112, 181, 220, 399, 409, 411, 424, 482, 618; IV 644, 648, 649.
Ohio, R., III 196, 197, 219, 220, 234, 236, 237, 238, 244, 247, 264, 265, 286, 295, 296, 297, 307, 308, 340, 341, 467; IV 167.
Okony, R., III 421.
Olcott, Simeon, Senator, III 549.
Olivier, Godefroy, IV 286.
O'Neil, Arthur, III 157, 160.
Opelousas, III 32, 126, 132, 170, 180, 215, 408, 418, 434, 436; IV 12, 134, 150, 153, 197, 298, 586.
Order of Immaculate Conception, II 141.
O'Reilly, Don Alexandro, II 136, 191, 265, 266, 284, 285, 291, 293, 295, 308, 311, 313, 324, 332, 336, 339, 350, 356; III 1, 3, 8, 18, 19, 23, 26, 41; IV 29, 41, 43, 44, 49, 53, 63, 68, 96, 99, 118, 119, 328, 428, 430, 432, 593, 594, 622, 625, 629.
d'Orgenoy, Lebreton, IV 19, 268, 272, 273, 297.
Orleans, Duke of, III 389, 390.
Orleans, Isle of, III 357.
Orleans, Territory, IV 4, 6, 16, 57, 6, 68, 72, 140. 168, 195, 224, 226, 238, 243, 245, 247, 248, 262, 264, 271, 326.
Orleans, Volunteers, IV 129, 149.
Orne, Jose, III 314.
Oroo, Ship, I 501.
Ortega, Jose, III 314.
Osages, III 176; IV 229.
d'Ossun, Marquis, III 119.
Ouachita, dist., II 355; III 170, 190, 215, 353, 354, 408, 456.
Ouachita, R., I 445.
Ouachitas, Indians, I 435, 459.
Oumas, declare in favor of Bienville, I 369, 409.
Oumas, concession, I 241.
Overton, Major, IV 497.
Pacific Ocean, III 532.
Packenham, Sir E., IV 416, 425, 432, 442, 468, 472, 473, 478, 537, 538.
Panama, Isthmus, III 519.
Panton, William, III 184, 185, ¬16, 317, 318, 319, 321.

Panuco, R. I 20.
Paper currency in Louisiana in 1723, I 467; II 21, 36, 51, 53, 105, 159.
Paris, Treaty of, II 92.
Paris, III 158, 448, 449, 451, 458, 460, 474, 481, 518, 529, 534, 546, 548, 560, 591.
Paris, Duvernay, I 241, 354.
Paris, Jacinto (commissary of war), III 125, 133.
Parisian, The, I 430, 438.
La Parisienne, French Privateer, III 373.
Parker, George, IV 400.
Parma, Duke of, IV 445, 446, 448, 452, 468, 470, 559.
Pascagoula Bay, I 60.
Pascagoula (parish), IV 243.
Pascagoula River, III 48.
Pascagoulas, I 241, 261, 515; II 28.
Pascagoula, mysterious music at I 383.
Pass Christianne, IV 349, 399, 401.
Pauger, Engineer, I 357, 364, 371.
Paulin, III 246.
Paulus, Peter, III 246, 257, 252.
Peace Treaty at Amiens between Spain, France and Great Britain, III 462.
Pearl River, IV 280, 421.
Peire, Major, IV 372, 373, 422, 433.
Pelican, Iberville's ship, R. I 32, 35.
Penalvert, y Cardenas, Louis de, III 334, 376, 378, 379, 407.
Penitentiary, State, IV 671.
Pennsylvania, Western and Whisky Insurrection, III 345.
Pensacola, I 243, 244, 247, 249, 255, 360, 457, 500; II 228, 232, 234, 263, 280; III 109, 111, 118, 130, 136, 137, 143, 145, 149,, 154, 162, 174, 175, 184, 213, 401, 412, 413, 421, 440, 441; IV 19, 69, 72, 76, 77, 87, 190, 221, 226, 241, 330, 332, 337, 338, 359, 372, 373, 384, 407.
Percy, Sir W. H., Capt. R. N., IV 350, 352, 353, 357, 358.
Perdido, River, I 247; III 530, 531, 539; IV 71, 239.
Perier, Governor, I 369, 372, 382, 383, 390, 392, 396, 397, 414, 423, 424, 434, 437. 440, 443, 448, 453, 456, 524; III 353.
Perret, Noel, III 588.
Perry, I 571.
Peru, III 394.

Petit, IV 17, 187, 284.
Petit, Joseph, II 303, 323, 337, 338, 343.
Petit Ougas, census 1745, II 28.
Petrony, Sheriff, IV 201.
Peytavin, Antoine, III 223.
Philadelphia, III 100, 102, 103, 109, 185, 204, 210, 222, 242, 246, 253, 315, 325, 326, 337, 359, 375, 384, 385, 423; IV 6. 306.
Philippe, Ship of war, I 243, 245.
Philippon's Plantation, IV 451.
Piatt, Col., IV 426, 433.
Pichon, III 543, 544.
Pickering, M., III 549, 551, 552, 557.
Pickett's History of Alabama, III 317, 319, 323.
Pierce, Franklin, Pres. U. S., IV 676.
Piernas Plantation, IV 417, 449, 450.
Piernas Canal, IV 459, 460, 463, 480.
Piernas, Don Pedro, Comm. of Spanish troops at Natchez, II 131, 241, 242, 243, 244; III 125, 133, 167, 311.
Pikle, III 130.
Pilié, L., IV 612.
Pin, II 127.
Pinckney, C. C., III 450, 451, 530, 541; IV 93, 326.
Pintado, Don Vincente, IV 19.
Piou of Nantes, I 233.
Piorias, III 382.
Piot de Launay, II 127, 192, 202, 375.
Pitman, Capt., III 168.
Pitot, IV 17, 297.
Pittsburg, III 100.
Place d' Armes, III 35.
Placentia, III 470.
Planters' Bank, IV 268.
Plaquemine Turn, II 33; III 417, 423.
Plaquemines, III 171, 184; IV 82, 196, 291, 524.
Plauché, E., III 589.
Plauché, Major, IV 409, 422, 427, 428, 433.
Poindexter, Mr., IV 251, 260, 262, 277.
Plumer, William, Senator, III 549.
Poeyfarré, III 20.
" Pointe aux herbes," I 351.
Pointe Coupee, I 241, 354, 423, 437, 469, 489, 516; II 101, 102, 131, 242, 355; III 29, 32, 101, 126, 127, 170, 215; IV 15, 110, 201, 205, 208, 210.

INDEX

Point Siguenza, III 139.
Police Regulations of Vaudreuil, II 361.
Pollock, Oliver, III 31, 100, 109, 113, 126, 222.
Pollock, IV 21.
Pompadour, Marquise de, I 47.
Pontchartrain, Count Louis Phelvpeaux, I 40, 41. 42, 49.
Pontalba, Commander at Pointe Coupee, II 59, 70.
Pontalba's (Memoir), III 410, 411, 445, 446.
Pontalba, Baroness, III 35.
Pope, Lieut., III 371.
Population, I 274, 365, 383, 454.
de Porneuf, III 311.
Port Louis, I 494.
del Portege, Don Juan Dorotheo, III 119.
Porter, Alexander, IV 272, 273.
Porter, Major, IV 129, 137.
Portillo, Felix, Capuchin Vicar, III 314.
Porto Rico, II 263; III 394.
Posey, Thomas, IV 282, 291.
Poupet, Pierre, II 127, 187, 337, 339, 343.
Power, Thomas, III 345, 358, 359, 365, 392, 395.
Poydras, Julien, III 133, 354; IV 19, 208, 210, 269, 271, 282, 286.
Pradel, Wm., II 188, 233, 234, 277.
Prairie du Chien, III 382.
Praslin, duc de, I 495; II 179, 202, 220, 225, 274; III 624.
Prat, of Superior Council, I 455.
Presidio del Norte, I 178, 180, 182, 236.
President's message 1803, III 548.
Prevost, Judge, IV 19, 68, 121.
Princeton, III 243.
Protest of Spain against Cession, III 543-545.
Protestants, III 276.
Prudhomme, Manuel, IV 273.
Public Property, IV 119.
Public Schools, Claiborne on, IV 204, 225.

Quebec, I 21, 22, 25, 204, 507; III 36, 49, 67, 69, 83, 102.
Quebec, Bishop of, II 80.
Quigual t anqui, Indian Chief, R. I 20; F. 18, 19.
Quincampoix, Rue, I 214.

Quincy, Josiah, IV 249, 250, 251, 262, 263.
Quito, III 385.

Raquet, I 455.
Randolph, John, III 493, 494, 571; IV 64, 66, 138.
Randolph, Thomas, III 561, 564, 570, 572.
Rapides, Parish, II 355; III 170, 215; IV 146, 150, 152.
Raynaud, Louis, IV 273.
Red River, I 18, 19, 40, 182, 444, 448; III 426; IV 83.
Red Shoe, Choctaw Chief, I 460, 462, 482, 503, 505, 520; II 25, 30, 41.
Redon, de Rassac, II 96.
Reggio, F. M., II 183; III 31.
Reggio, IV 424.
Regidores, III 4, 5.
Regnisse, I 481.
Reid, Aide de Camp, IV 433, 617.
Relf, Richard, IV 165, 345.
Religious Quarrels, II 69; IV 107.
Religion in Louisiana, I 357; III 58, 104.
Renault d'Hauterive, I 435.
Rendon, Francisco de, intendant, III 334, 371, 373.
Rennie, Col., IV 469, 470, 496.
Republic, Scheme of, II 281.
Revenue, III 180, 309.
del Rey, Felix, attorney general, II 320, 323, 324, 333, 337, 338, 342; III 8, 36.
Rey, IV 420.
Rhea, John, IV 231, 233, 248, 255, 279.
Rhode Island, III 242.
Ricard, Fryatin, I 420.
Rice, Price, I 557.
Richelieu, Duke of, I 493.
Richelieu, Cardinal, II 351.
Richmond, III 207.
Rieux, Vincent, III 130.
Rigolets, III 47; IV 348, 399, 496.
Rio Bravo, I 258; IV 111.
Rio Colorado, III 408.
Riots in New Orleans, IV 197.
Rivard, II 241.
Robertson, T. Bolling, Sec. of Terry., Gov., IV 228, 298, 637, 645.
Robertson, Col. James, III 262.

INDEX

Robertson's History of America, III 117.
Robertson, Colonel, II 97.
Robin, C. C., III 616.
Robinson, Dr. J. H., IV 320.
Robinson, Major Tully, IV 544.
Roche, II 183.
Roche, P., IV 612.
Rodriguez Canal, IV 422, 441, 445, 449, 463.
Rocheblave, II 90.
Rochefort, Renee de, I 379, 493.
de Rochemore, intendant commissary, I 492; II 83, 84; dismissed 85, 86, 87; departs 90, 95.
Rodney, III 570.
Rodriguez, de, clerk of Court, II 342, 343.
Rogers, Maurice, IV 219.
Roman, Gov. A. B., IV 19, 654, 655, 656, 658, 662.
de la Ronde, II 239.
Ronquillo, Juan, III 373, 384.
Ross, Senator, III 477, 479, 481, 488, 491, 503, 506.
Ross, Captain, IV 127, 131, 364, 422, 427, 433.
Rossard, Inspector of Police, I 381.
Rossart, Secy. of Council, I 455.
Rossard, his complaints of Leper's Bluff, 1727, I 381.
Rouffignac, IV 545.
Rousseau, II 44.
Rousseau, Captain, III 140, 141.
Rossin, Genesi, IV 273.
Rouvilliere, Honore Michel de, intendant commissary, II 58, 361; III 37.
Roux, II 75.
Royal Bank, I 201.
Rubi, Marquis of, II 231.
Rush, attorney general, IV 369.
Russia, Arbitration of, IV 520.

Sabine R., IV 76, 137, 150, 274, 299, 646.
St. Amand, his death, I 427.
St. Andrew, dist., III 406.
St. Auge, I 406.
St. Augustin, 228, 263; III 168, 289, 291.
St. Avid, III 589.
St. Bernard Bay, I 28, 258.
St. Bernard Parish, III 116; IV 398, 451, 524.
St. Catherine's Creek, I 429.
St. Charles Parish, I 354; II 355;
III 170, 215, 406; IV 398.
St. Clair, General, III 234, 235, 240.
St. Cloud, III 505, 506, 510, 521.
St. Cyr, III 534, 535.
St. Denis, Juchereau de, I 165, 182, 236, 239, 258, 277, 280, 418, 419.
St. Denis, Alcalde, III 31.
St. Domingo, I 438, 519; III 5, 108, 118, 309, 314, 344, 354, 433, 434, 437, 438, 440, 443, 475, 512, 515, 520, 580, 581, 594; IV 214, 220, 356, 365, 367, 406.
St. Fernando, dist., III 406.
St. Francis, III 57.
St. Francis River, III 243, 418.
St. Francisville, IV 241.
St. Geme, Capt., IV 582, 612.
St. Genevieve, III 23, 25, 170, 215, 223, 406.
St. Helena, IV 243, 284, 291, 298.
St. Ildefonso, Treaty of, III 445, 532, 534, 544, 545.
St. Jolo de Cuba, I 14.
St. James, III 170, 215.
St. Jean, IV 612.
St. John, I 354; III 170, 215; IV 260, 398.
St. John River, I 267.
St. Julien, III 506; IV 122.
St. Laurent, I 507.
St. Laurence R., III 176, 196.
St. Lette, II 127, 211, 274.
St. Louis, I 50, 56.
St. Louis, Cross of, I 263.
St. Louis (Post), III 23, 25, 170, 176, 215, 406; IV 81.
St. Malo, I 455.
St. Malo, I 241, 456, 502.
St. Marks, Flo., III 329.
St. Martin, Francois, IV 273, 274.
St. Martin, P., III 588.
St. Martin, P. B., IV 282, 286.
St. Mary's, IV 536.
St. Mary's R., III 157, 413.
St. Maxent, Gilbert Antoine de, III 98, 116, 127.
———, Daughters of, III 311.
St. Portais, II 183.
St. Reine, I 241, 354.
de St. Romes, IV 612.
Salary of Governors, II 158.
Salaries of Spanish Officers, III 6, 170.
Salamanca, III 178, 181.
St. Jago, IV 216, 219.
St. Rose, isl., III 139.

INDEX   xxi

St. Sebastian, IV 407.
St. Simon, Duc de, I 216.
Salcedo, Don Juan Manuel de, III 447 455, 576, 577, 591, 592, 599; IV 208.
de Sale, Lieutenant, II 233, 236.
Salins, I 496.
Salmon, Commissary, I 455, 458, 467, 468, 500, 514, 520, 521, 523; II 20.
Salverte de, I 440, 443, 456.
San Antonio, III 431; IV 89.
San Juan de Piedra, Albas Marquis, II 249, 254.
San Salvador, III 312.
Santa Cruzada, III 87.
Santa Fe, III 379, 380.
Sartines, I 494.
Saucier, I 508, 513.
Saunoy, I 283.
Sauve, III 605; IV 17, 58, 65, 67, 68, 109.
Sauve, Miss, IV 462.
Sauvolle, I 58, 59, 69, 73, 75, 77, 78, 79.
Savannah, III 149, 151, 401.
Savary (colored), made Captain, IV 406, 433.
Seahorse, Scho., IV 398, 399.
Sebastian, Benjamin, III 226, 243, 275, 279, 285, 286, 287, 346, 358, 359, 360.
Secession Convention, IV 690.
De Sedella, Father Antonio, III 269, 270, 271.
Senac, Father, burned alive by the Indians, I 487.
Serano, Don Manuel, assessor, III 315, 455, 456.
Serigny, I 243, 245, 246, 368.
Severne, I 489.
Sevier, Col. John, III 257, 258, 263.
Seville, III 44.
Shaumburgh, Col., IV 494, 495, 596, 597.
Shaw, Capt., U. S. N., IV 162, 166, 171.
Shelby, Gov. Kentucky, IV 345, 599.
Ship Island, I 37, 255, 278; II 79; IV 398.
Short, Payton, III 278.
Shreveport, IV 659.
de Sibeque, Titon, II 84.
Sibley, Dr., IV 79, 90, 203, 299, 301.
Sierra Leone, III 319.

Silk Worms in Louisiana in 1735, Ursuline Nuns teach the silk industry to orphans, I 469.
Silver River, I 445, 448.
Simon, a free black, I 480.
Skipwith, IV 563, 564, 565.
Slaves, I 242; III 302, 313, 325, 354, 355; IV 33, 229, 533.
Small Pox, I 457.
Smilie, III 570.
Smith, Henry, III 318.
Smith, Daniel, Brig. General, III 262, 263.
Smith, Robert, IV 233, 604.
Smugglers, I 466; II 147; IV 302, 369, 371.
Snipes, Major William, III 272, 274, 276.
Solis, III 349.
Someruelos, Marquis, Capt. General of Cuba, III 406, 593, 612.
Sophia, Brig, IV 350, 357, 358, 356.
Sopper, III 581.
Sorelle, Joseph, III 132.
Sorvidal, I 260.
Soto, Hernando de Soto, arrival in Florida, R., I 14; Expedition of, 15, 16; death of, 19, 21.
So. Carolina R., I 59.
South Carolina Company, III 272, 281, 287, 290, 291, 293, 294, 295, 296, 297, 298, 299, 300.
So. Carolina, III 420, 467, 482.
Soult, Marshal, IV 473, 474.
Stephen, colored, IV 131.
Spain, I 14, 22, 174, 238, 243, 244; II 88, 107, 110, 113, 126, 229, 240-243, 245, 247, 249, 254, 255, 260, 264, 269, 279, 282, 349; III 1, 15, 26, 27, 37, 43-46, 72, 81, 97, 100, 107-113, 116, 121, 131, 135, 136, 148, 151-164, 175, 181, 192-204, 207, 211-221, 224, 225, 229-241, 257-261, 279-292, 306, 307, 318-329, 334-345, 448-458, 464-471, 479-489, 495, 501, 519 545, 549, 553-599, 600-624; IV 1, 2, 6, 14, 15, 32, 33, 52, 69-75, 78-81, 84-87, 89, 91-99, 101, 107, 119, 127, 128, 131, 133, 135, 136, 137, 141, 146, 147, 150, 151-154, 159, 160, 203, 208, 234, 236, 241-243, 370, 372, 373.
Spaniards, I 19, 20, 40, 246, 382, 457, 523, 543; II 79, 114, 117, 126, 128, 144, 146, 165, 191, 213, 231, 251, 257, 266-268, 273, 285, 297, 300, 310, 316, 320, 322, 347; III 1, 26,

INDEX

30, 53, 126, 131, 136, 146, 148, 149, 177, 191, 319, 320, 347, 391, 392, 393, 403, 595, 596, 607, 615, 616; IV 76, 212, 338.
Spanish Capuchins, III 55, 56.
Spanish Domination in Louisiana, III 1-628.
Spanish Fleet, III 44, 142.
Spanish Language, III 7, 30, 47, 55, 60, 61.
Spanish Officers, IV 24, 29-31, 76, 77, 125, 130, 132.
Spanish Schools, III 378.
Spanish Minister, III 618.
Sparks, Colonel, IV 197.
Spotts, Lieut., IV 467.
Sprigg, Judge Superior Court, IV 68.
State Finances, IV 664.
Stay Law, enacted, IV 412.
Steele, Andrew, IV 231.
de Steuben, Baron, III 248.
Steamboat, arrival of the first one, IV 276, 277.
Stout, IV 312.
"Stung Serpent," his death, I 329, 342.
"Strawberry Plain," I 481.
Sugar, II 63, 86, III 348, 349, 435.
Sumter, III 492.
Superior Council, II 252, 279, 355, 364, 366, 368, 391, 392, 455; II 87, 111, 112, 130, 132. 189, 192, 203, 307, 445; III 2, 37, 49, 50, 61, 86. 307, 455.
Swann, Lieut, IV 169.
Swartwout, Samuel, IV 160, 171.
Swiss, I 470, 491, 500; II 71, 75.
Taensas Indians, II 103.
Talapouches, I 450, III 157, 158, 160, 161, 174, 175, 213, 329, 421.
Talleyrand, III 465, 501, 503, 505, 506, 507, 509, 510, 523, 530; his assurances of the right of deposit at New Orleans, III 473.
Tarascon, Santiago, III 132.
Tardiveau, III 238.
Tatergem, Francis, III 461.
Taylor, General, IV 670, 671.
Tchefuncta, IV 401, 416.
Tchoupitoulas Militia, II 234, 355.
Tchoupitoulas, I 354; III 170, 215.
Teche R., III 436.
Terrazas, Luis Lorenzo de, III 123.
Teuncin, Abbe. I 215.
Tennessee R., I 17.

Tennessee Company, III 291, 296, 482.
Tennessee, III 341, 345, 403, 618; IV 167, 307, 372, 376, 378, 388, 405, 519, 643.
Tennessee Riflemen, IV 414, 422, 429, 452, 453, 462, 465, 468, 472, 474, 503, 582, 610.
Tensas, La., I 61.
Terre aux Boeufs, III 116, 170, 215, 575; IV 221, 365, 434, 451.
Territorial Government of Louisiana, IV 107.
Tessier, Major, IV 544.
Texas, I 28, 40, 41; II 257, 260; III 76, 308, 408; IV 76, 80, 83, 87, 89, 299, 319, 647, 656, 657, 659, 666, 667, 689.
Thibodaux, State Senator, IV 272, 564, 565, 646.
Thomassin, II 192.
Thomas, Philemon, IV 286.
Thomas, Maj. Gen., IV 367, 405, 459, 461, 504, 557.
Thompson, N., IV 612.
Thompson's Creek, II 127.
Thornton, Col., IV 425, 478, 484, 485, 488, 489.
Tigouyou, III 121.
Tiverant, II 43.
Tobacco, I 273, 469; II 379; III 107, 425, 426.
Toledo, General, IV 320.
Tombigbee River, I 471, 484, 506; II 97; III 361, 362, 412; IV 89.
Tompkins, Gov. of N. Y., IV 389.
Tonti, Chev. de, R., I 23, 25, 39, 40, 69, 70.
de Tousard, Chevalier, French Consul N. O., IV 373, 374, 414, 580, 581.
Toussaint, III 453.
Tracey, Mr., in the Senate, III 549, 553, 556, 557.
Treaty of Aid la Chapelle, II 116; Fontainebleau, II 91; Ghent, IV 519, 525, 529, 580; Madrid, III 356-8; Paris, IV 524, 640; Utrecht, II 116.
Tremoulet's Coffee House, IV 345.
Trepagnier, IV 266.
Trinidad, III 470. IV 522.
Trinity, Catahoula Pa., I 445.
Trinity River, IV 89, 145.
Triton, (ship), I 519.
Troops, how distributed, II 56.

INDEX

Trudeau, Rene, IV 286.
Trudeau, II 87.
Tunicas, I 246, 259, 369, 459, 416, 424, 427, 428, 435, 436, 439, 443, 445, 459; II 50.
Tureaud, III 605.
Turner, Captain, IV 79, 87, 297.
Tuscany, III 440, 448, 452, 468, 536.
Tyler, IV 181.

Ulloa, Don Antonio de, II 130, 131, 142, 158, 164, 166, 173, 177, 181, 186, 209, 211; 215, 218, 229, 238, 253, 262, 275, 276, 301, 319, 323, 332, 337, 367; III 38, 40, 43, 393, 429, 624.
United States, III 112, 115, 117, 121, 157, 181, 192, 193, 221, 224, 225, 240, 241, 246, 260, 263, 267, 282, 285, 287, 291, 297, 299, 300, 306, 309, 340, 345, 355, 365, 371, 397, 399, 403, 405, 411, 414, 419, 450, 452, 459, 460, 464, 465, 474, 487, 491, 494, 498, 506, 516, 521, 524, 527, 536, 538, 540, 543, 546, 555, 562, 567, 569, 574, 576, 591, 601, 606, 619, 622; IV 221.
University, State, IV 135.
Unzaga, Don Luis de, III 30, 32, 44, 46, 56, 83, 85, 88, 90, 91, 97, 98, 99, 100, 102, 103, 104, 105, 106, 127, 156, 168, 170, 205, 216, 310.
Urissa, intendant, II 248, 249.
Urquhart, Thomas, IV 272, 273.
Urrutia, M. J. de, II 339; III 8, 36.
Ursuline Nuns, I 377, 380, 458; III 36, 47, 378; IV 112, 147.

Valdes, Don Antonio, II 221, 271; III 186, 198, 263, 271, 285.
Valdeterre, Dornot de, I 373, 376.
Valero, Marquis of, I 238.
Varnum, Rep., IV 39.
Vasconselos, de Silva, I 15.
Vattel's Law of Nations, II 335.
Vaudreuil, Marquis, I 523; II 17, 29, 57, 66.
Vaudreuil, Mme. de, II 61.
Vaugine, II 182.
De Velles, I 466.
Venezuela, La., III 116.
Vente, Curate de la, I 87, 88, 392.
Vera Cruz, I 249, 523; II 98, 427, 437, 442, 445; IV 15, 80, 315.
de Verbois, Chev., II 30.
Vergennes, Count d., III 119.

De Verges, Engineer, Memorial o Mississippi, II 30, 33.
Vermilion R., III 436.
Vernon, Ed., I 523.
Verret, J. B., III 589.
Verret, Andre, II 189, 235.
Versailles, I 494; III 171.
De Vezin, II 183.
de Vezin, Pierre Francois Olivier III 31.
Victor, General, III 471, 504, 577.
Vidal, Don Jose, commandant, III 397, 398, 404, 405.
Vidalia, III 398.
Viel, Etienne Bernard Alexandre, III 626.
Villamil, Joseph, III 627.
Villainville, I 438.
Villars, II 167; III 20, 106, 107, 114, 117, 118.
Villars, Marechal de, war ship, I 249.
Villemont., I 281, 282.
Villere, James, Major General, III 605, 610; IV 68-273, 322, 364, 417, 423, 450, 518, 633, 636, 646.
Villeré, Joseph, II 127, 187, 189, 234-237, 305-307, 320, 322, 328, 338.
Villeré, Madame, III 353.
Villeré, Major, IV 418, 420, 421, 433.
Villeré's Canal, IV 418, 421, 431, 461, 463, 488.
Vinache, III 618.
Vincennes, I 485, III 382
Virginia, I 520; III 107, 112, 113, 206, 225, 228, 238, 240, 250, 254, 266, 291, 295; IV 642, 643, 689.
Volante, Spanish Frigate, II 230, 243, 273, 278, 279; III 123.

Wabash (dist.), I 516.
Wabash Indians, I 405.
Wabash R., III 236.
Waldeck, Regiment, III 130.
Walker, Alexander, IV 474.
Walker, Joseph, IV 673, 675, 676.
Wallace, Caleb, III 226.
Wallingford, Lord, married daughter of J. Law, I 231.
Walnut Hills, III 296.
Walsh, Vicar General, IV 106, 112, 115.
Ward, Jno., III 281.
Washington, D. C., III 451; 458; 473, 475, 500, 501, 523, 534, 343, 547, 618; IV 17, 82, 274, 369, 585, 502.

INDEX

Washington, N. C., III 256, 342.
Washington, Texas, I 28.
Washington, G., President, III 272, 284, 300, 365, 420, 487; IV 299, 631.
Watkins, John, III 605; IV 19.
Watkins, Jones, IV 271, 272, 273, 274.
Watauga, III 112.
Watts, Miss., III 311.
Wax Tree, I 520; II 65.
Wells, Senator, III 551, 557.
Wells, up Delaware, III 482.
West Indies, III 435, 449.
Western States, III 158, 359, 360, 364, 365, 413, 415, 417, 424, 428, 459, 461, 473, 474, 479, 480, 484, 495, 548, 550, 572; IV 14, 341, 342, 345, 347, 395.
Western Company or Company of the Indies, founder I 192.
Wharton, III 243.
White Apple, Natchez Village, I 377.
White, E. D., IV 656, 657, 658.
White, Dr. James, his letter to Miro, III 258, 259, 260; described, 261, 262, 263.
White, Senator, III 482, 484, 549, 550, 551, 557.
White, Maunsell, III 607; IV 515, 612.
White, General, IV 301.
White River, R., I 18.
Wickliffe, Robert C., IV 680, 688.

Wikoff, IV 19.
Wilkinson, General, III 194, 199, 206, 213, 216, 223, 240, 247, 251, 257, 261, 275, 277, 280, 286, 293, 345, 346, 358, 359, 364, 365, 391, 392, 395, 396, 402, 405, 608, 618, 620; IV 14, 80, 81, 153, 160, 164, 173, 326, 385, 392, 393, 600, 602.
Williams, Robert, Gov. Mississippi, IV 88.
Willing, Capt., III 109, 113, 114.
Wilmot, Proviso, IV 672.
Wilson, Lieut, IV 30.
Winchester, General, IV 405.
Windward Isles, III 511.
Winter, Samuel, IV 273, 274.
Woodruff, Major, IV 521.
Woods, III 275.
Workman, Judge, IV 170, 171, 172, 175, 601.
Wren, Woodson, III 607.

Yazoo, dist., I 242, 273.
Yazoo Indians, I 61, 417, 418.
Yazoo River, I 240, 424, 459; III 147, 234, 243, 272, 288, 293, 294, 295, 361, 412.
Yellow Fever, III 375; IV 36, 38, 224, 676, 679.
You Dominique, IV 411, 450, 504, 582.

Zacatecas, III 373.
de Zillier, Baron, III 210.

www.ingramcontent.com/pod-product-compliance
Lightning Source LLC
Chambersburg PA
CBHW021821220426
43663CB00005B/96